GAME AI PRO 2

GAME AI PRO²

Collected Wisdom of Game AI Professionals

EDITED BY

STEVE RABIN

CRC Press
Taylor & Francis Group
Boca Raton London New York

CRC Press is an imprint of the
Taylor & Francis Group, an **informa** business

CRC Press
Taylor & Francis Group
6000 Broken Sound Parkway NW, Suite 300
Boca Raton, FL 33487-2742

Version Date: 20150312

International Standard Book Number-13: 978-1-4822-5479-2 (Hardback)

Visit the Taylor & Francis Web site at
http://www.taylorandfrancis.com

and the CRC Press Web site at
http://www.crcpress.com

Contents

Section II Architecture

Section III Movement and Pathfinding

Preface

It makes me proud to be able to deliver to you a brand new volume of *Game AI Pro*! After putting together books like this one for over a decade, I'm still humbled by the generosity of the authors to share their hard-earned knowledge with the game developer community. In this book, 47 authors have come together to bring you their newest advances in game AI, along with twists on proven techniques that have shipped in some of the most respected commercial games of the last couple years. In addition, we've scoured the latest game AI research from universities and offer you some of the most promising work.

Like most technological industries, the game industry is a whirlwind of new ideas, and the subfield of game AI is no exception. This book hits hard on the area of pathfinding optimization, showing several techniques that can beat a traditional A* search by one or two orders of magnitude. We dedicated a new section to search, giving an inside look into some of the best techniques for exploring a problem space. Another very special section in this book is on character behavior, where, among other wisdom, we detail three distinct areas of AI behavior within the award-winning game *The Last of Us*. In the area of tactics and spatial awareness, we have wisdom from the *Splinter Cell* series and the *Guild Wars* series, among others. Finally, we give you a tour of the most promising new twists on AI architectures and finish the book with a look into procedural content generation and analytics.

Over the last 5 years, game AI communities have really hit their stride and are truly supporting each other. In addition to the *Game AI Pro* book series, there are now annual conferences, both academic and developer-centric, held all over the globe. Organized by developers, there is the Game Developers Conference (GDC) AI Summit in San Francisco and the Game/AI Conference in Europe. Organized by academia, there is the AAAI Conference on Artificial Intelligence and Interactive Digital Entertainment (AIIDE) and the IEEE Conference on Computational Intelligence and Games. Outside of events, there are two communities that have also sprung up to help developers. The AI Game Programmers Guild is a free professional group with over 400 worldwide members (http://www.gameai.com), and there is a wonderful community of hobbyists and professionals at AiGameDev.com. We warmly welcome you to come hang out with us at any one of these conferences or participate in one of our online communities!

Acknowledgments

Game AI Pro² required a huge team effort to come together. First, I thank the five section editors for the excellent job they did in selecting, guiding, and editing the contributions in this book. The section editors were

- Neil Kirby—General Wisdom
- Alex Champandard—Architecture
- Nathan R. Sturtevant—Movement and Pathfinding; Applied Search Techniques
- Damián Isla—Tactics, Strategy, and Spatial Awareness
- Kevin Dill—Character Behavior; Analytics, Content Generation, and Experience Management

The wonderful cover artwork is courtesy of Sony Computer Entertainment America and Naughty Dog from the award-winning game *The Last of Us*. Three chapters covering techniques from this game appear in this book: Infected AI in *The Last of Us*, Enemy AI in *The Last of Us*, and Ellie: Buddy AI in *The Last of Us*.

The team at CRC Press and A K Peters have done an excellent job in making this whole project happen. I thank Rick Adams, Sherry Thomas, Kari Budyk, and the entire production team who took the contributions and carefully turned them into this book.

Special thanks to our families and friends who have supported us and endured the intense production cycle that required long hours, evenings, and weekends.

Web Materials

Example programs and source code to accompany the chapters are available at http://www.gameaipro.com.

General System Requirements

The following is required to compile and execute the example programs:

- DirectX August 2009 SDK
- DirectX 9.0 compatible or newer graphics card
- Windows 7 or newer
- Visual C++.NET 2012 or newer

Updates

Updates of the example programs and source code will be updated as needed.

Comments and Suggestions

Please send any comments or suggestions to steve.rabin@gmail.com.

Editors

Alex Champandard is the founder of AiGameDev.com, the largest online hub for artificial intelligence in games. He has worked in the industry as a senior AI programmer for many years, most notably for Rockstar Games where he worked on the animation technology of *Max Payne 3*. He regularly consults with leading studios in Europe, most notably at Guerrilla Games on the multiplayer bots for *KillZone 2* and *3*. Alex is also the event director for the Game/AI Conference, the largest independent event dedicated to AI in games.

Kevin Dill is a member of the group technical staff at Lockheed Martin Mission Systems and Training, the chief architect for Lockheed's Game AI Architecture, and the lead developer for the True Game-Based Learning project. Prior to coming to Lockheed, he worked as an AI engineer on seven published titles, ranging the gamut from strategy games (*Master of Orion 3*, *Kohan II: Kings of War*, and *Axis & Allies*) to simulation games (*Zoo Tycoon 2: Endangered Species* and *Zoo Tycoon 2: Marine Mania*) to action games (*Iron Man*) to open world shooter/adventure games (*Red Dead Redemption*).

Kevin is a prolific author and speaker and has spoken at the Game Developers Conference on several occasions. He has served as technical or section editor for five books, including the volume you hold in your hands, and has taught game programming and game AI at Boston University, Northeastern University, and Harvard University. He is also a veteran, having served for 4 years as an infantryman in the U.S. Army.

Damián Isla has been working on and writing about game technology for over a decade. He is president and cofounder of indie outfit Moonshot Games, purveyors of fun and innovative downloadable and mobile gaming fare. He is the creative director and project lead on *Third Eye Crime*, the innovative stealth/puzzle/telepathy game for PC and iOS. Before Moonshot, Damián was AI and gameplay engineering lead at Bungie Studios, where he was responsible for the AI for the mega-hit first-person shooters *Halo 2* and *Halo 3*. He also contributed to the AI on *Bioshock: Infinite*.

A leading expert in the field of artificial intelligence for games, Damián has spoken on games, AI, and character technology at the International Joint Conference on Artificial

Intelligence (IJCAI), at the AI and Interactive Digital Entertainment (AIIDE) Conference, and at SIGGRAPH and is a frequent speaker at the Game Developer's Conference (GDC). Before joining the industry, Damián earned a master's degree with the Synthetic Characters group at the Massachusetts Institute of Technology (MIT) Media Lab. He holds a BSc in computer science, also from MIT.

Neil Kirby is the author of *An Introduction to Game AI,* and his other publications include articles in volumes I, II, and IV of *AI Game Programming Wisdom*. He cowrote "Effective Requirements Traceability: Models, Tools and Practices" for the *Bell Labs Technical Journal*. His 1991 paper, "Artificial Intelligence without AI: An Evolutionary Approach" may well show the first use of what is now known as "circle strafing" in a game. His other papers and presentations can be found in the proceedings of the Game Developers Conference (GDC) from 1991 to the present as well as the 2003 Australian GDC.

Neil Kirby is a member of the technical staff at Bell Laboratories, the R&D arm of Alcatel-Lucent. He currently develops .NET solutions used to support requirements traceability. He also provides software architecture consulting services. His previous assignments have included building speech recognition software and teaching at the university level. He has been a judge of the Ohio State University's Fundamentals of Engineering Honors robot competition for many years on behalf of Alcatel-Lucent.

Neil Kirby cofounded the IGDA Foundation and serves on its board. He oversees the Eric Dybsand AI Memorial Scholarship to GDC that is awarded each year.

Neil holds a master's degree in computer science from Ohio State University. He lives with his spouse in central Ohio. There he chairs his local village planning commission and volunteers for the historical society.

Steve Rabin has been a key figure in the game AI community for over a decade and is currently a principal software engineer at Nintendo of America. After initially working as an AI engineer at several Seattle start-ups, he managed and edited seven game AI books in the *Game AI Pro* series and the *AI Game Programming Wisdom* series. He also edited the book *Introduction to Game Development* and has over two dozen articles published in the *Game Programming Gems* series. He has been an invited keynote speaker at several AI conferences, founded the AI Game Programmers Guild in 2008, and founded the Game Developers Conference (GDC) AI Summit, where he has been a summit adviser since 2009. Steve is a principal lecturer at the DigiPen Institute of Technology, where he has taught game AI since 2006. He earned a BSc in computer engineering and an MS in computer science, both from the University of Washington.

Nathan R. Sturtevant is a professor of computer science at the University of Denver, working on artificial intelligence and games. He began his games career working on shareware games as a college student, writing the popular Mac tank game *Dome Wars* in the mid-1990s, and returned to the game industry to write the pathfinding engine for *Dragon Age: Origins*. He has spoken at the Game Developers Conference (GDC) AI Summit twice, and his students have presented their games at the E3 college pavilion. Nathan is currently working on tools to help design more compelling puzzles for games.

Contributors

Tarn Adams is the creator of the cult classic *Dwarf Fortress* and cofounder of Bay 12 Games, along with his brother Zach. Tarn earned his PhD in mathematics from Stanford and BSc in mathematics from the University of Washington, Seattle, Washington.

Bobby Anguelov is a South African expat currently working as a senior programmer at Ubisoft, Montreal, Canada, primarily in the field of animation. Prior to joining Ubisoft, he worked as an AI/animation programmer at IO-Interactive. Outside of the game industry, he has worked in a variety of roles ranging from computer graphics lecturer to enterprise software consultant. Bobby holds an MS in computer science from the University of Pretoria, South Africa, with a focus on computational intelligence and computer graphics.

Mark Botta has been programming in the video game industry for 20 years. He started on the Sega Genesis and has created games for the PC and almost every generation of the Sony PlayStation and Microsoft Xbox. He has worked on side-scrollers, shooters, MMORPGs, and action, stealth, and horror games, including *Tomb Raider*, *Uncharted 3*, and *The Last of Us*. He has a wide range of game programming experience but specializes in AI. He earned his BSc in computer science from the University of California, San Diego. When not programming, he's exploring Los Angeles looking for the perfect iced tea.

Vadim Bulitko is a professor of computing science at the University of Alberta, Edmonton, Alberta, Canada. He has been working in the area of artificial intelligence for 19 years and in the area of video-game-related AI for 11 years. Vadim has published a number of journal papers on video-game-related AI as well as three book articles/chapters, including one in *AI Game Programming Wisdom 4*. Vadim has collaborated with BioWare for over 8 years and presented at CCP (Crowd Control Productions), Disney Imagineering, Lockheed Martin, and Google. Vadim chaired the Artificial Intelligence for Interactive Digital Entertainment (AIIDE) Conference in 2010 and 2011. He has been the head instructor for the University of Alberta's first undergraduate course on video games for the last 10 terms and taught video game AI at the graduate level over the last 13 years.

Phil Carlisle is a senior lecturer at the University of Bolton, Bolton, United Kingdom. He is also the owner of an indie studio called MindFlock Ltd., which he founded after over a decade in the game industry working on game characters and artificial intelligence. Phil has worked on numerous published games, primarily from the multimillion-selling *Worms* franchise.

Jérémy Chanut has a master's degree in computer science. Passionate about development and AI, he has been working as a software engineer at MASA Group since 2013, in the MASA LIFE team. As an intern, he worked on Recast/Detour and group navigation under the supervision of Clodéric Mars. He now focuses on software architecture in MASA LIFE while maintaining and updating his work on Recast/Detour.

Zhengxing Chen is currently a PhD student at Northeastern University College of Computation and Information Science, Boston, Massachusetts. His research focus is on game analytics and machine learning. He previously worked on interesting projects on embedded systems and mobile systems. As an undergraduate, he was part of the team that won 2nd prize for developing the *Virtual Costume Trial System*. Having experience in software development on mobile systems, he also published two mobile applications aiming to promote healthy habits.

Caroline Chopinaud received her PhD in computer science at the Pierre and Marie Curie University, Paris, France, in 2007, specializing in artificial intelligence. She joined MASA Group in 2008 as a developer of MASA LIFE, working on agent communications and the modeling of security and military behaviors. Caroline has since become head of R&D at MASA, in charge of innovation and the R&D team. She is mainly involved in research activities, in particular scientific monitoring and project building. She handles relations between MASA and academia. She published scientific papers in international conferences in the field of multiagent systems (ECAI, IAT, PAAMS, etc.).

Michael Dawe has been solving AI and gameplay problems in games since 2007, working on games such as *Kingdoms of Amalur: Reckoning*, *Dance Central Spotlight*, and *Grand Theft Auto 5*. He is a frequent speaker for the AI Summit at the Game Developers Conference, is a founding member of the AI Game Programmers Guild, and has written previously for the Game Programming Gems and Game AI Pro series. Michael holds an MS in computer science from DigiPen Institute of Technology, Redmond, Washington, as well as a BSc in computer science and philosophy from Rensselaer Polytechnic Institute, Troy, New York.

Etienne de Sevin earned his PhD in artificial intelligence at École Polytechnique Fédérale de Lausanne (EPFL), Switzerland, in 2006. During his research in several renowned labs, he designed, implemented, and evaluated cognitive architectures and real-time decision-making processes for autonomous nonplayer characters in order to populate virtual environments such as virtual cities or video games. He published several scientific papers in international conferences (AAMAS, CGI, CASA, etc.). He joined MASA Group as a research engineer in the R&D team in 2012.

Max Dyckhoff is an AI software engineer with 10 years of industry experience at Naughty Dog, Blizzard, Bungie, and Free Radical Design. His experience includes work on the AI of blockbuster titles such as *The Last of Us*, *Halo 3*, and *Halo Reach*. He has spoken on buddy AI, behavior trees, and knowledge representation at the Game Developers Conference and the Neural Information Processing Systems Conference. He holds a master of engineering in computer systems and software engineering from the University of York in the United Kingdom. He was born in Scotland, moved to the United States in 2006, and now lives in Santa Monica with his daughter. Currently, he is at Naughty Dog working on AI and other fun things for upcoming titles.

Leif Foged is currently a software engineer at Facebook, where he works on the Facebook Games Platform.

Andrew Fray is a ten-year veteran of the video game industry. He has worked on AI in many genres, including FPS and racing games. Andrew was the lead AI programmer on Codemasters' *F1 2010* and *F1 2011*. He has spoken at the Game Developers Conference (GDC) multiple times, as well as at other conferences. Andrew currently works for Spry Fox, making original digital games. You should follow him on twitter at @tenpn and read his blog at http://andrewfray.wordpress.com.

Stephen J. Guy is an assistant professor in the Department of Computer Science and Engineering at the University of Minnesota, Minneapolis, Minnesota. His research focuses on the areas of interactive computer graphics (real-time crowd simulation, path planning, intelligent virtual characters) and multirobot coordination (collision avoidance, sensor fusion, path planning under uncertainty). Stephen's work on motion planning has been licensed for use in games and virtual environments by Relic Entertainment, EA, and other companies; his work in crowd simulation has been recognized by best paper awards at international conferences. Prior to joining the University of Minnesota, he received his PhD in computer science in 2012 from the University of North Carolina at Chapel Hill with support from fellowships from Google, Intel, and the UNCF, and his BSc in computer engineering with honors from the University of Virginia in 2006.

Ian Horswill is associate professor of computer science at Northwestern University, Evanston, Illinois. His research interests include game AI, emotion, and cognitive architecture.

Éric Jacopin is a professor at the French military academy of Saint-Cyr where he headed the computer science research laboratory from 1998 to 2012; this includes teaching Turing machines, war games, and project management and the management of international internships for computer science cadets. His research has been in the area of planning for the past 25 years, not only from the viewpoint of artificial intelligence but also from everyday life perspectives. He received his PhD (1993) and his habilitation to direct research (1999) from the Pierre and Marie Curie University, Paris, France.

Ioannis Karamouzas is a research associate in the department of computer science and engineering at the University of Minnesota, Minneapolis, Minnesota. His research focuses on the development of motion planning algorithms for autonomous virtual humans, robots, and crowds of virtual characters. Prior to joining the University of Minnesota, Ioannis received his PhD in computer science from Utrecht University in the Netherlands, with a thesis that focuses in the area of motion planning for human crowd simulations. His doctoral work has been integrated into commercial gaming applications including driving simulators and pedestrian simulation suites. He previously earned an MSc in computer science from the University of Manchester in the United Kingdom and a BSc in applied informatics with honors from the University of Macedonia in Greece.

Kevin A. Kirst has specialized in artificial intelligence in the gaming and simulation industries since 2008. His previous work with companies including Crytek and Ubisoft has blessed him with the opportunity to be credited on two released titles (*Crysis 2* and *Tom Clancy's Splinter Cell: Blacklist*) as well as two unreleased titles. He is a graduate of Full Sail University in Orlando, Florida, The City Beautiful, where he once again resides. His current employment with RealTime Immersive, Inc., a subsidiary of Crytek, allows him the freedom and resources to continue growing, researching, and solving problems concerning AI development in the entertainment gaming, serious gaming, and simulation market spaces. Programming is his love; AI is his passion.

Sven Koenig is a professor in computer science at the University of Southern California, Los Angeles, California. He received his PhD in computer science from Carnegie Mellon University and is a fellow of the Association for the Advancement of Artificial Intelligence. Most of his research centers on techniques for decision making (planning and learning) that enable single agents (such as robots or decision-support systems) and teams of agents to act intelligently in their environments and exhibit goal-directed behavior in real time, even if they have only incomplete knowledge of their environment, imperfect abilities to manipulate it, limited or noisy perception, or insufficient reasoning speed.

Greg Lee is a PhD graduate of computing science at the University of Alberta, Edmonton, Alberta, Canada, and is currently working as the lead data scientist at FundMetric, Halifax, Nova Scotia, Canada. His PhD dissertation focused on the Sports Commentary Recommendation System (SCoReS), which automatically selects stories for a game by comparing features of the current game state to features of stories. Greg has published conference and journal papers on this subject, and SCoReS has been featured in popular science magazines and radio shows.

Mike Lewis has been working as a programmer in the game industry since early 2002, often with a focus on AI and related systems. He has lectured at the Game Developers Conference AI Summit and published a chapter in the first Game AI Pro book. Today, he calls ArenaNet home, where he plans to unleash bigger, better, and more entertaining AI on the world of massively multiplayer online gaming.

John Manslow started writing games on his Vic-20 as a teenager and gradually became more and more interested in smart AI. Having completed a degree and then a PhD in the subject, he joined Codemasters as the AI specialist in their R&D team, where he worked on several projects to bring next-generation AI to Codemasters' games. Since then, John has worked for several companies outside the industry but has remained focused on AI and statistical analytics.

Dave Mark is the president and lead designer of Intrinsic Algorithm, an independent game development studio in Omaha, Nebraska. He does consulting on AI, game design, and mathematical modeling for clients ranging from small indie game studios to AAA companies including EA, Sony Online Entertainment, and ArenaNet. Dave is the author of the book *Behavioral Mathematics for Game AI* and is a contributor to the *AI Game Programming Wisdom* and *Game Programming Gems* book series from Charles River Media and the first Game AI Pro book from CRC Press. He has also spoken at numerous game conferences and universities around the world on the subjects of AI, game theory, and psychology. He is a founding member of the AI Game Programmers Guild and has been a coadvisor of the Game Developers Conference AI Summits. Dave continues to further his education by attending the University of Life. He has no plans to graduate anytime soon.

Clodéric Mars has tried to make simulated characters behave "autonomously *and* as they are told to" for more than 6 years. At Golaem, he worked on a navigation engine used, for example, in a train passengers' simulation and a crowd simulation tool for animation and vfx. Now leading the developments of MASA LIFE, he is dedicated to make behavior authoring easy, fun, and accessible to game designers and field experts. Clodéric has a master's degree in computer science, with a specialization in AI. He spoke at the Paris Game/AI Conference 2011 and at the Game Developers Conference (GDC) 2014 AI Summit.

Travis McIntosh has worked at Naughty Dog, Santa Monica, California, for 9 years. He was lead programmer on *Uncharted 1*, *2*, and *3*, as well as *The Last of Us*. He has personally worked on gameplay systems as diverse as player control, cameras, AI, and animation. He is a devout Christian and lives with his wonderful wife, Vivien, and their son, Corin, in El Segundo, California.

Jan Müller studied computational visualistics at the University of Koblenz-Landau, Germany. During his master's thesis, he worked for the Fraunhofer Institute for Applied Information Technology near Bonn, Germany. The focus of his research was augmented and virtual reality as well as early prototypes of VR smart phone games. Among others, he published a research poster about image space constructive solid geometry at the Visualization 2005 conference. After graduating in 2005, he joined Crytek to work as a game and network programmer on *Crysis 1* and *Crysis 2*. In 2009, he joined the Fachhochschule Darmstadt as a guest lecturer teaching game development with CRYENGINE 2. In September 2010, he moved to Los Angeles, California, to work for Insomniac Games. There he was involved with the *Ratchet & Clank* franchise, *Fuse*, and *Sunset Overdrive* as a senior game programmer.

Alex Nash received his BSc in computer science from Yale University, New Haven, Connecticut, in 2004, his MS in computer science from the University of Southern California in 2006, and his PhD in computer science from the University of Southern California, Los Angeles, California, in 2012 for his dissertation on "Any-angle path planning." Since 2005, he has been performing mission-planning research and development for the information systems sector of the Northrop Grumman Systems Corporation. His research has been used on ground-based and embedded mission-planning systems for both manned and unmanned aerial vehicles.

Miguel A. Nieves has been programming games professionally for 10 years and is currently senior developer at Shenandoah Studio. Shenandoah Studio creates high-quality turn-based strategy war games from "Euro" board games. Working within the constraints of mobile and portable platforms, he has engineered creative and personality-driven characters in over half a dozen titles. In his latest release, *Desert Fox* (iOS), he uses the triune brain model of human brain evolution to develop six different AI generals. Check out earlier implementations of this architecture in *Drive on Moscow* and *Battle of the Bulge* available on Apple's App Store.

Truong-Huy D. Nguyen is currently working as a postdoctoral research associate at Northeastern University, Boston, Massachusetts. His research interests include, but are not limited to, artificial intelligence, data mining, and machine learning. His dream research outcomes are smart technologies that address all tedious and physically involved work, eventually allowing us to live lazily ever after. He enjoys playing both fast-paced sports games (*FIFA*, *Pro Evolution Soccer*) and take-your-time turn-based strategy games (*Fire Emblem* and the *Civilization* series) in his spare time. *Prison Break*, a puzzle game he created, won the Most Entertaining Game Award in a 24-hour game jam competition.

Sergio Ocio Barriales has been working in the game industry since 2005. He received his PhD from the University of Oviedo, Spain, in December 2010 with his thesis about hinted-execution behavior trees. He was an AI tech lead/AI programmer for 6 years at Ubisoft, working on the AI of *Driver: San Francisco* and *Tom Clancy's Splinter Cell: Blacklist*. He joined the AI team at id Software in May 2014.

Jeff Orkin is co-founder of Giant Otter Technologies. Previously, Jeff was the AI lead on *F.E.A.R.* and *No One Lives Forever 2* at Monolith Productions. He earned a PhD from MIT, where he researched artificial intelligence, natural language processing, and crowdsourcing in the MIT Media Lab's Cognitive Machines Group.

Graham Pentheny is a senior software engineer at Giant Otter Technologies, where he works with Dr. Jeff Orkin to develop innovative and engaging social simulations. Previously, he led AI and engine development at Subatomic Studios and is credited on the *Fieldrunners* tower defense games. He received his BSc in both computer science and interactive media and game development from Worcester Polytechnic Institute, Worcester, Massachusetts. In addition to game AI, he enjoys programming language design, ultimate frisbee, and music composition (grahampentheny.com).

Sergio Poo Hernandez is an MSc student in computing science at the University of Alberta, Edmonton, Alberta, Canada, focusing on interactive narratives and advised by Dr. Vadim Bulitko. His work and publication focus on how to use automated planning to generate content stubs that can be used along player modeling to ensure the player's emotional trajectory is as close as possible as the author intended.

Alejandro Ramirez is a PhD student in computing science at the University of Alberta, Edmonton, Alberta, Canada. He received his MSc in computing science from the University of Alberta in 2013, with a dissertation and publications focusing on artificial intelligence and video games, particularly on how to use automated planning to generate content stubs that could be later used along player modeling to increase the player's sense of agency and fun. Alejandro has also performed initial user studies and evaluations of these techniques with positive results.

Jeff Rollason currently heads up and is cofounder of AI Factory Ltd., Middlesex, United Kingdom, with some estimated 200 million users (including over 75 million Android downloads). AI Factory was founded in 2003 with the premise of creating modular AI and games that would be licensed to third parties. The business has been very successful with clients such as Microsoft, among other licensees, incorporating AI Factory game engines within software on consoles, PCs, in-flight entertainment, and mobile devices. His primary contribution is game AI. His education includes combined sciences BSc (1st) at Westfield College, University of London (UOL), and computer science MSc at University College London, UOL. His 17 years in academia included teaching core computer architecture courses at Kings College, UOL. His programs have also competed in computer tournaments for Chess, Go, and particularly Shogi (Japanese Chess), where his program *Shotest* twice ranked third in the world.

Andrea Schiel has more than 18 years of experience developing AAA games and has worked on most of the major EA Sports™ titles. A recognized specialist in AI, she leads the AI special interest group at EA™ and mentors other engineers in this field. Andrea has shipped over 25 titles on all major platforms and is currently working for BioWare Montreal™ on the *Mass Effect*™ franchise.

Magy Seif El-Nasr is an associate professor in the Colleges of Computer and Information Sciences and Arts, Media and Design at Northeastern University, Boston, Massachusetts. She is also the director of the Game Educational Programs and Research at Northeastern University and the director of the game design program in the College of Arts, Media and Design. She also directs the Game User Experience and Design Research Lab. Dr. Seif El-Nasr earned her PhD in computer science from Northwestern University, Evanston, Illinois. Magy's research focuses on interactive narrative, enhancing game designs by developing tools and methods for evaluating and adapting game experiences. Her work is internationally known and cited in several game industry books, including Programming Believable Characters for Computer Games (Game Development Series) and Real-time Cinematography for Games. In addition, she has received several best paper awards for her work. Magy worked collaboratively with teams at Electronic Arts, Bardel Entertainment, and Pixel Ante. She is also listed as an advisor for the Game for Health, Spa Play, in development by IgnitePlay.

Jeet Shroff comes from a background in AI, animation, and gameplay programming and direction, where he has worked as a programmer and realization director on game titles across multiple genres and studios for the last 10 years. His industry experience includes working at Avalanche Studios, Ubisoft (Montreal), and Electronic Arts, where he has worked on successfully shipped titles for major franchises such as *FIFA* and *Far Cry 3*. Currently, he is a lead character programmer at Avalanche Studios, where he is responsible for the development of AI, animation, and player mechanics for an unannounced open-world AAA title. Jeet holds a bachelor of mathematics in computer science from the University of Waterloo, Ontario, Canada, and has spoken on open-world AI behavior and design at the Game Developers Conference.

Fernando Silva is a software engineer at Microsoft ATG, providing engineering support to licensed game developers and internal groups, specializing in the Xbox One platform. He completed an undergraduate degree in computer science in real-time interactive simulation at DigiPen Institute of Technology, Redmond, Washington, where he minored in mathematics. Before Microsoft, he worked as a software engineer at Nintendo of America. In his free time, Fernando enjoys working on electronic projects with a focus on the Arduino platform, reverse engineering processes or devices, studying biological processes that can be applied to computer science, and most importantly dining.

Gillian Smith is an assistant professor at Northeastern University, Boston, Massachusetts, jointly appointed between the College of Computer and Information Science and the College of Arts, Media, and Design, and is a member of the Playable Innovative Technologies research group. She earned her PhD in computer science from University of California, Santa Cruz's Center for Games and Playable Media in 2012. Her research focuses on procedural content generation (PCG) and how humans—be they players or designers—can interact with it. She is particularly interested in the use of PCG to create new design experiences in the form of intelligent tools for designers and innovative game designs and has authored several articles on the subject. She is an associate editor for the *IEEE's Transactions on Computational Intelligence* and *AI in Games* and sits on the IEEE Computational Intelligence in Games Technical Committee. Her website is at http://www.sokath.com.

David Thue is a professor in the School of Computer Science at Reykjavik University, Reykjavik, Iceland. He has been working on the area of artificial intelligence for video games for 9 years, having published several related conference papers and two book chapters, one in *AI Game Programming Wisdom 4*. David has worked on AI-driven interactive experience management in the industry at Walt Disney Imagineering Research and Development and has presented at both BioWare and Lockheed Martin. He cochaired the International Conference on Interactive Digital Storytelling in 2011 and 2014 and has presented his work at the Artificial Intelligence for Interactive Digital Entertainment (AIIDE) Conference on five separate occasions (2006–2011). David teaches Reykjavik University's undergraduate course on video game design and development and also advises students on topics in game AI.

Tansel Uras is a PhD student in computer science at the University of Southern California, Los Angeles, California, working with Sven Koenig. Tansel received his BSc in computer science (with a minor in mathematics) in 2009 and his MSc in computer science in 2011 from Sabanci University, Istanbul, Turkey. Tansel is interested in incremental heuristic search, path planning, and game theory, among other topics. He developed a novel optimal path-planning approach (based on subgoal graphs) that was nondominated in the Grid-Based Path Planning Competitions in 2012 and 2013 and won a Best Research Assistant Award from the Computer Science Department at USC in 2014 for this achievement.

Martin Walsh has been in the industry for 10 years. In that time, he worked on *Rainbow Six: Lockdown* and then on *Splinter Cell: Conviction* as AI technical lead. On *Splinter Cell: Conviction*, he created a dynamic navmesh system that became a middleware at Ubisoft (used in titles such as *Assassin's Creed* and *ZombiU*) and was the subject of a Game Developers Conference (GDC) presentation in 2010. After leading the middleware team, Martin rejoined production to work as AI lead on *Splinter Cell: Blacklist.*

Rich Welsh graduated from Durham University, Durham, United Kingdom, in 2007 and went immediately into the game industry. From humble beginnings at a studio in his hometown of Newcastle, he has gone from strength to strength working on both gameplay and AI for the *Crackdown* and the *Crysis* series of games, as well as being part of the AI system development team for *CRYENGINE*. Presently, he is a senior gameplay programmer working at Ubisoft Massive on *Tom Clancy's The Division.*

Robert Zubek is a game developer and cofounder of SomaSim in San Francisco. Previously, he was a principal software engineer at Zynga, where he was on the founding teams of *CityVille* and *FarmVille 2*, the company's two large-scale social games. Prior to Zynga, he developed online game infrastructure at Three Rings Design and console games at Electronic Arts/Maxis. Before joining the industry, he specialized in artificial intelligence and robotics research. Robert holds a PhD in computer science from Northwestern University, Evanston, Illinois, where he also received his previous CS degrees.

Section I
General Wisdom

1

Game AI Appreciation, Revisited

Mike Lewis and Kevin Dill

1.1 Introduction

This book represents a collection of knowledge, advice, hard-learned wisdom, and insight gathered from across the community of developers and researchers who have taken an interest in game AI. With such a formidable lineup of expertise brought to bear on the subject, it may come as a surprise to learn that even the leading experts in the field of game AI find it challenging to define just what exactly that field comprises.

Concocting a reasonably concise definition of game AI is hard enough—let alone reaching consensus on that definition with the rest of the development community. Often, the question is evaded entirely. AI can be recognized when it is observed in action, so why bother trying to hem it in with a strict definition?

Unfortunately, this perspective does a fundamental disservice to the rest of the game community. Players, journalists, critics, and even other developers are often left with an incomplete idea of what exactly game AI is all about, what it can offer, and what is (and isn't) easy. A comprehensive analysis could fill a book by itself, but we will at least attempt to sketch out the boundaries of game AI here.

Music, classical art forms, film, theater, and even food all benefit from the idea of "appreciation courses." Without some foundational knowledge of how songs are composed or sculptures revealed within a block of marble, it can be difficult to truly grasp and enjoy what makes them so special. In this chapter, we will attempt to explore the field of game AI from a similar perspective.

1.2 What Is Game AI?

One of the first things established in any appreciation course is *vocabulary*. A shared lexicon makes communication much more fluid and much less error prone. Given that this is a book about game AI, it seems only natural to begin by defining the very term "game AI."

Although even the term "game" is notoriously difficult to pin down, we will assume that it is generally understood well enough. We are particularly interested in electronic computer games in that they are the most readily visible dwelling place for contemporary game AI. The important aspects of games that we consider in this chapter consist primarily of the gameplayer's *experience* as presented through the constraints of a *design*.

The design of a game is, loosely speaking, the setting and rules of the artificial "world" in which the game takes place—however abstract, fantastical, or realistic that world may be. A *designer* manages and sculpts the vision for how the game will operate, how the player is expected to interact with the game, and what sorts of experiences the player should be having while playing.

Typical components of the experience are things the player might observe (such as opponents, environments, and narrative moments), methods for interacting with the game itself, and *feedback* that provides information to the player about the consequences of those interactions.

Creating a game requires the use of a diverse array of tools, ranging from the purely artistic to the intensely technical. All of these tools are involved in enabling the vision of the game's design. AI is a particularly powerful part of that toolbox.

If game AI is a toolset, then when do those tools become necessary? Games can be (and occasionally are) created with no real "artificial intelligence" component. Clearly, it is not necessary to have particularly sophisticated AI to deliver an experience like Tetris. So when do these vision-enabling tools actually get deployed?

A key differentiator between games and some of the more common classical art forms is that games are inherently *interactive*. The player has some role, whether minor or central, in shaping the experience that unfolds during play. In more traditional arenas, participatory theater (such as improvisational comedy) invites the audience into an exchange with the performers. For games, there isn't necessarily a ready cast of human performers with whom to interact—and yet we still consider games *interactive*. Within this notion of interactivity lies an important signpost on the route to defining game AI.

Interaction can take on many forms. Strictly speaking, people interact with inanimate objects all the time. But interacting with other *people* is generally much more interesting than, say, turning on a light switch. While game experiences can be almost entirely mechanical and "inanimate" in a sense, many games seek to deliver something more compelling—something that seems more tangible, more relatable, more *real*.

We may be able to relate to characters or situations in a film or novel, but we can't interact with them. By contrast, our experience of a game is funneled through our interactions with the game universe. It is the sensation that something on the other side of the screen is almost *alive* that makes game AI unique and powerful. This feeling arises from observing the game "making decisions" about what happens next.

More broadly, game AI can be thought of as applied decision making, specifically in the context of games. Most often, this takes the form of an autonomous, decision-making agent (i.e., an NPC) in a virtual world. Game AI need not be limited to just these sorts of applications. For game AI practitioners, the goal is to use programmatic techniques to enable the computer to make effective decisions that support the experience they aim to create. These decisions might entail almost anything, from characters and their split-second reactions to in-game events, to sweeping changes to an entire set of game rules, based on models suggested by various algorithms [Schwab 14].

1.3 Fuzzy Border

Artificial intelligence as a field is expansive and encompasses quite a bit more than just games. It is worth noting that much of what is categorized as "AI" in nongaming spheres bears little resemblance to the typical technology used in games.

For example, academic AI commonly focuses on building a falsifiable scientific model of some cognitive processes. Popular reasoning packages from outside the game's domain, such as SOAR, ACT-R, and CoJACK, often take this approach. Changing the behavior of the AI requires refining and adjusting the cognitive model itself. While this approach is important for drawing sound conclusions from research and making verifiable predictions, it introduces a layer of abstraction between the game designer's intent and the AI's implementation. This added abstraction increases the required amount of development effort, because changes to the AI behavior cannot be made directly. Moreover, this abstraction introduces a significant computational cost, which can be prohibitive in many gaming applications.

For a game, we want to achieve a particular behavior to suit the design goals; how that behavior is arrived at is more or less inconsequential. More importantly, we want a simple set of controls with understandable and predictable effects, so that creating the desired experience is straightforward. Excess abstraction and complexity often serve to make it more difficult to attain the precise game experience that we want.

Another area of AI with considerable importance outside of games is machine learning. Allowing a computer to discover and tune its own solutions may sound appealing, but this approach frequently conflicts with the desire to create a specific sort of experience. Machine learning has been successfully applied in games, but mostly in limited subdomains, such as tuning paths taken by cars in racing games [Manslow 01]. Other uses include actual game design mechanics, which can be immensely entertaining and yet equally difficult to test [Barnes 02]. More recently, learning has been explored as a method for calibrating game balance [Tozour 13]. All too often, though, it poses a challenge that games simply don't need to address.

In a similar vein, many AI techniques (such as planning and utility-based reasoning) are designed to produce a high degree of *autonomy*. This characteristic enables AI agents to make sensible decisions in circumstances that were not directly anticipated by the developers. While autonomy in an AI agent can often be desirable, if it is not carefully constrained, it can lead to unpredictable behavior (sometimes referred to as "emergent behavior"). Whether or not this should be considered a positive outcome is hotly debated within the community, but ultimately, it depends highly on the game design and the nature of the experience we wish to create.

Authorial control and autonomy are fundamentally at odds, and it is up to each individual game designer to decide which side to favor and how strongly. Some games, like *The Sims*, thrive on autonomy—each individual character has almost complete freedom to act and even "live" within the game world. Some entire genres, such as real-time or turn-based strategy games, require a high a degree of autonomous behavior in order to deliver compelling opponents. On the other end of the spectrum, games like *World of Warcraft* have deliberately chosen to minimize autonomy. The AI in a typical *World of Warcraft* boss fight is very carefully hand-tuned to deliver a specific experience, but it is also extremely predictable.

One more area of burgeoning AI research is data mining. It is as yet unclear how much this field will overlap with game AI in the future. For the time being, though, there is only minimal intersection. In a few noteworthy cases, data mining is used to help calibrate and balance game designs (whether before or after shipping). However, the interaction between this data analysis and the resulting functionality of the game AI typically involves a significant element of human intervention. Much like with machine learning, there is a fundamental tension with the desire for authorial control, but still some significant potential.

Since the goals of game AI are so frequently different than those of other areas of AI research and application, the selection of techniques that appear in games naturally differs as well. As a general trend, game AI solutions favor simplicity, ease of tuning, and (to an extent, depending on the game) the ability to precisely control the resultant behaviors. While there can be considerable overlap with AI techniques from other fields, games are quite simply solving a different set of problems.

1.4 AI as the Nexus of Game Development

Game AI and game design are virtually inseparable—and indeed, many teams lean heavily upon hybrid design/engineering roles or even unify the "lead design" and "lead AI" roles entirely. As established previously, the entire purpose of game AI is to further the creation of compelling experiences. The nature and scope of those experiences depends entirely on the design vision of the game itself. Any healthy game development team will exhibit close interaction between design and programming, whether the roles are combined or not.

This relationship is no coincidence. For a large number of games, the design is itself expressed to the player through the medium of the AI. In order to communicate the nature of the game world and the agents within it, designers rely on AI, which in turn is brought to life in large part by programming efforts. Refining the behavior requires returning the focus to design, and the feedback and iteration loop perpetuates in this way.

Beyond just design, AI has ties to almost every part of the game development process. Models, sprites, textures, effects, animations, and other art assets define the visual language that AI agents can use to communicate with the player. Audio enables direct verbal interaction with the player. Even music can be dynamically selected and modified at run time in order to evoke specific reactions from the player.

Animation and AI exhibit a very similar relationship as AI and design. Much as the game design is largely expressed via the AI, the AI itself is largely expressed via animation. Animation is often the primary language by which the AI communicates its actions, its intentions, and its opinions and feelings to the player. The AI will only be perceived to be as good as the animations it uses. By the same token, all the fancy animations in the world are useless if the AI never chooses to use them or uses them poorly or inappropriately.

Another common tool for communication with the player is audio and particularly voice. Again, this is a case where the effectiveness of the audio is deeply tied to the power of the AI, and the perception of believability in the AI can be radically affected by careful voice work [Redding 09].

Physics systems are often vital to AI implementation, although the reverse is not true. That is, physics can provide information about the world (such as through raycasts) that the AI relies on to drive its decision-making processes. On the other side of the sense–think–act pipeline, physics often constrains the ways in which agents can interact with the game world. For instance, setting an actor's position by directly modifying its transform might violate the integrity of the physics simulation, so it becomes necessary to use the physical simulation to move that actor into place. This interplay can often lead to interesting problems, such as determining how to move an agent through the world to achieve a certain goal. As the complexity of these challenges grows, it becomes increasingly necessary to seek out novel solutions [Sunshine-Hill 14].

Even systems that are largely independent of the AI, such as rendering, can often be utilized by the AI to help portray intent. A common technique is the use of "tells"—graphical effects or very simple animations that are used to foreshadow upcoming actions on the part of the AI [Abercrombie 14]. One area that seems to have been less thoroughly explored is the interaction between AI and user interfaces. AI pathfinding has occasionally been used to show routing hints to the player. However, many more possibilities exist. For instance, UI elements could be selectively hidden or shown based on signals from the AI systems. Any UI offering a list of targets or objectives could be sorted or filtered based on intelligent criteria—deploying AI reasoning not necessarily in service of the computer's agents, but instead for the benefit of the human player.

For online games, AI can represent an interesting technical challenge. There are rarely one-size-fits-all solutions for replicating AI behavior on multiple distinct devices over a network. Making the AI behave in a consistent and timely manner on all relevant devices, while simultaneously trying to minimize both bandwidth and computational requirements, typically requires a considerable amount of effort. Even though bandwidth has increased dramatically since the early days of online gaming, a few bytes saved here and there can make a significant difference for games on cellular networks or with massive numbers of players.

Beyond the realm of what the player directly experiences, there is considerable potential for the use of AI in tools—both for developing games preship and for analyzing (and perhaps updating) them postrelease. While tools for debugging and observing AI are widely recognized as vital to creating sophisticated behaviors, it is far less common to see tools directly powered by (or even heavily supplemented by) AI systems. Notable exceptions do exist, and as data mining techniques are refined, it seems highly probable that deeply AI-bound tools will become more and more prevalent.

1.5 Frontiers of the Field

AI in games has, as a whole, been improving appreciably over time. What began as trivial pattern-based movement has evolved into spatial awareness and tactical reasoning. Opponents that once were limited to a single means of antagonizing the player can now cleverly take advantage of elements of the game world to invent new challenges on the fly. Even the presentation of an AI character's activities has melded into sophisticated animation and audio systems.

With all of this progress and with resources like this book filled with ever more powerful ideas and techniques, it may be tempting to assume that game AI has conquered the "easy stuff" already. And while some challenges are indeed understood well enough to have de facto standard solutions, it doesn't take much wandering off the beaten path to discover that the field of game AI contains very few truly "solved" problems. Even challenges with powerful theoretical solutions often become vastly more difficult when thrust into the ever more complex environments of contemporary games.

1.5.1 Pathfinding

Implementing a computer game featuring moving agents typically involves finding paths from one place to another through a (potentially complex) world space. Fortunately, efficient solutions to basic forms of the problem have existed since 1959 [Dijkstra 59], with notable improvements (in the form of A*) appearing less than a decade later [Hart 68].

The popularization of A* search has led to the widespread misconception that finding paths is a nonissue in modern games. It is certainly true that this algorithm and several noteworthy variants have had tremendous success in practical applications and will almost certainly remain a staple of pathfinding solutions for a long time to come. However, many games make concessions that enable A* to be particularly effective.

The spatial representation used by the game is a common area for such concessions. Navmeshes are almost ubiquitous in 3D games now, but they quickly begin to struggle if, say, the environment can be radically altered during gameplay in unpredictable ways. Solutions exist, but are not well understood or publicized, and are challenging to implement. (A large portion of them exist in middleware path-planning solutions and are regarded as trade secrets.) Even a static navmesh is fundamentally an approximation of space. It is not possible to guarantee shortest "real" paths when searching an abstract representation of approximate space.

On that note, most pathfinding techniques are only concerned with optimality in terms of distance and/or time; in other words, they are interested in finding the shortest or quickest route from point to point.

What if we want to have a group of agents split into several squads and follow the *four* "best" paths to a destination? What if we want one squad to pin the enemy in place, while another flanks them? What if agents want to find a path that minimizes their visibility to the enemy? What if the player can choose to place (or remove!) walkable areas at a whim? What if significant portions of the decision will change over time, such as when an agent wishes to use a slow-moving vehicle for temporary cover? What if the agent is an easily distracted puppy and prefers to bound to the left and the right as it walks?

Going further afield, what if an agent has many different ways to move around, such as jumping, flying, and swimming? How do all of those options get considered effectively?

How do we decide when to vault over an obstacle and when to simply go around? What if the agent is moving in three dimensions, such as a bird or dolphin? How do we decide where to place the agent vertically and when to change that position? What happens when the path space is crowded by other agents moving about? What if the path is meant for use by a snake (or spider, or elephant, or 18-wheeled truck) instead of a bipedal humanoid? How do we make the motion in these scenarios look convincing?

These are less well-trodden problems. Many game engines address at least some of them, and there are middleware vendors developing ever-increasingly impressive solutions. Yet many of the details are highly game specific, or even completely unsolved. As the sophistication of path requirements increases, so too does the likelihood of running into a truly difficult challenge.

When you play a game with AI characters that can move freely in the simulated world, try looking for cases where the AI favors "shortest" paths over more realistic or genuinely optimal paths. The AI characters taking such routes often lose all credibility. Players still spot completely pathological cases such as agents getting stuck against walls or running into each other in the wild. Watching game AI agents navigate their surroundings with a critical eye turns up plenty of opportunities for improvement.

Finding the shortest path is very close to a solved problem (in cases where the environment is sufficiently simple or amenable to an accurate search heuristic), but finding truly *great* paths remains an area of ongoing exploration.

1.5.2 Conversations

Games that offer the player the opportunity to engage in conversation with AI characters have traditionally encountered a series of nasty obstacles. Typically, game conversations are either purely scripted (e.g., the player may watch a noninteractive "cutscene" of the conversation) or, at best, powered by simple dialogue trees. This is almost entirely due to the difficulty of making genuine conversational interactions possible with an AI agent.

Dialogue trees remain popular but suffer from a geometric increase in the amount of necessary content as the degree of branching goes up. The more possibilities the conversation can explore and the longer the conversation might last, the more text must be written (and, perhaps, audio recorded) to cover all the options. As such, most dialogue trees stay quite limited and often seem artificially constrained to the player.

Developing better conversational interactions with AI quickly encroaches on natural language processing territory. Eventually, it becomes impractical to hand-author (and possibly record) all the dialogues possible. The extreme option is to parse the player's input on the fly and generate believable responses dynamically as well.

Tempting as this may sound, natural language processing is widely regarded as a highly difficult AI problem. While great inroads have been made in the area over the past decades, the natural language field as a whole still offers plenty of interesting challenges to tackle.

Intuitively, it seems that there must be some intermediate solutions between canned dialogue and full natural language conversation. While some approaches are available already, they typically rely on an enormous corpus of knowledge to operate—something that may not be practical to include in a game. Moreover, this knowledge base often comes from real-world data such as Internet resources, making it useless for an AI that is supposed to exist in, say, medieval Europe.

Some highly noteworthy exploration into conversations for games exists, and the results hold promise and excitement for anyone interested in better human/AI interactions [Evans 12, Orkin 07, Mateas 03, McCoy 13]. Even still, there is plenty of fertile ground for further investigation.

Any player who has complained about dialogue trees and their limited selection has felt firsthand the constraints of typical human/AI conversations. Even widely celebrated "chat bots" in the spirit of *ELIZA* [Weizenbaum 66] can be confounded or otherwise reveal their artificiality within the confines of relatively normal interactions.

Try listening to the conversations between "your" player character and other AI characters in a contemporary game. Every time something important cannot be said, every time something totally "wrong" is available as a choice, and every time you get bored of hearing the exact same dialogue dozens of times, think about the state of the art in human/AI interaction and where it might be pushed further.

1.5.3 Dynamic Storylines

As the cost of developing high-quality games continues to increase, it is more important than ever to maximize the value of every ounce of effort invested in a game's creation. The tension between the finite budget for developing a title and the amount of content the players expect from the final product requires careful balance. Budgets can only grow so large before it is simply impossible for a title to be profitable at the price points expected by consumers.

One way to address this problem is via *replayability*—if a title can be enjoyed multiple times without growing stale, the value to the player is increased, while the cost of producing that game remains fixed. Games like Tetris or chess are infinitely replayable, whereas a heavily narrative-driven, "cinematic" experience might only be worth playing through once. But what if we want to make a game that has a rich storytelling aspect *and* can be replayed many times?

There are many challenges in building a highly branching narrative with numerous opportunities for things to play out differently. In a sense, the problem closely resembles a more generalized version of the issue with dialogue trees. This is where dynamic storytelling enters the scene. Instead of hand-authoring all of the possible narrative states of the game, we use some AI to take on the role of storyteller.

The storyteller must manage pacing, tension, difficulty level, plot points, and so on, while simultaneously reacting in a believable and entertaining way to the player's decisions. This may even wind up feeding into the knowledge representation used by a dynamic conversation system, so that the player can converse with characters in the game world about what has been going on.

A crucial element of interactive storytelling is guiding the narrative toward critical moments and ultimately to a conclusion. This is difficult enough even without considering players who attempt to deliberately derail the story. As the players' freedom to interact with the game world increases, so do the number of possible outcomes of their actions. A major challenge with dynamic storytelling is to produce this guided narrative without feeling forced or jarring.

Steps have certainly been taken in this vein, such as the AI director in *Left 4 Dead* [Newell 08]. Even classic "choose your own adventure" style narratives can be considered a prototypical form of dynamic storytelling. There are two contrasting dynamic storytelling approaches represented here. For "choose your own adventure," the player selects a path through a preconfigured set of possible storylines. There is a strong sense in which the player is being told a story. On the flip side, AI director style systems focus on generating an interesting experience for the player to have; the story is emergent and may even only really become apparent once the player recounts that experience.

Both methods are completely valid, although the role of AI systems can be markedly different. (Indeed, the "choose your own adventure" book format predates sophisticated game AI.) In any event, there is a substantial amount of possibility in the field of dynamic storytelling, and the ultimate role of AI as storyteller is still being defined.

For anyone who has played a well-run pen and paper role-playing game, or even experienced a rousing session of "Let's Pretend," it isn't hard to find storytelling deficiencies in computer games. Eventually, someone playing is bound to try something that wasn't specifically accounted for in the game's construction. While this can lead to entertaining (albeit somewhat absurd) results, it more often leads to mild annoyance and disappointment.

When playing a highly narrative-driven game, take time to observe the ways in which player choices are handled. Note when choices are made available and the range of options provided. Try doing something that subtly (or wildly) clashes with the sorts of choices you are expected to be making. Anything that just doesn't quite "work" is likely to be a sign of the fringes of where computer-guided narrative has been taken. See if you can think of ways the developer could (practically and cost-effectively) extend the freedom of the player and the replayability of the game, without compromising narrative integrity.

1.5.4 Player Modeling

Software developers from across the tech sector often lament that we cannot intuit the true intentions of the player (or, more generally, the user). The available mechanisms for human/computer interaction are fundamentally limited. It should come as no real surprise that the full thought process of the human mind loses something in translation when crammed through the funnel of pushing keys and clicking mouse buttons.

A tremendous amount of effort goes into developing user experiences and researching how to streamline them. Most game studios are familiar with the routine of *usability testing*, where outside players are invited to play a game in development. By observing these players, the developer can glean huge amounts of valuable insight into where the game's user experience shines and where it needs improvement.

Generally, the feedback obtained from usability testing is only available during the development cycle of the game itself. Once the game ships, it is no longer viable to put eye-tracking hardware on each player or rig them up with electrodes. Outside of controlled, laboratory-style settings, we have a limited toolset for understanding how our players are thinking and how they are likely to behave.

Thankfully, the trappings of a high-tech behavioral science lab are not mandatory for analyzing player behavior. One increasingly popular technique is to harvest statistics from thousands or millions of players, collect them automatically via the Internet, and then comb through them for interesting revelations. Online games have been doing this extensively for years, although there is no strict reason why it could not be done for any game with access to a network connection.

Ultimately, the dream of collecting all these data is to build a *player model*. This is a statistical description of how players are likely to behave, often separating them into major groupings based on their play style. If this model is sufficiently accurate, it becomes possible not just to study player actions after the fact but also to predict *future* actions.

Once we have a mechanism for predicting player behavior, we can start customizing the game experience for each individual player based on the model. If a particular player is known to enjoy exploring large areas of the game world and collecting rare items, for example, the game can dynamically highlight similar opportunities for the player, or even generate new ones on the fly.

Much of this is already possible from a technical standpoint. In fact, games such as *League of Legends* exploit player modeling for, among other things, designing new content updates, which directly drive revenue streams [Lin 14]. However, the process is often long, arduous, and highly error prone.

Ideally, player modeling should be able to customize a game as it is being played, with response times measured in seconds—if not faster. Accomplishing this may seem like a predominantly mathematical task, but AI techniques for heuristically solving complex modeling problems are intensely promising.

Statistical modeling is still far more art than science and requires a substantial degree of expertise to apply effectively. Moreover, the challenges of gathering and processing millions of data points—sometimes millions *per day*—should not be underestimated. Turnaround time for player modeling is often measured in days—a far cry from the fractions of a second available during live gameplay.

While monetization opportunities are often the focus of research in this realm, there is plenty of fodder for improving the game experience itself. It can be tempting to limit our exploration of player modeling to simply trying to predict what a player wants or will do. A much more intriguing option is predicting what the player does not expect but will still be pleasantly surprised to discover.

Find any group of players discussing a particular game, and you're likely to find divergent opinions on the nature of the game experience itself. What if games could tailor themselves specifically to their individual audiences and deliver an excellent experience for everyone? One of the trickiest problems in game design is appealing to a broad enough audience to be financially successful without overtly diluting the purpose of the game itself. AI has the potential to significantly impact that balance.

1.5.5 Modeling and Displaying Emotion

The past several years have seen animation becoming an increasingly important element of game AI's presentation to the player. Without high-fidelity movement, it can be difficult to get AI agents to appear convincing and intelligent. While much progress has been made in animating humanoid bodies, there is still a lot of work to be done on the more subtle and powerful portrayal of emotions.

As early as the 1940s, it was noted that people tended to attribute emotions to animated shapes based purely on their spatial relationships and motions [Heider 44]. Until fairly recently, very few games could provide the visual fidelity required to do much more than this in terms of conveying emotion and intent.

Animation technology is already capable of incredible feats when it comes to facial details and expressions. Building a sufficient model of emotional state is also clearly well within reach, as *The Sims* demonstrated. The major source of difficulty lies in the realm of audio. Without the ability to modulate voices realistically, games often fall back on reusing voice assets in situations where they sound jarringly out of place.

Consider any moment when the immersion of a game experience has been broken by a character seeming stilted, robotic, or otherwise emotionally unrealistic. While carefully sculpted narrative moments and cutscenes can generally portray emotional state fairly well, the bulk of gameplay is often fraught with such moments of surreal absurdity. Modeling and displaying emotional richness will be essential to mitigating this in future games.

Advances in this area will unlock a vast amount of potential for AI characters and liberate game developers from the constraints of the fairly limited emotional palette currently available. Combined with dynamically generated dialogue and AI-assisted storytelling, emotional modeling represents a tremendous opportunity for creating games that are more immersive and convincing than ever before.

1.5.6 Social Relationships

Once AI characters are able to model and display emotions, we quickly run headlong into another difficult problem: what happens when two AI characters interact with each other? Delivering a believable scenario requires some degree of simulated social interaction. Some games have already experimented heavily with this [McCoy 13], but for the most part, relationships between AI characters have historically been rigidly scripted out by designers and writers.

What qualifies as a reasonable model of social behavior in a game might differ substantially from models used in more academic and scientific circles. A game's setting and narrative may only call for a limited number of interactions between AI characters, for instance, permitting the social model to be substantially simplified. On the other end of the spectrum, role-playing games or open-world "sandbox" games might benefit from fairly sophisticated simulations of social interaction.

As with emotions, however, modeling social behavior is not the end of the story. If the player doesn't have a way to observe the model's state and how it evolves during play, it may as well not exist. In fact, since the player has no way to understand why an NPC has made a particular choice, a hidden model can do more harm than good. The results of this social simulation will be most effectively portrayed when a variety of expressive options are available to an AI character. Generating dialogue, displaying emotional status, and selecting relevant animations will all be important parts of selling the social model to players.

1.5.7 Scale

Games are quite a bit different from many other realms of AI research in that they are constrained fairly heavily in terms of computational resources. A game might need to be playable on a cell phone, for instance. Even on more capable hardware, it is not uncommon for the lion's share of the resources to be dedicated to graphics and physics. By contrast, more traditional AI applications may have an entire machine—or network of machines—to themselves. Game AI systems are typically constrained to around ten percent of the available processing power, and even the most AI-intensive games rarely allow more than twenty percent. Moreover, many games require near-real-time interactivity with the player. The combined limitations on memory, CPU resources, and execution time can be fiendishly difficult to overcome.

Another important challenge for games is that they are typically pushing the performance of the host machine to the limit. Programming techniques that are marginally inefficient (e.g., creation of memory fragmentation, frequent cache misses) can easily add up to prohibitive performance problems, even if isolated systems are well within their defined limits.

The difficulties here lie more in engineering than theoretical AI techniques, although careful selection of techniques has a tremendous impact on the degree of ingenuity required. Understanding the time and memory requirements of various solutions is vital to selecting appropriate technical strategies.

Individual AI agents are becoming increasingly sophisticated. Decision-making techniques are often quite efficient in isolation, but the same is not always true for environmental awareness, perception, searches, dynamic state-space analysis methods, and so on. Gathering enough data to make an *informed* decision, or to execute that decision in a complex environment, can be costly.

Creating a small number of highly believable agents is challenging, but well within reach of modern game AI techniques. However, many games are increasingly vast in geographical terms, and others may call for huge numbers of agents interacting simultaneously. As AI agents proliferate, performance and memory usage become serious concerns.

It may be tempting to conclude that these challenges will eventually dissipate as computing hardware continues to advance. However, the slowing pace of CPU speed improvements and the ongoing difficulties surrounding effective use of massively parallel architectures dampen this hope substantially. Worse, history has shown that more powerful hardware tends to lead to a demand for correspondingly richer game experiences. For example, Damián Isla (AI developer on the *Halo* series) once remarked that *Halo 3* was actually able to do *fewer* line of sight checks than *Halo 2*, despite running on substantially more powerful hardware [Isla 09]. Environments had become so much more detailed and complex that the increased cost of an individual check outstripped the pace of Moore's law.

With these sorts of trade-offs facing developers on a routine basis, it is likely that scale will continue to be a source of interesting problems for quite some time to come.

1.5.8 Content Explosion

In the vein of practical challenges, the sheer quantity of hand-crafted assets and content used by even medium-scale contemporary games can be daunting. To move around the world convincingly, AI agents typically draw on a library of animations; more sophisticated movement requires a corresponding increase in the animation effort necessary to maintain a given level of desired fidelity.

Other types of assets can impose significant limitations on the expressivity of AI as well. If audio recordings are used for verbal communication, an AI character is restricted to "speaking" only the lines that have been recorded. Even without the limitation of voice-over recordings, hand-authored text for dialogue can represent a significant volume of content as well. For an AI agent to interact meaningfully with its surrounding world, the agent needs a selection of props and points of interest, as well as knowledge of how to make use of them. Such content can also proliferate quickly as world complexity increases.

In general, the so-called "content explosion" problem is becoming a substantial obstacle to the continued advance of game realism, fidelity, and richness. Every individual bit of detail that goes into the world leads to a combinatorial increase in the amount of content required to effectively make use of that detail from an AI perspective. Eventually, the cost of creating the content dwarfs the potential benefits of the addition itself, and reality slams headlong into a sort of upper bound on the sophistication of the game world.

Perhaps the most visible approach to addressing this problem (besides just accepting limited scope as a fact of life) lies in the realm of *procedurally generated content*. In essence, a computable algorithm is used to augment (or even supplant) direct human creativity. By relegating some portion of the content generation problem to an automated and repeatable process, the overhead of producing content can be diminished dramatically.

Procedural techniques have been used (with varying degrees of success) in areas such as world or map generation, storyline or "quest" creation, and even the dynamic emission of high-quality dialogue and narrative text. Animation already benefits from procedural augmentation, and research into broadening the applicability of procedural techniques to animation continues. Voice synthesis and recognition technologies advance at a rapid pace, offering the very real possibility of replacing human actors with computer voices in the not-so-distant future.

As an example of the sorts of challenges that procedural generation faces, though, voice synthesis becomes dramatically more difficult as the level of fidelity increases. Computers have been able to make rudimentary utterances for decades, and yet successfully portraying emotional cues—or even generating truly human-sounding voices—remains an area of ongoing research. To underscore the difficulty, the game *Portal* (which included an AI entity as a major character) modified the recordings of a human voice actor to sound synthesized, rather than trying to make a fully synthesized voice sound sufficiently human [Wolpaw 07].

In general, procedural content generation represents a promising but largely undeveloped frontier. While the theoretical benefits are considerable, it remains to be seen how much effort it will take to attain them.

1.5.9 The Unexplored

Beyond the relatively short list of difficulties enumerated here, there lies a vast realm of uncertainty. There is without a doubt a long list of questions that have yet to even be asked. In a very real sense, we have barely begun to scratch the surface of what game AI can do.

New forms of technology are constantly arriving on the scene, and a large portion of them can and will influence the direction of gaming in the future. Wherever these devices and mediums take us, game AI will be sure to follow close behind. For anyone with an interest in game AI, this is an exciting time. Not only do we have the opportunity to leverage a vast amount of existing technical capability and know-how, but we can also look forward excitedly to the games and AI of tomorrow.

1.6 Conclusion

With the proliferation of computer-powered games comes an ever-increasing desire to push the boundaries of the experiences those games can offer. As the seemingly limitless imagination of designers continues to generate fantastic new ideas for players to explore, there is no doubt that AI will play a powerful role in delivering those experiences.

Although many areas of game implementation are fairly well understood, there is still ample room for innovation and discovery. Game AI is no exception to this pattern. Developers have amassed a considerable body of formalized techniques and standard approaches to common problems—but many more challenges remain to be conquered.

The remainder of this book explores a diverse and rich slice of knowledge from contributors throughout the game AI community. The frontiers of game AI have advanced quickly over the past decades, and perhaps one of the most exciting possibilities created by books like this one is that any one of our readers could be instrumental in pushing those boundaries forward for games yet to come.

References

[Abercrombie 14] Abercrombie, J. 2014. Bringing bioShock infinite's Elizabeth to life: An AI development postmortem. *Lecture, Game Developer's Conference AI Summit 2014*, San Francisco, CA.

[Barnes 02] Barnes, J. and Hutchens, J. 2002. Testing undefined behavior as a result of learning. In *AI Game Programming Wisdom*, ed. S. Rabin. Boston, MA: Charles River Media.

[Dijkstra 59] Dijkstra, E.W. 1959. A note on two problems in connexion with graphs. *Numerische Mathematik* 1: 269–271.

[Evans 12] Evans, R. and Short, E. 2012. Beyond Eliza: Constructing socially engaging AI. *Lecture, Game Developer's Conference AI Summit 2012,* San Francisco, CA.

[Hart 68] Hart, P.E., Nilsson, N.J., and Raphael, B. 1968. A formal basis for the heuristic determination of minimum cost paths. *IEEE Transactions on Systems Science and Cybernetics SSC4* 4(2): 100–107.

[Heider 44] Heider, F. and Simmel, M. 1944. An experimental study of apparent behavior. *American Journal of Psychology* 57: 243–259.

[Isla 09] Isla, D. 2009. *Artificial Intelligence Panel*. Boston, MA: Post Mortem Group.

[Lin 14] Lin, J. 2014. *Keynote, New Economic Models and Opportunities for Digital Games*, York, United Kingdom.

[Manslow 01] Manslow, J. 2001. Using a neural network in a game: A concrete example. In *Game Programming Gems*, Vol. 2, ed. M. DeLoura. Boston, MA: Cengage Learning.

[Mateas 03] Mateas, M. and Stern, A. 2003. Façade: An experiment in building a fully-realized interactive demo. *Lecture, Game Developer's Conference 2003*, San Jose, CA.

[McCoy 13] McCoy, J., Treanor, M., Samuel, B., Reed, A., Mateas, M., and Wardrip-Fruin, N. 2013. Prom week: Designing past the game/story dilemma. *Proceedings of the Eighth International Conference on the Foundations of Digital Games,* Chania, Crete, Greece.

[Newell 08] Newell, G. 2008. Gabe Newell writes for edge. http://www.edge-online.com/features/gabe-newell-writes-edge/(accessed January 17, 2015).

[Orkin 07] Orkin, J. and Roy, D. 2007. The restaurant game: Learning social behavior and language from thousands of players online. *Journal of Game Development* 3(1): 39–60.

[Redding 09] Redding, P. 2009. Aarf! Arf arf arf: Talking to the player with barks. *Lecture, Game Developer's Conference 2009*, San Francisco, CA.

[Schwab 14] Schwab, B. 2014. AI postmortem: Hearthstone. *Lecture, Game Developer's Conference AI Summit 2014*, San Francisco, CA.

[Sunshine-Hill 14] Sunshine-Hill, B. 2014. Environmentally conscious AI: Improving spatial analysis and reasoning. *Lecture, Game Developer's Conference AI Summit 2014*, San Francisco, CA.

[Tozour 13] Tozour, P. 2013. From the behavior up: When the AI is the design. *Lecture, Game Developer's Conference AI Summit 2013*, San Francisco, CA.

[Weizenbaum 66] Weizenbaum, J. 1966. ELIZA—A computer program for the study of natural language communication between man and machine. *Communications of the ACM* 9(1): 36–45.

[Wolpaw 07] Wolpaw, E. 2007. Developer commentary. *Portal*. http://theportalwiki.com/wiki/Portal_developer_commentary (accessed January 17, 2015).

2

Combat Dialogue in *FEAR*

The Illusion of Communication

Jeff Orkin

2.1 Introduction

If the AI didn't say it, it didn't happen. This was the AI-design philosophy behind the squad behaviors in *FEAR*. There is no point in expending significant effort implementing complex AI if the player doesn't notice it. In developing *FEAR*, we found that having AI characters vocalize and commentate while executing squad behaviors is a highly effective means of bringing whiz-bang AI to the player's attention. While game developers typically remember *FEAR* for its Goal-Oriented Action Planning [Orkin 06], it is obvious from the reviews and forum chatter that the coordinated squad behaviors are what stood out for *gameplayers*.

2.2 From Barks to Dialogues

The guiding principle behind combat banter in *FEAR* is that whenever possible, AI characters should talk to each other about what they are doing. Rather than having an individual character react with a *bark*, multiple characters carry on a short dialogue that broadcasts mental state and intentions to the player.

Let's clarify this with barks from some prototypical first person shooter (FPS) gameplay situations. In the typical FPS, when you fire at an enemy, he cries out in pain. When an AI detects the player for the first time, he shouts, "There he is!" When the agent loses sight of the player, he exclaims, "Where did he go?!" When you land that headshot that takes out the enemy, he says … nothing, because he's dead. And dead men don't speak.

Why are the AI always "talking to themselves?" Often, these barks sound contrived, out of context, and fail to convincingly sell the situation to the player.

How can we improve upon these age old, tried and true, ever so familiar FPS tropes? In *FEAR*, where enemies were introduced in squads of 4 or 5, we turned each of these situations (and more) into a *dialogue* rather than a bark. We authored a variety of canned dialogues (sequences of 2 or 3 lines) that we could trigger when enough squad members were in proximity and some criteria was met.

Instead of having the enemy who got shot cry out in pain, someone else on the squad would yell, "What's your status?" The injured AI replies, "I'm hit!" or "I'm alright!" This dialogue serves multiple gameplay purposes. First, it tells the player that he hit someone. Second, it reinforces the illusion that AI are working together as a squad in a humanlike way. Lastly, it hints to the player the enemy's state of health.

When the AI are in pursuit as the player cunningly slips out of sight, they engage in a dialogue like in Figure 2.1, "Anyone see him?" "He's behind the tree!" The simple design task of tagging identifiable regions of space has a big bang for the buck. Stealthily crawling through the air ducts in *FEAR*, and hearing the enemy shout, "He's in the ceiling!", was certainly a memorable, "oh sh*t!" moment, for many players.

Dialogue can also be used to explain a lack of action to players. If you're firing at someone and they're not repositioning, they look like dumb, unintelligent, broken AI. But if you overhear the dialogue "Get out of there!" "I've got nowhere to go!" you can understand that the AI is aware of the threat, and wants to move, but can't find a better position to move to.

Similarly, if you find yourself in a stalemate with the AI, where no one is moving, it may feel like an AI failure. AI in *FEAR* kept track of regions of space where they observed comrades taking fire, or dying. They would refuse to move into these regions for some period of time, resulting in a dialogue between two squad members like "Advance!" "No f***ing way!"

In terms of production budget, this last point may be the most valuable of all. Dialogue can be used to create the illusion of behavior that has never even been implemented. In *FEAR*, enemy AI kept track of how many of their squad members had been killed. They could call out, "Man down!", "I've got two men down!", etc. When only the last squad member was left standing, he could call in reinforcements, "I need reinforcements!" In

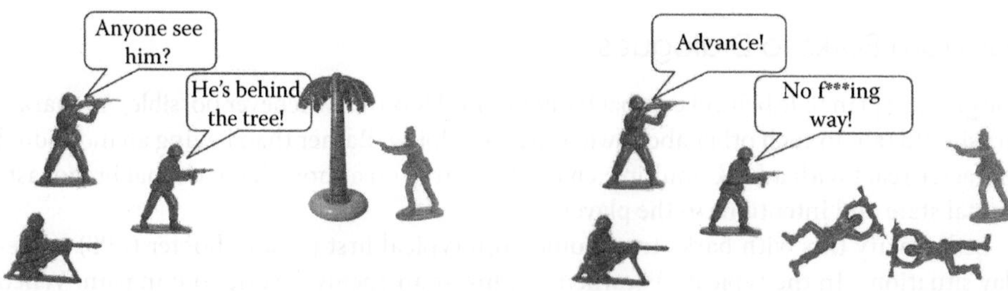

Figure 2.1

Dialogue works better than barks for conveying agent intelligence or even intelligence that doesn't actually exist. Dialogue convinces players that the AI is actually coordinating against them.

any FPS, it is likely that the player will see more enemies sooner or later, and if the player just heard, "I need reinforcements!" he is likely to draw the conclusion that these are the soldiers that the last guy called in. We never wrote any code for the AI to call in reinforcements, but the reviews said we did!

It's interesting to note that reverberations of what we pioneered in *FEAR* still echo today, with games like *The Last of Us* using similar dialogue tricks among the AI to intensify and polish the experience [McIntosh 15]. While it seems like such a simple trick, the impact it can make on players should not be underestimated.

2.3 Conclusion

We often fixate on animation as the primary means of AI expressing mental state. However, don't underestimate the power of language. As humans, we put ourselves on a pedestal due to our capacity for using language and judge other beings accordingly. Our perception of intelligence is elevated at a subconscious level when we see others who can use language effectively. Keep this in mind when designing behavior, especially social behavior. Use canned dialogue early and often. Impress your friends. Impress reviewers. And leave players with moments they'll never forget.

References

[McIntosh 15] McIntosh, T. 2015. Human enemy AI in The Last of Us. In *Game AI Pro²: Collected Wisdom of Game AI Professionals*, ed. S. Rabin. Boca Raton, FL: A K Peters/CRC Press.

[Orkin 06] Orkin, J. 2006. 3 states and a plan: The AI of F.E.A.R., *Game Developers Conference*, San Francisco, CA.

3

Dual-Utility Reasoning

Kevin Dill

3.1 Introduction

Utility-based approaches to decision making examine the situation in the game at the moment a decision is being made, calculate the *goodness* (which is often called things like utility, priority, weight, or score) of each option using a heuristic function, and then drive decision making using that value. This can be contrasted against purely Boolean decision-making approaches, such as the typical finite state machine (FSM) or behavior tree, which evaluate a series of black-or-white, yes-or-no questions in order to select an option for execution.

The advantage of utility-based AI is that it is better able to account for the subtle nuance of the situation when making its decision. In other words, in situations where more than one option is valid, utility-based AI will base its decision on an evaluation of the relative appropriateness and/or importance of each option instead of picking at random or simply taking the first valid option that it finds. At the same time, because the heuristic functions are hand-authored, the game designers retain reasonably tight control over the behavior of the AI and can thus better ensure that the player's experience will fit with their design.

One point that cannot be overemphasized is the importance of calculating each option's utility in game, at run time. It is not enough to assign fixed weights to the options a priori. Only by evaluating them based on the situation at the moment when the decision is being made can you achieve the responsive, dynamic behavior that utility-based AI promises.

3.2 Dual-Utility Reasoning

There are two common ways of using utility to make a decision. The first, which we will call *absolute utility*, simply evaluates each option and takes the one with the highest score. The second, *relative utility*, selects an option at random, but it uses the score of each option to define the probability that it will be selected. The probability for selecting an option (P_O) is determined by dividing the utility of that option (U_O) by the total utility of all options:

$$P_O = \frac{U_O}{\sum_{i=1}^{n} U_i} \tag{3.1}$$

This approach is referred to as *weight-based random* and is implemented as follows:

1. Add up the total weight of all valid options (i.e., those with a weight greater than 0).
2. Pick a random number between 0 and the total weight from step 1.
3. Go through the valid options one at a time and reduce the random number by the weight for each option. If the result is less than or equal to zero, pick this option. Otherwise, continue on to the next.

Relative and absolute utilities each have advantages and disadvantages. Absolute utility is best when you want to ensure that the AI always takes the most appropriate action available. Unfortunately, it can become predictable since, given a particular situation, it always does the same thing. In contrast, relative utility avoids the rigid predictability of absolute utility. By picking at random, it ensures a certain amount of variation, while still giving preference to the most appropriate choices. Nevertheless, while it *prefers* to pick good options, there is always some chance that an option with very low utility will be selected. This can easily make your AI look stupid. We can reduce the chance that a low-weight option will be selected by squaring the weights or eliminate it by screening out the lowest weight options, but this quickly becomes a balancing act that is hard to perfect and harder to maintain.

Dual-utility reasoning is an approach that combines absolute and relative utilities into a synergistic whole. It avoids the weaknesses of both approaches by combining them together and is also more flexible and expressive for the game designers.

The big idea is that rather than assigning a single utility value to each option, we assign two: a rank and a weight. *Rank* uses absolute utility to divide the options into categories, and we only select options from the best category. *Weight* is used to evaluate options within the context of their category. Once we've found the category with the highest rank, we select from among the options in that category using weight-based random.

The algorithm for actually selecting an option is as follows: First, go through all of the options and eliminate any that have a weight that is less than or equal to zero. These options can't be selected by the weight-based portion of the reasoner anyway, and eliminating them now makes the process simpler. In addition, this gives the designers a convenient way to mark an option as *invalid* or *inappropriate given current circumstances*. If an option shouldn't be selected, simply set its weight to zero and it will be rejected regardless of rank.

Second, find the highest *rank* among the options that remain, and eliminate any options whose rank is less than this. Again, what we are doing is finding the most important category and eliminating the options that don't belong to it.

Third, find the highest *weight* from among the options that remain, and eliminate options whose weight is less than some percentage of this. This step is optional, and the percentage that is used should be configurable on a per-decision basis. Conceptually, what we are doing is finding the options that really aren't all that appropriate (and thus have been given very low weight) and ensuring that the random number generator doesn't decide to pick them anyway. What remains are plausible (not stupid) options.

Finally, we use weight-based random to select from among those options that remain.

Once again, the four steps are as follows:

1. Eliminate the options with a weight of zero.
2. Find the highest rank category, and eliminate options that don't belong to it.
3. Find the best remaining option (i.e., the one with the highest weight), and eliminate options that are much worse (i.e., much lower weight) than it.
4. Use weight-based random to select from the options that remain.

As described earlier, the major strength of dual-utility reasoning is that it allows you to divide your options into categories and select from among those categories using absolute utility. Once this is done, we can use relative utility to pick from among the options within the best category in a random but reasonable way.

3.3 Dual-Utility Reasoning in *Zoo Tycoon 2*

In *Zoo Tycoon 2* [Blue Fang Games 04], the AI for both the animals and guests used dual-utility reasoning. Most of the time, the characters would select options based purely on their needs (i.e., their hunger need, entertainment need, and bathroom need). These options all had a rank of 0, but their weight would vary depending on the current situation.

There were times, however, when characters were in a specific situation that had a distinct set of behaviors, and only those behaviors were appropriate. For instance, if a koala climbed up a tree, then it would have a number of tree-climbing behaviors available (including some that allowed it to get out of the tree), and these behaviors would have a higher rank (typically around 5) to ensure that the animal didn't pick some other behavior and pop out of the tree unrealistically.

Taking it a step further, the *Marine Mania* expansion pack introduced the idea of marine animal shows. These were shows where the player could train dolphins to jump through hoops, seals to play with a ball, and so forth. It was very important that when one of these shows occurred, both the animals and an appropriate number of guests showed up so that the player was rewarded for their hard work training the animals. Furthermore, the behavior of the characters during the show was very heavily scripted. The animals would go through a specific sequence where they would come in to the show tank, swim over to the trainer, wait for the whistle, do their trick, go back to the trainer, get a treat, wait for the whistle again, do their next trick, and so forth. The guests had to come to the entrance, wait in line, go in and sit, react appropriately through the show, and then exit in a timely fashion.

In order to make sure that the right behaviors were picked at the right time, we simply gave them appropriate ranks (which were all between 98 and 102) so that the *best* action at any given moment would play. These ranks were coordinated by a simple FSM, although they could have been scripted or set in other ways.

Finally, there was one behavior that took precedence over every other behavior and that was dying. We didn't want any animals coming back from the dead, so the die behavior had a rank of 1,000,000, ensuring that it trumped anything else that might happen.

3.4 Conclusion

Utility-based AI is a term used to describe approaches that, rather than using purely Boolean logic, use a heuristic function to evaluate the appropriateness of each option given the moment-to-moment situation in the game and base their decision on the resulting score. These approaches typically either take the option with the highest score or use weight-based random to pick in a way that is nondeterministic but still gives a greater chance of being selected to the *best* options.

In this chapter we introduced the idea of dual-utility reasoning. This approach combines absolute and relative utilities. Absolute utility is used to divide the options into categories and ensure that only options from the most important or most relevant category will be selected. Once that is done, relative utility is used to pick at random from among the options within that category. This helps to prevent both the predictability of absolute utility and the occasional poor choices of relative utility. In addition, it provides a bit more flexibility and expressiveness to the game designers who are responsible for configuring the AI.

Reference

[Blue Fang 04] Blue Fang Games. 2004. *Zoo Tycoon 2*. Redmond, WA: Microsoft Games Studio.

4

Vision Zones and Object Identification Certainty

Steve Rabin

4.1 Introduction

Within games it is common for human AI agents to have a very simplistic vision model. This model usually consists of three vision checks performed in this order (for efficiency reasons): distance, field of view, and ray cast. The distance check restricts how far an agent can see, the field-of-view check ensures that the agent can only see in the direction of their eyes (not behind them), and the ray cast prevents the agent from seeing through walls. These reasonable and straightforward tests culminate in a Boolean result. If all three checks pass, then the agent can see the object in question. If any of the checks fail, the agent cannot see the object.

Unfortunately, this simplistic vision model leaves a very noticeable flaw in agent behavior. Players quickly notice that an agent either sees them or not. There is no gray area. The player can be 10.001 meters away from the agent and not be seen, but if the player moves 1 millimeter closer, the agent all of a sudden sees them and reacts. Not only is this behavior odd and unrealistic, but it is easy to exploit and essentially becomes part of the gameplay, whether intentional or not.

The solution to this problem is twofold. First, we eliminate the Boolean vision model and introduce *vision zones* coupled with a new concept of *object identification certainty* [Rabin 08]. Second, we must have the agent use the object identification certainty to produce more nuanced behavior.

4.2 Vision Zones and Object Identification Certainty

Human vision is not binary, which is the core problem with the simple vision model. There are areas where our vision is great and areas where our vision is not so great. Our vision is best directly in front of us and degrades with distance or toward our periphery. This can be approximated by using several vision zones, as shown in Figure 4.1.

However, if we are to abandon the Boolean vision model, then we have to introduce some kind of continuous scale. We can clearly use a floating-point scale, for example, from 0 to 1, but then the scale must *mean* something. What does a value of 0.3 or 0.7 mean?

While it's tempting to think of the scale as representing probability, this is a flawed approach. Does 0.3 mean that the agent has a 30% chance of seeing an object? That's not really what humans experience and it has odd implications. How often should an agent roll a die to check if it sees an object? If the die is rolled often enough, eventually the object will be seen, even if it has a very low value, such as 0.1. Additionally, this isn't much different from the Boolean vision model, but it has the added detriment that it's more unpredictable and probably inexplicable to the player (the player will have difficulty building a model in their head of what the agent is experiencing; thus, the AI's behavior will appear random and arbitrary).

A better interpretation of the [0, 1] scale is for it to represent an *object identification certainty*. If the value is a little higher than zero, the agent sees the object but just isn't sure what it is. Essentially, the object is too blurry or vague to identify. As the value climbs toward one, then the certainty of knowing the identity of the object becomes much higher. This avoids any randomness and is more consistent with what humans experience. The numbers within Figure 4.1 show the object identification certainty within each vision zone, on a scale of 0–1.

4.2.1 Vision Sweet Spot

Human vision is most acute directly ahead and many games modify the traditional vision cone to reflect this. Further, it has been found to produce better results in games when this sweet spot first widens and then narrows with distance, as shown in Figure 4.1. Variations of this widening and then narrowing of ideal vision have been in use in games for a long time [Rabin 08] and have recently been used in games such as *Splinter Cell: Blacklist* [Walsh 15] and *The Last of Us* [McIntosh 15].

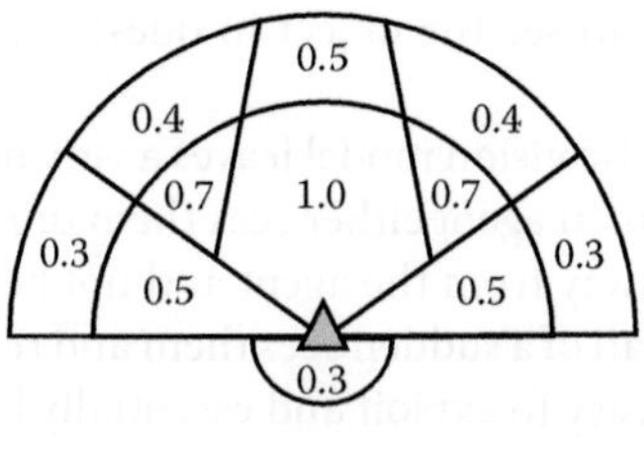

Figure 4.1

An example vision zone model with the associated object identification certainty values within each zone.

4.3 Incorporating Movement and Camouflage

If the zone values represent object identification certainty, then there are other aspects of an object that might affect this value other than location within a zone. For example, objects that are moving are much easier to spot than objects that are perfectly still. Additionally, objects are much harder to identify when they are camouflaged against their environment, because of either poor lighting or having similar colors or patterns to the background.

These additional factors can be incorporated into the vision model by giving an object a bonus or penalty based on the attribute. For example, if an object is moving, it might add 0.3 to its object identification certainty. If an object is camouflaged, perhaps it subtracts 0.3 from its object identification certainty. Therefore, if an object in the peripheral vision would normally have an object identification certainty of 0.3, then a camouflaged object in that same spot would essentially be invisible. Please note that the example zone value numbers and bonus/penalty values used here are for illustration purposes and finding appropriate numbers would depend on the particular game and would require tuning and testing.

4.4 Producing Appropriate Behavior from Identification Certainty

The final challenge is to figure out what the agent should do with these identification certainty values. With the simple vision model, it was simple. If the object was seen, it was 100% identified, and the agent would react. With this new vision model, it must be decided how an agent reacts when an object is only identified by 0.3 or 0.7, for example.

When dealing with partial identification, it now falls into the realm of producing an appropriate and nuanced reaction and selling it convincingly to the player. This will require several different animations and vocalizations. With low identification values, perhaps the agent leans in and squints toward the object or casually glances toward it. Note that as the agent adjusts their head, their vision model correspondingly turns as well. What once only had a 0.3 identification could shoot up to 0.8 or 1.0 simply by turning to look at it.

Another response to partial identification is to start a dialogue with the other agents, such as "Do you see anything up ahead?" or "I thought I saw something behind the boxes" [Orkin 15]. This in turn might encourage other agents to cautiously investigate the stimulus.

Deciding on an appropriate response to partial information will depend on both the game situation and your team's creativity in coming up with appropriate responses. Unfortunately, more nuanced behavior usually requires extra animation and vocalization assets to be created.

4.4.1 Alternative 1: Object Certainty with Time

An alternative approach is to require the player to be seen for some amount of time before being identified. This is the strategy used in *The Last of Us* where the player would only be seen if they were in the AI's vision sweet spot for 1–2 s [McIntosh 15]. Although not implemented in *The Last of Us*, the object identification certainty values from Figure 4.1 could be used to help determine how many seconds are required to be seen.

4.4.2 Alternative 2: Explicit Detection Feedback

A slightly different tactic in producing a more nuanced vision model is to explicitly show the player how close they are to being detected, as in the *Splinter Cell* series [Walsh 15]. *Splinter Cell* shows a stealth meter that rises as the player becomes more noticeable in the environment. This is a more gameplay-oriented approach that forces the player to directly focus on monitoring and managing the meter.

4.5 Conclusion

Vision models that push for more realism allow for more interesting agent behavior as well as allow for more engaging gameplay. Consider how your game's vision models can be enhanced and what new kinds of gameplay opportunities this might provide. However, be ready to address with animations, vocalizations, or UI elements how this enhanced model will be adequately conveyed to the player.

References

[McIntosh 15] McIntosh, T. 2015. Human enemy AI in The Last of Us. In *Game AI Pro²: Collected Wisdom of Game AI Professionals*, ed. S. Rabin. Boca Raton, FL: A K Peters/CRC Press.

[Orkin 15] Orkin, J. 2015. Combat dialogue in F.E.A.R.: The illusion of communication. In *Game AI Pro²: Collected Wisdom of Game AI Professionals*, ed. S. Rabin. Boca Raton, FL: A K Peters/CRC Press.

[Rabin 08] Rabin, S. and Delp, M. 2008. Designing a realistic and unified agent sensing model. In *Game Programming Gems 7*, ed. S. Rabin. Boston, MA: Charles River Media.

[Walsh 15] Walsh, M. 2015. Modeling perception and awareness in Splinter Cell: Blacklist. In *Game AI Pro²: Collected Wisdom of Game AI Professionals*, ed. S. Rabin. Boca Raton, FL: A K Peters/CRC Press.

5

Agent Reaction Time

How Fast Should an AI React?

Steve Rabin

5.1 Introduction

Modeling human behavior is a core aspect of game AI, which raises a very simple, yet important question: *How fast should an enemy AI react to seeing the player?*

Like many questions concerning human behavior, it is difficult to answer precisely and largely depends on context. Researchers have investigated human response time for over 100 years, trying to time the inner workings of the brain in an area of study known as mental chronometry [Posner 05].

However, if you want the quick and dirty answer to what should be used for an AI's reaction time, then let's just spill the beans. It's somewhere between 0.2 and 0.4 seconds, possibly longer depending on context. If you're curious as to which exact number to use and where these numbers come from, you'll need to read further!

5.2 Context Is Key

There are two primary situations, studied by cognitive psychologists and neuroscientists, which are commonly applicable to game AI and result in different reaction times:

1. *Simple reaction time*: An AI agent is aiming at a doorway, expecting an enemy to come through. When the enemy is finally seen, the agent pulls the trigger and the gun fires. We want to know the time between the enemy appearing in the agent's vision and the gun fired. This time period is modeling the time taken for the agent's brain to recognize the presence of the stimulus, the time to turn that recognition into a decision to fire, the time for the finger muscle to be told to contract, and the time to physically pull the trigger until the gun fires.
2. *Recognition or go/no-go time*: An AI agent is aiming at a doorway, expecting either a fellow teammate or an enemy to come through. When someone is seen in the doorway, the AI must recognize if it is a teammate or an enemy, then only pull the trigger if it is an enemy. What makes this more difficult than a simple reaction time is that the agent must discern between two different possible stimuli. We want to know the time between the enemy appearing in the agent's vision and the gun fired. This time period is modeling the time taken for the agent's brain to see the stimulus, the time to recognize it is an enemy, the time to turn that recognition into a decision to fire, the time for the finger muscle to be told to contract, and the time to physically pull the trigger until the gun fires.

It was recognized by Donders, a Dutch physiologist and ophthalmologist, in 1868 that a simple reaction time is faster than a go/no-go reaction time [Donders 69]. It has also been found that the weaker the intensity of the stimulus, the slower the reaction time [Luce 86].

A further complication with context is whether the AI agent is experiencing a momentary attentional lapse, which is common in humans and would cause much more variability in reaction times.

5.3 What Does Cognitive Research Tell Us?

Fortunately, researchers have determined average times for our two primary situations.

5.3.1 Simple Reaction Time

In the context of a simple reaction time, the mean time of college-age individuals for an auditory stimulus is 0.16 s and the mean time for a visual stimulus is 0.19 s [Kosinski 13]. Other research puts the mean time for a visual stimulus at 0.22 s [Laming 68]. This time is typically determined by telling the human subject to tap a button when a light stimulus changes state (for example, turns from off to on or from green to red). You can try this test yourself at http://www.humanbenchmark.com/.

These simple reaction time studies are most similar to an AI agent firing a gun when they are focused, expecting an enemy, and aiming directly at the enemy when it is seen. However, there are three caveats that would increase the time beyond ~0.2 s:

1. If the stimulus is weak, then the reaction time is slower [Luce 86], for example, seeing an enemy far away versus seeing an enemy close up.
2. If the AI agent must aim after seeing the enemy, then that added time must be factored in.
3. A lapse in focused attention, which is common in humans, would cause the reaction time to be much higher.

5.3.2 Recognition or Go/No-Go Time

In the context of having to differentiate between two different stimuli and only acting on one of them, the mean time for a visual stimulus is 0.38 s [Laming 68]. The stimuli typically used in this test are two-digit numbers, where the subject must push a button when the number is above 50 and not push the button when it is below 50. You can try a version of the go/no-go test yourself at http://cognitivefun.net/test/17.

Go/no-go time studies are most similar to an AI agent firing a gun when they are focused, expecting either an enemy or a friend, and aiming directly at the subject when it is seen. As with simple reaction time, the caveats that would increase reaction time also apply here.

5.3.3 Complex Cognitive Task Reaction Time

As you would expect, the more complex the cognitive task, the more time it typically takes. When faced with a choice between several items, choosing the best one will take longer than a go/no-go reaction time [Donders 69]. However, to get reasonable response time estimates for any unique complex task, a careful experiment with human subjects would need to be constructed and executed.

5.4 Conclusion

As you program your AI behaviors, you'll be forced to choose a reaction time for your agents. However, based on the context, you should use different reaction times.

The good news is that we are fairly confident that a simple reaction time should be around 0.2 s, while a go/no-go reaction time is around 0.4 s. From there, you'll need to add additional time to account for weak stimuli, more complex cognitive recognitions, additional movement time, or lapses in attention. As for picking the ideal reaction time for your particular game, it ultimately depends on the exact context and what feels right to the player.

References

[Donders 69] Donders, F. C. 1969. Over de snelheid van psychische processen [On the speed of psychological processes]. In *Attention and Performance: II*, ed. Koster, W. (Original work published 1868). Amsterdam, the Netherlands: North-Holland.

[Kosinski 13] Kosinski, R. 2013. A literature review on reaction time. Clemson, SC: Clemson University. http://biae.clemson.edu/bpc/bp/Lab/110/reaction.htm (accessed September 10, 2014).

[Laming 68] Laming, D. R. J. 1968. *Information Theory of Choice-Reaction Times*. London, U.K.: Academic Press.

[Luce 86] Luce, R. D. 1986. *Response Times: Their Role in Inferring Elementary Mental Organization*. New York: Oxford University Press.

[Posner 05] Posner, M. 2005. Timing the brain: Mental chronometry as a tool in neuroscience. *PLoS Biol* 3(2): e51. doi:10.1371/journal.pbio.0030051. http://www.plosbiology.org/article/info%3Adoi%2F10.1371%2Fjournal.pbio.0030051#pbio-0030051-b18 (accessed September 10, 2014).

6

Preventing Animation Twinning Using a Simple Blackboard

Michael Dawe

6.1 Introduction

Arguably, the most important aspect of an artificial agent in a game is the player perception of that agent. An agent acting intelligently can break the illusion of intelligence by looking awkward, silly, or robotic to the player. When a realistic game has many similar characters, as is frequently the case in open-world games, it can become quite likely for two or more characters visible to the player to begin playing the same animation simultaneously, a problem known as animation twinning. However, avoiding animation twinning is a relatively easy problem to solve, even for large character populations.

6.2 Animation Twinning

Animation twinning occurs when two agents play back the same animation at a close enough time so as to appear indistinguishable. It is easily noticeable to a player and breaks the illusion that a game is simulating actual persons, since real people never exhibit the exact same motions in real-world situations. Even when two agents have different appearances, the same animations playing on the two identical skeletons are quickly picked out as artificial by the human eye. While ideally agents would have a wide variety of animations to play, realistically, the available number is constrained by budgets and animator time. Additionally, if a game puts a large population of characters on screen, console loading times and memory overhead may become a factor in loading many different animations to be played back.

One practical solution is to introduce a delay in animation playback, as the same animation played back on two identical skeletons with such a delay looks much more natural. This solution is quick to implement and requires minimal animator time to ensure adequate differentiation among the animations a character can play in a particular situation. While locomotion animations probably cannot be delayed for gameplay reasons, most other ambient animations, such as eating a bagel or talking on a cell phone, will benefit from a short delay to prevent characters from looking mechanical and breaking the illusion of intelligence.

6.3 Animation Blackboard

Assuming a large population of agents (say, 30 or more being simulated at once), it is impractical for a single agent to query the animations of every other agent before playing an animation of its own. However, a single data structure available to all agents, such as a blackboard [Isla 02], can be used to store the relevant information in a manner that can be quickly checked for duplicates. When an agent needs to play an animation, the blackboard can be checked to ensure that no other character is playing the same animation within whatever time period is specified. Once an agent has permission, the blackboard is updated with the animation the agent has chosen to play.

The `AnimBlackboardEntry` definition in Listing 6.1 shows the information stored about every animation playing. First, each animation needs a unique identifier to be checked against. Practically, this can be any hashed value based off of the animation, carefully selected to avoid hash collisions. Next, the game time that the animation started playing at is stored, so we can allow characters to play the same animation after whatever amount of delay is appropriate. The world location where the agent is standing is useful in situations where characters must play the same animation due to many characters being on screen with a small number of animations to choose from, as players will have more difficulty noticing similar animations being played when they are separated in space. Finally, it is useful to separate animations into two categories: those which can easily be delayed for a significant amount of time (reading a book, eating a sandwich) and those which must not be delayed for very long (reacting to gunfire or an explosion). Agents that fail to react quickly to important stimuli will look just as odd as those that play identical animations.

Listing 6.1. `AnimBlackboardEntry` definitions.

```
enum AnimPriority {NORMAL, REACTION};

class AnimBlackboardEntry {
  Hash animId;
  unsigned int time;
  Vector3 worldLocation;
  AnimPriority priority;
};
```

Listing 6.2. `AnimBlackboard` definition.

```
class AnimBlackboard {
  AnimBlackboardEntry blackboard[32];  //Sized for population
  size_t front, back;//Treat array as a circular queue
  unsigned int priorityTimes[];//One per AnimPriority
};
```

Listing 6.3. `CanPlayAnim` function pseudocode.

```
bool AnimBlackboard::CanPlayAnim(Hash anim, Vector3 location) {
  For each entry
    If entry is too old, move the front of the queue up
      If entry isn't our anim, skip it
      If entry is our anim:
        If (now - entry.time) < min delay for entry.priority
          return false
  //Add the anim to the blackboard here, or do it afterwards
  return true
}
```

The `AnimBlackboard` definition in Listing 6.2 defines an array that will be used as a circular queue of `AnimBlackboardEntry` items. The size of the array will depend on the maximum number of agents needing to be animated simultaneously. Finally, the `priorityTimes` array stores the delay necessary before playing an identical animation.

When an agent needs to check if playing a particular animation is permitted, it can call `CanPlayAnim` as defined in Listing 6.3. Every call to `CanPlayAnim` walks from the front of the queue to the back. If the current entry is older than the maximum delay we care to enforce, the front of the queue can be pushed up to that entry, since it will never need to be checked against again. If an entry is found that we need to consider based on the time it was played, we compare the identifier of the animations and, if they match, return false if the time since that animation was played is within the delay period. Otherwise, the animation is allowed. Distance can also be considered here, if it was included in the `AnimBlackboardEntry` definition by allowing animations that would have been disallowed if they are far enough apart. If allowing animations based on distance, every entry in the blackboard must be checked. Once the animation has started to play, the agent must add it to the blackboard.

6.4 Delay Times and Animation Considerations

The amount of time animations should be delayed is subjective, but good results were found with a 1 s delay for normal animations and 300 ms for reaction animations. In general, the delay for normal animations is less critical than the delay for reaction animations, and the delay amount needs careful examination and adjustment. Too small of a delay (under 200 ms) produces indistinguishable differences, while too long of a delay (over 500 ms) results in characters not reacting quickly enough.

Also important in discussing the delay amounts is how the animations themselves can affect the delay needed, again impacting reaction animations more significantly. If the first half-second of a particular reaction animation has very little character movement, a delay less than that will still produce characters looking identical for a period of time. Work with the project animators to ensure enough variation in the first section of the animation and ensure consistency across a reasonable delay period, then experiment and adjust the timing based on what looks best.

While including the location an animation plays at is optional, it proved useful in situations where a population of over 20 characters all needed to play reaction animations simultaneously to get up from park benches and picnic tables in order to react to a threat. Despite having a number of animations to play considerably less than the population, the location information helped stop characters that were near to each other on screen from playing similar animations, which improved the overall appearance of the scene.

6.5 Conclusion

Characters playing simultaneous animations can look awkward, but it's simple to create a solution to avoid exact animation duplicates and performs well for large populations. While increasing the available number of animations for characters to play will always help reduce delays in playback, a short amount of time spent implementing this blackboard system will produce a marked difference in the appearance of the game, even with a relatively limited number of animations to choose from.

Reference

[Isla 02] Isla, D. and Blumberg, B. 2002. Blackboard architectures. In *AI Game Programming Wisdom*, ed. S. Rabin, pp. 333–344. Hingham, MA: Charles River Media.

Section II
Architecture

7

Possibility Maps for Opportunistic AI and Believable Worlds

John Manslow

7.1 Introduction

The state of a game world is the combination of the states of all the objects within it: the state of the player (his or her location, orientation, health, inventory, etc.), the states of all NPCs (nonplayer characters—their locations, emotional states, etc.), the states of inanimate objects (which doors are locked, which buildings have collapsed, etc.), and so on. Games usually simulate a game world in order to track the evolution of its state, perhaps using level-of-detail approximations for unobserved elements of game state to reduce the complexity of doing so.

This chapter will introduce the idea of maintaining probability and possibility distributions over some unobserved elements of game state rather than simulating their evolution explicitly. If such distributions are used correctly, they allow the artificial intelligence (AI) to defer decisions relating to unobserved elements of game state without the player realizing that anything unusual is happening. This makes it possible to identify opportunities for action that might otherwise have required the creation and execution of complex plans and hence to create opportunistic AI that appears much smarter than it actually is.

7.2 What Are Probability and Possibility Maps?

A probability map provides a mapping from game states to probabilities that represent the relative likelihoods of the game being in different states. For example, the location of a character in a village is part of the game state and can be approximated by discrete locations such as the character's home, the stables, the tavern, the well, the shop, and the stretches of road between them. A probability map can be used to associate these locations with probabilities so as to model the likely location of the unobserved character. The map might change with time of day so that the character is more likely to be found at home at night or in the tavern in the evening.

Possibility maps are simplified versions of probability maps that dispense with probability values and only map states to indications as to whether they are possible. A possibility map for a character in a village, for example, would be true for every location where the character could possibly be located and false everywhere else. Because possibility maps aren't concerned with the relative likelihoods of states, they are typically easier to use and better suited to applications that are concerned with creating the illusion of intelligence rather than level-of-detail approximations.

7.3 Using Possibility Maps

For an application of probability and possibility maps to be convincing, it is important that they are updated in a way that is consistent with the player's observations of the game's state. We will first consider how to do this for possibility maps because the mechanisms for updating them are easier to understand than are those for updating probability maps.

A possibility map must regularly be updated to propagate possibility information according to its propagation rules. The precise form of those rules depends on what the possibility map represents: if it represents the location of an NPC, for example, the propagation rules would reflect how the NPC moves around the environment. If an update would propagate possibility information into a state that would affect the player's observations, or the player makes an observation that determines a state that is marked as possible, the AI must immediately decide whether to put the game into that state. If it does decide to put the game into that state, all mutually exclusive states must be marked as impossible; if it decides not to put the game into that state, then that state must be marked as impossible.

The decision as to whether to put the game into a particular state is taken based on the AI's assessment of the state's desirability from a gameplay perspective except when it is the only possible state remaining, in which case the AI has no choice. A simple example of an element of game state that can usually be represented by a possibility map is the location of an NPC. Figure 7.1 shows a possibility map for the location of an NPC on a simple level where P represents the player's location, N the NPC's location, the Xs represent walls and the ?s represent possible locations of the NPC.

Initially, in Figure 7.1a, the player can see the NPC and hence there are no possible alternative locations for it. If the NPC moves east and the player remains stationary, the player loses sight of the NPC and the possibility map starts to track the NPC's possible movement, as represented by the question marks in Figure 7.1b. The progress of the question marks is determined by the map's propagation rules and, since the map represents the possible location of the NPC, the rules are simply set up to reflect its range of possible movement. Figure 7.1c shows

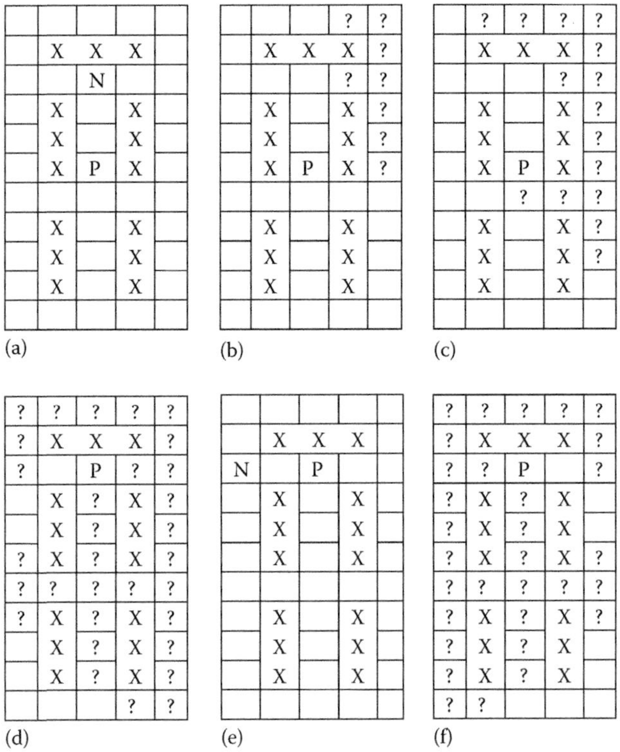

Figure 7.1

Possibility maps of an NPC's location. (a) A possibility map with a player looking north at an NPC. (b) The state of the possibility map a few seconds after the NPC moves out of sight to the east. (c) The state after a few more seconds. A melee attack from behind the player is now possible. (d) After the player moves north three squares, the AI can choose from a variety of melee and ranged weapon attacks. (e) The state of the map if the AI instantiates the NPC behind the player as the player turns to face east. (f) Possible locations for a second NPC that started in the same location as the first but moved west.

that, after several seconds, it becomes apparent that the NPC could've crept up behind the player and the AI has the opportunity to instantiate it and perform a melee attack.

If the AI chooses not to instantiate it and the player moves north three squares and starts to turn to the right, as shown in Figure 7.1d, the player will be about to observe two squares that are possible locations of the NPC. The AI must therefore decide whether to instantiate the NPC or to keep it hidden and continue propagating possibility information. It has a rich set of options if it chooses to instantiate it—it can instantiate it south of the player for a melee or ranged weapon attack, a couple of squares west of the player for a ranged weapon attack from behind, or to the east of the player for either a melee or ranged weapon attack. Figure 7.1e shows the state of the possibility map if the AI chose to instantiate it west of the player. If it chose not to instantiate it, the possibility map would look the same as in Figure 7.1d except that the two squares east of the player would be blank to indicate that the NPC cannot possibly be present at those locations.

In this example, the AI was forced to decide whether to instantiate the NPC when the player observed possible locations for it. It might also be the case that the player could infer the location of the NPC by other means, such as by hearing sounds that might be emitted when the NPC walks over noisy surfaces. If the player is out of earshot of the surfaces, then possibility information can propagate over them as if they didn't exist. If the player is within earshot, however, the surfaces block the propagation of possibility information and the AI would need to instantiate the NPC to allow it to cross. Similarly, if the NPC had no stealth capability, then the rules for propagating possibility information would've prevented locations adjacent to the player being marked as possible in Figure 7.1c and d and the AI would've needed to instantiate the NPC to get it close to the player. In general, the AI can choose to instantiate an NPC at any time though doing so prevents it from deferring decisions about the NPC's behavior and hence early instantiation is usually undesirable.

If the map in Figure 7.1 had contained two NPCs, their locations would've been represented by two independent possibility maps. The AI could create the illusion of finely coordinated movement between them by taking account of both their maps when deciding when and where to instantiate them. For example, assuming that both NPCs had started at the same location but the second moved west out of sight of the player, then the possibility map for the first NPC is as shown in Figure 7.1d, and the map for the second would be as shown in Figure 7.1f. As the player turns to the right, it is clear that the AI could instantiate an NPC almost anywhere and, in particular, could instantiate both NPCs to create the illusion of a planned coordinated attack from behind and to the side, from the front and to the side, from the front and from behind, and both from the front, both from the side, and both from behind. Note that, although the AI is technically cheating by using possibility maps, it always has to behave in a way that is consistent with the player's observations and hence a skillful player can often prevent the AI from springing these kinds of opportunistic traps by careful observation.

Figure 7.2 shows a level with a resource item—a health pack that can be used by NPCs—represented by an H. If the player initially observes the NPC, as shown in Figure 7.2a, and the NPC moves out of sight to the north, the possibility map will evolve as shown in Figure 7.2b. When it becomes possible for the NPC to have reached the health pack, the AI can either decide that the NPC should pick the health pack up immediately, in which case the possibility map is reset with the only possible location of the NPC being the location of the health

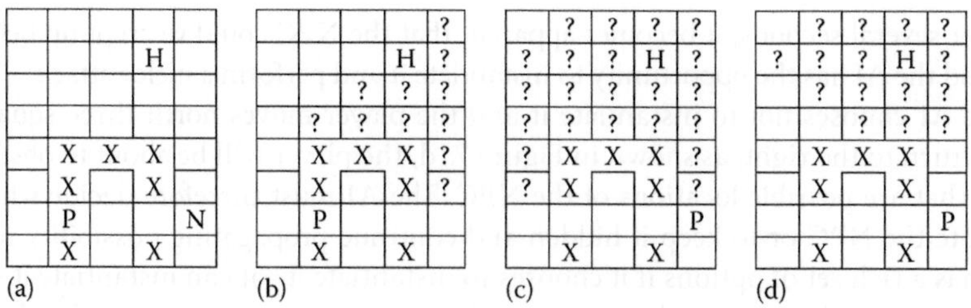

Figure 7.2

Possibility maps of an NPC's location with a health pack. (a) A possibility map with one health pack and a player facing an NPC. (b) The state of the map a few seconds after the NPC moves north out of sight of the player. (c) The state if the NPC did not pick up the health pack and the player moves three squares east. (d) The state if the NPC did pick up the health pack.

pack, or the AI can defer the decision. In order to defer the decision, the AI needs to fork the possibility map into two—one for the location of the NPC with the health pack and one for the location of the NPC without. The latter is simply a continuation of the original but the former is a new map with the only possible location of the NPC being the location of the pack.

If, as the NPC possibly reaches the health pack, the player moves east three squares, the possibility map for the NPC without the health pack, which is shown in Figure 7.2c, reveals that both melee and ranged weapon attacks are possible and the possibility map for the NPC with the health pack, which is shown in Figure 7.2d, shows that only a ranged weapon attack is possible. The AI therefore has the opportunity to choose between the lower health version of the NPC performing a melee or ranged weapon attack, the higher health version performing a ranged weapon attack, and keeping the NPC hidden. If the NPC is particularly effective in melee combat or ineffective at a distance, the benefits of deferring the decision about collecting the health pack are obvious.

Forking can be used to defer decisions in relation to a wide variety of actions—should an NPC pick up a key, unlock a door, flick a switch, buy a sword, etc.? It can, however, also result in a combinatorial explosion of possibility maps if the environment contains too many opportunities for action and the AI will usually have to make some decisions earlier than is strictly necessary simply to control the number of maps. Even deferring a decision for a short time, however, can be beneficial as the AI often has more information available to it when it comes to make the deferred decision than it would've had if it had not deferred the decision at all.

7.4 Updating Probability Maps

Like possibility maps, probability maps must also regularly be updated—this time to propagate probability information according to its propagation rules. The precise form of those rules depends on what the probability map represents: if it represents the location of an NPC, for example, the propagation rules would reflect the likelihood of the NPC moving from each location to every other. If an update results in nonzero probability in a state that would affect the player's observations, or the player makes an observation that determines a state that has nonzero probability, the AI must put the game into that state with the probability indicated by the probability map. If the game is put into the state, the probabilities of all mutually exclusive states are set to zero, but if the game is not put into the state, the probability of the state is set to zero. Normalization of the probability map must be maintained at all times—that is, the sum of the probabilities of all states must always be equal to one.

Consider, for example, a guard that's controlled by a state machine with the states patrolling from point A to point B, patrolling from point B to point A, eating, sleeping, and playing solitaire. Each of those states would be assigned a probability by the probability map and the map's propagation rules would provide probabilities for transitions between states and, perhaps, minimum times that the transitions should take. Table 7.1 gives some example transition probabilities, and Table 7.2 shows how the probability map evolves after the player sees the guard patrolling from point A to point B.

If the player entered the dining hall when the probability map had the values in the second to last row of Table 7.2, the AI would instantiate the guard in the eating state with probability 0.097. If the instantiation happened, the probability of the eating state would be set to one and the probabilities of all other states would be set to zero. If the instantiation did not happen, the probability of the eating state would be set to zero and the

Table 7.1 Transition Probabilities for a Guard

		Next State				
		A to B	B to A	Sleeping	Eating	Solitaire
Current state	A to B	0.00	1.00	0.00	0.00	0.00
	B to A	0.95	0.00	0.00	0.05	0.00
	Sleeping	0.04	0.00	0.95	0.01	0.00
	Eating	0.18	0.00	0.01	0.80	0.01
	Solitaire	0.50	0.00	0.50	0.00	0.00

Table 7.2 Probability Map for a Guard

Time	A to B	B to A	Sleeping	Eating	Solitaire
1	0.000	1.000	0.000	0.000	0.000
2	0.950	0.000	0.000	0.050	0.000
3	0.009	0.950	0.001	0.040	0.000
4	0.910	0.009	0.001	0.080	0.000
5	0.023	0.910	0.002	0.064	0.001
6	0.877	0.023	0.003	0.097	0.000
6 after observation	0.970	0.026	0.003	0.000	0.001

probabilities of the other states updated so that they still sum to one, as shown in the last row. In practice, state transition probabilities usually need to vary with time of day to produce realistic behavior. For example, the probabilities of transitioning from any state to the sleep state would be very high at night for a guard that was only working the dayshift.

Probability maps provide the AI with information about the relative likelihoods of different game states and that allows it to distinguish between states that are almost certain and others that are theoretically possible but highly unlikely. In this sense, they are more powerful than possibility maps. Unfortunately, it can be difficult to come up with transition probabilities that produce sensible behavior and, if the transition probabilities vary with time, the probability map will never stabilize. This means that the AI will, in principle, need to continue to update it regardless of how long it is since it was last affected by the player. These problems can be avoided by combining probability and possibility maps using the method described in the next section.

7.5 Combining Possibility and Probability Maps

A useful approximation to a normal probability map can often be achieved by combining a static probability map and a possibility map. A static probability map assigns probabilities to states but the probabilities are not propagated across the map according to transition probabilities as they are in a normal probability map. Instead, they represent the likelihoods of observing states when no previous observations have been made and a possibility map is used to ensure that only states that are consistent with the player's observations can be instantiated.

For example, Table 7.3 shows three static probability maps for a guard, the first to be used during the working day, the second at mealtimes, and the third at night. If the player

Table 7.3 Static Probability Map for a Guard

Time	A to B	B to A	Sleeping	Eating	Solitaire
Working day	0.495	0.495	0.001	0.003	0.001
Mealtimes	0.010	0.010	0.000	0.970	0.010
Night	0.002	0.002	0.990	0.003	0.003

observes the games room, the AI checks to see whether the possibility map indicates that it's possible for the guard to be in there and, if it is, the AI instantiates the guard with the probability specified by the static probability map after it's been adjusted so that the sum of the probabilities of all possible states is one. For example, in the unlikely event that it's mealtime and the player has just observed that the guard is not in the dining hall, then the guard must either be patrolling from A to B, patrolling from B to A, or playing solitaire—hence, the probabilities of those states are all 0.010/(1 – 0.970) = 0.333. If the player observes the games room, the AI would therefore instantiate the guard there with probability 0.333.

If the player left the area completely, it wouldn't take long for every state in the possibility map to be marked as possible, at which point, no further computation would be necessary until the player returned and made another relevant observation.

7.6 Factorizing Game State

The complete state of a game is an extremely complex multidimensional entity, and it is not realistic to expect to be able to create probability and possibility maps over the state in its entirety. Instead, it is necessary to factor the game state into independent elements and create multiple independent maps. Such elements must be independent in the sense that the state of one should not affect the probable or possible states of another. The most easily identifiable independent elements are usually the locations of NPCs, although they can become dependent when NPCs need to interact.

For example, if the guard in the earlier example had played poker rather than solitaire, then it would've been necessary for the AI to make sure that there was never only a single guard in the games room, thereby creating a dependency between the locations of guards. That problem could be solved by checking the probability and possibility maps of all guards when the player enters the games room to see if enough guards could be there for a game to be taking place and only instantiating them if that was the case. To guarantee that the AI always had a choice, however, it would need to make sure that no single guard ends up with the games room as his or her only possible location—something that could easily be achieved when deciding whether to instantiate guards elsewhere.

Shared resources create more serious dependencies. Consider, for example, a map with two NPCs and a health pack that can be taken by only one of them. As has already been described, as each NPC possibly reaches the location of the health pack, their possibility maps must fork and the game must maintain four possibility maps—two for each NPC, one to represent possible movement with the health pack and one without. When the AI decides to instantiate an NPC, it must decide whether it will be the version with the health pack or the one without and must remember that the health pack is with only one of the NPCs. The situation gets even more complicated if the health pack regenerates after a short time. In that case, it is possible for both NPCs to have picked it up but one of them could only have done so after it had regenerated. This situation can be modeled with additional forking to account for the order in which the NPCs picked up the pack and to allow for its regeneration time.

Another example of a shared resource that creates dependencies is a lift. Lifts create dependencies because, when one NPC moves the lift, it affects its availability for the others in an extremely complex way—the amount of time that an NPC's possibility map takes to propagate from one floor to the next via the lift depends on the location of the lift at the time the NPC possibly reaches it, the times other NPCs possibly reached it, and where they possibly left it—and all of that depends on deferred decisions that have not yet been made. In principle, this problem can also be solved by forking but it's probably better and certainly simpler to use an approximation such as to ignore the dynamics of the lift altogether and just propagate possibility information between floors with a slight delay.

If a suitable factorization of the game state cannot be found, a joint map can be created to model the probability or possibility of the combined state of multiple elements. This is effectively what is being done by forking; when, in the earlier example, an additional possibility map was created when the NPC could've picked up the health pack, the AI was dynamically creating a possibility map for the combined states of the location of the NPC and its health. The problem with this approach is that the number of states in a joint map grows exponentially with the number of elements of game state that it represents and hence joint maps can be excessively large and unwieldy. Some factorization is therefore always necessary for the successful application of probability and possibility maps.

7.7 Conclusion

This chapter has described probability and possibility maps and shown how they can be used individually and in combination to produce level-of-detail effects and allow the AI to defer decisions to create the illusion of highly intelligent, coordinated, and carefully planned behavior. Respect for the player's observational history ensures that this is achieved without the player noticing any inconsistencies and provides a way for players to limit the options of the AI through their own careful planning and observation.

8

Production Rules Implementation in *1849*

Robert Zubek

8.1 Introduction

This chapter presents implementation details of the production rule system used in the game *1849*. The system's main design goals were enabling quick iteration via a data-driven approach and good performance on a variety of hardware, down to significantly underpowered tablet devices.

First, we discuss the details bottom up, from the world model, through rule implementation, up to the overall rule system that manipulates them. Then, in the second half, we examine the performance consequences of these design choices, as well as lessons learned in the process of implementing the system.

8.2 Game Mechanics and Production Rules

1849 is a city building and management game for tablets, desktops, and the web. The fiction of the game is that gold has just been discovered in California, and player's task is to build gold mining towns and make money in the gold rush. The following is an overview of the game mechanics and simulation.

8.2.1 Game Mechanics

In terms of game mechanics, the game is a classic city builder, along the lines of early Impressions Games such as *Caesar* or *Zeus*. The main units of gameplay are as follows:

- *Buildings*, which the player places in town; they can be houses for residents or workplaces that produce resources or city benefits (such as fire prevention).
- *Resources* are created by buildings, either from nothing (such as farms producing wheat) or by consuming other resources (such as bakery consuming wheat and producing bread).
- *Workers* are the fuel powering all these buildings; they cannot be directly controlled by the player, but they can be influenced by providing them the resources they want.

The main feedback loops are set up such that workers power all buildings, but they are fickle and sensitive to what resources are available. As the town grows, more and more workers arrive looking for work, but they also demand more complex resources, and if they don't get what they want, they vote with their feet and leave, causing workplaces to shut down. Initially, their demands are simple, just food and drink, but soon, they start demanding increasingly processed resources, such as shoes, clothes, or newspapers. The player can either try to import those processed resources at a high cost or build out resource conversion buildings and manage their logistics. Much of the fun and difficulty of the game comes from the "spinning plates" feeling, of setting up these increasingly complicated resource production and conversion chains and then maintaining them and making sure that they are all running smoothly, that workers remain happy, and that the town's overall budget is trending in the right direction.

8.2.2 Game Simulation

The game simulation is implemented using a production rule system: all buildings run a collection of stand-alone rules that simulate the town's economy.

We can discuss them as a hierarchy of abstractions:

- Each building is a stand-alone rule executor for a set of rules.
- Each rule has some conditions that can match and produce some actions.
- Conditions typically involve queries about resources or the world, and actions typically involve resource modification and issuing side effects.
- Resource queries and modification bottom out in a data model optimized for specific types of context-sensitive access.

8.3 Rule System

Having introduced the layers of the system, let's discuss them bottom up.

8.3.1 Resources

The basic atomic unit of game economy is a *resource*. This is an `<id, amount>` tuple, such as "50 dollars" or "10 units of gold" or "50 units of stone." Everything that can be produced or consumed is a resource.

Most resources are concrete, like gold or stone or food. But there are also abstract resources such as people and map effects such as crime level.

When you build a house, and people move in, that's represented as the house gaining a "1 resident" resource—and later, when that resident gets a job, the workplace gains a "1 worker" resource as well (and the reverse happens when the resident moves out).

Map effects are things like crime, boredom, or fire risk. For example, every house creates a tiny amount of fire risk, say, "0.01 fire risk" per day, and this resource collects up in the world, and later causes fires, as we'll describe in a moment.

8.3.2 Resource Bins

Resources are not loose objects, rather, they're stored in bins. A resource bin contains a whole bag of resources and their amounts. There are three types of bins in the game.

First, *player's inventory* during a game session is stored in a bin. For example, the facts that I have $1000 in cash and 10 units of gold ready for trade are just two resource entries in my bin.

Second, each *board unit* (such as a building) has its own bin, which is its own inventory. For example, when a wheat farm grows wheat, it inserts a bunch of wheat units in its own bin. But those units are not yet usable by the player. There's a separate delivery step that has to happen, to deliver this wheat from the building to the player's inventory.

Finally, each *map tile* has a resource bin that's separate from any building that might sit on top of it. For one example, gold underground is represented as a gold resource inside that tile's bin, and it needs to be mined out of the ground and into the building's bin. For another example, fire hazard is a resource, conjured up and inserted into the world by wooden buildings.

8.3.3 Conditions and Actions

Since almost everything in the simulation is a resource, a lot of the game is based on resource conversions. Some simplified examples from our data definition files:

Ranch produces meat and leather, and shows an animated NPC at work:

```
"doWork":
  "outputs": ["unit 6 meat", "unit 6 leather"]
  "success": [
    "_ a-spawn-worker npc npc-farmer action ranch days 7"
  ]
```

Ranch delivers meat into storage, 20 units at a time:

```
"deliverWork":
  "frequency": "every 5 days",
  "checks": ["unit workers > 0"],
  "inputs": ["unit 20 leather"],
  "outputs": ["player 20 leather"],
  "success": [
    "_ a-spawn-walker npc npc-delivery
       to bldg-trade-store then return"
  ]
```

Cobbler brings leather from storage if it doesn't have any, consumes it, and produces shoes:

```
"bringMaterials":
  "checks": ["unit workers > 0", "unit leather < 2"],
  "inputs": ["player 8 leather"],
  "outputs": ["unit 8 leather"]
"doWork":
  "inputs": ["unit 2 leather"],
  "outputs": ["unit 3 shoes"]
```

But conversion rules don't have to be limited to just buildings bins—they also frequently interact with map tiles underneath and around:

Gold mine consumes gold from the map tiles underneath and produces gold in its own inventory, until all ground gold has been exhausted:

```
"doWork":
  "inputs": ["map 5 gold"],
  "outputs": ["unit 5 gold"]
```

Every wooden house produces a little bit of fire risk in the map tile underneath:

```
"produceFireHazard":
  "frequency": "every 7 days",
  "checks": ["map fire-hazard < 1 max"],
  "outputs": ["map 0.04 fire-hazard"]
```

Fire brigade consumes all fire risks from the map, within a given radius, using a special action:

```
"consumeMapResource":
  "frequency": "every 7 days",
  "checks": ["unit workers > 0"]
  "success": ["_ a-change-resource-in-area
              radius 5 res fire-hazard amount -1"]
```

As you can see, the fact that gold comes from underground, while food and other things are made in buildings, is not actually hard-coded anywhere in the engine. Right now, it's just a matter of convention. This means that you could rewrite the rules such that, for example, the cobbler makes shoes and inserts them underground inside the tile. You probably wouldn't want to, because nobody would be able to get at those shoes if they wanted them, but it's a possibility.

8.3.4 Rule Execution

As you can see from the previous examples, each rule consists of several elements. Here is the complete list:

- "Frequency": how often we check.
- "Checks": all of these have to be satisfied.
- "Inputs": if checks are satisfied, we check if desired inputs exist, and if so, they will be consumed.

Listing 8.1. Pseudocode for rule matching algorithm.

```
for each rule that should run at this point in time
    if all checks are satisfied
        if all inputs exist
            consume inputs
            produce outputs
            run success actions
        else
            run failedInputs actions
    else
        run failedChecks actions
```

- "Outputs": if inputs were consumed successfully, these will be produced.
- "Success": actions to run if this rule was applied successfully (neither checks nor inputs have failed).
- "FailedInputs": fallback actions to run if inputs were insufficient.
- "FailedChecks": fallback actions to run if checks failed.

The algorithm in pseudocode is listed in Listing 8.1. As we can see, "frequency" and "checks" both denote *conditions* in which the rule runs, "inputs" defines both *conditions* to be checked and related *actions* (consume inputs), while "outputs" and other fields define *actions* only. Frequency is pulled out separately as an optimization step (see next section).

8.4 Performance

Our production system is very efficient—in a town with many hundreds of entities, the rule engine's CPU consumption is barely noticeable in the profiler, even when running on rather underpowered tablets.

Most of the processing power is spent, predictably, on checking conditions. One of the design goals for this system was to make sure conditions can be checked quickly, ideally in constant or near-constant time, to help with performance.

We have three optimizations in place to help with this: flexible frequency of rule execution, a drastically simplified language for conditions and actions, and an efficient world model that is inexpensive to query.

8.4.1 Condition Checking Frequency

Production systems vary in how often the rules should be run. For example, we could run rules whenever something changes in the world, which in a game could be every frame, or maybe on a fixed schedule, such as 10 Hz, or on every game "turn" in a turn-based game.

In *1849*, the game's simulation is triggered off of game clock days (e.g., a farm produces wheat every 7 days), so we felt no need to run the rules too often. Our default frequency is once per day, and we made it easy to raise or lower the frequency as needed on a per-rule basis.

Here is an example of how frequency is specified—it's pulled out of the conditions definition into its own data field:

```
"produceFireHazard":
  "frequency": "every 7 days",
  "checks": ["map fire-hazard < 1 max"],
```

Finally, we implemented a very simple scheduler that keeps track of which rules are supposed to run when, so that they don't get accessed until their prescribed time.

8.4.2 Condition Definition Language

Many rule systems express conditions and actions in an expressive language such as predicate logic, so that the developer can make queries and assertions about entities as a class without committing to specific instances, and let the computer figure out to which entities those rules can be applied.

Here is a made-up example in a made-up predicate language:

```
If is-a(X,gold-mine) and is-a(T,map-tile) and
is-under(T,X) and contains(T,R,5) and is-a(R,gold)
=> Then increment(X,R,5) and increment(T,R,-5)
```

This kind of a rule would be very expressive and general. However, finding entities in the world that match this query can get expensive quickly: it's essentially a search problem. While numerous optimizations for inference systems are well known (e.g., the Rete algorithm [Forgy 82]), they're still not enough, given our desire to make conditions execute in constant or near-constant time.

Conditions and actions we use in our engine are not so generic. Instead, they are more contextual, which lets them be simpler. Once again, here is our gold mine example:

```
"doWork":
  "inputs": ["map 5 gold"],
  "outputs": ["unit 5 gold"]
```

Here, "map" and "unit" are like variables, in that they're not specific entities like "gold mine #52"—but they're also not free variables like X was in the previous example. Instead, they're contextually bound indexicals: "unit" refers to the entity that's currently executing this rule, "map" refers to all tiles underneath the unit, and "player" refers to the singleton entity that keeps player's city inventory.

In other words, instead of using objective representation and predicate logic, we use deictic representation [Agre 87], with variables that are already contextually bound at query time to particular entities. Game units typically only care about themselves and their immediate surroundings, so deictic representation is a perfect match.

This choice constrains our system's expressiveness, compared to a language with completely free variables and unification, but it drastically eliminates a huge search problem and associated costs.

8.4.3 Data Model

Most conditions are resource queries, and most actions are resource modifications. For example: check if there is gold underground, and if so, consume it and produce gold in my inventory; or check if I have any workers working here, and if there is gold in my inventory, and if so, deliver gold over to player's inventory, and so on.

As we described before, we store resources in resource bins, and those bins are attached to units, map tiles, and the player's data object. Each resource bin is implemented as a vector of 64 floating-point numbers, indexed by resource (because there are currently 64 resource types).

A resource query such as "unit gold > 5" then works as follows: first, we get a reference to the unit's own resource bin (via a simple switch statement), then look up resource value (an array lookup), and finally do the appropriate comparison against the right-hand side value (another simple switch statement). All this adds up to a constant-time operation. Similar process happens for update instead of a query.

A query such as "map gold > 5" is marginally more expensive, because it means "add up gold stored in all tiles under the unit and check if > 5". Fortunately, units are not arbitrarily large—the largest one is 2 × 2 map tiles—which means we execute at most four tile lookups, making it still a constant-time operation.

And as a fallback, we allow ourselves to cheat if necessary: both conditions and actions can also refer to a library of named built-in functions, and those can do arbitrary computation. For example, the fire brigade has a built-in action `a-change-resource-in-area` that consumes a pre-tuned amount of fire risk resource within its area of effect, but this operation is actually linear in map size. We use such actions rarely.

8.5 Lessons from *1849*

With the system overview behind us, we'll quickly go over what worked well in the process of building our game using this engine, and what, with the benefit of hindsight, we wish we had done differently.

8.5.1 Benefits

Performance was clearly a high point of the system, which can run cities with hundreds of active entities without breaking a sweat, even on comparatively underpowered tablet devices. We could probably push production rules even further, if the rendering subsystem had not claimed all available processor cycles already.

Also, as you can see from our examples, the rules themselves are specified in a kind of a domain-specific language, based primarily on JSON, with condition and action bodies expressed as strings with a specific syntax. They get deserialized at load time into class instances, following simple command pattern.

Exposing game rules as a DSL that can be loaded up with a simple restart, without rebuilding the game, had the well-known benefits of data-driven systems: decoupling configuration from code, increasing iteration speed, and ultimately empowering design.

8.5.2 Lessons

At the same time, we ran into two problems: one with how our particular DSL evolved over time, and one with production systems and how they matched the game's design.

The DSL was initially developed to support only queries such as "`<bin> <resource> <comparison> <value>`" or actions such as "`<bin> <resource> <delta>`".

These were appropriate for most cases, but we quickly found ourselves wanting to do more than just resource manipulation. For example, we wanted to start spawning workers to go dig up gold or carry it in wheelbarrows to the storage building—or even more mundane things, like playing sound effects or setting or clearing notification bubbles if a building is understaffed or can't get road access.

Over time, we added support for more types of actions, and a generic deserializer syntax, which supported actions such as "`_ a-spawn-worker npc npc-farmer action ranch days 7`". This was just syntactic sugar for a definition like `{"_type": "a-spawn-worker", "npc": "npc-farmer", "action": "ranch", "days": 7}`, and that in turn just deserialized into the class `ASpawnWorker` and filled in the appropriate fields.

In retrospect, we should have added support for custom or one-off conditions and actions from the very beginning; that would have saved us engineering time later on reworking parts of the system. Even in the most organized system design, there will *always* be a need for one-off functionality to achieve some specific effects, and all systems should support it.

Separately from this, we also discovered a representational deficiency, which came from a mismatch between one-shot and continuous processes. This is a deficiency we failed to resolve in time for shipping.

From the earliest points in the game's design, we operated under the assumption that resource manipulation is sparse and discrete, for example, every 7 days, the wheat farm produces 6 units of wheat or the bakery consumes 3 wheat and produces 5 bread. This lent itself perfectly to a rule system that triggers on a per-rule timer.

However, fairly late in the process, we realized that this kind of a discrete system was hard for our players to understand. Whether it was because we surfaced it poorly or because their expectations were trained differently by other games, our beta players had difficulty understanding the simulation and what was actually going on, because the activities were so sparse.

When we explored this further, we found that players reacted best when buildings looked like they operated continuously, for example, wheat farm producing wheat at velocity of 0.8 per day, and when its storage fills up, the surplus gets delivered.

Ultimately, we were able to produce much of the desired user effect by essentially faking it in the UI and in how we give feedback to the player. But had this happened earlier in development, we might have rewritten all of our rules to run much more frequently, to simulate continuous production, even at the cost of spending significantly more processing time on rule checks per second. Even better, we should have considered combining it with a form of parallel-reactive networks [Horswill 00], to help represent continuous processes, and hooked that up as part of the data model manipulated by the rule system.

8.6 Related Work

On the game development side, this implementation was very directly influenced by previously published implementation details of Age of Empires (AoE) [Age of Empires 97] and of the GlassBox engine used in SimCity [Willmott 12].

AoE was one of the earliest games to expose data-driven production systems. Their syntax is based on s-expressions, and rules might look something like

```
(defrule
  (can-research-with-escrow ri-hussar)
=>
  (release-escrow food)
  (release-escrow gold)
  (research ri-hussar))
```

The AoE system plays from the perspective of the player, that is, one rule engine is active per enemy player. The GlassBox rules, on the other hand, are much more granular and run from the perspective of each individual unit, for example,

```
unitRule mustardFactory
    rate 10
    global Simoleans in 1
    local YellowMustard in 6
    local EmptyBottle in 1
    local BottleOfMustard out 1
    map Pollution out 5
end
```

We were highly inspired by the design choices from GlassBox, especially the data model that organizes resources into bins, distributes those bins in the game world, and lets production rules check and manipulate them.

Finally, the representation of conditions and actions using a contextual language like "`unit gold > 5`" is related to the history of work on deictic representation, such as the implementation of game-playing AI for the game Pengi by [Agre 87] or reactive autonomous robots in [Horswill 00]. In particular, we decided against inference or queries with arbitrary free variables such as "`is(X,gold-mine) and has-workers(X)`". Instead, we replaced them with task-relevant indexicals, which made fast queries much easier to implement. The task of binding deictic variables can then be moved to a separate subsystem that can be optimized separately (in the Pengi example, it was done by simulating a visual attention system, but in our system, it's trivially easy, based on which entity executes the rule).

8.7 Conclusion

This chapter examined the implementation details of a production rule system used in the game *1849*. We started by examining the architecture of the system, followed by details of production rules and their components. As we demonstrate, a few specific simplifications enabled a very efficient implementation, suitable even for underpowered mobile devices.

References

[Age of Empires 97] Uncredited. 1997. *Age of Empires*. Developed by Ensemble Studios.

[Agre 87] Agre, P.E. and Chapman, D. 1987. Pengi: An implementation of a theory of activity. In *Proceedings of the AAAI-87*. Los Altos, CA: Morgan Kaufmann.

[Forgy 82] Forgy, C. 1982. Rete: A fast algorithm for the many pattern/many object pattern match problem. *Artificial Intelligence* 19: 17–37.

[Horswill 00] Horswill, I.D., Zubek, R., Khoo, A., Le, C., and Nicholson, S. 2000. The cerebus project. In *Proceedings of the AAAI Fall Symposium on Parallel Cognition and Embodied Agents*, North Falmouth, MA.

[Willmott 12] Willmott, A. 2012. GlassBox: A new simulation architecture. *Game Developers Conference 2012*, San Francisco, CA.

9

Production Systems

New Techniques in AAA Games

*Andrea Schiel**

9.1 Introduction

Production systems have been around since the 1940s and are now applied in a wide array of applications and ongoing research. AAA games bring a unique set of challenges to production systems; they require that AI systems be runtime efficient, deterministic, memory lean, and above all, implementable within the development cycle. Over the course of many of our titles, production systems have developed along different lines. This chapter tries to describe the majority of our more unique production systems, assuming that the reader has a basic knowledge of production systems. For readers who want to code their first production system, there is a list of references that describe basic production systems in more detail [Luger 93, Millington 09, Laird 12, Bourg 04] and these

* The author has worked at Electronic Arts for over 18 years on a variety of titles, in particular sports games. This chapter contains the insights from applying production systems to multiple AAA over many generations of consoles.

Table 9.1 Terms in Use in This Chapter

Term	Alternate
AI	AI agent or AI opponent system
Rule	Production, statement
LHS (left-hand side)	Precondition, conditional statement, if side
RHS (right-hand side)	Then side, action, postcondition
Rules database	Rules set, working set
Variable	Operator, assertion symbol, datum, working memory element, fact
Working memory	Input, assertion set, perceptions, knowledge, set of facts
Scripting language	Predicate logic, symbolic script
Matching stage	Rule binding, LHS evaluation, variable unification
Selection stage	Rule selection, conflict resolution
Execution stage	Act, RHS evaluation

should get you started. This chapter will step through some of the design choices you might make for a more advanced or specific system and presents some of the innovations in our AAA titles.

9.1.1 Terminology

Terminology surrounding production systems can be confusing since it varies depending on the source of the material. For clarification, Table 9.1 lists the terms in use in this chapter and some common alternate terms.

9.1.2 Design Considerations

Coding your own production system can be very rewarding but there are some choices that need to be made beforehand. Skipping one of these decisions has caused problems in development in the past and many of these can be found in postmortems on production systems:

- What decisions is the system trying to make? (scope and domain choice)
- How are rules represented? (rules representation)
- How will rules be authored?
- How does the left-hand side (LHS) evaluate? (matching systems)
- What happens if the AI fails to find a rule?
- What happens if there are multiple rules? (selection algorithms)
- Execution and the design of the right-hand side (RHS)
- How will the system be tuned?

The following sections go into more detail about each one of these points.

9.2 What Decisions Is the System Trying to Make?

Like any other architecture, production systems are good at certain tasks and not at others. If the decisions are particularly simple, a rules-based system is probably overkill. However, if the game doesn't break down into nice discrete states and the decisions need to reflect different scenarios, a production system (or variation thereof) would be appropriate. At a minimum, a production system can be used when

- AI decisions are based on a variety of factors and are not easily quantified
- The system needs to respond quickly to changes in state
- There is an *expert* with knowledge of the game that needs encoding and that knowledge doesn't break down into a nice algorithm
- The actions for the system are independent of each other

The key decision is which part of the game the production system should be applied to. For example, production systems could make decisions for only part of the AI's process: when to do a trick or execute specific plays—though even these more narrow scenarios still need to fit the aforementioned criteria. A more specific AI can help limit when the system runs, which will help contain the runtime cost, though spikes in performance can still be an issue.

Alternatively, the production system could run all of the AI's decision logic. This sort of system requires more extensive optimization, and memory may be an issue since the scope of the AI is broader. The same can be true if the AI is being used for all of the simulation. Production systems can also be used for non-AI logic—such as for a game analysis system like color commentary for a sports game or for a contextual help system. The scope of these applications are harder to determine and handling the case when no rule triggers can be critical.

Performance-wise, production systems have a heavier update cost than most decision trees or state machines. Memory is required, but not necessarily more than what might be needed for another AI system. The rules themselves tend to have a small footprint, but they do add up quickly as a *typical* AI agent can require 100–500 rules. Different applications or more narrow applications of the system may require fewer rules, of course. There is also a hidden workflow and tool development cost in that an expert needs to author the rules, be able to iterate on those rules, and debug behaviors.

9.3 Choice of Rules Representation

The way rules are described is probably the biggest difference between the way these systems are implemented in games, compared to those used in research and other industries. The actual scripting language varies between systems: in CLIPS [Riley 13], it's C; SOAR has its own symbolic language [Laird 12]; and in our games, the language is very specific for the domain that the rule is being used for. In larger production systems, the scripting language supports predicate logic and unification to allow more flexibility in deciding which rules are applicable. This is often expensive both to develop (if you're coding your own) and to run. Due to the cost of unification, there are algorithms like Rete [Schneider 02, Millington 09] that optimize the matching. The advantage of a full predicate calculus (like SOAR) is that the language is very flexible and can describe a large variety of scenarios.

In deterministic games, however, unification is often difficult to take advantage of, and when it is removed, the development of a rules representation can be simplified. Unification can make it difficult to optimize for the scale of the AI. In the majority of our games, a more custom, smaller, and specific language was used. The elements of the LHS are designed to reflect the game's perception and state variables and the RHS are called into the animation or lower systems.

Another detail we discovered is a little unusual; sometimes, designers wanted the ability to create temporary variables. These variables may not map to a variable in the perception system but are to represent some value the designers want to check, the most common being some type of counter. In systems with a working memory, this is trivial to implement, but if there isn't a working memory, a form of scratch memory or blackboard is needed to carry these temporary variables.

One caution here is that designers might attempt to use temporary variables to introduce state into the decision process itself. This should be discouraged and the solution is usually to sit down with the designer to assist them with building a better rule. Temporary variables have also been used to introduce randomness into the system—which could be another sign that the designer may need assistance with the development of the LHS of a rule (i.e., it is being selected too often or too little). Having useful operators for the LHS of rules or building in a weighting system for rule selection can help here. The types of operators (usually logical) will help determine how extensive the rules language will need to be.

9.4 Method of Rules Authoring

Full proprietary systems often support their own editor and in these cases, the authors are effectively scripting their rules. In addition, with the ability to read definitions at runtime, the evaluation of the rules can be a fantastic asset for debugging purposes. Live editing could also be possible but in one variant system we developed, the rules are recorded.

9.4.1 Recorded Rule System

Recording systems allow for rapid iteration on rules and for very quick authoring of rules. The author runs the game, puts the system into record mode, and the system will automatically record the state of the game. When the specific type of action occurs, the state of the game is associated with the action and becomes the LHS of the rule (the action is the RHS). The disadvantage of this system is that manual tweaking of the rules is limited.

For the LHS (the recorded part), the following are necessary considerations:

- What's being recorded: which game state variables are important?
- How important each game state variable is: a weight for each variable that modifies how much that variable applies when being matched. Lower weighted variables are less necessary for a match.
- The tightness of the matching for each variable: the range of values that would be tolerated for each variable.
- How far back in time is needed to be recorded to form the LHS—is it a snapshot right before the action or a time range before the action.

In our implementation, the LHS rules produce a score that is considered a match if it surpasses a given threshold value. The rules that match form the matched rules set and the rest of the system is a classic production system. That is, the actions (RHS) go through a stage of conflict resolution and whichever rules are left after selection then run their actions.

The disadvantage is that the system works best if the rules share a lot of the same LHS variables. By the same token, sharing a lot of LHS elements does make the Rete algorithm a good choice. However, since predicate calculus wasn't in use, a custom matching system was implemented.

Determining which game state variables are needed for the LHS is a challenge. Once this step is completed, the actual authoring is very quick. A useful aid here is the ability for the system to rewind and playback the rule and to identify, at runtime, which rules are being triggered, and specific for a rule, how each of the elements of the LHS matched.

9.4.2 More Typical Systems

Nonrecorded authoring utilizes a custom editor—though the best systems seem to be the ones that read in text files and effectively compile them into rules. However, this may allow for authors to create malformed rules (which they will have to correct), but it gives them the most freedom to use whichever text editor they prefer. As such, this is one of the more accessible approaches.

Alternatively, if the grammar is quite specific, a more symbolic or graphical editor can be used. In retrospect, many designers seem to dislike graphical editors but depending on the complexity, this is an option. How easy it is for designs to author the rules will have a direct impact on the efficiency of the workflow.

9.5 Choice of Matching System

On some platforms where we are constrained by runtime performance, and unification isn't being supported, optimization of the system's matching stage is required. In one case, this led to the development of a new system that is a departure from a true production system. In this variant, with a very large rules database, the matching system stops at the first rule matched. This turned the production system into a specialized rules-based system but it did open up some unique applications. This type of selection, a type of greedy selection, is described in Section 9.5.1.

9.5.1 Greedy Matching/Selection

As an example, let's start with 500 rules in our database, numbered 1–500. In any given update, the rule matching is capped at 1 ms. For up to 1 ms, process the LHS of the rules in order. If a match is made, exit early. If a match is not made, continue to the next rule. Once a match is made, selection has been effectively completed as well since there is only one rule. That rule's RHS is then executed.

This approach created the complication that the AI would always fire the same rule for the same state. This was solved by randomizing the order of the rules in the rules database. Figure 9.1 demonstrates how this works.

- *Step 1*: Rule 1's LHS is evaluated but it doesn't match. The system tries rule 2 and so forth until it matches rule 4. Rule 4's RHS is then executed. Before the next update, the rules database is randomly shuffled.
- *Step 2*: Several updates later when the same state occurs again, the database is now in a different order. The system starts with rule 300 (which doesn't match in this example). Finally, rule 87 matches/is selected. Its RHS is then executed. (This example assumes rule 4 was shuffled below rule 87).

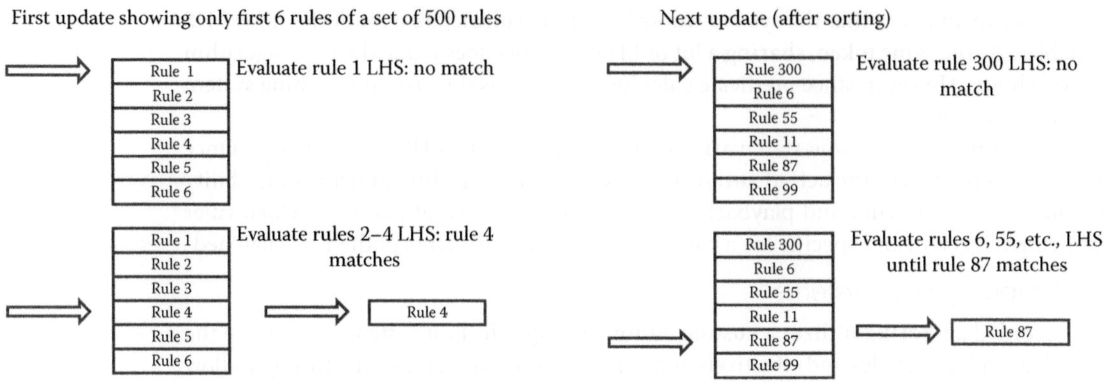

Figure 9.1

Greedy-based selection's first two updates (read left top to bottom, then right top to bottom).

This made the matching/selection processing extremely fast, allowing it to run very large rules databases on very limited platforms. In addition, we capped the matching so that only n numbers of rules were actually checked. This allows for the capping of a spike if all rules were not going to match. The capping is used because, like any list, the worst-case runtime is $O(n)$, which, again, can be prohibitive if n is large or a rule has an expensive LHS. It's worth noting that spikes can occur during matching (even with a cap) if a rule's LHS is very expensive to evaluate. This is mitigated by optimizing the LHS variables and by limiting the number of variables allowed for the LHS of a rule.

9.6 What Happens If the AI Fails to Find a Rule?

This may seem like a simple problem, but in practice, we've run into issues with the AI stalling. The first challenge is ensuring that it's obvious when the system fails to find a matching rule. The second challenge is to determine if that's acceptable. In some games, as long as the AI already has an action, it is fine if the AI doesn't find a new rule. In other games, this can lead to an AI standing absolutely still, or a factory not producing anything, or no tricks being performed, etc. As long as this is identified, a default rule could be the solution or additional rules to fill in the missing scenarios could be authored. In one unique case, backward chaining was used. This allowed the system to work out a sequence of steps to get to a matchable state. Backward chaining is beyond the scope of this chapter, but it is possible so long as the amount of back chaining is constrained.

9.7 What Happens If There Are Multiple Rules?

When there are multiple rules—that is, when greedy matching isn't in use—the matched rules need to undergo selection. The purpose of selection or conflict resolution is to ensure that the RHS of rules do not produce actions that conflict with each other but in some cases, it is also to scope down the number of rules. For example, in one system, when the set of matched rules is very large, only the first n rules are selected and this limits the number of RHS that execute and scales down the possible conflicts. If the RHS are kept as unique as possible, then the number of conflicting rules should be reduced since all rules would be able to run. We discovered it was important to track the number of times that a rule was executed (selected) since the selection algorithm was sometimes filtering out rules to the extent that they never were selected.

One system had the problem where for a few game states, a very large number of rules were always matched. The solution was to randomly select a subset, process these for conflicts (which were minimal), and then execute the subset. The random selection prevented a bias from creeping into the system from the selection algorithm (constraining the matching in this particular situation wasn't possible).

By contrast, in another system where a large number of matches occurred on a regular basis for many rules, a form of partially supervised training was the solution. The system supports a weighting of the LHS. When a rule is successful, its LHS weight is increased. If it fails, the LHS weight is decreased. This requires a selection algorithm that selects biased on a weight, a system that monitors the results of the RHS execution, and a method for the authors to tweak the amount of negative/positive feedback for the training system. The AI is then run many times in training mode against both itself and human players. After many games, the resulting database is locked and the result is a self-tuned rules database. The rules subset selected are the first *n* number of rules that matched—but not a random subset. Instead, since the subset reflects the result of training, the subset is the set of higher-performing rules.

This proves to be highly successful and it allows for the weeding out of bad rules. However, you will need to manually check for rules that are too highly rated and remove low-frequency rules. Low-frequency rules won't have as much reinforcement applied to their weights and will drift to the bottom. Likewise, you can boost the weight of a rule to increase its probability of selection if the expert feels a rule is being unfairly penalized.

9.8 Execution and the Design of the RHS

The RHS is the part of the system where an action can be taken as a result. It can be a flag, a setting of a variable, a message, or an event or any other form of implementation. In general:

- The RHS should be cheap as possible to execute
- As much as possible, the RHS should not preclude other RHS actions. That is, minimize the number of conflicts between the RHS if possible
- If implementing backward chaining, the RHS should be discretely identifiable and be reusable as a variable on the LHS
- The RHS should be able to support being called multiple times without restarting on every call or the LHS will need to check if a RHS action is already running
- There should be minimal dependency between RHS. If an RHS requires that another action runs before it, the rules need to enforce this, which adds additional checks to the LHS of the rules

Authoring of the RHS can be done in the same manner as the LHS or it can be distinct. In the example that follows, the RHS is generated during a recording session.

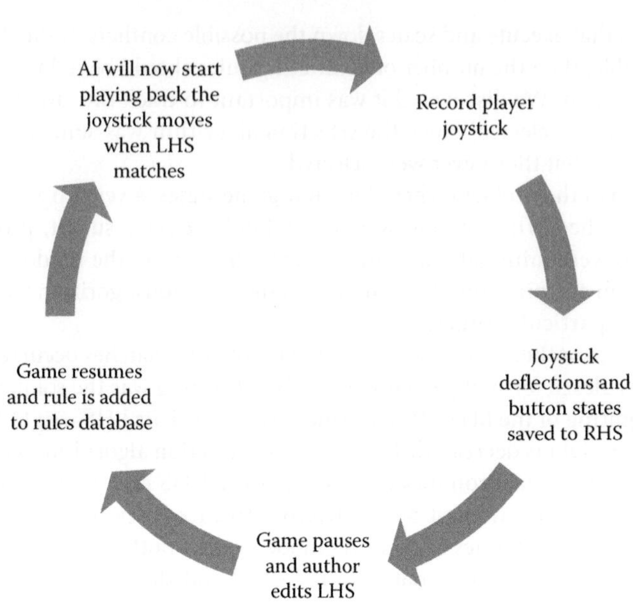

Figure 9.2

Recording the RHS.

9.8.1 More Complex RHS

One system records the joystick actions to produce the RHS of the rules, as shown in Figure 9.2. The execution for the RHS is simply a playback of the recorded joystick. This system allows a production system to be applied to a more complicated series of actions. It's very fast to author but it also requires a postediting stage so that authors can tweak the playback or discard bad recordings. Selection is also an issue since it isn't apparent when rules would be in conflict.

This is solved in two ways. In the first method, the rule is marked as unique so that if it matches, only that rule can be selected. In the second method, which applies to most of the rules, certain joystick maneuvers are identified and any rules that also hold these maneuvers are selected out. The authors could also watch the AI play, and if a rule is firing in the wrong scenario, the game can be paused, the rule opened for editing, and the LHS can be tweaked. The game then resumes but the production system reruns so that the author can ensure that their changes were appropriate. The final issue with this system is that if the player is what is being recorded, this will only work if the AI can use the data in the same way that the player uses it.

9.9 Debugging and Tuning

Several variants on how to author systems have been presented, but all of these need to be tuned and tested. Outside of the typical performance profiling, there are a couple of common key indicators that all of our systems have:

- Number of times a rule executes
- Success rate of executing the RHS

- Number of times a LHS variable matches
- List of rules that execute with a very high frequency
- List of rules that never execute

Another common debugging tool is to allow the RHS for a rule to be executed on demand—such that the behavior itself can be tuned or tweaked. Some systems support a complete reedit or rerecording of the RHS.

One implementation uses the selection step to train its AI. In training mode, the game is running with debug information available and the rules open for editing. If a rule is selected in training mode that the expert (designer) doesn't like, they can indicate that, and the system lowers the rule's weighting. Alternatively, the expert can pause the game and adjust the rule's LHS at runtime to ensure that the rule doesn't fire in that circumstance. They can likewise reward a given selection. This system requires a runtime editor for the rules and a way to reload the rules. Much more common is for production systems to log the results of matching and selection and have the *training* done offline.

In general, support for live editing can make iteration on the LHS of rules much easier. It can be difficult to author the constraints for the LHS of a rule for all possible scenarios—and having a way to edit and then rerun a scenario can help with this tuning immensely.

Logging and debug display of which rules are firing for a given AI is common. It helps to know which rules are creating the current behavior. Many systems support the graphical display for the test of the LHS variables. For example, if a variable is testing the range from one object to others, the debug might inscribe a circle to show what the radius/distance is set to.

9.10 Conclusion

Production systems have been used in a variety of published AAA titles and have proven themselves in many industries for some time now. All of the systems described are the results of the hard work of many engineers for different types of games over the course of many years. Some of these systems have evolved over time—almost all due to a practical constraint. Some are no longer production systems but all had their start with such a system and were usually developed initially over the course of 2 years.

A challenge all of these systems face is that they need to be very easy to iterate on and this has inspired new ways to author systems. Likewise, domain-specific systems have launched a variety of new ways to represent rules and to optimize matching outside of Rete and other classic algorithms. There is nothing inherently flawed with a more classic approach, but it is hoped that by presenting some of the techniques we use, readers might be inspired to think beyond the typical implementation and extend what is possible for these systems in their own games.

References

[Bourg 04] Bourg, D. M. and Seemann, G. 2004. *AI for Game Developers*. Sebastapol, CA: O'Reilly Media Inc.

[Laird 12] Laird, J. 2012. *The Soar Cognitive Architecture*. Cambridge, MA: Massachusetts Institute of Technology.

[Luger 93] Luger, G. F. and Stubblefield, W. A. 1993. *Artificial Intelligence Structures and Strategies for Complex Problem Solving*, 2nd edn. Redwood City, CA: The Benjamin/Cummings Publishing Company Inc.

[Millington 09] Millington, I. and Funge, J. 2009. *Artificial Intelligence for Games*. Boca Raton, FL: CRC Press.

[Riley 13] Riley, G. 2013. CLIPS: A tool for building expert systems. Sourceforge. http://clipsrules.sourceforge.net/ (accessed May 27, 2014).

[Schneider 02] Schneider, B. 2002. The Rete matching algorithm. *Dr. Dobbs Journal*. http://www.drdobbs.com/architecture-and-design/the-rete-matching-algorithm/184405218 (accessed May 27, 2014).

10

Building a Risk-Free Environment to Enhance Prototyping

Hinted-Execution Behavior Trees

Sergio Ocio Barriales

10.1 Introduction

Working on game technology is an iterative process. From game to game, we try to reuse as many systems as we can, but this leaves us in a situation where few substantial changes can be made to our already proven and solid solutions. At the same time, the creative nature of games is craving for changes, prototyping and testing new ideas, many of which come during production or even near the end of a project, when the risk of breaking things is at its peak. Can we do something to offer a risk-free environment to work on those potentially game changing ideas, or should we let them go?

Hinted-execution Behavior Trees (HeBTs) try to address this problem. The technology is an extension to the traditional behavior tree (BT) model that allows developers to dynamically modify the priorities of a BT based on some high-level logic; the new layer works in a plug-and-play fashion, which means it can be easily removed, leaving the base behavior untouched. This greatly reduces the inherent risk of changes.

In this chapter, we present the technology—which is a proven solution, successfully applied to the AI in *Driver: San Francisco*—then study how it works and show how HeBTs can be applied to real-world problems.

10.2 Explaining the Problem

Video games are a type of software that benefits from changes, and prototyping is necessary to develop fun. Building such experiences is a joint effort between programmers and designers. This is a two-way process: designers come up with ideas that are transformed into technology by programmers, but this technology, at the same time, refines the original idea and converts it into something feasible. This back-and-forth iterative process shapes what is going to be in the final game.

Let us focus in the technological aspect of the process. At a high-level, programmers produce black box systems with some tweakable parameters; game or level designers will use these black boxes to build what is going to be the final game. This workflow, which is shown in Figure 10.1, is very commonly used in the industry: ideas come from designers, who request the feature from engineering; after some implementation time, the new pieces are ready to use by design.

The key property of this type of process is that designers have very little control over what the new "box" is doing. In many situations, this is desirable, as programmers are the ones with the technical capabilities and designers do not need to worry about implementation details. However, it is worth noting that going from conception to being able to use the feature can be a long process and any change to a black box will restart the loop (i.e., generate another request that engineering will process and implement). Ideally, we would like design to be able to test or prototype new ideas faster, without going through engineering.

Although this scenario mitigates the potential long delays between conception and actual availability of features in game, it will most likely not be a feasible solution in most situations. The new workflow, as shown in Figure 10.2, could require working with very

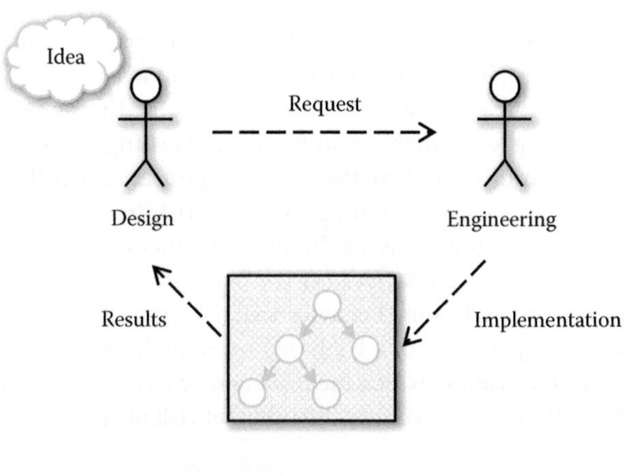

Figure 10.1

Traditional design/engineering collaboration workflow.

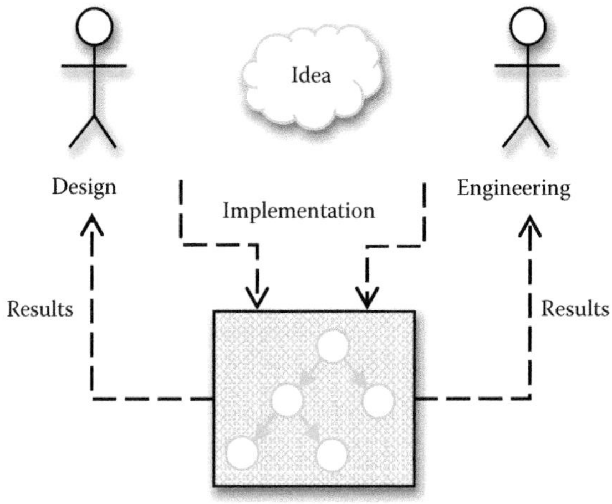

Figure 10.2

In an ideal world, both designers and engineers should have similar privileges when it comes to implementing and testing new ideas.

technical nonengineers that can manage, for example, modifying our BTs directly, which can be risky and produce more problems than benefits.

Another factor we have to take into account is that due to the complexity of video games, often new games use and improve previous games' codebases. This means we must be able to apply our solution to already existing code and technology.

The solution presented in this chapter, HeBTs [Ocio 10], is an extension to the traditional BT model. It tackles these problems and allows for fast and safe prototyping.

In the following sections, we will show how we can modify and manipulate an existing BT implementation to allow an extra high-level decision-making layer to dynamically change the priorities of certain sections of our behaviors.

10.3 Behavior Trees

The popularity of BTs has been growing steadily in the last 10 years and they have become a fundamental part of many games. In this section, we will cover the basics of what a BT is, as this knowledge is required to understand the rest of the chapter. Readers wanting to get better descriptions or some extra details about how a BT works should refer to [Isla 05, Champandard 08, Champandard 13] or the various materials available at AiGameDev.com [AIGameDev 15].

10.3.1 Simple BT

BTs are data-driven structures that can be easily represented in the form of a tree or graph. Nodes in a BT can be leaves or branches. Leaf nodes represent either an action or a conditional check, that is, nodes with a direct communication to the world. On the other hand, branch nodes do not perform any action but control the execution flow. In this category, we find nodes for control flow (selectors, sequences, parallels, etc.) or decorators.

Let us use a simple example, shown in Figure 10.3, to study how a BT works.

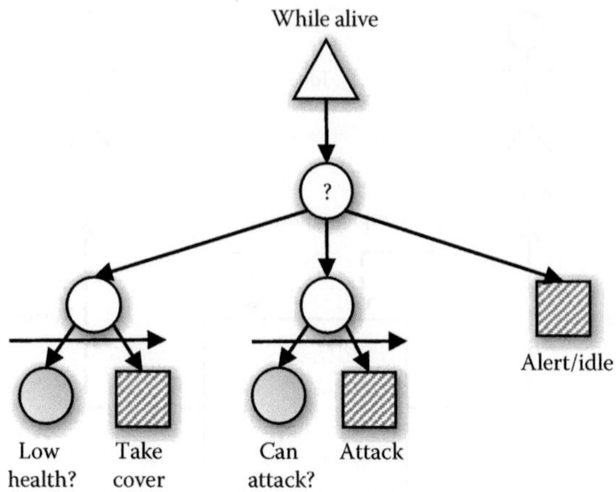

Figure 10.3

A simple BT.

In our example, we have modeled a very simple soldier behavior that will make the AI go and take cover if it is low in health, attack if it can, or just be alert (or idle) in any other case.

When a node is updated, it always returns a status value: "success," "failure," or "running." Return values are handled by parent nodes, which then decide what to do with this information. Thus, execution flow in a BT comes from its static structure (i.e., different branches will be activated in different orders all depending on what type of nodes we have used).

The most important node of the example tree is the selector (represented in the figure with a question mark). Selectors allow us to represent conditionals in a BT; translating it to what we could do in a programming language such as C++, selectors are the BT version of an "if-then-else" construction. It is this node's responsibility to decide what the AI is going to be doing at any given point. Priorities in the selector used in this example come from the order in which children of the selector are defined, that is, the leftmost node/branch is the highest priority and the rightmost, the lowest, resulting in static priorities.

Selectors try to pick the best possible child branch by testing each of them until one succeeds. In the example, we have represented two of the branches as sequences. A sequence is a special type of node that will run each of its children in order, succeeding if all the children succeed or failing otherwise. Due to this, sequences will very frequently be testing some preconditions as their first tasks and, if the preconditions pass, the actual actions can and will be run.

In the figure, our sequences have two children each: the first node is a condition node, or node that is just checking facts in the world; the second node is a proper action, or node that makes modifications in the state of the world.

Finally, we added a filter to our tree, which in the example is actually the root of the BT. The filter makes sure the behavior keeps running as long as the AI is alive.

For the sake of simplicity, we will continue using the example studied in the previous section, but the concepts presented in this chapter can be applied to BTs of any size.

10.3.2 Tree Complexity

The tree we are studying is very simple—it only has a handful of nodes—and making changes to it would be pretty straightforward. The problem is that, in a real-case scenario, trees can have dozens or hundreds of nodes and are not as easy to modify. There are some solutions to this, most of which involve having a good tool that allows us to work with the trees more easily (e.g., by expanding/collapsing branches or other UI improvements), but this does not remove the inherent complexity of the structure we are creating. Understanding the implications and side effects that a change might have in a complex tree is not trivial.

Going back to our example tree in Figure 10.3, let us say that at some point, we decide to bump the priority of the "attack" branch, because we want to model very brave (or, should we say, suicidal) soldiers that never retreat to take cover. In that situation, we would have to modify our tree, but that will make the "take cover" branch pretty much useless. What if, instead, we decide to only increase the priority of the attack in some circumstances?

Just by using the basic model, we can achieve this in a few different ways, like adding a new selector and duplicating some parts of the tree or by adding an extra precondition to the "take cover" branch, which is not that bad.

But, what if we would like the NPCs to attack for just 5 s then retreat and only do this for some specially flagged NPCs? Things can get complicated. In this case, we could end up with a tree similar to the one shown in Figure 10.4.

There are probably better ways to reorder the tree to accommodate for the new case, but the one presented in the figure is good enough to prove our point: modifying a BT to accommodate for new logic requires some thinking and always carries a risk.

In this chapter, we want to focus on a case like this one, particularly those in which we have to work with large BTs and where big changes are discouraged by deadlines or production milestones, but yet we need to keep iterating on our systems.

10.4 Extending the Model

BTs are a great technology, but they require good technical skills and hours of thinking to maintain them. The example of a change in the logic of a tree, studied in the previous section, showed how small changes in a simple tree can become difficult to understand very quickly. Logic changes are scary and, potentially, something we want to avoid, pleasing producers but hurting creativity.

In this section, we present a solution for these problems: HeBTs. The idea behind this extension is to allow extra layers of higher-level trees to run concurrently with our main tree and have the new logic dynamically modify priorities in the main BT.

10.4.1 Hint Concept

The main difference between a BT and a hinted-execution counterpart is that, while the execution flow in the former is defined by its own structure, HeBTs can reorder their branches dynamically to produce different results.

The system tries to imitate real-life command hierarchies, where lower-levels are told by higher-level ones what should be done, but, in the end, deciding how to do it is up to the individuals. In our system, the individual AI is a complex BT that controls the AI,

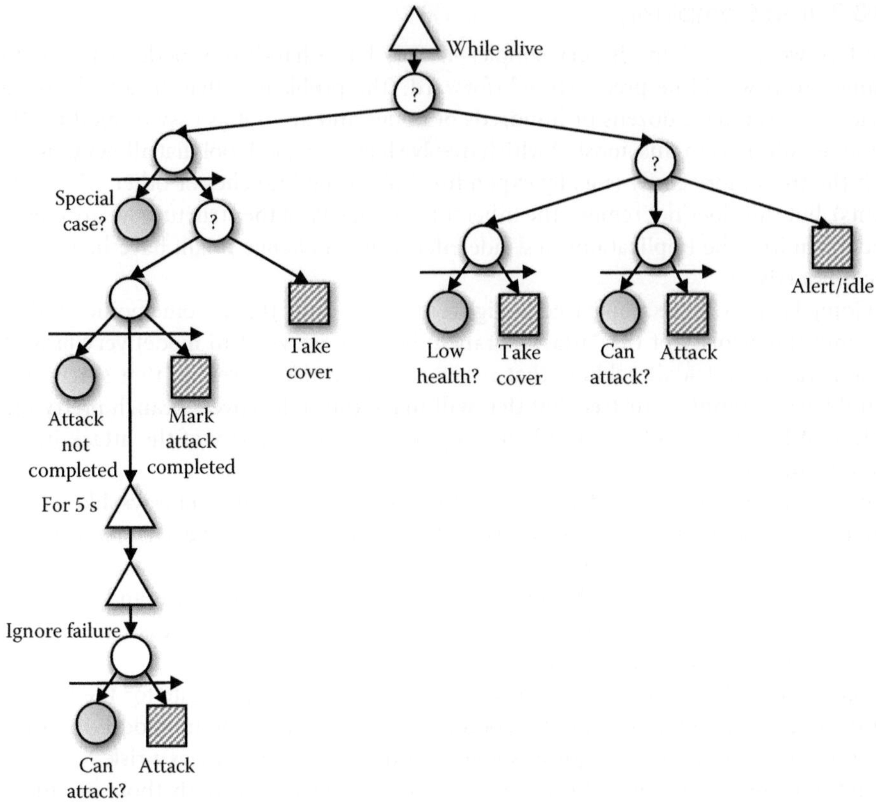

Figure 10.4

A more complex BT that adds special cases and extra checks.

so it behaves autonomously, but we want to open the higher-level layers to every member of the team, so they can test their ideas.

Nontechnical people will probably not be interested in how the AI works internally and will just want to tell it to do things (i.e., they just want to be able to order the AI to "kill an enemy," rather than "find a path to your enemy, then get closer, draw your weapon, and fire at your target, reloading your gun when you need to, etc."). These suggestions are called *hints* in the HeBT model.

A hint is a piece of information an AI can receive from a higher-level source and use it to produce an alternative behavior, as a consequence of a priority reorder. This means that an NPC, while maintaining its capability to respond properly to different situations, will take into account the requests coming higher in the command hierarchy to adapt its behavior to these petitions.

10.4.2 HeBT Selectors

Most of the decision making in a BT takes place in its selectors, which try different possibilities based on some priorities until a match is found.

In the simplest implementation of a selector, the priorities normally come from the order in which the branches were added to the selector node. So this means all of our priorities are *static*. HeBTs allow developers to change those priorities dynamically, resorting the branches associated to their selectors based on the information that a higher-level piece of logic has passed down to them. In order to do so, HeBTs introduce a new type of selector node.

Selectors, as composite nodes, have a list of children subbranches, each of which represents a possible action that a higher-level will, potentially, want the node to choose. We will talk further about these higher levels later on. In our new selectors, branches are assigned a unique identifier, which is assigned at creation time. This allows designers/engineers to name the branches and therefore create the hints that will favor each branch's execution.

Hints can be positive, negative, or neutral; if a hint is positive, the tree is being told to do something; if negative, it is being told not to do something; and, if neutral, the selector is not receiving the hint at all. Neutral hints are used to reset a priority to its default value.

The system works as follows: the AI is running a base BT (i.e., the one that contains all the logic for our game) and it can receive hints from a higher-level source. When a hint is received, the BT passes the information to all its selectors. The selectors will then recalculate the priorities of their branches.

For example, let us say we have a selector with five branches, named "A," "B," "C," "D," and "E." We have just implemented a HeBT system and our higher-level logic is telling us "D" and "E" are very desirable, but "A" is something we really should try to avoid. Figure 10.5 shows how the new selector would use this information.

The new selectors maintain four lists to control their children and their priorities. The first list just keeps track of the original priorities; the three extra lists store nodes that have been positively hinted (and thus, have more priority), nodes that have not been hinted (they are neutral), and nodes that have been negatively hinted (they have reduced priority). These extra lists are still sorted using the original order, so if two or more nodes are hinted, AIs will know which action is more important according to their original behavior.

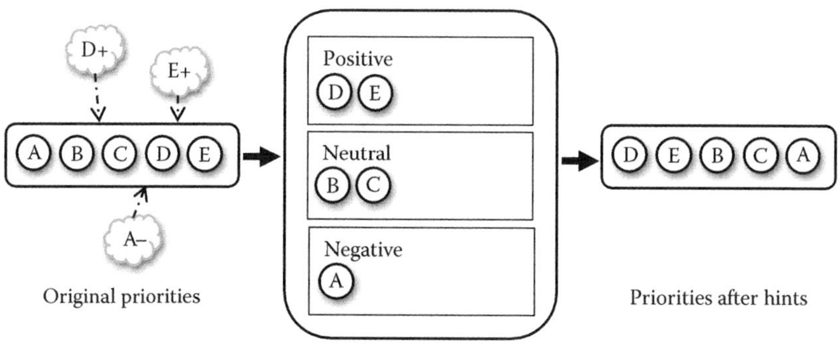

Figure 10.5

A HeBT selector sorts its children based on the hints it receives.

10.4.3 Hints and Conditions

With the modifications presented so far, we have made our trees capable of accepting hints and reordering the branches controlled by their selector nodes. It is up to tree designers to expose whatever logic they feel is important to expose to higher levels (i.e., to choose what hints the tree will accept).

As we have said, the execution flow in a BT is controlled by the type of nonleaf nodes we use and how we combine them. We can have many different type of nodes, but simplifying the traditional BT model, we could say most trees are collections of selectors and sequences, as shown in Figure 10.6.

Most of these sequences follow a basic pattern—shown in Figure 10.7—where some condition nodes are placed as the first children, followed by actual actions. This way, the actions will only get executed if these preconditions are met. If one of the conditions fails, the sequence will bail out, returning a failure, which will probably be caught by a selector that will then try to run a different branch.

This is not good for our hints in some situations, as the conditions could be making a hinted branch fail and not be executed. We can use the example shown in Figure 10.3 to illustrate this.

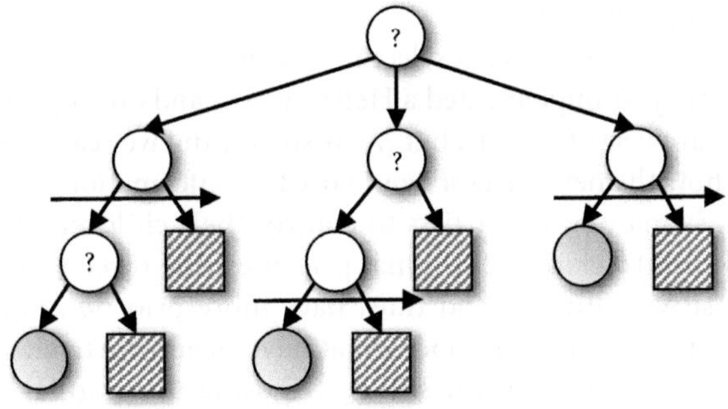

Figure 10.6

A basic BT can be seen as a series of selectors and sequences that control its execution flow.

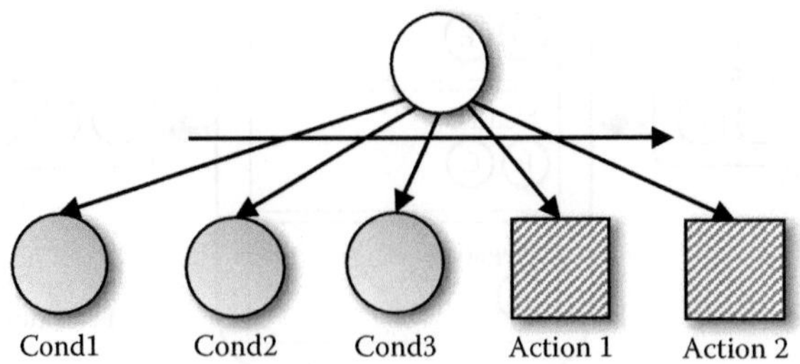

Figure 10.7

Basic sequence structure, where actions are preceded by a collection of preconditions.

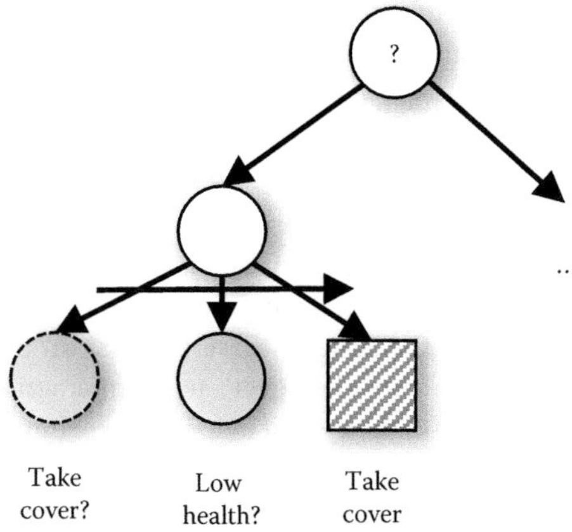

Figure 10.8

By using hint conditions, we can overcome problems caused by preconditions.

Let us say we have exposed the two first branches as hints. We will use the names "take cover" and "attack." Let us also say that we want to hint the AI to "take cover," by sending a positive hint to the tree.

The way we had defined our BT, the "take cover" branch already had the highest priority, so the selector does not really need to reorder its children (actually, it does reorder them, but this time, the order of the branches will not change). If we look closely at the first branch, we can see "take cover" is built as a sequence that checks a precondition (just as shown in Figure 10.7), called "low health?".

In the case where the AI has full health, the precondition will fail, making the sequence bail. The failure is ultimately propagated to the selector, which will run a different branch. Because we were hinting the AI to "take cover," we might be expecting it to take our suggestion into account, and not just ignore it blatantly.

So, we need a way to be able to ignore these preconditions *if that makes sense*, that is, if the condition is not really mandatory for the rest of the branch to be executed. In our example, we did not really need to be low on health to cover: this was just a design decision, probably trying to make the behavior more believable.

For that, HeBTs offer a *hint condition node*. This type of node is used to allow the BT to test if it is receiving a certain hint and what its type is (positive, negative, or neutral). We can modify our example's BT to modify the preconditions of the sequence, so our branch will look like what we show in Figure 10.8.

10.5 Multilevel Architecture

In the previous section, we introduced the concept of hints and how behaviors can be dynamically modified through them. These hints were sent to our trees by what we called "higher levels of logic."

Different approaches can be taken to implement these levels. For example, a quick and effective solution could be a layer of scripts that use the system to generate new behaviors.

However, the usage of scripts can make things harder to understand, as they normally require some technical background. A visual solution would be much more appropriate, as visualizing things is much simpler than learning a new language and its rules. Why not take advantage of the tools we have built to generate our base BTs, and expand it?

10.5.1 Behavior Controllers

BTs are constructed using a set of building blocks, among which we have actions; they are the nodes in charge of modifying the environment or the state of the AI instance itself. Depending on the granularity of the system, these actions can be more or less complex, ranging from subbehaviors, such as "take cover" to atomic actions such as "find cover spot." For users not interested in how the behaviors work—but just in the fact they do work—the coarser the granularity, the simpler the system will be for them.

Modifying a big BT can be complex and could require taking into account quite a lot of variables. Also, small changes in a tree could lead to undesirable behaviors, making AIs not work as expected. Because of this, we do not want new behaviors to be created from scratch; instead, we just want them to be flexible and malleable. So let us keep a base tree, maintained by engineers, and provide the team with the means to create new higher-level trees.

Higher-level trees use a different set of building blocks. Specifically, we will replace the action nodes with some new nodes that we call *hinters*. These nodes, as their name indicates, will send hints to the tree's immediate lower-level BT. The new trees will work on top of our base behavior, modifying it dynamically and allowing designers to prototype new ideas easily and safely, as the main BT is not modified permanently, thus reducing risks.

From now on, our AI instances will no longer be controlled by a single tree but by a number of layers of BTs. This set of trees is owned by a behavior controller. These controllers are in charge of maintaining the multiple levels of trees an AI can use and of running all of them to produce the final results.

A behavior controller works as a stack where we can push new trees. The top of the stack represents the highest level of logic, whereas the bottom contains the base BT. Every time we add a new tree, the controller informs the newly created high-level tree about what its immediate lower-level tree is, which will allow hints to be sent to the correct BT. This multilevel architecture is shown in Figure 10.9.

Once all the different trees have been created and registered with a behavior controller, it can run the final behavior. HeBTs are run from the top down, so higher levels are run first; this means that, by the time a tree is going to be executed, it would have already received all its hints, and their branches would be properly sorted. This process is shown in Figure 10.10.

By the end of each update, the AI will have run whatever action it has considered to have the higher priority, based on the information it has gathered from the environment *and* the hints it has received.

10.5.2 Exposing Hints to Higher Levels

High-level trees are built using a base BT to determine the hints that are available to them. When creating new trees, designers can name the branches of their selectors, which will

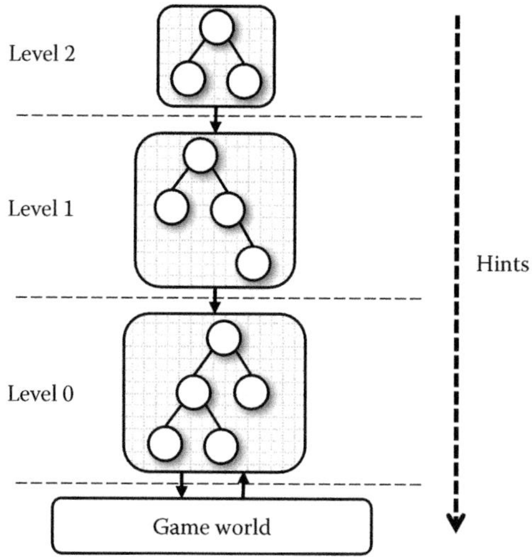

Figure 10.9

Multilevel structure of a HeBT.

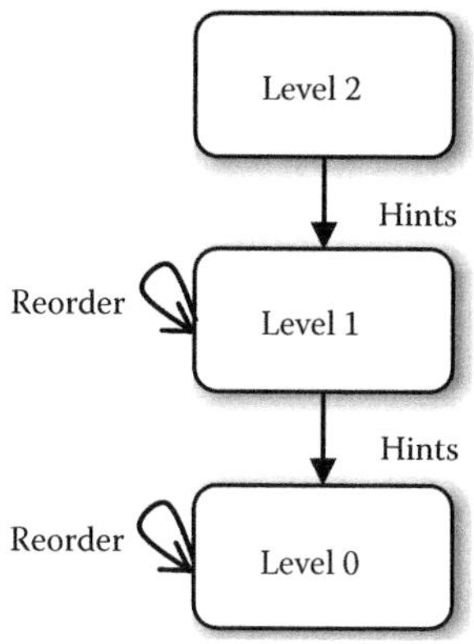

Figure 10.10

Each level in a HeBT will send hints to the level immediately below, causing the lower-level to reorder its priorities.

automatically expose the corresponding hints. In a similar way, if a condition hint is used anywhere in the low-level tree, the hint will automatically be exposed.

High-level trees cannot use actions; instead, they use hinters. Hinters allow trees to send any of the hints their lower-level trees are exposing to them, in order to produce new behaviors. Internally, they are very simple nodes: their logic is only executed once, and they bail out succeeding right after the hint has been sent.

It is important to note that hinters can send different types of hints, allowing us to send positive or negative hints. They can also set a hint back to neutral if necessary.

10.6 More Complex Example

So far, we have studied what a HeBT is and how it works internally. We have also been illustrating our exposition with a simple example. However, this example does not show the full potential of the system, so in this section, we will present an example that is closer to what we could find in a real game.

10.6.1 Prototyping New Ideas

There are many different ways to modify a behavior to obtain different responses from two AIs running the same logic. Some of them are even trivial to implement, such as the use of personality traits. However, adding more complex logic on top of an existing behavior starts getting complicated, especially if we do not want or cannot change the original BT.

In a real project, we are always subject to changes at any time, but new ideas and changes may pose a big risk to the project or require resources we cannot afford. As we saw, HeBTs allow us to generate this logic easily, just by using a high-level BT that will run on top of our base tree, guiding its normal execution toward what our new logic is suggesting should be done.

10.6.2 Base Behavior

Working on a new behavior requires that we have a base one working correctly, as it will define the way AIs in our game respond to different situations. In a real-life project, it would also have been thoroughly tested and optimized.

Let us say that for our example, our design team have decided the game needs some soldiers that

- Are able to patrol using a predefined route
- Detect the player as an enemy when they enter their cone of vision
- Attack the player once it is identified
- Try to find a cover position to keep attacking from it, if the agent takes damage

This behavior would be represented by a complex BT, and we show a simplified version of it in Figure 10.11.

Let us take a look at the base behavior. At a first glance, we can see there are three main branches controlled by a selector. We have named the branches "PATROL," "COVER," and "ATTACK;" this automatically exposes hints with the same names that can be used by a higher-level tree. The BT's root is a conditional loop that will keep the tree running until the AI is killed.

The first branch defines the agents' precombat behavior. In our case, we have chosen to have the soldiers patrol the area while they do not have an enemy. As we saw in a previous section, this condition might prevent the tree from behaving as expected when it receives the "PATROL" hint; to fix that, we have added a hint condition and put both condition nodes under a selector, which will allow us to enter the branch if either condition is true. It is also worth noting we have used a parallel node to run our conditions as an assertion (i.e., the conditions will be checked continuously to enforce they are always met); this way, the branch will be able to bail out as soon as the AI engages an enemy.

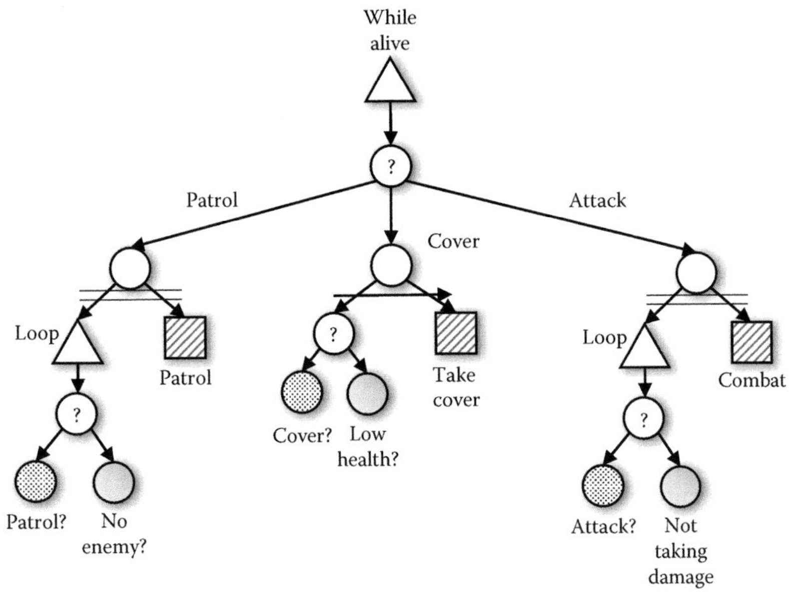

Figure 10.11

Simplified base BT our soldiers will run.

The second branch will make sure the agent takes cover when it is low on health. Similarly to the patrol branch, we have added a hint condition to make sure the tree will use hints properly.

Finally, the third branch is our combat behavior. Its structure is very similar to the "COVER" branch, with an assertion running to ensure combat is only triggered if we are not under fire (i.e., taking damage).

10.6.3 Prototype Idea

Once our AIs are able to run autonomously, in an ideal situation, most of the work for AI engineers will consist of debugging and polishing the behaviors. However, we could find ourselves in a situation when substantial changes to these behaviors are required, or maybe the team needs to keep testing new ideas to keep improving the game experience. This is where the power of HeBTs comes into play.

To demonstrate the capabilities of our new system, we will implement a "disguise" system just by adding a high-level tree to hint our base BT what should be done. The design for our feature is

- Players can wear the clothes of the enemies they kill, going unnoticed to other AIs if they do so.
- AIs should not recognize "disguised" players as enemies. However, they should react if the player damages them.

Basically, these changes would require gameplay and AI code modifications, and this new feature could not make it through to the final game. Because our game is using HeBTs, we could delegate the prototyping of new ideas to the design team or at least let them play with new thoughts with minimal technical supervision (if we have the appropriate tools for the job).

We must bear in mind that if we want to have a system that requires virtually no programming work to be extended, we must start from designing our base behaviors correctly. Also, building a complete set of tree nodes and conditions can facilitate things further down the line.

10.6.4 Creating a High-Level Tree

So, as designers, the idea behind our new system is that we want AIs to ignore players that are "in disguise." So, basically, we want to hint the base level to prefer patrolling. The first pass at the high-level tree would be very similar to the one shown in Figure 10.12.

This is, in a nutshell, what our high-level tree should look like. However, we still have to define our condition. We want to check if the player is disguised, but we do not have a condition that does that.

Our system must have defined a way for AIs to maintain some knowledge about the world. A common way to do this is by using blackboards. Let us say we do have such a system, where we can write information and from where we can get details about the state of the world. In this case, our condition would be transformed to an "is enemy in disguise?" condition that checks for that information in the blackboard. But, if we need to read this information from the blackboard, we must have set it somewhere first.

For the sake of simplicity, we will use a "broadcast" action that allows us to write a value to the system's blackboard. What we want to do is to let other AIs in the world (by adding this information to the blackboard) about the new status of the player as soon as one AI dies. Since our first pass at the high-level tree was already checking if the AI was alive, let us extend the tree to modify the blackboard properly. We show this in Figure 10.13.

The first thing we have done is add an extra sequence as the new root of our tree. The idea behind it is that we want to run the "alive branch" (on the left) first, but always have a blackboard update following it.

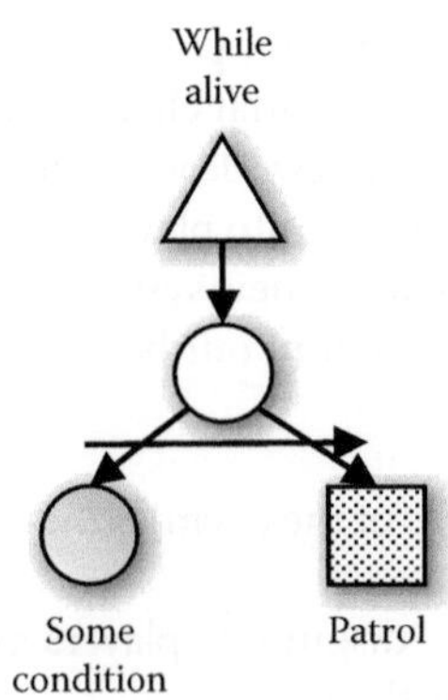

Figure 10.12

Basic idea behind the "disguise" system.

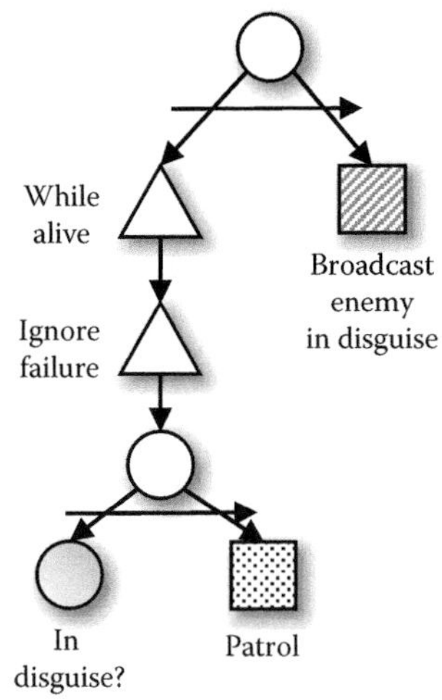

Figure 10.13

A first pass on a more complex high-level tree.

We have also added an extra decorator as a parent to our old sequence. The decorator's purpose is to ignore failures in the sequence, which will happen pretty frequently in our case (in fact, the sequence will fail every frame unless the player is in disguise); we never want the branch to fail, as it would break the root sequence.

So, with these changes, while the AI is alive, the tree will continue checking the blackboard to decide whether or not to hint the base BT to patrol; and, once the agent is dead, the blackboard will always be updated. When this happens, the remaining AIs will then have their blackboards updated, and they will start sending "PATROL" hints to their base BTs, causing those agents to ignore the player as intended.

Although this is a good first attempt at implementing the new feature, the tree is not completely correct yet, as AIs will not react to damage anymore if the player is disguised. To fix this problem, we need to clear the blackboard if an agent is under attack. The final high-level tree is shown in Figure 10.14.

In the final tree, we have added an extra selector that will catch whether the enemy has been attacked, clearing the disguise flag. The second branch of the selector is the same one our previous iteration had and, finally, the third branch is just making sure that, if nothing is going on, the "PATROL" hint is cleared.

10.6.5 Analyzing the Results

The key to this type prototyping is that the new logic is completely optional. We can just let the system know about it and see how the AI behaves with the extra feature or we can just remove the high-level tree, which will leave our original behavior untouched.

The base behavior requires minimal data changes, which are almost deactivated unless a high-level tree is used. Particularly, we have been using two types of base BT modifications: branch naming is a harmless change, as it does not affect the behavior at all; hint conditions do modify the original structure of the tree, but since they are straightforward

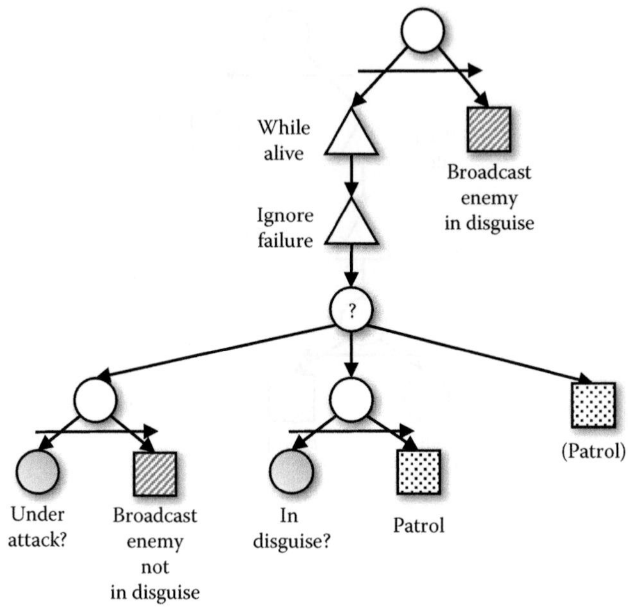

Figure 10.14

Final high-level tree that models the new feature.

flag (hint) checks, and the hints will never be enabled if a high-level tree is not present, it poses a very small risk. Hint conditions are also optional, and in some situations, we might not want to use them at all. Simply naming branches preemptively will expose dynamic priority control.

10.7 Other Applications

Over the course of this chapter, we have focused on the benefits HeBTs bring to quick and safe prototyping. These trees can also be used to help in other cases. In this section, we will present a couple of extra scenarios that can benefit from using HeBTs.

10.7.1 Adaptation

There are different ways to make our game more accessible to different types of players. Among them, we find the manual selection of a "difficulty level," which has been part of the game almost from the very beginning, or the adaptation of the difficulty level or situations to the player, which can allow us to offer a better and tailor-made experience to different groups of people.

HeBTs can help us offer different experiences to each player experience level and also allow us to modify things on the fly: we can define a different high-level tree per category and, in run-time, decide which one is most appropriate for our player. The base tree will recalculate its priorities based on the hints it is receiving and, hopefully, the player will enjoy our game better.

This is the approach Ubisoft's *Driver: San Francisco* used. In *Driver*, getaway drivers were able to adapt their route selection algorithm—which was controlled by a BT—by implementing a range of different high-level trees that could guide the route generation process [Ocio 12]. These high-level trees were called "presets," and they did things like making the route finder prefer straight routes (so casual players can catch the getaways easier) to zigzag routes or routes through dirt roads or alleyways.

10.7.2 Group Behaviors

Our hinted-execution model could also be used to create complex group behaviors based on command hierarchies. Hints would flow down the chain, allowing some AIs to have a better control over what others should do.

In a hint-based system, we would be able to create new links in our chain as high-level trees that are built on top of several base behaviors, rather than just one; in this case, each base tree would expose the orders that a particular class of AI can accept. Our higher-level tree would be able to broadcast hints to groups of AIs that are using the behaviors this level was based on.

An example of this would be a small army that has warriors, archers, and medics. A simplified version of their behaviors is shown in Figure 10.15.

We could use different generals, defining different high-level trees to create an intelligent army that obeys the orders we want to send. For instance, we could build a high-level AI that wants to attack with its archers first, holding off warriors and medics, and continuing with a melee-type attack that includes sending the medics along with the warriors to try and heal wounded units, and never allowing the units to retreat. The high-level tree that would control such behavior is shown in Figure 10.16.

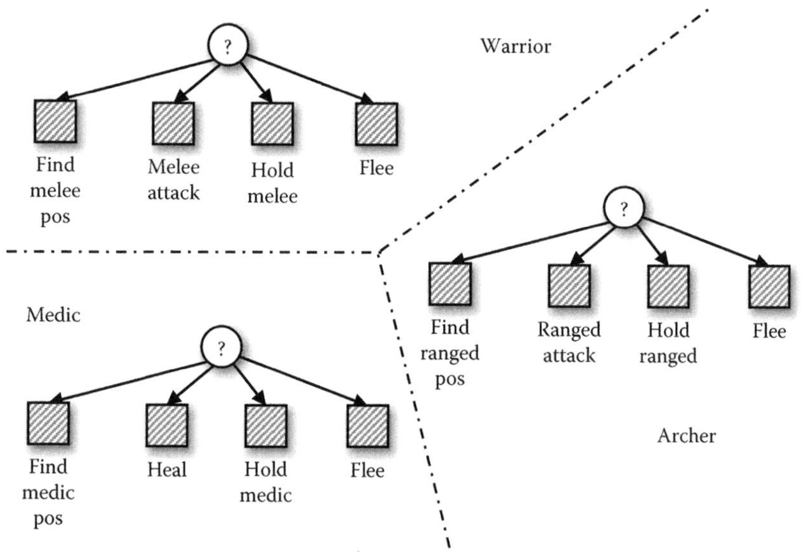

Figure 10.15

Base BTs controlling the different types of units in our army.

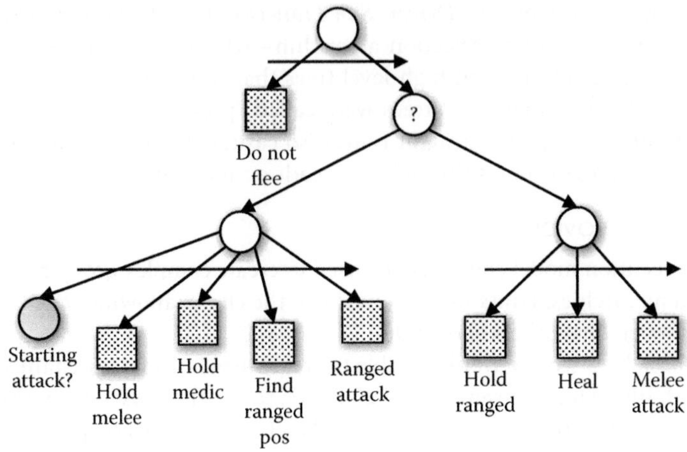

Figure 10.16

High-level tree that will define a tyrant high-level AI that never allows individuals to retreat.

Groups of units (as high-level entities) would also be controlled by HeBTs, so they could potentially receive hints too, producing a complex chain of command that can help us create more credible group behaviors.

10.8 Conclusion

BTs are a proven technology that has been used in many successful commercial games. However, as with any other technology, any change is risky, especially if these changes are made in the last stages of production.

HeBTs try to mitigate these risks by providing a way to do dynamic, revertible modifications to bigger, more complex BTs. These modifications are also controlled by another BT (that we call "high-level" BT), so we can still take advantage of the power and visual editing capabilities of the technology.

As we showed in this chapter, HeBTs help in many different problems, such as rapid prototyping, dynamic behavior adaptation, or group behaviors. In any case, risks are kept to a low, as we will never lose our base, tested behavior.

This technology is not hard to implement on top of an existing BT system and has also been used in an AAA game, *Driver: San Francisco*. HeBTs were key to the success of the game's AI, allowing its developers to adapt the behaviors of their getaway drivers to the skills of their players.

References

[AIGameDev 15] AIGameDev.com. http://www.aigamedev.com/.

[Champandard 08] Champandard, A. J. 2008. Getting started with decision making and control systems. *AI Game Programming Wisdom*, Vol. 4, pp. 257–263. Boston, MA: Course Technology.

[Champandard 13] Champandard, A. J. and Dunstan P. 2013. The behavior tree starter kit. In *Game AI Pro: Collected Wisdom of Game AI Professionals*. Boca Raton, FL: A K Peters/CRC Press.
[Isla 05] Isla, D. 2005. Handling complexity in the Halo 2 AI. In *Proceedings of the Game Developers Conference (GDC)*, San Francisco, CA.
[Ocio 10] Ocio, S. 2010. A dynamic decision-making model for game AI adapted to players' gaming styles. PhD thesis. University of Oviedo, Asturias, Spain.
[Ocio 12] Ocio, S. 2012. Adapting AI behaviors to players in driver San Francisco: Hinted-execution behavior trees. In *Proceedings of the Eighth AAAI Conference on Artificial Intelligence and Interactive Digital Entertainment (AIIDE-12)*, Stanford University, Stanford, CA.

11

Smart Zones to Create the Ambience of Life

Etienne de Sevin, Caroline Chopinaud, and Clodéric Mars

11.1 Introduction

To design "background nonplayer characters" that breathe ambient life into a virtual environment, we propose new concepts that facilitate the creation of *Living Scenes*. The aim is to generalize their use in video games as a way to improve the feeling of presence for the player. This chapter introduces the concept of *Smart Zones* used to design credible, consistent, and interactive ambient life, involving autonomous and adaptive NPCs.

11.2 Designing an Ambience of Life

Consider the following situation: *8 pm, the night is still young when our player arrives at a restaurant looking for his friends. As he enters the building, he sees dozens of clients eating, talking, and drinking. His friends, as they see him, made signs for him to join them. On the way, he meets a waiter asking him if he wants to order something.*

The problem we are trying to solve is how to quickly structure and design this ambience of life. Our answer: using a set of Living Scenes!

11.2.1 What Is a Living Scene?

A Living Scene is a set of nonplayer characters (NPCs) interacting with each other and with the players. Its aim is to give a feeling of life to a virtual environment, to give the player *a sense of being there*. To achieve this, the behaviors resulting from the Living Scene have to make sense in the context of the current setting, location, story, and actions of the player. Therefore, the living scene is located in the virtual environment, situated in time and reactive to the presence of the player.

Each NPC involved in a scene fulfills a *role*. Each role in the scene is defined by a set of *behaviors* that will be executed by the NPCs to achieve the scene. The behaviors assigned to the different roles are staged in order to execute the collective behavior expected for the scene.

Our aim is to split the design of ambient life in two: the individual behaviors level and the Living Scenes level. With such a distinction, game designers are able to focus separately on each level in order to create complex individual behaviors, as well as an explainable and consistent collective behavior. Furthermore, we introduce a role abstraction layer that enables reusability and allows a wide range of possible combinations.

Back to our restaurant example, we can extract three Living Scenes: the clients exhibiting behaviors related to the restaurant such as eating, talking, and drinking (Scene 1), the friends exhibiting specific reactive behaviors related to the presence of the player (Scene 2), and the waiter exhibiting an interactive behavior with the clients of the restaurant including the player (Scene 3).

In Scene 1, each NPC assumes the role of a client and has access to three individual behaviors: "eat," "talk," and "drink." These behaviors can be staged in a specific order, or chosen automatically by autonomous NPCs. In that case, the clients decide when is the best moment to drink, eat, or talk related to their current states and the global situation in Scene 1.

Scene 2 focuses on a part of Scene 1: the clients who are player's friends located at specific table in the restaurant. Each NPC in this scene assumes the same role of friend and has access to one more reactive behavior: "make a sign to the player to join them." They can also access the behaviors of a client such as "eat," "talk," and "drink."

Finally, in Scene 3, the unique NPC assumes the role of a waiter and can execute the "interact" behavior. This behavior is triggered when another NPC enters the scene (around the waiter). More precisely, when the player enters the scene, the waiter exhibits a complex interactive behavior to discuss with the player about his or her desire to drink or eat.

11.2.2 Performing Living Scenes through Smart Zones

To put a living scene into a virtual environment and to manage its execution, we propose to define a scene through a Smart Zone. A Smart Zone is a concrete representation of a Living Scene that can be located in the environment and executed in a stand-alone way to manage the lifetime of the scene. The concept of Smart Zones is inspired by *Smart Objects* [Kallmann 99], which is often used in video games for managing agent–object interaction such as in The Sims [The Sims 99].

The idea is to include the description, within Smart Zones, of all the characteristics of the Living Scenes and how the involved NPCs execute behaviors in order to play out the scene. Thus, when an NPC go into a Smart Zone, he or she has access to every characteristic of the scene, and a role is potentially assigned to the NPC, to be an actor of the scene. If required, he or she may have to execute a specific behavior according to the other NPCs playing in the scene. As Smart Objects manage the interactions between agents and objects, Smart Zones manage the individual and collective behaviors and their relation with the NPCs interacting within the zones. When the game is running, the Smart Zones will manage the "casting" from the available and skilled NPCs. Similar approaches, applying smart events to narrative for storytelling, have been described in earlier works [Stocker 10, Shoulson 11].

This approach leads to a decentralized control of the NPCs' behaviors in dedicated zones representing the Living Scenes. This is a way to reduce the complexity of the game control: it is not necessary to control the current situation as a whole; we can just focus on each Smart Zone instantiated in the environment. Moreover, because a Smart Zone embeds all the characteristics and information essential for the execution of the Living Scene, the control of the NPCs involved in a scene is easier: it is possible to assign, stage, and execute the NPCs' behaviors directly through the zone independently of the NPCs themselves.

11.3 Smart Zones in Practice

This section describes the definition and execution details of smart zones.

11.3.1 Definition of Smart Zones by Game Designers

To develop Living Scenes, game designers define Smart Zones in the game environment. Defining a Smart Zone means filling all the characteristics essential for the execution of the related Living Scene:

- The roles to be assigned to the NPCs
- The behaviors able to perform a role
- The orchestration of the scene by defining a sequence of behaviors
- The triggers for the scene activation
- The site of the scene (position, size, and shape)

The concepts of roles and behaviors are essential for the scene execution. The role is a way to assign a specific set of behaviors to an NPC that entered in a zone. A role is the main relation between an NPC and a scene. When an NPC assumes a role, he or she executes concretely the behaviors associated with the role in the scene. A behavior is a sequence of actions executed by the NPC during a given time interval. We decided to use these concepts because they are easily understandable and accessible for game designers. Moreover, these concepts are often used in storytelling and agent design in general.

In this way, the introduction of these concepts allows the design of the Living Scene in independent steps:

- The design of the individual behaviors
- The specification of the roles (defined by a set of behaviors)
- The organization of the Living Scene through the choice of the roles dedicated to the scene

Then, the most important part of the Living Scene design is the orchestration between the NPCs' behaviors in order to obtain a coherent collective behavior. Game designers can place behaviors of the NPCs into a timeline according to the roles, which leads to a sequence of behaviors for the Living Scene (or a part of the Living Scene) and describes the triggers to manage the starting of the scene.

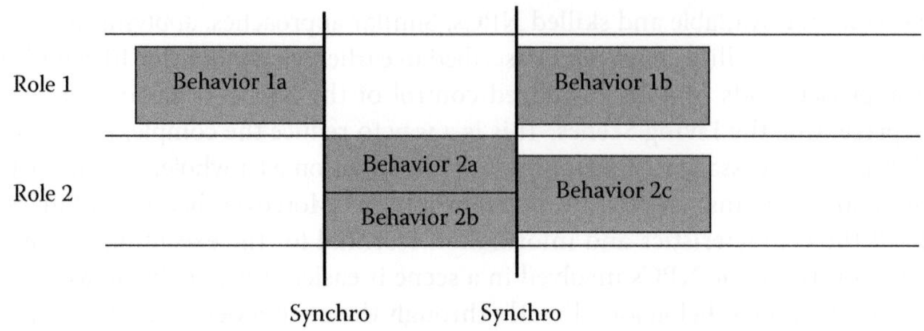

Figure 11.1

A timeline defining the orchestration of behaviors.

The timeline is organized as follows (see Figure 11.1):

- One row exists for each role.
- The behaviors are represented as boxes, and they have a beginning and an end. When several behaviors are placed at the same "time" in a single row, it means one of them will be chosen at runtime. This choice is specified by design (e.g., probability function) or automatically through the decision-making process of the NPC. This point leads to improve the variety of the observed behaviors.
- Synchronization points are used to trigger the beginning and ending of behaviors across several roles. They are added automatically after one behavior is added at the end of the timeline. However, the game designers can drag another behavior between two synchronization points to obtain specific behavioral sequences. For a given synchronization point, when all the behaviors executed by main roles end, it leads to the cancellation of the behaviors of all the other nonmain roles. For example, when the juggler finishes his or her performance, the spectators stop commenting or applauding and start congratulating (see Figure 11.6 in Section 11.4.2). If an NPC enters the Smart Zone during the execution of the Living Scene, he or she synchronizes his or her behavior with the current behavior executed by the main roles.

Finally, the game designers place the Smart Zones in the environment. The environment is considered as the "world zone" and includes all the Smart Zones. Smart Zones can overlap, in which case a priority order between the scenes must be defined. This order can be based either on the size of the zones or directly through priorities defined by the game designer.

In our example of a restaurant, each Living Scene is designed in the environment with a Smart Zone. Each Smart Zone defines the role (clients, friends, or waiter), the behaviors (drink, eat, ...), and the place of the scene in the environment. For instance, the orchestration between the behaviors in the third Smart Zone (to develop Scene 3) corresponds to a sequence of interactions between the waiter and the player in order to obtain a consistent collective behavior. The trigger of the Scene 3 consists in the entrance of an NPC in the zone. Finally, the Smart Zone to develop Scene 2 has priority on the Smart Zone to develop Scene 1.

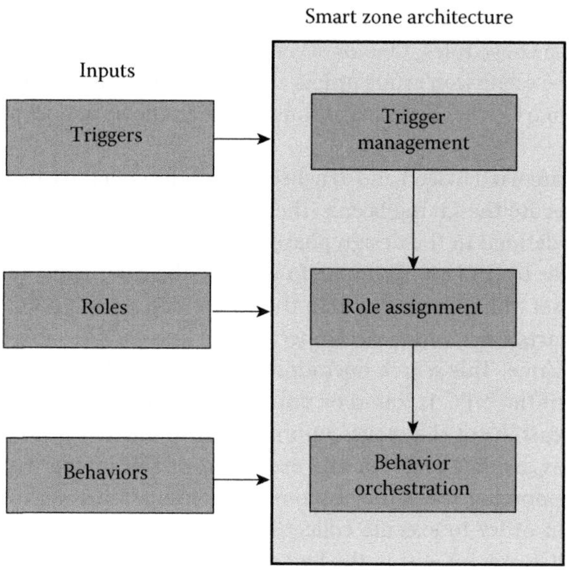

Figure 11.2

Runtime architecture of a smart zone.

11.3.2 Functioning of the Smart Zone Architecture

At runtime, when a Smart Zone is executed, it manages the lifetime of the Living Scene. In this section, we will present the runtime architecture (see Figure 11.2) for Smart Zones. It is made of several modules with different responsibilities. A Smart Zones will instantiate, start, execute, and stop a parameterized Living Scene and assign behaviors to NPCs.

11.3.2.1 Trigger Management

Triggers are a set of activation rules defining when a Living Scene should be started. Triggers can be the occurrence of a specific moment in time, the presence of a given NPC or player in a specific area, the beginning of an interaction with a particular object, or a combination of several of these rules.

This first module of the architecture aims to check whether the current situation allows the scene to be executed. The module takes as inputs the triggers defined for the scene and checks if all the trigger conditions are verified in the current situation. If that is the case, the next module steps in.

Let's consider, in our example, the waiter serving the player. The scene can start if and only if the two following trigger conditions are true: the waiter and another NPC are in the same zone at the same time, and it is after 8 pm.

11.3.2.2 Role Assignment

This module is responsible for the assignment of a role to each NPC present in the Smart Zone. An NPC has only one role in a scene. As described previously, a Smart Zone embeds a set of roles defined for the scene. In order to manage automatically the assignment of the roles, we define three subsets: main roles, supporting roles, and extras.

Main roles are essential for the execution of the scene. The scene itself revolves around characters fulfilling these roles. One or several NPCs can take main roles; they become the main actors. The scene won't start unless all the main roles are fulfilled with characters belonging to the Smart Zone. The scene is finished when the behaviors of all the main roles are finished.

The main roles are used to lead and synchronize all the collective behaviors. Main roles are essential to execute the Living Scene. The main role can be cast in two ways: either a particular NPC is defined in the design phase as a main actor for the Living Scene or the module should have to find an NPC able to endorse the role. Thus, the module chooses an NPC from the set of NPCs located into the Smart Zone. If no NPC is able to take the role, the module starts a dynamic search operation to find an NPC able to take a main role around the Smart Zone. This search operation uses an expanded zone, which is automatically extended until the NPC is found or until the expanded zone wraps the world zone. When the NPC is cast, he or she moves automatically to the Smart Zone.

Supporting roles are favorable for the execution of the Living Scene. Zero or more NPCs can take supporting roles; they become the supporting actors. They interact with the mains actors in order to execute collective behaviors. The supporting roles are first fulfilled by the NPCs present within the Smart Zone.

Finally, extra roles are optional for the realization of the Living Scene. Adding extras to a Living Scene allows the casting of numbers of nearby characters to execute "ambient" behaviors that will mostly react to the "main" set piece.

Let's illustrate these three sets of roles in a juggling show:

- The main role is the juggler; it triggers the start of the show.
- The supporting roles are the spectators.
- The extras are additional spectators as passersby, which are not mandatory for the show to be consistent, but that get involved because they are close to the show and interested from a distance.

The Role Assignment module needs to determine if a given character can fulfill a given role. This is why each created NPCs needs to be assigned a set of roles it can fulfill. The use of a role hierarchy can help to facilitate this assignment.

This role assignment step determines if the Living Scene can actually start. If at least all main roles can be cast, the runtime proceeds to the behavior orchestration. Then, each time an NPC enters the Smart Zone, the module determines if a role should be assigned to the NPC in the set of supporting or extra roles. If a supporting role is available, the role is assigned to the NPC. If all the supporting roles are fulfilled and if an extra role exists, the extra role is assigned to the NPC. If no extra role exists, the NPC does not join the Living Scene.

11.3.2.3 Behavior Orchestration

In practice, the "output" of a Living Scene is the execution of different behaviors by the involved NPCs. From the assigned role, an NPC is able to execute some behaviors defined for the role. This module is responsible for the assignment of a behavior to the NPCs, through the sequence of behaviors defined in a timeline (see Figure 11.1). The timeline orchestrates the roles of NPCs over time and synchronizes them in order to have credible individual and collective behaviors, including during a dynamic role assignment.

11.3.3 NPC Behaviors

To obtain a better ambience of life, we propose to take advantage of the principle of autonomy, by moving a part of the decision making to the NPC level.

11.3.3.1 Role Interruption

In the previous sections, we described a simple scenario where all participants of a Living Scene stay until all the main role behaviors end. The NPCs can also decide not to participate in a Living Scene according to their own goals. In this case, the Smart Zones do not entirely control the exit of the NPCs from the Living Scene, but they handle dynamic role assignments. Once more, the rules depend on the role:

- An NPC assigned to a main role can't leave the scene without stopping it if is not possible to recast the main role among other NPCs in the zone.
- When an NPC assigned to a supporting role leaves the scene, the role is cast automatically among extras and nonparticipants.
- NPCs with extra roles can leave as they wish without any incidence.

If the NPC decides to participate in a Living Scene, their behaviors are controlled by the timeline of the Living Scene. However, the selection between the NPC goals and the ones of Living Scene is based on priorities. If the priorities of goals are higher than the one of the Living Scene, the NPC can leave the scene. For example, if the hunger of a spectator is higher than its motivation of participating in the spectacle, it leaves the Living Scene and goes to eat.

11.3.3.2 Management of Overlapping Zones

As described previously, several levels of overlapping Smart Zones can result from their placement, which leads to a priority order of the scenes. The order can be defined through the relative sizes of the zones or directly by the game designers as a priority in the properties of the zones. These priorities are used by the NPCs to choose the best behaviors when they are located in several zones at the same time.

By default, the NPC chooses the behavior associated with the zone with the highest priority, but the NPC can also decide to execute a behavior from a zone with a lower priority for specific reasons, for instance:

- The behavior allows the NPC to achieve several Living Scenes at the same time
- The current internal state of the NPC allows him or her to execute the behavior but not the one from the zone with a higher priority
- The behavior allows the NPC to complete an individual goal

With such a degree of autonomy, an NPC can try to find a compromise between the roles of a scene and his or her goals.

11.4 Concrete Example

This section walks through an example scenario.

11.4.1 Scenario and the Smart Zones

The aim of this scenario example is to demonstrate how to create ambient life in a shopping street using multiple Living Scenes: "queue at the cash machine" (LS1), "spend time on a bench" (LS2), "buy interesting things at the shop" (LS3), "wait for the bus" (LS4), and "juggling show" (LS5).

The world zone is corresponding to the street, in which we define five specific Smart Zones to represent and manage these Living Scenes (see Figure 11.3):

- Smart Zone 1 (SZ1) is placed around the cash machine and triggered when an NPC enters the zone. The main role is the "cash taker" associated with the behavior "take cash" accessible when the NPC is the first in the queue. The supporting role is "queued" associated with the behavior of "wait for my turn." Several NPCs can take this role at runtime. No extra role is defined.
- Smart Zone 2 (SZ2) is placed around the bench and triggered when an NPC enters the zone. The main role is "dreamer" associated with the behavior "spend time." Several NPCs can take this role at runtime (depending on the size of the bench). No supporting or extra roles are defined.
- Smart Zone 3 (SZ3) is placed around the shop and triggered when the scenario is started. The main role is "merchant" associated with the behavior "sell things." The supporting role is "buyer" associated with the behaviors of "choose items," "buy items," and "wait for my turn." Several NPCs can take this role at runtime. No extra role is defined.
- Smart Zone 4 (SZ4) is placed around the bus station and triggered when an NPC enters the zone. The main role is "passenger" associated with the behaviors "buy a ticket," "wait for my turn," and "wait for the bus." Several NPCs can take this role at runtime. No supporting and extra role is defined.
- Smart Zone 5 (SZ5) is placed in the middle of the street and triggered every two hours. The main role is "juggler" associated with the behaviors "announce," "juggle," and "say goodbye." Only one NPC can take this role. The juggler NPC

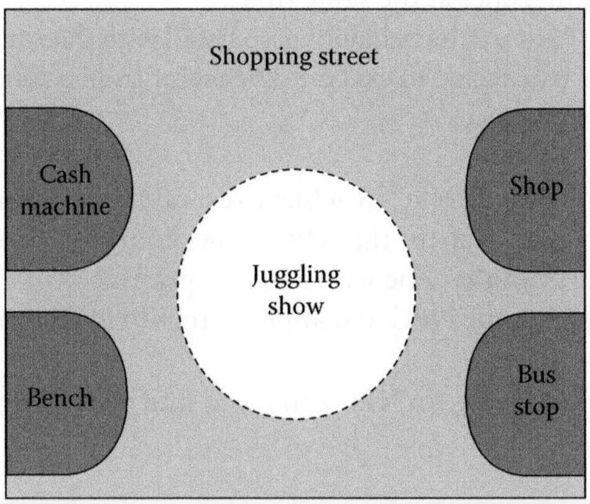

Figure 11.3

Schematic representations of the smart zones in our example.

is statically cast by the game designer before the beginning of the game. The supporting role is "spectator" associated with the behaviors "comment," "applaud," and "congratulate." Several NPCs can take this role. The extra role is "passerby" associated with the behavior "look from a distance."

By default, the NPCs that are in the world zone, take a default role of "wanderer," and can follow the default behavior of "wander" or "say hello" depending on the current situation. Thus, by default, they navigate randomly within the world zone from an activated Smart Zone to another (SZ1, SZ2, SZ3, and SZ4). To add some interaction between NPCs and the player, when an NPC meets another NPC, the behavior "say hello" can be executed.

When the first NPC enters, for example, SZ1, he or she is cast as a main role and then takes cash. Otherwise, the NPC entering in the zone is cast as a supporting role and stands in line in front of the cash machine. He or she takes cash when it is his or her turn (he or she is cast as the new main role). Similar operations occur for the other Smart Zones with the corresponding roles and behaviors.

11.4.2 Implementation in Unity3D

We have implemented the Living Scenes of the shopping street in Unity3D [Unity 14] and created the behaviors under MASA LIFE [MASA 14] using behavior trees [Champandard 08, Champandard 13]. We focus only on decisional behaviors and scene execution, and not on animation, navigation, and 3D design.

We created the roles and the associated behaviors for each Living Scene. The Smart Zones of the Living Scenes were placed in the environment of the shopping street (circles on Figure 11.4). We specified the characteristics of the Living Scenes through a dedicated

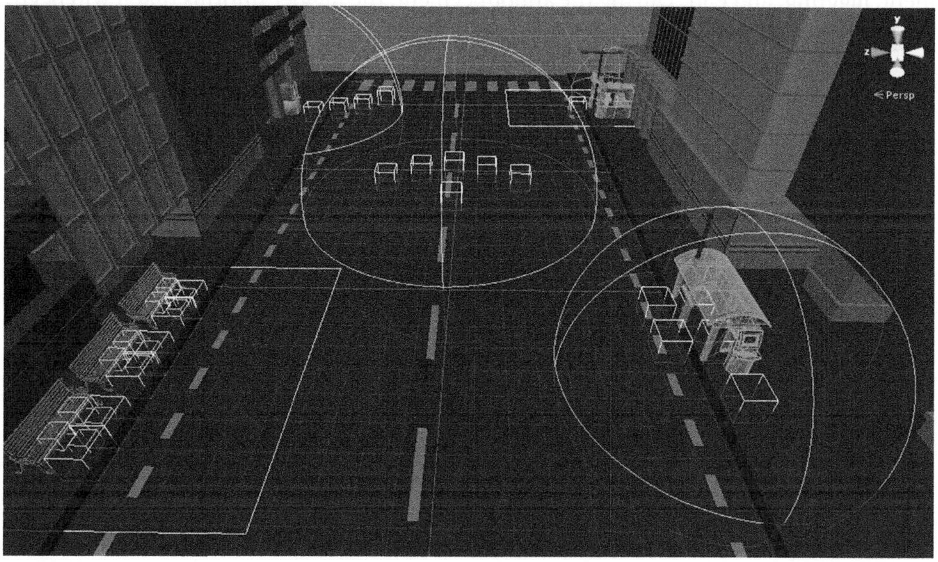

Figure 11.4

Instantiation of the shopping street example.

Figure 11.5

The shopping street example in Unity3D.

graphical interface in Unity3D by selecting the associated Smart Zones. Figure 11.5 illustrates the result of the Smart Zones execution in Unity3D.

Let's consider the juggling show scene. SZ5 defines five slots in which the spectators can take position to watch the show. Thus, five supporting roles are available in this specific case.

The timeline of the show defines the sequence of behaviors and their synchronization for the juggler and the spectators (see Figure 11.6). The show has three stages: announcement, juggling, and end. During the announcement, the juggler informs that it will begin the show soon (he or she executes the "announce" behavior).

The trigger for the scene is a given period. When the time comes, the juggler is automatically cast. In our example, the designer associates a particular NPC to the role of

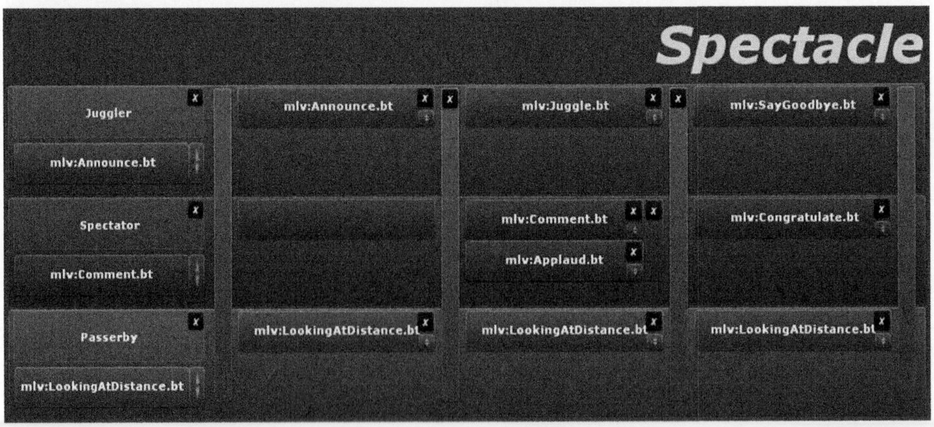

Figure 11.6

The timeline for the juggler spectacle.

juggler before runtime. The NPCs already in SZ5 when the scene is triggered are first cast as "spectators" if they can assume the role, until all the supporting roles are filled. The remaining NPCs cast as "extras" if they can assume the role. Moreover, NPCs interested in the show can go to SZ5 attracted by the announcement, and they are cast in the same way. They automatically adapt their behaviors to the corresponding stage of the show. During the juggling phase, the juggler juggles, and the spectators comment or applaud randomly. At the end of the show, the spectators congratulate the juggler, and the juggler says goodbye, and then the scene ends.

11.5 Conclusion

Living Scenes allow the execution of an ambience of life in video games with autonomous and less repetitive nonplayer characters exhibiting consistent, credible, and interactive behaviors. We propose a solution with Smart Zones to manage the NPCs' behaviors for the Living Scene execution and thus to move the complexity of the design into the zones. We implemented our solution into MASA LIFE and instantiated an example with Unity3D to test the Smart Zone concept, with positive results.

We demonstrated the prototype to game designers and their feedback is very encouraging. The model and the architecture seem to fit their needs to create ambience of life. Despite the simplicity of the scenario example presented in the previous section, the shopping street in Unity3D gives a good impression with less repetitive and more credible behaviors. Through this first implementation, we noticed that without the proposed model and architecture of Smart Zones to define and execute a Living Scene, the design of such an ambience would have been more complex.

This work is a part of the OCTAVIA Project, a research project funded by the French government (DGE). The main goal of the project is to propose an innovative tool to design and test scenes of ambient life involving interactive and autonomous nonplayer character in 3D environment. In this project, we plan to evaluate our solution design in order to validate its usability and whether our solution concretely simplifies the design of ambient life.

Although Smart Zones are an interesting and accessible approach to design Living Scenes, two main challenges need to be addressed to complete the solution: the integration of the player into a Living Scene with the impact of his or her actions on the scene; and the simplification of the design of the behaviors of autonomous NPCs in relation to Living Scenes, especially to allow NPCs to reason about Living Scenes.

Acknowledgments

This research is funded by the French government DGE within the OCTAVIA Project (PIA-FSN-2012) and supported by the cluster Cap Digital.

References

[Champandard 08] Champandard, A.J. 2008. Getting started with decision making and control systems. In *AI Game Programming Wisdom*, Vol. 4, pp. 257–264. Charles River Media, Hingham, MA.

[Champandard 13] Champandard, A.J. and Dunstan, P. 2013. The behavior tree starter kit. In *Game AI Pro: Collected Wisdom of Game AI Professionals*. A K Peters/CRC Press, Boca Raton, FL.

[Kallmann 98] Kallmann, M. and Thalmann, D. 1998. Modeling objects for interaction tasks. In *Proceedings of the Ninth Eurographics Workshop on Animation and Simulation (EGCAS)*, Lisbon, Portugal, pp. 73–86.

[MASA 14] MASA Group. 2014. MASA LIFE. http://www.masalife.net (accessed September 10, 2014).

[Shoulson 11] Shoulson, A. and Badler, N.I. 2011. Event-centric control for background agents. In *Lecture Notes in Computer Science*, Vol. 7069, pp. 193–198. Springer, Berlin, Germany.

[Stocker 10] Stocker, C., Sun, L., Huang, P., Qin, W., Allbeck, J.M., and Badler, N.I. 2010. Smart events and primed agents. In *Proceedings of the 10th International Conference on Intelligent Virtual Agents*, pp. 15–27. Springer-Verlag, Berlin, Germany.

[The Sims 99] The Sims. 1999. Electronic arts. http://www.ea.com/sims (accessed February 7, 2015).

[Unity 14] Unity Technologies. 2014. Unity 3D. https://unity3d.com/ (accessed September 10, 2014).

12

Separation of Concerns Architecture for AI and Animation

Bobby Anguelov

12.1 Introduction

There are two requirements for creating believable characters in today's games: the first is that characters need to make the correct decisions (artificial intelligence [AI]), and the second is that they need to look good when acting on those decisions (animation). With the heavy visual focus in today's games, it is fair to say that an AI system will live or die based on the quality of its animation system. Smart decisions won't matter much if the animation system can't execute them in a visually pleasing manner.

As we've improved the animation fidelity in our games, we've encountered a huge jump in the amount of content needed to achieve the required level of fidelity. This content refers to both the animation data, the data structures that reference the animation data, and the code required to control and drive those data structures. The biggest challenge facing us today is simply one of complexity, that is, how do we manage, leverage, and maintain of this new content in an efficient manner?

We feel that traditional techniques for managing this content have already reached their limits with the content volumes present in the last generation of games. Given the order of magnitude jump in memory between the last generation and the current-gen consoles, as well as the expectations of the audience, it is not unreasonable to expect a similar jump in the content volumes. As such, we need to take the time to evaluate and adjust our workflows and architecture to better deal with this increase in content and complexity.

In this chapter, we propose an architecture for managing the complexity of a modern animation system based on our experience developing for both last- and current-gen titles [Vehkala 13, Anguelov 13].

12.2 Animation Graphs

Before we discuss the higher-level architecture, it is worth giving a quick overview of modern-day animation systems. Animation graphs (animgraphs) are ubiquitous within the industry when it comes to describing the set of animations as well as the necessary chaining of these animations in performing in-game actions.

An animgraph is, in its simplest form, a directed acyclic graph wherein the leaf nodes are the animation sources (i.e., resulting in an animation pose) and the branch nodes are animation operations (i.e., pose modification such as blending). These sorts of animgraphs are commonly referred to as blend trees since they primarily describe the blends performed on a set of animations. Animation operations contained within a blend tree are usually driven through control parameters. For example, a simple blend between two animations will require a "blend weight" control parameter to specify the contribution of each animation to the final blended result. These control parameters are our primary means of controlling (or driving) our blend trees, the second mechanism being animation events.

Animation events are additional temporal hints that are annotated onto the animation sources when authored. They provide contextual information both about the animation itself and information needed by other systems. For example, in a walking animation, we might want to mark the periods in which the left or right foot is on the ground as well as when the game should trigger footstep sounds (i.e., contact period for each foot). Animation events are sampled from each animation source and then are bubbled up through the graph to the root. As these events bubble up through the graph, they can be also used by the branch nodes in their decision making, especially within state machine transitions. A simple blend tree describing forward locomotion for a character is shown in Figure 12.1, wherein we can control the direction and the speed of a character with the control parameters: "direction" and "speed."

In addition to blending, we also have the ability to select between two animations at branch nodes. For example, in Figure 12.1, we could replace the speed blend with a "select" node that will choose either the walk blend or the run blend based on the control parameter.

While a blend tree can perform all the necessary operations needed for a single action, it is extremely difficult to build a single blend tree to handle all the actions available to our characters. As such, we often wish to separate each action into its own blend tree and have some mechanism to switch between the actions. Often, these actions would have a predefined sequence as well as restrictions on which actions could

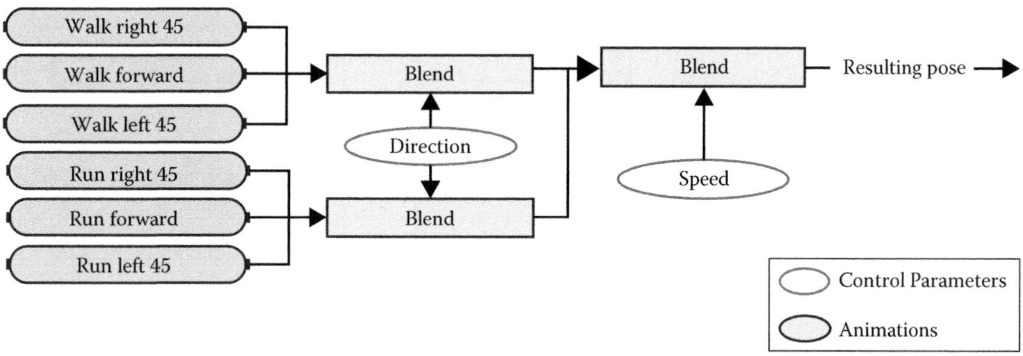

Figure 12.1

A simple blend tree describing forward locomotion.

be chained together, and so traditionally this switching mechanism between actions took the form of a state machine.

Within these state machines, the states would contain the blend trees, and the state transitions would result in blends from one blend tree to another. Each state transition would be based on a set of conditions which, once met, would allow the transition to occur. These conditions would also need to check animation-specific criteria like control parameter values, animation events, and time-based criteria like whether we reached the end of an animation. In addition, the states would also need to contain some logic for controlling and driving the blend trees (i.e., setting the control parameters values appropriately).

State machines were the final tool needed to allow us to combine all our individual actions in one system and so allow our characters to perform complex behaviors by chaining these actions together. Let's consider the simple example presented in Figure 12.1; since it only covered the forward arc of motion, we extend the direction blend to cover all directions, but we don't have any animation for when the character is idle and not moving. So we add this animation in another blend tree, which results in us needing a state machine to switch between the two blend trees. Now we realized the transitions between moving and idle don't look great, so we want to add some nice transition animations, which means that we need two more blend trees. Now we then realize that when stopping, it matters which foot of the character is planted, so we need two states to cover that and transitions that check the animation events in the walk animation. In the end, we end up with the state machine setup shown in Figure 12.2.

We can already see that for even the most basic setup, there is already a large degree of complexity present. Consider the fact that each blend tree might have its own set of control parameters that the code needs to be aware of and control, as well as all of the transition logic and state setup that needs to be created and driven. Now factor in that modern-day characters have dozens of available actions, each of which may require numerous blend trees as well as state logic for each and we now have a recipe for a complexity explosion, one which, unfortunately, has already occurred, and we now find ourselves trying to move forward through the fallout.

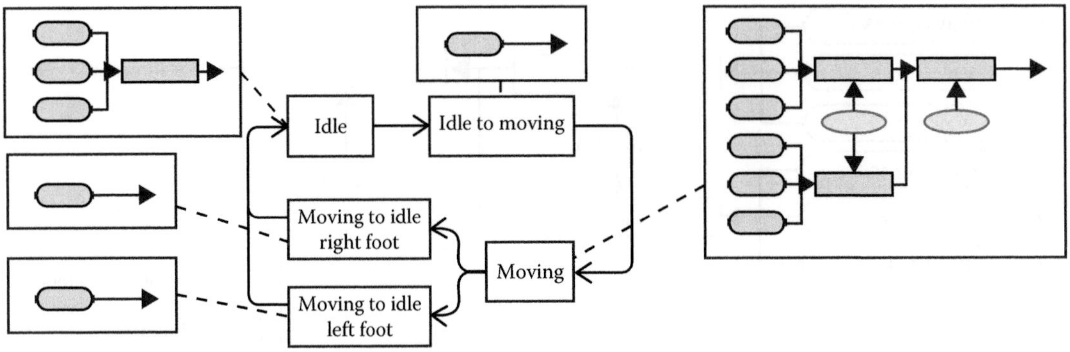

Figure 12.2

A simple animation state machine describing basic locomotion.

12.3 Complexity Explosion and the Problem of Scalability

To discuss the problem of scalability, we need to focus on the state machines described previously. Traditionally, a lot of developers would reuse the same state machine for driving both the animation and the gameplay state changes. This applies both to AI, where the state machine might take the form of a behavior tree or some other decision-making construct, as well as the player's state machine setup. We used the term state machine here, but this could be any sort of AI state change mechanic (behavior trees, planners, etc.). For simplicity's sake, from now onwards, we will use the term gameplay state machine to refer to any sort of high-level AI or player decision-making systems.

Reusing the high-level gameplay state machines for animation purposes is problematic for a variety of reasons, but the main issue is one of code/data dependency. As the blend graphs exist outside of the code base, they can be considered data and so are loaded at runtime as resources. With these blend graph resources, it is the responsibility of the game code to drive them by setting the necessary control parameters required by the graph. As such, the code needs to have explicit knowledge of these parameters and what they are used for. It is important to note that control parameters usually represent the animation-specific values (i.e., normalized blend values [0–1]), and so desired inputs need to be converted by the gameplay code into values that the animation system understands (e.g., the direction value in Figure 12.1 needs to be converted from degrees into a 0–1 blend value). In giving our code this explicit knowledge of the control parameter conversions, we've created a code/data dependency from our gameplay code to the blend tree resources meaning that whenever we change the blend trees, we need to change the code as well. The code/data dependency is pretty much unavoidable, but there is a lot we can do to push it as far away from gameplay code as possible, thereby reducing the risks resulting from it as well as allowing fast iterations.

The second biggest problem with reusing gameplay state machines is the asynchronous lifetimes of states, in that there isn't a one-to-one mapping between the gameplay states and the animation states. For example, consider a simple locomotion state from the gameplay's standpoint: a single state is usually enough to represent that a character is in motion, but on the animation side, we require a collection of states and transitions to actually achieve that motion. This usually means that we end up having animation only state machines embedded within the gameplay state machines, and over the course of a development cycle, the line between the two state machines becomes blurred. In fact, this is the main concern with the code/data dependency, since if we are required to make significant modifications to the blend trees, then the code needs to be adjusted as well and, unfortunately, this could end up affecting or even breaking the current gameplay since the two systems are so intertwined. Even worse, when animation and gameplay are so closely coupled, it can be tempting for a programmer to make direct use of information from the blend tree or make assumptions about the structure of the blend trees for gameplay decisions, which in pathological cases requires large portions of the gameplay code having to be rewritten when animation changes.

The example presented in Figure 12.2 is misleading: the idle state is a separate gameplay state. So if we were to create a simple gameplay state machine for a character with some additional abilities like jumping and climbing ladders, we might end up with a state machine setup similar to that in Figure 12.3.

There is already a significant degree of complexity in Figure 12.3, but even so, it doesn't show the full picture, as now the transitions between the gameplay states also need to contain and drive animation transitions. For example, when we transition between the idle and jump states, we somehow need to let the jump state know which animation state we are arriving from, so that we can choose the appropriate target animation state. Changing or adding animation transitions means we now need to modify the gameplay transitions in addition to all of the actual gameplay code and animation logic. As our system grows, maintenance and debugging starts to become a nightmare. The costs and risks associated with adding new states can be so high that it becomes nearly impossible to justify such change late in the development cycle. The best way to move forward and avoid this situation is to work toward loosening the couplings between the systems, and this is where a separation of concerns (SoC) architecture comes in.

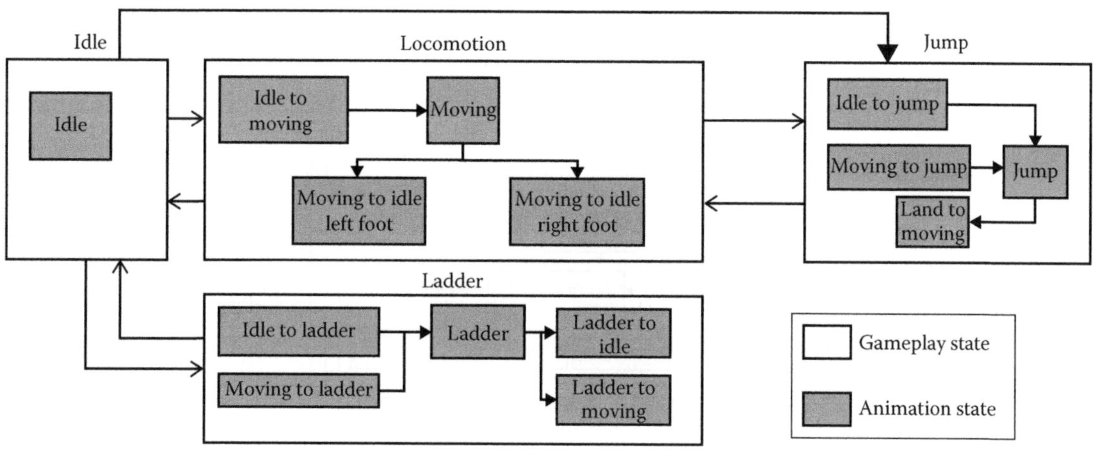

Figure 12.3

A combined gameplay/animation state machine for a simple character.

12.4 SoC

SoC is a principle that states that various systems that interact with one another should each have a singular purpose and thereby not have overlapping responsibilities [Greer 08]. It is already clear that this isn't the case for the state machine presented in Figure 12.3, as we have two distinct state machines and responsibilities intertwined together. So as a first step, we want to separate the animation state logic from the gameplay state logic. This is relatively easy, and, for many developers, this is already the case, in that their animation system supports animation state machines (e.g., *Morpheme*, *Mecanim*, *EmotionFX*). Unfortunately, the concept of animation state machines is not as common as one would imagine, and it was only in version 4 of both the Unity and Unreal engines that animation state machines were introduced. An animation state machine is simply a state machine at the animation system level, allowing us to define and transition between animation states as described in the previous sections. From this point on, we will use the term "animgraph" to refer to the combination of blend trees and state machines in a single graph.

Animation state machines can also be hierarchical in that the blend trees contained within a state can also contain additional state machines as leaf nodes. This allows for easy layering of animation results on top of one another but is not a feature that is available in all animation systems. For example, Natural Motion's *Morpheme* middleware is entirely built around the concept, while Unity's *Mecanim* only supports a single state machine at the root of an animgraph, but allows for the layering of multiple graphs on top of one another.

If we extract all the animation state machine logic from Figure 12.3, we end up with the state machine setup shown in Figure 12.4. As you can see, the animation state machine once separated out is still relatively complex but this complexity can be further simplified by making use of hierarchical state machines, with container states for each action (i.e., "jump" or "ladder"). The gameplay state machine is now free to only worry about gameplay transitions without having to deal with the animation transition, and it is now also possible, to some degree, to work on either system independently.

There is still a catch. While this initial separation goes a long way to help decouple the systems, we still have a coupling between the gameplay state machine and the animation system. We still need to have explicit knowledge of the control parameters

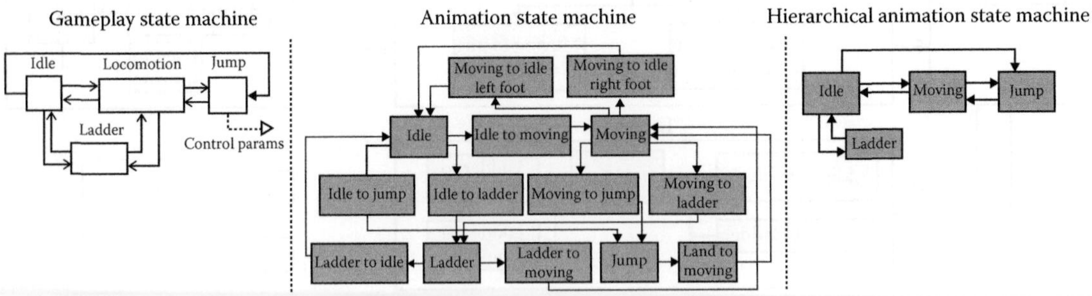

Figure 12.4

Separation of animation and gameplay state machines.

required to drive the state machine as well as explicit knowledge of the topology of the animgraph to be able to determine when states are active or when transitions have occurred/completed. This means that we still need a lot of code to drive and poll the animation system, and unfortunately this code still takes the form of some sort of state machine. It is surprising to note that only once we separated out the animation state machines from the gameplay state machines did we realize that we actually had three state machines that were intertwined: the gameplay state machine that controls character decision making, the animation state machine representing the states and possible transitions, and the animation driver state machine that acts as the interface between the gameplay and animation state machines. The fact that there was a hidden state machine goes a long way to highlight the danger posed by building monolithic systems.

Coming back to the animation driver state machine, its responsibilities are to inspect the animation state machine and provide that information back to the gameplay system. It is also responsible for converting from the desired gameplay control parameter values to values the animation system understands as well as triggering the appropriate animation state transitions when needed. In many cases, this driving code would also be responsible for any animation postprocessing required, that is, post rotation/translation of the animation displacement. As such, we still have a lot of different responsibilities within one system and we haven't really improved the maintainability or extensibility of our characters. To move forward, we need to pull all of this animation-specific code out of our gameplay systems, which will remove any remaining code/data dependencies we have between our animation data and gameplay code.

12.5 Separating Gameplay and Animation

To pull out the animation driving code, there are two things we can do, the first is relatively easy and goes a long way to simplify the gameplay code, while the second is significantly more invasive and time-consuming. So if you find yourself battling code/data dependencies toward the end of a project, the first technique might prove useful.

We mentioned that one of the key responsibilities of the animation driving code was to convert between high-level gameplay desires such as "move at 3.5 m/s while turning 53° to left" to the animation level control parameters, which might be something like "direction = 0.3 and speed = 0.24" (i.e., the blend weight values that will result in the required visual effect). To do the conversion between the gameplay values and the animation values, it is necessary for the gameplay code to have knowledge about the animations that are available, the blends that exist, what values drive what blends, etc. Basically, the driving code needs to have full knowledge of the blend tree just to convert a value from, for example, degrees to a blend weight. This means that if an animator modifies the blend tree, then the gameplay code might be invalidated and require code changes to restore the functionality. This means that any animgraph changes require both programmer and animation resources and a potentially significant delay before a build with both the code and data changes can be rolled out to the production team.

A simple way to get around this problem is to move all translation logic into the animgraph (i.e., directly feed in the higher-level gameplay values). Depending on your

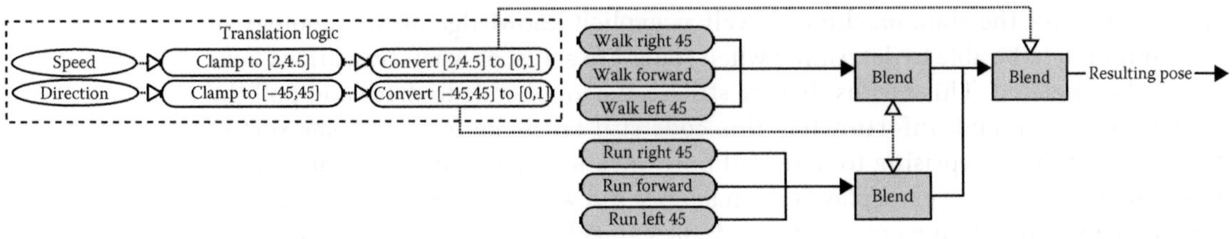

Figure 12.5

Moving control parameter translation logic to the animgraph.

animation system, this may or not be possible. For example, in Unreal 4, this is relatively trivial to do through the use of blueprints, while on Unity, there seems to be no way to perform math operations on control parameters within the graph. The benefits of moving the translation logic into the graph are twofold: first, gameplay code does not need any knowledge of the graph or the blends; all it needs to know is that it has to send a direction and speed values in a format it understands (i.e., degrees and m/s, respectively). In removing that dependency from the code and moving it into the animgraph, animators can now make drastic changes to the animgraphs without having to modify the gameplay code; in fact, they can even swap out entire graphs just as long as the inputs are the same, taking the setup shown in Figure 12.1 and moving all translation logic to the blend tree result in the setup shown in Figure 12.5.

In addition to the translation logic, we can also move a lot of other control parameter logic to the graph (e.g., dampening on input values so we get smooth blends to the new values instead of an instant reaction to a new value).

It is still important to note that gameplay code should probably be aware of the capabilities of the animation (i.e., roughly what the turning constraints are and what reasonable speeds for movement are, but it doesn't have to be explicit). In fact, it is usually gameplay that defines some of these constraints. Imagine that we have the setup in Figure 12.5 and gameplay decides we need the character to sprint; the gameplay team simply feeds in the faster velocity parameter and notifies the animation team. The animation team can now create and integrate new animations independently of the gameplay team. From a technical standpoint, moving the translation logic from the code to data removes one layer of coupling and brings us closer to the final SoC architecture we'd like.

The second thing we need to do to achieve the SoC architecture is to move all the animation driver state machine code from the gameplay state machine into a new layer that exists between the animation system and the gameplay code. In the classic AI agent architecture presented in [Russel 03], the authors separate an agent into three layers: sensory, decision making, and actuation. This is in itself an SoC design and one that we can directly apply to our situation. If we think of the gameplay state machine as the decision-making layer and the animation system as the final actuators, then we need an actuation layer to transmit the commands from the decision-making system to the actuators. This new layer is comprised of an animation controller and animation behaviors. Gameplay systems will directly interface with this new layer for any animation requests they have.

12.6 Animation Behaviors

An animation behavior is defined as a program that executes a specific set of actions are needed to realize a character action from a visual standpoint. As such, animation behaviors are purely concerned with the visual aspects of character actions, and they are not responsible for any gameplay state changes themselves. That is not to say they have no influence on gameplay, though. There is bidirectional flow of information between the gameplay systems and the animation behaviors, which will indirectly result in gameplay state changes, but these changes will not be performed by the behaviors themselves. In fact, we suggest the animation behaviors are layered below the gameplay systems (in your engine architecture), so that there is absolutely no way for the behaviors to even access the gameplay systems.

In describing animation behaviors, we feel it makes more sense to start at the animation system and slowly move back up to the gameplay system. As such, let's take a look at the example animgraph presented in Figure 12.6. We have a full-body animation state machine that contains all the full-body actions that our characters can perform. Within that state machine, we have a state called "locomotion," which, in turn, contains a state machine with the states necessary to perform locomotion. Each of these states represents additional blend trees/state machines.

Let's say that we wish to build a "move" animation behavior. For this behavior to function, it will need to have knowledge of the animgraph (especially the "locomotion" state machine), all the states contained within it, and the contents of each state. Once we've given the animation behavior all the necessary graph topological information, it will need to drive the state machine, which implies it requires knowledge about the needed control parameters and context thereof. With this knowledge, the animation behavior is ready to perform its task. This is achieved in three stages: "start," "execute," and "stop."

The "start" stage is responsible for ensuring that the animgraph is in a state in which the execute stage can proceed. For example, when starting to move from idle, we need to trigger the "idle to move" transition and wait for it to complete; only once that transition is complete and we are in the "move" state, we can move onto the "execute" stage. In the case of path following, we may also need to perform some pathfinding and path postprocessing here before the behavior can continue.

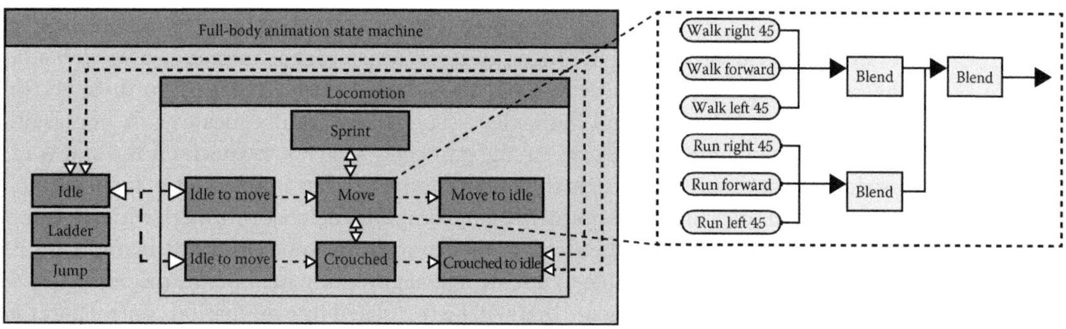

Figure 12.6

An example of a full-body animation state machine.

The "execute" stage is responsible for all the heavy lifting. It is responsible for driving the animgraph to generate the required visual result. In the context of locomotion, we would perform the path following simulation and set the direction and speed parameters needed to follow a given path. Once we detect that we have completed our task, we will transition over to the "stop" stage.

The "stop" stage is responsible for any cleanup we need to do as well as transitioning the animgraph to a neutral state from which other animation behaviors can continue. With our locomotion example, we would free the path and then trigger the "move to idle" transition in this stage and complete our behavior.

It is important to note that in the example given in Figure 12.6, the actual transition between "idle" and the "locomotion" state exists within the "full-body" state machine. This implies that both "idle" and "locomotion" need to know about the "full-body" state machine. Well, in fact, it turns out that all states in the "full-body" state machine need to know about it. This brings us to the concept of *animgraph views*. An animgraph view is an object that has knowledge of a specific portion of the graph as well as utility functions to drive that portion of the graph. From that description, animation behaviors are in fact animgraph views themselves with the exception that they have an execution flow. It is better to think of graph views as utility libraries and the animation behaviors as programs. Multiple behaviors can share and make use of a single graph view, allowing us a greater level of code reuse and helping to reduce the cost incurred when the animgraph changes. In our example, we would have a "full-body graph view" that would know about the topology of the "full-body state machine" and offer functions to help trigger the transitions between the states, for example, set full-body state (IDLE).

To execute a given task, animation behaviors require some instruction and direction. This direction comes in the form of an animation order. Animation orders are sent from the gameplay systems and contain all the necessary data to execute a given behavior. For example, if the gameplay systems want to move a character to a specific point, they would issue a "move order" with the target point, the desired movement speed, the character's end orientation, and so on. Each animation order has a type and will result in a single animation behavior (e.g., a "move order" will result in a "move behavior"). Animation orders are fire-and-forget, in that once an order is issued, the gameplay system doesn't have any control over the lifetime of the animation behavior. The only way that behaviors can be cancelled or have their orders updated is by issuing additional orders, as detailed in the next section.

In addition to the animation orders, we have the concept of *animation behavior handles* that are returned for each order issued. These handles are a mechanism through which the animation behaviors and gameplay systems can communicate with one another. Primarily, the handles are a way for the gameplay systems to check on the status of an issued animation order (i.e., has the order completed, has it failed, and, if so, why?). An animation handle contains a pointer to the animation behavior through which it can perform necessary queries on the state of the behavior. In some cases, for example, a player character, it is useful to be able to update a given program on a per frame basis (i.e., with the controller analog stick inputs that will be translated into animation control parameter settings by the behavior each frame).

We show a simple timeline representing the interaction between a gameplay system and an animation behavior for a simple "move" order in Figure 12.7. It is important to note

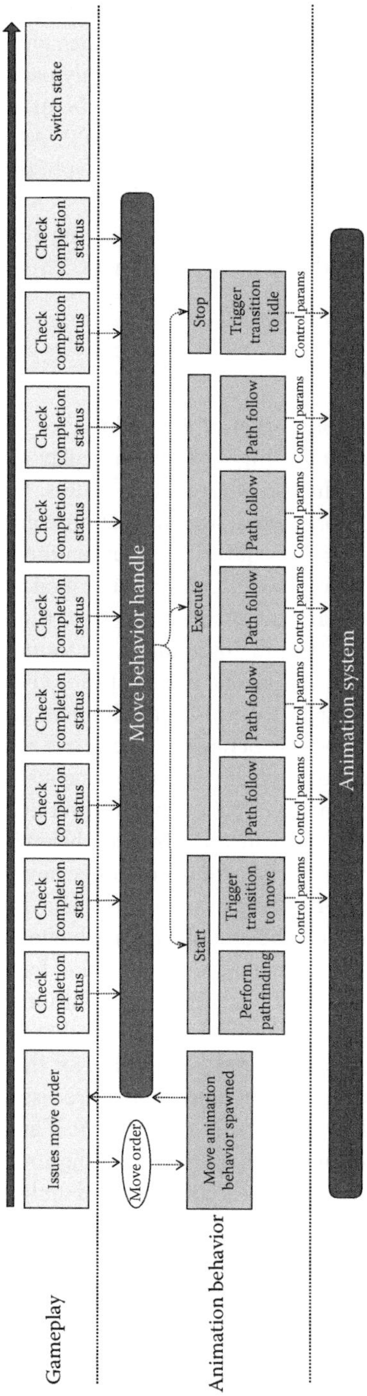

Figure 12.7

Timeline for an animation behavior.

how all communication between the animation behavior and the gameplay system occur through the animation handle.

In addition to the three update stages, animation behaviors also feature a post-animation update "postprocess" stage. This stage is mainly used to perform animation postprocessing such as trajectory warping but can also be used for post-physics/post-animation pose modification (i.e., inverse kinematics [IK]). As a note, IK and physics/animation interactions should ideally be performed as part of the animation update but not all animation systems support this.

Since we will have multiple animation behaviors covering all of a character's actions, we need some mechanism to schedule and execute them. This is where the animation controller comes in.

12.7 Animation Controller

The animation controller's main role is that of a scheduler for the animation behaviors. It is the primary interface used by the higher-level gameplay systems to issue requests to the animation system through the use of animation orders. It is responsible for creating and executing the animation behaviors. The animation controller also features animation behavior tracks (queues) used for layering of animation behaviors. For example, actions such as "look at," "reload," or "wave" can be performed on top of other full-body animations (e.g., "idle" or "walk"), and, as such, we can layer those actions on top of full-body actions at the controller level. In previous games, we found it sufficient (at least for humanoid characters) to have only two layers: one for full-body actions and one for layered actions [Anguelov 13, Vehkala 13]. We also had different scheduling rules for each track. We only allowed a single full-body behavior to be active at any given time, whereas we allowed multiple layered behaviors to be active simultaneously.

For the full-body behaviors, we had a queue with two open slots. Once a full-body animation order was issued, we would enqueue an animation behavior into the primary slot. If another full-body order was received, we would create the new animation behavior and first try to merge the two behaviors. Merging of animation behavior is simply a mechanism through which an animation order can be updated for a behavior. For example, if we issue a move order to point A, we would spawn a move animation behavior with the target A. If we then decided that point B is actually a better final position, we would issue another move order with point B as the target. This will result in another move animation behavior being spawned and merged with the original move behavior thereby updating its order; the second behavior is then discarded. Once the merge process completes, the behavior will then detect the updated order and respond accordingly. If an animation order results in a full-body animation behavior of a different type than the already queued behavior, we would have queued the new behavior to the second slot and updated it, but we would have also notified the original behavior to terminate. Terminating a behavior forces it to enter the stopping stage and complete. Once an animation behavior completes, it is dequeued and is not updated any more. This means that we can in essence cross-fade between two full-body actions allowing us to achieve greater visual fidelity during the transition.

The merging mechanism does have the requirement that all behaviors be built in a manner that supports order updating. While this manner of updating animation behaviors might seem strange at first, it has significant benefits for the gameplay code. The main one is that gameplay no longer needs to worry about stopping and waiting for animations to complete or how to transition between the different animation states, as this is all handled at the controller/behavior level. This transition micromanagement at the gameplay level is also extremely problematic when trying to delegate animation control between different systems, for example, when triggering an in-game cut scene, the cinematics system requires animation control of the character. When control is requested, the character could be in any animation state. The cinematic system needs to resolve that state in a sensible way, and this has been extremely difficult to achieve in the past without coupling unrelated systems (i.e., giving knowledge of the AI system to the cinematics system). With our approach, we can now delegate control to various systems without having to create any coupling between unrelated systems. For example, animation behaviors could be written for cinematics, and when the cinematics code takes control, it could issue those orders that would terminate existing orders and result in sensible transitions between orders. In fact, the cinematics system can even reuse the same locomotion orders that the AI is using, since they are entirely system agnostic. Imagine we needed to have an nonplayable character (NPC) climb a ladder in a cut scene. Instead of fully animating the cut scene, or trying to script the AI to climb the ladder, we could simply issue the animation order directly in the cinematics system without any knowledge of the AI or the current state of an NPC.

There is also an additional benefit of this approach on the animation side. If for whatever reason we have a barrage of orders from the gameplay systems, that is, behavior oscillation, our full-body queuing mechanism will simply overwrite/merge the queued behavior with whatever new behaviors it is ordered to perform. This greatly reduces the visual glitches that traditionally arise from these kind of gameplay bugs. On the downside, it does make those bugs harder to detect from a quality assurance (QA) perspective, as there is no visual feedback now, so we greatly recommend that you implement some sort of animation order spam detection.

When it comes to the layered behaviors, we can have any number of behaviors queued, and it is up to gameplay code to ensure that the combination makes sense. We also merge layered behaviors in the same manner as for the full-body behavior, giving us the same set of update capabilities.

There is one last thing to discuss when it comes to the scheduling of animation behaviors: behavior lifetimes. The lifetime of a behavior is not synchronous with that of the gameplay state that issued the original order. Once a behavior completes, it is dequeued, but we may need to keep the behavior since the handle may still be checked by gameplay code, which updates at a different frequency. The opposite may also be true, wherein a gameplay state issues an animation order that then completes without waiting for the order to complete. As such we decided to control animation behavior lifetime through the concept of shared ownership. A behavior is kept alive (in memory), while either a handle to it still exists or it is still on one of the animation controller update queues. This can be easily achieved through the use of an STL shared_ptr smart pointer. The final architecture across all system layers is presented in Figure 12.8. For more details on the controller/behavior architecture, readers are referred to [Anguelov 13].

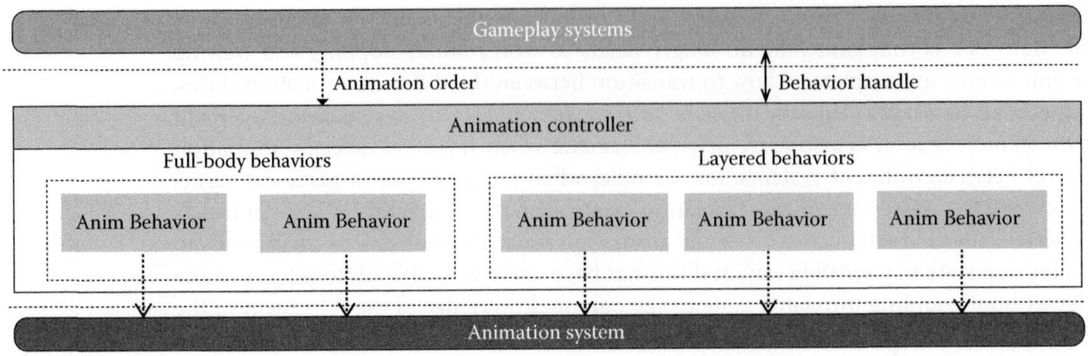

Figure 12.8

The final SoC architecture.

12.8 Benefits of an SoC Animation Architecture

Up until this point, we have discussed the SoC as a means to solving some existing problems. However, it is important to mention that there are some additional benefits in moving to an SoC architecture, which might not be immediately clear, and so we would like to highlight a few of them.

12.8.1 Functional Testing

The first clear benefit from this architecture is that systems can now be functionally tested in isolation. For example, if we wish to create some tests for the AI system, we can create a dummy animation controller that will receive orders and complete/fail them as desired without actually running any animation code. This will greatly simplify the task of debugging AI issues, as the animation code can be entirely removed from the equation. In the past with all the intertwined systems, we would never really be sure what the root cause of a bug was. This is also very true for animation testing. On a past project, we had built a stand-alone scripting system for testing the animation layer. This scripting system would issue the exact same orders as the AI, but allows us to build animation function tests in complete isolation. This was a massive win for us on previous projects when maintaining and verifying animation functionality, even across multiple refactoring phases of the gameplay code.

12.8.2 System Refactoring

Another huge benefit of this approach is that when we wish to make significant animation changes, it is much safer and easier to do so. This architecture allows us to replace character actions, one by one, without any risk of breaking the gameplay code. Furthermore, this approach allows us to perform nondestructive prototyping. When building a new version of an action, we can simply build a new behavior alongside the existing one and have a runtime switch to select between the two within the controller.

The beauty of this approach is that we can swap out behaviors at runtime without the gameplay code even being aware. If we combine this technique with the function testing mentioned earlier, it allows us to build a new version of an action and compare the two actions side by side (which alone is priceless), without having modified neither the original action nor the gameplay code. This allows us to rapidly prototype features with bare minimum functionality and expose them to the gameplay systems early on, all while building the final versions alongside them, allowing us to experiment and break actions without affecting the build.

12.8.3 Level of Detail

Being able to switch between behaviors at runtime without affecting gameplay allows us to leverage this to build a dynamic level of detail (LOD) system for the animation. In scenario's where the lifetime of characters is significant and AI updates are required even for offscreen characters (i.e., artificial life simulations), we require some mechanism to reduce or remove the cost of animation updates. If NPC locomotion was based on the animation (animation driven displacement), then this becomes relatively complex to achieve without a clear separation of the animation and gameplay systems.

With our approach, we can build several sets of cheap animation behaviors that can be dynamically swapped out at runtime based on a character's LOD level [Anguelov 13]. When we have an NPC at the highest LOD, we would want to run our default animation behaviors. As the character moves away and drops in LOD, we could exchange out some of the expensive layered behaviors with lightweight ones so as to reduce the cost. Once the character moves offscreen, then we can replace all animation behaviors with dummy behaviors that simply track the animation state needed to resume a high LOD behavior when needed.

For example, with locomotion, at the highest LOD, we would run the animation locomotion fully as well as having a layered footstep IK behavior enabled. At a medium LOD, we would replace the footstep IK behavior with a dummy behavior while keeping locomotion untouched. At the lowest LOD (offscreen), we would replace the locomotion with a simple time-based update on the given path, as well as estimating the velocity and state of the character (crouched, standing, etc.). Once this character comes back into view, we would simply swap back to the standard locomotion behavior and continue seamlessly. We suggest that you build separate behaviors for the different LODs, as this allows you to create "LOD sets" for different characters using various combinations of the behaviors. For example, you might not want to disable the footstep IK for huge characters even at medium LOD, since it may be more visible than for smaller characters.

12.9 Conclusion

In this chapter, we have presented an approach for decoupling your gameplay systems from your animation systems. We discussed the potential improvements to productivity and maintenance offered by this approach as well as provided advice on how to move toward a similar architecture.

References

[Anguelov 13] Anguelov, B. and Sunshine-Hill, B. 2013. Managing the movement: Getting your animation behaviors to behave better. *Game Developers Conference*. http://www.gdcvault.com (accessed May 11, 2014).

[Greer 08] Greer, D. 2008. The art of separation of concerns. Online article: The aspiring craftsman. http://aspiringcraftsman.com/2008/01/03/art-of-separation-of-concerns/ (accessed May 11, 2014).

[Russel 03] Russel, S.J. and Norvig, P. 2003. *Artificial Intelligence: A Modern Approach*, 2nd edn. Pearson Education, Englewood Cliffs, NJ.

[Vehkala 13] Vehkala, M. and De Pascale, M. 2013. Creating the AI for the living, breathing world of hitman: Absolution. *Game Developers Conference*. http://www.gdcvault.com (accessed May 11, 2014).

13

Optimizing Practical Planning for Game AI

Éric Jacopin

13.1 Introduction

Planning generates sequences of actions called plans. Practical planning for game artificial intelligence (AI) refers to a planning procedure that fits in the AI budget of a game and supports playability so that nonplayer characters (NPCs) execute actions from the plans generated by this planning procedure.

Jeff Orkin developed Goal-Oriented Action Planning (GOAP) [Orkin 04] as the first ever implementation of practical planning for the game [F.E.A.R. 05]. GOAP implements practical planning with (1) actions as C++ classes, (2) plans as paths in a space of states, and (3) search as path planning in a space of states, applying actions backwardly from the goal state to the initial state; moreover, GOAP introduced action costs as a search heuristic. Many games used GOAP since 2005, and it is still used today, for example, [Deus Ex 3 DC 13] and [Tomb Raider 13], sometimes with forward search, which seems easier to debug, as the most noticeable change.

In this chapter, we present how to optimize a GOAP-like planning procedure with actions as text files [Cheng 05] and forward breadth-first search (refer to Section A.2 of [Ghallab 04]) so that it becomes practical to implement planning. Actions as text files allow nonprogrammers to provide actions iteratively without recompiling the game project: nonprogrammers can modify and update the action files during game development and debugging. That is, planning ideas can be developed and validated offline. Moreover, if needed, C++ can always be generated from the text files and included in the code of your planner at any time during development.

Forward breadth-first search is one of the simplest search algorithms since it is easy to understand, extra data structures are not required prior to search, and short plans are found faster and with less memory than other appealing plan-graph-based planning procedures [Ghallab 04, Chapter 6]. Last, it is also a complete search procedure that returns the shortest plans; NPCs won't get redundant or useless actions to execute.

This chapter will first present the necessary steps before going into any optimization campaign, with examples specific to practical planning. Next, we will describe what can be optimized in practical planning, focusing on practical planning data structures that lead to both runtime and memory footprint improvements.

13.1.1 Required Background

The reader is expected to have a basic knowledge of GOAP [Orkin 04], predicate-based state and action representation [Cheng 05, Ghallab 04, Chapter 2], and basic search techniques (e.g., breadth-first search) as applied to planning [Ghallab 04, Chapter 4].

13.2 How Can You Optimize?

There are two main features to optimize in practical planning: time and memory. Ideally, we want to minimize both, but ultimately which one to focus on depends on the criteria of your game. Additionally, most algorithms can trade memory for time or vice versa.

13.2.1 Measure It!

Your first step is to get some code in order to measure both time and memory usage. The objective here is to instrument your practical planning code easily and quickly to show improvements in runtime and memory usage with respect to the allowed budgets.

Runtime measurement is not as easy as it sounds. Often, you'll get varied results even when the timings were performed under the same testing conditions. So an important aspect is to decide on a unit of time that has enough detail. Several timings under the same testing conditions should provide enough significant digits, with their numerical values being very close. If you're going to improve runtime by two orders of magnitude, you need to start with at least 4 significant digits. C++11 provides the flexible `std::chrono` library [Josuttis 13] that should fit most of your needs, but any platform-specific library providing a reliable high-resolution counter should do the job. Using microseconds is a good start.

With no (unpredictable) memory leak, memory measures are stable and must return the exact same value under the same testing conditions. The first step here is to measure memory overhead; for instance, an empty `std::vector` takes 16 bytes with Microsoft's Visual C++ 2013, while an empty `std::valarray` takes only 8 bytes if you can use it instead (they only store numeric values; they cannot grow but they can be resized), and there's no memory overhead for an instance of `std::array`, again if you can use it (they are C-style arrays: their size is fixed). The second step is to decide whether any measure is at all relevant; for instance, do you want to count distinct structures or the whole memory page that was allocated to store these structures?

Finally, you'll have to decide between using conditional compiling to switch on and off the call to measures, assuming the linker shall not include the unnecessary measurement code when switched off, or a specific version of your practical planner that shall have to be synchronized with further updated versions of the planner.

13.2.2 Design Valuable Tests!

The second step is to design a set of planning tests.

A first set of planning tests is necessary in order to confirm the planner generates correct plans, that is, plans that are solutions to the planning problems of your game. If your planner uses a complete search procedure such as breadth-first search, the correct plans should also be the shortest ones. By running your planner against these gaming problems, your objective is to show this planner can be used in your game. Do not consider only planning problems related to your game, because these problems certainly are too small to stress the full power of a GOAP-like planner. On one hand, a GOAP-like planner generates less than one plan per second per NPC on average, and on another hand, these plans are very short, say, at most four actions. Consequently, a second set of complex planning tests is needed to show any improvement in the optimization process. Runtime for such complex tests can be up to several minutes, whereas in-game planning runtime, it is at most several milliseconds. There are two kinds of complex tests: scaling tests and competition tests.

First, scaling tests provide an increasing number of one specific game object: box, creature, location, vehicle, weapon, and so forth. Solution plans to scaling tests can be short, and plan length is expected to be the same for all of the scaling tests; the idea is to provide more objects of one kind than would ever happen in a gaming situation so that the branching factor in the search space explodes, although the solution is the same. For instance, and this is valid for a forward state space GOAP-like procedure, take an in-game planning problem such that the goal situation involves only one box; assume that this box, say `box-1`, has to be picked up at one location and moved to another location. Then build an initial situation with increasing number of boxes: `box-2`, `box-3`, and so on, although `box-1` is still the only box that appears in the goal solution. As the planner can pick up one box, it shall try to pick up and then move each box until the goal solution, which only requires `box-1`, is reached.

Second, competition tests are complex problems whose objective is to swallow a lot of computing resources with the help of a high branching factor and a solution with a long sequence of actions [IPC 14]. For instance, it is now time to move several boxes to the final location. This requires that you allow for picking up and moving only one box at a time and do not impose priorities between boxes. There are consequently many solutions of the exact same length. Each of these solutions reflects the order in which the boxes reach the goal location, thus entailing a huge search space.

Of course, if any updated version of the planning code shows a performance decrease against these planning problems, then this update is not an improvement.

13.2.3 Use Profilers!

There is no way to escape the use of profilers.

With the first two steps, you are able to show your practical planner is usable for your game and that your latest code update is either an improvement or else a bad idea. But how are you going to improve more, avoid bad ideas, or discover unexpected and eventually fruitful paths? Runtime and memory profilers are here to help.

On the contrary to the quick and easy first two steps that both are matters of days, this third step is a matter of weeks and months. Either you use professional tools (e.g., Intel® VTunes™ and IBM® Rational® Purify Plus that both allow to profile source code and binaries) or else you'll need to develop specific in-game profiling tools [Rabin 00, Lung 11]. Using professional tools requires mastering them, while making your own definitively requires development time. Either way, an investment of time will need to be made.

By reporting where the computing resources go, these tools tell you where to focus your improvement effort, and this is invaluable. If, on this improvement path, you reach a point where no part of your code seems to stand out as a candidate for improvement, then, beyond changing the profiling scheme and counters and running the tests again, it might be time to settle down and think of your planning data structures and your planning algorithms.

13.3 Practical Planning Data Structures

From a far viewpoint, anything can be optimized, from parsing the action text files to the data structure holding the solution to the planning problem. There is also the planning domain (how actions are encoded) and the planning problems (how states, either initial or goal, are encoded) using properties of your game world [Cheng 05, pp. 342–343]. For instance, you may not wish to represent the details of navigation from one location to another (e.g., navigating into a building, unlocking, and opening doors, avoiding obstacles) or the necessary actions to solve a puzzle in the planning problem; instead, encode only one action that magically reaches the goal location or magically solves the puzzle; then, delegate the execution of this action to a specific routine. Our focus here is different.

From a closer viewpoint, we learn from computational complexity that time complexity cannot be strictly less than space complexity [Garey 79, p. 170]; that is, at best, the computation time shall grow (with respect to a given parameter, e.g., the number of predicates) as the amount of memory needed for this computation, but never less. Consequently, you can design better algorithms to achieve better runtimes, but you can also design better data structures and start with shrinking memory: use as less memory as you can and use it as best as you can [Rabin 11].

First, make sure to choose the smallest structure that supports the features you need. Then, avoid multiple copies of these structures by storing information only once, and share it everywhere it is needed [Noble 01, pp. 182–190]. For instance, the action text files may contain several occurrences of the same identifier; when reading the first occurrence of this identifier, push it in an `std::vector` and share its position:

```
std::vector<Identifier> theIdentifiers;

size_t AddIdentifier(Identifier& id)
{
    size_t position = theIdentifiers.size();
    theIdentifiers.push_back(id);
    return position;
}
```

Of course, the next occurrence of id in the text file must not be pushed at the back of theIdentifiers but must be retrieved in theIdentifiers in order to share its position. So you may want instead to hash identifiers in an std::unordered_map, storing an integer value at the hashed position, and increment this value each time a new identifier is added to the table:

```
std::unordered_map<Identifier, size_t> theIdentifiers;

size_t AddIdentifier(Identifier& id)
{
    size_t position = theIdentifiers.size();
    theIdentifiers[id] = position;
    return position;
}
```

Lookup and sharing is then achieved through an iterator:

```
size_t shared_position;
std::unordered_map<Identifier, size_t>::iterator it;

it = theIdentifiers.find(id);
if (theIdentifiers.end() == it)
   shared_position = AddIdentifier(id);
else
  shared_position = it->second;
```

When the parsing of the action text file ends, we know exactly how many distinct identifiers are in the action text file and thus can allocate an array and move the identifiers from the hash table to their position in the array. More space can be saved as soon as we know the number of distinct identifiers: that is, use an unsigned char, instead of size_t in the aforementioned code, to share the positions when there are less than 256 identifiers for your planning problems, and so on.

Finally, consider a custom memory allocator (even for the STL [Isensee 03]) to access memory quicker than the classical memory allocation routines (e.g., malloc). Several high-performance memory allocators are available [Berger 14, Lazarov 08, Lea 12, Masmano 08] with various licensing schemes. Try them or any other one before embarking into developing your own.

Assuming that predicates can share their position to other planning data structures, the rest of this section discusses the use of the sharing pattern [Noble 01, pp. 182–190] to actions, plans, and states.

13.3.1 Actions

An action is made of two sets of predicates, in the spirit of IF/THEN rules [Wilhelm 08]: the set of preconditions predicates and the set of postcondition predicates (effects). A predicate can only occur in both sets if and only if it is negative (prefixed by not) in one set and positive in the other set. For instance, the positive predicate hold(gun) can appear as a precondition of the action Drop if the negative predicate not(hold(gun)) is one of its effects; accordingly (i.e., symmetrically), hold(gun) can be an effect of the action Take if not(hold(gun)) is one of its preconditions.

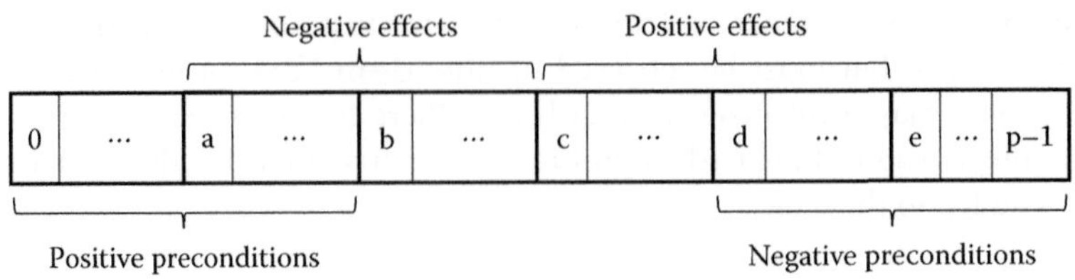

Figure 13.1

Action predicates occur only once when preconditions and effects overlap.

Assume an array of shared positions of predicates, ranging from 0 to (p – 1). Then the action predicates can be ordered in the array so that they occur only once:

- Let a, b, c, d, e, and p such that $0 \leq a \leq b \leq c \leq d \leq e \leq (p-1)$.
- [0, a – 1] is the range of positive preconditions.
- [a, b – 1] is the range of positive preconditions that occur as negative effects.
- [b, c – 1] is the range of negative effects.
- [c, d – 1] is the range of positive effects.
- [d, e – 1] is the range of positive effects that occur as negative preconditions.
- [e, p – 1] is the range of negative preconditions.

Consequently, preconditions are in the range [0, b – 1] and in the range [d, p – 1], and effects are in the range [a, e – 1] as illustrated in Figure 13.1.

For instance, the positive predicate `hold(gun)` of the action `Drop` shall occur in the range [a, b – 1], whereas it shall occur in the range [d, e – 1] for the action `Take` (which is detailed in a following section).

Moreover, an action has parameters that are shared among its predicates; for instance, both the actions `Drop` and `Take` have an `object` as a parameter for the predicate `hold`. If we further constrain all predicate parameters to be gathered in the set of parameters of an action, then all predicate parameters only need to be integer values pointing to the positions of the parameters of their action; the type `unsigned char` can be used for these integer values if we limit the number of parameters to 256, which is safe.

13.3.2 Plans

A GOAP-like plan is a totally ordered set of actions. An action is uniquely represented by an action identifier, for example, `Drop`, and its parameters (once they all have a value), which is called the action signature, for example, `Drop(gun)`. An action signature is a good candidate for sharing its position in an array. Consequently, a plan is an array of shared positions of action signatures.

As plans grow during the search, using an `std::vector` is practical, while keeping in mind the memory overhead for `std::vectors`. Assume the 16 bytes of Visual C++ 2013, at most 256 action signatures, and a maximum plan length of 4 actions [F.E.A.R. 05]: `std::array<unsigned char,4>` (4 bytes) can safely replace `std::vector<unsigned char>` (at least 16 bytes and at most 20 bytes for plans of length 4). Assuming 65,535 action signatures and a maximum plan length of 8 actions, then `std::array<short,8>` still saves memory over `std::vector<short>`.

13.3.3 States

The planning problem defines the initial and the goal states. Forward breadth-first search applies actions to states in order to produce new states, and hopefully the goal state. Indeed, if the preconditions of an action, say `A`, are satisfied in a state, say `s`, then the resulting state, say `r`, is obtained by first applying set difference (–) with the negated effects of `A` and second to `s` and then by applying set union (+) with the positive effects of `A`: `r` = (`s` – (negative effects of `A`)) + (positive effects of `A`).

States are made of predicates, and as for actions, it is obvious to substitute predicates by their shared positions.

Set operations can be easily implemented with the member operations of `std::set` or `std::unordered _ set`. The memory overhead of these STL containers is of 12 bytes for the former and 40 bytes for the latter with Visual C++ 2013; if you want to store all generated states in order to check whether the resulting state `r` has previously been generated, then 1000 states means 12 kb or else 40 kb of memory overhead.

Set operations can also be implemented with bitwise operations where one bit is set to 1 if the predicate belongs to the state and set to 0 otherwise. `std::bitset` provides the bitwise machinery so that a 1000 states over (at most) 256 predicates would require 32 kb.

Runtime measurement can help you make the final decision, but combining the two representations provides an interesting trade-off. For instance, you may want to use an `std::array`, which has no memory overhead, to represent a state and convert it to an `std::bitset` when computing the resulting state; then, convert the resulting state back to an `std:array`. In this case, 10 shared positions of predicates in a state on average means 10 kb for a 1000 states, which is less than 12 kb, while 32 kb would allow for the storing of more than 3000 states.

13.4 Practical Planning Algorithms

Runtime profiling should report at least the two following hot spots for forward breadth-first search with actions as text files: (1) checking which predicates of a given state can satisfy the preconditions of an action and (2) unifying the precondition predicates of an action with predicates of a given state in order to assign a value to each parameter of this action (consequently, we can compute the resulting state).

13.4.1 Iterating over Subsets of State Predicates

First, consider the following description for action `Take`, stated with simple logic expressions (conjunction and negation) and written with keywords (`:action`, `:parameters`, `:preconditions`, `:effects`), a query mark to prefix variable identifier, and parenthesis, to ease parsing and the reading of the action:

```
(:action Take
    :parameters (location ?l, creature ?c, object ?o)
    :preconditions (not(hold(?object, ?c))
                    and at-c(?l, ?c)
                    and at-o(?l, ?o))
    :effects (not(at-o(?l, ?o)) and hold(?object, ?c))
)
```

Assume the shared positions of the predicates of the action Take are the following:

Predicate	Shared Position
at-o(?l, ?c)	3
at-c(?l, ?o)	7
hold(?object, ?c)	9

If predicates are shared in the order they are read from the action file, the values of these shared positions means at-o(?l, ?o) is the third predicate that was read from the file, while at-c(?l, ?c) and hold(?object, ?c) were the seventh and ninth, respectively. With these shared positions, the array (refer to Figure 13.1) representing the 3 predicates of the action Take is shown in Figure 13.2.

Second, consider the following initial state:

```
(:initial (at-c(loc1, c1) and at-c(loc1, c2)
          and at-c(loc2, c3) and at-c(loc3, c4)
          and at-o(loc1, o1) and at-o(loc1, o3)
          and at-o(loc3, o4) and at-o(loc5, o2)
          and at-o(loc5, o5))
)
```

For instance, the action represented by the action signature Take(loc1,c1,o1) can be applied to the initial state because all its preconditions are satisfied in the initial state. But there are four more actions that can be applied to this initial state, represented by the four following action signatures: Take(loc1,c1,o3), Take(loc1,c2,o1), Take(loc1,c2,o3), and Take(loc3,c4,o4).

We can first note that each positive precondition identifier must match at least one state predicate identifier. Second, we can note that no state predicate identifier can be a negative precondition identifier. When these two quick tests pass, we can further test the applicability of an action, pushing further the use of the predicate identifiers.

To test the applicability of action Take in any state and in particular in the initial state earlier, we can sort the predicates of the state according to their identifier (refer to Figure 13.2). It is consequently possible to test only 20 pairs (4 instances of at-c × 5 instances of at-o) of predicates from the initial states instead of the 36 pairs (choosing any two elements in a set of 9 elements = (9 × 8)/2 = 36 pairs), which can be built from the initial state.

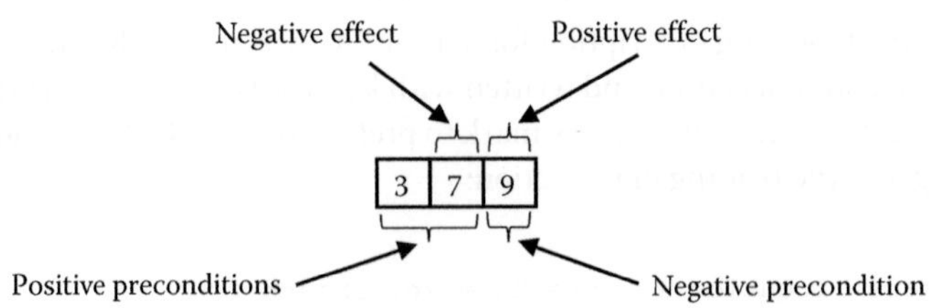

Figure 13.2

Three predicates of the action Take. Based on the key in Figure 13.1, this three-digit array can be decoded as a = 1, b = c = d = 2, and e = p = 3.

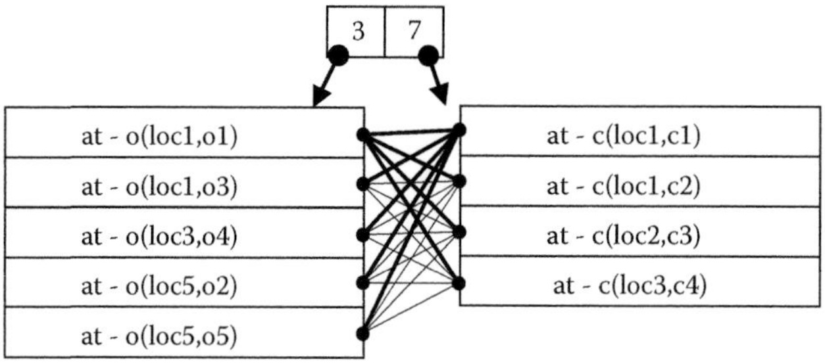

Figure 13.3

Sorting state predicates with respect to their identifiers.

In Figure 13.3, the top array containing three and seven represents the positive preconditions of action `Take`. We then iterate over the predicates of the initial state. If an initial state predicate has the same predicate identifier as a precondition predicate, then this initial state predicate is pushed at the back of the appropriate column. If the identifier of an initial state predicate does not correspond to any identifier of a precondition predicate, then this initial state predicate is ignored. Finally, iterating in both columns, we can make pairs of predicates as indicated in Figure 13.3.

Note that if the language of the actions file allows predicates with the same identifier but with a different number of parameters, then the number of parameters must also be checked to build both columns in Figure 13.3.

There are various ways of achieving the iterations over both columns. For instance, we begin by forming the two-digit number made by the size of the columns in Figure 13.3: 54. Then we start with the two-digit value 00 and increase the rightmost digit; when this value reaches 4, we rewrite the two-digit number to 10 and increase it until the rightmost digit reaches 4 again. We then rewrite this number to 20 and so on until 54 is reached. This procedure builds the following list of two-digit numbers: 00, 01, 02, 03, 10, 11, 12, 13, 20, 21, 22, 23, 30, 31, 32, 33, 40, 41, 42, and 43. Alternatively, we can start from 43 and decrease until 00 is reached, thus producing the two-digit numbers of the previous list in the reverse order. Each of these 20 two-digit numbers can be used to access a position in both columns in order to make a pair of state predicates. The iterating procedure in Listing 13.1 works for any number of positive preconditions.

13.4.2 Recording Where the Action Parameters Occur in the Action Predicates

The procedure in Listing 13.1 generates tuples such that each state predicate identifier matches the identifier of a precondition predicate. Consequently, the unification procedure need only checking whether the state predicate parameters unify with the action parameters.

We know from Figure 13.3 that the positive precondition predicate whose shared position is 3, that is, `at-o(?l,?o)`, is unified with state predicate `at-o(loc5,o5)`, and then the parameter `?l` of action `Take` gets the value `loc5`, and the parameter `?o` of action `Take` gets the value `o5`. The positive precondition predicate whose shared position is 7,

Listing 13.1. Iterating procedure to find all pairs of state predicates.

```
For each predicate of the current state
  Push the predicate back to the list which corresponds to its identifier
End For each;
Make the number n with as many digits as there are non-empty lists;
Set each digit of n to 0;
Repeat
  Access each of the lists with respect to the digits of n and
    make the tuple of predicates of s;
  Increase the least significant digit of n by 1;
  For each digit d of n, starting with the least significant digit,
    If the digit d is equal to the size of the dth list Then
      If d is the most significant digit of n Then
        Break the enclosing For each loop;
      End if;
      Reset digit d to 0;
      Increase digit (d+1) of n by 1
    Else
      Break the enclosing For each loop;
    End if;
  End For each;
Until the value of n is made of the size of the n lists.
```

that is, `at-c(?l,?c)`, with the parameter `?l` equal to `loc5`, must now unify with state predicate `at-c(loc3,c4)`. This fails because `loc3` is different from `loc5`.

The idea is to record all the positions where an action parameter occurs in positive precondition predicates and then check that the parameters at these positions in the state predicates have the same value. For instance, the parameter `?l` of action `Take` occurs as the first parameter of both positive precondition predicates. If the values at these positions in the state predicates are equal (which can be trivially achieved by testing the value of the first position against all other positions), then we can check for the equality of the occurrences of the next parameter. Recording the positions can be achieved once for all when parsing the action files.

13.5 Conclusion

A Visual C++ 2013 project is available from the book's website (http://www.gameaipro.com), which implements a practical planner with the features (i.e., actions as text files and forward breadth-first search) and the data structures and algorithms described in this chapter.

Although planning is known to be very hard in theory, even the simplest planning algorithm can be implemented in a practical planner, which can be used for your gaming purposes, providing you focus on shrinking both memory and runtime requirements.

Quick runtime and memory measurement routines, as well as relevant testing and systematic profiling, can hopefully help you succeed in making planning practical for your gaming purposes.

References

[Berger 14] Berger, E. 2014. The hoard memory allocator. http://emeryberger.github.io/Hoard/ (accessed May 26, 2014).

[Cheng 05] Cheng, J. and Southey, F. 2005. Implementing practical planning for game AI. In *Game Programming Gems 5*, ed. K. Pallister, pp. 329–343. Hingham, MA: Charles River Media.

[Deus Ex 3 DC 13] Deus Ex Human Revolution—Director's Cut. Square Enix, 2013.

[F.E.A.R. 05] F.E.A.R.—First Encounter Assault Recon. Vivendi Universal, 2005.

[Garey 79] Garey, M. and Johnson, D. 1979. *Computers and Intractability: A Guide to the Theory of NP-Completeness*. New York: W.H. Freeman & Co Ltd.

[Ghallab 04] Ghallab, M., Nau, D., and Traverso, P. 2004. *Automated Planning: Theory and Practice*. San Francisco, CA: Morgan Kaufmann.

[IPC 14] International Planning Competition. 2014. http://ipc.icaps-conference.org/ (accessed May 28, 2014).

[Isensee 03] Isensee, P. 2003. Custom STL allocators. In *Game Programming Gems 3*, ed. D. Treglia, pp. 49–58. Hingham, MA: Charles River Media.

[Josuttis 13] Josuttis, N. 2013. *The C++ Standard Library*. Upper Saddle River, NJ: Pearson Education.

[Lazarov 08] Lazarov, D. 2008. High performance heap allocator. In *Game Programming Gems 7*, ed. S. Jacobs, pp. 15–23. Hingham, MA: Charles River Media.

[Lea 12] Lea, D. 2012. A memory allocator (2.8.6). ftp://g.oswego.edu/pub/misc/malloc.c (accessed May 26, 2014).

[Lung 11] Lung, R. 2011. Design and implementation of an in-game memory profiler. In *Game Programming Gems 8*, ed. A. Lake, pp. 402–408. Boston, MA: Course Technology.

[Masmano 08] Masmano, M., Ripoli, I., Balbastre, P., and Crespo, A. 2008. A constant-time dynamic storage allocator for real-time systems. *Real-Time Systems*, 40(2): 149–179.

[Noble 01] Noble, J. and Weir, C. 2001. *Small Software Memory: Patterns for Systems with Limited Memory*. Harlow, U.K.: Pearson Education Ltd.

[Orkin 04] Orkin, J. 2004. Applying goal-oriented action planning to games. In *AI Game Programming Wisdom 2*, ed. S. Rabin, pp. 217–227. Hingham, MA: Charles River Media.

[Rabin 00] Rabin, S. 2000. Real-time in-game profiling. In *Game Programming Gems*, ed. M. DeLoura, pp. 120–130. Boston, MA: Charles River Media.

[Rabin 11] Rabin, S. 2011. Game optimization through the lens of memory and data access. In *Game Programming Gems 8*, ed. A. Lake, pp. 385–392. Boston, MA: Course Technology.

[Tomb Raider 13] Tomb Raider—Definitive Edition. Square Enix, 2013.

[Wilhelm 08] Wilhelm, D. 2008. Practical logic-based planning. In *AI Game Programming Wisdom 4*, ed. S. Rabin, pp. 355–403. Boston, MA: Course Technology.

SECTION III

Movement and Pathfinding

14

JPS+
An Extreme A Speed Optimization for Static Uniform Cost Grids*

Steve Rabin and Fernando Silva

14.1 Introduction

Jump point search (JPS) is a recently devised optimal pathfinding algorithm that can speed up searches on uniform cost grid maps by up to an order of magnitude over traditional A* [Harabor 12]. However, by statically analyzing a map and burning in directions to walls and jump points, it is possible to dramatically speed up searches even further, up to *two orders of magnitude* over traditional A*. To illustrate the difference in speed on a particular 40 × 40 map, A* found an optimal solution in 180.05 ns, JPS in 15.04 ns, and JPS+ in 1.55 ns. In this example, JPS+ was 116x faster than traditional A*, while remaining perfectly optimal.

Both JPS and JPS+ use a state-space pruning strategy that only works for grid search spaces where the cost of traversal is uniform with regard to distance. This chapter will explain in detail how JPS+ works and the exact specifics on how to implement it. JPS+ was first unveiled on June 2014 at the International Conference on Automated Planning and Scheduling (ICAPS); however, one of the authors of this chapter (Steve Rabin) independently invented the improved algorithm for storing directions to walls and jump points a month before Harabor's initial publication. For consistency, the terms in this chapter will be from the original ICAPS paper [Harabor 14].

The code from this chapter, along with a full source demo, can be found on the book's website (http://www.gameaipro.com).

14.2 Pruning Strategy

JPS gets its tremendous speed from pruning the search space at runtime. This exploit exists because open areas in grids can be visited multiple times through equivalent paths. Consider a uniform cost grid space of 2×5 that contains no walls, as in Figure 14.1. Now consider how many optimal paths exist from the bottom left to the top right of this search space. Figure 14.1 shows that there are four identical cost paths. In many problems, traditional A* will redundantly check the same nodes along these paths to verify that a shorter path cannot be found. This is wasted work; with the ideas behind JPS+, we can avoid it.

JPS has a clever method for systematically choosing a single route through these equivalent paths. Figure 14.2 shows how JPS searches from the start node, visiting each node only once. That is, JPS will only consider the successors of a state in the direction of the arrows; all other successors are ignored. Of the total JPS speedup over A*, this pruning strategy accounts for roughly 50% of the speed improvement.

To understand this strategy in more detail, consider the node east of the center node in Figure 14.2. This is a node visited straight (nondiagonally) from the parent. Nodes visited straight from their parent only have successors that continue on in that same direction. In this case, the node east of the center node only considers the node to the east as a possible neighbor (pruning from considering the other seven directions).

Now consider the node northeast of the center node in Figure 14.2. This is a node visited diagonally from the parent. Nodes visited diagonally only consider three neighbors in the diagonal direction. The node northeast of the center node only considers nodes to the north, northeast, and east as possible neighbors (pruning from consideration the northwest, west, southwest, south, and southeast nodes).

JPS has another trick where it only puts relevant nodes, called *jump points*, on the open list. Since the open list is a bottleneck in traditional A*, a dramatic reduction in nodes on

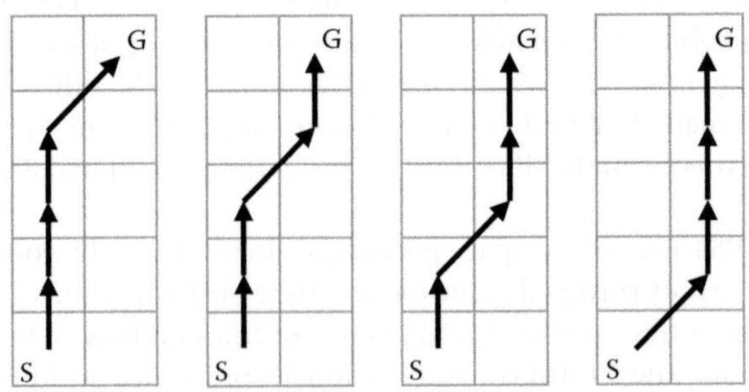

Figure 14.1

Four equivalent and optimal paths exist from the start node to the goal node.

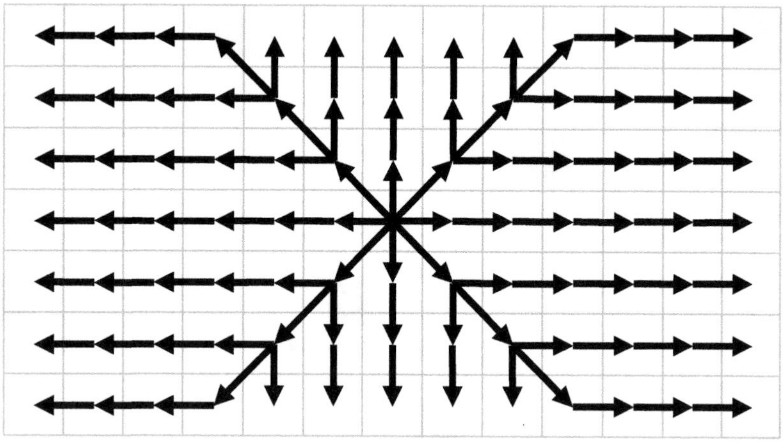

Figure 14.2

Systematic pruning rules keep nodes from being visited multiple times.

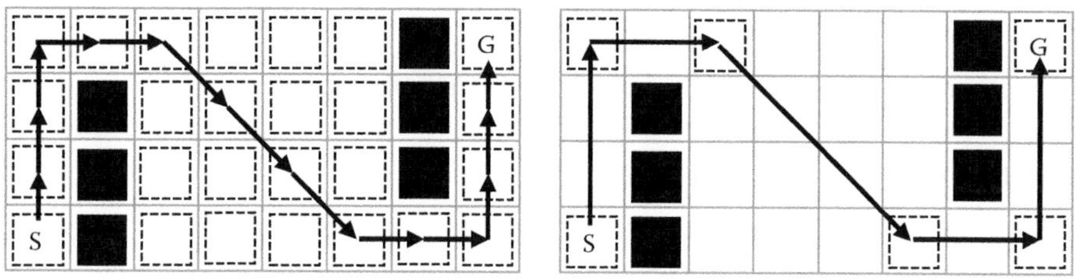

(a) Traditional A*: nodes placed on the open list

(b) JPS: jump point nodes placed on the open list

Figure 14.3

Nodes put on the open list in (a) traditional A* versus (b) JPS.

the open list results in a tremendous runtime savings. This second trick accounts for the other 50% speedup over traditional A*. Figure 14.3 illustrates the difference in the number of nodes that get placed on the open list.

Assuming that these two general ideas are understood, the rest of this chapter will provide a detailed explanation of how to correctly and efficiently implement them.

14.3 Forced Neighbors

There are certain cases where the pruning strategy from Figure 14.2 fails to visit a node due to walls in the search space. To address this, JPS introduced the concept of *forced neighbors*. Figure 14.4 shows the eight forced neighbor cases. Forced neighbors only occur when traveling in a straight or *cardinal* direction (north, south, west, or east). Forced neighbors are a signal that the normal pruning strategy will fail and that the current node must consider additional nodes.

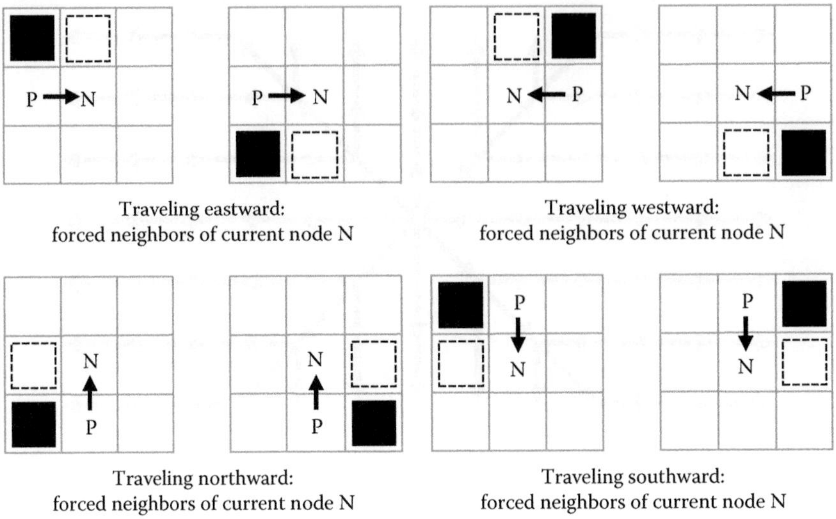

Figure 14.4

The eight forced neighbor cases. Forced neighbor nodes are outlined with a dashed line. Node P is the parent node and node N is the current node being explored. Note that forced neighbors are dependent on the direction of travel from the parent node.

14.4 Jump Points

Jump points are another concept introduced by JPS. Jump points are the intermediate points on the map that are necessary to travel through for at least one optimal path. JPS+ introduces four flavors of jump points: *primary*, *straight*, *diagonal*, and *target*.

14.4.1 Primary Jump Points

Primary jump points are easy to identify because they have a forced neighbor. In Figure 14.4, the primary jump points are the current node, N, for each situation shown. In Figure 14.5, we introduce a new map that shows the primary jump points, given the travel direction from the parent node.

Note that a node is only a primary jump point when traveling to the node in the direction indicated. So the same node can both be a jump point and not a jump point depending on the direction of travel during the search. Given that jump points only occur when traveling in a cardinal direction, there are four possible jump point flags for each node.

14.4.2 Straight Jump Points

Once all primary jump points have been identified, the straight jump points can be found. The straight jump points are nodes where traveling in a cardinal direction will eventually run into a primary jump point for that direction of travel (before running into a wall), as shown in Figure 14.6.

Note that a node can be both a primary and straight jump point for each direction of travel. Think of straight jump points as directions on how to get to the next primary jump point for that direction of travel.

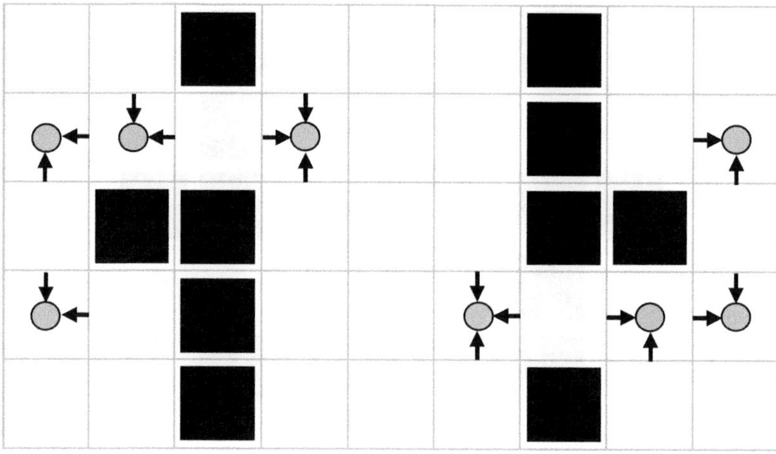

Figure 14.5

Primary jump points due to forced neighbors. Nodes marked with a circle are the jump points. The arrow direction indicates the direction of travel from the parent node for that node to be a jump point in that direction of travel.

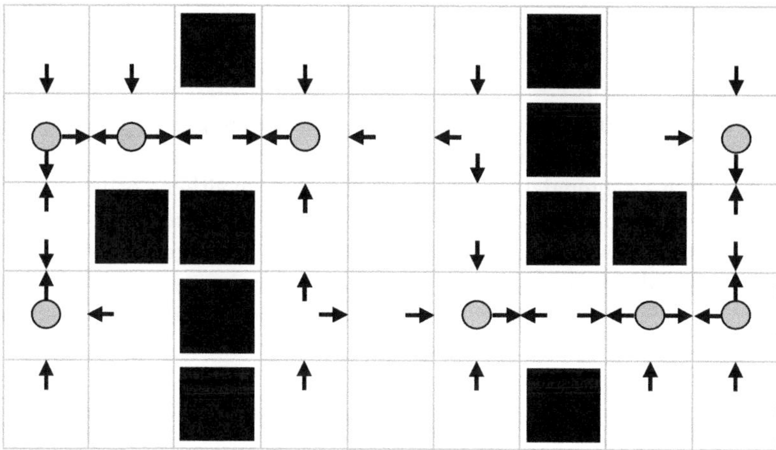

Figure 14.6

Straight jump points point to primary jump points. Primary jump points are marked with a circle. Straight jump points are any node with an arrow in it.

Figure 14.7 is a more detailed version of Figure 14.6 where the arrows have been replaced with distances. The distances indicate how many nodes away is the next primary jump point for that direction of travel. However, there is a very tricky thing going on in Figure 14.7 that wasn't apparent in Figure 14.6. The distance values aren't the distance to just any primary jump point, but only to primary jump points *in that direction of travel.* For example, the node on the very bottom left has a distance value of 3 in the up direction.

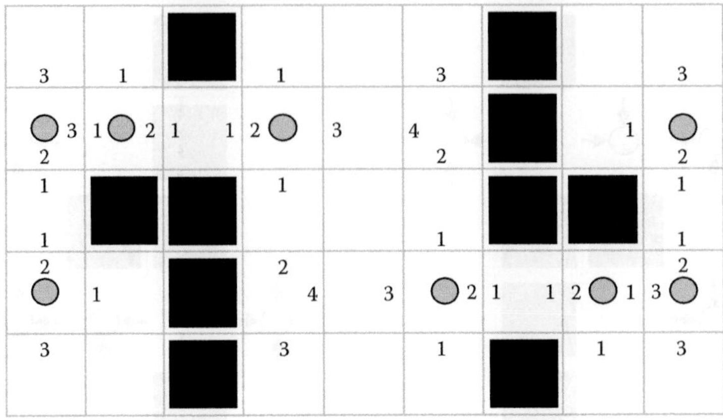

Figure 14.7

Straight jump points are marked with a distance indicating how many nodes away the next primary jump point is for that direction of travel.

It looks as if it should be a 1, but the primary jump point in the node above it is not a primary jump point *for that direction of travel* (double check Figure 14.5 to confirm). The actual primary jump point for traveling up is 3 nodes above.

14.4.3 Diagonal Jump Points

After straight jump points and their respective distances to primary jump points have been identified, we need to identify diagonal jump points. Diagonal jump points are any node in which a diagonal direction of travel will reach either a primary jump point or a straight jump point *that is traveling in a direction related to the diagonal direction* (before hitting a wall). For example, a node with a diagonal direction moving northeast is only a diagonal jump point if it runs into a primary or straight jump point traveling either north or east. This is consistent with the pruning strategy introduced in Figure 14.2.

As we did with straight jump points, we need to fill diagonal jump points with distances to the other jump points. Figure 14.8 shows our map with the diagonal jump points filled in.

14.5 Wall Distances

The information built up in Figure 14.8 is very close to the finished preprocessed map, but it needs wall distance information to be complete. In an effort to minimize the memory required for each node, we will represent wall distances as zero or negative numbers. Any node direction that is not marked with a straight or diagonal distance will be given a distance to the wall in that direction. Figure 14.9 shows the completed map where every node has distances for all eight directions. Additionally, we have deleted the primary jump point markers since they were only used to build up the distance map and are not needed at runtime.

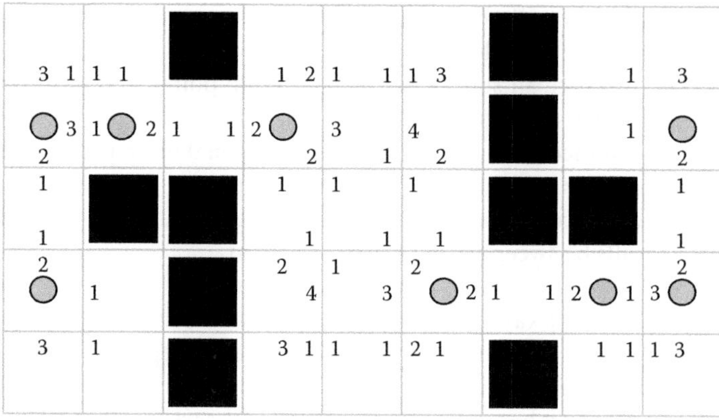

Figure 14.8

Diagonal jump points filled in with distances to primary and straight jump points.

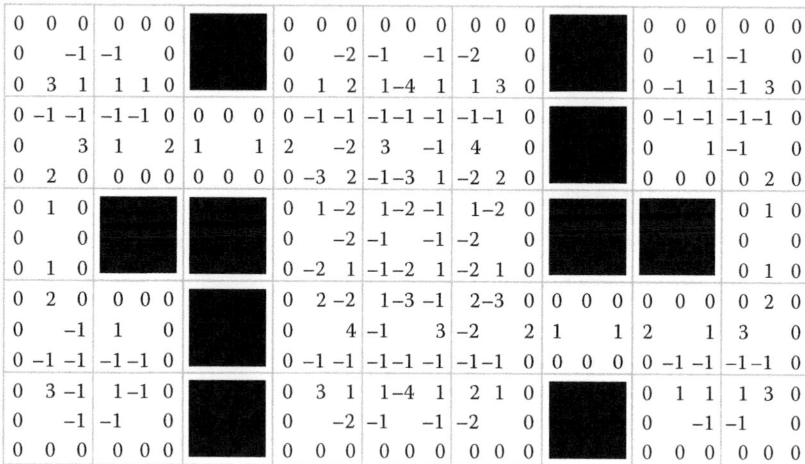

0 0 0 0 0 0 0 0 0 0 0 0 0 0 0 0 0 0 0 0 0 0 0 0
0 -1 -1 0 0 -2 -1 -1 -2 0 0 -1 -1 0
0 3 1 1 1 0 0 1 2 1 -4 1 1 3 0 0 -1 1 -1 3 0
0 -1 -1 -1 -1 0 0 0 0 0 -1 -1 -1 -1 -1 -1 -1 0 0 -1 -1 -1 -1 0
0 3 1 2 1 1 2 -2 3 -1 4 0 0 1 -1 0
0 2 0 0 0 0 0 0 0 0 -3 2 -1 -3 1 -2 2 0 0 0 0 0 2 0
0 1 0 0 1 -2 1 -2 -1 1 -2 0 0 1 0
0 0 0 -2 -1 -1 -2 0 0 0
0 1 0 0 -2 1 -1 -2 1 -2 1 0 0 1 0
0 2 0 0 0 0 0 2 -2 1 -3 -1 2 -3 0 0 0 0 0 0 0 0 2 0
0 -1 1 0 0 4 -1 3 -2 2 1 1 2 1 3 0
0 -1 -1 -1 -1 0 0 -1 -1 -1 -1 -1 -1 -1 0 0 0 0 0 -1 -1 -1 -1 0
0 3 -1 1 -1 0 0 3 1 1 -4 1 2 1 0 0 1 1 1 3 0
0 -1 -1 0 0 -2 -1 -1 -2 0 0 -1 -1 0
0 0 0 0 0 0 0 0 0 0 0 0 0 0 0 0 0 0 0 0 0 0 0 0

Figure 14.9

Wall distances added to all unmarked directions. Walls are either zero or negative and represent the distance to a wall (discard the negative sign).

14.6 Map Preprocess Implementation

As a practical matter, the complete precomputed map in Figure 14.9 can be created with the following strategy:

1. Identify all primary jump points by setting a directional flag in each node.
2. Mark with distance all westward straight jump points and westward walls by sweeping the map left to right.
3. Mark with distance all eastward straight jump points and eastward walls by sweeping the map right to left.

4. Mark with distance all northward straight jump points and northward walls by sweeping the map up to down.
5. Mark with distance all southward straight jump points and southward walls by sweeping the map down to up.
6. Mark with distance all southwest/southeast diagonal jump points and southwest/southeast walls by sweeping the map down to up.
7. Mark with distance all northwest/northeast diagonal jump points and northwest/northeast walls by sweeping the map up to down.

Listing 14.1 provides an example of the sweep to compute westward numbers in step 2. Similar code must be written for the other three sweep directions in steps 3–5. Listing 14.2 provides an example of the sweep to compute southwest numbers as part of step 6. Similar code must be written to compute southeast, northeast, and northwest numbers.

Listing 14.1. Left to right sweep to mark all westward straight jump points and all westward walls.

```
for (int r = 0; r < mapHeight; ++r)
{
    int count = -1;
    bool jumpPointLastSeen = false;

    for (int c = 0; c < mapWidth; ++c)
    {
        if (m_terrain[r][c] == TILE_WALL)
        {
            count = -1;
            jumpPointLastSeen = false;
            distance[r][c][West] = 0;
            continue;
        }

        count++;

        if (jumpPointLastSeen)
        {
            distance[r][c][West] = count;
        }
        else //Wall last seen
        {
            distance[r][c][West] = -count;
        }

        if (jumpPoints[r][c][West])
        {
            count = 0;
            jumpPointLastSeen = true;
        }
    }
}
```

Listing 14.2. Down to up sweep to mark all southwest diagonal jump points and all southwest diagonal walls.

```
for (int r = 0; r < mapHeight; ++r)
{
    for (int c = 0; c < mapWidth; ++c)
    {
        if (!IsWall(r, c))
        {
            if (r == 0 || c == 0 || IsWall(r-1, c) ||
                IsWall(r, c-1) || IsWall(r-1, c-1))
            {
                //Wall one away
                distance[r][c][Southwest] = 0;
            }
            else if (!IsWall(r-1, c) && !IsWall(r, c-1) &&
                (distance[r-1][c-1][South] > 0 ||
                 distance[r-1][c-1][West] > 0))
            {
                //Straight jump point one away
                distance[r][c][Southwest] = 1;
            }
            else
            {
                //Increment from last
                int jumpDistance =
                    distance[r-1][c-1][Southwest];

                if (jumpDistance > 0)
                {
                    distance[r][c][Southwest] =
                        1 + jumpDistance;
                }
                else
                {
                    distance[r][c][Southwest] =
                        -1 + jumpDistance;
                }
            }
        }
    }
}
```

14.7 Runtime Implementation

The genius of the preprocessed map is that it contains many of the decisions required for the search, thus making the runtime code much simpler and faster than traditional JPS. For example, the recursive step from JPS is completely eliminated and only jump points are ever examined.

The pseudocode in Listing 14.3 is the complete JPS+ runtime algorithm. However, there are several aspects that need clarification. The first is the `ValidDirLookUpTable`. This table is used to only consider directions in the spirit of Figure 14.1. For example, if traveling in a diagonal direction such as northeast, the directions east, northeast, and north

Listing 14.3. Complete runtime pseudocode for JPS+.

```
ValidDirLookUpTable
    Traveling South: West, Southwest, South, Southeast, East
    Traveling Southeast: South, Southeast, East
    Traveling East: South, Southeast, East, Northeast, North
    Traveling Northeast: East, Northeast, North
    Traveling North: East, Northeast, North, Northwest, West
    Traveling Northwest: North, Northwest, West
    Traveling West: North, Northwest, West, Southwest, South
    Traveling Southwest: West, Southwest, South

while (!OpenList.IsEmpty())
{
    Node* curNode = OpenList.Pop();
    Node* parentNode = curNode->parent;

    if (curNode == goalNode)
        return PathFound;

    foreach (direction in ValidDirLookUpTable
             given parentNode)
    {
        Node* newSuccessor = NULL;
        float givenCost;

        if (direction is cardinal &&
            goal is in exact direction &&
            DiffNodes(curNode, goalNode) <=
            abs(curNode->distances[direction]))
        {
            //Goal is closer than wall distance or
            //closer than or equal to jump point distance
            newSuccessor = goalNode;
            givenCost = curNode->givenCost +
                        DiffNodes(curNode, goalNode);
        }
        else if (direction is diagonal &&
                 goal is in general direction &&
                 (DiffNodesRow(curNode, goalNode) <=
                 abs(curNode->distances[direction]) ||
                 (DiffNodesCol(curNode, goalNode) <=
                 abs(curNode->distances[direction]))))
        {
            //Goal is closer or equal in either row or
            //column than wall or jump point distance

            //Create a target jump point
            int minDiff = min(RowDiff(curNode, goalNode),
                              ColDiff(curNode, goalNode));
            newSuccessor =
                GetNode (curNode, minDiff, direction);
            givenCost = curNode->givenCost +
                (SQRT2 * minDiff);
        }
```

```
        else if (curNode->distances[direction] > 0)
        {
            //Jump point in this direction
            newSuccessor = GetNode(curNode, direction);
            givenCost = DiffNodes(curNode, newSuccessor);
            if (diagonal direction) {givenCost *= SQRT2;}
            givenCost += curNode->givenCost;
        }
        //Traditional A* from this point
        if (newSuccessor != NULL)
        {
            if (newSuccessor not on OpenList or ClosedList)
            {
                newSuccessor->parent = curNode;
                newSuccessor->givenCost = givenCost;
                newSuccessor->finalCost = givenCost +
                    CalculateHeuristic(newSuccessor, goalNode);
                OpenList.Push(newSuccessor);
            }
            else if(givenCost < newSuccessor->givenCost)
            {
                newSuccessor->parent = curNode;
                newSuccessor->givenCost = givenCost;
                newSuccessor->finalCost = givenCost +
                    CalculateHeuristic(newSuccessor, goalNode);
                OpenList.Update(newSuccessor);
            }
        }
    }
}
return NoPathExists;
```

must be considered. If traveling in a cardinal direction, continued movement in the cardinal direction plus any possible forced neighbor directions plus the diagonal between the forced neighbor and the original cardinal direction must be considered. For example, if traveling east, the directions east plus the possible forced neighbors of north and south plus the diagonals northeast and southeast must be considered. The actual distances in each node will further clarify if these are worth exploring, but this is a first-pass pruning. Figure 14.10 shows an example computed path where you can see the directions considered at each node based on the `ValidDirLookUpTable`.

Consider another important clarification regarding the middle conditional in the for loop to create a target jump point (Listing 14.3). The need for this is subtle and nonobvious. When approaching the goal node, we might need a *target* jump point (our fourth type of jump point) between the current node and the goal node in order to find a path that is grid aligned to the goal. This arises only when traveling diagonally, the direction of travel is toward the goal node, and the distance to the goal node in row distance or column distance is less than or equal to the current node's diagonal distance to a wall or jump point. The newly synthesized target jump point will be constructed by taking the minimum of the row distance and the column distance to the goal node and continuing travel diagonally by that amount. If the goal node is directly diagonal in the direction of travel, this new target

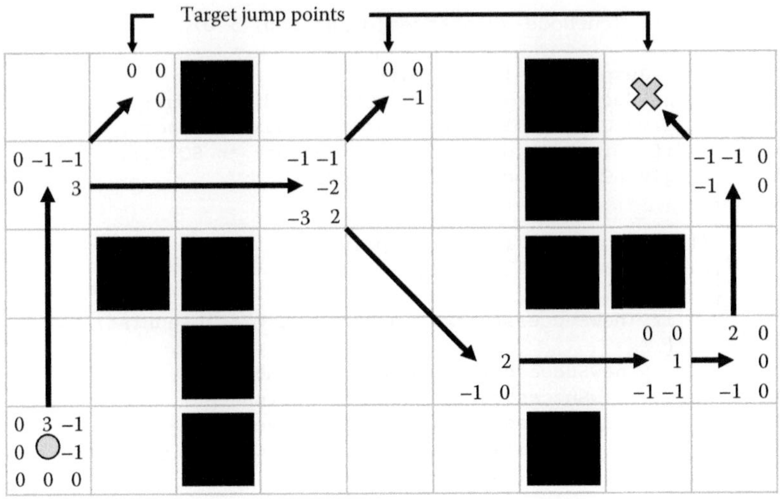

Figure 14.10

Runtime search from bottom left node to top right goal node. Only node distances used in the search are included in the figure. Note that three target jump points are created along the top row based on potential intermediate routes to the goal.

jump point will be equal to the goal node. Otherwise, this target jump point is a possible intermediate jump point between the current node and the goal node. Figure 14.10 shows an example computed path where three target jump points are created at runtime.

To appreciate the speed of JPS+, consider the search in Figure 14.10. Only 10 nodes are even considered during the entire search with 7 of them being absolutely necessary for an optimal path. Contrast this with traditional JPS that would look at every node on the map during its recursive step. Additionally, since all wall information is stored in the grid cells themselves as distances, this data structure is extremely cache friendly since neighboring rows or columns aren't constantly checked for the existence of walls. The cumulative result is that JPS+ does very little runtime processing and considers an extremely limited number of nodes. This accounts for the tremendous improvement over traditional JPS.

In order to achieve good results with JPS+, it is advised to use a heapsort algorithm for the open list, preallocate all node memory along with a dirty bit for cheap initialization, and use an octile heuristic [Rabin 13]. If you have between 1 and 10 MB of extra memory available, you can achieve a ~10x speed increase by using a bucket-sorted priority queue for the open list. Create a bucket for every 0.1 cost and then use an unsorted preallocated array for each bucket. If you use a LIFO strategy in each bucket, the final path won't be more than 0.1 worse than optimal and it will be blazing fast. For A*, this data structure would require 10 to 100 MB, but JPS+ puts far fewer nodes on the open list, which makes this optimization much more practical.

14.8 Conclusion

JPS+ takes a great deal of the runtime computation from JPS and stores it directly in the map. As a result, the algorithm is up to an order of magnitude faster than traditional JPS and two orders of magnitude faster than a highly optimized A*. The trade-off for this speed is that the map is static (walls can't be added or removed), the map must be preprocessed with eight numbers stored per grid cell, and the map is a uniform cost grid.

The degree of speed gains is directly proportional to the openness of the map. If the map contains large open areas, JPS+ is extremely fast and will achieve up to two orders of magnitude speed improvement over A*. If the map is intensely mazelike consisting primarily of jagged diagonal walls, then JPS+ is more conservatively around 20% faster than traditional JPS and about 2.5x faster than a highly optimized A* solution.

References

[Harabor 12] Harabor, D. and Grastien, A. 2012. The JPS pathfinding system. In *Proceedings of the Fifth Symposium on Combinatorial Search (SoCS)*, Niagara Falls, Ontario, Canada. Available online at: http://users.cecs.anu.edu.au/~dharabor/data/papers/harabor-grastien-socs12.pdf (accessed September 10, 2014).

[Harabor 14] Harabor, D. and Grastien, A. 2014. Improving jump point search. In *International Conference on Automated Planning and Scheduling (ICAPS)*, Portsmouth, NH. Video available at: https://www.youtube.com/watch?v=NmM4pv8uQwI (accessed September 10, 2014).

[Rabin 13] Rabin, S. and Sturtevant, N. 2013. Pathfinding architecture optimizations. In *Game AI Pro: Collected Wisdom of Game AI Professionals*. A K Peters/CRC Press, Boca Raton, FL.

15

Subgoal Graphs for Fast Optimal Pathfinding

Tansel Uras and Sven Koenig

15.1 Introduction

Paths for game agents are often found by representing the map that the agents move on as a graph and using a search algorithm, such as A*, to search this graph. Pathfinding in games needs to be fast, especially if many agents are moving on the map. To speed up path planning, maps can often be preprocessed before games are released or when they are loaded into memory. The data produced by preprocessing should use a small amount of memory, and preprocessing should be fast if it is performed at runtime.

In this chapter, we present *subgoal graphs*, which are constructed by preprocessing maps that are represented as grids. Subgoal graphs use a small amount of memory and can be used to find shortest paths fast by ignoring most of the grid cells during search. We describe several variants of subgoal graphs, each being a more sophisticated version of the previous one and each requiring more preprocessing time in return for faster searches. Even though subgoal graphs are specific to grids, the ideas behind them can be generalized to any graph representation of a map.

Table 15.1 summarizes the results from the original paper on subgoal graphs [Uras 14] on maps from the video games *Dragon Age: Origins*, *StarCraft*, *Warcraft III*, and *Baldur's*

Table 15.1 Comparison of Subgoal Graph Variants on Game Maps

Subgoal Graph Variant	Preprocessing Time (s)	Memory Used (MBytes)	Runtime of A* on Subgoal Graphs Rather Than Grids	Optimal?
Simple subgoal graphs	0.022	1.172	24 times faster	Yes
Two-level subgoal graphs	2.031	1.223	71 times faster	Yes
N-level subgoal graphs	2.195	1.223	112 times faster	Yes

Note: The average runtime of A* is 12.69 ms on these maps.

Gate II [Sturtevant 12]. The two-level subgoal graph (TSG) entry was one of the nondominated entries in the Grid-Based Path Planning Competitions 2012 and 2013. That is, if another entry was faster, it either was suboptimal or required more memory.

15.2 Preliminaries

We assume that the map is represented as a uniform-cost eight-neighbor grid with obstacles consisting of contiguous segments of blocked cells. The agent moves from grid center to grid center and can move to an unblocked cell in any cardinal or diagonal direction, with one exception: we assume that the agent is not a point and, therefore, can move diagonally only if both associated cardinal directions are also unblocked. For example, in Figure 15.1, the agent cannot move diagonally from B2 to A1 because A2 is blocked. The lengths of cardinal and diagonal moves are 1 and $\sqrt{2}$, respectively.

A* is a commonly used algorithm for pathfinding. It is an informed search algorithm that uses a heuristic to guide the search to find paths faster. The heuristic estimates the distance between any two locations on the map and, in order for A* to find shortest paths, needs to be admissible, that is, never overestimate the distance between two locations [Hart 68].

One common heuristic used when solving pathfinding problems is the Euclidean distance, which is the straight-line distance between two locations. For instance, the Euclidean distance between s and r in Figure 15.1 is $\sqrt{5^2+2^2}=5.39$. The Euclidean

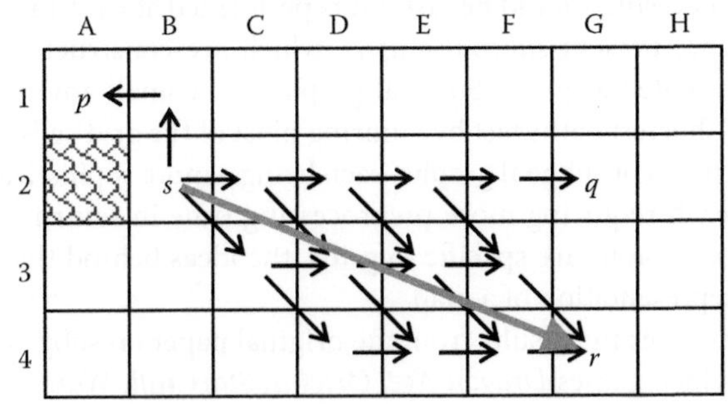

Figure 15.1

Shortest paths from *s* to some other cells on an eight-neighbor grid and the straight line between *s* and *r*.

distance is guaranteed to be admissible on maps with uniform traversal costs since the shortest path between two locations cannot be shorter than the straight line between them.

On eight-neighbor grids with uniform traversal costs, however, there is a more informed heuristic. The octile distance between two cells on the grid is the length of a shortest path between (that is, between their centers) assuming there are no obstacles on the grid. On a grid with no obstacles, the shortest path between two cells contains moves in only two directions. For instance, in Figure 15.1, all shortest paths between s and r contain exactly two diagonal moves toward the southeast and three cardinal moves toward the east. Therefore, the octile distance between two cells can be computed by simply comparing their x and y coordinates to figure out exactly how many diagonal and cardinal moves would be on a shortest path between them if the grid had no obstacles. For instance, the octile distance between s and r is $3+2\times\sqrt{2}=5.83$.

The octile distance is guaranteed to be admissible on eight-neighbor grids with uniform traversal costs since the shortest path between two cells cannot be shorter than on a grid with no obstacles. It is more informed than the Euclidean distance because the octile distance between two cells cannot be smaller than the Euclidean distance but is sometimes larger. Searching with a more informed heuristic means that the search typically performs fewer expansions before it finds a path and is then faster.

15.3 Simple Subgoal Graphs

Simple subgoal graphs (SSGs) are an adaptation of visibility graphs to grids. Visibility graphs abstract continuous environments with polygonal obstacles. The vertices of a visibility graph are the convex corners of obstacles, and the edges connect vertices that are visible from each other. The length of an edge is equal to the Euclidean distance between the vertices it connects. To find a shortest path between given start and goal locations in a continuous environment, one simply adds the vertices for them to the visibility graph, connects them to all vertices visible from them, and searches the resulting graph for a shortest path from the start vertex (which corresponds to the start location) to the goal vertex (which corresponds to the goal location). Figure 15.2 shows an example of a visibility graph and a path found by searching this graph. If an optimal search algorithm is used to search this graph (such as a suitable version of A* with the

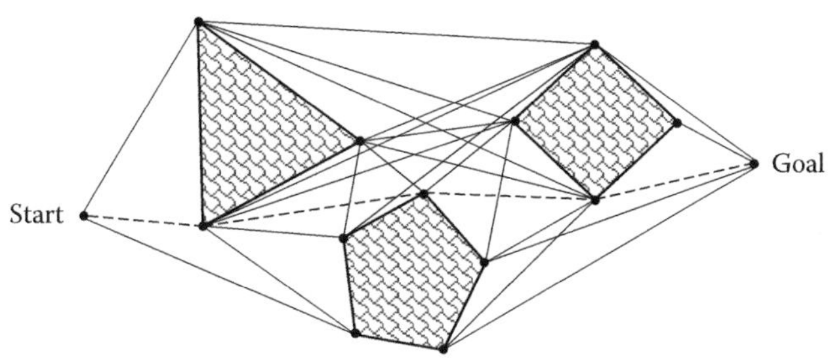

Figure 15.2

A visibility graph and the shortest path between the start and goal vertices.

Euclidean distance as heuristic), the resulting path is also a shortest path from the start location to the goal location in the continuous environment.

SSGs, on the other hand, abstract grids. The vertices of an SSG are called subgoals and are placed at the convex corners of obstacles on the grid. The edges connect subgoals that satisfy a certain connection strategy that we describe later. The length of an edge is equal to the octile distance between the vertices it connects. To find a shortest path between given start and goal cells on a grid, one can use the following steps: First, vertices are added to the SSG for the start and goal cells. Then, edges are added to connect them to the other vertices using the given connection strategy. Finally, the resulting graph is searched with A* with the octile distance as heuristic. The resulting high-level path is a series of subgoals connecting the start and goal vertices. One can then connect the subgoals on this high-level path on the grid to obtain a shortest low-level path on the grid.

Visibility graphs have strengths that SSGs aim to preserve. For instance, they can be used to find shortest paths and can be precomputed and stored. Visibility graphs also have some weaknesses that SSGs aim to fix. For instance, they can result in search trees with high branching factors, which is bad for both memory consumption and search time. The construction of visibility graphs can also be time consuming since one needs to perform visibility checks between all pairs of vertices. Even if preprocessing time is not an issue, visibility checks need to be performed when connecting the start and goal vertices to the visibility graph at runtime, namely, from the start and goal vertices to all other vertices of the visibility graph.

15.3.1 Constructing Simple Subgoal Graphs

Similar to visibility graphs, SSGs place subgoals at the corners of obstacles. Formally, we say that a cell s is a subgoal if and only if s is unblocked, s has a blocked diagonal neighbor t, and the two cells that are neighbors of both s and t are unblocked. For instance, in Figure 15.1, B1 is a subgoal because A2 is blocked and both A1 and B2 are unblocked. The idea is the same as for visibility graphs, namely, that one can use the convex corners of obstacles to navigate around them optimally.

We now introduce the concept of *h-reachability*. We say that two vertices of a graph are h-reachable if and only if there is a shortest path between them whose length is equal to the heuristic between them. H-reachability is a generalization of the concept of visibility in visibility graphs. Since visibility graphs abstract continuous environments, the heuristic used is the Euclidean distance. Thus, two vertices in a continuous environment are h-reachable if and only if they are visible from each other. Therefore, edges in visibility graphs connect exactly the h-reachable vertices.

Now, we discuss how h-reachable subgoals are connected. Since SSGs abstract grids, we use the octile distance as heuristic, and the length of an edge is equal to the octile distance between the subgoals it connects. Figure 15.3 shows an SSG constructed by connecting all h-reachable subgoals.

We now explain three properties that a connection strategy should possess and check whether the strategy of connecting h-reachable subgoals satisfies them:

1. *Edges are easy to follow on the grid*: If two cells on the grid are h-reachable, we can navigate from one cell to the other by moving in only two directions, as discussed in the preliminaries. This certainly makes it easier to follow h-reachable edges (edges that

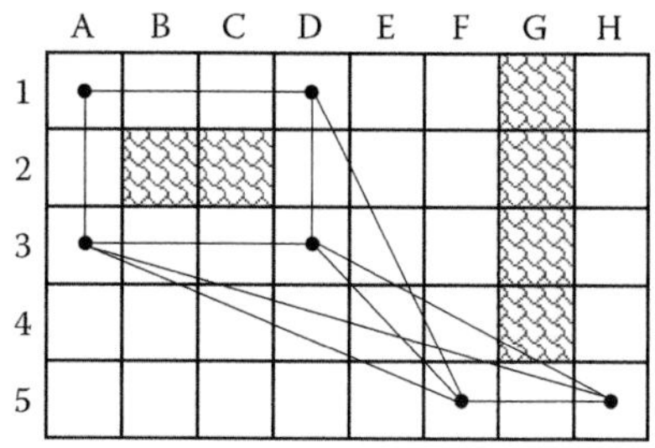

Figure 15.3

An SSG constructed by connecting all h-reachable subgoals.

connect two h-reachable cells) compared to doing an A* search on the grid between the two subgoals they connect since we know how many cardinal and diagonal moves to make in which directions. All we have to figure out is the order of the moves.

2. *Searches find shortest paths*: Adding edges between all h-reachable subgoals (plus the start and goal cells) also allows us to find shortest paths on the grid. The proof follows from the observation that, if two cells are not h-reachable, then there must be an obstacle that makes the path between the two cells longer than the octile distance between them. This obstacle introduces a subgoal that can be used to optimally circumnavigate it [Uras 13].
3. *Search trees have low branching factors*: Unfortunately, with this connection strategy, SSGs can have many more edges than the corresponding visibility graphs. For instance, in Figure 15.3, D3 and H5 are not visible from each other, but they are h-reachable.

The branching factors are a deal breaker for us, so we need to modify our connection strategy. H-reachability is still a valuable concept that will be used later when we generate two-level subgoal graphs from SSGs.

Fortunately, it is easy to address this issue. Consider the edge between D3 and H5 in Figure 15.3. This edge corresponds to the grid path D3-E4-F5-G5-H5. But there is already a subgoal at F5, and there are edges in the SSG between D3 and F5 and between F5 and H7. The sum of the lengths of these two edges is equal to the length of the edge between D3 and H5. Therefore, the edge between D3 and H5 is redundant and can be removed from the SSG without affecting the optimality of the resulting paths. When we remove all such redundant edges from the SSG in Figure 15.3, we end up with the SSG in Figure 15.4. We call the remaining edges *direct-h-reachable* edges and the subgoals they connect direct-h-reachable subgoals.

Formally, we say that two cells are direct-h-reachable if and only if they are h-reachable and none of the shortest paths between them pass through a subgoal. Direct-h-reachable edges are easier to follow than h-reachable edges. As mentioned before, h-reachable edges are easy to follow because we know exactly how many cardinal and diagonal moves we have to make in each direction. The problem is that we have to figure out the order of the moves. This is not the case for direct-h-reachable edges. Observe that, in Figure 15.1, all shortest paths between *s* and *r* cover a parallelogram-shaped area. As an equivalent definition of direct-h-reachability, we say that two cells are direct-h-reachable if and only if the parallelogram-shaped area between them does not contain any subgoals and that the

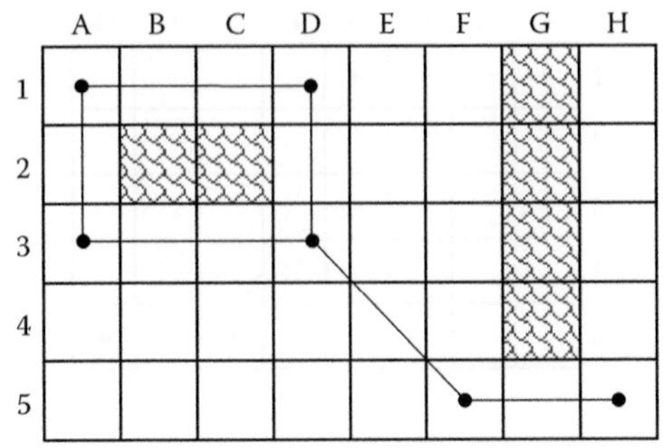

Figure 15.4

An SSG constructed by connecting all direct-h-reachable subgoals.

movement inside the parallelogram-shaped area is not blocked. Therefore, when following direct-h-reachable edges, we can make the cardinal and diagonal moves in any order. The equivalence of the two definitions follows from the observation that obstacles that block movement in the parallelogram-shaped area between two cells either introduce subgoals in the parallelogram-shaped area (meaning that the two cells are not direct-h-reachable) or block all shortest paths between the two cells (meaning that the two cells are not even h-reachable) [Uras 13].

The definition of parallelogram-shaped areas is also useful for showing that the branching factors of the search trees generated when using SSGs are lower than when using visibility graphs. If the movement inside the parallelogram-shaped area between two cells is not blocked, then the straight line between the two cells cannot be blocked either, which means that they must be visible from each other. Therefore, every direct-h-reachable edge in an SSG corresponds to a straight-line edge in the visibility graph. The converse is not true. For instance, in Figure 15.4, A3 and F5 are visible from each other but not direct-h-reachable.

To summarize, SSGs are constructed by placing subgoals at the corners of obstacles and adding edges between subgoals that are direct-h-reachable. Section 15.3.3 describes an algorithm to identify all direct-h-reachable subgoals from a given cell.

15.3.2 Searching Using Simple Subgoal Graphs

Once an SSG has been constructed, it can be used to find shortest paths between any two cells on the grid. Given a start cell and a goal cell, we connect them to their direct-h-reachable subgoals using the algorithm described in the next section. We then search the resulting graph with an optimal search algorithm, such as a suitable version of A* with the octile distance heuristic, to find a shortest high-level path. We then follow the edges of this path by simply moving in the direction of the next cell on the high-level path, to find a shortest low-level path on the grid. This process is illustrated in Figure 15.5.

There are some subtle points to the algorithm. If either the start or goal cell is a subgoal, we do not need to identify the subgoals that are direct-h-reachable from them since they are already in the SSG. Also, since the algorithm described in the next section finds only the subgoals that are direct-h-reachable from a given cell, it might not connect the start cell to the goal cell if they are direct-h-reachable but neither of them is a subgoal. In this case, we might not be able to find a shortest path between them. Before connecting the

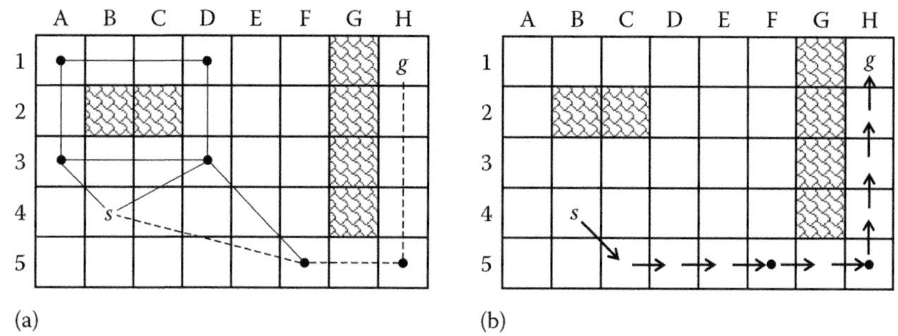

Figure 15.5

Connecting the start and goal cells to the SSG and finding a shortest high-level path on the resulting graph (a). Then, following the edges on this high-level path to find a shortest low-level path on the grid (b).

start and goal cells to the SSG, we therefore first generate a possible shortest path between them (for instance, by first moving diagonally and then moving cardinally). If the path is not blocked, we return it as the shortest path. Otherwise, the start and goal cells cannot be direct-h-reachable, and we therefore search using the SSG as described earlier.

15.3.3 Identifying All Direct-H-Reachable Subgoals from a Given Cell

Being able to identify all direct-h-reachable subgoals from a given cell quickly is important both during the construction of SSGs and when connecting the start and goal cells to SSGs. The algorithm we propose is a dynamic programming algorithm that identifies all direct-h-reachable cells from a given cell *s* and returns all subgoals among them. Figure 15.6 shows an example.

Our algorithm uses clearance values. The clearance value of a cell *s* in a direction *d*, called *Clearance*(*s*, *d*), is the maximum number of moves the agent can make from *s*

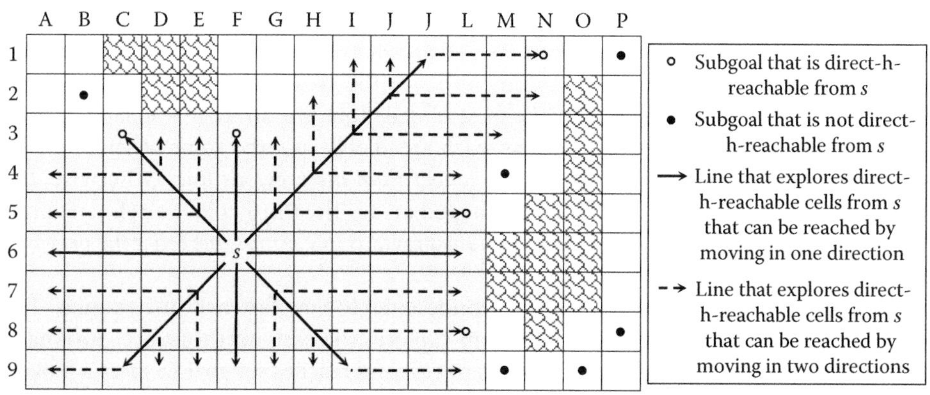

Figure 15.6

Identifying the direct-h-reachable area around *s* (shown in gray), which contains all direct-h-reachable subgoals from *s*.

toward *d* without reaching a subgoal or being blocked. For instance, the east clearance of *s* in Figure 15.6 is 6 because M6 is blocked. The north clearance of *s* is 2 because F3 is a subgoal. Clearance values can be either computed at runtime or be precomputed, although the algorithm does not benefit much from storing clearance values in diagonal directions. The algorithm works in two phases:

The first phase identifies all direct-h-reachable cells from *s* that can be reached by moving in only one direction. This is achieved by looking at the clearance values of *s* in all eight directions to figure out if there are direct-h-reachable subgoals in these directions. For instance, since the north clearance of *s* in Figure 15.6 is 2, the algorithm checks the cell 2 + 1 moves north of *s*, F3, to see if it is a subgoal. In Figure 15.6, the first phase determines that C3 and F3 are direct-h-reachable subgoals from *s*.

The second phase identifies all direct-h-reachable cells from *s* that can be reached by a combination of moves in a cardinal and a diagonal direction. There are eight combinations of cardinal and diagonal directions that can appear on a shortest path between two direct-h-reachable cells, and each of them identifies an area. Figure 15.6 shows these combinations, divided by the solid lines emanating from *s* in eight directions. The algorithm explores each area line by line (using the dashed lines in Figure 15.6). Assume that it is exploring the area that is associated with cardinal direction *c* and diagonal direction *d*. For each cell that is direct-h-reachable from *s* by moving toward *d*, it casts a line that starts at that cell and travels toward *c*. It starts with the line closest to *s* and continues until all lines are cast.

We now present three rules to determine how far each line extends. The first rule is simple: *a line stops when it reaches a subgoal or directly before it reaches an obstacle*. This is so because the additional cells the line would reach cannot be direct-h-reachable from s according to the definition of direct-h-reachability. Otherwise, the parallelogram-shaped area between s and the next cell the line would reach contained a subgoal or obstacle. The second rule follows from the following observation: if cell *t* is direct-h-reachable from cell *s*, then any cell *u* that lies in the parallelogram-shaped area between *s* and *t* is also direct-h-reachable from *s*. This is so because the parallelogram-shaped area between *s* and *u* is a subarea of the parallelogram-shaped area between *s* and *t* and, therefore, does not contain any subgoals and the movement inside the area is not blocked (since *s* and *t* are direct-h-reachable). Therefore, the area of cells that are direct-h-reachable from *s* is a union of parallelogram-shaped areas, each area between *s* and some other cell. This results in the second rule: *a line cannot be longer than the previous line*. Otherwise, the area cannot be a union of parallelogram-shaped areas. The third rule is a refinement of the second rule: *a line cannot be longer than the previous line minus one cell if the previous line ends in a subgoal*.

The algorithm uses these rules to determine quickly how far each line extends. For instance, in Figure 15.6, when the algorithm explores the east–northeast area around *s*, the first line it casts travels along row 5 toward east and reaches subgoal L5 after 5 moves. Since the first line ends in a subgoal, the second line can only travel 5 − 1 = 4 moves and stops before reaching subgoal M4, which is not direct-h-reachable from *s*. Instead of explicitly casting lines, the algorithm can use the clearance values of the cells in which the lines originate. Listing 15.1 shows pseudocode that uses the clearance values.

Listing 15.1. Identify all direct-h-reachable subgoals in an area.

```
GetDirectHReachable(cell s, cardinal dir. c, diagonal dir. d)
    SubgoalVector list = {};
    int maxLineLength = Clearance(s,c);
    int nDiagMoves = Clearance(s,d);
    for int i = 1 … nDiagMoves
        s = neighbor of s toward d;
        l = Clearance(s,c);
        if (l < maxLineLength)
            maxLineLength = l;
            s' = the cell l+1 moves away from s toward c;
            if (s' is a subgoal)
                list.add(s');
    return list;
```

15.4 Two-Level Subgoal Graphs

Searches using SSGs are faster than searches of grids because SSGs are smaller than grids and searching them expands fewer cells on average. In a way, SSGs partition the cells into subgoals and nonsubgoals, and the search ignores all nonsubgoals other than the start and goal cells.

Two-level subgoal graphs (TSGs) apply this idea to SSGs instead of grids. TSGs are constructed from SSGs by partitioning the subgoals into local and global subgoals. The search ignores all local subgoals that are not direct-h-reachable from the start or goal cells, allowing us to search even smaller graphs. TSGs satisfy the following property, called the *two-level property* (*TLP*):

> The length of a shortest path between any two (local or global) subgoals s and t on the SSG is equal to the length of a shortest path between *s* and *t* on the graph consisting of all global subgoals of the TSG plus s and t (and all edges between these subgoals in the TSG).

In other words, if we remove all local subgoals except for *s* and *t* (and their associated edges) from the TSG, then the length of a shortest path between *s* and *t* does not change.

This property guarantees that TSGs can be used to find shortest paths on grids [Uras 13]. Figure 15.7 shows an SSG and a TSG constructed from the SSG. Observe that the subgraph of the TSG consisting of A1, D1, D3, and H5 contains the shortest path between A1 and H5. Also, observe that the edge between D3 and H5 is not direct-h-reachable. During the construction of TSGs, h-reachable edges can be added to the graph if this allows classifying more subgoals as local subgoals.

15.4.1 Constructing Two-Level Subgoal Graphs

Constructing TSGs from SSGs is different from constructing SSGs from grids. When constructing SSGs from grids, we identify some cells as subgoals and connect them with a connection strategy that allows them to be used to find shortest paths on the grids. This is possible because grids have structure, and visibility graphs provide some intuition for exploiting it.

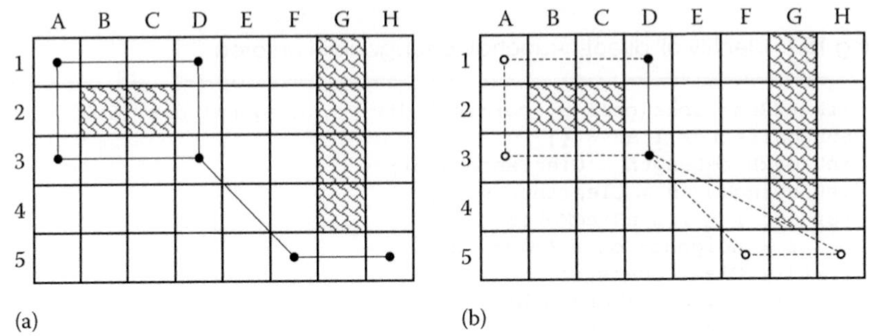

Figure 15.7

An SSG (a) and a TSG constructed from the SSG (b). Hollow circles indicate local subgoals, and solid circles indicate global subgoals.

On the other hand, there is little structure to exploit when constructing TSGs from SSGs. Therefore, we start by assuming that all subgoals are global subgoals. At this point, the TLP is satisfied since the TSG is identical to the SSG. We then iterate over all global subgoals and classify them as local subgoals if doing so does not violate the TLP. We are allowed to add edges between h-reachable subgoals if doing so helps to preserve the TLP and allows us to classify a global subgoal as a local subgoal.

The question remains how to determine quickly whether a subgoal *s* can be classified as a local subgoal. The straightforward method is to check if removing *s* from the TSG increases the length of a shortest path between two other subgoals that are not h-reachable (if they are h-reachable, we can simply add an edge between them). It is faster to check if removing *s* from the TSG increases the length of a shortest path between two of its neighbors that are not h-reachable, because any path that passes through *s* must also pass through its neighbors. The process of removing *s* in this way is called a contraction [Geisberger 08]. Listing 15.2 shows pseudocode for constructing a TSG from an SSG.

For each global subgoal *s*, we accumulate a list of edges that would need to be added to the TSG if *s* were classified as a local subgoal. We iterate over all pairs of neighbors of *s*. If there exists a pair of neighbors such that all shortest paths between the two neighbors pass through *s* and the neighbors are not h-reachable, then *s* cannot be classified as a local subgoal because doing so would violate the TLP. Otherwise, we classify *s* as a local subgoal and add all necessary edges to the TSG.

SSGs do not necessarily have unique TSGs since the resulting TSG can depend on the order in which the subgoals are processed. For instance, in Figure 15.7, if D1 were a local subgoal and A3 were a global subgoal, the resulting TSG would still satisfy the TLP. No research has been done so far on how the order in which the subgoals are processed affects the resulting TSG.

15.4.2 Searching Using Two-Level Subgoal Graphs

Search using TSGs is similar to search using SSGs. We start with a core graph that consists of all global subgoals and the edges between them. We then connect the start and goal cells to their respective direct-h-reachable (local or global) subgoals. Next, local subgoals

Listing 15.2. Constructing a TSG from an SSG.

```
ConstructTSG(SSG S)
    SubgoalList G = subgoals of S; //Global subgoals
    SubgoalList L = {}; //Local subgoals
    EdgeList E = edges of S;
    for all s in G
        EdgeList E+ = {}; //Extra edges
        bool local = true; //Assume s can be a local subgoal
        for all p, q in Neighbors(s) //Neighbors wrt E
            d = length of a shortest path between p and q
                (wrt E) that does not pass through s or any
                subgoal in L;
            if (d > c(p,s) + c(s,q))
                if (p and q are h-reachable)
                    E+.add((p,q));
                else //s is necessary to connect p and q
                    local = false; //Can't make s local
                    break;
        if (local)
            G.remove(s); //Classify s as a local subgoal
            L.add(s);
            E.append(E+); //Add the extra edges to the TSG
    return (G, L, E);
```

that are direct-h-reachable from the start or goal cells using edges not in the core graph are added to the graph. Once a high-level shortest path from the start cell to the goal cell is found on this graph, we follow its edges to find a low-level path on the grid. We might have to follow edges between cells that are h-reachable but not direct-h-reachable. This means that we have to identify the order of cardinal and diagonal moves, which can be achieved with a depth-first search. Figure 15.8 shows an example of this search graph. The number of subgoals excluded from the search can be much larger for larger TSGs.

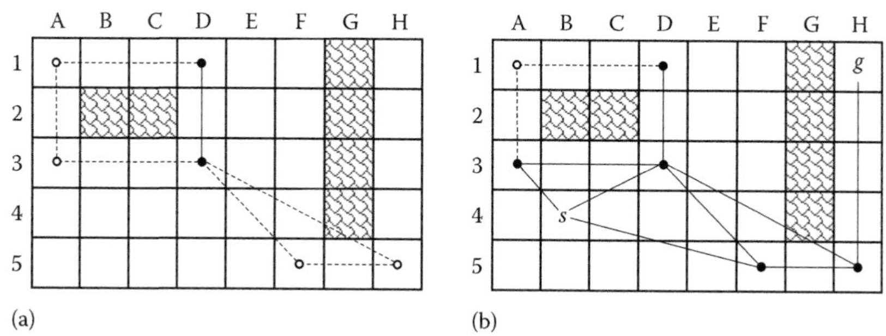

Figure 15.8

A TSG (a) and a search using this TSG (b). The graph that is searched consists of the solid circles.

15.5 N-Level Graphs

We now generalize the ideas behind the construction of TSGs to be able to generate graphs with more than two levels from any given undirected graph [Uras 14].

Observe that only the terms "subgoal" and "h-reachable" are specific to subgoal graphs in the partitioning algorithm shown in Listing 15.2 and can be replaced by the terms "vertex" and "a property *P* that all extra edges need to satisfy," making the partitioning algorithm applicable to any undirected graph. The lengths of the edges added to the graph should always be equal to the lengths of shortest paths on the original graph between the two vertices they connect. We need to specify a property *P* that all extra edges need to satisfy. Otherwise, all vertices of a graph can be classified as local by adding edges between all vertices, which would create a pairwise distance matrix for the graph. *P* should be chosen such that the extra edges can easily be followed on the original graph and the branching factors of the search trees do not increase too much. H-reachability satisfies these criteria for subgoal graphs, although other properties could exist that would result in even faster searches. If it is hard to come up with such a property, one can always choose *P* such that no extra edges are added to the graph, resulting in fewer vertices being excluded from the search. *Two-level graphs* can be constructed by applying the general version of the partitioning algorithm described in Listing 15.2 to any undirected graph. Figure 15.9 shows an example with an undirected graph with unit edge costs and a two-level graph constructed from the undirected graph without adding extra edges.

The general version of the algorithm described in Listing 15.2 partitions the vertices of an undirected graph into local and global vertices. Call local vertices *level 1 vertices* and global vertices *level 2 vertices*. Level 2 vertices and the edges between them form a graph, and one can apply the general version of the algorithm described in Listing 15.2 to this graph to partition the level 2 vertices into level 2 and level 3 vertices. Figure 15.10 shows an example of a *three-level graph*, constructed from the two-level graph shown in Figure 15.9 by partitioning its level 2 vertices into level 2 and level 3 vertices.

One can keep adding levels to the graphs by recursively partitioning the highest-level vertices until they can no longer be partitioned. Adding more levels to the graph means

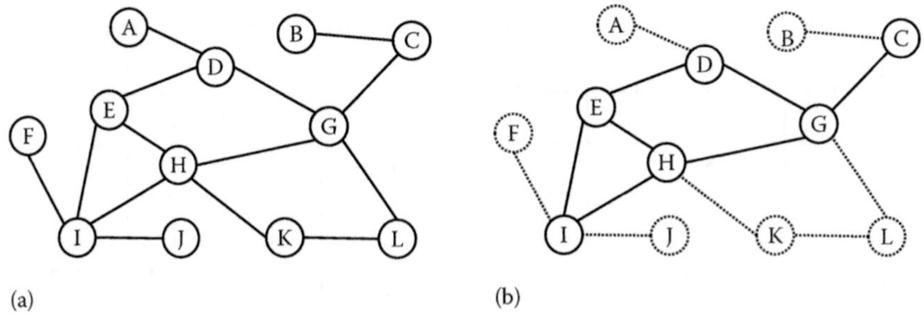

Figure 15.9

An undirected graph with unit edge costs (a) and a two-level graph constructed from the undirected graph without adding extra edges (b). Solid circles indicate global vertices, and dashed circles indicate local vertices.

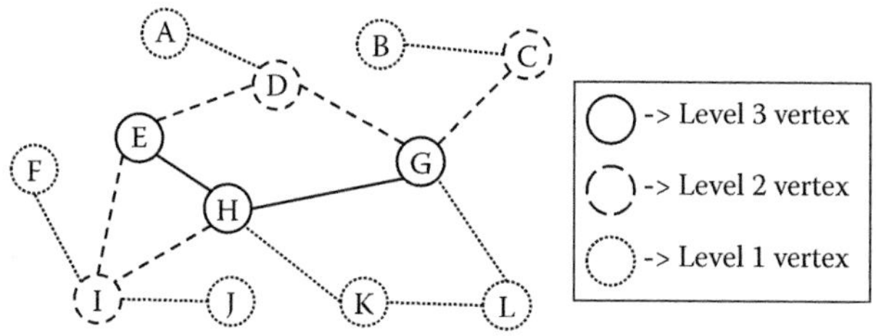

Figure 15.10

A three-level graph constructed from the undirected graph in Figure 15.9.

that the graphs that are searched are getting smaller but also that one needs to spend more time constructing the graph for each search.

Once an n-level graph has been constructed, it can be used to find shortest paths between any two vertices of the original graph. Call the graph consisting of all highest-level vertices (and the edges between them) the *core graph* since it appears in every search. When using a two-level graph to find a shortest path between given start and goal vertices, one adds them to the core graph and searches the resulting graph with an optimal search algorithm to find a high-level path. When using a three-level graph to find a shortest path between given start and goal vertices, one also adds any level 2 vertices that are neighbors of the start or goal vertices. This process is illustrated in Figure 15.11. Listing 15.3 shows pseudocode to determine which vertices need to be added to the core graph when using n-level graphs, for any value of N. This algorithm needs to be called for both the start and goal vertices. When this algorithm is called for an SSG, it creates an n-level subgoal graph.

SSGs are essentially *two-level grid graphs.* If one were to allow the addition of extra edges between direct-h-reachable vertices of the grid graph, the general version of the algorithm described in Listing 15.2 could classify all subgoals as level 2 vertices and all nonsubgoals as level 1 vertices [Uras 14], although it could take a long time to run and the extra edges between direct-h-reachable cells could require a lot of memory to store. The construction of SSGs, as described previously, avoids these issues by exploiting the structure of grids and by only storing direct-h-reachable edges between subgoals. Direct-h-reachable edges that are not stored are reconstructed

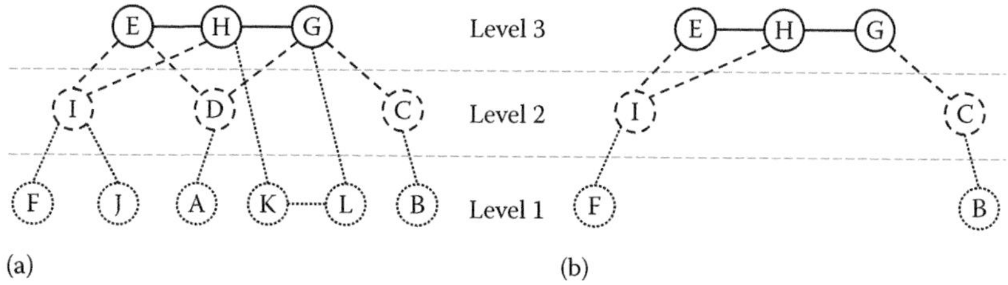

Figure 15.11

The three-level graph from Figure 15.10 with vertices rearranged in layers (a) and the graph searched for a shortest path between vertices F and B of the three-level graph (b).

Listing 15.3. Identifying which vertices need to be added to the core graph during search.

```
IdentifyConnectingVertices(vertex s, Graph G, int graphLevel)
    VertexList open = {s};
    VertexList closed = {};
    while (open != {})
        vertex p = open.getVertexWithSmallestLevel();
        open.remove(p);
        if (p.level == graphLevel)
            break;
        if (!closed.contains(p))
            closed.add(p);
            for all neighbors q of p in G
                if (q.level > p.level && !closed.contains(q))
                    open.add(q);
    return closed;
```

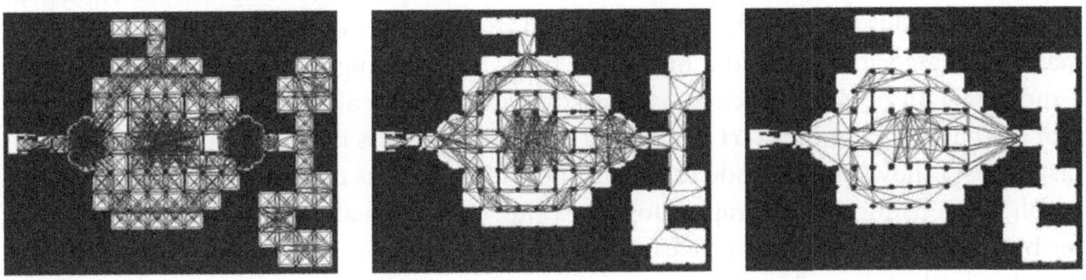

(a) (b) (c)

Figure 15.12

An SSG (a), TSG (b), and a five-level subgoal graph (c). Only the highest-level subgoals and the edges between them are shown.

before a search when connecting the start and goal cells to the SSG or when checking if the start and goal cells are direct-h-reachable. Figure 15.12 shows an SSG, a TSG, and a five-level subgoal graph (six-level grid graph).

The ideas behind n-level graphs are also closely related to contraction hierarchies [Geisberger 08], where the vertices of a graph are first ordered by "importance" and then iteratively contracted, starting from the least important vertex. Contracting a vertex v means replacing unique shortest paths between the neighbors of v that go through v by shortcut edges. The resulting graphs are searched with a bidirectional search algorithm, where the forward search uses only edges leading to more important vertices and the backward search uses only edges coming from more important vertices. Vertex contraction is used during the construction of n-level graphs whenever the level of a vertex is decreased. In essence, n-level graphs are contraction hierarchies where there are constraints on adding new edges to the graph but each level is not limited to contain only one vertex.

15.6 Conclusion

Subgoal graphs are generated by preprocessing grids and can be used to significantly speed up searches on grids, with little memory overhead. The ideas behind them apply to any undirected graph, although it might need some ingenuity to figure out a suitable property that all extra edges need to satisfy. We have, so far, only tested n-level graphs on grids.

Acknowledgments

The research at USC was supported by NSF under grant numbers 1409987 and 1319966. The views and conclusions contained in this document are those of the authors and should not be interpreted as representing the official policies, either expressed or implied, of the sponsoring organizations, agencies or the U.S. government.

References

[Geisberger 08] Geisberger, R., Sanders, P., Schultes, D., and Delling, D. 2008. Contraction hierarchies: Faster and simpler hierarchical routing in road networks. *Proceedings of the International Workshop on Experimental Algorithms,* Provincetown, MA, 319–333.

[Hart 68] Hart, P., Nilsson, N., and Raphael, B. 1968. A formal basis for the heuristic determination of minimum cost paths. *IEEE Transactions on Systems Science and Cybernetics* 4(2):100–107.

[Sturtevant 12] Sturtevant, N. 2012. Benchmarks for grid-based pathfinding. *Transactions on Computational Intelligence and AI in Games* 4(2):144–148.

[Uras 13] Uras, T., Koenig, S., and Hernandez, C. 2013. Subgoal graphs for optimal pathfinding in eight-neighbor grids. *Proceedings of the International Conference on Automated Planning and Scheduling,* Rome, Italy, 224–232.

[Uras 14] Uras, T. and Koenig, S. 2014. Identifying hierarchies for fast optimal search. *Proceedings of the AAAI Conference on Artificial Intelligence*, Quebec City, Quebec, Canada, pp. 878–884.

16

Theta* for Any-Angle Pathfinding

Alex Nash and Sven Koenig

16.1 Introduction

One of the central problems in game AI is finding short and realistic-looking paths. Pathfinding is typically divided into two steps: discretize and search. First, the **discretize** step simplifies a continuous environment into a graph. Second, the **search** step propagates information along this graph to find a path from a given start vertex to a given goal vertex. Video game developers (and roboticists) have developed several methods for discretizing continuous environments into graphs, such as 2D regular grids composed of squares (square grids), hexagons or triangles, 3D regular grids composed of cubes, visibility graphs, circle-based waypoint graphs, space-filling volumes, navigation meshes, framed quad trees, probabilistic road maps, and rapidly exploring random trees [Björnsson 03, Choset 04, Tozour 04].

Due to its simplicity and optimality guarantees, A* is almost always the search method of choice. A* is guaranteed to find shortest paths on graphs, but shortest paths on graphs are not equivalent to shortest paths in the continuous environments. A* propagates information along graph edges and constrains paths to graph edges, which artificially constrains path headings. Consider Figures 16.1 and 16.2, in which two different continuous environments have been discretized into a square grid and a navigation mesh, respectively. The shortest paths on the square grid and the navigation mesh (Figure 16.1) are longer than the shortest paths in the continuous environment (Figure 16.2) and are unrealistic looking due to either a heading change in free space or a heading change that does not *hug* a blocked cell.

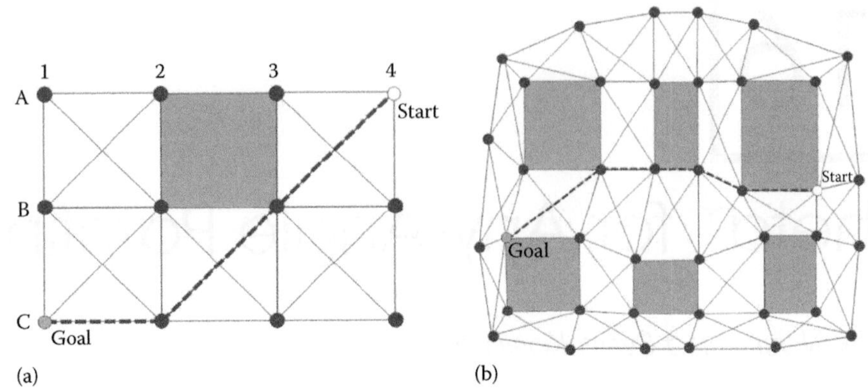

Figure 16.1

Grid paths: square grid (a) and navigation mesh (b). (Adapted from Patel, A., Amit's game programming information, 2000, Retrieved from http://www-cs-students.stanford.edu/~amitp/gameprog.html, accessed September 10, 2014.)

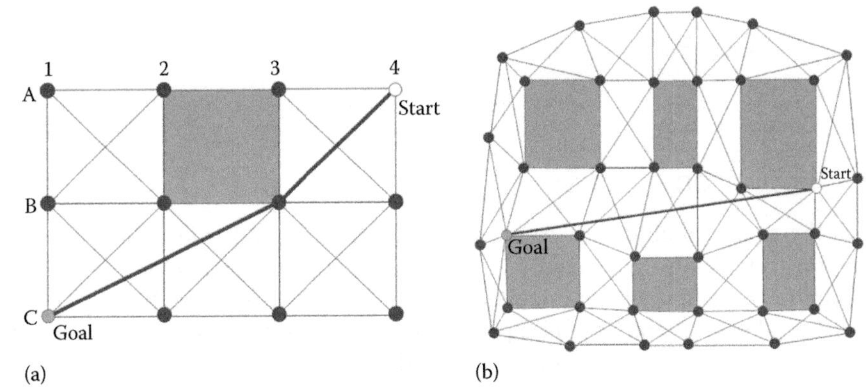

Figure 16.2

Any-angle paths: square grid (a) and navigation mesh (b). (Adapted from Patel, A., Amit's game programming information, 2000, Retrieved from http://www-cs-students.stanford.edu/~amitp/gameprog.html, accessed September 10, 2014.)

The fact that A* paths can be long and unrealistic looking is well known in the video game community [Rabin 00]. The paths found by A* on eight-neighbor square grids can be approximately 8% longer than the shortest paths in the continuous environment [Nash 12]. The typical solution to this problem is to use a postprocessing technique to shorten the A* paths. One such technique is to remove vertices from the path, such that they look like *rubber bands* around obstacles (A* PS). This technique shortens paths such that all of the heading changes on the path *hug* a blocked cell.

However, choosing a postprocessing technique that consistently shortens paths is difficult because there are often several shortest paths on a given graph, and a

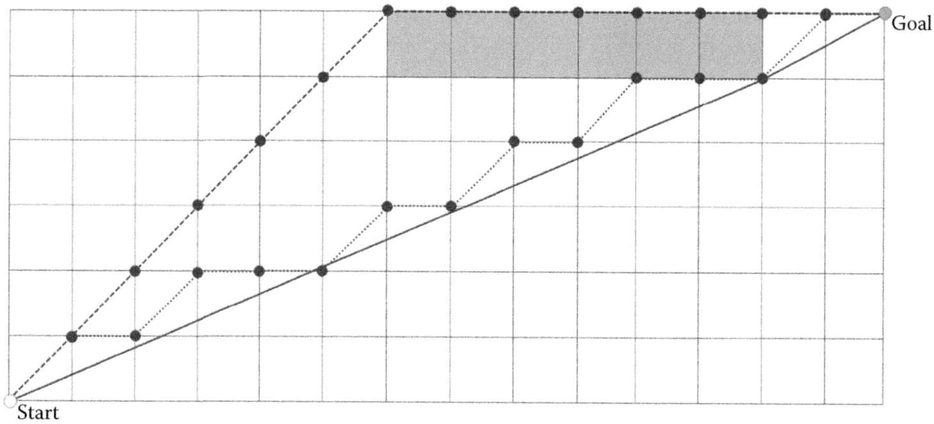

Figure 16.3

A* paths with different postprocessing techniques.

postprocessing technique typically shortens some of them more effectively than others. For example, A* with the octile distance heuristic finds paths very efficiently on eight-neighbor square grids. (The octile distance is the shortest distance between two vertices on an eight-neighbor square grid with no blocked cells.) However, these paths are often difficult to shorten because the search tends to find paths in which moves in the diagonal directions appear before moves in the cardinal directions (for the tie-breaking scheme explained in the next section). The dashed path in Figure 16.3 depicts this behavior.

On the other hand, A* with the straight-line distance heuristic finds paths that are of the same lengths as those found by A* with the octile distance heuristic, albeit more slowly due to additional vertex expansions. However, paths found using the straight-line distance heuristic are often shortened more effectively because they tend to follow the shortest paths in the continuous environment. The dotted path in Figure 16.3 depicts this behavior. In general, postprocessing techniques do improve paths, but they provide trade-offs between path length and runtime that are difficult to chose between, and they do not address the fundamental issue, namely, that the search only considers paths that are constrained to graph edges [Nash 07, Ferguson 06].

We address this issue by describing a different approach to the search problem, called any-angle pathfinding. Specifically, we describe Theta*, a popular any-angle pathfinding algorithm. The development of Theta* was motivated by combining the desirable properties of A* on two different discretizations of the continuous environment:

- *Visibility graphs*: Visibility graphs contain the start vertex, the goal vertex, and the convex corners of all blocked cells [Lorzano-Perez 79]. A vertex is connected via a straight line to another vertex if and only if it has line of sight to the other vertex, that is, the straight line from it to the other vertex does not pass through a blocked cell or between blocked cells that share a side. Shortest paths on visibility graphs are also shortest paths in the continuous environment. However, pathfinding is slow on large visibility graphs since the number of edges can be quadratic in the number of vertices.

- *Grids*: Pathfinding is faster on grids than visibility graphs since the number of edges is linear in the number of cells. However, shortest paths on grids can be longer than shortest paths in the continuous environment and unrealistic looking since the path headings are artificially constrained to grid edges [Nash 07].

Theta* combines the desirable properties of these pathfinding techniques by propagating information along graph edges (to achieve short runtimes) without constraining paths to graph edges (to find short *any-angle* paths).

Theta* is easy to understand, quick to implement and provides a good trade-off between path length and runtime. It quickly finds short and realistic-looking paths and can be used to search any Euclidean graph. The pseudocode for Theta* is very similar to the pseudocode for A*, and both pathfinding algorithms have similar runtimes. Despite this, Theta* finds paths that have nearly the same length as the shortest paths in the continuous environments without the need for postprocessing techniques.

16.2 Problem Formalization

For simplicity, this article focuses on eight-neighbor square grids in which a 2D continuous environment is discretized into square cells that are either blocked (gray) or unblocked (white). Vertices are placed at cell corners rather than cell centers, and paths are allowed to pass between diagonally touching blocked cells. Neither of these two assumptions are required for Theta* to function correctly. Our goal is to find a short and realistic-looking path from a given start vertex to a given goal vertex (both at the corners of cells) that does not pass through blocked cells or between blocked cells that share a side.

In the following pseudocode, s_{start} is the start vertex of the search, and s_{goal} is the goal vertex of the search. $c(s, s')$ is the straight-line distance between vertices s and s', and `lineofsight(s, s')` is true if and only if they have line of sight or, synonymously, they are visible from each other. *open.Insert*(s, x) inserts vertex s with key x into the priority queue *open*. *open.Remove*(s) removes vertex s from *open*. *open.Pop*() removes a vertex with the smallest key from *open* and returns it. For A*, we break ties among vertices with the smallest key in the open list in favor of vertices with the largest g-value. This tiebreaking scheme can reduce the runtimes of A*, especially when used with the octile distance heuristic. Finally, $neighbor_{vis}(s)$ is the set of neighbors of vertex s that have line of sight to s.

16.3 A* Algorithm

Theta* builds upon A* [Nilsson 68], and thus we introduce it here. The pseudocode for A* can be found in Figure 16.4. A* uses heuristic values (h-values) $h(s)$ for each vertex s that approximate the goal distances and focus the search. A* maintains two values for every vertex s: the g-value and the parent. The g-value $g(s)$ is the length of the shortest path from the start vertex to s found so far. The parent *parent*(s) is used to extract the path after the search terminates. Path extraction is performed by repeatedly following parents from the goal vertex to the start vertex. A* also maintains two global data structures: the open list and the closed list. The open list *open* is a priority queue that contains the vertices to be considered

```
1  Main()
2      open: = closed: = ∅;
3      g(s_start) := 0;
4      parent(s_start) : = s_start;
5      open.Insert(s_start, s_start) + h(s_start));
6      While open ≠ ∅ do
7          s: = open.Pop();
8          if s = s_goal then
9              return "path found";
10         closed: = closed ∪ {s};
11         foreach s' ∈ neighbor_vis(s) do
12             if s' ∉ closed then
13                 if s' ∉ open then
14                     g(s') : = ∞;
15                     parent(s') : = NULL;
16                 UpdateVertex(s, s');
17     return "no path found";
18 end
19 Update Vertex(s,s')
20     g_old: = g(s');
21     ComputeCost(s, s');
22     if g(s') < g_old then
23         if s' ∈ open then
24             open.Remove(s');
25         open.Insert(s', g(s') + h(s'));
26 end
27 ComputeCost(s,s')
28     /* Path 1 */
29     if g(s) + c(s, s') < g(s') then
30         parent(s') := s;
31         g(s') := g(s) + c(s, s');
32 end
```

Figure 16.4

Pseudocode for A*.

for expansion. For A*, we break ties among vertices with the smallest key in the open list in favor of vertices with the larger g-value. This tiebreaking scheme can reduce the runtimes of A*, especially when used with the octile distance heuristic. The closed list `closed` is a set that contains the vertices that have already been expanded. A* updates the g-value and parent of an unexpanded visible neighbor s' of vertex s (procedure **ComputeCost**) by considering the path from the start vertex to s [$= g(s)$] and from s to s' in a straight line [$= c(s, s')$], resulting in a length of $g(s) + c(s, s')$ (Line 29). It updates the g-value and parent of s' if this path is shorter than the shortest path from the start vertex to s' found so far [$= g(s')$].

As noted by Rabin [Rabin 00], A* paths often appear as though they were constructed by someone who was drunk. This is both because the paths are longer than the shortest paths in the continuous environment and because the path headings are artificially constrained by the grid. As we mentioned earlier, postprocessing techniques can shorten A* paths but are often ineffective. This is because A* only considers paths that are constrained to grid edges during the search and thus cannot make informed decisions about other paths. Theta*, on the other hand, also considers paths that are not constrained to grid edges during the search and thus can make more informed decisions during the search.

16.4 Theta* Algorithm

The key difference between Theta* and A* is that Theta* allows the parent of a vertex to be any visible vertex, whereas A* requires the parent to be a visible neighbor. So, the pseudocode for Theta* is nearly identical to the pseudocode for A*. Only the procedure ComputeCost is changed; the new code can be found in Figure 16.5. We use the straight-line distance heuristic $h(s) = c(s, s_{goal})$ to focus the search. Theta* is identical to A* except that Theta* updates the g-value and parent of an unexpanded visible neighbor s' of vertex s by considering the following two paths in procedure ComputeCost, as shown in Figure 16.5.

- *Path 1*: As done by A*, Theta* considers the path from the start vertex to s [$= g(s)$] and from s to s' in a straight line [$= c(s, s')$], resulting in a length of $g(s) + c(s, s')$ (Line 41).
- *Path 2*: To allow for any-angle paths, Theta* also considers the path from the start vertex to parent(s) [$= g(parent(s))$] and from $parent(s)$ to s' in a straight line [$= c(parent(s),s')$], resulting in a length of $g(parent(s)) + c(parent(s),s')$, if s' has line of sight to $parent(s)$ (Line 36). The idea behind considering Path 2 is that Path 2 is guaranteed to be no longer than Path 1 due to the triangle inequality if s' has line of sight to $parent(s)$.

Theta* updates the g-value and parent of s' if either path is shorter than the shortest path from the start vertex to s' found so far [$= g(s')$]. For example, consider Figure 16.6, where B3

```
33 ComputeCost(s,s')
34     if lineofsight(parent(s),s')then
35         /* Path 2 */
36         if g(parent(s)) + c(parent(s),s')< g(s')then
37             parent(s') := parent(s);
38             g(s') := g(parent(s)) + c(parent(s),s');
39     else
40         / * Path 1 */
41         if g(s) + c(s,s')< g(s')then
42             parent(s'):= s;
43             g(s'):= g(s) + c(s,s');
44 end
```

Figure 16.5

Pseudocode for Theta*.

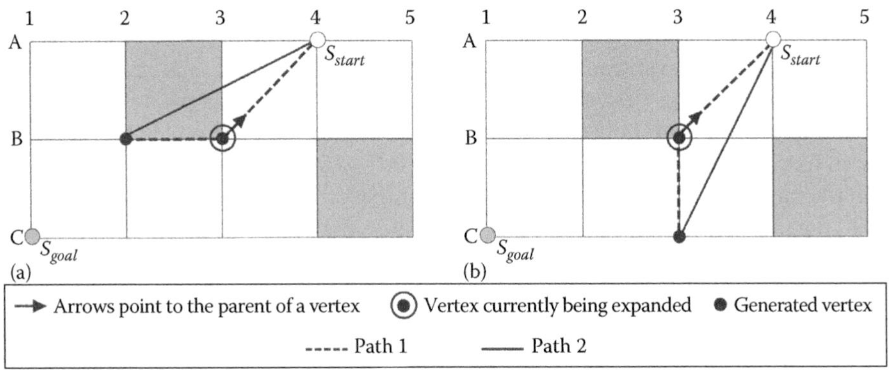

Figure 16.6

Theta* updates a vertex according to Path 1 (a) and Path 2 (b).

(with parent A4) gets expanded. The Path 1 rule is used when generating B2 because it *does not* have line of sight to A4. This is depicted in Figure 16.6a. The Path 2 rule is used when generating C3 because it *does* have line of sight to A4. This is depicted in Figure 16.6b.

Figure 16.7 shows a complete trace of Theta*. Arrows point from vertices to their parents. The concentric circles indicate the vertex that is currently being expanded and solid circles indicate vertices that have already been generated. The start vertex A4 is expanded first, followed by B3, B2, and C1.

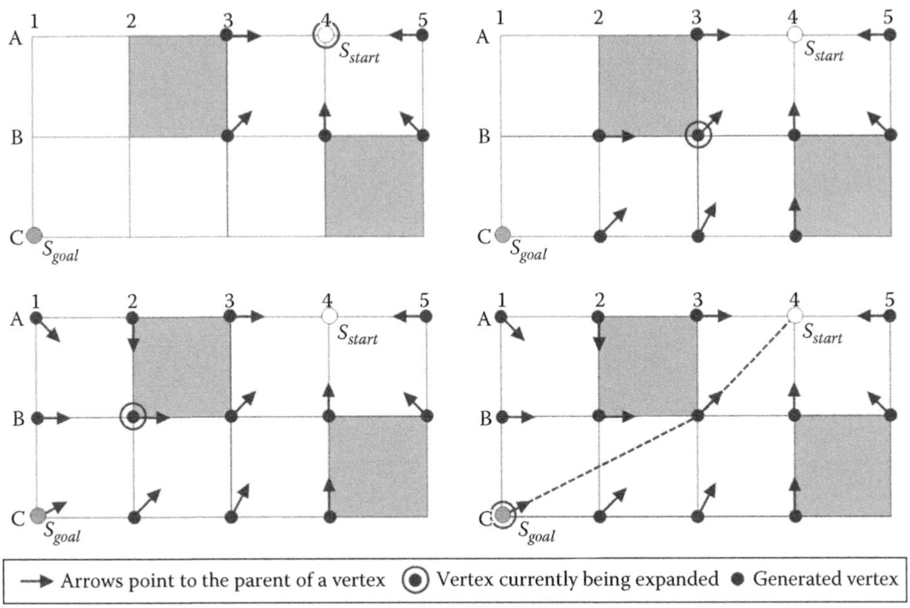

Figure 16.7

Example trace of Theta*.

16.5 Theta* Paths

While Theta* is not guaranteed to find shortest paths in the continuous environment (for the reasons explained in the work of Nash et al. [Nash 07]), it finds shortest paths in the continuous environment quite frequently, as demonstrated in Figure 16.8. We performed a search from the center of the grid to all of the vertices in the grid. In Figure 16.8a, A* PS found the shortest path in the continuous environment from the center of the grid to each shaded dot. Similarly, in Figure 16.8b, Theta* found the shortest path in the continuous environment from the center of the grid to each shaded dot. There are far more shaded dots in Figure 16.8b than Figure 16.8a.

Figure 16.9 compares a Theta* path (bottom) and an A* path (top) on a game map from BioWare's popular RPG *Baldur's Gate II*, which has been discretized into a 100 × 100 eight-neighbor square grid. The Theta* path is significantly shorter and appears more realistic than the A* path. Furthermore, most postprocessing techniques are unable to shorten the A* path into the Theta* path since the A* path circumnavigates blocked cells in a different way.

16.6 Analysis

Researchers have performed experiments comparing the path lengths and runtimes of A*, A* PS, and Theta* using eight-neighbor square grids that either correspond to game maps or contain a given percentage of randomly blocked cells [Nash 12, Yap 11, Sislak 09]. The relationships between the lengths of the paths found by A*, A* PS, and Theta* are relatively consistent. The Theta* paths are approximately 4% shorter than the A* paths. The A* PS paths are approximately 1%–3% shorter than the A* paths depending on the type of environment and the heuristic (e.g., straight-line distance or octile

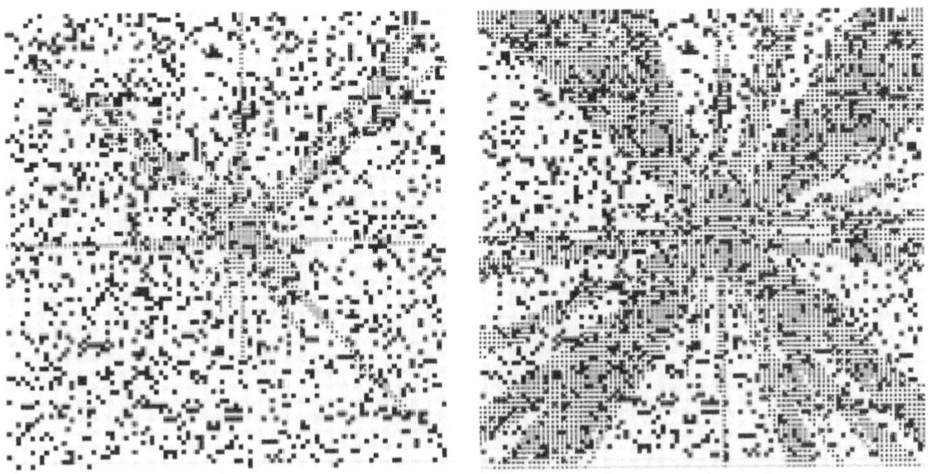

(a) (b)

Figure 16.8

Shortest paths found by A* PS (a) and Theta* (b).

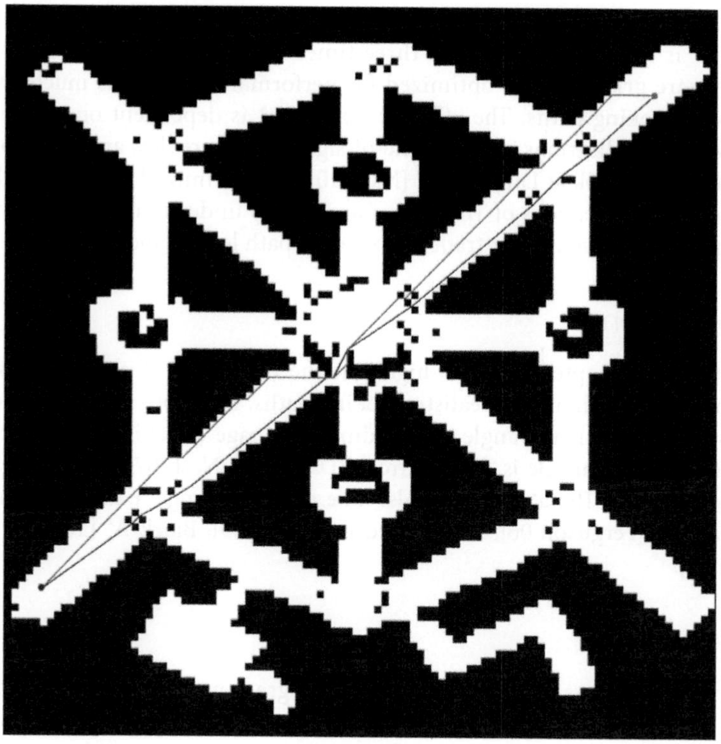

Figure 16.9

Theta* path (bottom path) versus A* path (top path).

distance heuristic). The shortest paths in the continuous environment are approximately 0.1% shorter than the Theta* paths.

The relationships between the runtimes of A*, A* PS, and Theta* are less consistent. This is because the results vary significantly with different experimental setups (such as grid size, placement of blocked cells, locations of start and goal vertices, *h*-values, and tiebreaking scheme for selecting a vertex among those with the smallest key in the open list). Currently, there is no agreement on standard experimental setups in the literature. We therefore broadly average over all reported results to give the reader an approximate idea of the efficiency of Theta*. Theta* is approximately two to three times slower than A* with the octile distance heuristic and approximately two times *faster* than A* PS with the straight-line distance heuristic. The significant difference in runtime between A* with the octile distance heuristic and A* PS with the straight-line distance heuristic is due to a large difference in the number of vertex expansions. However, highly informed heuristics, such as the octile distance heuristic on grids, do not exist for many discretizations of continuous environments, such as navigation meshes. If A*, A* PS, and Theta* all use the straight-line distance heuristic, then Theta* might find shorter paths faster than A*, and A* PS.

In general, Theta* provides a good trade-off between path length and runtime. On the one hand, Theta* is orders of magnitude faster than standard implementations of

A* on visibility graphs and finds paths that have nearly the same length. On the other hand, Theta* is approximately two to three times slower than versions of A* on eight-neighbor square grids that are optimized for performance but finds much shorter and more realistic-looking paths. The efficiency of Theta* is dependent on efficient line-of-sight checks. For applications in which line-of-sight checks are slow and thus a bottleneck, we suggest taking a look at Lazy Theta* [Nash 10] and Optimized Lazy Theta* [Nash 12]. These are optimized versions of Theta* that are easy to understand, quick to implement, and often provide an even better trade-off between path length and runtime.

16.7 Conclusion

We hope that this chapter serves to highlight the usefulness of any-angle pathfinding for efficiently finding short and realistic-looking paths. For more information on Theta*, we suggest visiting our any-angle pathfinding web page [Koenig 14] and reading the publications that this article is derived from [Daniel 10, Nash 07, Nash 12, Nash 13]. If you are interested in Theta*, you may also like other any-angle pathfinding algorithms such as Field D* [Ferguson 06], Accelerated A* [Sislak 09], Block A* [Yap 11], and Anya [Harabour 13].

Acknowledgment

The research at USC was supported by NSF under grant numbers 1409987 and 1319966. The views and conclusions contained in this document are those of the authors and should not be interpreted as representing the official policies, either expressed or implied, of the sponsoring organizations, agencies or the U.S. government.

References

[Björnsson 03] Björnsson, Y., Enzenberger, M., Holte, R., Schaeffer, J., and Yap, P. 2003. Comparison of different grid abstractions for pathfinding on maps. *Proceedings of the International Joint Conference on Artificial Intelligence*, 1511–1512.

[Choset 04] Choset, H., Hutchinson, S., Kantor, G., Burgard, W., Lydia, K., and Thrun, S. 2004. *Principles of Robot Motion.* MIT Press, Cambridge, MA.

[Daniel 10] Daniel, K., Nash, A., and Koenig, S. 2010. Theta*: Any-angle path planning on grids. *Journal of Artificial Intelligence Research*, 39, 533–579.

[Ferguson 06] Ferguson, D. and Stentz, A. 2006. Using interpolation to improve path planning: The Field D* algorithm. *Journal of Field Robotics*, 23(2), 79–101.

[Harabor 13] Harabor, D. and Grastien, A. 2013. An optimal any-angle pathfinding algorithm. *Proceedings of the International Conference on Automated Planning and Scheduling*, Rome, Italy, 308–344.

[Koenig 14] Koenig, S. 2014. Project "Any-angle path planning". Retrieved from http://idm-lab.org/project-o.html (accessed September 10, 2014).

[Lorzano-Perez 79] Lozano-Perez, T. and Wesley, M. 1979. An algorithm for planning collision-free paths among polyhedral obstacles. *Communication of the ACM*, 22, 560–570.

[Nash 07] Nash, A., Daniel, K., Koenig, S., and Felner, A. 2007. Theta*: Any-angle path planning on grids. *Proceedings of the AAAI Conference on Artificial Intelligence*, 1177–1183.

[Nash 10] Nash, A., Koenig, S., and Tovey, C. 2010. Lazy Theta*: Any-angle path planning and path length analysis in 3D. In *Proceedings of the AAAI Conference on Artificial Intelligence*, 147–154.

[Nash 12] Nash, A. 2012. Any-angle path planning. PhD dissertation, University of Southern California, Los Angeles, CA.

[Nash 13] Nash, A. and Koenig, S. 2013. Any-angle path planning. *Artificial Intelligence Magazine*, 34(3), 85–107.

[Nilsson 68] Nilsson, N., Hart, P., and Raphael, B. 1968. Formal basis for the heuristic determination of minimum cost paths. *IEEE Transactions on Systems Science and Cybernetics*, 4(2), 100–107.

[Patel 00] Patel, A. 2000. Amit's game programming information. Retrieved from http://www-cs-students.stanford.edu/~amitp/gameprog.html (accessed September 10, 2014).

[Rabin 00] Rabin, S. 2000. A* aesthetic optimizations. In *Game Programming Gems*, ed. DeLoura, M., 264–271. Charles River Media, Hingham, MA.

[Sislak 09] Sislak, D., Volf, P., Pechoucek, M., Suri, N., Nicholson, D., and Woodhouse, D. 2009. Accelerated A* path planning. *Proceedings of the International Conference on Autonomous Agents and Multiagent Systems*, 375–378.

[Tozour 04] Tozour, P. 2004. Search space representations. In *AI Game Programming Wisdom 2*, ed. Rabin, S., 85–102. Charles River Media, Hingham, MA.

[Yap 11] Yap, P., Burch, N., Holte, R., and Schaeffer, J. 2011. Block A*: Database-driven search with applications in any-angle path-planning. *Proceedings of the AAAI Conference on Artificial Intelligence*, 120–125.

17

Advanced Techniques for Robust, Efficient Crowds

Graham Pentheny

17.1 Introduction

To date, crowds in games are usually driven by static pathfinding combined with localized steering and collision avoidance. This technique is well understood and works well for small or moderate crowd sizes that are sparsely distributed in their environment. As crowd density increases and the agents' goals converge, this approach falls apart. In situations like this, agents fight the rest of the crowd to follow their ideal path as closely as possible, seemingly ignoring all other possible routes.

Congestion maps provide a simple means of modeling aggregate behavior in large crowds of tens or hundreds of thousands of agents. Combined with *vector flow fields*, congestion maps can be used to elegantly handle large variations in path travel times due to congestion and crowding from other agents in the scene. Agents controlled by this technique appear to be more aware of their surroundings, reconsidering their current path choice if a less-congested alternative exists.

17.2 Pathfinding's Utopian Worldview

Current solutions for pathfinding compute paths in an idealized environment. They compute the shortest distance path from the current agent position to its goal through a given environment as if no other agents existed. Some variations of common pathfinding approaches such as Partial Refinement A* [Sturtevant 05] repeatedly perform partial path calculations to account for changes in the environment. This is ideal for rapidly changing environments as much of a full path calculation is likely to never be used before it is necessary to repath. Despite adeptly handling changes to the open areas in the environment, Partial Refinement variants of A* operate on the principle that the only obstacles in the environment are static and binary. Either the agent can move through a given location or it can't. These approaches cannot handle situations where certain path directions are obstructed by large groups of other agents, because they do not consider other agents in their calculations. This can be thought of as optimizing for total path length, rather than for the actual travel time. In an empty environment, the travel time is simply the distance inversely scaled by the agent's velocity. However, in a crowded world, other agents increase the travel time through certain points in the environment.

Collision avoidance algorithms attempt to avoid other agents in the local vicinity by either restricting or augmenting the agent's velocity. These techniques are well suited for avoiding localized collisions and are often used to complement idealized pathfinding. Collision avoidance algorithms, however, fail to account for situations where movement is significantly impacted by other agents. Collision avoidance helps avoid other agents that may obstruct travel along the ideal, shortest path, but does not deviate the path direction. In games using this dual-layered pathing and collision avoidance approach, repathing occurs only when the collision avoidance solver pushes the agent far enough away from their current, ideal path so that it no longer remains the ideal movement direction. The implications of this are most easily seen in the following example, illustrated in Figure 17.1.

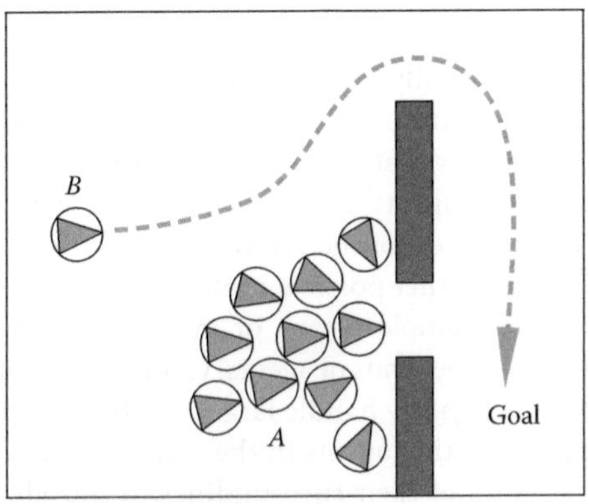

Figure 17.1

Two groups of agents attempting to reach a shared goal. The dashed line indicates the time-optimal path for agent *B*.

In this scenario, the agents are attempting to reach a common goal. There are a large number of agents in group *A*, and therefore they will take a considerable amount of time to move through the lower opening. Because all agents follow their ideal shortest path, both groups attempt to move through the lower opening. The agent marked as "*B*" in this example could path through the upper unobstructed opening, resulting in a shorter travel time to its goal. This alternative path is indicated as a gray dashed line in Figure 17.1. With just path planning and collision avoidance, agent *B* will consider the alternative path only when its collision avoidance moves the agent close to the upper opening. Only then, when the agent's shortest path is through the upper opening, will it consider this alternative route.

Both approaches that compute individual paths, and those like flow fields that aggregate pathfinding information across a group, suffer from this lack of contextual awareness. These algorithms are designed to minimize the total path distance, as this is a measurable and easily optimized metric. Alternatively, full movement-planning approaches involve predicting and planning movement for all agents through the scene and solving for collisions and congestion over their entire respective paths. These approaches can be too resource intensive to compute for large numbers of agents in real time. Additionally, motion planning does not account for future environmental or goal changes that may affect the computed movement information. As such, motion planning is only seen in situations requiring high-quality movement for small numbers of agents.

17.3 Congestion Map Approach

The solution we propose is a hybrid of static, idealized pathfinding, with a simplification of motion planning. The approach computes aggregate crowd density and movement across the environment and then compares that to the idealized path direction and movement. This information, called a *congestion map*, is then used to augment pathfinding computations by discouraging movement through crowded areas. Congestion maps offer significant advantages over *direction maps* (DMs) [Jansen 08], an approach we will compare later in this chapter.

This approach is based on the observation that moving against or across a crowd is much more difficult than movement aligned with the flow of the crowd. Additionally, the more densely crowded an area is, the more time it will cost to move through.

Because information on crowd dynamics is computed for groups of agents as a whole, the computational complexity is far less than that of full motion planning. Combined with aggregate pathfinding techniques such as flow fields, this approach scales well to large numbers of agents, making it ideal for large crowd simulations.

17.4 Augmenting Path Planning with Congestion Maps

The first step in the process is to compute the aggregate crowd density across the environment. For each agent in the scene, we record its current velocity and position. We then use the agent positions to construct an agent influence map [Champandard 11] across the environment space. This is used as an estimation of agent density, where larger influence values correspond to a denser crowd at that position. Conversely, lower values indicate more sparsely distributed agents.

Velocity information is plotted and distributed over the environmental space in the same manner. In addition, we compute a rolling average of the agent velocity vectors, providing a map of the average velocity of the crowd at each point. For clarity, both the average velocity and the crowd density information are referred to collectively as a "congestion map." The congestion map indicates areas that are likely to experience increased travel costs due to crowd congestion.

The congestion map information is then used as a means of computing path traversal cost in a heuristic pathfinding algorithm, such as A*. Crowd density alone could be interpreted as a traversal cost; however, this would cause agents moving together at a uniform velocity to unnecessarily avoid each other. Instead, we use the aggregate crowd velocity information to ensure that we only add traversal costs when necessary. Using an unmodified pathfinding algorithm, we begin to compute the ideal path from the agent to the goal. In the pathfinding process, we use the congestion map to augment the computed traversal cost from one step in the path to the next. This is done by computing the difference in the aggregate crowd velocity and the agent's ideal path velocity. The scalar magnitude of this vector difference is then scaled by the crowd density value, resulting in the "congestion penalty" for that movement. Pseudocode for computing the traversal cost is shown in Listing 17.1. The congestion penalty can then be easily integrated into existing calculations as an additional path traversal cost. Furthermore, because the crowd congestion penalty is never negative, it maintains heuristic admissibility in the path planner.

As agents move through the scene, they use the congestion map to augment their pathfinding queries. This ensures that they will favor paths that offer the shortest travel time, even if they are not the shortest in distance. Each agent performs a traditional pathfinding query, or an aggregate pathfinding pass is performed in the case of using flow fields. The normal behavior of the heuristic path planner uses the "congestion map" information to choose paths with lower costs and thus minimal travel times. Alternatively, if a congested path still remains better than any alternative, the path planner will correctly choose the congested path.

Listing 17.1. Traversal cost computation using the congestion map information.

```
float congestionPenalty(Vec2 ideal,
                        Vec2 aggregate,
                        float density)
{
    //Projection of aggregate onto ideal, represented
    //as a scalar multiple of ideal.
    float cost = Vec2.dot(ideal, aggregate);
    cost /= ideal.mag() * ideal.mag();

    //If cost is > 1, the crowd is moving faster along the
    //ideal direction than the agent's ideal velocity.
    if (cost >= 1) return 0.0f;

    //Cost is transformed to be positive,
    //and scaled by crowd density
    return (1 - cost) * density;
}
```

The final step in the process involves adding in local collision avoidance. While the congestion map will help deal with macrolevel collision avoidance, we still rely, albeit far less, on collision avoidance algorithms to resolve local agent collisions.

17.5 Path Smoothing

Because the congestion coefficients are used by the pathfinder as traversal cost values, unmodified path-smoothing algorithms will not maintain this information. Path smoothing relies on line-of-sight collision checks to determine whether a waypoint in a path is considered redundant and can be removed. This process creates a final, smoothed path containing the minimal number of waypoints necessary to accurately guide the agent through the static obstacles in the environment to its goal. Because the heuristic for skipping path nodes only considers line of sight, it will not produce smoothed paths that respect congestion map information.

Smoothing of paths computed with congestion map information involves comparing the movement cost of smoothed routes. Classic path-smoothing approaches assume the movement cost in the world is invariant and thus optimize for the shortest total path distance. To incorporate the congestion map information, the path-smoothing algorithm must compare the ultimate time cost of moving along both paths. To accurately compare two potential smoothed versions of a path, the smoothing algorithm must produce a heuristic that accounts for both the traversal cost and total distance of each. The heuristic estimates the total travel cost for a path by computing the line integral along path direction over the congestion penalty function. This can be easily computed over a discretized world (such as a grid) by computing the sum of each step's movement distance scaled by its corresponding traversal cost. The result of this summation (more generally of the line integral) constitutes the overall traversal cost for a path. The path-smoothing algorithm can use this value as a heuristic, allowing it to accurately compare two potential smoothed paths.

17.6 Flow Fields with Congestion Maps and Theta

In dense crowd simulations, many agents will be considering movement in a shared space. Additionally, many agents may share a set of goal destinations. As such, pathfinding approaches that exploit this uniformity across the agent population are ideal. Flow fields provide these benefits, as they unify pathfinding information for all agents with a shared goal. Flow fields compute ideal path directions for every discretized point in a given world. This provides constant computation and look-up cost for paths for any number of agents with a shared set of goals. The increased pathfinding complexity of congestion map aware algorithms amplifies the benefits of flow fields for large crowds. When using flow fields with congestion maps, the special path-smoothing considerations can be combined into the flow vector calculation process.

Flow fields are generated by back-propagating ideal path directions from the goal position using an unbounded Dijkstra's algorithm. While this is efficient and easily implemented for simple applications, it does not offer smoothed paths. Additionally, adding smoothing as a postprocess step (as in single-source pathfinding) does not scale well to large crowds due to the number of line-of-sight calculations required. These restrictions make the Theta* [Nash 07, Nash 15] algorithm ideal for generating flow fields.

Theta* operates identically to Dijkstra's algorithm when generating flow fields; however, it performs path-smoothing calculations as paths are being constructed. As Theta* creates a path link between two nodes *A* and *B*, it performs a line-of-sight check between the new node *A* and the parent of the previously expanded node *B*. This line-of-sight check then exists through the remainder of all path calculations and can be reused in subsequent path-smoothing calculations. The line-of-sight check can also incorporate congestion map information by computing and memoizing the path traversal cost via the process defined in the previous section. Theta* combined with these path cost calculations allows it to efficiently generate congestion map aware flow fields. Please see the chapter on Theta* in this book for more details on Theta* [Nash 15].

17.7 Current Alternatives

Current crowd dynamics solutions generally involve two layers: pathfinding and local collision avoidance. These approaches offer a few noteworthy benefits. They produce high-quality movement and avoidance on small scales and are well understood and researched by the community. There are many open-source and off-the-shelf implementations of these techniques, and they integrate well into existing technology. A popular choice for many games is the combination of A* with velocity obstacle [van den Berg 08] approaches such as ORCA [van den Berg 09] or ClearPath [Guy 09]. These offer an enticing combination of fast, inexpensive pathfinding with robust, high-quality collision avoidance.

In high-density crowd situations, solely relying on local collision avoidance and idealized pathfinding will cause agents to pile up at popular, shared path waypoints. Collision avoidance algorithms only help avoid local collisions in the pursuit of following the ideal path. Often games rely on these algorithms to divert agents to less-congested, less-direct routes in high-density situations. In certain situations, collision avoidance can lead to this desired behavior, though it is always a side effect of the system and not a deliberate consideration.

Work has been done in incorporating aggregate crowd movement and crowd density into pathfinding computations [van Toll 12, Karamouzas 09, Jansen 08]. Approaches that augment pathing via crowd density [van Toll 12, Karamouzas 09] do not take into account the aggregate movement or direction of movement of the crowd. This leads to overcorrection of the phenomenon illustrated in Figure 17.1.

Congestion maps are similar in many ways to existing cooperative pathfinding algorithms, such as "DMs" [Jansen 08], but differ in a few key respects. DMs use average crowd motion over time to encourage agents to move with the flow of the crowd. Because of this, many of the oscillations present in the congestion map approach are smoothly resolved. Conversely, this temporal smoothing prevents DMs from quickly and accurately reacting to changes in the environment and crowd behavior. Both congestion maps and DMs apply the aggregate crowd movement information to the path planning process in much the same way; however, congestion maps handle agents of varying size and shape, while DMs traditionally assume homogeneity. The final major difference between DMs and congestion maps is that congestion maps weight movement penalties proportional to the density of the crowd. Without taking density into account, DMs display overly pessimistic pathing behavior, where agents are encouraged to path around sparse groups of agents blocking the ideal path.

17.8 Benefits

Congestion maps offer an effective way of enhancing crowd behavior at scale. Compared to motion planning approaches that predict movement and interactions of all agents in a given time interval, congestion maps are an inexpensive addition to established character movement systems. Additionally, the simplicity of congestion maps makes them easy to implement and optimize.

Congestion maps augment agent pathfinding to work as it should. Instead of optimizing for minimal path distance, path planners using congestion maps correctly optimize for path travel time. This ensures agents will consider less-crowded alternative routes that may be slightly longer but ultimately faster than the ideal path.

Though congestion maps can be added to any existing path planning system, flow fields are ideal for exploiting the benefits of this approach. Using Theta* to generate flow fields results in drastically fewer line-of-sight checks, as their results can be shared across path calculations. Theta* minimizes the impact of the increase in path-smoothing computations with congestion maps, without reducing the technique's effectiveness.

17.9 Drawbacks

Despite the many benefits congestion maps offer, they are not a replacement for full motion planning. Congestion maps are a reactive, macrolevel collision avoidance technique. Changes to crowd density over time are not taken into account when augmenting unit paths. As such, an agent may avoid a congested area along its ideal path that, by the time the agent would reach that area, would no longer be congested. This can lead to agents appearing to "change their mind" as congestion eases in specific locations. Conversely, an agent can begin moving toward a location that is not currently congested, but that will become so once the agent reaches the area. This will cause the agent to change directions toward a longer, less-congested path. Depending on the application of the congestion map approach, these behavioral flaws may be acceptable, as they mimic the fallibility of human path planning. In other applications, their impact may be negligible.

Due to the dynamic nature of crowd density, congestion maps are best suited for highly dynamic environments and techniques. As crowd density changes, existing paths become less ideal in both distance and traversal time. This necessitates replanning existing paths to account for changes in the environment. Hierarchical discretization helps alleviate some of the costs of consistent repathing by shrinking the search space, speeding up individual pathfinding computations.

Finally, by their nature, congestion maps weaken the heuristic used for search, increasing the cost of path planning. Again, hierarchical methods or weighted A* can be used to reduce this overhead [Jansen 08].

17.10 Performance Considerations

Congestion maps compute crowd density and aggregate information across the entire environment. This requires discretizing the continuous space at some granularity. As the resolution of the congestion map data increases, the memory required to store the congestion data also increases. Additionally, the cost of computing blended moving averages of aggregate crowd movement vectors increases with the resolution of the congestion map.

Despite holding information for every position in the environment, the congestion map doesn't need to correspond directly to the existing world discretization. In fact, the congestion map resolution can be much smaller than the world discretization resolution and still maintain much of its effectiveness. However, the coarser the congestion map resolution, the more likely agents will exhibit strange behavior, such as avoiding areas that don't need to be avoided. The overall macrolevel behavior will be correct and consistent; however, individuals may show odd patterns of behavior.

17.11 Future Work

Hysteresis can be added to the system to prevent agents from oscillating between potential paths quickly due to rapid changes in congestion information. With hysteresis, an agent will remain on its current path until the congestion values have surpassed a certain value for a certain amount of time. Likewise, the agent will not consider a shorter path until that path has been uncongested for a certain amount of time. These time intervals and congestion thresholds are user defined, offering high-level control over the behavior of the agents in the scene. Additional realism is obtained by authoring congestion coefficient levels and time delays as random distributions over specific value ranges.

Because the congestion map only offers a snapshot of the current crowd density and aggregate velocity, it is not perfectly accurate to the realities of the agents' theoretically ideal behavior. This inaccuracy is introduced as a means of improving runtime performance and simplifying implementation details. Computing the full crowd density over time would allow the path planner to more accurately compute traversal cost. With this method, the path planner can base the traversal cost on the crowd state at the time when the agent would be at the considered position in its path. This is similar to motion planning approaches, in that each agent must know the expected behavior of the other agents in the scene to compute an ideal path. Because they only require computing aggregate agent behavior, congestion maps evaluated over time intervals may also prove to be less computationally expensive than full motion planning.

17.12 Conclusion

A combination of static, idealized pathfinding and localized collision avoidance algorithms are often used to simulate crowds in games. While effective for small numbers of sparse agents, these approaches lack consideration of the effects of crowd dynamics on agents' path planning calculations.

Congestion maps introduce context awareness to the path planning system and allow individual agents to react to the agents around them on a large scale. Together with Theta*, congestion maps can generate ideal pathing information for an entire environment in the form of a vector flow field. By maximally reusing shared path computations, flow fields help reduce the cost of smoothing individually computed paths.

Adding congestion maps to a path planning system allows agents, in situations of high crowd density, to find alternative, longer paths that will ultimately take less time to follow.

This is a behavior not previously possible without expensive motion planning approaches, which provides opportunities for games to create more compelling, realistic, and interesting crowds.

References

[Champandard 11] Champandard, A. 2011. The mechanics of influence mapping: Representation, algorithm and parameters. http://aigamedev.com/open/tutorial/influence-map-mechanics/ (accessed June 1, 2014).

[Guy 09] Guy, S., Chhugani, J., Kim, C., Satish, N., Lin, M., Manocha, D., Dubey, P. 2009. ClearPath: Highly parallel collision avoidance for multi-agent simulation. *Proceedings of the Eurographics/ACM SIGGRAPH Symposium on Computer Animation (2009)*, pp. 177–187.

[Jansen 08] Jansen, M. and Sturtevant, N. 2008. Direction maps for cooperative pathfinding. *Proceedings of the AAAI Conference on Artificial Intelligence and Interactive Digital Entertainment.*

[Karamouzas 09] Karamouzas, I., Bakker, J., and Overmars, M. 2009. Density constraints for crowd simulation. *Proceedings of the ICE Games Innovations Conference*, pp. 160–168.

[Nash 07] Nash, A., Daniel, K., Koenig, S., and Felner, A. 2007. Theta*: Any-angle path planning on grids. *Proceedings of the AAAI Conference on Artificial Intelligence*, pp. 1177–1183.

[Nash 15] Nash, A. and Koenig, S. 2015. Theta* for Any-Angle Pathfinding. In *Game AI Pro^2: Collected Wisdom of Game AI Professionals*, ed. S. Rabin. A K Peters/CRC Press, Boca Raton, FL.

[Sturtevant 05] Sturtevant, N. and Buro, M. 2005. Partial pathfinding using map abstraction and refinement. *Proceedings of the National Conference on Artificial Intelligence*, July 2005, Vol. 5, pp. 1392–1397.

[van den Berg 08] van den Berg, J., Lin, M., and Manocha, D. 2008. Reciprocal velocity obstacles for real-time multi-agent navigation. *IEEE International Conference on Robotics and Automation*, 1928–1935.

[van den Berg 09] van den Berg, J., Guy, S., Lin, M., and Manocha, D. 2009. Reciprocal n-body collision avoidance. *Proceedings of the International Symposium on Robotics Research.*

[van Toll 12] van Toll, W., Cook IV, A., and Geraerts, R. 2012. Real-time density-based crowd simulation. *Computer Animation and Virtual Worlds*, 23, 59–69.

18

Context Steering

Behavior-Driven Steering at the Macro Scale

Andrew Fray

18.1 Introduction

Steering behaviors are extremely common in the games industry [Reynolds 87, Reynolds 99]. Their popularity is with good cause, promising a fast-to-implement core with emergent behavior from simple components.

However, steering behaviors are not suited for some types of game. When the player can pick out and watch individual entities, collision avoidance and consistent movement become very important. Achieving this can cause behavior components to balloon in size and become tightly coupled. Entity movement then becomes fragile and hard to tune.

In this chapter, we'll outline how you can identify the games for which steering behaviors aren't a good fit and describe a new approach for those problems called *context steering*. Context steering behaviors are small and stateless and guarantee any desired movement constraint. When used to replace steering behaviors on the game *F1 2011*, the codebase shrunk by 4000 lines, yet the AI were better at avoiding collisions, overtaking, and performing other interesting behaviors.

18.2 When Steering Behaviors Go Bad

A steering behavior system is used to move an entity through a world. The system consists of multiple child behaviors. During each update, the child behaviors are asked for a vector representing how they would like the entity to move. The vectors are combined to produce a final velocity. That's really it; the simplicity of the system is one of its strengths.

Note that the behavior vectors can be either a desired final velocity or a corrective force to the current velocity. This chapter will show behavior output as a final velocity. It doesn't change the arguments either way, but it makes the diagrams easier to arrange and understand.

Imagine an entity with free movement on a 2D plane. The entity cares about avoiding *obstacles* and chasing *targets*. At the instant of time shown in Figure 18.1, there are two possible targets in the scene and one obstacle.

What's the ideal result here? Assuming our only concern on choosing a target is distance, the entity should move toward target A. However, there's an obstacle in the way, so moving toward target B would be best. Can that decision emerge from small simple behaviors?

We start with two simple steering behaviors: *chase*, for approaching targets, and *avoid*, for not hitting obstacles. Our avoid behavior sees the nearby obstacle and returns a velocity to avoid it. The chase behavior knows nothing about obstacles and so returns a velocity toward the nearest target, target A.

The behavior system combines these behaviors. Let's assume they're just averaged for now, although you can use more complex combination techniques. The final vector is very close to 0, and the entity hardly moves. Players are not going to think this is an intelligent entity!

Steering behavior systems have evolved some Band-Aids to deal with this situation over the years. Here's a few ways this stalemate might be solved:

We could add *weighting* to our behaviors, so avoid heavily outweighs chase when there is an obstacle nearby. Now the entity has a strong northward velocity, but at some point, it will reach equilibrium again. We've only succeeded in moving the problem, at the cost of a new weighting parameter. That parameter will invariably need tweaking any time we change any of the affected behaviors.

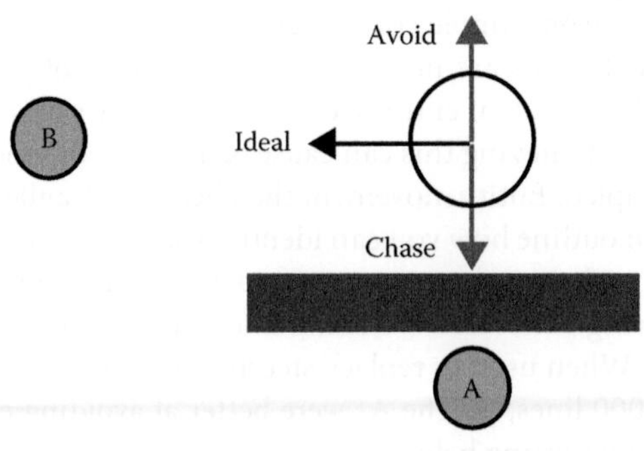

Figure 18.1

Entity layout, ideal path, and first path.

We could add *prioritization*, so avoid is the only behavior that runs when near obstacles, but then movement near obstacles is very single minded, and not very expressive.

Finally, we could add some *awareness* of obstacles to the chase behavior. It could raycast to reject targets that don't have a clear path or pathfind to all targets and select the one with the shortest path. Both of these introduce the concept of obstacles into chase, which increases coupling. In most game engines, raycasts and pathfinds are going to be either expensive or asynchronous, both of which introduce different types of complexity. This makes chase neither "small" nor "stateless."

There doesn't seem to be a good way to fix this.

This may sound like a forced example, but it's based on a real experience. In *F1 2010*, our equivalent of the avoid behavior had to be incredibly robust, which meant it often demanded to run frequently and in isolation, dominating how the opponent cars moved. To put some expressiveness back into the AI, we extended the avoid behavior over and over again to make it avoid in intelligent ways, coupling it to multiple other behaviors and making it monolithic. By the end, it had decomposed into an old-school sequence of if/else blocks with a thin steering behavior wrapper and was a maintenance nightmare.

18.2.1 Flocks versus Groups

If steering behaviors are so broken, why are they so popular? Because not all games expose the right conditions to make the problems apparent. Steering behaviors are a statistical steering method. Most of the time, they will give you mostly the right direction. How often they give you inconsistent or bad results, and how bad that is for the player, is a per-game decision.

It's no coincidence that the most famous application of steering behaviors is flocking [Reynolds 87]. In flocking, the user is typically an external observer of many entities moving as a semicohesive group. The group seems to have lifelike properties and unpredictable but believable behavior. Really, the "entity" here is the flock, not the individual. The size of the flock can hide the odd inconsistent movement or collision of individuals.

In the racing genre, the player is often inside the "flock," wheel to wheel with AI cars. Here, inconsistent movements can be glaring and immersion breaking. They can result in missed overtaking opportunities, poor overtake blocking, or at worst collisions with other cars. Steering behaviors were not a good fit for *F1*.

18.2.2 Lack of Context

We now understand what steering behavior failure looks like and what types of games that matters for. But we don't yet know *why* steering behavior systems have this flaw. Once we understand that, we can design a solution.

A single steering behavior component is asked to return a vector representing its decision, considering the current state of the world. The framework then tries to merge multiple decisions. However, there just isn't enough information to make merging these decisions possible. Adding prioritization or weighting attempts to make merging easier by adding more information to the behavior's result, but it translates to louder shouting rather than more nuanced debate. By making chase aware of obstacles, we can make it produce more sensible results, yet this is just special casing the merge step. That is not a scalable solution.

Sometimes, the reasons why a behavior didn't want to go any other way—the *context* in which the decision was made—is just as important as the decision itself. This is a particular problem for collision avoidance behaviors, because they can only communicate in the language of desired velocity, not undesired velocity.

18.3 Toward Why, Not How

Returning a decision, even with some metadata, just isn't going to work. Instead, what if we could ask a behavior for the context in which it would make the decision, but skip the actual decision step? If we could then somehow merge all those contexts, some external behavior-agnostic processor could produce a final decision, fully aware of everything.

The context of avoid could be, "I feel moderately strongly we shouldn't go south," and the chase context could be, "it's a little interesting to go west and quite interesting to go south." It's a holistic view rather than a resolute decision. The framework then waves a magic wand and combines these contexts, revealing that the ideal decision is to go west.

The end result is as if chase was aware of obstacles and disregarded its favorite target because it was blocked, yet the individual behaviors were focused only on their concerns. The system is emergent and has consistent collision avoidance and small stateless behaviors.

18.3.1 Context Maps

The context steering framework deals in the currency of *context maps*. Imagine everything the entity cares about in the world projected onto the circumference of a circle around the entity, as shown in Figure 18.2. It's like a 1D image, and in fact, many of the tricks we'll show you later in the chapter follow from this image metaphor.

Internally, the context map is an array of scalar values, with each slot of the array representing a possible heading, and the contents of the slot representing how strongly the behavior feels about this heading. How many slots the array has is the "resolution" of the context map. (If you're already wondering if you need huge resolutions to have decent movement, then relax. I'll show you later why you need many less than you think.) By using this array format, we can easily correlate and merge different context maps and go from slots to headings and vice versa. This is our data structure for arbitrating between different behaviors.

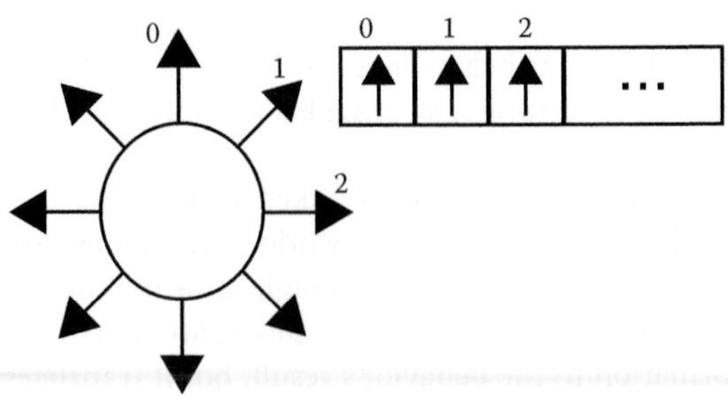

Figure 18.2

Mapping headings to context map slots.

In each frame, the framework will ask every behavior for two different context maps: the *danger* map and the *interest* map. The danger map is a view of everything the behavior would like to stay away from. As you'd suspect, the interest map is everything the behavior would like to move toward.

18.4 Context Maps by Example

What does our previous entity example look like, rewritten to use context maps? We can translate it by thinking about the information that informed the old behavior's decision and storing that information in the correct context map.

18.4.1 Chase Behavior

The chase behavior wants the entity to move toward targets, preferring near targets to far. However, choosing the best target requires making a decision, and we don't want to do that. So we're going to write all the targets into the interest map, with farther targets represented with lower intensity.

We could take a vector directly toward a target, translate that into a map slot, and write only into that slot. That captures that moving toward the target is desirable. However, we can also write over a range of slots, centered on the target with configurable falloff to zero. This captures that passing the target but just missing it is also an interesting thing to do, even if not the best. There's a lot of power and nuance in how this falloff works, giving you a lot of control over how the entity moves.

All this can be done with a quick for-each over all targets, some tuning constants, and no state. The resultant interest map is shown in Figure 18.3.

18.4.2 Avoid Behavior

The avoid behavior wants the entity to keep at least a minimum distance away from obstacles. We're going to render all obstacles into the danger map, in a very similar for-each loop to chase. The intensity of an obstacle in the danger map represents the distance to the obstacle. If the obstacle is beyond the minimum distance, it can be ignored. Again, falloff around the obstacle can be used in an interesting way. Here, it represents the heading

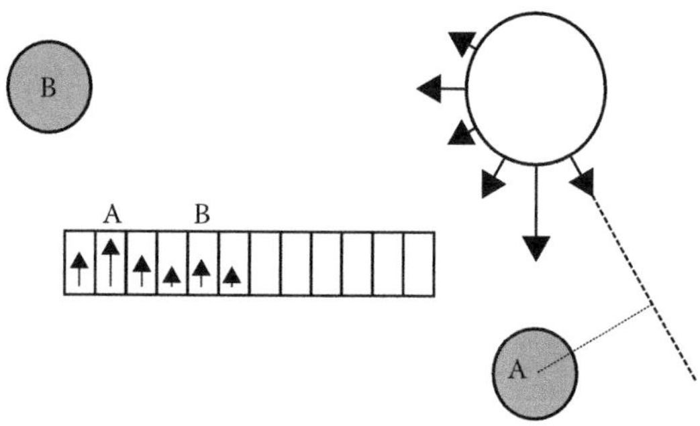

Figure 18.3

Chase behavior, writing into interest map.

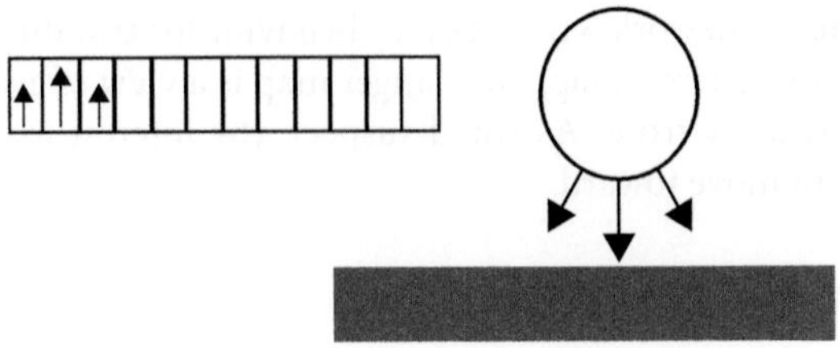

Figure 18.4

Avoid behavior, writing into danger map.

required to pass it without reentering the exclusion zone around it. This behavior is also stateless and small. The avoid behavior is shown in Figure 18.4.

18.4.3 Combining and Parsing

The output of each behavior can be combined with others by comparing each slot across multiple maps and taking a maximum. We could sum or average the slots, but we're not going to avoid a particular obstacle any more just because there's another obstacle behind it. We already must avoid the first obstacle, and that obscures any danger from the second. Through combining, we can reduce all output to a single interest and danger map pair.

The next step processes the maps, boiling down the entire shared context into a single final velocity. How this happens is game specific; the racing game example will have its own implementation.

First, we traverse the danger map to find the lowest danger and mask out all slots that have higher danger. In our example, there are some empty slots in the danger map, so our lowest danger is zero, and therefore, we mask out any slot with nonzero danger, shown in Figure 18.5(i). We take that mask and apply it to the interest map, zeroing out any masked slots (ii). Finally, we pick the interest map slot with the highest remaining interest (iii) and move in that direction (iv). The speed we move is proportional to the strength of interest in the slot; a lot of interest means we move quickly.

The final decision here is the correct decision. It is emergent—preserving collision avoidance while chasing a sensible target—yet we did it with small, stateless, and decoupled behaviors. It is the promise of steering behaviors at the macro scale.

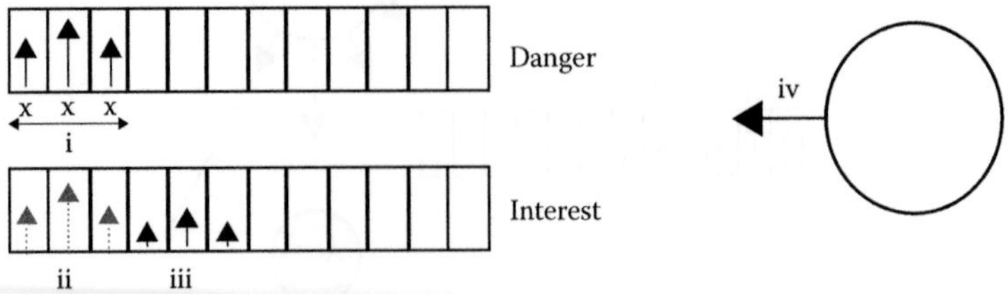

Figure 18.5

Processing the final maps.

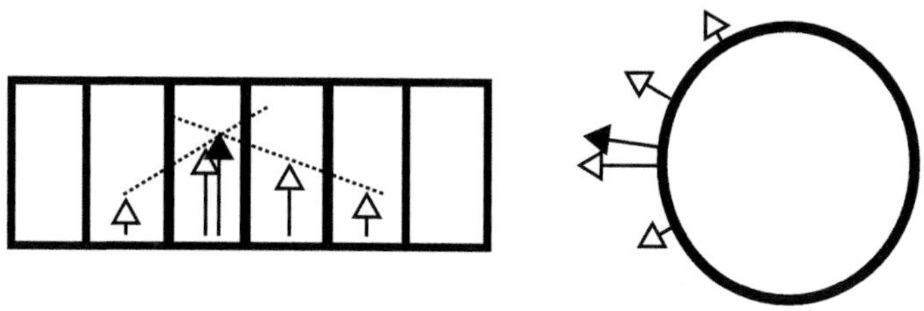

Figure 18.6

Subslot calculations.

18.4.4 Subslot Movement

You might initially think the context map is too limiting a system. The entity will always be locked to one of the slot directions, so either you need a bucketful, which sounds expensive, or you are stuck with robotic entities that can only move in very coarse directions.

It turns out we can keep the slot count low, for speed, and yet have movements in a continuous range. Once we have our target slot, we can evaluate the gradients of the interest around it and estimate where those gradients would have met. We then back-project this *virtual* slot index into world space, producing a direction to steer toward, as shown in Figure 18.6.

18.5 Racing with Context

Context steering doesn't just work for 2D entities on a plane. In fact, it is easily portable to any decision made in 1D or 2D space. Let's look at how the context steering for *F1* was implemented and how it differs from the entity example.

18.5.1 Coordinate System

We could pretend race cars moved with freedom in 2D space, but they don't. In *F1*, a low-level driver system followed a hand-placed *racing line* spline, braking for corners and accelerating down straights. The behavior system only needed to manage position on the track, rather than driving. This was done with a scalar left or right offset from the racing line. That's one of our dimensions. Although the driver will brake for corners for us, the behavior system must handle collision avoidance, so it needs to be able to slow down for emergencies. How much we want to slow down, if at all, is another scalar making our second dimension.

You can visualize the context map as a cross section of the track, with each slot representing a specific offset of the racing line, as shown in Figure 18.7. The map scales with the width of the track, with the left and right edges of the map lining up with the track edges. The racing line doesn't always map to the same slot; it will sweep from one edge of the map to the other as it moves across the track. In this and the following figures, the AI car is white.

18.5.2 Racing Line Behavior

The racing line behavior maps interest all across the track, with a peak around the racing line. It never quite reaches zero no matter how wide the track is. We only want to create a

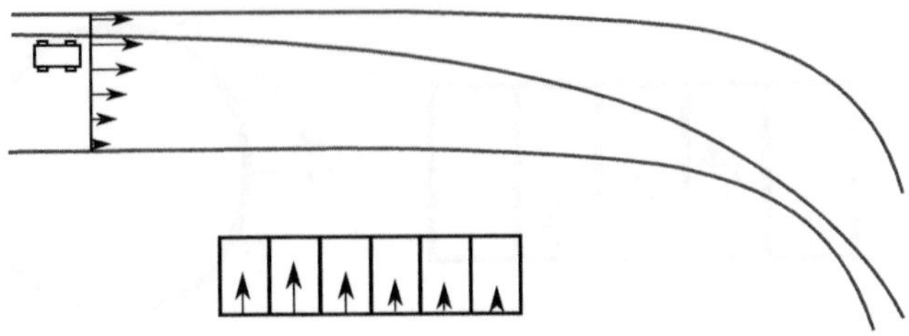

Figure 18.7

Racing line writing into interest map.

differential from slot to slot, so if the car is trapped at a far edge of the track by traffic, it always has an idea of which way is closer to the racing line and can tuck in tightly.

The behavior will write the most interest at the racing line, but never very much. Being able to reach the racing line should be good, but we want lots of room to be expressive about other interest map behaviors, while still having that important differential across the whole map.

18.5.3 Avoid Behavior

For an open-wheel racer, collision avoidance is paramount. Any type of connection (side to side or front to back) would be catastrophic. The avoid behavior evaluates all cars in the vicinity and writes danger into the map corresponding to the other car's racing line offset, with intensity proportional to the presented danger, as shown in Figure 18.8. Evaluating the danger of a car is complex. If a car is in front but at racing speed, then you should ignore them—writing danger for them will only make overtaking difficult. However, if a car is substantially below racing speed, you may need to take evasive action, so should write danger. Cars alongside are always considered dangerous. This is a good benefit of using the racing line as a coordinate system: the behavior system can be aware of a stationary car around a corner, where a raycasting approach might not see it until after the corner has been turned.

We've already seen how context steering can guarantee collision avoidance, but it can also be used more subtly. *F1* wrote high danger into the map over the width of the other car, but also a decreasing skirt of danger at the edges. This kept a minimum lateral separation between cars. The driver personality fed into this, writing wider skirts for drivers that were more cautious.

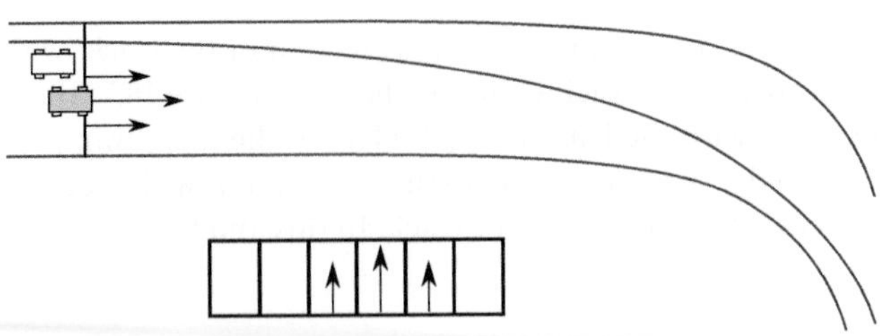

Figure 18.8

Avoid behavior written into the danger map.

18.5.4 Drafting Behavior

These two behaviors are enough for collision avoidance around a track, but it would make for quite a dull race. *F1* had four or five other behaviors that made the AI more expressive, but we'll just cover the drafting behavior.

Drafting happens when one car follows another closely and at high speeds. The trailing car doesn't need to do so much work to push air out of the way, so it can match the leading car's speed without using as much energy. At the right moment, the spare energy can be used to overtake.

F1's drafting behavior evaluated all the cars in front of the AI and scored each for "draftability." Cars going fast and near to us would score lots of points. Then the behavior would write pyramids of interest into the context maps at the corresponding racing line offset of each car, with more interest for more draftable cars, as shown in Figure 18.9.

18.5.5 Processing Context Maps

Now we have a pair of complex maps, with danger and interest in different places. How do we go from that to an actual movement? There are probably a few ways to do this that produce good consistent movement, but this is how *F1* did it.

First, we find the slot of the danger map corresponding to the car's current position on the track, shown in Figure 18.10(i). Then we walk left and right along the map, continuing as long as the danger in the next slot is less than the current. Once we cannot expand any

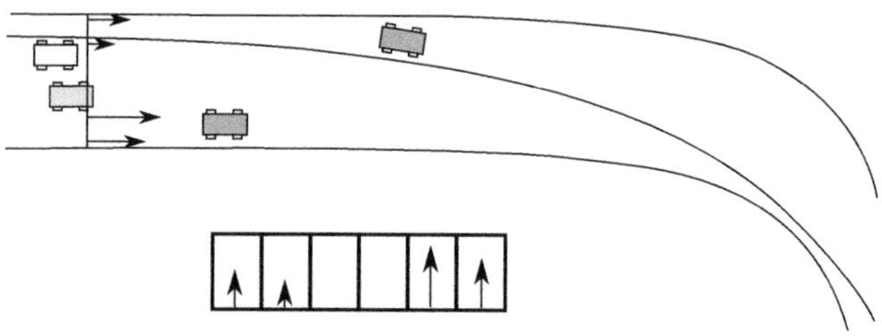

Figure 18.9

Draft behavior writing into interest map.

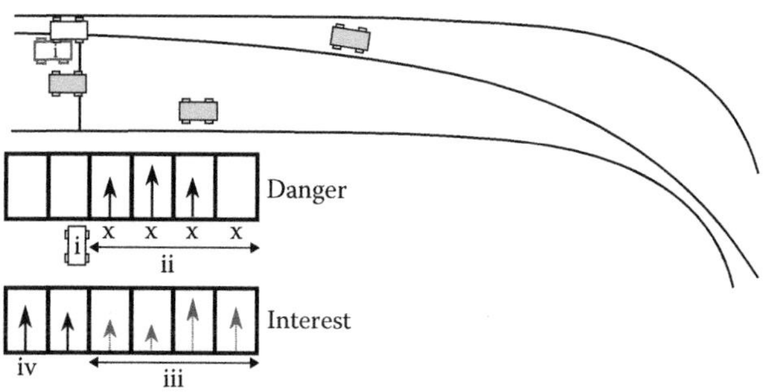

Figure 18.10

Processing the maps for a final racing line offset.

more, we mask all slots we can't reach (ii). We apply the mask to the interest map (iii) and pick the highest remaining slot (iv). The resulting movement picks the car in the far right of the figure to draft, avoiding the nearer car because it can't be reached without a collision.

This approach avoids moving into higher danger, which might represent a physical obstacle. It also stops us remaining in high danger because of high interest when there's an obvious escape route. Once we have all valid movements, it picks the most interesting of those movements.

To find out if we need to do emergency braking, we look at the highest danger across the planned journey from our current slot to the most interesting. If any slot is over some threshold of danger, we ask for braking with intensity proportional to the danger strength. We use a threshold because some danger can be informative without being a real issue, a developing situation to be aware of rather than a problem.

18.6 Advanced Techniques

There are several improvements we can make to the simple implementations outlined. These improvements are often easier to implement and maintain than their steering behavior counterparts, because they work at the level of the context map, not the individual behavior components.

18.6.1 Post-Processing

To avoid sharp spikes or troughs, we can apply a blurring function over the context maps after the behaviors have acted. As it's a global effect, it's easy to tweak and cheap to implement.

The chase behavior from our original steering behaviors example suffers from flip-flopping if the closest target oscillates back and forth between two choices. We can fix this with per-behavior hysteresis, but that adds state and complexity to behaviors. Context steering allows us to avoid flip-flopping much more easily. We can take the last update's context map and blend it with the current one, making high values emerge over time rather than instantly. This is a kind of global hysteresis that requires no support from the behaviors at all.

18.6.2 Optimizations

The overall complexity of the system is dependent on your implementation, but everything we've outlined here is linear in memory and CPU in proportion to the context map resolution. Doubling the size of the map will require twice as much memory and probably be twice as slow.

On the other hand, halving the map will double the speed. Because the system can still provide consistent collision avoidance and continuous steering even with a low-resolution map, you can construct a very granular level-of-detail controller to manage system load. Entities far from the player can be allocated small maps, producing coarser movements but requiring less system resources. Entities near the player can have more resolution, reacting to very fine details in the map. It's not very common to find an AI system that can be tweaked as subtly as this without compromising integrity.

Since the context maps are essentially 1D images, we can further optimize them using techniques from graphics programming. We can use vector intrinsics to write to and process the map in chunks, providing a massive speed up. *F1* shipped like that, and although it made the guts of the processing harder to read, the payoff was worth it. We did that late in the project, when the implementation was nailed down.

Because the behaviors are stateless, and context maps merge easily, we can multithread them or put them on a PS3 SPU. You might also consider doing the behaviors and processing in a compute shader. Be sure to profile before and after, because some behaviors may be so simple that the setup and teardown costs of this kind of solution would be dominant. Batching behaviors into jobs or structuring the whole system in a data-orientated way is also possible. Doing this with more stateful and coupled steering behaviors would be difficult.

18.7 Conclusion

Steering behaviors remains extremely useful in many situations. If your game has individual entities that will be closely watched by the player and a world with strong physical constraints, steering behaviors can break down. For games that can be represented in two dimensions, context steering offers strong movement guarantees and simple, stateless, decoupled behaviors.

References

[Reynolds 87] Reynolds, C. 1987. Flocks, herds and schools: A distributed behavioral model. *International Conference and Exhibition on Computer Graphics and Interactive Techniques,* Anaheim, CA, pp. 25–34.

[Reynolds 99] Reynolds, C. 1999. Steering behaviors for autonomous characters. *Game Developers Conference,* San Francisco, CA.

19

Guide to Anticipatory Collision Avoidance

Stephen J. Guy and Ioannis Karamouzas

19.1 Introduction

Anticipation is a key aspect of human motion. Unlike simple physical systems, like falling rocks or bouncing balls, moving humans interact with each other well before the moment of actual collision. This type of forethought in planning is a unique aspect to the motion of intelligent beings. While physical systems (e.g., interacting electrons or magnets) show evidence of oriented action at a distance, the intelligence humans show in their paths is a unique phenomenon in nature, and special techniques are needed to capture it well.

In games, the act of computing paths that reach a character's current goal is typically accomplished using some form of global planning technique (see, e.g., [Snook 00, Stout 00]). As a character moves along the path toward its goal, it still needs to intelligently react to its local environment. While, typically, there are not computational resources available to plan paths that account for every local detail, we can quickly modify a character's path to stay free of collisions with any local neighbors. In order to keep this motion looking realistic and intelligent, it is important that our characters show clear anticipation even for this local collision-avoidance routine. Consider, for example, the scenario shown in Figure 19.1, where two agents pass each other walking down the

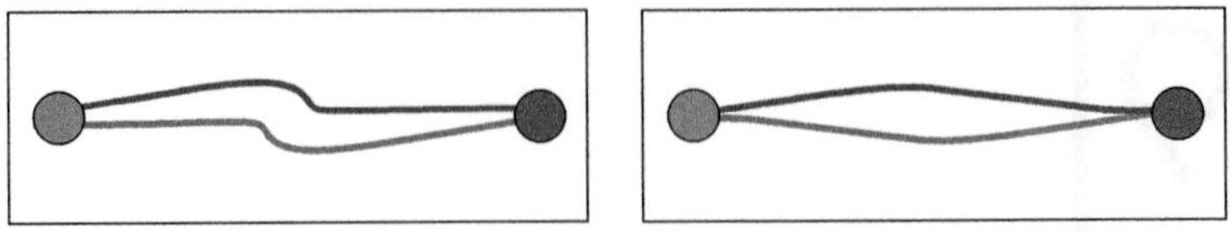

Figure 19.1

(a) Simple reactive agents versus (b) anticipatory agents. Anticipatory agents exhibit smooth and efficient motion as compared to simple reactive agents.

same path. On the left, we see the result of a last second, "bouncy-ball" style reaction—the characters will get to their goals, but the resulting motion does not display much anticipation. In contrast, the right half of the figure shows our desired, humanlike behavior, where characters are able to anticipate the upcoming collision and efficiently adapt their motions early on.

In this chapter, we will present the key ideas needed to implement this type of high-quality, anticipatory collision avoidance for characters in your game. After explaining the main concepts, we will provide a step-by-step explanation of a modern anticipatory collision-avoidance algorithm and discuss how to optimize its implementation. We will also walk through the approaches taken by modern systems used in commercial games and explain how they relate to the algorithm presented here.

19.2 Key Concepts

Before presenting our avoidance model, we need to cover some key foundational concepts. The collision-avoidance system we describe here is *agent based*. This means that each animated character a user may encounter in the current scene, no matter how complex, is described by a simple abstract representation known as an agent. Each agent has a few variables that store the state of the corresponding animated character. The exact variables used will vary from different implementations, but common agent states include position, velocity, radius, and goal velocity.

Each agent is expected to update its state as part of a larger game loop. We assume that each agent has an individual goal velocity that represents its desired speed and direction of motion, typically set by external factors such as an AI planner or a player's input. Each time through the game loop, our task will be to compute collision-avoidance behaviors for each agent. The approaches we will discuss are anticipatory, updating the positions of each agent by finding new velocities that are free of all *upcoming* collisions. In the following, we detail each variable in the agent state and give complete code for quickly determining if two agents are on a collision course.

19.2.1 Agent State

Listing 19.1 provides the complete state of each agent. Each variable is stored as an array across all the agents.

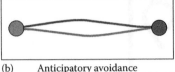

Listing 19.1. Arrays of agent state variables.

```
x = []     /* array of agent positions */
r = []     /* array of agent radii */
v = []     /* array of agent velocities */
gv = []    /* array of agent goal velocities */
```

- *Radius (float)*: We assume that the agent moves on a 2D plane and is modeled as a translating disc having a fixed radius. At any time, the center of the disc denotes the position of the agent, while the radius of the disc defines the area that is occupied by the agent and that other agents cannot step into. By choosing a larger disc than the one defined by the shoulder–shoulder distance of the animated character, we can allow larger separation distances between agents while they pass each other. In contrast, if the radius is smaller than the visualization radius, the animation engine should be able to account for such a difference (e.g., by rotating the upper body).
- *Position (2D float vector)*: A simple 2D vector of the agent's x and y position is needed to locate the agent.
- *Velocity (2D float vector)*: The agent moves across the virtual world with a certain velocity. In the absence of any other agents, this velocity is the same as the goal velocity. Otherwise, the agent may have to adapt its current velocity to ensure a collision-free navigation.
- *Goal velocity (2D float vector)*: At any time instant, the agent prefers to move toward a certain direction at a certain given speed. Together, these two components define the agent's goal velocity (for instance, a velocity directed toward the agent's goal having a unit length). In most games, the goal velocity is passed to the agent by a global navigation method or directly by the player.

19.2.2 Predicting Collisions (Time to Collision)

To exhibit intelligent avoidance behavior, an agent must be able to predict whether and when it is going to collide with its nearby agents so that it can adapt its velocity accordingly. We can use the concept of a time to collision (denoted τ) to reason about upcoming interactions. Specifically, a collision between two agents is said to occur at some time $\tau \geq 0$, if the corresponding discs of the agents intersect. Consequently, to estimate τ, we extrapolate the trajectories of the agents based on their current velocities. Then, the problem can be simplified into computing the distance between the extrapolated positions of the agents and comparing it against the sum of the combined radii of the agents.

More formally, given two agents A and B, a collision exists if

$$\left\|(x_B + v_B\tau) - (x_A + v_A\tau)\right\| = r_A + r_B. \tag{19.1}$$

Here, to estimate the extrapolated positions of the agents, we assume that the agents move at constant speed. Even though such an assumption does not always hold, it practically works very well for predicting and avoiding upcoming collisions, especially in the short run. Squaring and expanding (19.1) leads to the following quadratic equation for τ:

$$(v \cdot v)\tau^2 + 2(w \cdot v)\tau + w \cdot w - (r_A + r_B)^2 = 0 \tag{19.2}$$

where

$w = x_B - x_A$

$v = v_B - v_A$

For ease of notation, let $a = v \cdot v$, $b = 2(w \cdot v)$ and $c = w \cdot w - (r_A + r_B)^2$. Then, the aforementioned equation can be solved following the quadratic formula, allowing us to estimate the possible time to collision between the two agents: $\tau^{\pm} = \left(-b \pm \sqrt{b^2 - 4ac}\right)/(2a)$. Note that since b is a factor of 2, by setting $b = -w \cdot v = w \cdot (v_A - v_B)$, the solution can be simplified as $\tau^{\pm} = \left(b \pm \sqrt{b^2 - ac}\right)/a$, allowing us to save a couple of multiplications.

If there is no solution ($b^2 < ac$) or only one (double) solution ($b^2 = ac$), then no collision takes place and τ is undefined. Otherwise, two distinct solutions exist leading to three distinct cases:

1. If both solutions are negative, then no collision takes place and τ is undefined.
2. If one solution is negative and the other is nonnegative, then the agents are currently colliding, that is, $\tau = 0$.
3. If both solutions are nonnegative, then a collision occurs at $\tau = \min(\tau^+, \tau^-)$.

In practice, one does not need to explicitly account for all these cases. Assuming that the agents are not currently colliding, it suffices to test whether τ^- is nonnegative. Otherwise, τ is undefined. The code for computing the time to collision between two agents is given in Listing 19.2.

19.2.3 Time Horizon

It is typically not necessary (or realistic) for an agent to worry about collisions that are very far off in the future. To account for this, we can introduce the notion of a *time horizon* that represents the furthest out point in time after which we stop considering collisions. In theory, an agent can try to resolve all potential collisions with other agents that may happen in the future. However, such an approach is computationally expensive and unrealistic, since game-controlled avatars and NPCs can drastically change their behaviors well before the predicted collision happens. As such, given a certain time horizon t_H (e.g., 3 s), an agent will ignore any collisions that will happen more than t_H seconds from now. This not only reduces the running time but also leads to more convincing avoidance behavior.

Note that the time horizon can vary between agents, increasing the heterogeneity in their behaviors. An aggressive agent, for example, can be modeled with a very small time horizon (slightly larger than the time step of the simulation), whereas a large time horizon

Listing 19.2. Function to compute the time-to-collision (τ) between two agents i and j.

```
function ttc(i,j):
    r = r[i] + r[j]
    w = x[j] - x[i]
    c = dot(w, w) - r * r
    if (c < 0):      //agents are colliding
        return 0
    v = v[i] - v[j]
    a = dot(v, v)
    b = dot(w, v)
    discr = b*b - a*c
    if (discr <= 0):
        return INFTY
    tau = (b - sqrt(discr)) / a
    if (tau < 0):
        return INFTY
    return tau
```

can be assigned to an introvert or shy agent. Some examples of varying the time horizon are shown in the following section.

19.3 Prototype Implementation

Armed with the concepts of agent-based simulations, goal velocities, time horizons, and an efficient routine to compute the time to collision between two agents, we can now develop a full multiagent simulation algorithm, complete with anticipatory collision avoidance between agents. After providing method details, and code, we'll show some simple example simulations.

19.3.1 Agent Forces

At any given time, an agent's motion can be thought of as the result of competing forces. The two most important forces on an agent's path is a driving force, which pushes an agent to its goal, and a collision avoiding force, which resolves collision with neighboring agents in an anticipatory fashion. Typically, an agent's driving force is inferred from its goal velocity. If the agent is currently moving at its desired direction and speed, no new force is needed. However, if the agent is moving too fast, too slow, or in the wrong direction, we can provide a correcting force that gradually returns an agent back to its goal velocity with the following equation:

$$F_{goal} = k(v_g - v) \tag{19.3}$$

where

v_g is the agent's goal velocity
k is a tunable parameter that controls the strength of the goal force

If k is too low, agents lag behind changes in their goal velocity. If k is too high, the goal force may overwhelm the collision-avoidance force leading to collisions between agents.

In the examples later, we found that a k of 2 balances well between agents reaching their goal and avoiding collisions.

If an agent is on a collision course with any of its neighbors ($\tau \geq 0$), it will also experience a collision-avoidance force. The magnitude and direction of this avoidance force will depend on the predicted time until the collision and the expected point of impact, as detailed in the next section. The sum of all of the collision-avoidance forces from the agent's neighbors along with the goal-directed driving force will determine the agent's motion.

As part of the overall game loop, each agent performs a continuous cycle of sensing and acting with a time step, Δt. A time step begins with an agent computing the sum of all the forces exerted on it as outlined earlier. Given this new force, an agent's velocity, v, and position, x, can be updated as follows:

$$\begin{aligned} v &+= F * \Delta t \\ x &+= v * \Delta t \end{aligned} \tag{19.4}$$

which is a simple application of Eulerian integration, with the current force updating the agent's velocity and the new velocity updating the agent's position. A small time step, Δt, can help lead to smoother motion; in the examples later, we use a Δt of 20 ms.

19.3.2 Avoidance Force

Each agent may experience a unique avoidance force from each of its neighboring agents. Because this force is anticipatory in nature, it is based on the expected future positions of the agents at the time of collision rather than on the agents' current positions. The avoidance force is computed in two steps with the direction of the avoidance force being computed separately from the magnitude.

19.3.2.1 Avoidance Force Direction

To compute the direction of the avoidance force, both agents are simulated forward at their current velocity for τ seconds. The direction of the avoidance force is chosen to push the agent's predicted position away from its neighbor's predicted position as illustrated by the gray arrows in Figure 19.2a. By extrapolating an agent along their current velocity, the avoidance direction that an agent A experiences from a neighboring agent B can be computed efficiently as follows:

$$dir = (x_A + v_A * \tau) - (x_B + v_B * \tau) \tag{19.5}$$

19.3.2.2 Avoidance Force Magnitude

The magnitude of the avoidance force is inferred from the time to collision τ between the two agents. When τ is small, a collision is imminent, and a very large avoidance force should be used to prevent the collision. When τ is large, the collision will take place far in the future, and the avoidance force should have a small magnitude, vanishing to a value of zero at the time horizon t_H. There are many functions with these two properties. Here, we propose the function $(t_H - \tau)/\tau$ that is fast to compute and smoothly

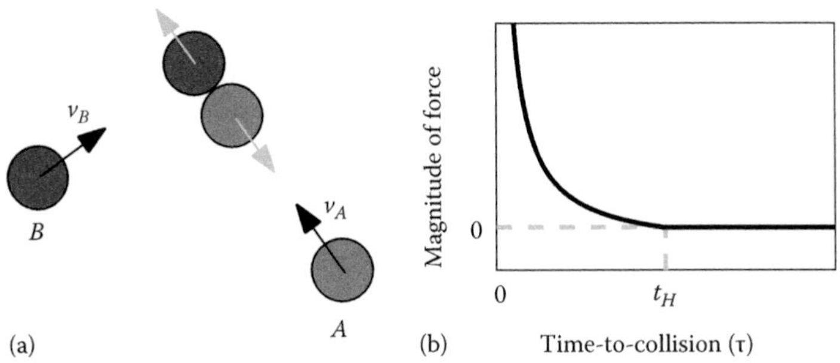

Figure 19.2

Computing the avoidance force. When agents are on a collision course ($\tau > 0$), an avoidance force is applied. (a) The *direction* of the force (gray arrows) depends on the relative positions at the moment of the predicted collision. (b) The *magnitude* of the force is based on how imminent the collision is (as measured by time to collision τ).

drops the force to zero as τ approaches t_H (see Figure 19.2b). This means the final avoidance force can be computed as

$$F_{avoid} = \frac{(t_H - \tau)}{\tau} * \frac{dir}{\|dir\|} \tag{19.6}$$

19.3.2.3 Corner Cases

If two agents are already colliding, the time to collision is zero, and the magnitude of the force is undefined. This condition can be quickly detected by comparing the distance between two agents to the sum of the radii. One option is to use a special nonanticipatory force to push colliding agents away from their current positions. In practice, we find the following simple trick to be sufficient: if two agents are colliding, shrink their radius for this one time step to just under half the distance between the agents. Most collisions between agents are quite small, and this will prevent the collision from getting any worse.

Additionally, agents who are very close and moving toward each other will have a very small time to collision. Following Equation 19.6, these agents will have very high (near infinite) avoidance forces that would dominate the response to all other neighbors. To avoid this, we can cap the maximum avoidance force to a reasonable value (we use 20 in the examples later).

19.3.2.4 Code

Listing 19.3 gives complete pseudocode implementing the collision-avoidance algorithm outlined in this section. The supplemental code corresponding to this chapter on the book's website (http://www.gameaipro.com) provides complete python code for this algorithm, including a simple scenario where agents move with heterogeneous velocities and directions on a 2D plane.

19.3.3 Runtime Performance

The aforementioned algorithm is fast to compute, and optimized implementations can compute avoidance forces for thousands of agents per frame on modest hardware. The main bottleneck in performance is actually determining an agent's neighbors. A naïve implementation might, for each agent, iterate over all other agents to see if they are on a collision course, resulting in quadratic runtime complexity. However, the pseudocode in Listing 19.3 illustrates a more efficient approach, pruning the search for nearest neighbors before computing any forces to only consider agents within a certain sensing radius (e.g., the distance that the agent can travel given its time horizon and maximum speed). The proximity computations in the pruning step can be accelerated using a spatial data structure for nearest neighbor queries, such as a *k*-d tree or a uniform grid. By selecting a fixed maximum number of neighbors for each agent, the runtime will be nearly linear in the number of agents.

19.3.4 Parameter Tuning

Any collision-avoidance method has tunable parameters that affect the behavior of the different agents. For example, agents with larger radii will move further away from their neighbors (perhaps looking more shy), and agents with a larger goal velocity will move faster

Listing 19.3. A time-to-collision-based avoidance algorithm.

```
//Precompute all neighbors for all agents (Section 19.3.3)
for each agent i:
    find all neighbors within sensing radius

for each agent i:
    F[i] = 2*(gv[i]-v[i]) //Compute goal force (Eqn. 19.3)

    for each neighboring agent j:
        //Compute time-to-collision (Section 19.2.2)
        t = ttc(i,j)

        //Compute collision avoidance force (Section 19.3.2)
        //Force Direction (Eqn. 19.5)
        FAvoid = x[i] + v[i]*t - x[j] - v[j]*t
        if (FAvoid[0] != 0 and FAvoid[1] != 0):
            FAvoid /= sqrt(FAvoid.dot(FAvoid))

        //Force Magnitude (Eqn. 19.6)
        mag = 0
        if (t >= 0 and t <= tH):
            mag = (tH-t)/(t + 0.001)
        if (mag > maxF): mag = maxF
        FAvoid *= mag

        F[i] += FAvoid

//Apply forces (Eqn. 19.4)
for each agent i:
    v[i] += F[i] * dt
    x[i] += v[i] * dt
```

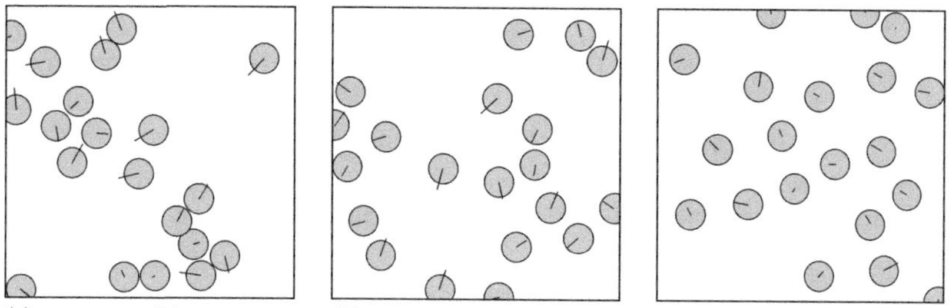

Figure 19.3

Effect of time horizon. Changing the time horizon, t_H, has a strong affect on an agent's behavior. (a) With a too small value of t_H, agents come very close and sometimes collide. (b) A moderate value of t_H produces high-quality anticipatory motions. (c) If t_H is too large, agents separate out in an unnatural way and may not reach their goals.

(looking more hurried or impatient). For an anticipatory method, one of the most important parameters to tune is the time horizon, as it has a strong affect on an agent's behavior.

Figure 19.3 shows the effect of varying the time horizon. In this scenario, every agent is given a goal velocity of moving in a random, predetermined direction at 1.5 m/s. With a very small time horizon of 0.1 s (Figure 19.3a), agents do not show any anticipation in their motion, do not avoid each other until collisions are imminent, and can even overlap. With too large a time horizon of 20 s (Figure 19.3c), agents avoid too many collisions and separate out much more than necessary, slowing the progress to their goals. Using a moderate time horizon of 4 s, the agents avoid all collisions while following their goals and show clear anticipatory motion (Figure 19.3b).

As mentioned before, the time horizon can be varied on a per-agent basis. Agents who are aggressive or impulsive can be given a smaller time horizon, and will perform many last minute avoidance maneuvers. Agents who are shy or tense can be given a larger time horizon and will react far in advance of any potential encounters.

19.4 Advanced Approaches

The collision-avoidance routine outlined earlier can provide robust, collision-free avoidance for many agents and works well in a wide variety of scenarios. However, recent work in crowd simulation and multiagent collision avoidance has gone beyond just modeling robust collision avoidance and focused on closely reproducing human behavior and providing rigorous guarantees on the quality of the motion.

19.4.1 Human Motion Simulation

Many assumptions we made in deriving the previous algorithm are unrealistic for modeling real humans. Our proposed model, for example, assumes that agents can see forever, know perfectly the radii and velocities of all of their neighbors, and are willing to come indefinitely close to any neighbors. Recent work such as the predictive avoidance method (PAM) provides some guidelines to making a more realistic model [Karamouzas 09].

19.4.1.1 Personal Space

Each agent in PAM has an additional safety distance that prefers to maintain from other agents in order to feel comfortable. This distance, along with the radius of the agent, defines the agent's personal space. When computing the time to collision to each of its nearest neighbors, an agent in PAM tests for intersections between its personal space and the radius of its neighbor. This creates a small buffer between agents when they pass each other.

19.4.1.2 Field of View

Agents in PAM are not allowed to react to all the other agents in the environment, but rather are given a limited field of view in which they can sense. Often, the exact orientation of an agent is unknown, but we can generally use the (filtered) current velocity as an estimate of an agent's facing direction. PAM agents use a field of view of ±100°, corresponding to the angle of sight of a typical human, and discard any agents who fall outside of this angle.

19.4.1.3 Distance to Collision

In PAM, agents reason about how far away (in meters) the point of collision is—defining a distance-to-collision, rather than a time-to-collision, formulation. This distance to collision is used to control the magnitude of the avoidance force. If the predicted collision point between two agents is closer than is allowed by an agent's personal space ($d_{\min}$), the magnitude of the avoidance force rises steeply to help create an "impenetrable barrier" between agents. If the distance is further away than some maximum distance ($d_{\max}$), the avoidance force will be zero. Between $d_{\min}$ and $d_{\max}$, the magnitude is shaped to reduce jerky behavior.

19.4.1.3 Randomized Perturbation

In PAM, some perturbation is introduced in the collision-avoidance routine to account for the uncertainty that an agent has in sensing the velocities and radii of its nearby neighbors. Such perturbation is also needed to introduce irregularity among the agents and resolve artifacts that arise from perfectly symmetrical patterns (e.g., two agents on antipodal positions having exactly opposite directions). This perturbation can be expressed as a force that is added to the goal and collision-avoidance forces.

Figure 19.4a provides an illustration of the concept of an agent's personal space and limited field of view. Figure 19.4b shows how the magnitude of the avoidance force falls off as a function of distance to collision. Finally, a simulation of two PAM agents was used to create the anticipatory avoidance example shown in Figure 19.1b.

19.4.2 Guaranteed Collision Avoidance

Rather than trying to closely mimic the limitations of human sensing and planning, some researchers have focused on providing mathematically robust, guaranteed collision-free motion between multiple agents. The optimal reciprocal collision avoidance (ORCA) algorithm is one such approach, which is focused on decentralized, anticipatory collision avoidance between many agents [van den Berg 11].

The ORCA method works by defining a set of formal constraints on an agent's velocity. When all agents follow these constraints, the resulting motion is provably collision-free,

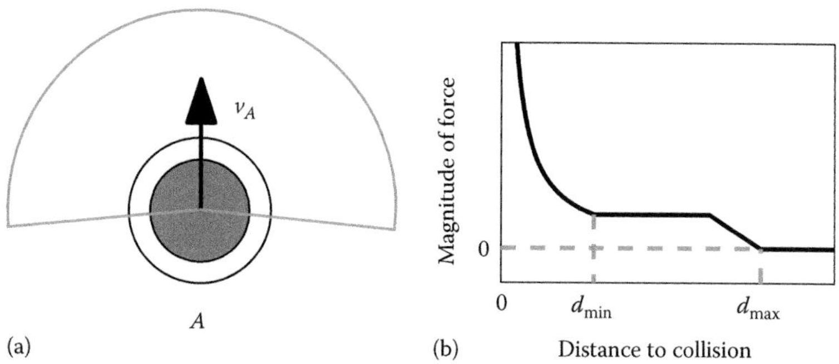

Figure 19.4

PAM agents' parameters. (a) Here, agents have a limited field of view and an extended soft personal space past their radius (dashed circle). (b) The magnitude of the avoidance force is a function of the distance to collision that rises sharply when this distance is less than d_{min} (the radius of the personal space) and falls to zero at some user-defined distance threshold d_{max}.

even with no communication between agents. In games, this formal guarantee of collision avoidance can be important, because it allows a high degree of confidence that the method will work well in challenging scenarios with fast-moving characters, quick dynamic obstacles, and very high density situations that can cause issues for many other avoidance methods.

Unlike PAM and the time-to-collision-based approach, which both use forces to steer an agent, ORCA is a velocity-based approach directly choosing a new velocity for each agent, at each time step. The idea of a velocity space can help illustrate how ORCA works. Unlike normal world space (Figure 19.5a) where each 2D point represents a position, in velocity space, each 2D point represents an agent's (relative) velocity. So the origin in

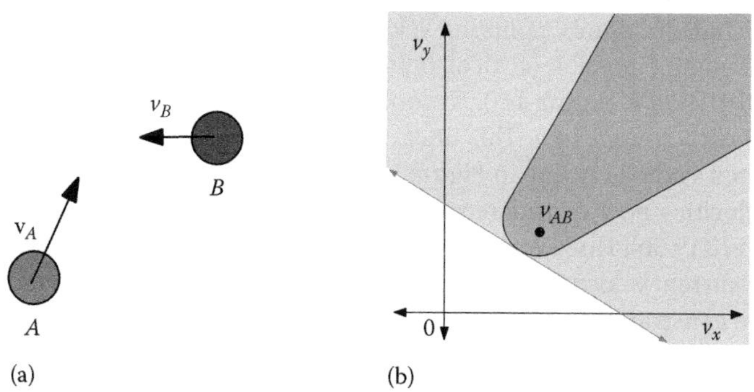

Figure 19.5

ORCA collision avoidance. (a) The world space shows the true position and velocities of two agents on a collision course. (b) Agent A's velocity space. The dark-shaded region shows the RVO (forbidden relative velocities), and the gray line shows a linear approximation of this space used by ORCA resulting in a larger forbidden region (both the light- and dark-shaded regions).

velocity space, for example, represents an agent moving at the same speed as its neighbor. We can now designate the set of all velocities that lead to a collision before a given time horizon as forbidden and prevent agents from choosing those velocities for the next time step. This set of forbidden velocities is commonly called a velocity obstacle (VO). Figure 19.5b illustrates an agent's velocity space and shades as gray the velocities that are forbidden. Because these forbidden velocities are based on future collisions, ORCA is a fundamentally anticipatory technique.

Conceptually, ORCA can be thought of as each agent on each time step, computing the VO for each of its neighbors and choosing a velocity outside the union of all VOs that is closest to its goal velocity. Unfortunately, directly implementing such an approach does not lead to great results. In practice, ORCA presents two important improvements to this simple approach in order to get efficient, stable motion. These changes derive from the key concepts of reciprocity and linearization.

In this context, *reciprocity* means the sharing of the collision-avoidance responsibility between two agents. Imagine Agents A and B on a collision course (as in Figure 19.5a). If A chooses a velocity outside of the VO, that means it has resolved the collision completely on its own and B does not need to respond anymore. Likewise, if B avoids the entire collision, A should do nothing. Both agents choosing velocities outside the VOs will overly avoid the collision resulting in inefficient motion and can ultimately lead to distracting oscillations in an agent's velocity. ORCA resolves this issue through the use of reciprocity, allowing each agent to avoid only part of the collision with the knowledge that the neighboring agent will resolve the reminder of the collision (a simple solution is to split the work 50–50 between the two agents). This modified set of forbidden velocities, which only avoid half of the collision, is known as a reciprocal velocity obstacle (RVO), which is illustrated as the dark-shaded region in Figure 19.5b.

When there are multiple neighbors to avoid, each neighbor will cast a separate RVO onto the agent's velocity. The agent should choose a new velocity outside the union of all these RVOs that is as close as possible to its goal velocity. Unfortunately, this is a complex, nonconvex space making it difficult to find an optimal noncolliding velocity. Potential approaches include randomly sampling velocities (as is implemented in the original RVO library) or testing all possible critical points that may be optimal (as implemented in ClearPath and HRVO [Gamma 14]). In contrast, ORCA avoids this issue by approximating each RVO with a single line. This linear approximation is called an ORCA constraint and is illustrated as the gray line in Figure 19.5b. The result is an overapproximation with many new velocities now considered forbidden (i.e., both the dark- and the light-gray regions in Figure 19.5b). However, the linearization is chosen to minimize approximation error near the current velocity, allowing ORCA to work well in practice. Because the union of a set of line constraints is convex, using only linear constraints greatly simplifies the optimization computation resulting in an order of magnitude speedup and allows some important guarantees of collision-freeness to be formally proved [van den Berg 11].

In some cases, the ORCA constraints may overconstrain an agent's velocity leaving no valid velocity choice for this time step. In these cases, one option is to drop constraints from far away agents until a solution can be found. When constraints are dropped in this manner, the resulting motion is no longer guaranteed to be collision-free for that agent, for that time step. However, in practice, this typically results in only minor, fleeting collisions.

A complete C++ implementation of the ORCA algorithm is available online as part of the RVO2 collision-avoidance library (http://gamma.cs.unc.edu/RVO2/). This implementation is highly optimized, using a geometric approach to quickly compute both the RVOs and the ORCA constraints for every agent. The library then uses a randomized linear programming approach to efficiently find a velocity near the goal velocity that satisfies all the ORCA constraints. Using this optimized approach, ORCA can update agents' states nearly as quickly as force-based methods, while still providing avoidance guarantees.

19.4.3 Herd'Em!

ORCA, and methods using similar geometric principles, has been integrated into many different computer games, both free and commercial. One freely available game that makes use of the library is *Herd'Em!* (http://gamma.cs.unc.edu/HERDEM/) [Curtis 10]. *Herd'Em!* simulates a flock of sheep and allows the user to control a sheepdog in an attempt to herd the sheep into the pen on the left side of the screen (Figure 19.6). The game uses a simple boids-like approach with one force pulling agents toward each other, one force encouraging some separation, and another force aligning the agents toward the same velocity. The new velocity as a result of these three forces is used to provide a goal velocity to ORCA. The ORCA simulation is set with a small time horizon, so that the flocking behavior is only modified when a collision is very imminent. This allows agents to flock nicely, while still guaranteeing collision avoidance.

The guaranteed avoidance behavior is very important once a user is added in the loop. In *Herd'Em!*, every sheep feels an additional repulsive force away from the direction of the dog. As the user controls the dog by dragging it quickly around the screen, the dog can have a very high velocity. It is also common for users to try to stress the system by steering

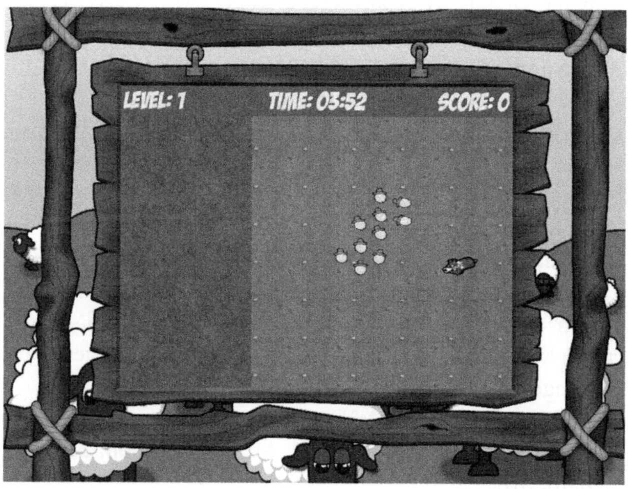

Figure 19.6

ORCA in practice. The game *Herd'Em!* combines a simple flocking method with ORCA to provide guaranteed collision avoidance of the characters under a wide variety of user inputs. (Courtesy of Dinesh Manocha, © 2012 University of North Carolina, Wilmington, NC. Used with permission.)

as many sheep as possible into a small corner. In both cases, the guaranteed avoidance of ORCA allows the simulation to remain collision-free despite the challenging conditions.

19.5 Conclusion

While anticipation in an agent's motion is a wide-ranging topic, this chapter has covered many of the most important concepts to get started understanding the many exciting new developments in this area. Agent-based modeling, force-based versus velocity-space computations, time-to-collision calculations, time horizons, and goal velocities are all concepts that are central to a wide variety of character planning and navigation topics. While the code in Listing 19.3 provides good collision-avoidance behaviors in many situations, there is still room for improvement and exploration.

One exciting area of recent interest has been applying anticipatory collision-avoidance techniques to robots [Hennes 12]. An important consideration here is to robustly account for the uncertainty caused by imperfect sensing and actuation. Other interesting challenges include incorporating an agent's anticipation into its character animation or adapting techniques such as ORCA to account for stress, cooperation, and other social factors. We hope the concepts and algorithm we have detailed in this chapter provide readers with a solid starting point for their own experimentations.

References

[Curtis 10] Curtis, S., Guy, S. J., Krajcevski, P., Snape, J., and D. Manocha. 2010. HerdEm. University of North Carolina, Wilmington, NC. http://gamma.cs.unc.edu/HERDEM/. (accessed January 10, 2015).

[Gamma 14] Manocha, D., Lin, M. et al. 2014. UNC GAMMA group's collision avoidance libraries, University of North Carolina, Wilmington, NC. http://gamma.cs.unc.edu/CA/and http://gamma.cs.unc.edu/HRVO (accessed September 10, 2014).

[Guy 15] Guy S. J. and Karamouzas, I. 2015. Python implementation of the time-to-collision based force model. Game AI Pro Website. http://www.gameaipro.com (accessed February 7, 2015).

[Hennes 12] Hennes, D., Claes, D., Meeussen W., and K. Tuyls. 2012. Multi-robot collision avoidance with localization uncertainty. In *Proceedings of the 11th International Conference on Autonomous Agents and Multiagent Systems*, pp. 147–154.

[Karamouzas 09] Karamouzas, I., Heil, P., van Beek, P., and M. H. Overmars. 2009. A predictive collision avoidance model for pedestrian simulation. In *Motion in Games, Lecture Notes in Computer Science 5884*, eds. A. Egges, R. Geraerts, and M. Overmars, pp. 41–52. Springer-Verlag, Berlin, Germany.

[Snook 00] Snook, G. 2000. Simplified 3D movement and pathfinding using navigation meshes. In *Game Programming Gems*, ed. M. DeLoura, pp. 288–304. Charles River Media, Hingham, MA.

[Stout 00] Stout, B. 2000. The basics of A* for path planning. In *Game Programming Gems*, ed. M. DeLoura, pp. 254–263. Charles River Media, Hingham, MA.

[van den Berg 11] van den Berg, J., Guy, S. J., Lin, M., and D. Manocha. 2011. Reciprocal n-body collision avoidance. In *Springer Tracts in Advanced Robotics*, Vol. 70, eds. C. Pradalier, R. Siegwart, and G. Hirzinger, pp. 3–19. Springer-Verlag, Berlin, Germany.

20

Hierarchical Architecture for Group Navigation Behaviors

Clodéric Mars and Jérémy Chanut

20.1 Introduction

It is now fairly common to find autonomous human-like characters that are able to navigate in 3D environments, finding paths and avoiding collisions while exhibiting convincing navigation behavior. In the past few years, several major publications have been applied successfully to games: we now have well-tested recipes to generate navigation meshes (nav meshes), compute paths, have pedestrians follow them, and avoid collisions in a convincing way.

However, we still fall short when it comes to group navigation. Like real groups, we want virtual humans to be able to walk down roads with their group of friends. Like real ones, virtual soldiers should be able to patrol while staying in formation. And like real ones, virtual tourists should be able to enjoy a tour of the Mont Saint-Michel following their guide's umbrella.

The aim of this chapter is to provide a base recipe to implement a group navigation system. The first two sections form an introduction, presenting the different kinds of group navigation and the basics of navigation behaviors. The next section presents our proposed hierarchical architecture, and the following sections present different aspects of its design.

20.2 Group Navigation

Taxonomy can be a daunting word, but classification can help establish a common understanding. Reading the navigation simulation literature, three main categories of approaches can be found: flocks, formations, and small "social" groups.

20.2.1 Flocks

A flock is, by definition, a group of birds traveling together. Flocking strategies for navigation can be applied for other animal species as well as humans (e.g., school children crossing the street to the swimming pool).

Entities in a flock travel at roughly the same speed and form a cohesive group without strict arrangement. Figure 20.1 showcases such a flock; you can notice that entities are not facing in the same direction and are not evenly distributed. Generally, an entity in a flock will follow independent local rules to stay in the group. While the term is primarily associated with a large number of entities, the same kind of strategy can be used for groups of only a few members.

Reynolds popularized flocking simulation in what must be the two most cited articles in the field, making their implementation a well-known subject [Reynolds 87, Reynolds 99].

20.2.2 Formations

While flocks emerge from a set of individual rules enforcing the general cohesion of the group, formations are a kind of group arrangement where members enforce a set of strict top-down rules. The first and most important one is the formation's spatial arrangement, that is, the relative positions of members; it is designed for tactical, aesthetic, or other specific purposes. Most of the time, a formation gets much of its usefulness from allocated fields of fire and sight, which is why orientation is also enforced [Dawson 02].

Figure 20.1

A flock of navigating entities.

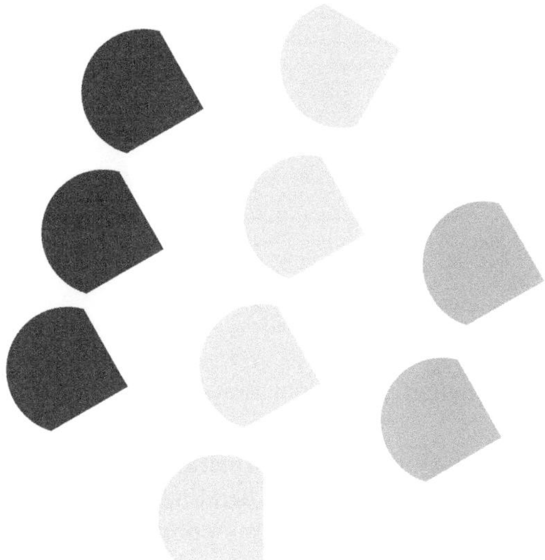

Figure 20.2

A formation of navigating entities.

The last rule is to assign entities having the right role to the right slot: archers at the back, foot soldiers facing the enemy.

Figure 20.2 showcases a formation of nine entities in three layers dedicated each to a specific role, represented by the entities' colors. As formations are important for real-time strategy games, interesting and working solutions have been known for some time: Dave Pottinger, who worked on the *Age of Empire* series, presented his in a Game Developer Magazine article, which is now available for free at Gamasutra.com [Pottinger 99].

20.2.3 Social Groups

Beyond amorphous flocks and rigid formations, groups that are more common in our everyday lives are small and their spatial configuration is the result of social factors and crowd density.

In two different surveys focusing on those small social groups, the authors showed that there are more groups than single pedestrians in urban crowds and that groups of more than four are very rare [Peters 09, Moussaïd 10].

Furthermore, it appears that the formation assumed by the observed groups is influenced both by the lateral clearance to nearby obstacles and by the need of social interaction between members of the group.

These two surveys show that social groups tend to follow three preferred formations depending on the density of the crowd. When motion is not constrained (i.e., when obstacles are far and the crowd density is low), a group tends to adopt an abreast formation that facilitates dialog between its members (leftmost formation on Figure 20.3).

When facing navigation constraints, the group compacts the formation to reduce its frontal width. And, when the lateral space between members becomes too thin, that is, when members are shoulder to shoulder, the formation is staggered. The bending of the

Figure 20.3

Social navigation formations, from left to right: abreast, V-like, lane.

group is, most of the time, forward (V-like formation—in the middle in Figure 20.3) to maintain good communication. A backward bending (inverted-V-like or wedge formation) would be more flexible moving against an opposite flow but seems to be less usual. As the crowd density increases, groups tend to form a tight lane (rightmost formation of Figure 20.3).

Another observation found in these studies is that groups tend to avoid collisions with other pedestrians or with obstacles while remaining together, but if needed, they are able to split and merge back afterward.

In the following section, we introduce a way to efficiently include the group navigation process into a software architecture.

20.3 Navigation Pipeline Architecture

Before delving into topics specific to group behaviors, in this section, we will give a quick overview of what we call *navigation behavior* and the *navigation pipeline* that makes it possible to combine them.

20.3.1 Navigation Behaviors

Typically, a navigation behavior is responsible for computing velocity changes from

- Higher-level individual orders
- Other entities (e.g., neighbors to take into account for collision avoidance)
- And, generally, the state of the world (nav mesh, scene geometry, etc.)

As illustrated in Figure 20.4, this input is usually a path to follow. Paths are computed to reach a target, which is selected by some decision-making code. It then outputs orders driving a locomotion engine that actually makes the entity move.

This architecture supports partial updates. For example, the navigation behavior and the following components can be updated on their own by reusing the previous navigation orders. This allows a compromise between costly components that do not require high reactivity (such as decision making or path finding) and cheaper ones that benefit from a high update frequency (e.g., physics or animation) [Mononen 10, RecastDetour 14].

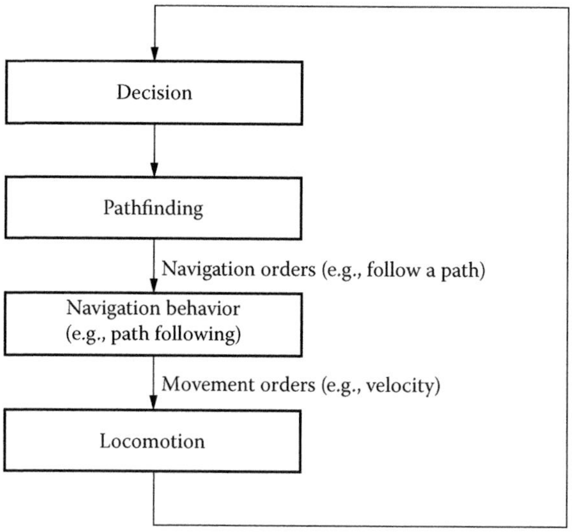

Figure 20.4

Typical character update loop involving navigation.

20.3.2 Navigation Pipeline

In real-life scenarios, entities exhibit different navigation properties and are able to handle several types of orders and constraints:

- An entity can reach a target
- Wounded and thus not walking straight
- While it is avoiding obstacles

In order to model this kind of complex behavior, we use a *navigation pipeline*: a sequence of navigation behaviors.

At runtime, the behaviors are updated sequentially, each considering the state of the entity as well as the orders output by its predecessor in the pipeline. In practice, each behavior "corrects" the orders of the previous one.

Consider the "wounded" behavior in the pipeline of Figure 20.5. The previous behavior computes a velocity that makes the entity follow a path. The "wounded" behavior will use this desired velocity as an input and compute a new one that is close to it by applying some noise function. In turn, the "collision avoidance" behavior will correct the orders to avoid future collisions. As the last behavior in the pipeline, it has the last word on the actual decision.

This architecture comes with two great benefits: modularity and reusability. In the case of groups, member entities behaviors need to take into account both the collective goals, for example, flock or stay in formation, and the individual goals, for example, avoid collisions early or minimize deviation from initial trajectory. Modeling these as navigation behaviors and using the navigation pipeline architecture gives us a flexible framework to fulfill these requirements.

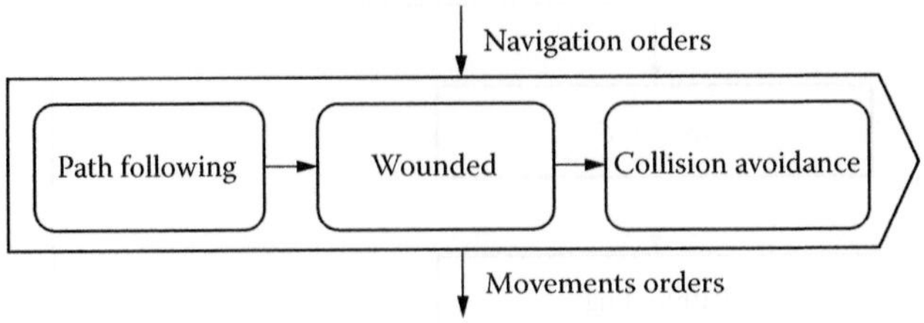

Figure 20.5

A navigation pipeline using three navigation behaviors.

In the following sections, we'll see how the navigation pipeline can be used to model the described group navigation behaviors.

20.4 Group to Members Relationship Model

While some behaviors might be decentralized, in order to manage groups in a context where we need to make them go from A to B, top-down decision making is needed [Musse 01]. A group-level process will be able to make the group move while each of its members follows. Two very different approaches can be used:

1. Make one of the group members the leader.
2. Introduce a virtual entity representing the group itself.

The two following sections will describe the two approaches through their use in the technical literature; the third will describe how we propose to implement an entity hierarchy.

20.4.1 Leader

When trying to enforce a strict equivalence between simulated entities and actual characters, many approaches rely on a leader–followers approach. With such an approach, one member of the group is the leader and the others are the followers. The leader takes responsibility for the whole group's navigation [Loscos 03, Qiu 10].
Implementation using a navigation engine for independent entities is straightforward:

- The leader is similar to any entity.
- The followers maintain a reference to their leader and follow its decisions.

However, the leader cannot reuse the exact same navigation process as an independent entity. Its navigation must take into account the bulk of the whole group as well as the different locomotion constraints of its followers. It is also better to differentiate the leader's own attributes (position, orientation and velocity) from the group's [Millington 06]. Taking all these constraints into account makes the decision-making process of the leader very different from those of the other members.

20.4.2 Virtual Group Entity

Noting that the leader-based approach has several flaws, a growing proportion of architectures chose to move the group "anchor" from the leader to a virtual group entity [Karamouzas 10, Schuerman 10, Silveira 08]. This virtual entity is similar to any other simulated entity but does not have a visual or physical representation. In such an architecture, the group members are identical to one another. The group entity creates a one-level-deep hierarchy of entities. This approach can be taken a step further to create groups of groups and so on [Millington 06, Schuerman 10], allowing a more structured crowd.

Such hierarchical separation of responsibility leads to a cleaner software architecture as well as arguably simpler behaviors, but it is also slightly more complex to implement. In the following section, we'll describe the design choices we made when doing this.

20.4.3 Hierarchical Entity Architecture

In our architecture, we build upon the virtual group entity approach to create a hierarchy of entities (see Figure 20.6). Everything is an entity and is handled in the same way in our navigation loop; groups are composites of entities.

This hierarchy allows us to differentiate the group from the individual. An individual is the most basic entity we can have in our simulation. Groups, on the other hand, are entities containing other entities. It is a fairly standard implementation of a composite pattern.

Navigation behavior algorithms need information about the entity they are working on (position, velocity, orientation, etc.). They could take these from the entity, but the situation is more complicated when working with groups, because a group's properties depend on its entities. The way to define this relationship can be tricky to get right; here are the key ideas:

- The group's position can be computed from the members as their barycenter.
- Its bulk can also be computed either as a radius or as an oriented bounding box.
- Its orientation is tricky to define from the members; the best course of action is to tie it to the group's velocity or to have specific navigation behaviors handle the group's rotation [Millington 06].
- Its maximum speed, acceleration, and other movement limits need to be computed from the entities so that they are able to follow the group. For instance, the maximum speed of the group should be below the smallest of the members' maximum speeds. It is also important to consider that the maximum rotation rate of the group needs to take into account the maximum speed of its members and the width of the group.
- Finally, its velocity is independent, as we want the entities to "follow" the group.

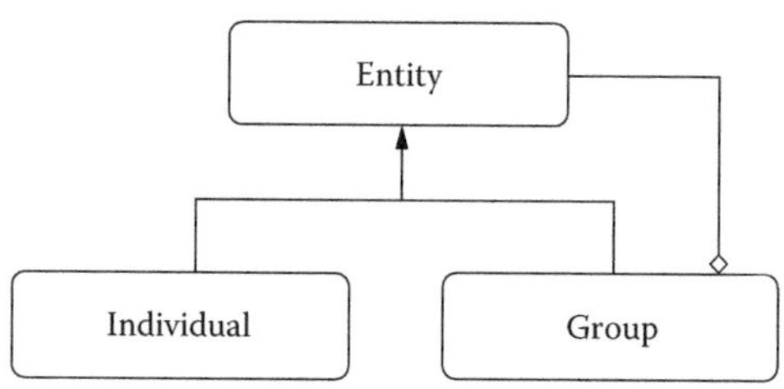

Figure 20.6

Entity hierarchy.

As we mentioned, a navigation behavior only relies on its "orders," the state of the world, and the state of the following entities:

- The one it is working on
- Its parent and/or children, used, for example, by formation slots assignment (discussed later)
- Its geometrical neighbors, used, for example, by collision avoidance

This means that it is easy to make the entities' navigation processes completely independent from one another by keeping the previous simulation update state as a read-only input. Thus, allowing easy multithreading.

One drawback is that the entity hierarchy has to be static from the point of view of the navigation behaviors. In other words, a navigation behavior cannot split or merge groups. The preferred approach to control groups' creation and membership changes is to treat the group hierarchy as an external parameter akin to a path planning target. A higher-level control layer is in charge of organizing groups; the navigation behavior should be resilient to these changes when they occur between updates.

This architecture can be used to create hierarchies with more than one level. This allows a complex structure and choreography for groups of entities with no actual additional cost.

One pitfall can be observed in deep hierarchies, however. Group members only take into account orders computed by the group during the previous simulation update, thus introducing a tiny delay. When adding layers of hierarchy, the delay grows linearly with its depth. We believe that this is not a real-world problem as a deep hierarchy does not have many use cases.

20.5 Pathfinding

One of the reasons to introduce group navigation is to factorize a costly aspect of navigation: pathfinding. As the members of a group are expected to follow the same high-level path through the environment, a single query should be sufficient for the whole group.

The most important aspect of group-level path planning is to choose how to take the bulk of the group into account. Contrary to a single entity where its bulk is static and thus is a hard constraint, a group may be able to reconfigure itself in order to pass through narrower corridors.

Therefore, the query has to be tuned in order to

- Prefer paths on which the group, in its current spatial configuration, can navigate
- Allow the use of narrower passages, for which the group can be reconfigured, if necessary

This means that the cost of falling back to a narrower spatial configuration needs to be comparable to the cost of taking a longer path [Bayazit 03, Kamphuis 04, Pottinger 99].

Once the path is computed, the path-following process provides local steering orders resulting in the entity following the path. In some works, the group-level path-following computation is also responsible for environment-aware formation adaptation, allowing the formation to change when the clearance to obstacles changes [Bayazit 03, Pottinger 99].

20.6 Emergent Group Structure

In most modern navigation engines, the simulated entities are autonomous, with their behavior relying on local "perception" to take action, not on an external choreographer. With this approach in mind, it is possible to design decentralized navigation behaviors to comply with group constraints.

20.6.1 Boids and Derivatives

At the core of Reynolds' work [Reynolds 87, Reynolds 99], three steering forces allow entities to flock. For a given entity in the group, separation makes it move away from close neighbors, alignment makes it go in the same direction as other members, and cohesion makes it move toward the group's anchor. The combination of these simple forces allows the emergence of a simple flocking behavior.

Given the nature of this model, it is simple to add new forces or to change the relative importance of forces (e.g., more or less repulsion) to better control the structure of the group. One example of such adaptation is the addition of a force modeling the desire for members of small social groups to keep all group members in their field of view for communication purposes [Moussaïd 10]. Another example is the modulation of members' attractivity to better take into account social relations [Qiu 10].

20.6.2 "Local" Formations

With the same strictly decentralized approach and by taking inspiration from molecular crystals, some formation control can be applied using an attachment site method. Each entity defines several attachment sites indicating, relatively, where its neighbors are supposed to be. When navigating, group members locate the nearest available site among their neighbors' and steer toward it.

The resulting formation arrangement is a direct result of the attachment sites position and it can scale to any number of group members. But, as the attachment rules are local, no control on the overall shape is possible; it is a good fit, though, for modeling social groups [Balch 00].

20.6.3 Implementing an Emergent Group

To get an idea of how such an emergent group structure can be implemented using our hierarchical architecture (see Figure 20.7), let us consider Boids' flocking behavior. In the by-the-book approach, given an initial velocity, the group will move cohesively in some direction. But, an adaptation is needed to control the group's movement.

Usually, a special entity is added: orders are given (e.g., a path to follow) to this leader, who "drags" the rest of the group around. Using our approach, no physical leader is needed. The group entity is the high-level order recipient and executor, and the group members use its position and velocity as an input for their cohesion and alignment behaviors.

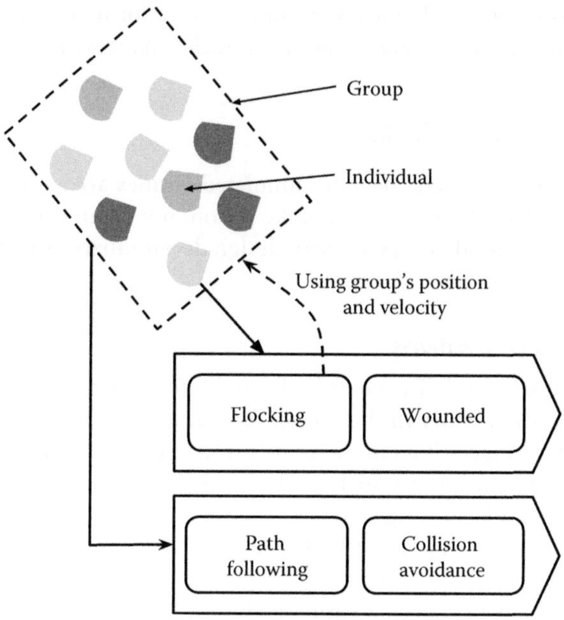

Figure 20.7

Flock architecture in our hierarchical group architecture.

The algorithm unfolds as follows during each update (the order of these is not important):

- The group updates its position and current velocity based on its members and then computes a new velocity based on a given path.
- Group members compute their new velocity based on the group's position (cohesion), the group's velocity (alignment), and the other members' relative positions (separation).

20.7 Choreographed Formations

While groups whose members are implementing local rules can exhibit convincing behavior, they cannot take into account the group as a whole and thus are not fully controllable. If exact group arrangement is needed, some of the behavior must be delegated to a higher level of control [Musse 01]. In this section, we will study the three steps needed to make a group stay in a given formation: formation design, slot assignment, and formation following.

20.7.1 Formation Design

In the context of navigation, a formation is the specification of the spatial arrangement of the members of a group. As we focus on pedestrians walking on the ground, each slot of the specification has a 2D position; two properties might be added, an orientation and a role (i.e., which kind of entity should be assigned to each slot). The slots are defined relative to the group's own position and orientation. The slots specification can come from different sources for different use cases, such as military doctrine, artistic choices, or even survey results.

The number of slots should match the number of entities in the group. If not, simple techniques can be used to select the used slots or create needed slots [Silveira 08].

20.7.2 Slots Assignment

Before our entities can navigate as a group, each of them must be assigned slot. This might seem trivial but should be implemented with care to avoid congestion between members of the same group; this will affect the credibility of the simulation. The greedy approach of each member being assigned the closest slot doesn't always work: the entities might have to cross each other's paths and the last entities might have to circle around the group to get to their slots [Dawson 02, Millington 06].

The best solution would be to globally minimize the distance the entities are covering to get to their slots but its implementation would lead to an $O(n!)$ complexity as every permutation would have to be tested.

One solution works well when no specialized slots are defined: The general idea is to sort the slots spatially then sort the members in the same way and assign the ith entity to the ith slot [Mars 14].

20.7.3 "Blind" Formation Following

The most basic approach to formation following is to have members no longer be responsible for their steering: members are placed on relative coordinates around the group's position [Pottinger 99]. This solution is fine if the group steering is robust.

Implementing this approach using our architecture is straightforward:

- The group updates its position and current velocity based on its members and then computes a new velocity based, for example, on a given path. Finally, it assigns a slot to each group member. It is also possible and often desirable to extend the group's navigation behavior with collision avoidance.
- Group members retrieve their slots and set their position accordingly.

One potential evolution of this approach is to assign group members a simple behavior that can compute and apply the necessary velocities for reaching their slot's position.

This makes it possible to customize the velocity application phase, taking into account characteristics such as maximum speed or acceleration or delegating it to an external system (e.g., locomotion).

When using this strategy, it is important to extrapolate the slot position to make it nonreachable in a single simulation update. This will contribute to avoid motion jolts [Karamouzas 10, Schuerman 10]. In practice, a simple extrapolation of the slot position using the group velocity over a time period greater than the frame duration is enough. This computation also handles gracefully nonmoving groups, as their velocity is null.

Additionally, the extrapolation time period can be controlled to define the "cohesion" of the formation, a small value for a tight formation a larger one for a very "loose" formation. The farther the target is, the less it will impact the member velocity.

20.7.4 Autonomous Formation Following

In most instances, members of a formation do not follow orders blindly. Instead, they have an autonomous strategy to stay in formation. This is especially true when simulating small social groups, where the formation is more of an emergent feature than a strict rule. Furthermore, it allows entities to break formation to pass through tight corridors and around small obstacles [Silveira 08].

This use case is where our architecture shines. The same strategy as before can be applied and, to enhance the individuality of the members, their behavior can be extended with (as shown in Figure 20.8)

- Collision avoidance, so that groups do not have to micromanage everything to avoid collisions between their members
- Specific behaviors, allowing entities to have "subgoals," for example, attraction to store fronts
- Specific velocity noise functions, to give them "personality"

While the same collision avoidance behaviors can be used by the entities whether they are part of a group or not, they must be adapted. As a matter of fact, collision avoidance algorithms, such as Reciprocal Velocity Obstacle [van den Berg 08], try to enforce a safe distance to obstacles and other entities that might forbid close formations [Schuerman 10].

To mitigate this issue, a member's behavior needs to either differentiate between its peers (other members of the group) and the other entities or to be adapted when it is part of a group by, for example, only considering imminent collisions.

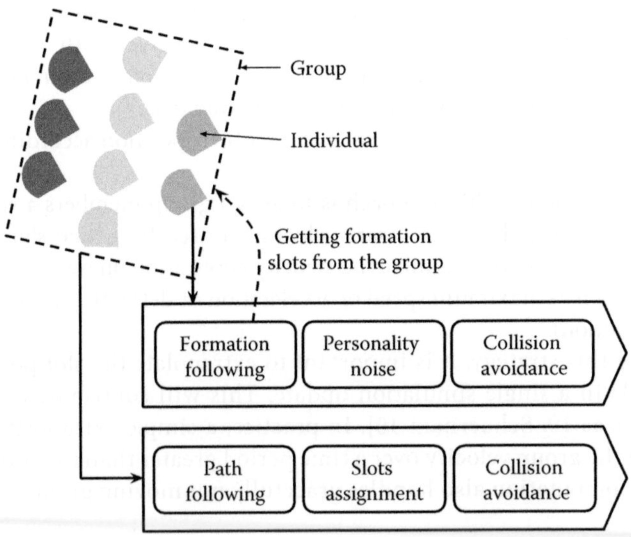

Figure 20.8

Autonomous formation following.

20.8 Group Collision Avoidance

In real life, groups tend to stay coherent when navigating between obstacles and among other pedestrians, which is why it is interesting to use group-level collision avoidance. Many existing algorithms for entities can be applied directly or adapted for group-level collision avoidance. As we noted earlier, the main difference between groups and single entities is that their bulk is not a hard constraint. The spatial configuration of a group can be adapted to occupy less frontal space, less longitudinal space, or both.

20.8.1 Velocity Correction

Existing collision algorithms such as RVO can be applied by considering the bulk of the group as a disc. The resulting collision avoidance is very conservative as the disc is, most of time, greatly overestimating the real footprint of the group [Schuerman 10, van den Berg 08].

To get better results, navigation behaviors of this family can be adapted to reason on the group's oriented bounding box [Karamouzas 04, Karamouzas 10, Peters 09].

20.8.2 Formation Adaptation

As discussed for path following, groups can spatially reconfigure themselves to change their bulk; this idea can be applied for better collision avoidance.

Consider a couple, walking side by side in a corridor: a simple formation. When another pedestrian arrives in the opposite direction, the couple will form a lane, reducing their frontal bulk, allowing the crossing. This is an instance of formation adaptation.

In RVO-like collision avoidance algorithms, several candidate velocities are computed around the current velocity, the ones leading to future collisions are pruned and the remaining one closest to the desired velocity is kept. The same approach can be used for formation adaptation [Karamouzas 10]:

- Define a set of formations the group can use and its preferred one (cf. Section 20.2.3 for social groups).
- At each time step, interpolate a number of candidate formations from the group's current state to the formations of the initial set.
- For each candidate formation, do an RVO-like evaluation outputting its "best" velocity and time to collision.
- Compute a cost for each candidate that take into account those values and the distance to the preferred formation.
- Take the lowest cost.

It is important to limit the number of candidate formations to preserve the performance of the algorithm. The original work uses a set of five formations and interpolates three candidates to each one of them, thus evaluating 15 in total.

Those group-level navigation methods allow the group to take responsibility for a part of the collision avoidance and more easily preserve the group cohesion. They can be easily implemented in our architecture as group behaviors and combined with finer granularity entity level steering.

20.9 Conclusion

In this chapter, we introduced a hierarchical architecture for group navigation, and we have shown how it can be used to fulfill different use cases, flocks, formations, and social groups, leveraging existing work. We proposed a generic framework to design and implement group navigation. A similar architecture was already implemented as a part of the Golaem SDK [GolaemSDK 14] and it is our plan to implement it in the open source navigation engine Recast/Detour [RecastDetour 14].

Externalizing some of the tricky collaborative decision making to a virtual group entity is one of the major design choices we made. Such "choreographer" entities are also a good pattern to apply when a high degree of control is needed over a group of individuals: traffic management around a door, group discussions, tactical synchronization, combat pacing, etc. Moreover, as we have shown in the context of navigation, this centralized decision-making method does not come at the cost of the individuality of each entity's behaviors.

References

[Balch 00] Balch, T. and Hybinette, M. 2000. Social potentials for scalable multi-robot formations. In *IEEE International Conference on Robotics and Automation*, San Francisco, CA, pp. 73–80.

[Bayazit 03] Bayazit, O., Lien, J., and Amato, N. 2003. Better group behaviors in complex environments using global roadmaps. In *Eighth International Conference on Artificial Life*, Department of Computer Science, Texas A&M University, College Station, TX, pp. 362–370.

[Dawson 02] Dawson, C. 2002. Formations. In *AI Game Programming Wisdom*, ed. Rabin, S., pp. 272–282. Charles River Media, Hingham, MA.

[GolaemSDK 14] Golaem SDK. 2014. Available from: http://golaem.com/ (accessed July 10, 2014).

[Kamphuis 04] Kamphuis, A. and Overmars, M.H. 2004. Finding paths for coherent groups using clearance. In *ACM SIGGRAPH/Eurographics Symposium on Computer Animation*, Copenhagen, Denmark, pp. 19–28.

[Karamouzas 04] Karamouzas, I. and Overmars, M. 2004. Simulating human collision avoidance using a velocity-based approach. In *VRI-PHYS 10: Seventh Workshop on Virtual Reality Interactions and Physical Simulations*, Eurographics Association, Copenhagen, Denmark, pp. 125–134.

[Karamouzas 10] Karamouzas, I. and Overmars, M. 2010. Simulating the local behaviour of small pedestrian groups. In *17th ACM Symposium on Virtual Reality Software and Technology*, Hong Kong, China. Center for Advanced Gaming and Simulation, Utrecht University, Utrecht, the Netherlands, pp. 183–190.

[Loscos 03] Loscos, C., Marchal, D., and Meyer, A. 2003. Intuitive crowd behaviour in dense urban environments using local laws. In *Proceedings of the Theory and Practice of Computer Graphics*, Manchester, U.K., p. 122.

[Mars 14] Mars, C. 2014. Simple formation assignment. *GDC 2014 AI Summit*, San Francisco, CA.

[Millington 06] Millington, I. 2006. *Artificial Intelligence for Games*, pp. 41–202. Morgan Kaufmann, San Francisco, CA.

[Mononen 10] Mononen, M. 2010. Navigation loop. In *Paris Game/AI Conference 2010*, Paris, France.

[Moussaïd 10] Moussaïd, M., Perozo, N., Garnier, S., Helbing, D., and Theraulaz, G. April 2010. The walking behaviour of pedestrian social groups and its impact on crowd dynamics. *PLoS ONE*, 5(4):e10047.

[Musse 01] Musse, S. and Thalmann, D. 2001. Hierarchical model for real time simulation of virtual human crowds. *Transactions on Visualization and Computer Graphics*, 7(2):152–164.

[Peters 09] Peters, C., Ennis, C., and O'Sullivan, C. 2009. Modeling groups of plausible virtual pedestrians. *IEEE Computer Graphics and Applications*, 29(4):54–63.

[Pottinger 99] Pottinger, D. January 1999. Implementing coordinated movement. Available from: http://www.gamasutra.com/view/feature/3314/implementing_coordinated_movement.php?print=1 (accessed May 21, 2014).

[Qiu 10] Qiu, F. and Hu, X. 2010. Modeling dynamic groups for agent-based pedestrian crowd simulations. In *IEEE/WIC/ACM International Conference on Web Intelligence and Intelligent Agent Technology*, Toronto, Canada, pp. 461–464.

[RecastDetour 14] Recast/Detour. 2014. Available from: https://github.com/memononen/recastnavigation (accessed July 10, 2014) and https://github.com/masagroup/recastdetour (accessed July 10, 2014).

[Reynolds 87] Reynolds, C. 1987. Flocks, herds and schools: A distributed behavioral model. In *ACM SIGGRAPH '87 Conference Proceedings*, Anaheim, CA, pp. 25–34.

[Reynolds 99] Reynolds, C. 1999. Steering behaviors for autonomous characters. In *Proceedings of Game Developers Conference*. Miller Freeman Game Group, San Francisco, CA, pp. 763–782.

[Schuerman 10] Schuerman, M., Singh, S., Kapadia, M., and Faloutsos, P. 2010. Situation agents: Agent-based externalized steering logic. In *International Conference on Computer Animation and Social Agents*, University of California, Los Angeles, CA.

[Silveira 08] Silveira, R., Prestes, E., and Nedel, L. 2008. Managing coherent groups. *Computer Animation and Virtual Worlds*, 19(3–4):295–305.

[van den Berg 08] van den Berg, J., Lin, M., and Manocha, D. 2008. Reciprocal velocity obstacles for real-time multi-agent navigation. In *International Conference on Robotics and Automation*, Pasadena, CA, pp. 1928–1935.

21

Dynamic Obstacle Navigation in *Fuse*

Jan Müller

21.1 Introduction

Climbing over obstacles like walls, ledges, or ladders plays a supporting role in video games: they are not usually central to the experience, but they stand out when done poorly or omitted entirely. There are, of course, exceptions to the rule, games like *Mirror's Edge* [EA 08] or *Tomb Raider* [CD 14] that make the climbing sections, so called *traversal*, the core gameplay element. Traversal makes the AI navigation more complicated: it requires additional markup and programming for the AI to understand how to mount a ladder or jump over a wall, not to mention special animation states to control their location as they jump, vault, climb, or swim. As a result, video games with very complex or varied AI characters tend to avoid climbing altogether. Instead, AI navigation [Snook 00] is usually limited to finding paths on a continuous mesh [Mononen 12], where the actors can walk or run everywhere they need to go.

Traversal is hard enough if we have consistency between obstacles, that is, if all jumps are the same length and all walls the same height, so that there is a single solution to any locomotion problem. What if it is more complicated? What if there are hundreds of different volumes placed by either a designer or a content creation tool, each with different attributes and the AI has to decide which ones to consider based on the real time context? In the game *Fuse* [IG 13], from Insomniac Games, four hero agents with different abilities fight cooperatively. Of those four actors, up to three can be under AI control at any given time. Furthermore, we had a complex and highly varied environment, making locomotion more challenging. In contrast to many games with cooperative NPCs, we wanted to make our AI characters follow the same rules as a human player. They aren't tougher to kill, can't teleport to keep up with the player, and need to be able to follow the same gameplay mechanics with regard to activities like climbing a ladder or manning a turret. It is crucial for the game balance that the AI plays as well as a human—not better or worse. The rule we ended up with is "50/50," meaning that half of the total damage is dealt by human players and the other half should be dealt by the AI (assuming that at least two of the four heroes are AI controlled, of course).

To make things even more challenging for the AI, *Fuse* features the *leap* ability, which allows human players to switch from their current character to any of the other heroes that isn't already being controlled by another human player. The game does not restrict leaps to any specific time or place; you can leap in the middle of combat just as easily as during a traversal section. Furthermore, players can drop in or out of the game at any time, and all of this has to work in a peer-to-peer online environment.

The result of all of this is that there can be no cheating. Whatever the human player is capable of doing, the AI has to be able to do it too. Whatever situation the human player is in, he or she can leap to another character (or drop out of the game), leaving the AI to deal with it. This circumstance leads to volatile AI characters that must be able to function smoothly when they initialize halfway through a nontrivial traversal section. Imagine waking up to find yourself hanging one-handed from a ledge 50 ft above the ground, while your enemies are firing semiautomatic rifles at you and a teammate is in need of medical attention down at the bottom. In such a context, the AI cannot rely on markup alone, but needs to evaluate dynamically changing traversal paths at runtime.

21.2 Fuse Traversal Setups

Fuse has numerous, wide-ranging traversal sections. To give players a break between fights, the protagonists will often have to climb obstacles like a mountain side or sewage pipes below a medieval castle in India. These setups usually have three or four possible ascents, which intersect at various points. In addition to the complexity of the ascent itself, there are often enemy bots or turrets that can shoot at you during the climb. When a character is hit, he or she can fall down to the ground and become incapacitated. If that happens to the player, the AI has to be able to find a path down to revive him.

On the content-authoring side, these traversal setups are represented as a group of volumes with different markup options. The most common types of such volumes are vertical pipes and horizontal ledges, as well as variations of those such as ladders. Depending on their attributes and the situation, you can perform different climb animations. For example, you might hang from a ledge and traverse with your hands or mount it to stand on top of it. Connections between volumes may be explicitly marked in the places where they intersect or overlap, or they are implicitly allowed through jump and drop thresholds. To determine whether an actor, be it human or AI controlled, can jump from one ledge to the next, we match their attributes and then perform distance and collision tests between the two points closest to each other. Additionally, we place custom clues that connect the navigation mesh between the start and end of the traversal section. These elements

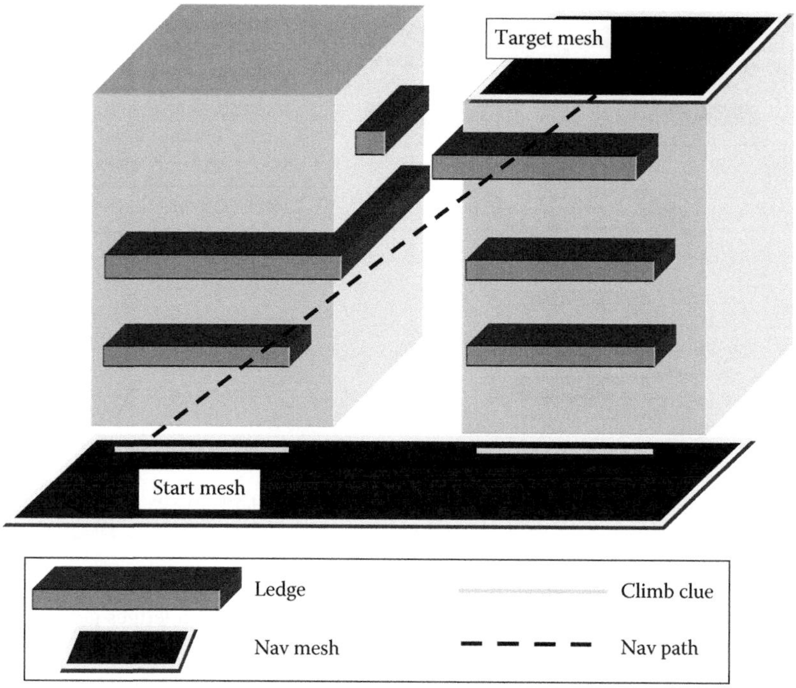

Figure 21.1

A traversal section with ledge markup and navigation path between two meshes.

together provide enough information for the AI to parse the traversal and generate a climb path procedurally. For a typical traversal section in *Fuse*, refer to Figure 21.1. For simplicity's sake, we exclude vertical elements, like pipes or ladders. However, their connections within the climb mesh work the same way as the horizontal elements.

The navigation path in Figure 21.1 connects two disjoint navigation meshes. It creates a link between the start and the end point of the traversal. The path is a straight line between these two climb clues, since the navigation system has no further information about the connecting climb.

21.3 Climb Mesh Generation

The first step of the procedural traversal system is to generate the climb mesh. It collects all possible traversal elements from a group of traversal volumes and creates connections between them. Each connection can link to multiple other traversal elements, but the most common case is that there are no more than one or two connections per node. The system first considers touching or overlapping volumes, which explicitly link two elements together. If two elements touch each other at their end points, they share one merged node in the climb mesh and create explicit connections. For example, if a ledge touches a pipe at a cross section, they share a node at their intersection that forms edges to the start and

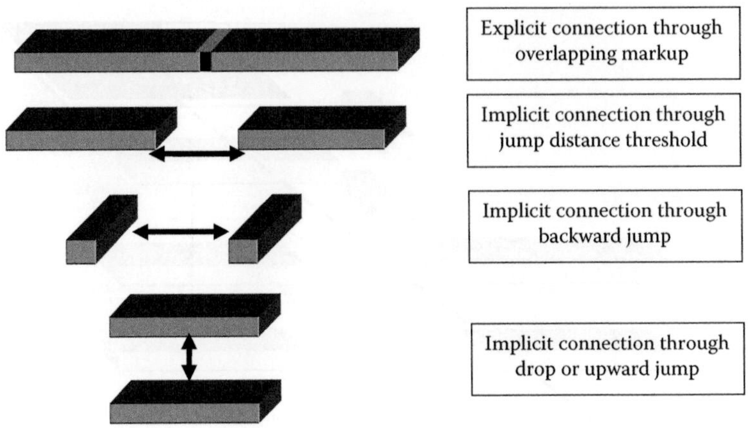

Figure 21.2

Possible connections between two ledge elements in the climb mesh.

end of the ledge as well as the pipe element. If two ledges intersect at their end points, they form an explicit connection between them. Examples of two ledges generating links between each other can be seen in Figure 21.2.

Once all explicit connections have been generated, the system searches for implicit links like jumps or drops. Players can jump between two elements at any time, as long as certain distance and angle thresholds are not exceeded. For simplicity's sake, the *Fuse* AI considers such transitions in the climb mesh only from the end points and between the center points of the volume markup, although other transitions would be possible. Thus, for every traversal element, the algorithm tests three nodes for implicit links to nearby elements. Alternately, you can generate these links at fixed intervals, for example, one per meter, but that has an impact on both the mesh complexity and the parsing resolution. We discuss those implications in the section on generating a virtual controller input (VCI).

The node connections are stored in the climb mesh. Cyclic connections are allowed and are resolved in the path generation step by marking already visited nodes. At this level of abstraction, the actual animation that moves a character from one climb element to the next does not matter. That means a connection between two elements could result in a jump animation for one character and in a swing animation for another. Only the type and distance of the connection, as well as line of sight tests between its elements, are considered. Figure 21.3 illustrates the climb mesh that the example in Figure 21.1 would generate, including all of its nodes and connections.

21.3.1 Path Following on Climb Meshes

As mentioned before, the climb meshes are independent from our navigation system, which only knows about the existence of the traversal, not its layout. When an actor needs to pass through a traversal section, the navigation system returns a path that includes two special clue edges that connect the start and end points of the climb. The clue edges are placed by the level designer and represent the traversal section within the navigation system.

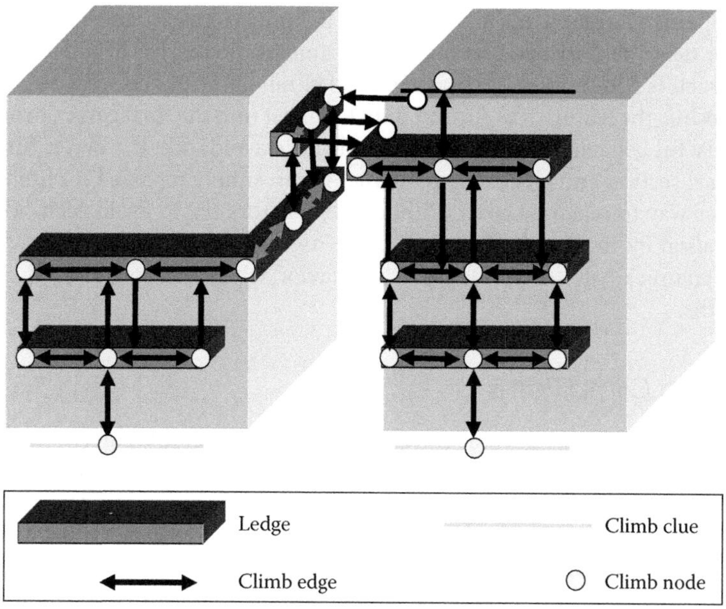

Figure 21.3

The fully generated climb mesh with all possible transition edges.

It does not store any further information about the climb elements or connections. The navigation system only knows the distance between two climb clues and that a climb has to happen to move the character from edge A to B and continue the path from there.

Within the climb mesh, the closest point from the climbing actor on the custom clue is added as the initial climb node. From there, the traversal system triggers a secondary path query that follows the traversal nodes between the start and end clues. Path following on climb meshes utilizes a standard A* search. It searches from the initial climb node and iterates through the neighboring edges, starting with the least-cost candidate, meaning the closest to the target node. Each step of the pathfinding parses the links from the current node to connected nodes in the climb mesh, marking those it already visited as closed. When a path to the target node is reached, then all nodes of that path are returned as a set of 3D vectors. The result is the shortest path on the climb mesh that connects two custom clues on the navigation mesh.

21.3.2 Caveats of the Climb Path Generation

The traversal system in *Fuse* does not consider different costs per traversal element and does not store how long specific animations take to play back. The edge costs are generally normalized within the climb mesh and increased only if other bots use the same climb elements on their path. This means that the shortest path does not necessarily take the least amount of time. However, since there are usually only a few routes to choose from in *Fuse*, avoiding other characters is of higher importance than finding the shortest-time path.

At one point during development, there was a plan to support combat during climbing. This involved shooting from climb elements as well as being incapacitated by hits. If this were to happen to the player while he or she was hanging from a ledge, the character would hang on for dear life until another teammate came to the rescue. In order to allow this, the AI characters had to be able to parse partial climb paths to and from any location on the mesh. While the feature was cut and didn't make it into the final game, it enabled us to add other useful behaviors such as dynamic obstacle avoidance. If a player turns around on a traversal section and blocks the path, the AI can simply reparse the climb mesh and find another way to reach its goal. Without it, AI actors try to avoid each other during path generation by increasing the costs of the used climb edges. But the system is not updating dynamically based on the player's behavior, which can lead to traffic jams along blocked paths.

21.4 Parsing Climb Paths

The second part of the procedural traversal system is the climb parser. The hero AI in *Fuse* shares about half of its implementation with the player controlled characters. This is possible by splitting hero character states into drivers and processors: drivers are responsible for the state input and transition logic. For human players, this means interpreting controller inputs and context into animation parameters. For AI actors, these transitions are controlled by their behaviors and VCI. While drivers are fundamentally different between human and AI characters, the state processors can be shared. The state processor interprets driver updates and communicates with the animation tree of the character. The reuse of hero state processors means that the hero AI automatically inherits all traversal animations from the player characters.

The climb parser generates the VCI for AI-controlled characters. The state transition logic then compares the input data against animation thresholds to determine when, for example, a ledge climb animation can transition into a jump to a nearby pipe. Once the first traversal state has been initialized, the AI behavior strictly follows the VCI and the current state's transition logic. Thus, during the traversal, there is no decision making in place beyond following the VCI, adhering to the state transitions thresholds (including terminating states like the death of the character), and checking against collision with geometry and other characters.

21.4.1 Generating Virtual Controller Input

To generate VCI, the climb parser first resolves the climb path as a Bézier spline curve [DeBoor 78, Farin 97]. Curves in Bézier form are defined as a set of four control points that span a curve between each other. A Bézier spline is a continuous set of such curves that form a smooth, higher-order shape. Such splines can be straight lines, only spanning between two points, but also complex curves with dozens or hundreds of control points. Using the path points as input data for a Bézier curve automatically interpolates the path and creates better results than the raw input data with 90° turns. The reason for this is that the additional curve points add angular momentum to the path. A simple example is a 180° turn around 2 corners: in its raw form, the path is only as long as the total length of its three sides and incorporates two sharp, 90° turns. A spline following the same control points however will extrude the curve to avoid sharp angles, which adds length and curvature to the path.

This is important because the system projects the VCI target on that curve at a fixed distance of 2.8 m ahead of the AI actor from its current position on the spline curve. A traversal move resolution of 2 m gave the best results for the climb animations in *Fuse* but might differ in other games. Many transitional animations move the character by roughly this distance and need to trigger ahead of a directional change to look smooth. The projection distance is the length of the diagonal of a $2 \times 2\ m^2$ square, which is roughly 2.8 m. That also means that the climb parser is not accurate if there are multiple intersections within a 2 m radius (plus a certain margin for error) and generally speaking chooses the closest one. For example, if there were two vertical pipes intersecting a ledge 1 m apart, the parser would pick the closest one (based on the approach direction). This occurs because the Bézier curve doesn't follow the raw path data precisely, so when two elements are close together, the algorithm can't tell which one was originally on the A*-generated path. Regardless, this doesn't necessarily impact the result. When this happens in *Fuse*, it always appears correct if the parser chooses the closest element.

The 3D vector between the current actor position on the spline curve and the projected VCI target is the VCI vector as depicted in Figure 21.4. The parser generates input strength values for all three axes relative to the character. Those input values are then tested against thresholds for different transitions. A transition in this sense does not necessarily mean jumping or climbing to another element but also transitioning from an idle animation to a climb animation on the existing one. Each climb state has individual thresholds in its transition functions that define the points where characters can switch from one state

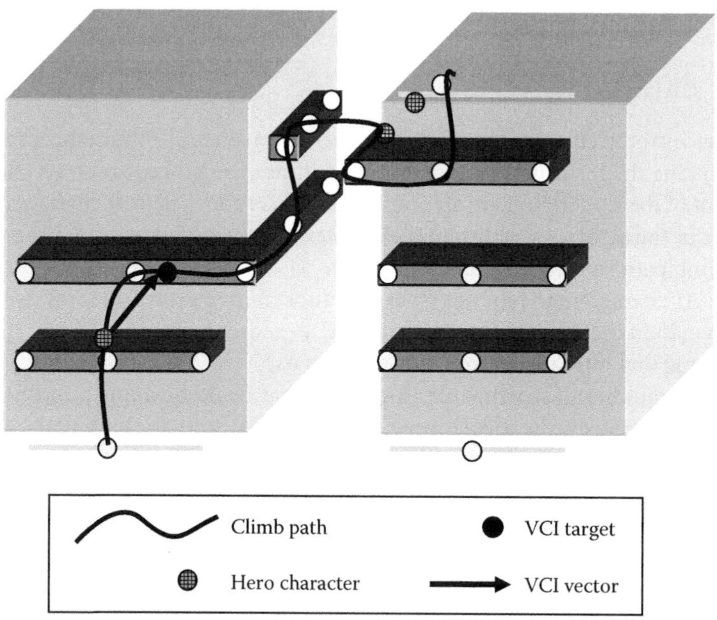

Figure 21.4

The VCI generates a 3D vector between the current actor position and the immediate, projected target position.

to another. For example, if the input vector mostly points to the relative right of the character while he or she is hanging from a ledge, he or she will start climbing to the right. If the character gets into the proximity of a pipe element and the input vector points to the right and top, he or she will transition to the vertical climb animation, attach to the pipe, and start climbing upward. This sequence of traversal animations ends when a terminating state is reached. Examples for such states are mounting the top of a wall or dropping from a ledge back onto the navigation mesh. The system also supports depth transitions such as jumping backward between two parallel ledges on opposing walls or flipping over the top of a flat wall.

There are a limited number of entry states for traversal sections, such as mounting a ladder or jumping up to a ledge above the initial climb node. This makes the transition from walking or running to climbing relatively predictable. The most common case has the VCI vector pointing up or down at the traversal start. In that case, the climb could start by attaching to a ladder or jumping up or down to a ledge. Once the traversal state has been initialized, the VCI target is projected forward on the climb path as described. The state treats the VCI data the same way it would interpret human controller input and matches the values against transition thresholds. In the example in Figure 21.4, the initial jump-up state would transition to a ledge hang state, which would be followed by another jump, since the VCI mostly points upward. Once the character reaches the second ledge, the VCI would point to the relative right side of the character, which leads to a ledge move animation. The character would follow the climb path until eventually reaching the final ledge and playing a mount animation at the top of the traversal section. That state would terminate the climb so that we can return the AI to the navigation mesh.

21.5 Conclusion

This chapter introduced an approach to generating traversal climb meshes from markup and to following the resulting climb paths at runtime. The procedural traversal system is independent of the underlying animation states and is robust against changes in the locomotion sets of the actors. In addition, the chapter demonstrated how VCI can be utilized to parse climb paths along a Bézier spline curve. Using climb paths in combination with VCI allows AI characters to handle traversal setups in much the same way as they would normal navigation meshes. It also allows the AI to share the same traversal markup and transition logic that human-controlled characters use.

There are a number of worthwhile extensions that could be applied to this approach: as mentioned previously, the algorithm can be modified so that climb paths can be generated between any two locations within the climb mesh. This allows dynamic obstacle avoidance and path replanning. Games with mid-climb combat elements would especially benefit from those features.

Furthermore, using Euclidean distance as the edge cost worked well for *Fuse*, but might not be accurate enough for more complex climbing setups. If this approach is implemented for a game with very long or complex traversal segments, then the climb path generation should consider animation playback times to accurately detect the shortest path.

References

[CD 14] Crystal Dynamics. 2014. *Tomb Raider* [PC, Xbox 360, PS3]. Redwood City, CA.

[DeBoor 78] de Boor, C. 1978. *A Practical Guide to Splines*. Springer Verlag, New York.

[EA 08] Electronic Arts DICE. 2008. *Mirror's Edge* [Xbox 360]. Stockholm, Sweden.

[Farin 97], Farin, G. 1997. *Curves and Surfaces for Computer Aided Geometric Design*, 4th edn. Academic Press, San Diego, CA.

[IG 13] Insomniac Games. 2013. *Fuse* [Xbox 360, PS3]. Burbank, CA.

[Mononen 12], Mononen, M. 2012. Recast and Detour, a navigation mesh construction toolset for games. http://code.google.com/p/recastnavigation/ (accessed July 21, 2014).

[Snook 00] Snook, G. 2000. Simplified 3D movement and pathfinding using navigation meshes. In *Game Programming Gems*, pp. 288–304. Charles River Media, Newton, MA.

Section IV
Applied Search Techniques

22

Introduction to Search for Games

Nathan R. Sturtevant

22.1 Introduction

Search techniques are broadly used outside of video games, but search is not widely used in current video games, outside of its ubiquitous use in path planning. As a result, many books about artificial intelligence (AI) in games do not usually dedicate significant resources to describing general search techniques and their application. However, the use of search appears to be growing, and thus a section of this book is dedicated to search-specific techniques. The purpose of this chapter is to give some introduction and justification of why and when search will be a useful technique. As the importance and use of AI in games grows, particularly with the availability of parallel cores for computation, we expect that the role of search in games is also going to increase.

22.2 Illustrative Example

To illustrate the role and potential power of search, consider a battle in a role-playing game (RPG) where a nonplayer character (NPC) in the player's party has the choice of using several weapons to attack an enemy. There are a range of approaches that can be used when this NPC decides which weapon to use.

The simplest approach offloads the choice onto the human player, by asking them to equip a default weapon or specifying simple decision rules that help the NPC make the decision. While this might be strategically interesting for the human, it isn't interesting from an AI perspective.

The next approach is based on static analysis of the situation. The designer in charge of the AI might craft a number of rules or even build a more complicated decision tree or behavior tree to author the behavior of the NPC in battles. If the battles are relatively simple, or the NPC faces relatively uniform challenges, this approach can be sufficient. But, because it relies on static analysis, the resulting behavior can be brittle when the NPC is faced with new or unforeseen situations. Note that the input to this static analysis is a state of the game, and the output is one or more actions to be applied.

We can now introduce a basic search approach. Instead of using static analysis, we could build into our game engine the ability to query the expected damage by any weapon against any foe. Since the engine already has the ability to simulate the attack, it just needs a flag to determine whether to apply the damage from the attack or to simulate the damage and return the expected value. After doing this for all possible attacks, the NPC can, for instance, choose the attack that has the highest expected damage. In many ways, this is far simpler than the previous static analysis, because nothing needs to be hand authored for this to work. If a particular weapon is ineffective against a particular enemy, the NPC will know not to use it, and if an enemy is vulnerable to a particular weapon, the NPC will surely use that weapon. This is a 1-ply analysis, because it searches one step into the future.

The drawback of this approach is that by taking the action that maximizes damage, it ignores other resource considerations. Consider, for instance, a weapon that has a limited number of death strikes that will immediately kill an opponent. This power should obviously be saved for use against strong opponents, but the search would not discriminate between easy and hard foes. The approach can be generalized by mixing static analysis with search. Instead of choosing the attack that maximizes damage, the best action will balance the short-term damage to an opponent against the long-term use of resources. So, a static evaluation function must be designed to evaluate the result of a 1-ply search. The static evaluation function will need less sophistication than without the search, as some of the information normally captured in the evaluation function will now be captured in the search. In this example, the role of the static analysis shifts. Instead of suggesting actions, the static evaluation must evaluate states after an action has been taken.

Now, suppose that the designers change the parameters of the game, shifting the damage done by all types of weapons and introducing new weapon buffs. Any AI designed around a static evaluation would have to be completely retuned, and information about the new weapon damages and buffs would have to be added to the AI logic. But, with the 1-ply search, significantly fewer changes are needed. Changing the game engine immediately enables the AI to reason with the new weapon models. The static evaluation may have to be retuned to balance the new buffs, but this is relatively small in comparison.

Unless the search considers all possibilities, there is always the chance that it will miss something important in the future, whether it is the next battle immediately after this one or the boss at the end of the level. But, practically speaking, even a small amount of search will capture dynamics that are difficult to capture in a static evaluation function.

This can easily be generalized to deeper search. In general, the stronger and more exhaustive a search becomes, the weaker the static evaluation function can be. But, there are diminishing gains from search relative to its cost. Each game will have its own sweet spot where the intelligence of the AI is balanced against the resources required to achieve that performance.

22.3 Basic Search Requirements

In order to apply search to a game, there are a few requirements that must usually be met. In general, search begins with the *state* of the world. This doesn't have to be the full state of everything going on everywhere, but the state must capture everything that is of interest to the AI. The state is usually composed of a set of variables and their values. This might include all characters in a battle and their stats, such as health and inventory, but could also include an arrangement of puzzle pieces on a board.

Given the state of the world, you need some way to search over different states of the world through the application of valid *operators*. Operators can vary wildly between different types of games or different parts of the same game. In our battle example, different operators might attack with different weapons. But, in a puzzle game, operators might correspond to moving different pieces of a puzzle around. Because the available operators might change based on the state of the world, it is usually useful to have a function that can return the valid operators in a given state.

The final piece needed for search is the ability to *apply* a valid operator to a given state. This is the only step that actually changes the state of the world. Sometimes, it is useful to be able to *undo* operators to extract the parent of a particular state, but this isn't possible in all state spaces.

These three pieces are the basic foundation of many types of search. There are other distinctions, such as whether the search is adversarial, whether the world is deterministic or stochastic, whether actions are taken simultaneously or sequentially, and whether characters have full knowledge of the world. Each of these distinctions require different types of search, something we will not cover here, but it is worth mentioning that search can also be exhaustive in nature (such as A* or a breadth-first search) or local (such as a genetic algorithm or hill-climbing approach). Each type of algorithm has its own strengths and weaknesses.

Because search techniques tend to look at large numbers of states, it is important that these operations are efficient. If the state is too large, the number of operators is too large, or the cost of applying operators is too expensive, search may not be the best approach, or a more efficient representation might be necessary.

22.3.1 Efficient State Representation

There are significant advantages when the search representation corresponds exactly to the representation used by the game engine. This ensures that any reasoning done by the AI matches exactly with the world. But, sometimes, the world is too complicated to simulate exactly for search. The classical example for this is in path planning. It is often the case that movement restrictions for game characters are defined by the physics engine, which performs collision checking and other tasks that influence path following and locomotion. But, planning directly in the physics engine is usually too expensive. Thus, many path planning representations are an abstraction of the physical world that is more suitable for search than the physics engine. The drawback of this abstraction is that when the abstraction does not correspond with the real world, strange behavior results, such as characters that get caught on world geometry when trying to move around the world.

Despite this, there are many ways in which abstraction can simplify and decompose the world, making it feasible for planning. In our RPG example, for instance, the physical movement of characters might be abstracted in order to eliminate the need for path planning during search. In a real-time strategy game (RTS), battles could be abstracted instead of simulated to allow for higher-level planning. The selection of operators can also abstract the choices available. Instead of allowing any character to attack any opponent with any weapon, the operators might only allow a choice between melee and ranged attacks. Choosing an appropriate abstraction of the world is important for controlling the cost of the search and the quality of the results.

Once the world is defined appropriately for search, there are additional techniques for reducing the cost of search. One important technique is to avoid storing multiple copies of the state of the world. Operators are usually much smaller than the world state, and so it is easier to store a sequence of operators than a sequence of states. This is particularly efficient when it is possible to *undo* operators, as a depth-first search can then just keep a single copy of the world state along with a stack of operators in the search. It is also important to avoid memory allocations during search. As much as is possible, data structures for providing legal operators should be preallocated, and runtime memory allocation should be avoided.

22.4 Alternate Uses of Search

When search capabilities are well integrated into a game engine, we have used them to support many other necessary functions of a game. For instance, the search engine can be used to determine what parts of the game graphical user interface (GUI) should be activated. This works when the search engine is able to produce a set of valid operators that correspond to GUI elements that a human player can interact with. Such elements are often enabled or disabled depending on the state of the game, and custom logic is often written to do this. But, the search code already encodes this knowledge with the available operators. Thus, instead of using custom logic for the GUI, the GUI can just query the search engine to determine what GUI elements should be activated. Related to this, the search engine can provide the ability for users to undo their actions or replay games by storing the sequences of operators that were used during the game.

In a similar manner, a search engine can be used to build a dynamic tutorial for a game. Tutorials, particularly in puzzle games, often have simple puzzles for players to solve. If the search engine is able to solve these puzzles automatically, then the tutorial does not have to use a fixed set of puzzles for training. Instead, the search engine can be used to find solutions and train users. Similarly, if players appear to be stuck, a search engine can be used to find solutions and suggest moves for players.

Finally, search engines are useful for debugging purposes, as even a simple depth-first search can quickly reach a large range of states, potentially exposing unintended consequences of the game design or other bugs.

22.5 Bottlenecks for Search

Search is not a universal antidote to underperforming AI; many compelling games have been created without using search. Thus, it is worth noting the situations when search might not be appropriate.

Many optimization problems are more suited to be solved by linear programming (LP). In these types of problems, the question often isn't what particular action to take, but, for instance, how to allocate resources along a continuous spectrum. LPs can also be used to compute action probabilities for games of imperfect information, although non-LP methods can also be used for this problem.

The value of search is also limited when it is very costly to apply operators, when the number of legal operators is very large, or when the static evaluation of states is difficult. In many cases, these difficulties can be overcome through the use of abstraction, although it isn't always apparent what form of abstraction will result in the best behavior. But, broadening use of search in games will help reveal the best abstractions for achieving high performance. The following chapters in this book will illustrate new and interesting ways to apply search for a variety of games.

22.6 Conclusion

The goal of this chapter was to provide a basic background on search techniques to introduce the chapters in the general search section of this book. The astute reader will find many of the ideas in this article reflected in the following chapters in this section. We hope that it will provide a valuable framework for thinking about search and its applications.

23

Personality Reinforced Search for Mobile Strategy Games

Miguel A. Nieves

23.1 Introduction

The design philosophy central to the critical acclaim and success of the strategy war game *Battle of the Bulge* (iOS) was that every move can be used to express personality as well as skill. Despite being based on a board game, determining how the AI should play proved to be quite complex. The plethora of rules, units, map characteristics, and nondeterministic outcomes led to an explosion of game states. Since the game was new, no established strategies existed. This, coupled with the processing and memory limitations of mobile development, made searching to a win state impossible.

Too often, a win state is the focus of development and "personality" is expressed using a random range of positive, but suboptimal choices. In an attempt to win, some choose to skew less visible odds in the computer's favor. Some developers navigate a quagmire of numeric optimization of their state evaluator. These approaches are fundamentally attempting to solve the wrong problem. It is not "How do I win?", but "How do I play?"

Freed of the focus to win, other decision-making metrics can be explored. These data-centric methods are mixed with traditional tree-search approaches to create a personality-centric informed search. The overall architecture is surprisingly similar to the triune model of human brain evolution. This model combines instinct, experience, and prediction in a simple and intuitive way that supports agile development methodologies.
This chapter will describe how we:

- Used the triune brain model as a guide to perform a personality-based tree search
- Created visible development goals, enabling greater stakeholder confidence
- Started making decisions quickly using utility for personality-based decisions
- Simplified game state for faster iteration
- Created adaptive behavior that doesn't assume an opponent personality
- Removed hand tuning by allowing the AI to breed
- Understood how personality can be expressed via optimization

While this chapter's focus is on optimizing for personality in turn-based strategy games, these techniques are applicable to problems with a large number of potential states and no clear dominant strategy.

23.2 Turn-Based Strategy War Games Based on "Euro" Board Games

Euro-style board war games mix strategy, chance, and complex rules to keep wins close, but just out of reach until the very end. This makes them very engaging but difficult to quickly score or evaluate for equivalency. Like many board games, *Battle of the Bulge* is played by moving pieces on a map, except that each piece and map location are associated with detailed stats and rules. Units may also attack each other, but combat is nondeterministic. Thus, a "good" move can still fail and cause a player to reevaluate their plans. Determining victory is often multifaceted and can occur instantly due to accumulated points and positioning or can occur after a fixed number of turns.

The general flow of a game is as follows:

Day Start → Some Number of Player Turns → Day End Rules/Victory? → Next Day Start

Each player turns consists of the following:

Turn Start → Special Rules Decision → Movement Decision → Combat(s) → Movement after Combat Decision → Turn End → Next Player Turn

There are many factors that make the analysis of this game complex. Player turns do not always alternate, but the opposing player cannot move until the first player has finished. Movement rarely involves a single game piece or unit. For each unit, there are many potential destinations, multiple paths, and even side effects from moving at all. Sometimes, additional movement decisions are needed after combat. Additionally, many action permutations yield the same outcome. This results in a huge branching factor even before exploring enemy counter moves!

Before, during, and after each move, there are numerous, potentially dynamic, rules that must be referenced or cross-referenced to determine legality. Every space may contain both friendly and enemy units and even those units have changing statistics. Past actions may influence the turn flow. These factors all contribute to a game state that is expensive to store, copy, and compare for equivalence.

Not being able to reach a significant terminal state puts a lot of pressure on the state evaluator. An overworked state evaluator is difficult to maintain and becomes even more complex when game designs are asymmetric. Without significant time spent studying and playing, what constitutes a good move remains subjective. Designers rarely have the answer, even for their own game system. Most often, their answers require expensive analysis, further slowing an already laden system.

Perhaps, there are some lucky developers who do not have to answer to timelines, CPU restrictions, or dwindling budgets, but that is not our situation. Our stakeholders need quantitative results to justify the budget we request of them. These are not villains, but real people who feel betrayed when their AI expert doesn't deliver something up to their undefined metric of "good." To them, it doesn't matter how little processing power a user's device has or how many times the game designers changed the rules out from under the AI. What matters is that a challenging game is released, on time, and is profitable enough that everyone can still keep doing what they love. Fortunately, there is a solution, and one that looks shocking like... *the human brain*! Don't laugh... okay, laugh a little bit, but bear with me and you'll see how remixing traditional techniques and optimizations for mobile come together to create a smarter personality-driven opponent.

23.3 Evolution and the Triune Brain

The triune brain model posits three brains emerged in succession during the course of evolution and are now nested one inside the other in the modern human brain: a "reptilian brain" in charge of survival functions, a "limbic brain" in charge of memories and emotions, and the "neocortex," in charge of abstract, rational thinking [Dubac 14]. While this model has been criticized as an oversimplification in the field of neuroscience [Smith 10], it makes an interesting metaphor in creating our personality-driven architecture.

We build these three brains, shown in Figure 23.1, into a loosely coupled, tunable, informed search algorithm capable of expressing personality as well as skill. The number of moves, permutations, and game states war games generate make it essential to find ways to only explore the moves that matter. A good start is to use a search algorithm like alpha–beta, for improved tree pruning over minimax. However, more aggressive methods are needed to prune the tree to one that can be explored by mobile hardware. An interpretation of Occam's razor is that if there is a good reason to make an assumption, then do so even if is not always true [Birmingham 77].

This is where our other two brains can provide information on what it thinks is important and what the player thinks is important. Our reptile brain provides move ordering via tunable utility-based heuristics. The limbic brain records and recalls player metrics gathered from other play sessions to understand the past. And the search function in the neocortex brings all this information together to determine, through the lens of the state evaluator, likely counter moves.

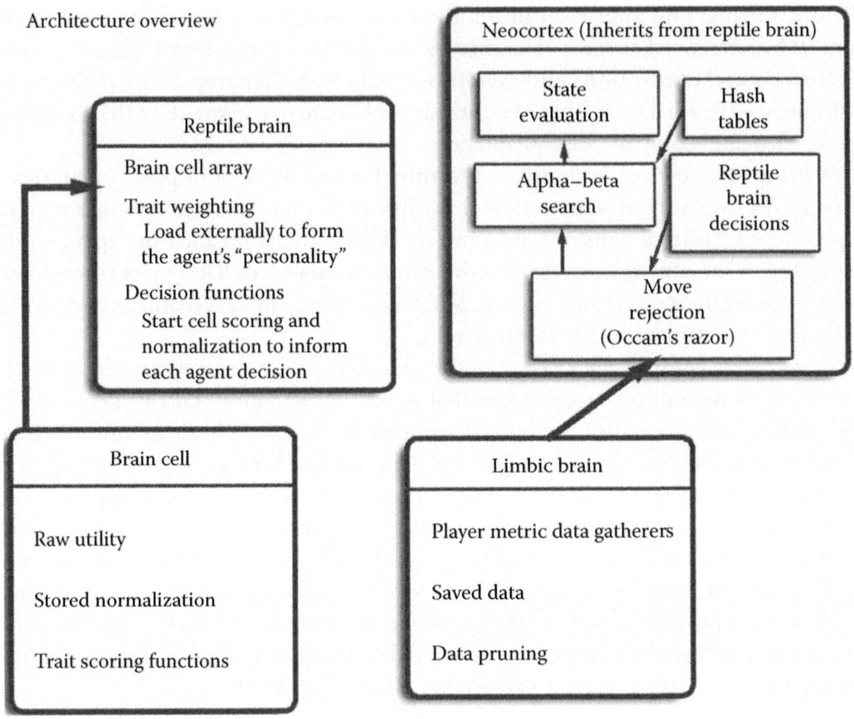

Figure 23.1

Architecture overview for triune brain-modeled AI.

23.4 Personality First

Many developers try to create the perfect player first, then down tune to create personality. This prioritization discounts the great wealth of expression players have on each of their chosen battlefields. Within every game, there are very different ways to play. Thinking about opponents you've personally faced in games, what makes Mary different from Sue is how she might approach the problem, what she thinks is important, and her temperament during play. What sort of characteristics make up how they choose moves? Does she carefully consider each move or brashly jump on any potentially victorious outcome? What does she consider a win? Building in these metagame aspects can help create AI opponents that "feel" like human players. Play becomes richer because strategies are formed not just within the game rules, but in how another will react to those rules.

The personality in the triune architecture comes from the reptile brain. In this brain, we create utility functions that explore only "one" aspect of play. Think of what a player considers before a move. "I'd be a real jerk if I moved here" is a valid heuristic. We look for these factors in the same way you'd score the space that would yield the highest point gain. The goal is to find the move that exemplifies that single aspect. These decisions may or may not take in account counter moves; the goal is to make each determination in near linear time.

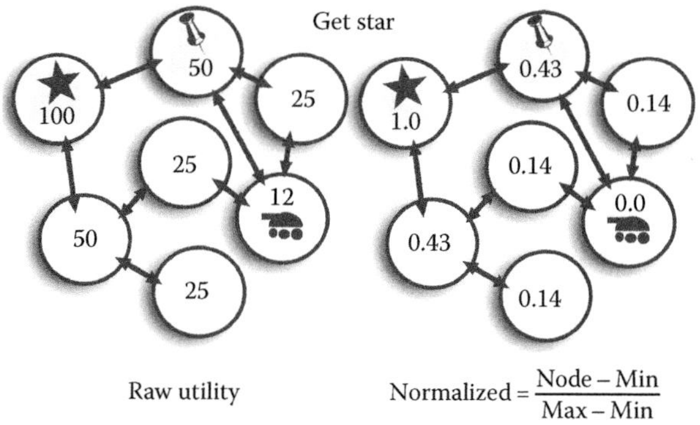

Figure 23.2

Sample output for the "get star" trait.

In the following examples, each circle represents a space that can be moved to. Arrows indicate how spaces are connected. The tank is the player's location and the other graphics are features of the space. Raw utility is a number system we have made up to help quantify the world.

Consider Figure 23.2. If we only care about the star, then what are the best spaces to be in? These are evaluated with raw and normalized utility. Now, what if we do not want to be near a tack? States are evaluated with this metric in Figure 23.3. We now have two utility functions, one for moving toward the star and another for avoiding a tack.

Here, we've created two *wildly* different number systems! How do we determine what to do? We use normalization [Mark 08]. There are lots of different ways to express the quality of a space, but normalized values are easy to compare and combine, as shown in Figure 23.4. Best of all, they are easy to scale.

Personality is created in a consistent way when you scale the normalized outcome of each utility function. It also helps if you keep in mind archetypes [Ellinger 08] when building your utility function. Archetypes are bold behaviors that can be described by a single

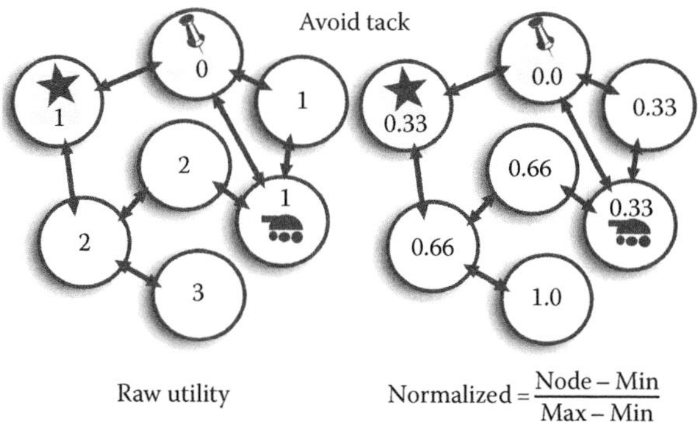

Figure 23.3

Using a different numeric basis for other traits still works when normalized.

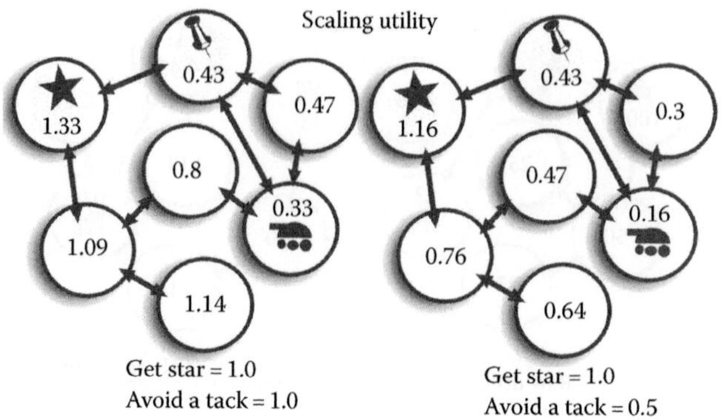

Figure 23.4

Scale and combine normalized values to achieve a unique personality.

word, such as "coward," "defender," or "psycho." While this may use a few different types of data, it still has a singular focus. It may help to think of each of these utility functions as personality traits. Testing each trait in isolation reveals new ways to think about how a player might move through the game. It also presents the chance to think critically about what information is important to interesting decision making.

In adjusting values for different traits, traits can even be scaled by negative numbers. A trait may have a corresponding and interesting opposite. This is because as the traits are combined, the scaling is relative. Scaling a trait A by 5 and trait B by 10 is the same as scaling trait A by 0.2 and trait B by 0.4. Conversely, if you have a several conflicting traits and scale them all the same, the move choice will be similarly conflicted and indecisive. It's very important for archetypes to be clear and obvious.

These hand-tuned values should be loaded externally to start, but as more traits are added, the "test, tweak, repeat" method becomes quite time consuming. AI versus AI play can be used at this point to validate potential agents, but before running off to build our genetic algorithm, we should move on to our neocortex.

23.5 Neocortex

The neocortex is where all the gathered data is used. For now, the development of the limbic brain will not help as much as the gains from early performance testing and more competitive play. The neocortex is the most traditional portion of this architecture. It starts with a lightly optimized implementation of alpha–beta search. For now, this should be kept independent of the reptile brain. The key features needed early on is the ability to control the number of plies (turns) explored and a set of counters to help determine which decisions get made the most. For now, the only optimizations focus on greatly reduce processing time. When optimizing any tree-search algorithm, the major hot spots are likely to be

- Legal move generation
- Path finding
- Copying game state
- The state evaluator

With a game state as complex as required by war games, transposition tables are your best friends. Initially, this may seem daunting, but these lookup tables don't have to be complete. We create them so they capture only enough information to determine if duplicate processing is about to happen. If units A and B want to go to space Z, unit A could move first then B, or B first then A. The end result is an identical state of "AB in Z" or "BA in Z." That's not so bad, but if we only looked at one of those states, we'd be twice as fast. What if there are three units in space:

"ABC in Z," "ACB in Z," "BAC in Z," "BCA in Z," "CAB in Z." What if you also were exploring Space Y?

The trick to getting this working for complex games turned out to be surprisingly simple. A string much like the aforementioned examples is generated and hashed. This creates a unique number and is added to other hashes to create a final master hash. So the string "unit A to Z" might create a hash of 42 and "unit B to Z" might create a hash of 382561. Add the two numbers together for the final move's hash. If the combination comes up again, the code knows not to reexplore that branch. Care must be taken if XOR is used to combine these hashes. If two units have the same value and move to the same space, they will XOR to 0. This can cause false positives (hash collisions) that would be difficult to identify.

Lookup tables can be exploited when dealing with legal move generation as well. In our case, we had three units that could move during a turn, but the first unit could invalidate a move by the second. It was much faster to store the initial legal moves and then check if a previous move would make a current move illegal. This type of lookup table also speeds up path finding. By storing the best path found, expensive path creation only happens once. Using the ply count as our index lets us keep tables small and searches fast.

Simplifying data became essential when attempting to keep track of game states. Initially, we experimented with copying the entire state at every decision point. Copies are made so we can speculate along a decision branch and perfectly return to that point and to try a new decision. With each game having hundreds of pieces, each with multiple mutable attributes, it was expensive to copy all states (unlike a chess board of 64 integers). Since alpha–beta is a depth-first method of searching, we didn't feel memory pressure despite the massive size of state, but the system struggled as it processed tens of thousands of copies. This only seemed to get worse as games progressed.

The first step was removing as many copies as possible by tracking and unwinding the changes using the same mechanisms developed for player level undo. This drastically reduced the copies, but it did not remedy the late game slow down. Some planning algorithms reduce their game state to (action, result) pairs. Building on this concept, the only data copied with the final game state was the action list changes from the initial decision point and the score provided by the state evaluator. In the late game, this took the number of actions copied per state from several thousand to a few dozen. The initial copy of game state is also simplified down to only what is needed for rejecting, applying, and scoring future moves.

23.6 State Evaluation

The neocortex's state evaluation is focused on raw numeric values. Even with asymmetric games, it is initially important to keep state scoring as symmetric as possible. Numbers like army health (normalized), spaces owned, special rules spaces owned, points scored, and if the state is a win, loss, or draw are a good place to start. Each unit's distance from the goal or enemy line is good for keeping units moving. If any strategies are revealed during the reptile brain tests that are easily quantifiable, include those as well (e.g., unit type A is more likely to win in combat if unit type B is also present). It is important to keep the state evaluator as close to linear or polynomial time as possible since this will be run several thousand times during search.

The next step is to verify the neocortex in isolation by having it find the best decision for a 1-ply search. This is also a good baseline for performance testing. While you should allocate resources as needed to improve game code, it is important to determine acceptable wait times for decisions. The 1-ply search should be relatively fast and its data can be used to improve the ordering of the moves searched in the multi-ply search.

However, the primary method of optimization is in the application of Occam's razor to the move space. Aggressive move rejection or "chopping" prevents wasting time on useless or redundant moves. This becomes especially important as more plies are processed and impacts all other problem hotspots in our search performance. Consider the size of the searches:

10 Moves for P1 → 10 Counter Moves for P2 = 100 Game States Processed
2 Moves for P1 → 10 Counter Moves for P2 = 20 Game States Processed
2 Moves for P1 → 2 Counter Moves for P2 = 4 Game State's Processed
10 Moves for P1 → 10 Counters for P2 → 10 Counter-Counter Moves for P1 = 1000 States
2 Moves for P1 → 10 Counters for P2 → 2 Counter-Counter Moves for P1 = 40 States
2 Moves for P1 → 2 Counters for P2 → 2 Counter-Counter Moves for P1 = 8 States

Random move chopping provides a baseline for the real-world processing savings, but we can bring intelligence and personality to our move removal. The chopping function itself will be run even more than the state evaluator so it's important not to load it down with too much logic. The chopping function scores each legal move for basic factors like terrain, distance for the origin, and current owner.

At this point, we can finally add the value of the move as decided by the reptile brain! Before kicking off the alpha–beta search, we use the reptile brain to score what it thinks are the best moves. This time, instead of using the legal move range of a unit, we pretend the unit can reach *every* space. We let the reptile brain rank every space then store the normalized value. Finally, we apply a scaling factor in the chopping function that allows the other numeric factors to break ties.

CAUTION: If there is an instant win space, ensure its utility doesn't stomp out the expression of the other spaces. If the win space score is 10,000, but all other spaces score <100, linear normalization puts yields 1.0 and <0.009. Work to keep the final number ranges within reason, to get the most expression from the reptile brain.

As in the examples earlier, the amount you chop can be asymmetric, externally loaded, and even dynamic. Using the reptile brain to guide the chopping function allows its personality to be expressed and converts a downside of chopping to your advantage. If the reptile brain is "aggressive," it will likely remove nonaggressive moves. Unfortunately, this could mean a potential good move could be missed. Also, since we only have a limited time with our games before they need to ship; it is very likely there is a style of play that we have not accounted for. Fortunately, since our function is dynamic, and our evaluator robust, we can add the final piece of the puzzle.

23.7 Limbic Brain

One of the amazing things about the human brain is our ability to learn. As game developers, one constant is that players will always surprise us. So, we aren't reliant on anecdotal data; we use metrics to learn how players play to improve their experience. In marketing, this might be used to determine which ad experience provides the best return and click through rates. We can use this to build a model of player behavior and guide our agents to interrupt emerging strategies.

Our implementation of the limbic brain is similar to "heat maps" as seen in shooters. Since our games are turn based, the major difference is the use of time. When a player makes a move is just as important as what move that player makes. The data we want to gather should not necessarily be related to previous evaluation functions. We must assume the player has a better idea of what makes a space or move valuable. We record each time a player makes a move or passes through a space. It doesn't matter if the move led to the player's win or loss, the goal is to interrupt an emerging dominant strategy. This data can be used right away, but it is important to scale its effect based on sample size.

The most valuable place for this data is the minimizing player's chopping function, specifically where the AI must guess which move a human opponent will make. Alpha–beta assumes optimal play by both sides. This is less reliable on shallow searches, especially when the quality of the terminal state evaluation is ill defined. Since the inclusion of the reptile brain, the chopping function would have only assumed our opponent played with the same personality. The inclusion of actual player data lets the AI learn from past actions and start to model its opponent.

This model can do more than reduce counter moves. Integrating the limbic brain data back into the reptile brain creates a new heuristic. This heuristic scores where the player moves the most during the next turn. By including ownership/defense of player-valued spaces in the state evaluator, soon the AI appears to use human strategies for itself. We updated the chopping function to always include one player-valued space.

23.8 Evolution and the Genetic Algorithm

Each of these systems can be developed largely independently to start, but as seen with the addition of the limbic brain, they add a great deal of value to each other when used together. As in the triune brain model, these systems help each other and become more interconnected. Ideas from one brain feed solutions to others. These systems can be leveraged to optimize and even produce higher quality results.

Even with personality traits as guides for the reptile brain, it becomes time consuming to hand tune values. This is especially true when looking for "perfect" play or when games take a long time to play. We taught our code to tune itself using a genetic algorithm. The reptile brain already loads values externally, so they can be evaluated through scoring the outcome of a few AI versus AI games. Playing several games is important because it reduces "lucky dice" in games with nondeterministic play. It also gives you a better idea of the AI's actual abilities. Since the state evaluator gives us more information than win or loss, the final state evaluation gives a good indication of fitness of a strategy. Early on, we only tune one AI at a time so there is a fixed point of comparison. This helps narrow the search space since you are likely to have multiple floating-point values in your AI's chromosome.

23.9 AI Chromosomes

Genetic algorithms work by combining, mutating, and testing a set of values on a problem space. The chromosome contains those values. In our case, a sample chromosome might look like the following:

Aggression = 0.5, LimbicBrainValue = 0.2, SpaceGain = 0.2, Seek_Pie = 1.0
Or encoded, this would be: 0.5|0.2|0.2|1.0.

The key with encoding is to create a flexible enough data structure that makes it easy to import values into the reptile brain. Because this isn't a structure needed for performance, compactness isn't as important as readability and exportability. Dictionaries work well here, and a few small variables let the chromosome keep some information about itself. In our chromosome, we stored the following:

Genes (Dictionary[string, float]) → These values will get changed and mutated.
Best & Worst Score (Float) → Indicators of the range of fitness.
Total games (Integer) → How many games has this chromosome played.
Total Sore (Float) → Combined fitness of all games played.
Average Score (Float) → Could be calculated, but occasionally nice to have around.

There are a few really great tutorials on best settings and trade-offs when creating your genetic algorithm [Buckland 02]. One alteration to mutation that is especially helpful when dealing with floating-point-style chromosomes is to modify instead of entirely replacing a gene. This way, the floating-point value being mutated goes up or down based on a maximum random amount you specify. All gene values should be kept within a certain range to ensure readable data is fed to the reptile brain.

The tiny size of each chromosome makes them easy to keep in memory. This can be leveraged to provide quality debug output of all the chromosomes tested. Early in development, this is essential since AI on AI games will likely expose game-breaking bugs. We saved each generation separately so we could view the propagation of chromosomes and separately saved a master list of all chromosomes sorted by a meaningful metric like highest average fitness. That metric has a tendency to hide big losses with big wins, so a better metric is a winner with the smallest best-to-worst score range.

Reviewing the gene values of winning chromosomes provides further insight and validation into your creation of reptile brain heuristics. In the example earlier, the "Seek_Pie" gene was set to our maximum value of 1.0. As a developer, my love of pie may have blinded me to actual winning strategies. The genetic algorithm, at some point, may mutate a "Seek_Pie" gene to a lower value. If this is the case, it may turn out that these heuristics may need to be reworked or avoided in the future. Conversely, heuristics that may not have seemed as valuable could turn out to be very useful.

23.10 Conclusion

There are many approaches to improving the number and quality of game states searched via alpha–beta or similar search algorithm. Simplifying games states, creating transposition tables, throttling, and move ordering alone does not make for smarter or more interesting opponents. In looking to our own brain's evolution, we have created an AI that can play with personality, plan ahead to the future, and even predict ways to interrupt player strategies. Parallels to our own biology make it easy to explain to stakeholders. It can be evaluated with concrete goals and feature sets. Lastly, it reduces the amount of hand tuning usually required by utility-based systems by leveraging the power of genetic algorithms.

This system has evolved with and powered the AI of *Battle of the Bulge* (reptile brain), *Drive on Moscow* (triune brain), and *Desert Fox* (optimized triune brain). While the game systems are similar, each game has wildly different rules, maps, and units for each scenario. Each game grew in complexity, and the number of game states with it. While not explicitly a general game player, the triune brain system has the flexibility to deal with each new situation without major architecture reworking. By focusing on personality rather than winning, and data collection over code crunching, interesting AI opponents are created even in the face of complex game systems.

References

[Birmingham 77] Birmingham, J.A. and Kent, P. 1977. Tree-searching and tree-pruning techniques. In *Advances in Computer Chess 1*, ed. M.R.B. Clarke, pp. 89–107, Edinburgh University Press, Edinburgh, U.K., ISBN 0-852-24292-1 [reprinted in *Computer Chess Compendium*, D.N.L. Levy (ed.), pp. 123–128, Springer, New York, 1989, ISBN 0-387-91331-9].

[Buckland 02] Buckland, M. 2002. *AI Techniques for Game Programming*. Premier Press Game Development, Cengage Learning PTR. http://www.ai-junkie.com/ga/intro/gat1.html (accessed September 10, 2014).

[Dubac 14] Dubac, B. 2014. The evolutionary layers of the human brain. http://thebrain.mcgill.ca/flash/d/d_05/d_05_cr/d_05_cr_her/d_05_cr_her.html (accessed September 10, 2014).

[Ellinger 08] Ellinger, B. 2008. Artificial personality: A personal approach to AI. In *AI Game Programming Wisdom 4*, S. Rabin, Ed. Charles River Media, Hingham, MA.

[Mark 08] Mark, D. 2008. Multi-axial dynamic threshold Fuzzy Decision Algorithm. In *AI Game Programming Wisdom 4*, S. Rabin, Ed. Charles River Media, Hingham, MA.

[Smith 10] Smith, C. 2010. The triune brain in antiquity: Plato, Aristotle, Erasistratus. *Journal of the History of the Neurosciences*, 19:1–14. doi:10.1080/09647040802601605.

24

Interest Search

A Faster Minimax

Jeff Rollason

24.1 Introduction

Minimax has been the dominant paradigm for many board games for so long, able to deliver either good or perfect solutions to many game problems. Such is this success that in many primary areas of human game intellect the best play is based on minimax-based AI. However, minimax has its limitations, and in some domains with great combinatorial complexity, minimax has been replaced by Monte Carlo tree search (MCTS) as the preferred solution. Where unscripted MCTS is rolling out to terminal nodes (the expected case), it sadly depends on spending most of its time assessing junk variations in the simulation phase in order to finally pick a "best" move. Note that in this case, only a small fraction of MCTS moves will likely fall inside the selection/expansion tree. This is a surrender to the complexity of the problem domain, determining that it is not possible to address the domain by exploring just meaningful game variations. If we look back at minimax, the situation is better, but actually still largely quite poor. If you randomly freeze a minimax search for a typical chess program, you will find that most variations explored will be largely in the range of poor to junk.

Interest search is another way to look at minimax pruning and allows the search to concentrate on meaningful variations. This method radically impacted the fortunes of the shogi program *Shotest*, which twice ranked #3 in the Computer Shogi Association (CSA) world championships in Japan, making it the all-time highest ranked western shogi program ever. Even basic implementations of this method yield a 5× speedup for chess, with no net loss of strength. For shogi this yield was 14×. This chapter details this method and how it was used for chess and shogi.

24.2 Background

A key observation the author made from early days in working in chess is that, despite good move ordering, much of the time was spent searching variations that, to the human observer, were obviously pointless. Having just one absurd move in a branch would be followed by an expensive subtree of variations to assess that move. To an extent, alpha–beta and related methods help reduce the overhead by creating more cutoffs in these bad variations. However, this was still not enough, particularly for quiet positions, where the large bulk of the search was still dominated by exploring poor variations. This characteristic cannot have been lost on early chess developers so early work in minimax for chess originally divided primarily into two camps:

1. Fast full-width search that attempted to explore all variations, pruned by alpha–beta and related methods to optimize the tree (Shannon type A)
2. Selective search, which likely spent more time in evaluation, but restricted the number of moves searched through heuristic forward pruning (Shannon type B)

If selective search could reliably reduce the number of nodes explored, then this could be traded for deeper search. Naturally selective search came at a price, requiring heuristic assessments during search. If the cost of this was less than the saving caused by narrower search, and if this avoided missing moves that should be explored, then selective search could search deeper and therefore be stronger. Since it would also have access to slower evaluation, it would also be able to have better terminal node evaluation.

Hope and logic in those early days suggested that (2) would win out as the idea of move selection that depended on trying to explore every possible combination of move plays surely could not be the way to deliver the best possible play. However, history has shown that method (1) appeared to quickly dominate and the method of forward pruning simply was unable to compete.

24.3 Rethinking Selective Search

An issue with selective search is that as soon as you restrict the moves list to some subset, even though the confidence that any one list will have all the moves it needs might be high, that once this gets multiplied in a multimove variation, the risks geometrically increase. Even with a 99% confidence in any one moves list, after 10 plies, the chance that the key variation may have been missed is still 10%. To achieve 99% certainty within any one list would alone be very hard and to achieve it would probably mean that there was no selective search saving. You might as well search a few more moves, slightly faster, and be 100% certain that you had examined the key variation.

I think the flaw here is that trying to find the magic compromise where you sacrifice some small portion of all moves in each list to narrow the tree is perhaps doomed to failure. Trying to assess viability in terms of individual moves lists (with perhaps some peeking at previous plies in order to keep choices relevant) is probably a too limited way to look at being selective.

24.4 Selection by Variation: Interest Search

When assessing snapshots from a chess alpha–beta search, the key disappointment is not just that an absurd move was tried, but that the search then followed up such moves with comprehensive follow-ons to validate or reject that move. Intuitively wacky moves do not merit the same thorough examination as moves that are more obviously sound.

That reveals what the goal could be: Dubious moves do not warrant the same level of examination, so that as soon as a variation introduces such a move, the willingness to devote time exploring the variation should diminish.

This is the underlying principle the drives interest search. (It should be noted that this principle also drives the selection and expansion phase of MCTS, but not the simulation phase, where most moves are usually selected.)

24.5 Quantifying the Interest Search Idea

Interest search passes down a value through the branch indicating how interesting that branch is. For aesthetic reasons, a high value might obviously have been chosen to indicate "high interest," but actually, this is inverted and the value actually represents "interest cost," so that a high value means that the variation is already expensive, perhaps because it is already deep into the tree or that it includes mediocre moves.

This value is passed down the tree and is used to determine when a branch ends, completely replacing the usual "iterate by depth" by "iterate by interest," where the interest threshold increases with each iteration. Search paths full of highly interesting moves get explored at depth, whereas poor variations are terminated at shallow depths. Once a variation contains one very poor move, it uses up a high proportion of its interest value, so that it only receives limited follow-on search. The same impact might be achieved by a variation containing two mediocre moves, which net may generate the same high value of one very poor move. This is intuitively a reasonable idea.

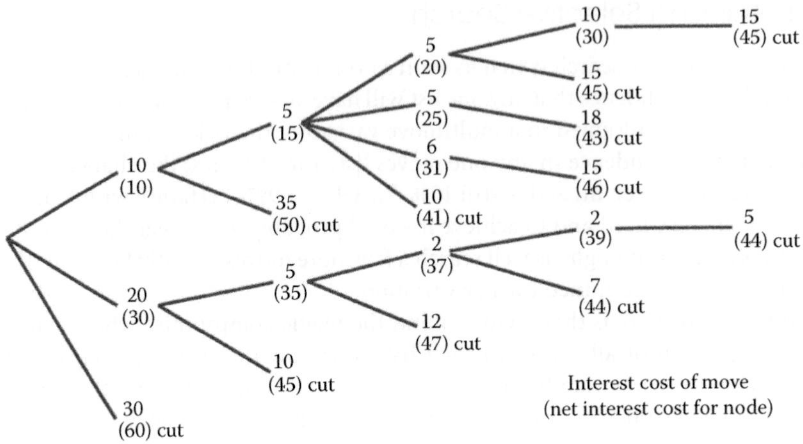

Figure 24.1

An interest search tree with an interest threshold of 40.

Figure 24.1 shows how this principle might impact the structure of a tree search, terminated on interest cost rather than depth. The upper number shows the interest cost of that move and the lower number the net interest cost of that branch. As you move left and down, the lower number increases in value. When its value exceeds the interest threshold, a cutoff occurs.

24.6 Classifying the Moves in Terms of Interest

This idea earlier could be managed in wide variety of ways, unlike alpha–beta, which has just one exact definition. The description given here is the method used on AI Factory's Treebeard chess. A more comprehensive implementation follows later, for Japanese chess (shogi).

At each ply, a full plausibility analysis is performed, to achieve an expected ordering of moves. This delivers a score for "how good a move is likely to be" but in addition, a second value is calculated for how "interesting" a move is. If a move is "good," then it is also interesting, but it might also be very interesting because it forces a reply.

Our Treebeard chess has a relatively simple set of criteria, each of which adds a value to the interest. A simplified overview of this is as follows:
For each move the plausibility analysis evaluates (separate from static terminal evaluation) the following:

1. Interest is initialized to 1000/number of legal moves.
2. If in check, value increases += 1000 (function of number of replies).
3. Move is in the transposition table += 25.
4. Ply1 existing previous iteration best move += 100.
5. Killer move += 100.
6. Move is voted global "best reply" to previous move in branch += 100.
7. Best follow-on from previous move 2 plies ago += 100.

8. Pawn attacks piece += f(value piece).
9. Value of capture += f(value of capture).
10. We give check. += 100, more if our previous ply was also check.
11. Attack pieces, extra if fork += f(value of piece).
12. Moving a piece under attack += f(value of piece).
13. Capture checking piece += 100.
14. Promotion += 100.
15. Diminish interest if beyond iteration depth.
16. Move piece that is target of pin/tie += f(value of pin/tie).
17. Move is best noncapture += 100.

The interest value, which is higher for more interesting moves, is finally added to the plausibility score, so that interesting moves have an increased chance of selection. Therefore, move ordering is a combination of how good a move is and how interesting it is.

Within the search, once a move has been selected for assessment, its net interest cost is calculated as K/(move interest), so this converges to "K" for the least interesting move (where "K" is an arbitrary constant, picked solely to fit the word size of the target hardware; if using floating point this might simply be 1.0) and reduces to near zero for extremely interesting moves.

At the point that a move may be selected for search, the following calculation is made:

```
net_Interest = total_Path_Interest + total_Interest_This_Ply
             + interest_This_Move
```

where

`total_Path_Interest`	The net interest cost of the branch leading to this ply
`total_Interest_This_Ply`	Net interest cost of all previous moves explored at this ply
`interest_This_Move`	The interest cost of the move to be considered

This is then compared to the "iteration interest limit" and if it is greater, then a cutoff occurs and no further moves are explored at this node. This iteration interest limit simply increases the limit for each iteration as each iteration is executed.

If a cutoff does not occur, and the move is searched, then "`net_Interest`" becomes the new "`total_Path_Interest`" passed on for the next ply.

24.7 Does This Work?

If you follow through the idea given earlier in a thought experiment, it is not hard to observe that this appears to have a very serious flaw. If you test a move that appears to result in a very strong outcome a few plies later, then the opponent could avoid this outcome by exploring a move with a high interest cost, so that it cuts off before the outcome is reached. Indeed, this destroys the search, which quickly descends into poor play. The key here is to separate the interest tally for different search parities—that is, for each player in the game.

To make this work, you need to track separate interest cost for each of the two search parities. Now, the search cannot avoid an opponent variation outcome by attempting to insert a dull move to force an early cutoff. However, this does not stop each side avoiding horizon events. The search could find that a "good" move actually leads to disaster, so avoids the good move by searching a "bad" move that causes an earlier cutoff. This is actually not so different to the existing defect that minimax already has. The difference is that minimax would allow time to be wasted exploring the "bad" move, whereas interest search will cut it off earlier.

Note that if side A has run out of interest but side B has not, then A might cause a termination, but this is after side B having just moved. So A forcing a cutoff will leave B with the advantage of last move.

24.8 Performance of Interest Search for Treebeard Chess

From testing, the addition of interest search resulted in a 20× speedup in search time (500 games) but with only a 41% win rate as there was some inevitable loss of critical moves. If the number of iterations was increased to achieve strength parity, then the net speedup was 5×, as shown in Table 24.1.

Note that this method makes no absolute limit on any one moves list. If the previous branch contained high interest moves, then at the current depth, there will be the option to potentially explore all moves. Note also that in follow-on iterations, the best moves will have already become hash and best reply choices, so they will be promoted in interest value. With the increased interest threshold of the next iteration, then new moves will be considered throughout the tree for examination, not just the usual terminal node extension you normally get with iterated minimax.

Our implementation of interest search for chess could undoubtedly be optimized. With more attention, we would expect that a 10× speedup or more is likely. We have not needed to explore this as our chess already easily fulfils what it needs to, as the mobile version, from its Elo rating, appears to be already stronger than 99.5% of online players on chess.com.

However, this method was actually primarily developed at length with our shogi program, where the optimization was vital as shogi grows combinatorially faster than chess.

24.9 Applying Interest Search to Japanese Chess (Shogi)

Shogi is a much greater challenge than chess as is combinatorially explosive. To start, the average number of moves is nearer 80 rather than 35 for chess but can easily peak at 200 moves near the end game. The reason for this is that pieces captured can be replayed on the board (9 × 9) on any square as a move (a drop), so that if many pieces have been captured,

Table 24.1 Comparing the Performance of Search with and without Interest Search for Chess

		Result for A Compared to B		
Player A	**Player B**	**Time Used**	**Win%**	**Comment**
Interest ON	Interest OFF	20× faster	41	
Interest ON	Interest OFF	5× faster	50	Rebalanced win rate
Interest ON	Interest OFF	Equal time	72	Rebalanced time

the number of legal moves goes up. This makes the game very challenging as pieces are never eliminated from play, so that swapoff exchange simplifications are not possible.

The core mechanism to drive this is essentially the same as for chess earlier, but backed by a much more comprehensive and sensitive plausibility analysis, with 48 separate components. Among the more significant additions are as follows:

1. Move to a square that is now safer (less attacks) than it was at root ply.
2. Move is now legal but not legal at root ply (i.e., a new move).
3. Index into various positional arrays to credit better squares or desirable target squares.
4. Various context-sensitive credits, including moves to defend against threatened mates.
5. Negative plausibility: Penalize moves that in previous branches were searched before the best alpha was actually found.

These complex terms mean that each move may get multiple credits as each move performs multiple roles. Such moves are more likely to be ordered high in the search list. The complexity of this also makes it more likely that few moves will have the same score as they will likely each have at least some differentiating value.

However, such is the nature of the game shogi that this is not enough, as most of the time multiple drops will be possible. For example, the move list might contain 40 possible drops by a rook. This could easily flood the top of the moves list with multiple alternative rook drops, all of which look equally good, but clearly, it would not make sense to explore all of these before trying some other kind of move.

Therefore to address this, the plausibility needs to dynamically modify the score and interest value to change the move ordering, to diminish selection of moves similar to those already played.

24.10 Dynamic Calculation of Score and Interest

As each move is searched, the list of existing unsearched moves is updated depending on how similar they are to the move just played.

These similarity checks penalize the following matching criteria, to different degrees:

1. Dull moves that have no tactical component.
2. Vacate moves that avoid some tactical threat such as a capture.
3. Vacates per square. This is like (2) but counts separately for each square.
4. Unsafe moves that are expected to result in some loss.
5. Moves by piece type.
6. Mate threats.
7. Checks.
8. Move from square and move to square.
9. Drop move.
10. Blocking move.
11. Attacking move that creates a new threat.
12. Discovered attack.

This then changes the move ordering by score so that the next move to be considered may have changed from what otherwise might have been selected. That new move will also have a modified interest value.

24.11 Impact of Interest Search on Shogi

Note first that the aforementioned reordering still applies, even if interest search is not in use. Also, the search control is not "naked" if the interest search is switched off as the program will already have the usual move ordering mechanisms such as killer, hash, history heuristic, best reply, and best follow-on tables. It also has a number of other pruning methods to contain the tree search, as follows:

1. Razoring (prune by comparing to beta)
2. Gamma pruning (prune by comparing to alpha)
3. Alpha fail pruning (stop selection of the next move if too many moves fail to replace alpha)

The aforementioned are necessary to limit the search that otherwise would be very slow.

Comparing this to chess, it is clear that with shogi, interest search is eliminating more critical lines than chess as simply switching off interest search decimated the performance (threshold initialized for similar depth), dropping to a 8.3% win rate, but 119× faster (see Table 24.2). With rebalancing by adding more iterations to restore a 50% win rate, the speedup was still 14× the speed of search with no interest search. If we rebalanced time taken, then interest search manages a healthy 90.5% win rate.

24.12 Analysis

The behavior of this type of search was intuitively much more natural to my own perception of what AI search should be doing. I was always uneasy that minimax on its own felt more like a theorem prover than AI. Determining a move primarily from variations that humans could never consider did not feel like AI.

However, justifying the underlying basis of why AI methods are actually valid can be hard. Large tree searches cannot be easily visualized or intuitively understood. Minimax search, although in its core foundation is easy to understand, is harder to comprehend once you are considering vast numbers of nodes.

A consideration in assessing the validity of interest search is that its concentration on plausible variations reduces the chance of suspect evaluation results arising from obscure random variations. For example, when exploring a complete space with full-width

Table 24.2 Comparing the Performance of Search with and without Interest Search for Shogi

		Result for A Compared to B		
Player A	Player B	Time Used	Win%	Comment
Interest ON	Interest OFF	119× faster	8.3	
Interest ON	Interest OFF	14× faster	50	Rebalanced win rate
Interest ON	Interest OFF	Equal time	90.5	Rebalanced time

minimax, any possible odd-ball position might be reached, and among these, some may manage to deliver a high evaluation value that causes a beta cutoff, simply because the evaluation is unable to reliably assess all random positions thrown at it. This will expose the terminal evaluation weaknesses by exposing it to positions that it was probably never designed for.

Interest search avoids the chance of this by ensuring that it only explores highly plausible search lines, which may contain a very limited number of odd-ball moves. Therefore, the evaluation is mostly only exposed to positions that a human player might consider "reasonable." This is a healthy premise as it is otherwise an unfortunate impediment that without selective search, the evaluation needs to not only be plausible in reasonable positions but also provide meaningful comparative assessments with the larger bulk of absurd positions as well. Without this handicap, the evaluation can be freed to only needing to comparatively assess a narrow set of related reasonable positions, rather than the wider spectrum of absurdity.

This may not be obvious, but actually, the map of the tree explored by this method will likely resemble the map of an MCTS tree, with exploration concentrated to explore "better" lines of play. The driving mechanism to achieve this is somewhat different, but with a likely similar end product.

It is hard to reliably project the full practical consequences of this method, but Treebeard chess has a great following, being by far the most played chess on Android, and is also used in Microsoft's MSN chess, so therefore probably the most played chess program on the planet. It is rated strongly for its agreeable humanlike style (see online reviews of "Chess Free AI Factory"), which may well be the end consequence of its use of interest search. The programs and related methods used are discussed in an online periodical [AIF 14] and previous paper [Rollason 00].

24.13 Other Games

MCTS is now becoming a preferred paradigm to minimax in combinatorially complex games, but interest search may offer a widening of the net that minimax can cope with. Its advantage is that it offers the possibility of providing near-proven best plays, whereas MCTS only offers a probability of best play. It also offers an analysis that confines positions being analyzed to being more reasonable than minimax on its own and much more reasonable than MCTS.

It should be noted that there is no reason why interest search could not also be applied to the MCTS simulation phase. This might offer a much faster MCTS if less time is spent considering very low quality lines of play.

24.14 Conclusion

Without interest search, *Shotest* would not have been able to twice rank #3 in the World Computer Shogi Championships in Japan. Although my program had other important evaluation features that contributed well to its performance, it is very clear that without interest search that I would have been very lucky to even make the top 20.

The methodology of this seems to be applicable to any minimax program that has more than a trivial plausibility analysis. It risks missing variations that regular minimax would pick up but the vast volume of what it rejects will certainly be very poor. The loss of key variations will have been traded by much more available time that can be used to explore high probability branches. Empirically, this has worked very well in both chess and shogi and there is no obvious reason why this would not work in other games.

Note also that this method avoids the forced geometric discrete stepping associated with iteration in minimax. In the latter, the chance to progress for more analysis is severely restricted by the large jump in time needed for each new iteration. With interest search, you can set the size of each progression, so that each step might be quite small. This can even be dynamically changed between moves, which might be much more effective if small steps where the search is struggling to pin down the right line of play. The key here is that the option is available, whereas iteration by depth is hardwired and inflexible.

Finally, note that this single currency of "interest" to control search offers all kinds of flexibility to modify how interest is assigned per move. This gives the developer the chance to dynamically select between shallow bushy or deep sparse trees, as they see fit. There is a great deal to explore here. This method has served the author well for some 18 years and, as yet, they have not found any other paradigm to replace it for supporting minimax.

References

[AIF 14] AI Factory Newsletter. 2003–2014. Currently 46 articles on game AI. www.aifactorynewsletter.co.uk (accessed September 10, 2014).

[Rollason 00] Rollason, J. 2000. SUPER-SOMA—Solving tactical exchanges in Shogi without tree searching. In *Lecture Notes in Computer Science*, ed. G. Goos, J. Hartmanis, and J. van Leeuwen. LNCS 2063. Springer, Berlin, Germany, ISSN 0302-9743.

25

Monte Carlo Tree Search and Related Algorithms for Games

Nathan R. Sturtevant

25.1 Introduction

This chapter is designed to introduce a number of recent algorithms, developed academically for game AI, primarily in board and card games. However, these algorithms also have significant potential in other video game genres, which we also explore here. This chapter is an expansion of a talk from the GDC 2014 AI Summit. We will introduce four different, but related, algorithms that can be used to create more dynamic and adaptable AI for games. With the description of each algorithm, we will provide examples of contexts where it would be most useful.

25.2 Background

To begin, we introduce a number of classifications between algorithms and other similar concepts that will be used repeatedly in this chapter.

A first important distinction is whether an approach plays strictly in an *online* manner or it also simulates actions *offline* (i.e., not player facing) before finally taking actions online. An online AI is one that gains experience and knowledge about the world strictly from making actions that are player facing. Most generally, an offline AI either ships with a static strategy or performs simulations at runtime that the player cannot see to determine the best action. In particular, we want to distinguish algorithms that require the ability to take and evaluate actions in an offline world before actually performing them in the online world.

The algorithms described in this chapter are *bandit algorithms* because the decisions they make are modeled by n-arm bandits (slot machines). The general n-arm bandit problem is to find the slot machine (a one-armed bandit) that has the best payoff. This is done by trying different bandits and looking at the resulting payoff. So, the assumption is that an action can be taken, and it will then be immediately associated by some reward or payoff. The primary difficulty in this problem is to balance exploiting the current-best slot machine with exploring to make sure that another slot machine doesn't have a better payoff. This problem describes an online slot machine because we pay each time we play a machine. In an offline problem, we would be able to simulate the slot machines offline without cost to find the best one before taking an action in the real world.

These algorithms also can be described as *regret-minimizing algorithms*. Loosely speaking, regret-minimizing algorithms guarantee that you will not regret using the algorithms instead of selecting and always playing one of the n-arm bandit strategies. Note that the quality of this guarantee depends on the strategies that correspond to each of the arms of the bandit. If these strategies are all poor, there is no guarantee that these algorithms will do any better.

Finally, these algorithms all use the notion of *utility* for evaluating states of the game. We use this instead of something like the chance of winning because the goal of an AI in many games is not to win, only to create the perception that it is trying to win. In doing so, the goal is usually to create a compelling experience for the human player. If we give high utility to the actions that help create a compelling experience, then in maximizing utility, the AI will be achieving the desired behavior.

Because it is simple and easy to illustrate, we demonstrate several algorithms using rock–paper–scissors (RPS) first before progressing to real-world examples that are more suited to each algorithm. To review, RPS is a two-player simultaneous game where each player chooses either rock, paper, or scissors. Paper beats rock, scissors beats paper, and rock beats scissors. RPS is usually played repeatedly. For our purposes, we assume that we get a score of 1 if we win, 0 if we draw, and −1 if we lose.

Given this background, we can now introduce our first algorithm.

25.3 Algorithm 1: Online UCB1

The first algorithm we describe, UCB1 [Auer 02], is a simple online bandit algorithm; it is deterministic and easy to implement. A naïve implementation of UCB1 is not perfectly suited for RPS, but after introducing this simple approach, we show to modify our strategies to improve the approach. Slight modifications to UCB1 have recently been proposed to give better regret bounds [Auer 10], but in practice the algorithm is quite robust, even when we break theoretical assumptions about how the algorithm should be used.

We demonstrate UCB1 by using it to play RPS. In our first approach, we assign each action (rock, paper, and scissors) to one of the arms of our slot machine, yielding a three-armed bandit. For each arm, UCB1 maintains the average payoff achieved when playing that arm, as well as the number of times each arm was played. Each time we are asked to make an action, we compute the value of each arm, $v(i)$, according to the formula in the following equation, where $x(i)$ is the average utility when playing arm i, $c(i)$ is the count of how many times we've played arm i, and k is a constant for tuning exploration and exploitation:

$$v(i) = x(i) + \sqrt{\frac{k \ln(t)}{c(i)}} \tag{25.1}$$

When asked to make an action, UCB1 plays the arm that has the maximum value of $v(i)$. The value, $v(i)$, is composed of two parts. The first part is an exploitation component, suggesting that we play the arm with the maximum average payoff. The second component is an exploration component. The more an arm is played, increasing $c(i)$, the smaller this value will be. The more other arms are played, the large the value will be. When payoffs are between 0 and 1, it is suggested that k should have the value 2. In practice, k can be tuned to achieve the desired balance between exploration and exploitation. When first starting, all arms are played once to get initial experience, although this could be preinitialized before ship. These actions are player facing, so it is important to avoid taking bad actions too many times.

We illustrate the resulting behavior in Table 25.1 when playing against a player that always plays rock for $k = 2$. For each action, we show the number of times the action was played ($c(i)$), the average utility of that action ($x(i)$), and the value ($v(i)$) that UCB1 would compute for that action. At time steps 0, 1, and 2, UCB1 has unexplored actions, so it must first explore these actions. At time step 3, the value of paper is $1+\sqrt{2 * \ln 3/1} = 2.48$. Paper is played because this is the best value of any action and continues to be until time step 7. During this time the value of paper decreases because $c(i)$ increases, while the value of scissors and rock increases because t increases. At time step 7, UCB1 finally stops exploiting paper and explores rock to see if playing rock can achieve a better outcome.

If we use UCB1 as an AI to play RPS, it will play in a relatively predictable manner, because there is no randomization. Thus, there are many sequences of actions that will

Table 25.1 Using UCB1 to Select the Next Action and Simulate the Resulting Situation in Order to Evaluate Which Next Action Is Best

	Rock			Paper			Scissors		
Time	$c(i)$	$x(i)$	$v(i)$	$c(i)$	$x(i)$	$v(i)$	$c(i)$	$x(i)$	$v(i)$
0	**0**	**0**	∞	0	0	∞	0	0	∞
1	1	0	0.00	**0**	**0**	∞	0	0	∞
2	1	0	1.18	1	1	2.18	**0**	**0**	∞
3	1	0	1.48	**1**	**1**	**2.48**	1	−1	0.48
4	1	0	1.67	**2**	**1**	**2.18**	1	−1	0.67
5	1	0	1.79	**3**	**1**	**2.04**	1	−1	0.79
6	1	0	1.89	**4**	**1**	**1.95**	1	−1	0.89
7	**1**	**0**	**1.97**	5	1	1.88	1	−1	0.97

be able to exploit the AI behavior. In the preceding example, playing the sequence P, S, R repeatedly will always win. This, of course, may be a desirable behavior if we want to reward the player for figuring this out. Because UCB1 will keep exploring its actions, it will never completely rule out playing bad actions. Thus, it may not be wise to assign a poor action to an arm of the bandit, as it will be played regularly, albeit with decaying frequency. Finally, note that if the opponent starts playing predictably (such as playing the sequence R, P, S repeatedly), this will never be noticed by the AI and never exploited.

To combat these shortcomings, we propose a slightly more interesting way of assigning actions to the arms of the bandit. Instead of letting the arms correspond to low-level actions in the world, we can have them correspond to strategies that are played, where each strategy is well designed and safe to play at any time. For instance, the nonlosing strategy (Nash equilibrium) in RPS is to play randomly. So, this should be the first possible strategy. If we wish to discourage repeated sequences of play, we can have other arms in the bandit correspond to imitation strategies, such as playing the same action the opponent played in the last round or playing the action that would have lost to the opponent in the last round. These strategies will be able to exploit repetitive play by the opponent. Taken together, we know that UCB1 will always default to a reasonable strategy (random) if its other strategies are losing. But if an opponent is playing in a predictable manner, it will be able to exploit that behavior as well.

Sample JavaScript code is included on this book's website (http://www.gameaipro.com), and a simplified portion of the code showing the main logic for implementing UCB1 is shown in Listing 25.1. This code is generic, in that it relies on a separate implementation of functions like `GetActionForStrategy`. Thus, it is simple to change out strategies and see how the play changes.

25.3.1 Applying to Games

While the previous example makes sense for a simple game like RPS, what about more complicated games? At the highest level, for UCB1 to be applicable, the decisions being made must be able to be formulated as bandit problems, with a set of available actions or strategies that result in known utility after they are sampled in a game. Given this restriction, here are several examples of how UCB1 can be used in other scenarios.

First, consider a fighting game like *Prince of Persia*, where enemies have different styles of fighting. There may be a general well-designed AI that works well for many players. But a small percentage of players are able to quickly defeat this general strategy or might learn to do so through the game. Perhaps a second AI is a good counter for these players, but isn't as well tuned for the other players. Instead of shipping a static AI that will fail for some percentage of the players, UCB1 could, at each encounter, be used to choose which AI the human should face next. The utility of the AI could be related to how long it takes the human to dispatch the AI. If the human is always defeating a certain AI quickly, UCB1 will start sending the alternate AI more often and in this way adapt to the player. If it is taking the player too long to defeat the alternate AI, then the first AI would be sent more often instead.

UCB1 works well here because neither AI strategy is fundamentally poor, so it can't make really bad decisions. Additionally, there are many small battles in this type of game, so UCB1 has many opportunities to learn and adapt. In some sense, UCB1 will work

Listing 25.1. An implementation of UCB1 in javascript.

```
function GetNextAction()
{
    if (init == false)
    {
        for (var x = 0; x < numActions; x++)
        {
            count[x] = 0;
            score[x] = 0;
        }
        init = true;
    }
    for (var x = 0; x < numActions; x++)
    {
        if (count[x] == 0)
        {
            ourLastStrategy = x;
            myLastAction = GetActionForStrategy(x);
            return myLastAction;
        }
    }

    var best = 0;
    var bestScore = score[best]/count[best];
    bestScore += sqrt(2*log(totalActions)/count[best]);
    for (var x = 1; x < numActions; x++)
    {
        var xScore = score[x]/count[x];
        xScore += sqrt(2*log(totalActions)/count[x]);
        if (xScore > bestScore)
        {
            best = x;
            bestScore = xScore;
        }
    }
    ourLastStrategy = best;
    myLastAction = GetActionForStrategy(best);
    return myLastAction;
}

function TellOpponentAction(opponentAct)
{
    totalActions++;
    var utility = GetUtility(myLastAction, opponentAct);
    score[myLastAction] += utility;
    count[myLastAction]++;
}
```

well for any game with these two properties. In a shooter, UCB1 might be used to decide whether to deploy a team with bold or cautious AI players. The bold AI would quickly be killed by a player holed up with a sniper rifle, while the cautious AI might sneak up on such a player. This is a natural situation where using UCB1 to balance the types of AI deployed could improve the player experience.

Oftentimes, there is hesitation to apply adaptive algorithms, as players might coerce them to adapt one way in order to exploit them in a key moment with a counterstrategy. This is less likely to be successful when all arms of the bandit are reasonable strategies. But the length of time that the AI plays in a certain way can be limited by only learning over a limited window of play or by weighting recent encounters more than earlier ones. Then, within a few encounters, the AI will be able to adapt back toward another strategy.

This approach would not work well for something like weapon selection in a role-playing game (RPG), because the AI would spend a lot of time trying to attack with poor weapons. It would also not work well when choosing individual attacks in a fighting game, because there are situations where some attacks make no sense or when multiple attacks must be balanced randomly to prevent complete predictability. (We note that sometimes this is desired, so that players can experience the joy of learning to defeat a particular opponent. But it is not always desired of all opponents.) A final shortcoming of this approach is that it learns more slowly because it doesn't consider retrospectively what might have happened if it did something different. In some games, like RPS, we can evaluate what would have happened if we used a different strategy, and we can use that to improve our performance.

25.4 Algorithm 2: Regret Matching

Regret matching [Hart 00] is another online algorithm that is just slightly more complicated than UCB1, but it can produce randomized strategies more suited to games where players act simultaneously or where the AI needs to act in a more unpredictable manner. Regret matching works by asking what would have happened if it had played a different action at each time step. Then, the algorithm directly accumulates any regret that it has for not playing different actions that were more successful. By accumulating this regret over time, the algorithm will converge to strong behavior or, more technically, a correlated equilibrium. We won't cover the theoretical justification for the algorithm here; besides the original paper, the interested reader is referred to the *Algorithmic Game Theory* book [Blum 07].

Regret matching works as follows. For each possible action, the algorithm keeps track of the regret for that action, that is, the gain in utility that could have been achieved by playing that action instead of a different one. Initially, all actions are initialized to have no regret. When no actions have positive regret, we play randomly. Otherwise, we select an action with a biased random in proportion to the positive regret of each action. Each time we take an action, we retrospectively ask what the utility of every alternate action would have been if we had taken it during the last time step. Then, we add to the cumulative regret of each action the difference between the payoff we would have received had we taken the other action and our actual payoff from the action we did take. Thus, if another action would have produced a better payoff, its regret will increase, and we will play it more often.

We illustrate regret matching in RPS, with our bandit arms corresponding to playing each of our actions: rock, paper, and scissors. Initially, we have no accumulated regret and play randomly. Suppose that we play rock and lose to the opponent playing paper. Assuming we get 1 for winning, −1 for losing, and 0 otherwise, our regret for not playing scissors (and winning) is increased by (1 − (−1)) = 2. Playing paper would have tied, so we accumulate regret (0 − (− 1)) = 1. We have not accumulated any positive or negative regret for playing rock. Thus, in the next round, we will play scissors with probability 2/3 and paper with probability 1/3. Suppose that in the next round we play scissors and draw against an opponent playing scissors. Then, our regret for not playing rock will increase by 1, since playing rock would have increased our utility by 1. Our regret for playing paper is decreased by 1, since we would have lost if we had played paper. Thus, our regrets are now 1 for rock, 2 for scissors, and 0 for paper. In the next round, we will play rock with probability 1/3 and scissors 2/3. Note that the algorithm can be improved slightly by computing regret using the expected utility of the action that was taken (according to the probability distribution that determines play) instead of using just the utility of the action that was taken. As with UCB1, regret matching can use strategies instead of actions as the bandit arms.

The code included on the book's website implements regret matching for both actions and strategies. You can play against both to observe play, and you can also try to exploit the algorithm to get a feel for its behavior. Simplified JavaScript code for regret matching can be found in Listing 25.2. The key property that the algorithm needs to run is the ability to introspectively ask what would have happened if other actions were played. Additionally, we need to know the utility that would have resulted for those actions. If this cannot be computed, then regret matching is not an applicable algorithm.

In practice, there are several changes that might be made to ensure better play. First, instead of initializing all regrets to 0, the initial values for the regret can be initialized to produce reasonable play and influence the rate of adaptation. If, in RPS, all initial regrets are set to 10, the algorithm will start adapting play in only a few rounds. But if all initial regrets are set to 1000, it will take significantly longer for the program to adapt. Related to this, it may be worthwhile to limit how much negative regret can be accumulated, as this will limit how long it takes to unlearn anything that is learned.

Finally, regret matching can be used both as an offline or online algorithm when the game has two players and the payoffs for each player sum to zero. Regret matching is the core algorithm used recursively for solving large Poker games [Johanson 07]. In this context, the game is solved offline and the static strategy is used online, although slight modifications are needed for this to work correctly.

25.4.1 Applying to Games

Once again it is natural to ask the question of how this approach can apply to more complicated video games, instead of a simple game like RPS. We provide two examples where the algorithm would work well and one example where it cannot be applied.

Our first example is due to David Sirlin in situations he calls "Yomi" [Sirlin 08]. Consider a two-player fighting game where one player has just been knocked down. This player can either get up normally or get up with a rising attack. The other player can either attack the player as they get up or block the anticipated rising attack. This situation looks a lot like RPS, in that both players must make simultaneous decisions that will then result

Listing 25.2. An implementation of regret matching in javascript.

```
function GetNextAction()
{
    if (init == false)
    {
        for (var x = 0; x < numActions; x++)
            regret[x] = 0;
        init = true;
    }
    for (var x = 0; x < numActions; x++)
    {
        lastAction[x] = GetActionForStrategy(x);
    }

    var sum = 0;
    for (var x = 0; x < numActions; x++)
        sum += (regret[x]>0)?regret[x]:0;
    if (sum <= 0)
    {
        ourLastAction = floor(random()*numActions);
        return ourLastAction;
    }
    for (var x = 0; x < numActions; x++)
    {
        //add up the positive regret
        if (regret[x] > 0)
            chance[x] = regret[x];
        else
            chance[x] = 0;
        //build the cumulative distribution
        if (x > 0)
            chance[x] += chance[x-1];
    }
    var p = random();
    for (var x = 0; x < numActions; x++)
    {
        if (p < chance[x])
        {
            ourLastStrategy = x;
            ourLastAction = lastAction[x];
            return ourLastAction;
        }
    }
    return numActions-1;
}
```

```
function TellOpponentAction(opponentAct)
{
    lastOpponentAction = opponentAct;
    for (var x = 0; x < numActions; x++)
    {
        regret[x] += GetUtility(lastAction[x], opponentAct);
        regret[x] -= GetUtility(ourLastAction, opponentAct);
    }
}
```

in immediate payoff (damage). Here, regret matching would be applied independently in each relevant context, such as after a knockdown, to determine how to play at that point. During play, the AI will appropriately balance its behavior for each of these situations to maximize its own payoff.

In these situations, the AI has the potential to balance attacks far better than a human player and, as a result, might be almost unbeatable. (Conversely, identifying the current situation properly might be too error prone to result in good play.) AI players using regret matching for their strategies can be given more personality or a preferred playing style by biasing their utility. If we want a player that likes to punch, we simply give more utility for performing punches, even if they are unsuccessful. This fools the AI into performing more punch actions, because it will maximize utility by doing so.

In this context, regret matching can also be used offline prior to shipping the game to build a single strong player via self-play. This player would not adapt at runtime but would still randomize its behavior at runtime, resulting in play that cannot be exploited.

For our second example, we go from very low-level character control to high-level strategic decision making. Suppose that we are playing multiple rounds of a game like *Starcraft* against an opponent and we must decide what sort of build tree to use at the beginning of the game—optimizing for rushing or some other play styles. We can use regret matching for this purpose if we are able to introspectively evaluate whether we chose the best strategy. This is done by looking to see, after the match was complete, whether another strategy would have been better. For instance, we might evaluate the building selection and resource distribution of our opponent after 3 min of play (before either team has a chance to see the other team and adapt their resulting play). If we see that we might have immediately defeated the opponent had we chosen to follow a rush strategy, we then accumulate regret for not rushing.

To give an example where regret matching will not work well, consider again a fighting game like *Prince of Persia*, where we might be choosing what sort of AI to send out against the human player. Once the AI acts in a way that influences the human behavior, we can no longer ask what would have happened if we had sent different AI types. Thus, we will not be able to use an algorithm like regret matching in this context.

25.5 Algorithm 3: Offline UCB1

The algorithms introduced thus far primarily act in an online manner, without considering the implications of their actions beyond the feedback collected *after* every action is taken. This means that they are best used when the strategies or actions taken will always be reasonable, and the main question is how to balance these actions in order to provide a compelling gameplay experience. But this isn't always possible or desirable. In many situations, we need an algorithm that will reason to rule out bad actions and never take them. To do this, we perform offline simulations of actions in the world before deciding on a final action to take.

To discuss possible options concretely, move away from RPS and use the same example found in the introductory chapter to this section of the book—a simple role-playing game (RPG) battle. In that chapter, we discussed how a one-step search combined with a strong evaluation function would produce reasonable play. (The evaluation function should return the utility for the AI in that state.) The drawback of that approach is that we must write the evaluation function and tune it for high-quality play. The first new idea here is that it is much easier to write an evaluation function for the end of the game than for the middle of the game. So, if we play out a game to the end using some strategy (even random), we can often get a better evaluation than we would by trying to write an evaluation function after a 1-ply search. We demonstrate this using an RPG battle, where the AI is controlling a nonplayer character (NPC) spellcaster that has a fighter companion. The spellcaster will primarily use ranged attacks from a magical staff but can occasionally cast either a healing spell or an area attack such as a fireball.

Previously, we discussed how bandit algorithms can use both low-level actions and high-level strategies as the arms for the bandit. Here, we will combine these ideas together. We will use the primitive actions as the arms for our bandit using UCB1. But instead of actually taking actions online in the world, we simulate the actions internally. Then, instead of just applying a utility function to evaluate the best action, we continue by using a high-level strategy to simulate actions through the end of the current battle.

This is illustrated in Figure 25.1. The NPC must act using one of these three actions: healing, attacking with a staff, or casting a fireball. UCB1 selects an action to play and then simulates the rest of the battle using some default strategy. When the battle is over, we must compute the utility of the resulting state, for instance, returning the total health in our party after the battle finishes (perhaps adding some bonus for every party member that is still alive). This evaluation resembles what would be used in a 1-ply search, but the evaluation is much easier than before because we don't have to evaluate every

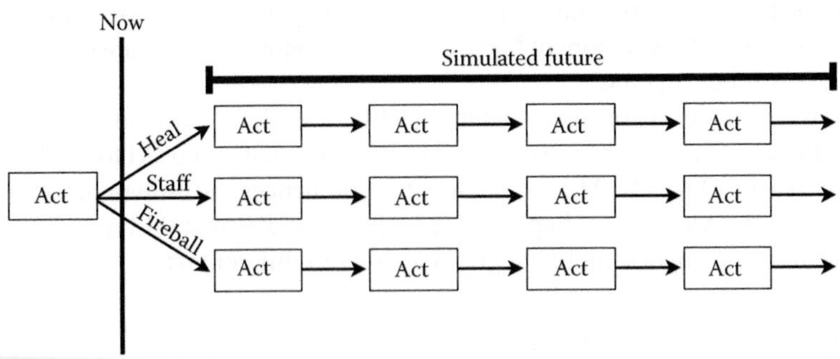

Figure 25.1

Using UCB1 to select the next action and simulate the resulting situation in order to evaluate which next action is best.

situation possible in the battle; we are restricted to only evaluating states where one team is defeated. Instead of trying to predict the outcome of the battle, we just need to evaluate if our party survived and compute the utility how many resources we have left. Suppose that casting a fireball would use all available manna and allow no other spells to be cast through the remainder of the battle. In the short term, this might seem good, but in the long term, the inability to cast healing may cause us to lose the battle. Being able to simulate the battle to its end will reveal this expected outcome.

Now, we might do this once per action and then select the best action, but there is often significant uncertainty in a battle, including randomness or other choices like the selection of what enemies to target. Thus, instead of just simulating each move once, it is valuable to simulate moves multiple times to get better estimates of the final outcome. If we sample every top-level action uniformly, we waste resources simulating bad strategies and lose out on gaining more information about strategies that have similar payoffs. This is where UCB1 shines; it will balance playing the best action with exploring actions that look worse in order to ensure that we don't miss out on another action that works well in practice. It should be noted that if we are going to simulate to the end of the battle, our default strategy also must provide actions not only for the AI player but also for all other players in the battle.

We show high-level pseudocode for using UCB1 in this manner in Listing 25.3. This code just provides the high-level control of UCB1 using the definition of `GetNextAction()` defined previously in Listing 25.1. In the previous example, this function was called each time an action was needed for play. Now, this is called as many times as possible while time remains.

After generalizing this approach to the UCT algorithm in the next section, we will discuss further the situations where this algorithm could be used in practice.

Listing 25.3. Pseudocode for using UCB1 to control simulations for finding the next best move. This code uses the `GetNextAction()` method from Listing 25.1 for playing actions.

```
function SimulateUCB()
{
    while (time remains)
    {
        act = GetNextAction();
        ApplyAction(act);
        utility = PlayDefaultStrategy();
        UndoAction(act);
        TellUtility(act, utility);
    }
    return GetBestAction();
}

function TellUtility(act, utility)
{
    totalActions++;
    score[act] += utility;
    count[act]++;
}
```

25.6 Algorithm 4: UCT

UCB1 as described in the last section is a 1-ply search algorithm in that it only explicitly considers the first action before reverting to some default policy for play. In practice there can be value in considering several actions together. For instance, there may be two spells that, when cast together, are far more powerful than when used alone. But if they must be cast from weakest to strongest to be effective, a 1-ply algorithm may not be able to find and exploit this combination of spells. By considering the influence of longer chains of actions, we give our AI the ability to discover these combinations automatically. The generalization of UCB1 to trees is called UCT [Kocsis 06]; this is the final algorithm we present in this chapter. UCT is the most popular specific algorithm that falls into the general class of Monte Carlo tree search (MCTS) algorithms.

UCT extends the use of UCB1 in the previous section by building a dynamic tree in memory, using the UCB1 algorithm to direct the growth of the tree. UCT builds a nonuniform tree that is biased toward the more interesting part of the state space. The longer the search, the larger the tree, and the stronger the resulting play.

Over time, researchers have converged on describing UCT and MCTS algorithms via four stages of behavior. The first stage is selection, where the best moves from the root to the leaves of the in-memory tree are selected according to the UCB1 rule at each node. The second stage is expansion, where new nodes are added to the UCT tree. The third stage is simulation, where some default policy is used to simulate the game. The final stage is propagation, where the value at the end of the simulation is propagated through the path in the UCT tree, updating the values in the tree.

We walk through an example to make these ideas concrete. In our example, a spell-casting AI is allowed to cast two spells back to back, after which the normal battle will continue. We assume that a gas cloud can be ignited by a fireball to do additional damage. Figure 25.2 shows the root of a UCT tree for this situation with three children, one child for each spell that can be cast. The nodes in black (nodes 1, 2, and 3) are in the tree prior

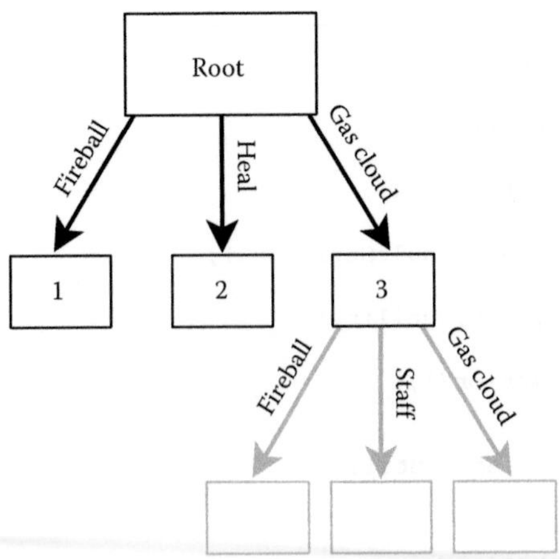

Figure 25.2

UCT selection and expansion phases.

to starting our example. The selection phase starts at the root and uses the UCB1 rule to select the next child to explore according to the current payoffs and number of samples thus far. This is repeated until a leaf node is reached. In this case we select the third spell and reach the leaf of the tree. Each time we reach the leaf of the tree, we expand that node, adding its children into the tree. Since we haven't seen these new nodes before, we select the first possible action and then continue to the simulation phase.

In Figure 25.3 we show the simulation phase. Starting after the fireball action, we use some policy to play out the game until the current battle is over. Note that in this simulation we will simulate actions for all players in the battle, whether or not they are on our team. When we reach the end of the battle, we score the resulting state. Then, we modify the UCB1 values at the root, state 3, and state 4, updating the number of simulations and average utility to take into account the result of this simulation. If there are two players in the game, nodes that belong to the opposing player get different utilities than those belonging to the AI. Following what is done in the minimax algorithm, this is usually just

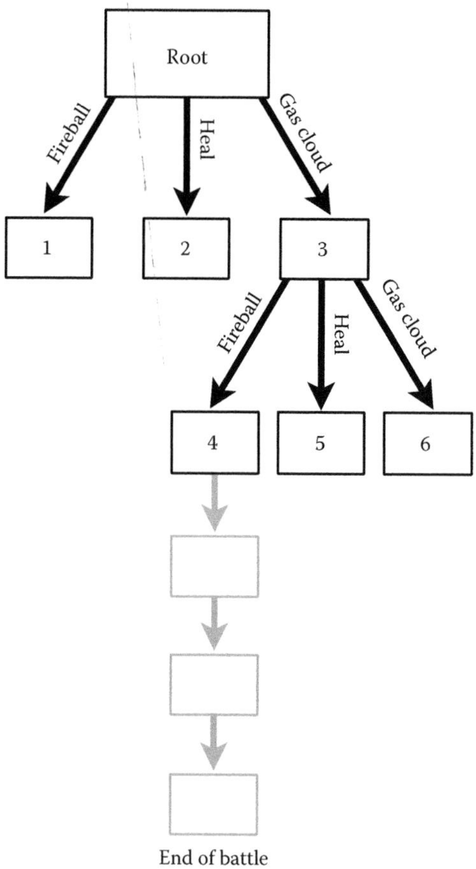

Figure 25.3

UCT simulation and propagation phases.

the negation of the score of the AI player. If there are multiple competing players, different utilities should be backed up for each player [Sturtevant 07].

This entire process should be repeated many times. The more it is repeated, the better the resulting strategy. In practice, what would usually happen in an example like this one is that initially the fireball would be preferred, as it immediately causes significant damage. But as more simulations are performed and the tree grows, the strategy of a gas cloud followed by a fireball emerges, as this combination is much more effective than a fireball followed by a gas cloud.

Pseudocode for a recursive implementation of UCT is shown in Listing 25.4. The top-level code just repeatedly calls the selection rule until the time allotment runs out. The tree selection code uses the UCB1 rule to step down the tree. Upon reaching the end, it expands the tree and then simulates the rest of the game. Finally, the counts and utilities for all nodes along the path are updated.

Listing 25.4. Pseudocode for UCT.

```
function SimulateUCT()
{
    while (time remains)
    {
        TreeSelectionAndUpdate(root, false);
    }
    return GetBestAction();
}

function TreeSelectionAndUpdate(currNode, simulateNow)
{
    if (GameOver(currNode))
        return GetUtility(currNode);
    if (simulateNow)
    {
        //Simulate the rest of the game and get the utility
        value = DoPlayout(currNode);
    }
    else if (IsLeaf(currNode))
    {
        AddChildrenToTree(currNode);
        value = TreeSelectionAndUpdate(currNode, true);
    }
    else {
        child = GetNextState();//using UCB1 rule (in tree)
        value = TreeSelectionAndUpdate(child, false);
    }

    //If we have 2 players, we would negate this value if
    //the second player is moving at this node
    currNode.value += value;
    currNode.count++;
    return value;
}
```

25.6.1 Important Implementation Details

Those who have worked with UCT and other MCTS algorithms have shared significant implementation details that are important for improving the performance of UCT in practice.

First, it is very important to look at the constant that balances exploration and exploitation when tuning UCT. If this constant is set wrong, UCT will either explore all options uniformly or not sufficiently explore alternate options. We always look at the distribution of simulations across actions at the first ply of the UCT tree to see if they are balanced properly in relation to the payoffs.

As memory allocation can be expensive, it is worthwhile to preallocate nodes for the UCT tree. A simple array of data UCT nodes is sufficient for this purpose. Although many implementations of UCT add new nodes to the tree after every simulation, the process of adding new nodes can be delayed by requiring a node to be visited some minimum number of times before it is expanded. This usually saves memory without significantly degrading performance.

After simulation, a final action must be selected for execution. This action shouldn't be selected using the UCB1 rule, as there is a chance it will sample a bad move instead of taking the best one possible. Two common approaches are to choose the action that was sampled the most or to choose the action that has the highest payoff. In some domains, these alternate strategies can have a large influence on performance, but in others, both are equally good, so this should be tested in your domain.

UCT works best in games or scenarios that are converging. That is, the games are likely to end even under a fixed strategy or under random play. If a game isn't converging, the game simulations may be too expensive or too long to return meaning information about the game. Thus, it is common to do things like disable backward moves during simulations; in an RPG, it might be worth disabling healing spells if both parties have them available. The quality of the simulations can have a significant impact on the quality of play, so it is important to understanding their influence.

25.6.2 UCT Enhancements and Variations

There is a large body of academic researcher's work looking at modifications and enhancements to UCT and MCTS algorithms. While we can't discuss all of these in detail, we highlight a few key ideas that have been used widely.

- In games like Go, the same action appears in many different parts of the game tree. This information can be shared across the game tree to improve performance [Gelly 07].
- In some games the simulations are too long and expensive to be effective. But cutting off simulations at a shallower depth can still be more effective than not running simulations at all [Lorentz 08].
- There are many ways to parallelize the UCT algorithm [Barriga 14], improving performance.

At the writing of this chapter, a recent journal paper [Browne 12] catalogs many more of these improvements, but there has also been significant new work since this publication.

25.6.3 Applying to Games

UCT and MCTS approaches are best suited for games with discrete actions and a strong strategic component. This would include most games that are adaptations of board games and games that simulate battles, including tabletop-style games and RPGs. The last 10 years of research has shown, however, that these approaches work surprisingly well in many domains that would, on the surface, not seem to be amenable to these techniques. Within a decade or two, it would not be surprising to find that minimax-based approaches have largely disappeared in favor of UCT; chess is currently one of the few games where minimax is significantly stronger than UCT approaches. In fact, MCTS techniques have already found their way into commercial video games such as *Total War: Rome II*, as described in the 2014 Game/AI Conference. We believe that they could be very effective for companion AI in RPGs.

The main barrier to applying UCT and MCTS approaches in a game is the computational requirements. While they can run on limited time and memory budgets, they are still more expensive than a static evaluation. Thus, if simulation is very expensive or if the number of available actions is very large, these approaches may not work. But, even in these scenarios, it is often possible to abstract the world or limit the number of possible actions to make this approach feasible.

25.7 Conclusion

In this chapter, we have presented four algorithms that can be used in a variety of game situations to build more interesting and more adaptive AI behavior. With each algorithm, we have presented examples of possible use, but we suspect that there are many more opportunities to use these algorithms that we have considered. Most of these algorithms are based in some way on UCB1, a simple and robust bandit algorithm.

We hope that this work will challenge the commercial AI community to explore new approaches for authoring strong AI behaviors. If nothing else, we add four more techniques to the toolbox of AI programmers for building game AI.

References

[Auer 02] Auer, P., Cesa-Bianchi, N., and Fischer, P. 2002. Finite-time analysis of the multi-armed bandit problem. *Machine Learning* 47:235–256.

[Auer 10] Auer, P. and Ortner, R. 2010. UCB revisited: Improved regret bounds for the stochastic multi-armed bandit problem. *Periodica Mathematica Hungarica* 61:55–65.

[Barriga 14] Barriga, N., Stanescu, N., and Buro, M. 2014. Parallel UCT search on GPUs. *IEEE Conference on Computational Intelligence and Games*, Dortmund, Germany, pp. 1–7.

[Blum 07] Blum, A. and Mansour, Y. 2007. Learning, regret minimization, and equilibria. In *Algorithmic Game Theory*, ed. N. Nisan, pp. 79–102. Cambridge University Press, Cambridge, U.K.

[Browne 12] Browne, C., Powley, E., Whitehouse, D., Lucas, S., Cowling, P., Rohlfshagen, P., Tavener, S., Perez, D., Samothrakis S., and Colton, S. 2012. A survey of Monte Carlo tree search methods. *IEEE Transactions on Computational Intelligence and AI in Games* 4(1):1–43.

[Gelly 07] Gelly, S. and Silver, D. 2007. Combining online and offline knowledge in UCT. *International Conference on Machine Learning. ACM International Conference Proceeding Series,* Corvallis, OR, pp. 273–280.

[Hart 00] Hart, S. and Mas-Colell, A., 2000. A simple adaptive procedure leading to correlated equilibrium. *Econometrica* 58:1127–1150.

[Johanson 07] Johanson, M., 2007. Robust strategies and counter-strategies: Building a champion level computer poker player. Master's thesis, Department of Computing Science, University of Alberta, Edmonton, Alberta, Canada.

[Kocsis 06] Kocsis, L. and Szepesvári, C. 2006. Bandit based Monte-Carlo planning. In *European Conference on Machine Learning*, pp. 282–293. Springer, Berlin, Germany.

[Lorentz 08] Lorentz, R. 2008. Amazons discover Monte-Carlo. *Computers and Games* 5131:13–24.

[Sirlin 08] Sirlin, D. 2008. Yomi layer 3: Knowing the mind of the opponent. http://www.sirlin.net/articles/yomi-layer-3-knowing-the-mind-of-the-opponent.html (accessed September 15, 2014).

[Sturtevant 07] Sturtevant, N. 2007. An analysis of UCT in multi-player games. *Computers and Games* 5131:37–49.

26

Rolling Your Own Finite-Domain Constraint Solver

Leif Foged and Ian Horswill

26.1 Introduction

Constraint programming is a kind of declarative programming. Rather than specifying *how* to solve the problem using some specific algorithm, the programmer provides a description of *what* a solution would look like. Then, a domain-independent search algorithm finds a solution using the description.

For example, suppose you are building a rogue-like or a dungeon crawler and you want to decide what items and enemies to put in what rooms. You probably know something about what you want in the rooms. You might want the number of enemies to be in a certain range and the amount of supplies to be in some other range, so that the level is balanced. You may also want to limit the number of goodies in a particular room, restrict certain key items to only appear in certain kinds of rooms like choke points, or outlaw having enemies in adjacent rooms.

You could probably write an *ad hoc* algorithm to do that and get it to work eventually, but it would take a fair amount of your time, time that could be better spent on other things. And it could have some very subtle bugs like making unsolvable levels once every 700 runs or going into an infinite recursion every 3000 runs. And you might get the algorithm debugged just in time for your design lead to tell you there's some new constraint you need to enforce, so you need to do it all over again.

Another example would be character or vehicle creation, either for generating NPCs or for use in the UI for the player character. You know a character needs some armor, a weapon, some skills, and so on, subject to some compatibility restrictions (e.g., evil mages can't wear the Divine Armor of Archangel Bruce) and some limit on build points. Again, you could roll your own algorithm, and it might be more efficient than an off-the-shelf algorithm for general constraint satisfaction, but it could be a time-consuming nightmare to debug. With the off-the-shelf algorithm, you already know it works. Provided it's fast enough for your needs, you can just code it up and move on to other issues.

This chapter will show you how to implement your own simple constraint solver. We will talk about the most common type of constraint satisfaction problem, finite-domain problems, and a simple and reasonably fast technique for solving them.

26.2 Simple Example

To simplify the presentation, we will use a simpler example than the aforementioned ones. Imagine you are generating a level for a tile game. There are 16 blocks and 6 possible colors for each block, as shown in Figure 26.1.

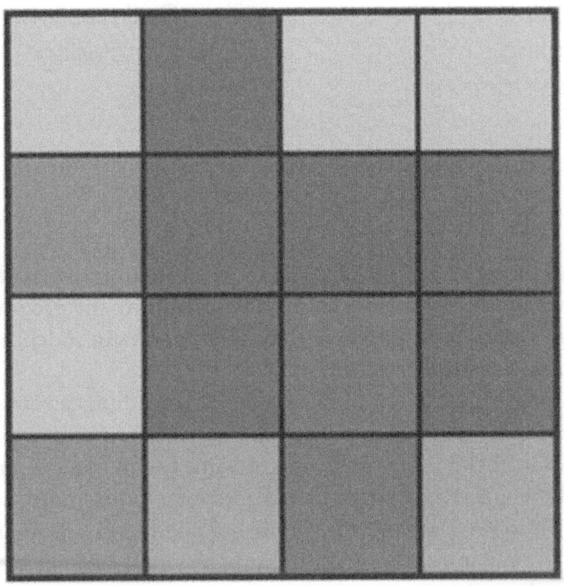

Figure 26.1

A possible level for our tile-based game.

And you need to select colors for the initial configuration, subject to some set of restrictions. For example, we might want to ensure that all six colors appear somewhere, no color appears on more than four tiles, and certain adjacent tiles have to have the same color. So we have a set of choices (the color of each individual block) and a set of restrictions on those choices. In constraint programming parlance, choices are known as *variables* and restrictions are known as *constraints*. The set of possible values for a given variable is called its *domain*. In this case, our variables have six different possible values (colors), so this is a *finite-domain* constraint satisfaction problem.

Finite-domain constraint satisfaction problems (CSPs) are the most widely studied and best understood constraint problems. In practice, the domains need to be not just finite, but small, so they tend to involve things like enums, booleans, or small integers. Finite-domain methods aren't practical for floats, even though there are technically only a finite number of 32-bit IEEE floats. Finite-domain CSPs are often used for solving configuration problems, such as generating puzzles or game levels. More broadly, they are useful for many of the things random number generators are used for in games today, but offer the ability to filter out classes of obviously bad outputs.

Here are some examples of constraints we can efficiently implement with a finite-domain constraint solver:

- Two specific blocks must have the same color.
- Three specific blocks must each have different colors.
- Some specific blocks must be blue.
- Some specific blocks cannot be green.
- Any two diagonal blocks must have different colors.
- At most four blocks of the same color.
- At least three red blocks.

All of these constraints share a common theme: as we *narrow* the possible values (colors) for one variable (block), we (often) also narrow the possible values of other variables involved in the same constraint. For instance, if two blocks are required to have the same color, then forcing one block to be red forces the other to be red as well. We will return to this idea shortly and discuss how exploiting the specific relationships between variables often enables us to dramatically speed up our algorithm.

We will structure the remainder of this article by starting with a simple brute-force algorithm and progressively making it faster and more sophisticated. Our primary focus is on making the code and explanations intuitive and clear, but we will occasionally shift gears to discuss practical performance optimizations.

26.3 Algorithm 1: Brute Force

There are 16 blocks and 6 possible colors for each block. For each block, we will assign a variable (`v1`, `v2`, etc.) to hold its color, as shown in Listing 26.1.

In the case of our block game, there are 16 possible tiles with 6 choices each, or 2,821,109,907,456 total possible levels. Even with relatively simple constraints, it may take quite a long time to discover an assignment of colors to blocks that satisfies them all.

Listing 26.1. An iteration of all possible assignments of colors to blocks.

```
foreach color for v1
   foreach color for v2
      foreach color for v3
         ...
            foreach color for v16
               if ConstraintsNotViolated()
                  return [v1, v2, v3, ... v16]
```

Even worse, it's easy to find situations that will cause this algorithm to exhibit worst-case performance. Suppose we always try colors in the same order, say blue, green, yellow, etc. So the first color considered for any block is always blue. If we have the constraint that the first two blocks have different colors, that is, `v1 != v2`, then for the first time through the two earlier outer loops, we have `v1 = v2 = blue`, which is already a violation of the constraint. But the algorithm won't notice because it doesn't check for constraint violations until it gets all the way into the innermost loop.

Worse, when it does find the constraint violation, it won't jump back up to the outer loops, but rather blindly run all the inner loops to completion. So it will mechanically grind through all 78 billion possible color assignments for blocks `v3` through `v16` before considering a different color for `v2`, which was the actual source of the problem.

26.4 Algorithm 2: Backward Checking

There are some obvious optimizations to the brute-force approach. The simplest is **backward checking**. Each time we make a choice about a block's color, we verify that it's at least consistent with the other block colors we've chosen so far. If it's not, we can skip the evaluation of any additional nested loops and go directly to the next possible color for the current block. This gives us an algorithm like the one shown in Listing 26.2.

This approach is much better. It avoids the problem of exhaustively trying values of irrelevant variables when an already inconsistent set of choices has been made.

Listing 26.2. An iteration of all possible assignments of colors with backward checking.

```
foreach color for v1
   if ConstraintsNotViolated()
      foreach color for v2
         if ConstraintsNotViolated()
         foreach color for v3
            if ConstraintsNotViolated()
               ...
                  foreach color v16
                     if ConstraintsNotViolated()
                        return [v1, v2, v3, ... v16]
```

But unfortunately, it only checks that the choice we just made is consistent with the choices we've already made, not with future choices. Suppose instead of constraining the first two blocks to have different colors, we instead constrain the *first and last* blocks to be the same color and then add the constraint that no more than two blocks may be blue. Again, on our first pass through the two outer loops, the first two blocks get assigned blue. That doesn't violate any constraints *per se*. But since the first and last blocks have to have the same color, the last block must also be blue and will violate the two-blue-blocks constraint when we get around to assigning a color to the last block.

So choosing the first two blocks to be blue really does violate the constraints; the algorithm just won't detect it until it tries to assign a color to the last block. So once again, we end up trying 78 billion combinations before we give up and fix the bad choice we made at the beginning.

26.5 Algorithm 3: Forward Checking

To fix this new failure case, we need to detect when a choice we're making now precludes any possible choice for some other variable we have to assign in the future. More generally, we'd like to be able to reason about how the choices we've made so far *narrow* our remaining choices.

We can do this by explicitly representing the *set* of remaining candidates for a given variable rather than just a single value. We start by assuming any variable can have any value. When we choose a value for a variable, we're really just narrowing its set of possible values to a single value. If there is a constraint between that variable and some other variable, then we can usually narrow the set of possibilities for the other variable. This not only reduces the number of choices we need to explore but also lets us know when we've made an impossible set of choices.

Let's walk through an example in detail. To keep things simple, let's assume that we only have 4 blocks, so four variables, `v1`, `v2`, `v3`, and `v4`. Our constraints will be that

- Variables `v1`, `v2`, and `v3` must all have *different* values from one another
- Variables `v2` and `v4` must have the *same* value

We can represent this with the graph in Figure 26.2. Box nodes represent our variables, along with their possible values (R, G, B, C, M, and Y), circle nodes represent the constraints between them, and the edges specify which variables participate in which constraints.

As before, we start by picking a value for one of the variables. So, again, we assign `v1` the first color, blue (B), which means removing all other possible values, shown in Figure 26.3.

At this point, our previous algorithm would blindly pick a color for `v2`. In fact, it would make `v2` be blue, which violates the inequality (`!=`) constraint. But we can do better. We can *propagate* the value of `v1` through the graph to restrict the values of the other variables in advance. In this case, we know that `v1` can only be blue, but `v2` and `v3` have to be different from `v1`, so we can **rule out** blue for each of them, as shown in Figure 26.4.

But wait—there's more! Since `v2` and `v4` are joined by an equality constraint, `v4` can't have any value that `v2` doesn't have (or vice versa). So `v4` can't be blue either! This is shown in Figure 26.5.

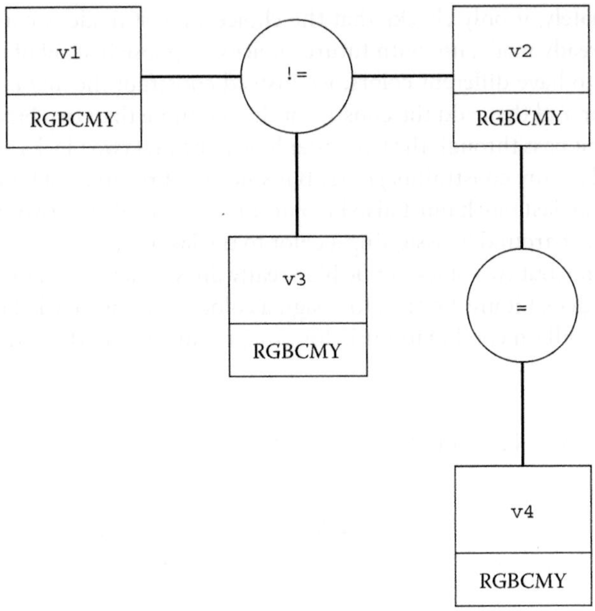

Figure 26.2

A graphical representation of the problem's variables and constraints.

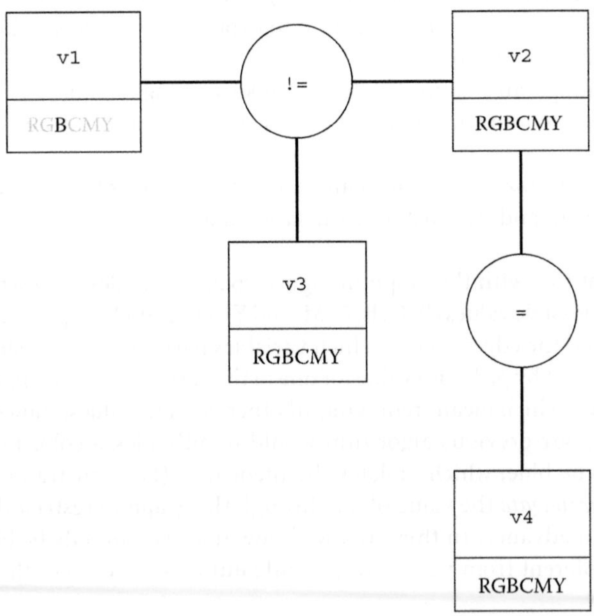

Figure 26.3

Variable `v1` is assigned blue (B), with all other color possibilities removed from `v1`.

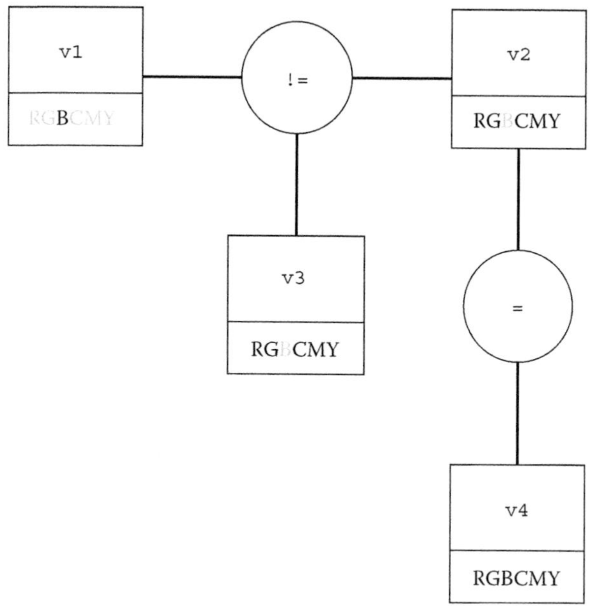

Figure 26.4

The value of `v1` is propagated through the graph, causing blue (B) to be removed from `v2` and `v3` due to the inequality constraint.

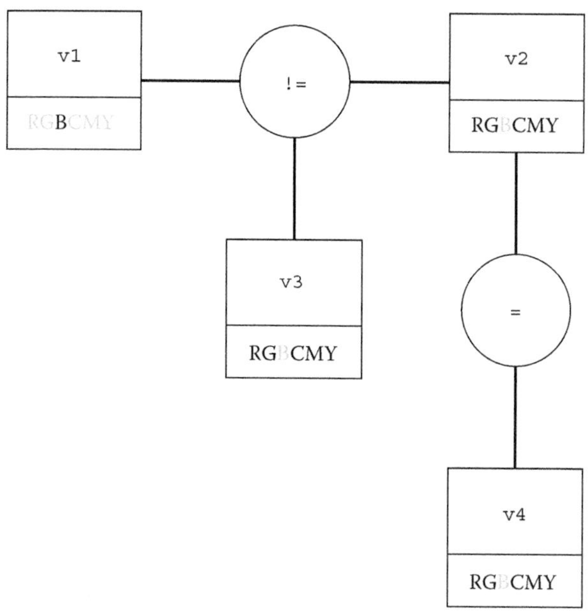

Figure 26.5

Constraints are further propagated to remove blue (B) from `v4`, due to the equality constraint between `v2` and `v4`.

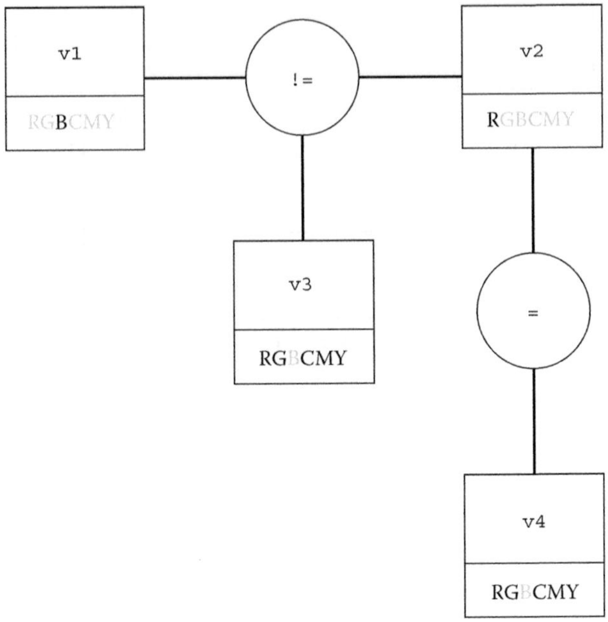

Figure 26.6

The variable v2 is assigned red (R).

Now that there are no changes left to propagate through our constraints, we can resume our earlier algorithm and select a value for v2. Since we already removed blue (B) from its set of possible values, we will try red (R), shown in Figure 26.6.

Once again, we can propagate this choice through our constraints. Since `v4 = v2` and we just decided v2 was red, we effectively forced v4 to be red. Moreover, since `v3 != v2`, we can remove red from the possible values for v3, shown in Figure 26.7.

At this point, we just have one variable left, v3, and we've narrowed it to only four possibilities. We try one of them, say, green (G), shown in Figure 26.8.

Again, we propagate it through the constraint network. In this case, that means ruling out green as a possible color for v1 and v2. But since we'd already ruled out green for each of them, we don't have to take any further action. So we know we have a valid solution.

26.6 Detecting Inconsistencies

That worked out very well for us, but here's an example where it doesn't work out as well. Suppose we're choosing colors for our four blocks, but we can only use three colors, and we have two different inequality constraints, such that every pair of blocks has to have different colors, except for v1 and v4, shown in Figure 26.9.

This problem is perfectly solvable, but it requires choosing the same color for both v1 and v4. Unfortunately, search algorithms don't know that. So suppose it chooses blue for v1 and propagates (ruling out blue for v2 and v3), shown in Figure 26.10.

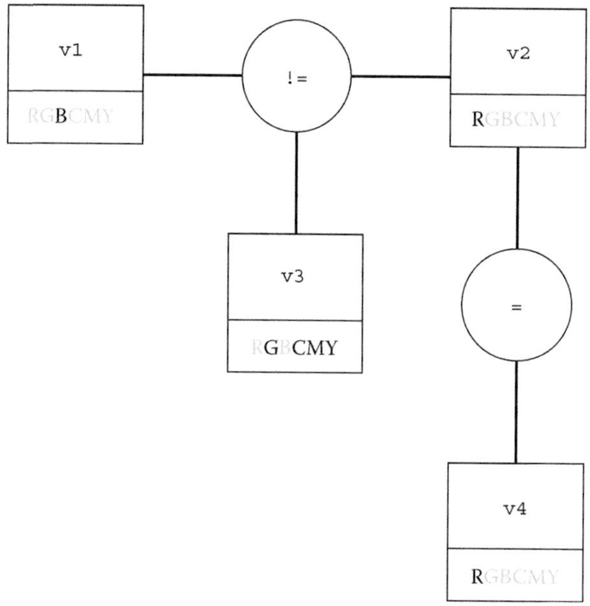

Figure 26.7

The variable v4 is now red (R) due to the equality constraint between v2 and v4. Further, red (R) can be removed from v3's possibilities due to the constraint v3 != v2.

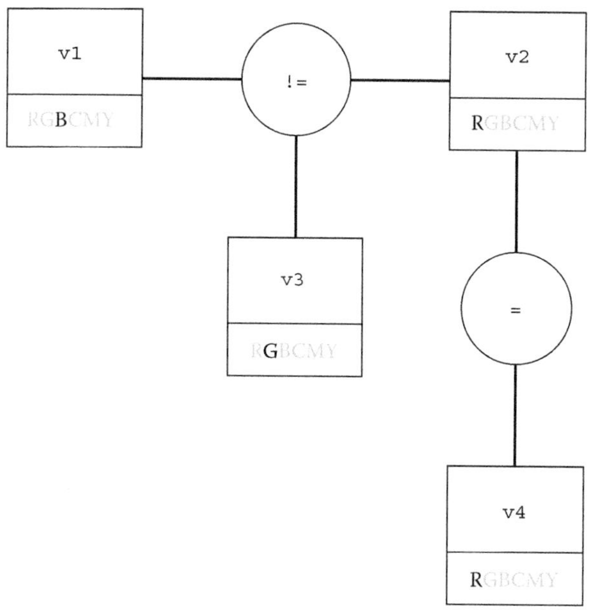

Figure 26.8

The variable v3 is chosen as green (G). From previous steps, v1 is blue (B), v2 is red (R), and c4 is red (R). This is a valid solution since it meets all constraints.

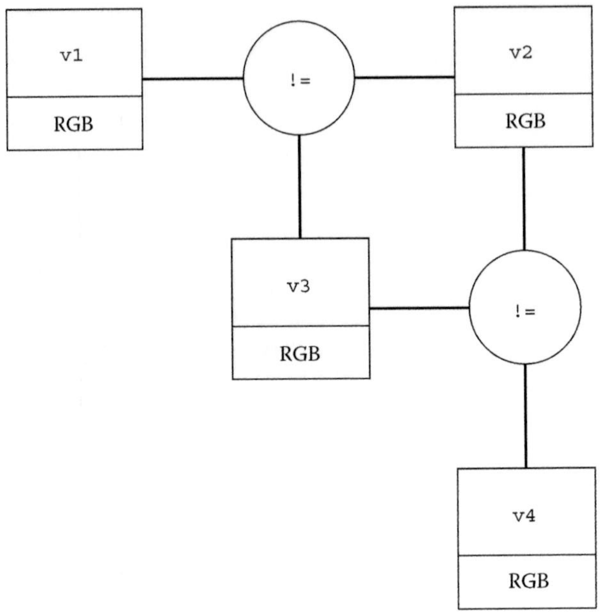

Figure 26.9

Only three colors allowed, with two different inequality constraints.

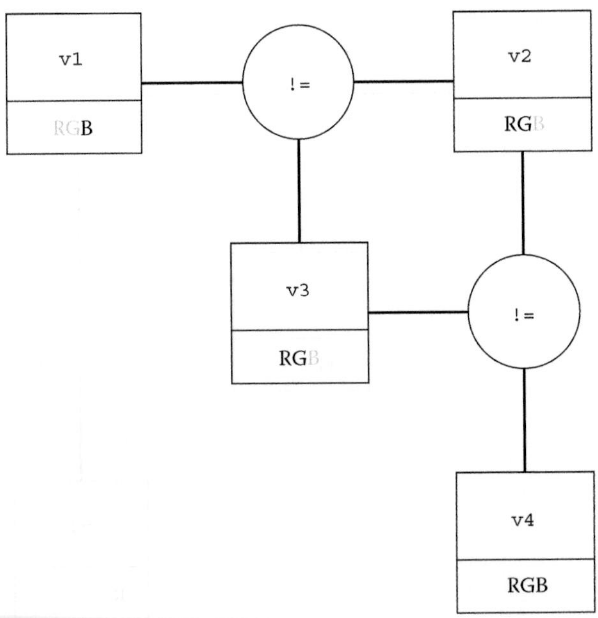

Figure 26.10

The variable `v1` is assigned blue (B) and the constraint is propagated such that blue (B) is ruled out for `v2` and `v3`.

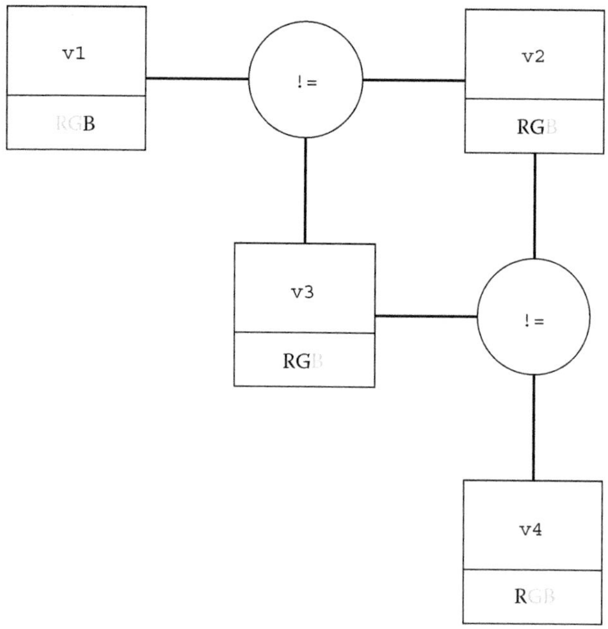

Figure 26.11

The algorithm choose red (R) for v4.

So far so good, but now suppose that for whatever reason, the algorithm chooses red for v4, as shown in Figure 26.11.

Now we have a problem when we propagate. First, v4 tells v2 and v3 that they can't be red. But that means they've both been narrowed down to one choice (green), shown in Figure 26.12.

This violates both the inequality constraints, but the algorithm hasn't noticed this yet. Instead, it blindly continues to propagate the constraints. In this case, both v2 and v3 were just narrowed, so their narrowed values need to get propagated through the network. Let's say it propagates v3 first. Since it's been narrowed to just green, it removes green from the possible values for the other nodes. That's not a problem for v1 and v4, but for v2, green was all that was left, as seen in Figure 26.13.

We've narrowed the possible values for v2 to the empty set, meaning there's no possible value for v2 that's compatible with the values we've assigned the other variables. That means the last choice we made (assigning red to v4) *necessarily* leads to a constraint violation given the choices made before it (in this case, assigning blue to v1), and so we need to choose a different color for v4.

That's all well and good, except that in the meantime we've gone and changed the values of v2 and v3. So when we decide v4 can't be red, we need to set everything back to the way it was just before we chose red for v4. In other words, we need to implement *undo*.

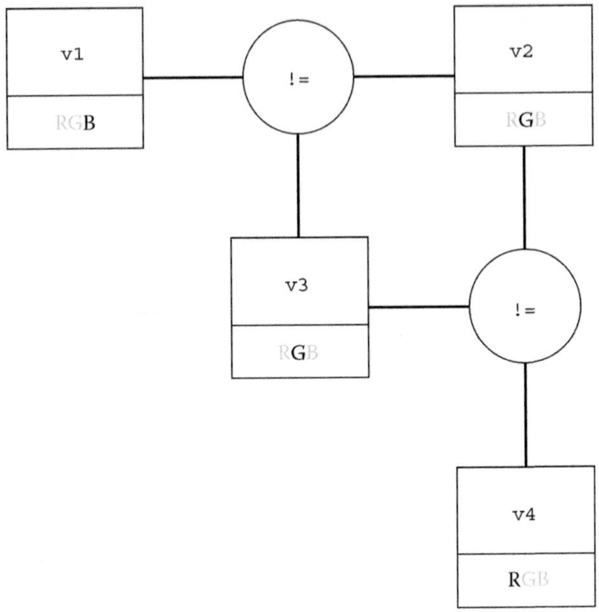

Figure 26.12

The variables v2 and v3 have been narrowed down to green (G), since they can't be red (R) due to v4.

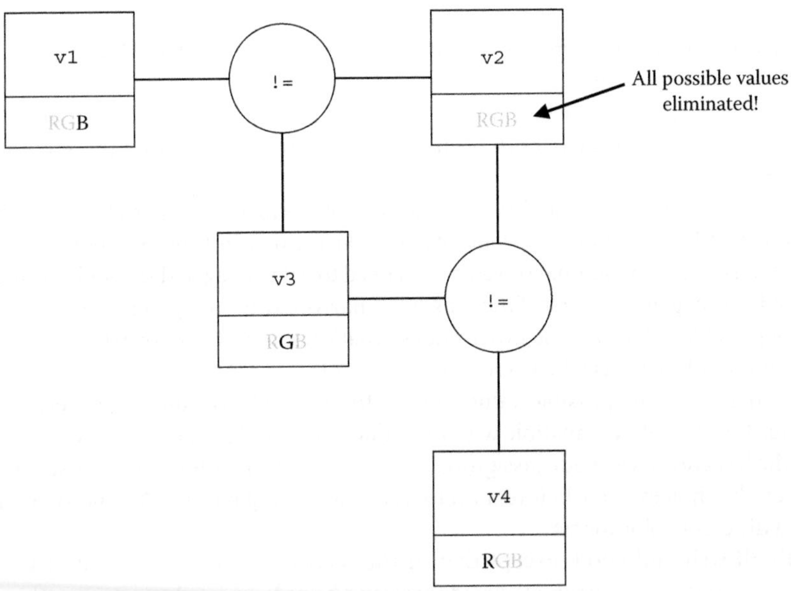

Figure 26.13

The variable v3 was marked as green (G) and then propagated constraints, removing green (G) from v2. Now there are no possible values left for variable v2.

26.7 Algorithm 4: Forward Checking with Backtracking and Undo

Implementing undo for variables is pretty much like implementing undo for a word processor. We keep our undo information in a stack. Every time we modify a variable, we add an entry to the undo stack with the variable and its old value. When we want to undo a set of changes, we pop entries off the stack, setting the specified variables to the specified old values, until the stack is back to the depth it had had before we started changing things.

Listing 26.3 shows the basic outline of the algorithm for using constraint propagation: instead of just checking the constraints, we propagate updates through the constraints. If propagation ever narrows a variable to the empty set, it fails and returns false. We then undo any variable modifications we'd done and move on to try another value.

`PropagateConstraints` is a subroutine that takes a variable as input and propagates any changes through any constraints applied to that variable. Those constraints in turn further attempt to narrow other variables they are applied to and propagate those changes. So, as expected, this leads to a natural mutually recursive algorithm, shown in Listing 26.4.

This propagation algorithm is a variant of Mackworth's arc consistency algorithm #3 (AC-3) [Mackworth 77].

26.8 Gory Implementation Details

So, how can we take this conceptual idea of narrowing possible choices to variables and propagating constraints and implement it a programming language like Java or C#? A complete solver implementation is included on the book's website (http://www.gameaipro.com), and it's also hosted at https://github.com/leifaffles/constraintthingy. For the sake of brevity, we have tried to capture the main implementation strategies in the text, but the source code is much more liberal with comments and explanatory text.

An unfortunate side effect of our previous implementation is that creating new constraints involves modifying the solver's main propagation subroutine (in `Narrow`). Additionally, we'd like to make it possible to use the solver without having to remember to modify the undo stack and propagate constraints as we iterate through possible choices for blocks.

Listing 26.3. An iteration of possible colors with forward checking and backtracking.

```
foreach possible color for v1
   mark1 = undoStack.depth
   narrow v1 to just the selected color
   if PropagateConstraints(v1)
      foreach remaining color v2
         mark2 = undoStack.depth
         narrow v2 to just the selected color
         if PropagateConstraints(v2)
            foreach remaining color v3
               …
         RollbackTo(mark2)
   RollbackTo(mark1)
```

Listing 26.4. The mutually recursive constraint propagation algorithm.

```
bool PropagateConstraints(variable v)
    foreach constraint c applied to v
        if !Narrow(c)
            return false
    return true

bool Narrow(constraint c)
    if c is an equality constraint:
        ...
    else if c is an inequality constraint:
        ...
    ...
    foreach changed variable v:
        if !PropagateConstraints(v)
            return false
    return true
```

The most intuitive approach is to simply have a class for variables and a class for constraints. In the variable class, we will implement the main loop over the variables' possible values as an iterator over the finite domain in a method named `Colors`. Additionally, we will use a special method `SetValues` to narrow a variable's possible values, which will automatically save the old values on the undo stack and automatically propagate constraints. We demonstrate this in Listing 26.5.

Constraints will also be modeled as a class, as shown in Listing 26.6. They have an abstract method, `Narrow`, which each individual type of constraint will override to provide its own constraint-specific implementation of narrowing.

The simplest example of a constraint is equality. In practice, equality constraints are usually implemented by aliasing the two variables together, as is typically done in the unification algorithm. Then a change to one variable automatically changes the other. However, we write it here as a propagated constraint because it makes for a clear example.

As expected, implementing an equality constraint involves providing an implementation of `Narrow`. If there is a value that is in one variable's set of possible values and not in the other, it can *never* satisfy the constraint. So, any values that aren't in the *intersection* of the two variable's possible values shouldn't be considered. We implement this in `Narrow` in Listing 26.7 by computing the set intersection and calling `SetValues` on each value with this set (which, in turn, propagates these new values through more constraints).

A somewhat more complicated example is an inequality constraint. Like many constraints, inequality isn't able to narrow anything until one of the variables is narrowed to a unique value. But once one of the variables is constrained to a single value, we can definitively rule that value out for the other variable, shown in Listing 26.8.

One last example of a common constraint is a *cardinality constraint*. These constraints state that within some set of variables, at most (at least) a certain number of variables can (must) have a particular value. For example, in one of the preceding examples, we said that at most two blocks could be blue. We can implement such a constraint in a manner similar to the inequality constraint: we scan through the variables affected by the constraint,

Listing 26.5. Declaration of the variable class.

```
class Variable {
   public FiniteDomain Values {get; private set;}

   public bool SetValues(FiniteDomain values) {
       if (values.Empty) {
         return false;
       }else if (Values != values) {
           UndoStack.SaveValues(this, _values);
           Values = values;
           if (!PropagateConstraints(this))
               return false;
       }
       return true;
   }

   IEnumerable<Color> Colors() {
       int mark = UndoStack.Depth;
       foreach (var color in Values) {
           if (SetValues(color)) {
               yield color;
           }
           UndoStack.RollbackTo(mark);
       }
   }
   ...
}
```

Listing 26.6. Declaration of the constraint class.

```
abstract class Constraint {
   public abstract bool Narrow();
   ...
}
```

Listing 26.7. Implementation of an equality constraint.

```
class EqualityConstraint {
   Variable a;
   Variable b;

   public override bool Narrow() {
       var intersection = Intersect(a.Values, b.Values);
       return a.SetValues(intersection) &&
              b.SetValues(intersection);
   }
}
```

Listing 26.8. Implementation of an inequality constraint.

```
class InequalityConstraint {
   Variable a;
   Variable b;

   public override bool Narrow() {
       if (a.IsUnique && !b.SetValues(SetSubtract(b.Values,
                                                   a.Values)))
             return false;
       if (b.IsUnique)
          return (a.SetValues(SetSubtract(a.Values,
                                          b.Values)));
   }
}
```

counting the number that has been constrained to just the specified value. If it's less than the maximum allowed, we don't need to do anything. If it's more than the maximum, we fail. But if it's exactly the maximum, then we remove the value from the candidates for any remaining variables, as shown in Listing 26.9.

An "at least" constraint is implemented similarly, but rather than monitoring how many variables can only have the specified value, it monitors how many haven't yet ruled it out. If that number goes below a threshold, then we fail, and if it reaches exactly the threshold, we force all remaining variables that can have the value to be exactly the value, shown in Listing 26.10.

Listing 26.9. Implementation of an "at most" constraint.

```
class AtMostConstraint {
   Variable[] variables;
   FiniteDomain constrainedValue;
   int limit;

   public override bool Narrow() {
      int valueCount;
      foreach (var v in variables)
         if (v.Value == constrainedValue)
            valueCount++;
      if (valueCount > limit)
         return false;
      else if (valueCount = limit)
         foreach (var v in variables)
            if (v.Value != constrainedValue
                && v.SetValue(SetSubtract(v.Values,
                                          constrainedValue))
                return false;
      return true;
   }
}
```

Listing 26.10. Implementation of an "at most" constraint.

```
class AtLeastConstraint {
   Variable[] variables;
   FiniteDomain constrainedValue;
   int limit;

   public override bool Narrow() {
      int valueCount;
      foreach (var v in variables)
         if (v.Value.Includes(constrainedValue))
            valueCount++;
      if (valueCount < limit)
         return false;
      else if (valueCount = limit)
         foreach (var v in variables)
            if (v.Value.Includes(constrainedValue)
               && v.SetValue(constrainedValue)
               return false;
      return true;
   }
}
```

26.9 Extensions and Optimizations

Surprisingly, this covers the basics of every part of the solver. You could load this code up and it would work. This section focuses on simple optimizations to the algorithm.

26.9.1 Finite-Domain Representation

We were pretty vague about how finite domains actually get implemented in the solver. These can be implemented any way you like subject to the restriction that operations on them have *value semantics*. While using a standard hash set data type such as C#'s `HashSet<T>` may seem appealing, it is ultimately impractical because such structures are expensive to copy (which must be done every time its value is modified since the undo stack must be able to restore a variable to a previous value at any point in time).

We strongly recommend implementing finite domains as fixed-size bit sets. For instance, for many problems, these can be implemented entirely with 32- or 64-bit integers (e.g., using a bit for each color.) This makes key operations like intersection extremely efficient to implement with bit-wise operations, as shown in Listing 26.11.

We have many of these operations implemented in the source code of our solver (in the `FiniteDomain` type). A great reference for bit hacks is the *Hacker's Delight* [Warren 12].

Listing 26.11. Implementation of set operations as bit-wise operations.

```
int Intersect(int a, int b) {return a & b;}
int SetSubtract(int a, int b) {return a & ~b;}
bool IsUnique(int a) {return a != 0 && (a & (a-1)) == 0;}
```

Listing 26.12. Implementation of queued narrowing operations ("constraint arcs").

```
class ConstraintArc {
   public Constraint Constraint;
   public Variable Variable;
   public bool Queued;
}

Queue<ConstraintArc> WorkList;

bool ProcessWorkList() {
     while(WorkList.Count > 0) {
           ConstraintArc arc = WorkList.Dequeue();
           arc.Queued = false;
           if(!arc.Constraint.Narrow(arc.Variable))
                return false;
     }
     return true;
}

class Variable {
    public bool SetValues(FiniteDomain values) {
       if (values.Empty) {
           return false;
       } else if (Values != values) {
           UndoStack.SaveValues(this, _values);
           Values = values;
           QueueConstraints();
       }
       return true;
    }

    IEnumerable<Color> Colors() {
       int mark = UndoStack.Depth;
       foreach (var color in Value) {
           if (SetValues(color) && ProcessWorkList()) {
               yield color;
           }
           UndoStack.RollbackTo(mark);
       }
    }
}
class EqualityConstraint {
    Variable a;
    Variable b;
    public EqualityConstraint(Variable a, Variable b) {
       this.a = a;
       this.b = b;
    }

    public override bool Narrow(Variable v) {
       FiniteDomain intersection =
           Intersect(a.Values, b.Values);
```

```
        if (v == a) {
            return a.SetValues(intersection);
        } else {
            return b.SetValues(intersection);
        }
    }
}
```

26.9.2 Constraint Arcs and the Work Queue

Another practical optimization is avoiding unnecessarily narrowing the same constraints and variables twice.

We create a global queue that we will use to queue up narrowing operations for constraints and variables. These queued operations are called *constraint arcs* because they represent the outgoing edges from constraints to the variables they touch. Representing these explicitly enables us to keep a bit on each constraint arc that we can test to see if the arc is already queued and avoid requeueing it. Listing 26.12 shows what this all looks like in code.

Further optimizations can be made by passing more information along in the queue. One possibility is to pass `Narrow` both the variable that changed and also its previous value. This can allow constraints like `AtMost` to determine when the change made to the variable is irrelevant to the constraint, since `AtMost` only cares when the specific value it's tracking is removed from the variable.

26.9.3 Randomized Solutions

Often games would like to be able to run the solver repeatedly and get different answers. So far, our algorithm has been completely deterministic. With a very small tweak and without compromising the ability of the solver to enumerate all solutions, we update our algorithm to iterate over the possible values of a variable in a random order:

```
foreach (var color in shuffle(Values)) {
    ...
}
```

26.9.4 Variable Ordering

For more constrained problems, it's not uncommon to narrow a variable to the empty set (resulting in a failure) deep into the solver algorithm with a large undo stack. Unfortunately, if the responsible choice point was one of the first choices the algorithm made, it will take a long time before it gets around to reconsidering those initial choices because the initial assumption is that it was the *last* choice that was responsible.

This means that the *order* that we visit variables in can greatly affect performance. One option is to visit the most constrained variables before the least constrained variables. The intuition here is that more constrained variables are more likely to be narrowed to the empty set of values, and so we should figure that out up front instead of in a deep inner loop of the solver.

26.10 Conclusion

Constraint solvers are appealing for certain kinds of common tasks in procedural content generation (PCG) and game programming more generally. They let the programmer solve the problem with a minimum of fuss, and changes can be made to the constraints without having to modify and redebug some piece of custom code. That said, it must be stressed that constraint solvers ultimately rely on search algorithms and so can take exponential time in the worst case.

Simple constraint solvers such as the one described here are appropriate for use in game on "easy" problems, where the solver is being used to introduce variety by generating different random solutions each time the game is played. *Easy* problems have a lot of solutions, so the solver doesn't have to work very hard to find one. This usually means having relatively few constraints per variable. As the number of constraints per variable increases, the set of possible solutions usually decreases and the solver has to do a lot more work.

For "difficult" constraint satisfaction problems, that is, problems with large numbers of variables (large search spaces) but very few solutions, a more sophisticated solver, such as an answer-set solver [Smith 11], is more appropriate. However, these solvers, while capable of solving much more sophisticated problems, are generally designed for offline use. So they would be more appropriate for use in a design tool or in the build pipeline.

Happy hacking!

References

[Mackworth 77] Mackworth, A.K. 1977. Consistency in networks of relations. *Artificial Intelligence*, 8:99–118.

[Smith 11] Smith, A.M. 2011. Answer-set programming for procedural content generation: A design-space approach. *IEEE Transactions of Computational Intelligence and AI in Computer Games*, 1:3.

[Warren 12] Warren, H. 2012. *Hacker's Delight.* Addison-Wesley Professional, Boston, MA.

Section V
Tactics, Strategy, and Spatial Awareness

27

Looking for Trouble

Making NPCs Search Realistically

Rich Welsh

27.1 Introduction

Searching is so second nature to us that apart from the inconvenience of having misplaced something, we're naturally able to effectively track down missing items. What thought processes do we go through while we're searching? How can we take these and apply them to our nonplayer characters (NPCs) in order to make them appear more realistic when they're searching? If you're searching for answers to these questions, then look no further!

27.2 Types of Searching

The main focus of this chapter is to outline the way in which NPCs search for hostile targets in a title that I am unable to name. Since the target in this game is a player character, the target will be referred to as "the player"; however, in terms of implementation, this could be any target that is hostile to the NPC. The assumption is also made that the player is actively hiding from hostile NPCs. Despite these assumptions, a lot of the principles described here are suitable for almost any type of search. With that in mind, there are two main types of search that can occur in the game.

27.2.1 Cautious Search

A cautious style of searching is one in which the NPC has been alerted, but does not know whether their target is hostile. This style of searching is generally used when the NPC has been alerted by a stimulus without any knowledge of the source, for example, if a player throws a bottle to draw attention and lure an NPC. While the NPC is aware of the noise, they are unaware of whether the source is a friend or foe.

27.2.2 Aggressive Search

An aggressive search is one where the NPC knows about the target they are searching for and, at the very least, that their target is a hostile one. In most cases, the NPC will have previously seen the player and the player will have successfully evaded the NPC. However, any NPC that has knowledge of their target should employ this style of search—this includes reinforcement NPCs who have just entered the engagement or NPCs who have been informed of their hostile target by an ally.

27.3 Triggering a Search

The first key to making a search seem realistic is triggering it at the right time and telegraphing that transition to the player. Since the player is usually still nearby when the search is triggered, it is likely that they are still able to see or hear the NPCs who are about to hunt for them. Therefore, a poor decision on starting the search will be obvious to the player.

While it may not seem as important as the search itself, telegraphing the transition into a searching state to the player is vital to get right in order for players to be able to identify what will and will not cause NPCs to react. In most games, this transition is signaled by some dialogue and occasionally an accompanying animation.

27.3.1 Initial Stimulus-Based Trigger

An initial stimulus-based trigger is one in which the NPC goes from an unaware state into a searching state due to an indirect stimulus such as a sound. If the NPC is able to see the target directly, then they would enter a combat state rather than search, so in this situation the player must have created some kind of stimulus that was sensed without a direct line of sight to the player.

Stimuli received by NPCs can be divided into two categories. *Hostile stimuli*, such as gunfire and explosions, will trigger an aggressive search response. Although the target isn't known, it is assumed to be hostile from the type of stimulus received. *Distraction stimuli* on the other hand, for example, a bottle being thrown or a prop being knocked over, will trigger a cautious search.

27.3.2 Losing a Target

This method of triggering a search is one in which the NPCs had a direct line of sight to the target at some point—whether the player just briefly dashed across the NPC's field of view or ran away when spotted or actively engaged in combat. When losing sight of a target, NPCs have knowledge of the last position and direction in which they were moving. Normally, if it were a person watching a target leave, they would be able to estimate the location of the target after losing sight. Simply using the target's last known velocity to estimate a current position after a time can cause problems however, as characters (especially players) don't move in perfectly straight lines.

One common problem with extrapolating a position in this manner arises when trying to then map that extrapolated position to a navigable position. Without testing against navigable surfaces (which can range from being a simple navmesh raycast through to a full-blown physics request), it is impossible to guarantee that such a naïve method won't have generated a position inside a prop or outside of the world. A far simpler solution to this problem is to simply allow the NPC to "know" the position of their target for a few seconds after losing sight of them—the exact number can be tweaked to suit the feel of the game, but around 2–3 s gives a reasonably realistic feel. This is both a cheap and effective way of giving the AI a human sense of "intuition" and has been used in a number of high-profile titles, including the *Halo*, *Crysis*, and *Crackdown* series of games.

27.4 Phases of Searching

When performing the actual search in the game, both the cautious and aggressive searches follow the same phases. The differences between the two come from the speed at which the character moves, the animations that they play, and the rate at which they abandon the search (see Table 27.1 for a summary of the differences).

27.4.1 Phase 1

When you're searching for something, the most sensible place to start looking is the last place that you saw it. The same principle should be applied here when NPCs are searching for their target. Whether it's a cautious or an aggressive search, the first phase should be to check the last known position in what can be described as a "narrow" search.

It is worth noting that while implementing phase 1, it is important to consider how many NPCs should be able to simultaneously investigate the search location. This also may vary between a cautious style and an aggressive style of searching.

27.4.1.1 Cautious

In the case of a stimulus that has drawn the NPC's attention, the NPC should either move up until they have line of sight with the stimulus position or move as close to the position as possible. A suitable animation (such as an animation that makes the character look around or report the incident over a radio) can then be played. Often with a cautious search, once the initial position of the stimulus has been investigated, there is no further need to progress into the second search phase.

In a cautious first phase, limiting the number of NPCs who move to investigate can dramatically change the feel of your game. By allowing only a single NPC, it gives the player the option to peel targets away from a group in order to take them out separately

Table 27.1 Differences between Cautious and Aggressive Searching Modes

	Cautious	Aggressive
Movement speed	Walk	Run
Animations	Slow, glancing around	Weapon raised, more alert
Abandon search	After initial location searched (phase 1 only)	After all locations searched or time limit reached (phases 1 and 2)

or sneak past them more easily. This also makes it possible for emergent interactions between the NPCs to take place—for example, the NPC going to investigate could play an audio clip to any nearby allies saying that he's going to check out the disturbance, and they could reply with an acknowledgment. If that character doesn't return within a certain time, a new stimulus could be generated at his position that attracts allies to see why he hasn't returned.

Any NPCs who weren't allowed to investigate the source should lose interest in the search and return to their standard behaviors.

27.4.1.2 Aggressive

When searching aggressively, NPCs know that they are engaging a hostile target; thus, they should be much more alert as they approach and their movement should reflect that. For example, they might run until they're able to establish a line of sight with the target's estimated position and then slow to walk more cautiously up to that position. This gives the appearance that while they are trying to track their target down, they are also aware of the potential danger that they're facing.

Unlike the cautious first phase, all NPCs who are involved in this search should stay in the first phase until either the search is completed or phase 2 is started. These NPCs should look as if they're assisting without starting to sweep—this can be achieved by having them cover their colleagues by aiming their weapons, moving into cover or more tactical positions nearer to the search target's last known position, or just playing suitable animations.

In the aggressive first phase, allowing multiple NPCs to all investigate simultaneously can allow the characters to appear more coordinated—however, a limit should still be placed to prevent every NPC from clustering at the same point (a limit of 2 or 3 characters searching simultaneously works well). Upon reaching their target destination, suitable animations and audio can be played, and all other NPCs who are participating in the search should be informed that the phase will now be advanced.

27.4.2 Phase 2

The second phase is a much broader search, with characters sweeping the area to try and locate the target after the first phase failed to locate them. This doesn't really apply for the cautious search, as after investigating the initial position of the stimuli, the search should finish (however, this is ultimately a design decision to be made to best suit your game).

It is important in this phase to have some kind of search coordinator that NPCs register with, as the search needs to be performed as a group. Each participant in the second phase of a search will request a new search spot to investigate from the coordinator and move until either they reach that position or have a clear line of sight to it. This behavior will be repeated until the search coordinator runs out of search spots or reaches a time limit.

27.4.2.1 Generation of Search Spots

These searching behaviors were originally designed to work with the CryENGINE AI system, which utilizes a tactical point system (TPS) [Jack 13]. The behaviors operate on a set of discrete points. Although there are other systems that can be used to describe search areas within the game (such as occupancy maps [Isla 06]), these data can always be reduced to a set of points on which these behaviors will operate.

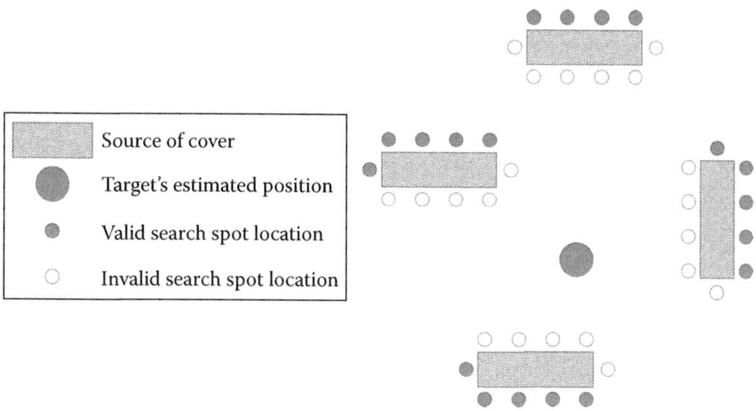

Figure 27.1

Search spot generation.

As soon as an aggressive style search is initiated, the search coordinator should start building up a list of search spots. A search spot is a location that could potentially be hiding the player and as such will need to be investigated.

Commonly, a location that provides cover for a character also obscures that character from sight. This allows cover positions to be used as a basis for generating search spots. Similarly, a system such as a TPS could be used to generate locations in a radius around the target's last known position that would obscure the target from view.

An example of search spot generation can be seen in Figure 27.1. In this example, cover is used as the basis for generating search spots. Any cover that is obscured from the target's estimated position is used to create a search spot. If there aren't enough points generated by using cover, then random positions on the navigation mesh that are hidden from the estimated position can be used to increase the number of search spots, for example, adding points that are around corners or in alleys.

27.4.2.2 Performing the Search

After the search spots have been generated and the search coordinator has a list of them, it's time for the NPCs to begin their broad phase 2 search. This works as follows:

A new search spot should be requested from the search coordinator. If the coordinator does not return a search spot (this could be because there are no more spots available or because a time limit has been reached), then the character should return to their regular behavior. If a spot is available, then the coordinator should calculate the best spot for the search, mark that spot as being "in progress," and return it to the NPC. The character should then move toward the spot with their weapon raised, playing alerted "glancing around" animations.

As the NPC is moving, line of sight checks should be done to all unsearched spots that are within its field of view (including the current target search spot). By having all searching NPCs test against all unsearched spots that they can potentially see, spots are quickly removed from the coordinator. This prevents different characters from searching an area that has already been swept, as in Figure 27.2.

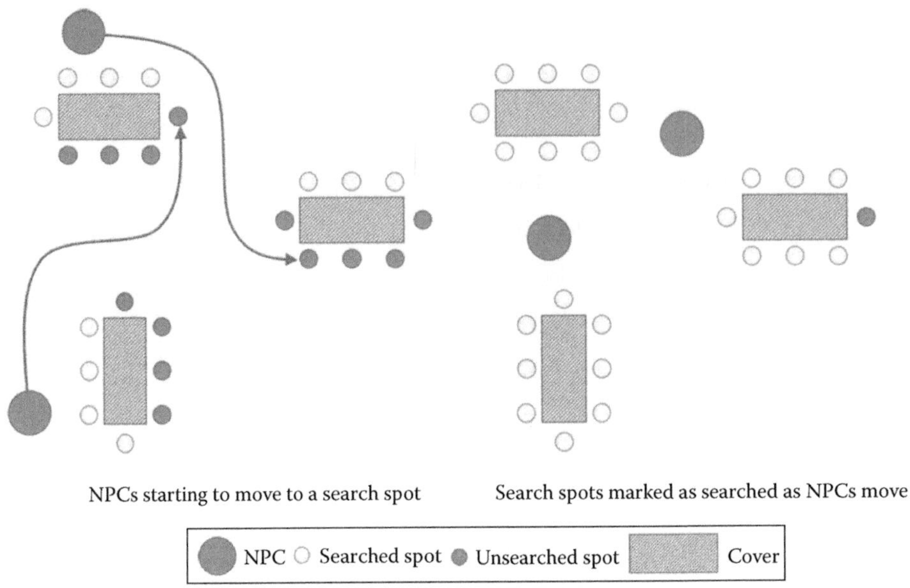

Figure 27.2

Search spots becoming marked as searched as NPCs move.

There are two issues with this approach that need to be addressed, however. First, raycasts are expensive. To address this issue, deferring or timeslicing these raycasts is a good option. Unless the characters are moving extremely fast, a raycast every 1 or 2 s to each unsearched spot will be enough to invalidate any that the character passively searches while moving toward their target spot.

The second issue that can arise with this method is that the coordinator's pool of search spots can be depleted very quickly if a lot of spots are in areas visible to characters. Rather than allow multiple NPCs to search the same spot, the best way to solve this problem is to ensure that the initial pool of spots is large enough to accommodate a suitably lengthy search. Alternatively, if the search needs to continue but all spots have been marked as searched, the coordinator could mark the oldest "searched" points as unsearched once more and allow the search to continue or increase the search radius and rerun the generation step once more to provide a new, larger pool of search spots.

27.4.2.3 Selecting the Best Search Spot

When the coordinator is asked to select the best search spot to return for an NPC, it first needs to check whether any of the search spots that it has stored in the search list are currently free to be searched. Any spots that are in progress are no good, since that would lead to two NPCs moving to the same spot at the same time. Similarly, any spots that have been marked as already searched should be ignored.

Once the unavailable spots have been eliminated, the remaining spots should be scored and the most suitable for the requesting NPC returned. This scoring of potential points is often used in AI systems for tactical positioning in order to help determine which potential position will be the most attractive option for an AI. A good example of how to score points can be seen in *Killzone's* Tactical Positioning system [Straatman 05]. If no spots are available or if the search has exceeded it's time limit, then the system returns NULL and the NPC should abandon the search.

When scoring the spots, the most important two weights should be the distance of the spot from the target's estimated position and the distance of the spot from the NPC's current location. However, as several NPCs will be drawing from the same pool of points, this leads to characters favoring search spots in areas localized around themselves. By adding an extra weight for the distance of the search spot from the player's actual current position, it gives the AI the illusion of human intuition and shapes the search pattern gently in the correct direction. The weighting for distance to target actual location should be quite subtle compared to the other two weights, so as not to make the NPCs all immediately flock to the target. This would both break the illusion of intuition and make the game feel unfairly stacked against the player.

27.4.3 Improving Phase 2 Search: Gap Detection

While moving toward their target search spot, it is important to keep the characters animated in order to keep them looking as if they are actively searching an area—not just mindlessly pathing from point to point.

The obvious way to handle this is simply to layer sweeping or glancing animations on top of the movement. This can result in glances that seem random or unmotivated, however. The realism of the NPCs and the effectiveness of their search can both be increased by adding gap or corner detection to their searching movement, as shown in Figure 27.3. By using long raycasts both perpendicular to the character's path direction and slightly ahead of the character, upcoming gaps can be detected on either side of the path. The character then has the option to turn and look into the gap, which will potentially invalidate search spots that would otherwise require further investigation. The character can pick

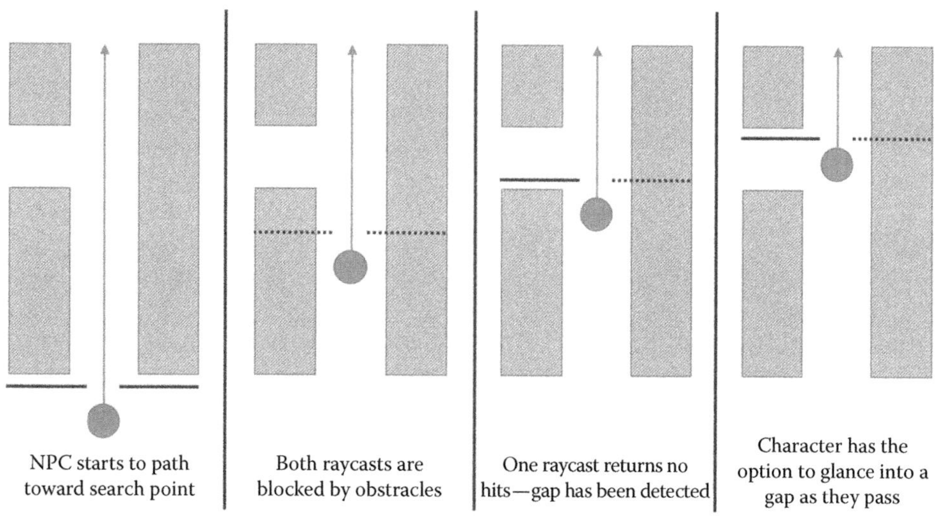

NPC starts to path toward search point
Both raycasts are blocked by obstracles
One raycast returns no hits—gap has been detected
Character has the option to glance into a gap as they pass

Figure 27.3

Gap detection.

randomly between going over to look, an animated turn, and a head-only glance, so that not every character passing by a gap will react in the same way.

27.4.4 Ending the Search

There are two ways that a search can end: either the target is successfully located by an NPC or the search is called off and the target is considered lost. With the latter, it will ultimately be the decision of the search coordinator as to whether the search should stop. When either no more search spots are valid to be searched or a time limit is reached, NPCs should naturally filter back to their regular behaviors in their own time. Although they are operating as a group, stopping all NPCs simultaneously looks very strange, giving the impression that they are operating under one hive mind.

27.5 Conclusion

This chapter examined the subtleties of NPC searching. First, the type of searching must be determined, either as a cautious search or an aggressive search, based on the triggering event. Then the search proceeds in two phases. The first phase attempts to find the source of the triggering event directly by going to its last known position. Once successfully investigated, a cautious search will complete, while an aggressive search will proceed to phase 2. In phase 2, new search spots will be generated and investigated, with NPCs sharing information over recently searched spots. If the player was not uncovered during these searches, then the NPCs should naturally return back to their previous tasks.

As a practical matter of effectiveness, there were several key tricks introduced that make the search behavior look more natural. First, if the NPC loses sight of the target, it should cheat and continue to know the target's position for 2–3 s, as if continuing to pursue by intuition. Second, within phase 2, it's important to generate enough search spots so that the search doesn't end prematurely. Lastly, the search behavior will appear much more natural if you implement gap detection and have the NPCs exhibit various glancing animations.

References

[Isla 06] Isla, D. 2006. Probabilistic target tracking and search using occupancy maps. In *AI Game Programming Wisdom 3*, ed. S. Rabin. Hingham, MA: Charles River Media.

[Jack 13] Jack, M. 2013. Tactical position selection: An architecture and query language. In *Game AI Pro: Collected Wisdom of Game AI Professionals*, ed. S. Rabin. New York: A K Peters/CRC Press.

[Straatman 05] Straatman, R. and Beij, A. 2005. Killzone's AI: Dynamic procedural tactics. http://www.cgf-ai.com/docs/straatman_remco_killzone_ai.pdf (accessed September 10, 2014).

28

Modeling Perception and Awareness in *Tom Clancy's Splinter Cell Blacklist*

Martin Walsh

28.1 Introduction

With many games incorporating stealth elements and generally trying to increase fidelity, having solid perception and awareness models for nonplayer characters (NPCs) is becoming increasingly important. This chapter discusses four types of perception and awareness that were modeled in *Tom Clancy's Splinter Cell Blacklist*: visual, auditory, environmental, and social/contextual. Before jumping in, we'll present the four characteristics that we believe these models need to display to be successful: fairness, consistency, good feedback, and intelligence.

28.1.1 Fairness

In a game with stealth, getting detected can be the difference between success and the player throwing their controller across the room, especially if it felt unfair. Having models that *feel* fair is key, it is also one of the most difficult things to achieve since both the models themselves and how fair they are in a given situation are extremely subjective.

28.1.2 Consistency

As a player, you need to have some idea of what the AI will perceive and how they will react so you as the player can strategize and improve; so the AI's behavior needs to be somewhat predictable. This is in contrast to actual humans who vary in terms of what they perceive and how they react and, as a result, tend to be very unpredictable. Note that predictability does not mean repetitiveness; we need, for example, to get similar distances and timing for reactions every time, but the animations and barks (short vocal clips) need to be different; otherwise, immersion is broken very quickly.

28.1.3 Good Feedback

While consistency is essential, good feedback is also required to help the player understand the AI's behavior. The player must be able to "read" or understand what the AI is doing and why they are doing it. Similar to what is mentioned earlier, it's a difficult balance between readable feedback and something that looks and feels human. Getting the right barks and animations is important, as well as having enough variety.

28.1.4 Intelligence

Finally, if your opponents feel dumb, it isn't satisfying to beat them. But not being dumb does not necessarily mean being smart; it means always being plausible.

Now that we've covered the four key components for success, let's examine the models themselves.

28.2 Visual Perception

Any game where the player can hide, or break line of sight (LOS), requires some type of visual perception model. Commonly, we refer to this as a vision cone, and while a cone does a good job of modeling what the NPC can see directly in front of him, it does a poor job of modeling many other aspects of vision. The two most glaring examples are peripheral vision and vision at a distance. It's pretty obvious why a cone doesn't model peripheral vision well, but for vision at a distance, we need to dive a bit deeper.

Before we do, we will examine the difference between perception and awareness. On *Splinter Cell*, we used the following definition of awareness and perception: awareness is a set of discreet mental states (levels of awareness) that represent an increasingly more detailed understanding of the thing being perceived and that can be reached progressively over time through sensory perception.

When you first perceive something, you only start to become aware of it. In other words, if you see something moving in the distance, all you can really say is, "I see *something* over there." What's key here is you don't know exactly what you see; that potentially takes more time and depends on many factors such as what you expect to see, lighting, and the amount of time you see it for. Many games, including *Blacklist*, abstract all of that into a progress bar that, while analog in nature, only represents two binary states for the NPC: "I don't see anything suspicious" or "that's enemy #1 over there!" Some games (including *Splinter Cell*) include a third, intermediate, state where the NPC knows he saw something and will go to investigate (usually at some percentage of the progress bar). See Figures 28.1 through 28.3 for a description of how we did this on *Blacklist*.

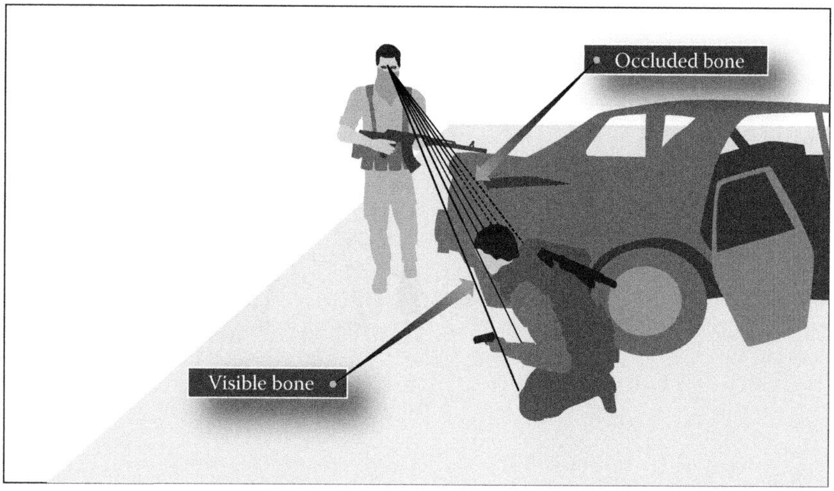

Figure 28.1

On *Blacklist*, we raycast to eight different bones on the player's body. Depending on the stance, it takes a certain number of visible bones to kick off detection. In this case, the player stance is "in cover" that requires more than the two bones that are currently visible so detection has not yet begun.

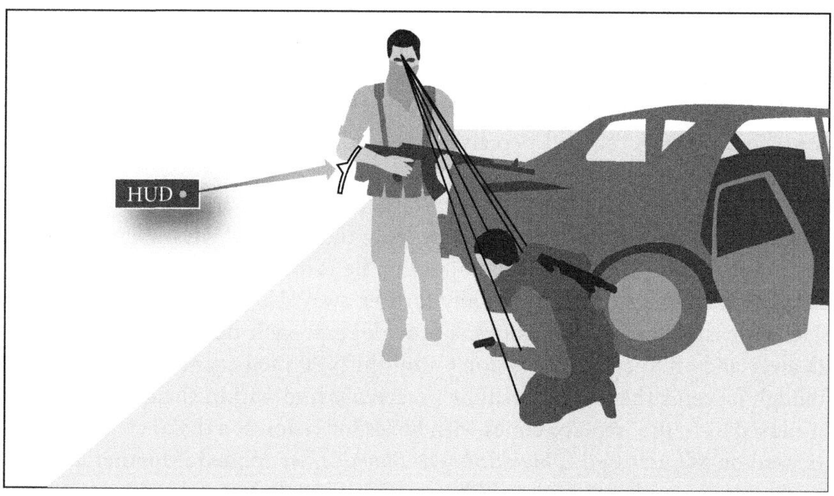

Figure 28.2

Once enough bones are visible to the NPC, the detection process starts and a timer kicks off. The full range of the timer is defined by the detection shape the player is in (Figure 28.3), and the actual value used is arrived at by scaling linearly inside that range based on the current distance to the player. The timer is represented by the growing HUD element that provides feedback to the player that defines his window of opportunity to break LOS or kill the NPC to avoid detection. Once the detection HUD is full, the player is detected.

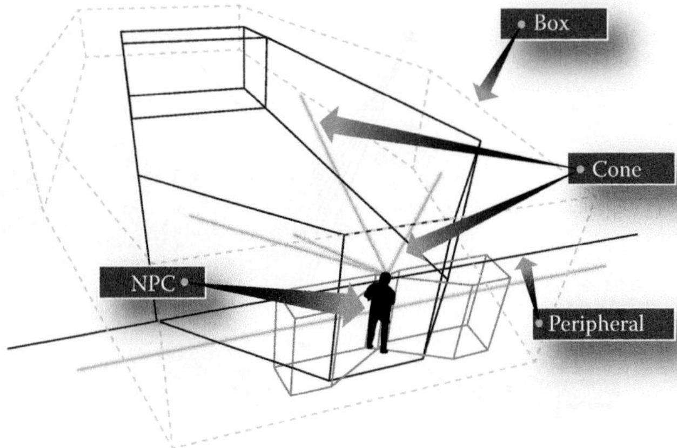

Figure 28.3

This debug drawing represents the detection shapes in *Blacklist*. The coffin-shaped box can be seen, as well as the standard vision cone that defines the area directly in front of the NPC where the player should get detected quickly. The most inclusive shape the player is in defines the range of the detection timer.

The point is that AI developers try to combine the concepts of seeing something and being aware of what we see into a single concept modeled essentially using vision shapes and a timer. On *Blacklist*, when the player is inside of a vision shape of the NPC, unobstructed and lit, a timer kicks off, which is scaled based on the distance to the player, lightness of the player, NPC state, etc., and when that timer reaches 0 (or the progress bar is full), the NPC immediately does two things: he *perceives* the player and becomes *aware* of him as a threat. This abstraction forces us to compromise: we need to define the area where the NPC should perceive *and* become aware of the player within some reasonable time.

Getting back to the vision cone, the reason a cone doesn't model vision at a distance well is that a cone expands as it moves away from the NPC, which implies that as things get further away from the NPC in the direction he is looking, he tends to perceive, and become aware of, things that are laterally farther away. Up to a certain distance that is plausible, but past that distance, it doesn't provide reasonable behavior. If the player is far enough away and off to one side, we don't want the NPCs to become aware of them at all, even though it seems they should still be perceiving him within their field of view. This insight caused us to first replace cones with boxes for vision at a distance; this is the solution we used on *Splinter Cell Conviction*. On *Blacklist*, we refined it further and replaced our standard boxes with coffin-shaped boxes (Figure 28.3) that expand up to a point like a cone and then start to contract as they continue to move further away from the NPC, which gives us the effect we want.

It's important to note that no solution is perfect. All of the variations described have a threshold (the edge of the vision shape). If the player is 1 cm outside of that threshold, then the NPC will stand there forever without seeing the player. One centimeter inside and the player will be detected within a couple of seconds at most. This is a direct result of the way the model is abstracted and the need to match the NPC state to the feedback we display to the player (in this case the detection HUD).

On *Splinter Cell*, we arrived at our solution through many hours of playtesting and designer tweaking. For different games, the right solution may be different and it's impossible to have a single solution that gives the expected results for everyone all the time. Even if we had a perfect model of vision, a player may feel that in a certain case, an NPC should have seen him when he didn't and vice versa. This is not fixable since even in real life we can be surprised when we think someone is looking right at something and doesn't see it (anyone who watches sports with referees can attest to that). What's important is to provide a consistent model, with good feedback, that fits the expectations of the players of your game.

28.3 Environmental Awareness

Environmental awareness is a broad term. At the very basic level, the navmesh or navigation graph provides environmental awareness. It tells the NPC which parts of the environment are walkable and whether two parts of the environment are connected. Other common parts of the model include cover representation and interactive objects like doors or switches. All of these give the NPC some knowledge about his environment that helps him interact with it better and appear more intelligent because of this. The two things we focused on modeling beyond these basics in SC were changes to objects in the environment and the connectivity of the environment.

28.3.1 Connectivity

In the first *Splinter Cell* games, there were very few active NPCs. This meant that, once in combat, finding a cover that (when peeked out) gave LOS on the player was relatively easy and taking that cover was enough to give the impression that NPCs were aware of their environment on a basic level. Starting with *Conviction*, we had 12 active NPCs and some very tight areas. This meant that often many NPCs could not find cover with LOS on the player because in many situations there were more NPCs than available covers. These NPCs ended up staring at the player through walls since they couldn't get a direct LOS but had nothing better to look at.

To solve this problem, we initially thought about pathfinding to the player and having the NPC look at some visible point along that path to give the impression that he is looking at where the player may be coming from instead of staring at a wall. While this could work in some cases, it has a couple of major drawbacks: it's often hard to find the right point to look at, and in our game the player could take paths that were not walkable or accessible to NPCs. For example, if the area the NPC is in is only directly connected to the player's area by a window, the pathfinding solution would have him staring in the wrong direction since it would not take that window into account. And even if it did, there could be multiple windows or doors; so picking the one along the shortest path would have all NPCs in that area covering the same choke point, which is not what we wanted. We realized that what we needed was a way to model the connectivity of the environment (i.e., which areas, or rooms, are connected to which other areas through which choke points).

It is important to note that this model maps better to an indoor environment with well-defined areas and choke points than it does to wide open spaces. However, in practice, even our outdoor environments could be broken down into areas separated by choke points although defining those areas and chokes is less obvious outdoors.

To achieve this we created a model we called Tactical Environment Awareness System (TEAS) (Figure 28.4). This system subdivided the world into areas (defined by subnavmesh areas) and defined the connections between those areas. So, for example, if two rooms are connected by a door and a window, each room would have its own *subnavmesh* (essentially a subset of the triangles of the navmesh), and these would be connected to each other by two choke nodes: one representing the window and the other the door.

One question that should immediately come to mind is, "How are these areas and connections generated?" This process on *Conviction* worked as follows. First, the level designer (LD) would subdivide the navmesh into subnavmeshes by tagging the triangles for each area using our navmesh tool (every triangle had to belong to at least one subnavmesh). Note that the LD could tag triangles directly since our "base navmesh" was hand-authored to precisely fit to the contours of the structural geometry (all static props and dynamic objects would then automatically cut the navmesh). He would then create special overlap triangles to define the choke area (if it was walkable, like a door). These triangles were members of both subnavmeshes. Finally, the LD would place the choke nodes above the overlap triangles in the walkable case and above an area with no navmesh (like in a window) in the nonwalkable case. These choke nodes came with a red and a blue position node attached. The LD would place one of the position nodes above navmesh in area A and one in area B. This was sufficient to tell the system that area A is connected to area B through the choke node. There could be multiple choke nodes

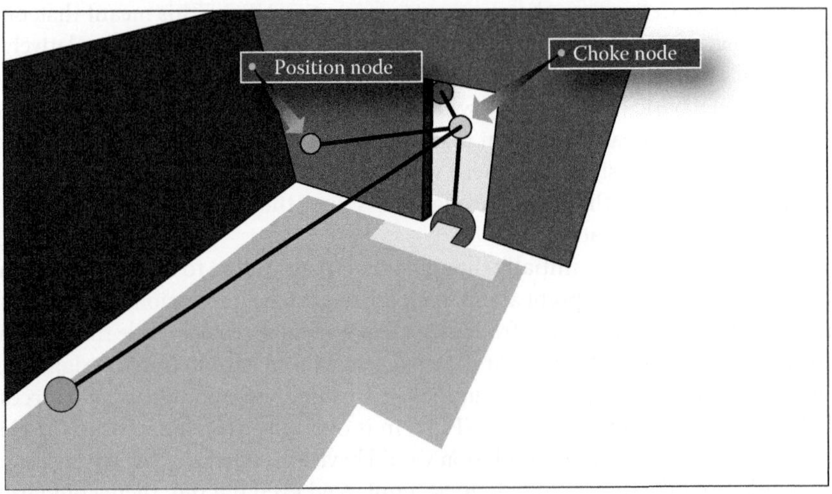

Figure 28.4

An example of TEAS in *Blacklist*. Assume we are looking at a door that leads from a hallway to a room. You can see the position node outside the room connected to the choke node, which is connected to the position node inside the room. This indicates that the area outside the room is connected to the area inside through the choke (a door in this case). You can also see the second position node attached to the choke node that can be used as a fallback position.

connecting two areas, one for each distinct choke point. Additionally, the LD had the option of adding multiple red or blue position nodes. The reason for this was that position nodes served two purposes. On top of defining which area was linked to the choke node, they also served as backup positions for covering that choke, so their position was important. If the NPC could not find suitable cover with LOS on the choke node, he knew he could always fall back to a position node that was a good open position with LOS. Finally, the LD would place an area property node above a triangle in the area. This node contained metadata for the area including the size of the area, the number of NPCs that should enter that area for search or combat, and the type of area (open balcony or closed room).

This system added substantial depth to our NPC tactics. They could now reason about player location with respect to the environment and act accordingly. For example, they could know that the player was hiding in a small room that is a dead end and cover the only way out instead of rushing in to their death. In the case with two rooms (areas A and B) connected by a door and a window, it meant that NPCs in area A who couldn't get LOS on the player in area B and didn't want to enter his area could intelligently cover the door and window leading to the player's area. In other words, NPCs who couldn't get LOS on the player always had something intelligent to do, which was important for our game since the player could outflank the NPCs in combat and see them through walls using his goggles. There is nothing worse than feeling smart by outflanking an NPC just to realize that he's just sitting there staring at a wall.

We made a lot of improvements to this system on *Blacklist* including autogenerating choke nodes and the special overlap triangles and adding a bunch of error checking in the editor to try to determine if the LD missed some linking opportunities or had linked two areas improperly. One thing we could have done but never got around to was autogenerating the subnavmesh areas themselves. We could have done this by allowing the LDs to place choke nodes where we couldn't autogenerate them first (i.e., narrow areas with no door objects), then generating the overlap triangles, and finally using flood fill to tag all the remaining triangles.

28.3.2 Changed Objects

The system we used for detecting and reacting to changes in environmental objects (doors, windows, lights, etc.) was very simple, but it is worth mentioning since it gave us more bang for our buck than any other system. In fact, a few of the reviews for the game brought up the fact that NPCs noticed doors that had been opened or light switches that turned off [Metro 13].

In *Splinter Cell*, when an object changed state from its previously known state, it would create an event with a lifetime. The first NPC to witness that event would claim it and potentially do a minor investigation depending on his state and other factors. Theoretically, the player could use this tactically to distract the NPC, but mostly it was there to give the impression of intelligence. Obviously, the key to making something like this work is selling the reaction with good feedback. If the NPC just looks like he randomly walked to the door the player left open, you get no sense of the fact that he noticed an open door; so the NPC needs to announce it, but in a way that feels realistic. We did this by having very obvious reaction animations where the NPC would stop and look at the area around the door, combined with more subtle barks where the NPC would ask introspectively, "Did I leave that door open?" after which he would walk through the door playing a "sweep" (look left–right) animation. This works very well but can lead to problems with immersion: the more specific a dialog line is, the more memorable it is, and the more immersion breaking it is when you hear that line repeated.

On *Blacklist* we did a major overhaul of our barks system, and one thing we did to address this issue was to create a three-tiered bark system that worked as follows: tier 1 barks were the very specific barks like the one mentioned earlier, tier 2 barks were more generic (e.g., "Did I leave that open?") that could apply to a door or window, and tier 3 barks were completely generic (e.g., "Huh?"). The idea was that we would cycle through the tier 1 barks first so the player would get the specific barks the first few times something happened, then we would drop to tier 2 and finally tier 3, so as the player got used to the NPC behavior and didn't need the specific barks, he would get the generic ones (which had a larger pool) and never hear the same memorable line twice.

28.4 Auditory Perception

Auditory perception for us is pretty simple: every audio event has a radius and priority; if an NPC is in range of the event, he will hear it and react differently based on the event, who else is in range, and his current state. On *Conviction*, we had two major problems with our auditory events: the first was accurately calculating the audio distance and the second had to do with the fairness of getting detected by NPCs you don't see because of events you don't directly control (details in the next section).

28.4.1 Calculating Audio Distance

In a game where creating sounds (e.g., by running) can get you detected, it is important to accurately calculate the audio distance of events. Using Euclidian distance is obviously not good enough since that would mean the player would be heard through walls. Initially, we used our sound engine, but it was not optimized for calculating arbitrary sound distance, and some calls were insanely expensive. A second issue with using the sound engine was that if the audio data weren't built (which happened often), it created all kinds of false detection bugs, which made testing difficult. The solution we ended up with made use of TEAS described earlier. Remember that TEAS is a connectivity graph that represents areas connected through choke points.

To calculate sound distance, we would get the "area path" from the source (event location) to the destination (NPC location). This would give us a shortest path represented by a series of areas (let's call it list A with n areas $A_0 \ldots A_{n-1}$) starting with the room containing the source and ending with the room containing the destination. In the trivial case where the source and destination are in the same room, we just used Euclidian distance; otherwise, we used the following equation:

$$\begin{aligned}\text{Total distance} = {} & \text{dist}(\text{source, closest choke leading to } A_1) \\ & + \text{dist}(\text{closest choke leading to } A_1, \text{closest choke leading to } A_2) \\ & + \cdots + \text{dist}(\text{closest choke leading to } A_{n-1}, \text{destination})\end{aligned} \tag{28.1}$$

Now let's say the sound was made in area A and the NPC is in area D and those areas are connected in the following way: area A is connected by *window1* to area B, area B is connected by *door2* and *window2* to area C, and area C is connected by *door3* to area D, with the extra information that *window1* is closer to *door2* than *window2*. Then the total distance would be $\text{dist}(source, window1) + \text{dist}(window1, door2) + \text{dist}(door2, door3) + \text{dist}(door3, destination)$. Although this is clearly a rough approximation, in practice, the results were accurate enough that we made the switch and never looked back.

28.4.2 Auditory Detection Fairness

The second problem we faced with auditory events is actually a general problem: it can feel unfair to be creating events that get noticed by guards you can't see, especially if you don't know that they are reacting to an event you created. This problem occurred often in internal reviews. Our creative director would often complain about being detected for no reason. For example, he'd be running down a hallway with no NPC in sight and all of a sudden hear an NPC say, "Hey, who's there!?!" Sometimes it was due to a bug, but often if we paused and used the free cam to show him where the NPC who heard him was, it usually made sense to him why he got detected. However, that didn't stop him from complaining the next time, and he was right to complain because ultimately it's irrelevant what the NPC *should* be able to hear. The player can't pause the game and free-cam, so it just ends up feeling unfair.

One important thing we learned here, as with tuning vision, is that it's only important what's plausible from the player's point of view—it really doesn't matter what the NPC *should* see or hear; it's what the player *thinks* the NPC can see and hear. This is a really important distinction. It implies that in the case of player perception versus simulation accuracy, player perception should win. This is not an absolute statement, however, and in the solution we will present, we'll show how this is actually limited by plausibility. However, first, let's look at a solution that we rejected.

To solve the fairness issue, we could have gone with the brute force solution of tuning down auditory event distances to make them more forgiving. This would have solved the unfairness problem but would have led to other issues: namely, it would feel ridiculous if you can see a guard in front of you, and you're sprinting toward him, but he can't hear your footsteps until you're very close. Not only would that make him seem unresponsive, but in our case, it would actually break the game since we had "insta-kill takedowns" if you got the jump on an NPC; so a player could just sprint through the map stabbing everyone in the back.

There's actually a big problem that we're trying to solve here: for two NPCs at the same distance from you (with one just around the corner), it can feel fair getting detected by the one that you see and unfair by the one you don't. To solve this problem, we considered having some HUD feedback for sound, which may have helped, but design wanted minimal HUD, so in the end we solved this in two ways.

The first thing we did was that NPCs that are offscreen, but far enough away from the player that it was plausible they didn't hear him, have their hearing reduced for certain events by ½. The result was that the game instantly became more fun and our creative director stopped complaining. We ended up applying this to some indirect visual events as well, such as seeing an NPC get shot. This is actually a good example of balancing plausibility versus fairness. Imagine the case where you are on one side of a corner and an NPC is right around the corner (a few feet from you). If you run and make noise, it still feels unfair if you get detected by the NPC you don't see, *but* if he didn't react and then you rounded the corner, it would feel ridiculous that he didn't hear you! Therefore, we still needed to pick a distance where this case leads to a plausible result even if it may feel unfair to the player (at least until he realizes where the NPC is), which is why we couldn't just reduce hearing completely for all offscreen NPCs.

The second thing we did was to provide better feedback to the player. We mentioned earlier how we overhauled our barks system with the "three-tiered" strategy, and this is one area where that had a big impact. We created a lot of very specific barks to put in tier 1 (like "I think I heard footsteps"); tier 2 had more generic barks like "I think I heard someone over there," down to tier 3's "I think someone's over there." The results, again, were that the player got the feedback they needed the first few times they were heard (so in this case, they realized that running created footstep noise) and then got the more generic versions to avoid repetition when the explicit ones were no longer necessary.

28.5 Social/Contextual Awareness

The last type of awareness I want to discuss is social and contextual. We've lumped these two together for a couple of reasons. First, the idea behind them is similar. You want the NPCs to appear aware of social and contextual events that are happening around them, and you want future NPC behavior to be affected by past events. Second, we'll look at these together because we didn't really have an overarching model for either of these. We did have a group behavior system that made modeling social awareness easier, but in general, the awareness came through in the design of the group behaviors themselves, not as a direct result of the system, and the rest was done with some clever tricks. So this section will be more like a "tips and tricks for giving the impression of social and contextual awareness" as opposed to a detailed description of a model.

Before presenting the tricks we used, we'd like to define what we mean by "contextual event" and give a couple of reasons for actually trying to model this in the first place since many games don't do this at all.

A contextual event is an event whose meaning changes based on context. So, for example, in *Splinter Cell*, if a searching NPC spots a dead body for the first time, he will get very agitated and call for help. On the other hand, if that same NPC spots a dead body in the middle of a war zone, he will ignore it. The event is the same ("see dead body"), but the context is different. Another example described in the following section is seeing the player. On *Splinter Cell*, seeing the player in the open was different from seeing the player in an unreachable area (like a rooftop) or seeing him in a dead end. Again, the event is the same ("see player"), but the reactions, barks, and behaviors are different. Perhaps more to the point, seeing a player on a rooftop for the first time is different from seeing him on that same rooftop again after he massacred five NPCs from there last time he was seen. In this case, the reactions and behaviors will be completely different (the NPCs will call out that he's back on the roof and immediately run to safety instead of trying to engage). So the event "see player" is actually interpreted as "see player again on rooftop after massacre" due to the context.

Social awareness is a subset of contextual awareness; if an NPC is engaged in a conversation with someone or waiting for someone to return, he will treat certain events (e.g., or lack of events—if he's expecting a response) very differently from the situation where he is just in the proximity of another NPC.

On *Splinter Cell*, we modeled this for two reasons:

1. To make NPCs seem more intelligent (you spend more time observing them than in most games)
2. To create antiexploits in the form of group behaviors

We'll give two examples that use group behaviors followed by a trick we used to solve a common social/contextual awareness problem: the disappearing NPC problem.

28.5.1 Social Awareness: Conversation

In most games, if you interrupt two NPCs talking, either it breaks the conversation or the conversation restarts robotically. On *Blacklist*, when NPCs are in a conversation, they are actually in a group behavior. The group behavior system takes control of all NPCs involved and gets to be first to handle any event received by any of those NPCs; so, for example, when a minor event occurs, the behavior gets the opportunity to handle it. In this case, it can pause itself and have the NPCs branch into a group investigation with the possibility of resuming the conversation after the investigation is complete. This allows us to do some interesting stuff, like having the NPC discuss the event received in context before investigating, maintain awareness of each other during the investigation, and branch seamlessly back into the conversation if the investigation does not yield anything. This was made possible by the fact that, for every conversation, our dialog writers wrote custom breakout and rejoin lines and also blocked out each conversation. When restarted, the rejoin line would be played and then the conversation would resume at the beginning of the current dialog block.

Here is an example of how a conversation that's interrupted by a minor event plays out in *Blacklist*:

1. The NPCs are discussing a football match on TV.
2. The player creates a minor event (footsteps, whistle, etc.).
3. The NPCs hear the event.
4. The system handles the event and branches to the "ignore minor event" behavior, with the lines:
   a. "Hey, did you hear that?"
   b. "Yeah, must've been the TV, now what were you saying…" (custom rejoin line)
5. The system then resumes the conversation only to be interrupted by a second event.
6. "Hey that wasn't the TV; you better go check it out!"

At this point the NPCs branch into a two-man investigation with the conversation on pause. Note how they delivered their lines in context and demonstrated awareness of what activity they are engaged in and what happened previously.

There are two possible outcomes to this investigation that could cause this scenario to continue: either the NPC finds nothing and they return to the conversation with a line like "Guess it was nothing. So what were you saying?" or the NPC gets killed silently during the investigation. In that case, the group behavior system receives the "NPC died" event that allows it to handle the event in context. The result is that the behavior waits a bit and then sends an investigation event to the NPC who's still alive near the location where the NPC was killed. He will branch into this second investigation with a line like "Hey, are you ok over there? Talk to me!" at which point the group behavior will end and he will do a systemic investigation at that location.

All of this really gives the impression that the NPCs are aware of their current situation and have some model of what has happened in the recent past and also who is around them and what they might be doing.

28.5.2 Contextual Awareness: Unreachable Area

Depending on where the player is, and what the situation is, the AI may not be able to, or want to, engage in direct combat. In this example I'll describe a situation that arises frequently in *Blacklist* (the player in an unreachable area) and how we deal with it. First, note that this situation can easily become an exploit; so when we deal with it, we are actually trying to solve two problems:

1. Remove the exploit. We don't want the player to be able to sit on a rooftop and shoot the AI like fish in a barrel.
2. React in a believable and readable way. We want the player to understand what the AI is doing and why. This makes them seem more intelligent for understanding the situation and also allows the player to adapt.

This is actually a situation that arises in many games: the player finds a spot where he has a big tactical advantage. This is exacerbated when the player has traversal moves the AI doesn't and can reach areas the AI can't get to. In *Splinter Cell*, there are really only three things the AI can do to deal with the player in this scenario: shoot back (which is not a good option since the player has the advantage), throw a grenade (this is not always easy to pull off since they have to land the grenade in a hard to reach area, but it's very effective when it works), and fall back (this is effective as an antiexploit but can be frustrating to the player if it's not called out).

To tackle this scenario, we used a combination of the group behavior system and TEAS. TEAS allows us to reason about the environment; so we know that the player is in an unreachable area (no valid area paths to the player) and what type of area it is, thanks to the markup in the area node. Therefore, in the scenario being described, TEAS allows us to know that the player is on a small, unreachable rooftop. The group behavior system then selects the appropriate behavior to kick off, in this case the "unreachable above" behavior. The mechanism for this selection works as follows: when no group behavior is running, the group behavior system is constantly looking for a trigger to kick off the most appropriate group behavior. The event "player seen" gets mapped to the event "player seen on unreachable rooftop" based on the criteria mentioned earlier. This event and some other checks (e.g., certain group behaviors should not be repeated) cause the group behavior system to select the most appropriate group behavior (which is mapped to its respective contextual event, "player seen on unreachable rooftop" in this case). The scenario proceeds as follows:

1. The player starts shooting at the AI from the unreachable rooftop.
2. Once his location is known, we kick off the "unreachable above" group behavior.
3. NPC A: "He's hiding up there! Toss a frag and flush him out!"
4. NPC B: "I'm on it! Give me cover fire!"
5. NPC A and other NPCs cover fire and NPC B throws the frag.

At this point, a few different things could happen, but we'll describe two of them. In the first case, the player gets off of the roof undetected and something similar to the following plays out after a few seconds:

1. NPC A: "Do you think he's still up there?"
2. NPC B: "I doubt it. Let's spread out and search the area!"
3. NPCs transition to search.

If the grenade throw is not successful and the player starts firing back and killing them, the following proceeds:

1. NPC A: "Forget it! Fall back! Fall back!"
2. NPC A covers fires while the other NPCs run for protective cover.
3. NPC B provides cover while NPC A falls back.

So you can see that we've been able to deal with this exploit in a way that preserves the lives of the NPCs, makes them seem aware, and gives the player the feedback they need. One important thing to note is that the dialog lines aren't callouts but a discussion. This has the effect of making the behavior seem much more natural as opposed to just being a means of giving information to the player [Orkin 06, Orkin 15].

28.5.3 Disappearing NPC Problem

We'll conclude this section by discussing our solution to a common problem: the disappearing NPC problem. The problem goes something like this: there are a bunch of NPCs guarding an area. The player starts stealthily taking them out one by one. At the end, there are only a couple of NPCs left, and unless they find a dead body, they are oblivious to the fact that an area that was crawling with their buddies is now an empty wasteland.

As mentioned earlier, we have a solution for the specific case when the NPCs are currently engaged in a conversation, but what about the general case where they are just near each other? Before discussing our solution, it's interesting to think about what we're trying to model. The idea here is that NPCs should be aware of the presence of other NPCs because they are seeing or hearing them at regular intervals. They should then become aware of the fact that they are no longer seeing and hearing those NPCs, get suspicious, and investigate. Trying to model this directly would be a lot of work for not a lot of gain. You'd have to create events for hearing and seeing NPCs, store a history of those events per NPC, and then detect the fact that the NPC is no longer receiving those events.

We chose a much simpler and cheaper solution. If NPC A has been in earshot (sound distance-wise) of NPC B for 10 seconds and then for 5 more seconds after he stops making noise (i.e., once he's dead), then we generate an investigation event. This event has a pretty long cooldown to avoid repetition and exploits. This gives us the result we want: if two NPCs are in the same general area and you kill one of them and if the other NPC is still in that area after a few seconds, he will become suspicious because he is no longer hearing/seeing the NPC that was just in his vicinity.

28.6 Conclusion

As you can see, the success of these models depends largely on a combination of picking the right abstraction and clever design. The goal is not so much to get an accurate model as it is to get one that feels fair to the player and allows you to provide good, consistent feedback, all while maintaining the illusion that the NPCs are human (plausibility). It's a difficult balance that requires a lot of playtesting, iterations, and working closely with design, animation, and dialogue. Hopefully, this chapter has brought those points home and given you some useful tips and tricks, which we arrived at through many hours of playtesting and iterating, that you can apply to your project.

References

[Metro 13] Metro.co.uk. 2013. Splinter cell: Blacklist—Sneaky compromise. http://metro.co.uk/2013/08/15/splinter-cell-blacklist-review-sneaky-compromise-3925136/ (accessed July 11, 2014).

[Orkin 06] Orkin, J. 2006. 3 States and a plan: The AI of F.E.A.R. *Game Developers Conference*, San Jose, CA.

[Orkin 15] Orkin, J. 2015. Combat dialogue in F.E.A.R.: The illusion of communication. In *Game AI Pro²: Collected Wisdom of Game AI Professionals*, ed. S. Rabin. A K Peters/CRC Press, Boca Raton, FL.

29

Escaping the Grid

Infinite-Resolution Influence Mapping

Mike Lewis

29.1 Introduction

One of the central elements of any robust AI system is *knowledge representation*. This encompasses a wide variety of techniques and mechanisms for storing and accessing information about an AI agent's perception of the world around it. The more powerful the knowledge representation, the more effective the AI can be.

A common form of knowledge representation involves measurable (or computable) quantities that vary throughout a region of space. The set of techniques for handling this sort of information is generally referred to as *spatial analysis* or *spatial reasoning*. One of the many powerful tools used in spatial reasoning is the *influence map*.

This chapter will look at the limitations with a traditional 2D influence map and introduce the concept of an infinite-resolution influence map. With this new representation, we'll then explore the issues of propagation, queries, handling of obstacles, and the third dimension.

29.2 Influence Mapping

To construct and use an influence map, three elements are typically involved. First, there must be some kind of *value* that varies throughout a spatial environment. Second, there is sometimes a *propagation method* by which these values change through space and/or time. Finally, there must be a *query mechanism*, which allows the AI system to examine and reason about the values stored in the influence map.

Classical influence mapping is generally performed on a regular 2D grid; more complex variants can also use arbitrary graphs, such as a navigation mesh (navmesh). In either case, the important element is not the representation of space, but the fact that space exists and is relevant to determining some value.

Propagation methods vary by application. For instance, a map used to represent the probability of an enemy occupying a given area (occupancy map) might use a simple combination of setting high values when an enemy is spotted and allowing values to decay and "spread outward" to nearby points over time. A more complex example is a visibility map, wherein the value of the map changes based on how well each point can be "seen" by a particular agent.

Some applications need not perform any propagation at all, such as tactical maps that store the instantaneous locations of various agents. Such maps can be queried directly for as long as their information is deemed up to date, and when the map becomes stale, it can simply be wiped and recomputed from scratch.

In any case, propagation generally consists of two elements: *placement* and *diffusion*. Placement is the mechanism by which new, known values are stored in the influence map. Diffusion is the process that allows influence to spread out, blur, smear, or otherwise travel across the influence map. Diffusion may occur over time or range smoothly across some distance from the nearest "placed" value, and so on.

See Figure 29.1 for an example of an influence map representing the AI's "guess" at the probability of a player being in a particular grid cell. Note that each cell contains a value from 0 to 9 and that these values increase toward areas where the player was last seen. Observe how the obstacles (dark squares) interact with the propagation of the influence.

Queries of the influence map are typically straightforward. Given a point in space (or a relevant point in the representational graph), determine the value of the influence quantity at that point. There may be some value in retaining historical data, so an agent can appear to "remember" recent influence states. A similar but more difficult trick is predicting future influence states, usually by simulating additional time-based propagation.

One final technique worth mentioning is *breadcrumbing*. In this mode, influence is deposited and diffused across the map in an ordinary fashion. When the map is updated, rather than resetting the values and recalculating them based on the relevant placement and diffusion rules, the old values are *decayed* by a given proportion. The new influence values are then added "on top of" the old values. This yields a sort of historical heat map. For example, rather than showing where agents are located *right now*, a bread-crumbed influence map can show where agents have generally tended to concentrate or travel routinely over a given span of time.

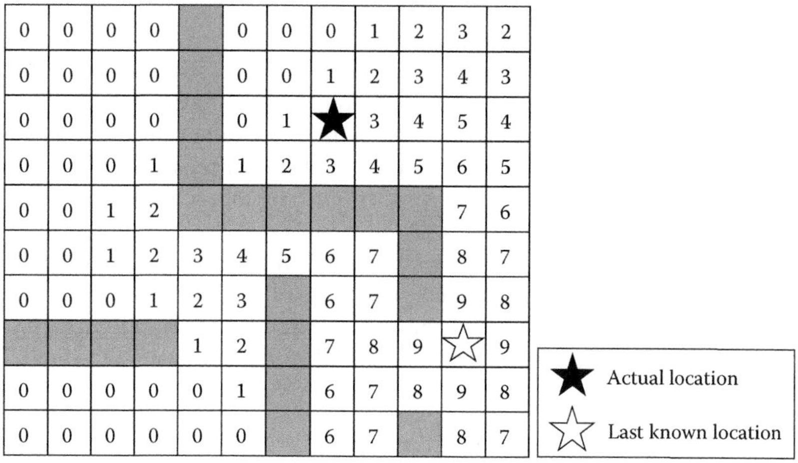

Figure 29.1

This map illustrates the AI's best guesses about the player's location.

29.3 Limitations

Representing a large, finely detailed world as a grid is often cost prohibitive. A graph might help, but even then, the trade-off between resolution and performance must be carefully examined. In many cases, the difficulty of using a graph is not justified, given that they do not solve the resolution issue, and can even compound the performance problems if not managed carefully, due to the need for nontrivial mappings between points in space and nodes in the graph.

Not only are large grids expensive in terms of memory, but they can also consume a vast amount of CPU time during propagation. Each cell must be updated with *at least* the surrounding eight cells worth of influence value, and even more cells become necessary if propagation must reach beyond a point's immediate neighbors. For many applications, this might entail processing hundreds of cells each time a single cell is updated. Even though grid lookups are constant-time operations, the propagation phase can easily become an issue.

One potential approach to mitigate this problem is to use subgrids to minimize the number of cells involved; this can be done in a few flavors. For instance, a quadtree can be established, and empty nodes of the tree can have no associated grid. Another technique is to store small grids local to relevant AI agents or other influence-generating points in the world.

Unfortunately, the quadtree approach requires constantly allocating and freeing grids as influence sources move about. Localized grids can avoid this problem, but at the cost of making propagation and lookups substantially trickier. Both techniques perform worse than a giant, fixed grid when influence must be tracked uniformly across a very large area, for example, due to having agents covering an entire map.

29.4 Point-Based Influence

Consider that most influence sources can be considered point based. They deposit a defined amount of influence onto the map at their origin point and then potentially "radiate" influence outward over a limited range. This spread of influence can occur instantaneously, or over time, or both. For instantaneous propagation of influence, a simple *falloff function* is sufficient to describe the influence value contributed by the influence source at a given location on the influence map.

If the falloff function for a point is well defined, there is no need to represent the influence of that source in a discretized grid. Instead, influence at a *query point* on the influence map is simply equal to the value of the falloff function. Suppose the falloff function is a simple linear decay out to radius r, as described in the following equation:

$$f(x) = 1 - \frac{x}{r} \quad \text{for } x \le r \tag{29.1}$$

The influence value ranges smoothly from 1 to 0 as the distance from the origin increases. For a 2D influence map, the equivalent falloff function is expressed in Equation 29.2, based on an influence source at the point (x_0, y_0):

$$f(x,y) = \max\left(1 - \frac{\sqrt{(x-x_0)^2 + (y-y_0)^2}}{r}, 0\right) \tag{29.2}$$

Naturally, influence maps with only one influence source are rather boring. On the plus side, adding in multiple influence sources is trivial: just add the values of the falloff functions. In formal notation, the computation looks like the following equation:

$$g(x,y) = \sum_i f_i(x,y) = \sum_i \max\left(1 - \frac{\sqrt{(x-x_i)^2 + (y-y_i)^2}}{r_i}, 0\right) \tag{29.3}$$

One highly useful observation is that the influence falloff function need not be trivial and linear; any differentiable function will suffice. (The importance of the ability to compute well-defined partial derivatives of the falloff function will be explored in a later section.) In fact, each individual influence source can use any falloff function desired; the value of the influence at a point remains the sum of the falloff functions for each individual influence source.

Another useful addition to this recipe is the ability to scale individual influence sources so that they do not all contribute the exact same maximum value (of 1, in this case). This is easily demonstrated in the linear falloff model as shown in the following equation:

$$g(x,y)=\sum_i \max\left(s_i\left(1-\frac{\sqrt{(x-x_i)^2+(y-y_i)^2}}{r_i}\right),0\right) \tag{29.4}$$

Given this set of tools, it is possible to replicate and even improve upon the discretized mechanisms typically used for influence mapping. Note that the value of the influence map can be queried at any arbitrary point with unlimited resolution; there is no loss of detail due to plotting the influence value onto a grid. Further, memory requirements are linear in the number of influence sources rather than increasing quadratically with the size and resolution of the grid itself.

Nothing comes for free, though; in this case, the cost of performing a query increases dramatically from $O(1)$ to $O(n)$ in the number of influence sources. Dealing with non-trivial topologies and obstacles is also significantly trickier, although, as will be explored later, some effective solutions do exist. There is also the matter of performing believable time-based propagation of influence, which is not immediately supported by the falloff function model as described. Last but not least, only one type of query has been detailed thus far; queries such as "find the point in a given area with the lowest (or highest) influence value" have not been considered.

Thankfully, all of these issues can be addressed well enough for practical purposes. Together with some optimizations and some mathematical tricks, this elimination of grids yields *infinite-resolution influence mapping.*

29.5 Making Queries Fast

Perhaps the most worrisome of the limitations of the influence mapping model described thus far is the need for comparatively expensive calculations for each query. Fixing this shortcoming is straightforward but takes some careful effort.

A key observation is that, in most practical cases, the vast majority of influence sources will not be contributing any value at an arbitrary query point. In other words, most of the influence sources can be completely ignored, drastically reducing the cost of a query.

The general idea is to use a *spatial partitioning structure* to make it possible to trivially reject influence sources that cannot possibly have an impact on a particular query. From among the many different partitioning schemes that have been developed, there are a few that seem particularly promising.

Voronoi diagrams are an appealing candidate. Constructing a Voronoi diagram optimally costs $O(n\log n)$ time in the number of influence sources, using the canonical *Fortune's algorithm* [Fortune 86]. The difficulty here is that it is often important for multiple influence sources to *overlap* each other, which fundamentally contradicts the purpose of a Voronoi diagram (i.e., to separate the search space such that each source is in exactly one *cell*).

Search trees are another category of techniques with great potential. Quadtrees are perhaps the most popular of these methods, but there is an even better option available: the *k*-d tree [Bentley 75].

Intuitively, a *k*-d tree is fairly simple. Each node in the tree has a *splitting axis*, a *left-hand branch*, and a *right-hand branch*. The splitting axis determines how the descendants of the tree node are organized. If the splitting axis is *x*, for example, all points in the left-hand branch have an *x* coordinate less than the parent node, and all points in the right-hand branch have an *x* coordinate, which is greater than that of the parent node.

A *k*-d tree is considered *balanced* if it has a (roughly) equal number of nodes in the left-hand branch as in the right-hand branch. Constructing a balanced *k*-d tree is relatively easy. Given a set of points, recursively perform the following procedure:

1. Pick an axis for the splitting axis.
2. Sort all of the input points along this axis.
3. Select the median of the input points from the sorted list.
4. This median node is now considered a *k*-d tree node.
5. Recursively apply this method to all points in the first half of the sorted list.
6. The resulting node becomes the left-hand node of the parent found in step 4.
7. Recursively apply this method to all points in the latter half of the sorted list.
8. The resulting node becomes the right-hand node of the parent found in step 4.

The splitting axis generally alternates between levels of the tree; if a given node is split on the *x*-axis, its two children will be split on *y*, and so on. Other methods for selecting a splitting axis exist but are generally most useful in fairly extreme cases. Experimentation is always encouraged, but for most uses, a simple alternation scheme is more than sufficient. A very simple *k*-d tree constructed in this manner is illustrated in Figure 29.2. The corresponding tree-style arrangement is shown in Figure 29.3.

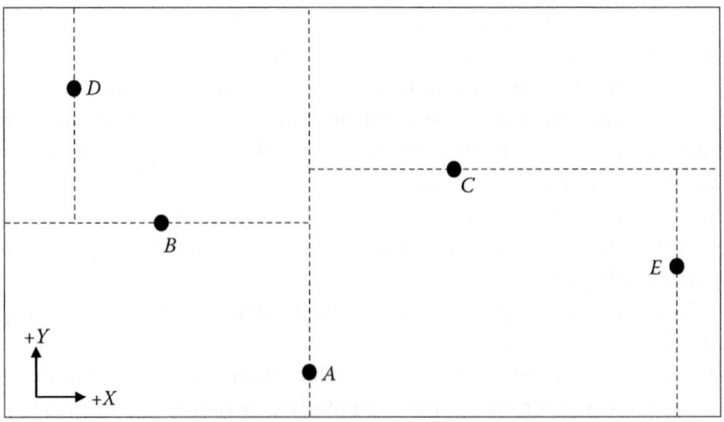

Figure 29.2

The points in this space have been partitioned into a *k*-d tree.

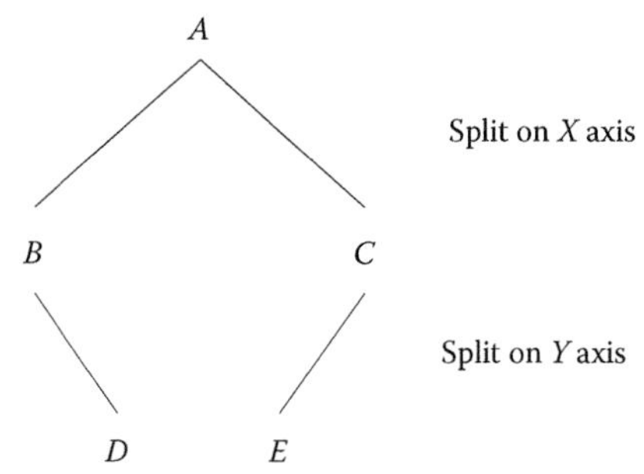

Figure 29.3

This is the same *k*-d tree as Figure 29.2, visualized as a tree structure.

Using this structure, the worst-case search time for points lying in a given range is known to be $O\left(2\sqrt{n}\right)$ for 2D *k*-d trees with *n* points [Lee 77]. The lower bound on search time is *O*(*logn*) given that *k*-d trees are fundamentally binary trees.

With these characteristics, the application of a *k*-d tree can substantially increase the performance of the infinite-resolution influence map. However, constructing the *k*-d tree represents a nonzero overhead, largely due to the need for sorting points along each axis. The number of queries desired, frequency of influence source position updates, and number of influence sources must all be carefully considered to determine if this data structure is a net win. As always, performance profiling should be conducted rigorously during such evaluations.

Once the influence source points are partitioned into a *k*-d tree, it is necessary to perform a *range query* on the tree to find influence sources that can potentially affect a given location of interest. The implementation of a range query is simple but has a few subtleties that merit careful investigation.

A range query begins at the root node of the *k*-d tree and recursively walks the branches. If the query region lies in the negative direction (i.e., left or down) from the *k*-d tree node's associated influence source point, the *left* branch of the tree is explored. If the region lies in the positive direction (i.e., right or up), the *right* branch is explored. If at any time the space bounded by a branch cannot possibly overlap the query area, the entire branch and all of its descendants can be ignored. A sample implementation is provided in Listing 29.1.

Note that it is not sufficient to check if the query location lies closer to the left or right branch. Due to the potential for the query area to overlap the splitting axis represented by the *k*-d tree node, it is important to include branches of the tree that *might* intersect the query area. The final two `if` checks in Listing 29.1 represent this logic; since they are not mutually exclusive conditions, no `else` is present.

29.6 Temporal Influence Propagation

An interesting characteristic of traditional influence maps is the ability to propagate influence values through the map over time. This behavior can be replicated in the infinite-resolution approach. Once again, the cost comparison between a grid-based propagation method and the infinite-resolution method will vary widely depending on the application.

Listing 29.1. Example C# implementation of a k-d tree range query.

```
void FindPointsInRadius (
    KdTreeNode node,
    float x,
    float y,
    float radius,
    ref List<KdTreeNode> outpoints
) {
    if (node == null)
        return;

    float dx = x - node.x;
    float dy = y - node.y;
    float rsq = (dx * dx) + (dy * dy);
    if (rsq < (radius * radius))
        outpoints.Add(node);

    float axisdelta;
    if (node.SplitAxis == SplitAxis.X)
        axisdelta = node.x - x;
    else
        axisdelta = node.y - y;

    if (axisdelta > -radius) {
        FindPointsInRadius(
            node.Left, x, y, radius, ref outpoints
        );
    }

    if (axisdelta < radius) {
        FindPointsInRadius(
            node.Right, x, y, radius, ref outpoints
        );
    }
}
```

The number of influence sources, relative density, complexity of obstacles on the map, and so on will all contribute to the performance differences. While temporal propagation is certainly possible in the grid-free design, it is not always an immediate performance win.

To accomplish propagation of influence over time, two passes are needed. In the first stage, new influence sources are generated based on each existing source. These are generally organized in a circle around each original source, to represent spatial "smearing" of the values. A decay function is applied to the old source, and influence is spread evenly among the new sources, to represent falloff occurring over time and conservation of influence as it radiates outward, respectively.

On subsequent timesteps, this procedure is repeated, causing each point to split into a further "ring" of influence sources. If splitting a source would cause its contribution to the influence map to drop below a tuned threshold, the entire point is considered to have *expired* and the source is removed from the map completely.

It is possible to approximate this result by adjusting the falloff function, for example, to a Gaussian distribution function centered on the influence source point. This reduces the number of sources involved but introduces a complication that will be important later on when considering obstacles.

Once influence sources have been added, a simplification step is performed. The goal of this step is to minimize the number of k-d tree nodes required to represent the influence present on the map. It must be emphasized that this simplification is *lossy*, that is, it will introduce subtle changes in the values of the influence map. However, these changes are generally very minor and can be tuned arbitrarily at the cost of a little bit of performance.

Simplification is accomplished by looking at each node in the k-d tree in turn. For each node, the number of nearby nodes is queried. A *neighbor* is a node close enough to the test node to contribute influence, based on the limiting radius of the applicable falloff function. If too few neighbors exist, the test node is allowed to exist unmodified.

However, if more than a certain number of neighbors are found, their *centroid* is computed by independently averaging the x and y coordinates of each neighbor. The total influence at the centroid is then sampled. If this value is sufficiently large, all of the neighbors (and the test node) are pruned from the k-d tree and replaced by a *new* influence source node that attempts to replicate the contributions of the neighbors.

The net effect of this procedure is that tightly clustered groups of nodes can be replaced by smaller numbers of nodes without *excessively* disturbing the overall values in the map. (Note again that some loss is inevitable, although for some use cases, this simplification method can actually produce very pleasing effects.)

29.7 Handling Obstacles and Nontrivial Topologies

While this method works nicely on plain, flat, empty geometry, it lacks a critical component for dealing with *obstacles*, that is, areas of the influence map where values should not propagate. There is also no consideration of more interesting topologies, for instance, where the influence propagation distance is not strictly linear.

As described, things quickly break down when considering influence propagation, because it is important to conserve "energy" as influence spreads outward. Influence that hits an obstacle should not simply vanish, but rather "bounce off" and appear to flow *around* the boundary of the obstruction.

Fortunately, a pretty convincing effect can be implemented with relatively minor adjustments to the propagation/simplification technique. During propagation, before placing a new influence source, the new point is queried to determine if that point is obstructed. If not, the point is placed as normal. If so, the point is not placed at all. Once the set of valid points is established, each one is given a fraction of the original influence source's energy, based on the number of points that were ultimately placed.

This allows influence propagation to flow smoothly through narrow corridors, for example. The result closely resembles something from a fluid dynamics simulation, where tighter constraints cause influence to move faster and farther, as if under higher pressure. By splitting influence points explicitly into new sources, it is possible to guide this "flow" through unobstructed regions of geometry, rather than uniformly outward, as would occur if the falloff function were simply replaced with a Gaussian distribution or similar function.

Another way to visualize this procedure is to consider an influence source as a cellular automaton. In the propagation step, the automaton distributes the energy it carries into a

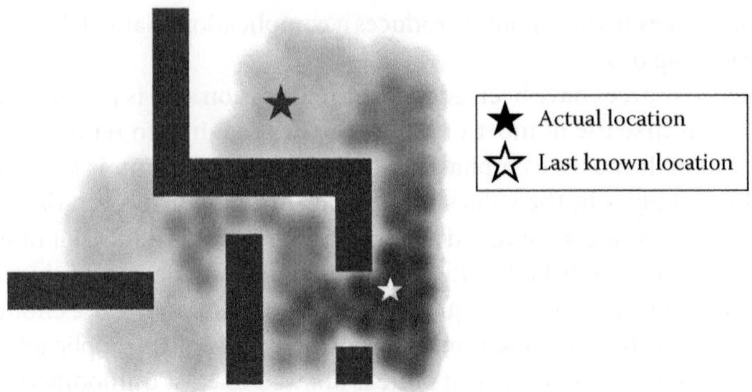

Figure 29.4

This map illustrates grid free, obstacle-aware influence propagation.

number of descendants in the surrounding (nonoccluded) space. During the simplification step, automata are resampled so that those sharing a sufficient amount of space in the world are collapsed into a single "cell." Additionally, automata that have lost too much energy due to decay or splitting are considered to have gone extinct.

If this cellular automata concept is plotted onto a grid, the result looks remarkably similar to that illustrated earlier in Figure 29.1. Allowing the influence sources to move freely rather than being truly cell based yields the effect shown in Figure 29.4, which offers a snapshot view of how infinite-resolution influence mapping handles obstacles during propagation.

Each influence source in this image is propagating a short, linear distance. However, *in totality*, the influence values will range smoothly and fluidly around obstacles, as the figure shows. By carefully controlling the placement of propagated influence nodes, it is possible to represent any spatial characteristics desired.

The methods leading to these results are directly inspired by similar techniques used in the computer graphics world, most notably *photon mapping* [Jensen 01]. In turn, more generalized statistical techniques such as *kernel density estimation* [Rosenblatt 56] are important ancestors of infinite-resolution influence mapping. These approaches provide both the foundations of the methods described in this article as well as ample opportunities for exploring the technique further.

Although it can initially seem limiting to use simple (even linear) falloff functions for representing influence sources, the vast body of prior research in the aforementioned areas should offer some reassurance that nontrivial problem spaces can be very effectively handled using such straightforward mathematical processes.

29.8 Optimization Queries

Influence mapping is valuable for far more than just acting as a mapping of spatial coordinates to arbitrary numbers. Besides just testing the value at a point, there are several other types of query that are commonly employed. In mathematical terms, these are all reducible to *local optimization queries*.

For instance, it might be useful to know the location (and value) of the point of lowest (or highest) influence, within a given area. Looking for such a lowest value is known as *local minimization*, and looking for the highest value is similarly referred to as *local maximization*. More generally, optimization within a restricted input domain is known as *constrained optimization*.

A tremendous volume of research has gone into optimization problems of various kinds. Fortunately, if the influence falloff function is carefully selected (i.e., continuously differentiable), the infinite-resolution influence map optimization problem becomes fairly straightforward.

For some types of optimization problems, there are known techniques for analytically finding an exact solution. Some require processes that are fairly difficult to automate, however. In practice, it is usually adequate to rely on *iterative* approximations to optimization queries, which are much easier to implement in the general case and typically more than fast enough for real-time use.

Specifically, the *gradient descent* optimization method [Cauchy 47] can yield local minima or maxima in a relatively short number of iterations, provided that the function being optimized is continuously differentiable. In essence, gradient descent is performed by looking at a random starting point and computing the slope of the function at that point. Based on that slope, the algorithm moves down (or up) the gradient defined by the function's curve or surface. This is repeated until further steps fail to yield improvements, indicating that a local optimum has been found.

There is a considerable tuning caveat to this technique, which is selecting the distance up (or down) the gradient to travel between steps. Different applications might find very different optimal values for this stepping. It is advisable to calibrate this value using a realistic sample set of influence sources. Optionally, the distance can be "guessed at" by examining the magnitude of the function at the current sample point and attempting to dynamically increase or decrease the step size accordingly.

Gradient descent in two dimensions simply requires partial differentiation of the candidate function and can also be generalized to three dimensions easily enough. The question is, what is the candidate function being optimized? In this case, the influence contribution function is defined again in the following equation:

$$g(x,y) = \sum_i \max\left(s_i \left(1 - \frac{\sqrt{(x-x_i)^2 + (y-y_i)^2}}{r_i} \right), 0 \right) \quad (29.5)$$

Recall that this boils down to adding up several individual functions. Conveniently, the derivative of such a summation is equal to the sum of the derivative of each function in turn. This can be succinctly expressed as in the following equation:

$$g'(x,y) = \sum_i f_i'(x,y) \quad (29.6)$$

So all that is necessary to compute the derivative of the influence map function itself is to sum up the derivatives of the influence functions for each contributing influence source.

The partial derivative of the influence function with respect to x is given by Equation 29.7. Similarly, the partial derivative with respect to y is given by Equation 29.8. The vector describing the slope of the influence function is then equal to Equation 29.9:

$$\frac{d}{dx} f_i(x,y) = \frac{-s_i(x - x_i)}{r_i\sqrt{(x-x_i)^2 + (y-y_i)^2}} \tag{29.7}$$

$$\frac{d}{dy} f_i(x,y) = \frac{-s_i(y - y_i)}{r_i\sqrt{(x-x_i)^2 + (y-y_i)^2}} \tag{29.8}$$

$$\left(\frac{d}{dx} f_i(x,y),\ \frac{d}{dy} f_i(x,y)\right) \tag{29.9}$$

Note that the influence function is defined to fall off to 0 outside the effective radius of each influence source. This logic must also be included when computing the values of the partial derivatives. In this case, it is sufficient to check the distance from the test point to the influence source beforehand and simply skip the source if its contribution would be zero.

Once this slope at a point can be computed, the gradient descent algorithm can be used to find nearby local optima. Queries for local minima or maxima can be accomplished by performing gradient descent and constraining the distance from the query point to a given radius (or other area). The algorithm for minimization is demonstrated in Listing 29.2. Note that this is an approximation only and will not necessarily find the

Listing 29.2. A pseudocode implementation of gradient descent for a local minimum.

```
maxRadius = searchRadius + NODE_MAX_RADIUS
nodeList = FindNodesInRadius(searchPoint, maxRadius)
minimum = InfluenceAtPoint(searchPoint, nodeList)

for (STEP_LIMIT) {
    if (minimum <= 0.0)
        break;

    gradientXY = GradientAtPoint(searchPoint, nodeList)
    newSearchPoint = searchPoint - (gradientXY * SCALE)
    newSum = InfluenceAtPoint(newSearchPoint, nodeList)

    if (distance(newSearchPoint, originalPoint) > maxRadius)
        break;

    if (newSum < minimum) {
        searchPoint = newSearchPoint;
        minimum = newSum;
    }
}
minimumPoint = searchPoint;
```

true optimal point in a given range without some additional modifications. However, in practice, it works well enough for general use.

Modifying this code for maximization is straightforward: each search step should check for *increasing* values of influence, and the new search point should be found by adding the scaled gradient vector instead of subtracting it.

Of course, the provided equations work only for the linear falloff function defined earlier; again, though, any falloff function can be used provided that it is continuously differentiable. If doing a lot of manual calculus is not appealing, any suitable mathematics package (including several online web sites) can be used to find the partial derivatives of a substitute falloff function [Scherfgen 14]. It is worth noting that more complex falloff functions may be substantially more expensive to compute and differentiate than the linear model.

29.9 Traveling to the Third Dimension

Thus far, influence mapping has been considered only in the context of flat, 2D geometry. While influence maps can be applied to more complex terrain, they often struggle to cope efficiently with overlapping vertical areas, such as multiple floors in a building. Potential solutions for this problem include manually marking up horizontal regions of a map, thereby creating smaller influence maps on each floor of the building, for example.

It is not difficult to find "pathological" cases where 3D geometry simply does not lend itself well to grid-based influence mapping. For games utilizing a navigation mesh, the basic technique can be loosely applied to navmesh polygons instead of squares in a grid. However, this generally equates to a loss of resolution, and a measurably more expensive propagation phase, since mesh adjacency information must be used to spread out influence instead of trivial grid cell lookups. Moreover, if the environment does not lend itself to the use of a navmesh, influence mapping in a cube-based grid is even more problematic in terms of memory and computation time.

For the 2D case, removing grids and location-based networks has a number of advantages. In the 3D case, avoiding voxelization of the world space makes infinite-resolution influence mapping an intriguing possibility. However, it is important to note that the propagation techniques discussed earlier will become accordingly more expensive in three dimensions, due to the increased number of influence sources generated during each propagation step.

Getting the infinite-resolution technique to work in three dimensions is pretty simple. The *k*-d tree data structure generalizes to any number of dimensions—in fact, the name stands for "*k*-dimensional tree." Adding a third dimension is simply a matter of adding another splitting axis option when partitioning points into the tree.

Point-based influence is also simple to generalize to three dimensions. The linear, distance-based falloff function is adjusted to compute distance based on all three coordinates instead of only two. Summation of contributing influence sources works exactly as in two dimensions.

Temporal propagation can be appreciably more expensive due to the extra points needed to effectively spread influence out over time. However, aggressive simplification and careful tuning can mitigate this expense. For very geometrically sparse environments, one alternate option is to increase the radius of an influence source as it spreads, rather than adding new points. Note that this might complicate k-d tree construction and traversal, however, due to the increased maximum effective radius of any given influence source.

Last but not least, optimization queries can also be carried forward into the third dimension with relative ease. The partial derivative of the falloff function with respect to z follows the same pattern as the first two derivatives, and as with computing the influence value itself, computing the slope (or *gradient*) of the influence function is just a matter of summing up the partial derivatives for each axis.

29.10 Example Implementation

A complete implementation of the 2D form of infinite-resolution influence mapping can be found on this book's website (http://www.gameaipro.com/). The demo is written in C# for simplicity. While it should not be considered a performance benchmark, the speed is appreciable and illustrates the potential of the technique to provide a powerful alternative to grid-based approaches.

The demo is divided into two sections. One displays a raw influence map with a variable number of influence sources placed in a configurable pattern (or randomly). This view includes the ability to perform optimization queries (specifically minimization) against the generated influence map and can show the gradient descent algorithm in action. The second section of the demo shows how temporal propagation works, including moving influence around a simple set of obstacle regions.

All code in the demo is thoroughly commented and includes some tricks not covered in detail here. It is worth repeating that this example is written for clarity rather than performance, so an optimized C++ version may look substantially different.

While the influence mapping techniques illustrated are not (to the author's knowledge) presently in use in games, the foundational mathematics is certainly highly proven in other spheres, again notably including computer graphics in the form of photon mapping. Examination of the demo code is strongly encouraged, as an animated visual demonstration is far more illustrative than simple descriptions in prose.

29.11 Suitability Considerations

Infinite-resolution influence mapping is not a drop-in improvement for standard grid-based techniques. Before applying it to a particular problem space, it is important to consider several factors that may heavily affect performance and suitability. Although there are no hard and fast rules for these considerations, careful planning up front can be invaluable.

29.11.1 Influence Source Density

Due to the use of a k-d tree to store influence source points, the density of sources can be a major factor affecting performance. While having a few dozen points in close proximity is no issue, scaling to thousands or tens of thousands of overlapping influence sources would pose a significant challenge. Note that many thousands of sources are easily handled if they are spatially distributed such that most sources do not overlap; this allows the k-d tree to ignore a larger proportion of nodes that cannot possibly be relevant to a given query.

29.11.2 Query Point Density

If the locations of queries against the influence map are relatively well distributed and sparse, infinite-resolution techniques may be very well suited. However, as queries tend to cluster or repeatedly sample very small areas, the cost of recalculating the influence contributions (and, even more so, of performing optimization queries) can become prohibitive. Use cases that need to issue large numbers of queries in dense proximity are likely better served using a grid-based approach.

29.11.3 Update Frequency

One of the most expensive steps of the infinite-resolution method is rebuilding the *k*-d tree. When updates to the influence map can be batched and performed in a single pass, the cost of propagation, simplification, and *k*-d tree reconstruction can be significantly amortized. However, if updates need to occur very frequently, or in a series of many small, independent changes, the costs of keeping the data structures up to date may be come problematic.

29.11.4 Need for Precise or Extremely Accurate Results

Fundamentally speaking, infinite-resolution influence mapping works by discarding information and relying on statistical approximations. These approximations tend to lead to subtly less precise and less accurate results. For cases where the production of exact influence values is important, grid-based methods are almost certainly preferable.

29.12 Conclusion

Influence mapping is a remarkably effective tool for knowledge representation in game AI. Traditionally, it has been confined to 2D grids and relatively simple connected graphs, such as navigation meshes. Representing large, fine-grained, and/or 3D spaces is typically very difficult if not outright impractical for influence maps. Escaping these limitations is deeply appealing.

Truly 3D, freeform influence mapping can be a remarkably powerful tool. This power, as is often the case, comes at a cost. While the infinite-resolution method is certainly very efficient in terms of memory storage, it can become highly costly to query and update influence maps created in this fashion.

As with any such performance trade-off, there will be situations where infinite-resolution influence mapping is useful and other cases where it is not applicable at all. Care should be taken to measure the performance of both techniques within the context of a specific use case. Like all game AI techniques, this one has its limitations. Given the right circumstances, though, it can be a very powerful tool in any AI developer's arsenal.

References

[Bentley 75] Bentley, J. L. 1975. Multidimensional binary search trees used for associative searching. *Communications of the ACM* 18(9): 509.

[Cauchy 47] Cauchy, A. 1847. Méthode générale pour la résolution des systèmes d'équations simultanées. *Compte Rendu des Séances de L'Académie des Sciences XXV, Vol. Série A* 25: 536–538.

[Fortune 86] Fortune, S. 1986. A sweepline algorithm for Voronoi diagrams. In *Proceedings of the Second Annual Symposium on Computational Geometry*, Yorktown Heights, NY, pp. 313–322.

[Jensen 01] Jensen, H. W. 2001. *Realistic Image Synthesis Using Photon Mapping*. Natick, MA: A.K. Peters.

[Lee 77] Lee, D. T. and Wong, C. K. 1977. Worst-case analysis for region and partial region searches in multidimensional binary search trees and balanced quad trees. *Acta Informatica* 9(1): 23–29.

[Rosenblatt 56] Rosenblatt, M. 1956. Remarks on some nonparametric estimates of a density function. *The Annals of Mathematical Statistics* 27(3): 832.

[Scherfgen 14] Scherfgen, D. 2014. Online derivative calculator. http://www.derivative-calculator.net/ (accessed January 17, 2015).

30

Modular Tactical Influence Maps

Dave Mark

30.1 Introduction

A large portion of the believability of AI characters in shooter and role-playing games (RPGs) comes from how they act in their environment. This often goes beyond *what* the character elects to do and gets into *where* the character decides to do it. Certainly, technologies such as traditional pathfinding and automatic cover selection provide much of this illusion. However, there is another layer of "spatial awareness" that, by helping to inform the decision process, can provide even more of the appearance of intelligence in game characters. Much of this stems from the character not only being aware of the static environment around it (i.e., the fixed level geometry) but also being aware of the positioning of other characters—both enemy and ally—in their immediate area. This is often done through the use of influence maps.

Influence mapping is not a new technology. There have been many articles and lectures on the subject [Tozour 01, Woodcock 02]. This article does not give a complete overview of how to construct and use them. Instead, we present an architecture we developed for easily creating and manipulating influence maps in such a way that a variety of information can be extracted from them and used for things such as situation analysis, tactical positioning, and targeting of spells. Additionally, while influence maps can be used on a variety of scales for things such as strategic or ecological uses—for example, the positioning of armies on a map or guiding the habitats and migrations of creature—this article will primarily focus on their use in tactical situations—that is, positioning in individual or small group combat. Note that many of the techniques, however, can be adapted for use in higher level applications.

This architecture was originally developed for the prototypes of two large, online RPG games. However, it can apply to many types of games including first-person shooters, RPGs, or even strategy games where multiple agents need to appear aware of each other spatially and act in a cohesive manner in the game space.

The in-game results that we achieved from utilizing this architecture included the following:

- Positioning of "tank style" defenders between enemies and more vulnerable allies such as spellcasters
- Determining the relative threat that an agent was under at a given moment
- Determining safe locations to evade to or withdraw to
- Identifying and locating clusters of enemies for targeting of area of effect spells
- Identifying locations for placement of blocking spells between the caster and groups of enemies
- Maintaining spacing from allies to avoid agents "bunching up"
- Determining when there enough allies near a prospective target to avoid "piling on"

30.2 Influence Map Overview

Tactical influence maps are primarily used by individual agents to assist in making tactical and positional decisions in individual or small group combat. The influence map doesn't actually provide instruction—it only provides information that is used by the decision-making structures of the agents. One particular advantage to using influence maps is that they can represent information that all characters could potentially have knowledge of. By calculating and storing this information once for all characters, it prevents the expensive and possibly redundant calculation of information by each individual agent. For example, an influence map that represents where people are standing in a room is information that could potentially be common knowledge to those people. By calculating it once and storing it for all to access as needed, we save the time that would be involved in each agent processing that information on its own. An additional benefit is that, although the decisions are still being made by the individuals, by using shared information about the battlefield, some sense of emergent group behavior can result.

While a simple (x, y, z) coordinate is sufficient for describing the location of an object or agent in a space, an influence map gives a coherent way of describing how that object affects that space—either at that moment or possibly in the near future. It helps to answer questions such as the following:

- What could it hit?
- How far could it attack?
- Where could it move to in the next few seconds?
- What is its "personal space?"

While some of these seem like they could be answered with a simple direction vector (and they can), the advantages gained by the influence map are realized when multiple agents are affecting the space. Rather than dealing with the n^2 problem of calculating multiple distance vectors between agents, we can look at the influence map and determine where the combined influence is. Now we can ask group-based questions such as "what could *they* hit?" or "where is it crowded?"

Additionally, the questions needed by game agents are often not "where is this," but rather "where is this *not*." The questions now become

- Where can they *not* hit?
- Where can I *not* be reached in the next few seconds?
- Where will I *not* be too close to people?

The basic form of the influence map is to divide the space into sections—most often a grid—and assign values to the cells. The values of the cells can represent a wide variety of concepts such as "strength," "danger," "value," or anything else that can be measured. Typically, a value has a locus that the "influence" radiates out from. For example, an agent that has a certain strength in its local cell may radiate influence out to a certain radius with the influence declining as the distance from the agent increases (see Figure 30.1). In some

					0.05	0.09	0.12	0.13	0.12	0.09	0.05					
			0.02	0.10	0.16	0.21	0.24	0.25	0.24	0.21	0.16	0.10	0.02			
		0.02	0.12	0.20	0.27	0.33	0.36	0.38	0.36	0.33	0.27	0.20	0.12	0.02		
		0.10	0.20	0.29	0.38	0.44	0.48	0.50	0.48	0.44	0.38	0.29	0.20	0.10		
	0.05	0.16	0.27	0.38	0.47	0.55	0.60	0.63	0.60	0.55	0.47	0.38	0.27	0.16	0.05	
	0.09	0.21	0.33	0.44	0.55	0.65	0.72	0.75	0.72	0.65	0.55	0.44	0.33	0.21	0.09	
	0.12	0.24	0.36	0.48	0.60	0.72	0.82	0.88	0.82	0.72	0.60	0.48	0.36	0.24	0.12	
	0.13	0.25	0.38	0.50	0.63	0.75	0.88	1.00	0.88	0.75	0.63	0.50	0.38	0.25	0.13	
	0.12	0.24	0.36	0.48	0.60	0.72	0.82	0.88	0.82	0.72	0.60	0.48	0.36	0.24	0.12	
	0.09	0.21	0.33	0.44	0.55	0.65	0.72	0.75	0.72	0.65	0.55	0.44	0.33	0.21	0.09	
	0.05	0.16	0.27	0.38	0.47	0.55	0.60	0.63	0.60	0.55	0.47	0.38	0.27	0.16	0.05	
		0.10	0.20	0.29	0.38	0.44	0.48	0.50	0.48	0.44	0.38	0.29	0.20	0.10		
		0.02	0.12	0.20	0.27	0.33	0.36	0.38	0.36	0.33	0.27	0.20	0.12	0.02		
			0.02	0.10	0.16	0.21	0.24	0.25	0.24	0.21	0.16	0.10	0.02			
					0.05	0.09	0.12	0.13	0.12	0.09	0.05					

Figure 30.1

Influence radiating out from the location of a single agent to a radius of 8 units.

implementations, this is the result of influence propagation that takes place over time. In our system, we simply evaluate the influence of individual cells as a function of distance from the locus.

In many implementations, including ours, when multiple agents are placed in an area together, the values that they radiate are added together so that a combined influence is created. By looking at the values of the cells, we can determine how much *combined* influence is in any given location. If the agents are closer together, the influence between them is higher than if they are farther apart. Because the influence decreases over distance, as you move away from the agents, you will eventually arrive at a location where their influence is 0. In Figure 30.2, you can see two agents who are close enough together that their influence overlaps. Note that, while each agent has a maximum influence of 1.0 (as in Figure 30.1), the area where they overlap significantly shows influences greater than 1.0.

					0.05	0.09	0.12	0.13	0.12	0.14	0.14	0.12	0.13	0.12	0.09	0.05					
			0.02	0.10	0.16	0.21	0.24	0.27	0.34	0.37	0.37	0.34	0.27	0.24	0.21	0.16	0.10	0.02			
		0.02	0.12	0.20	0.27	0.33	0.39	0.49	0.56	0.60	0.60	0.56	0.49	0.39	0.33	0.27	0.20	0.12	0.02		
		0.10	0.20	0.29	0.38	0.44	0.58	0.70	0.78	0.82	0.82	0.78	0.70	0.58	0.44	0.38	0.29	0.20	0.10		
	0.05	0.16	0.27	0.38	0.47	0.60	0.77	0.90	0.98	1.02	1.02	0.98	0.90	0.77	0.60	0.47	0.38	0.27	0.16	0.05	
	0.09	0.21	0.33	0.44	0.55	0.74	0.93	1.08	1.16	1.20	1.20	1.16	1.08	0.93	0.74	0.55	0.44	0.33	0.21	0.09	
	0.12	0.24	0.36	0.48	0.60	0.84	1.06	1.24	1.31	1.33	1.33	1.31	1.24	1.06	0.84	0.60	0.48	0.36	0.24	0.12	
	0.13	0.25	0.38	0.50	0.63	0.88	1.13	1.38	1.38	1.38	1.38	1.38	1.38	1.13	0.88	0.63	0.50	0.38	0.25	0.13	
	0.12	0.24	0.36	0.48	0.60	0.84	1.06	1.24	1.31	1.33	1.33	1.31	1.24	1.06	0.84	0.60	0.48	0.36	0.24	0.12	
	0.09	0.21	0.33	0.44	0.55	0.74	0.93	1.08	1.16	1.20	1.20	1.16	1.08	0.93	0.74	0.55	0.44	0.33	0.21	0.09	
	0.05	0.16	0.27	0.38	0.47	0.60	0.77	0.90	0.98	1.02	1.02	0.98	0.90	0.77	0.60	0.47	0.38	0.27	0.16	0.05	
		0.10	0.20	0.29	0.38	0.44	0.58	0.70	0.78	0.82	0.82	0.78	0.70	0.58	0.44	0.38	0.29	0.20	0.10		
		0.02	0.12	0.20	0.27	0.33	0.39	0.49	0.56	0.60	0.60	0.56	0.49	0.39	0.33	0.27	0.20	0.12	0.02		
			0.02	0.10	0.16	0.21	0.24	0.27	0.34	0.37	0.37	0.34	0.27	0.24	0.21	0.16	0.10	0.02			
					0.05	0.09	0.12	0.13	0.12	0.14	0.14	0.12	0.13	0.12	0.09	0.05					

Figure 30.2

The combined influence from two agents can be greater than the influence of a single agent alone.

If the same process is performed for enemy agents and then inverted (i.e., allies are positive influence and enemies are negative), a topography is created that goes beyond a binary "ours" and "theirs." It can also express ranges from "strongly ours" to "weakly ours" based on the total value in cells. The resulting map, such as the one in Figure 30.3, can give a view of the state of any given location on the map as well as the orientation of the forces in an entire area. Behaviors can then be designed to take this information into account. For example, agents could be made to move toward the battlefront, stay out of conflict, or try to flank the enemy.

Other information can also be represented in influence maps. For example, environmental effects such as a dangerous area (e.g., due to a fire, a damaging spell, or a pending explosion) can be represented and taken into account by the game agents in the same way that they can process information about the location of other agents.

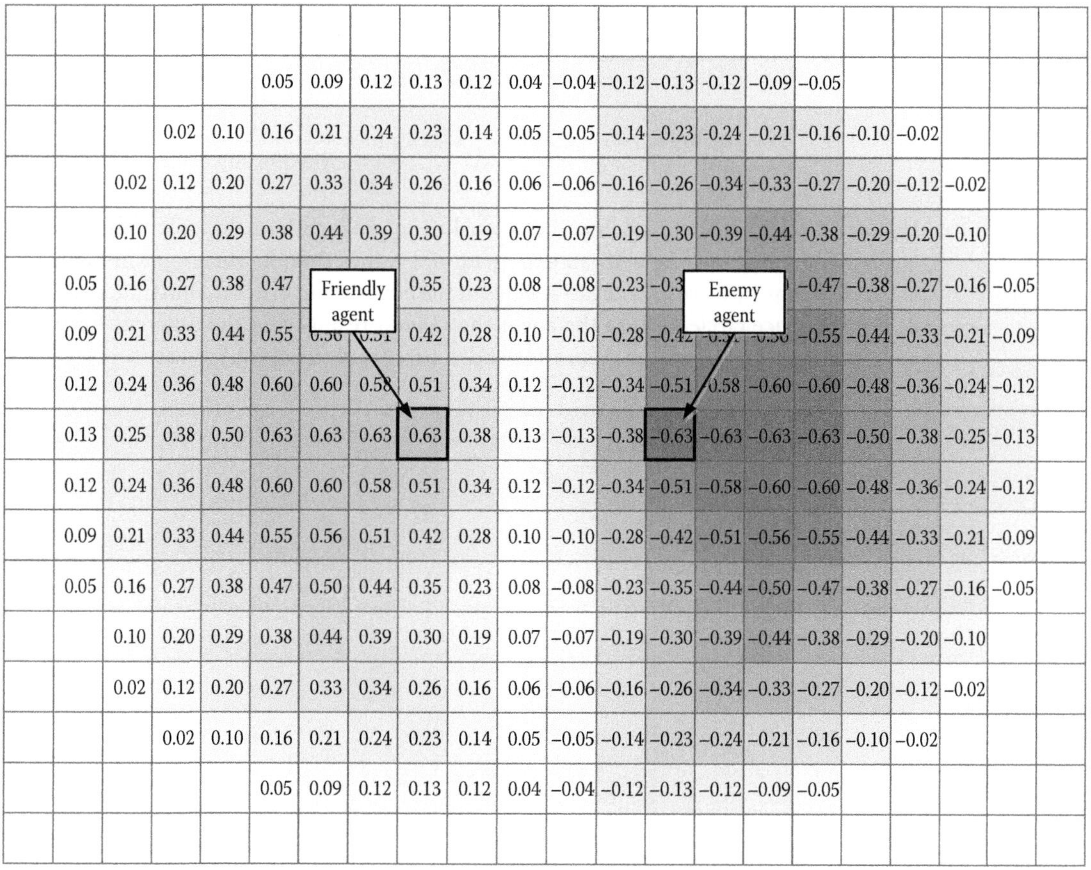

					0.05	0.09	0.12	0.13	0.12	0.04	−0.04	−0.12	−0.13	−0.12	−0.09	−0.05					
			0.02	0.10	0.16	0.21	0.24	0.23	0.14	0.05	−0.05	−0.14	−0.23	−0.24	−0.21	−0.16	−0.10	−0.02			
		0.02	0.12	0.20	0.27	0.33	0.34	0.26	0.16	0.06	−0.06	−0.16	−0.26	−0.34	−0.33	−0.27	−0.20	−0.12	−0.02		
		0.10	0.20	0.29	0.38	0.44	0.39	0.30	0.19	0.07	−0.07	−0.19	−0.30	−0.39	−0.44	−0.38	−0.29	−0.20	−0.10		
	0.05	0.16	0.27	0.38	0.47	[illegible]	[illegible]	0.35	0.23	0.08	−0.08	−0.23	[illegible]	[illegible]	[illegible]	−0.47	−0.38	−0.27	−0.16	−0.05	
	0.09	0.21	0.33	0.44	0.55	[illegible]	[illegible]	0.42	0.28	0.10	−0.10	−0.28	[illegible]	[illegible]	[illegible]	−0.55	−0.44	−0.33	−0.21	−0.09	
	0.12	0.24	0.36	0.48	0.60	0.60	0.58	0.51	0.34	0.12	−0.12	−0.34	−0.51	−0.58	−0.60	−0.60	−0.48	−0.36	−0.24	−0.12	
	0.13	0.25	0.38	0.50	0.63	0.63	0.63	0.63	0.38	0.13	−0.13	−0.38	−0.63	−0.63	−0.63	−0.63	−0.50	−0.38	−0.25	−0.13	
	0.12	0.24	0.36	0.48	0.60	0.60	0.58	0.51	0.34	0.12	−0.12	−0.34	−0.51	−0.58	−0.60	−0.60	−0.48	−0.36	−0.24	−0.12	
	0.09	0.21	0.33	0.44	0.55	0.56	0.51	0.42	0.28	0.10	−0.10	−0.28	−0.42	−0.51	−0.56	−0.55	−0.44	−0.33	−0.21	−0.09	
	0.05	0.16	0.27	0.38	0.47	0.50	0.44	0.35	0.23	0.08	−0.08	−0.23	−0.35	−0.44	−0.50	−0.47	−0.38	−0.27	−0.16	−0.05	
		0.10	0.20	0.29	0.38	0.44	0.39	0.30	0.19	0.07	−0.07	−0.19	−0.30	−0.39	−0.44	−0.38	−0.29	−0.20	−0.10		
		0.02	0.12	0.20	0.27	0.33	0.34	0.26	0.16	0.06	−0.06	−0.16	−0.26	−0.34	−0.33	−0.27	−0.20	−0.12	−0.02		
			0.02	0.10	0.16	0.21	0.24	0.23	0.14	0.05	−0.05	−0.14	−0.23	−0.24	−0.21	−0.16	−0.10	−0.02			
					0.05	0.09	0.12	0.13	0.12	0.04	−0.04	−0.12	−0.13	−0.12	−0.09	−0.05					

Figure 30.3

An allied agent spreading positive influence and an enemy one spreading negative influence can show a "neutral zone" where the influence crosses 0.0.

30.3 Propagation

As we have alluded to earlier, influence can be propagated into the map from each agent. One way of propagating influence into a map is to walk through the cells surrounding the agent. For each cell, the influence is determined by using the distance from the agent to the center of that cell passed through a response curve that defines the propagation decay of the distance. For example, the formula for linear propagation of influence is shown in the following equation:

$$\text{Influence} = \text{MaxValue} - \left(\text{MaxValue} \times \frac{\text{Distance}}{\text{MaxDistance}}\right) \tag{30.1}$$

Note that influence propagation does not have to be a linear formula. In fact, different types of influence propagation might be better represented by other response curves. Another common type is an inverse polynomial defined by a formula similar to the one shown in the following equation:

$$\text{Influence} = \text{MaxValue} - \left(\text{MaxValue} \times \frac{\text{Distance}}{\text{MaxDistance}}\right)^2 \tag{30.2}$$

Figure 30.4 shows the difference between linear propagation, the polynomial formula earlier, and a similar one with an exponent of 4 rather than 2. The graph in Figure 30.4 shows both the positive and negative sides of the equation in order to illustrate the "shape" of the influence circle around the agent that would result from the different formulas—specifically, the falloff of the values as the distance from the agent increases.

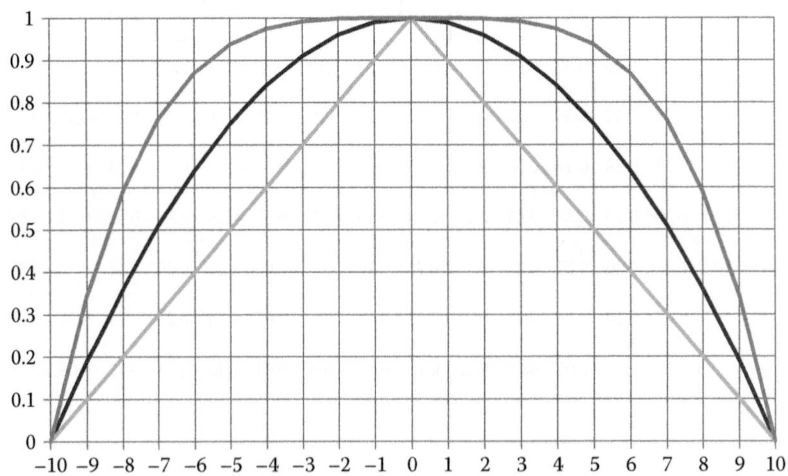

Figure 30.4

The shapes of a sample of propagation formulas centered on the agent: linear (inside) and two polynomial curves with exponents of 2 (middle) and 4 (outer).

The important thing to remember when selecting formulas is that the response curve simply shapes the propagation of the influence as it spreads away from the agent's location. Note that there is nothing stating that the value must be at its maximum at the location of the agent. For example, a catapult is fairly innocuous at close range but has a ring of influence that it projects at its firing range. An influence map designed to represent this threat would be at its highest point in a ring surrounding the catapult rather than at its actual location.

All of the aforementioned propagations of threat assume no barriers to sight or movement around the agent. Certainly, that is not the case in many game environments. In those cases, other methods of propagation need to be employed. If the influence that is being spread is entirely based on line of sight (such as the threat from a guard or someone with a direct fire weapon), it is often enough to simply not propagate influence to locations that cannot be seen by the agent.

If the influence is meant to represent the potential threat of where an agent could possibly move—for instance, "what could that tiger bite in the next 3 seconds?"—the path distance between the agent and the location in question could be used. This helps solve situations where, for example, the tiger is on the other side of fence. Yes, it is close to the target location, but it is not a threat because it would take a while for the tiger to move *around* the fence. The solution here is often simply to swap the linear distance calculation code with a call to the pathfinding system to return a distance. Since many such queries are likely to be made over the course of an influence map evaluation, a common solution is to precompute cell path-distances for a large set of cells using an undirected Dijkstra search starting from the agent's location. Either way, the costs in run-time performance and engineering effort alike are nonnegligible.

30.4 Architecture

There are different types of maps in our architecture. Some of them are the base maps for holding various types of information. Others are created at run time and stored for use in the repetitive task of populating the main maps. Still others are temporary in nature for use in combining the data into usable forms. The following sections describe each type of map.

30.4.1 Base Map Structure

The most important type of map structure is base map. The definition of this map is what determines the definitions of all the other maps to follow.

Maps are defined as rectangular areas so that they can be stored and accessed as a 2D array (or similar structure). The base map typically covers the entire level. In the case of maps where there are rigidly defined areas that are to be processed separately (e.g., the inside of a building), then a map could theoretically be smaller than the entire game level. It is often preferable, however, to attempt to simply combine maps into large areas due to complications of propagating influence from the edge of one map to an adjacent map. As you will see in the *working maps* section, it is usually easier to simply store the base map information in as large a chunk as possible.

Each map is a regular square grid. While the dimensions of the influence map are determined by the game map that it is to be used on, the cell granularity is more subject to adjustment. In general, they should be a size that would represent approximately the minimum granularity that you would want characters to position at, target at, etc. For example, if you want characters to "think in terms of" 1 m for where to stand, your cell sizes would be 1 m as well.

Because a small change in the granularity of cells can result in a massive change in the number of cells (and therefore the memory footprint and calculation time), a balance must be struck between the fidelity of the actions and the resources available to you. Suffice to say, there is no "right answer" for any of these values. They will have to be chosen based on the game design and the restrictions on processing power that might be in place.

30.4.2 Types of Base Maps

We use two types of base maps in our game. The first, and most common, is a map representing the physical location of characters—what we call a "proximity map," or simply "prox map." This map goes beyond showing the physical location at the moment—the influence radiated by the agents also shows where that agent could get to in a short period of time. Therefore, each agent's presence in the location map is represented by a circle, centered on their current location and spreading out in a circle of decreasing value until 0 is reached (see Section 30.4.3). A proximity map that contains multiple agents would show not only their current locations but also where those agents could reach in short order. The higher the value of a cell, the closer that cell is to one or more agents and the higher the likelihood of it being influenced by an agent.

The second type of map is the "threat map." This differs from the location map in that it represents not where an agent could go, but what it could potentially threaten. This may differ significantly depending on the game design. A game that involves only melee combat may have a significantly different set of demands for a threat map from a game involving gunfire with unlimited (or at least functionally unlimited) ranges. As we will see in the next section, the architecture supports different ranges of threat in the same game.

In the case of a melee unit, the threat map functions in a manner similar to the proximity map earlier, with the highest threat value propagated from the agent at the agent's location and with the threat decreasing with distance to zero. In the case of ranged units, the threat influence may take the form of a ring of influence surrounding the agent's location, as in the catapult example cited earlier. If a cell is being threatened by more than one agent, it is possible (even likely) that the threat value at that location will be greater than that generated by a single agent alone.

There will be one base map of each type (proximity and threat) for each faction in the game—often at least two factions (i.e., "us vs. them"). This allows us to pull information about either enemies or allies and combine them as necessary.

30.4.3 Templates

One problem with the calculation of influence propagation is the significant number of repetitive calculations that are needed. While they may seem trivial at first, we will soon realize that the calculations mount quickly as the number of agents increases. The most obvious fix is to limit the number of cells filled by only calculating cells in the square defined by our propagation radius. That is, if the radius of influence is 10 cells, only attempt to propagate into the cells that are within 10 vertically or horizontally from the agent—there's no point in iterating through the potentially hundreds or thousands of cells that are outside that range. However, the major stumbling block is that the distance calculations between cells—even in the small area—involve many repetitive square root calculations. When multiplied by dozens—or even hundreds—of characters, these calculations can be overwhelming.

The best optimization that eliminates the repetitive distance and response curve calculations is gained through the use of "templates." Templates are precalculated and stored maps that can be utilized by the influence map engine to "stamp" the influence for agents into the base map. We precalculate and store templates of various sizes at start-up. When it comes time to populate the map (see Section 30.5), we select the appropriate size and type of map and simply add the precalculated influence values in the template into the map at the appropriate location. Because the propagation has already been calculated in the template, we eliminate the repetitive distance and response curve calculations and replace them with addition of the value of the template cell into a corresponding cell on the base map.

As we alluded to earlier, this "stamp" method does not work when there are significant obstacles to movement in the area—particularly for proximity maps. For those situations, it would be necessary to calculate the path distance and then determine the influence value for that location.

The number and type of templates that we need depends on a number of factors:

- What does the base map represent?
- What is the possible range of values that we would use to look up the correct template?
- What is an acceptable granularity for that range of values?

As we go through the three types of templates, we will see how these values determine how many templates we need and what they represent.

Note that the influence in each of these templates is normalized—that is, the range of values is between 0 and 1. This is largely because we are defining the *shape* of the influence curve only at this point. When it comes to usage of the templates, we may often use these simple normalized curves. However, as we will explain shortly, we may want to multiply the "weight" of the influence that an agent has. By leaving the templates normalized, we can make that decision later as needed.

We utilize two different types of templates—one for proximity maps and one for threat maps. We use different templates because the propagation formula differs between them. If we were using the same formula, the templates would be identical and this differentiation would not be needed.

The first type of template is used for location maps. A location template represents what was discussed earlier in this article—where can the agent get to quickly? As mentioned in the propagation section earlier, the formula for location templates should be a linear gradient with a formula as shown in Equation 30.1.

If our map granularity was 1 m (meaning a cell was 1 m^2), our maximum speed in the game was 10 m/s, and our refresh time on maps was 1 second, and our maximum map size would be a radius of 10 m. This allows us to propagate influence out to how far an agent could get in the amount of time between map updates (1 s). Therefore, our maximum template size would be a 21 × 21 grid (10 cells on either side of the center row or column).

In order to support agents that would move at slower speeds, we must create templates that radiate out to different ranges, however. If there was a slower agent that only moved at 5 m/s, we would need one for that speed. In an RPG where there could be many different types of characters with many different movement speeds, we may want to have 1 template for each integer speed from 1 to 10.

Constructing templates for threat maps—the second type of template—would be similar. However, there are a couple of changes. First, threat maps are best calculated with a polynomial formula that reflects that the threat is similar across most of the distance and only drops off as it reaches its furthest point. Equation 30.3 shows a formula that we often use for this—a polynomial with an exponent of 4:

$$\text{Influence} = \text{MaxValue} - \left(\text{MaxValue} \times \frac{\text{Distance}}{\text{MaxDistance}}\right)^4 \tag{30.3}$$

The template is looked up by using the maximum range of the threat of the agent. An RPG character with a spell range of 30 m, for example, would need a map that was 61 × 61. On the other hand, a primarily melee character with a range of 2 m would use a significantly smaller map.

As with the speeds earlier, there needs to be a map that approximately matches the threat range of the agent in question. If you have only a small number of very specific characters and abilities, then certainly create templates to match. If there is a wider variety that would necessitate more sizes of maps, use discretion in how to create them. Because of the potentially great variety and differences between threat ranges, it might not be advisable to create one template for each measurement unit (in our example, each meter). Instead, templates can be created at specified intervals so as to give coverage adequate enough to provide a template that is at least roughly similar to the needs of the agent.

The third type of template is the personal interest map. Rather than being used to propagate influence into the base maps, these templates are specifically designed to apply to other maps in order to determine what an agent might be interested in. We will discuss the application of these maps later. As with location and threat templates, depending on the game design, it is often advisable to have multiple sizes of these maps as well so the appropriate size can be applied as needed without calculation.

30.4.4 Working Maps

Working maps are temporary maps that are used to assemble data from the main maps and templates. Working maps can be of any size but they are usually smaller than the main map because they only are used for the data directly relevant to a decision. They will always be as large as the largest template used for the decision. Most often, the working maps will be centered on the agent location (Figure 30.5).

The rationale behind working maps is that, when we are assembling combinations of map information, we will often be iterating over the relevant portions of the required maps to add or multiply their values. There is no point in iterating over the entire level if we are only interested in values that are close to the agent requesting the information. By creating a working map and copying the necessary values from

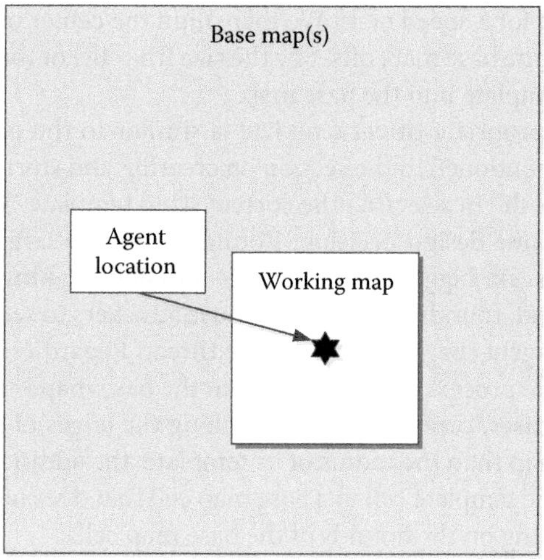

Figure 30.5

A working map is a temporary, small map centered on an agent used to assemble and process information from multiple maps in the local area.

the base maps into it (through addition or multiplication), we limit the iterations necessary and the memory footprint needed.

Because working maps are discarded immediately after use, in a single-threaded environment, there will only be one working map in existence at a time. In order to eliminate the issue of repeatedly creating and destroying these arrays often, it is often a good idea to create a single, larger, working map and preserve it for continual use.

30.5 Population of Map Data

Because the base maps must draw their information from the world data—namely, the positions and dispositions of the agents—they must be updated on a regular basis. For the games we have used this system on, we updated tactical influence maps once per second. However, any frequency can be selected based on the needs of the game, the period between think cycles for your agents, and the processing power available. For tactical movement, we would not recommend updating them any faster than 0.5 s (game characters will not need data much faster than that) or any less often than every 2 s (the data will get too stale between updates).

On each update, the map is first zeroed out—no data is carried over from one pass to the next. We then iterate through the population of the game world, and, for each agent, we apply—or "stamp"—their influence onto the appropriate maps for their faction based on their location. Assuming that we are using both proximity and threat maps, this means that each character is registering its influence on the two maps corresponding to its faction.

For the proximity map, we select the proximity template that most closely corresponds to the agent's maximum speed. That is, if an agent's maximum speed was 4 m/s, we would select the template that matched this. (If we had used integer speeds from 1–10, this would simply be the template for a speed of 4.) We then align the center of the template with the corresponding cell on the base map, offset by the size (in cells) of the template, and add the cell values from the template into the base map.

Looking up the appropriate threat template is similar to the process for the location templates earlier. As mentioned in the section on creating and storing templates, however, there may be more "slush" in selecting the correct sized template. Whether you round up or down is purely a game design decision. Rounding up to a larger threat template will cause their ranges to seem bigger than they are—possibly making attackers stay farther away. On the other hand, rounding down may cause attackers to seem that they don't realize the danger of the agent that is projecting the threat. Regardless, once the appropriate template is selected, the process of applying it into the base map is identical.

Note that in both cases, care must be taken along the edges of the map. If an agent is closer to the edge of map than the radius of its template, the addition process will attempt to apply the value of the template cell to a base map cell that does not exist. This is avoided simply by range checking on the bounds of the base map cells.

One possible addition to this process is that we may want different agents to exert different levels of influence into the map. For example, a weak character with a threat range of 10 needs to be represented differently than a strong character with an identical threat range. We need a representation that the area around the stronger character is more dangerous than around the weaker character.

Because the templates are normalized to 1.0, we can simply add a magnitude to the process of adding the influence to the map. If the stronger character was three times as powerful as the weaker character, we would simply need to pass a strength value of 3 into the function and the values in the template would be multiplied by 3 as it is stamped into the threat map. Therefore, the value of the influence of the stronger character would start at 3 and drop to 0 at the maximum range.

30.6 Information Retrieval

Once information is in the base maps, it can be retrieved in different ways depending on the needs at the time. While we will address specific use cases in the next section, the process is the same for most applications.

30.6.1 Values at a Point

The simplest form of information is retrieving the value of one map or a combination of maps at a specified point. For example, if an agent wanted to know the amount of enemy threat at its location, it could simply retrieve the value of the threat map cells for each faction that it considers an enemy. These are simply added together and returned to the agent for its consideration. Again, more use cases will be covered in the next section.

30.6.2 Combinations of Maps

Much as we applied templates into the base maps, we can lift information out of the base maps into working maps. The process is essentially the reverse of how we applied templates into the base map. We do this so that we can easily combine the map information for the area of interest without having to worry about processing the entire map.

In addition to simply passing the map into the functions to be modified, we also can pass in a modifier that dictates a magnitude for the modification. For example, rather than simply constructing a working map that consists of the values in MapA plus the values in MapB, we can specify that we want the values in MapA plus 0.5 times the values in MapB. The latter would yield a different output that might suit our purposes better at the time. In words, it would read "the influence of MapA plus *half* of the influence of MapB." By doing so, we can craft "recipes" for how an agent is looking at the world—including priorities of what is important to consider.

By including basic functions for adding and multiplying maps into the map class, we can construct a simple syntax that assists in building a working map that includes the information that we need. Each function takes a map and processes it into the working map according to its design and parameters if necessary. This is how we achieve the modularity to be able to construct a variety of outputs in an *ad hoc* manner.

For example, our code could look like the following:

```
WorkingMap.New(MyLocation);
WorkingMap.AddMap(EnemyLocationMap(MyLocation), 1.0f);
WorkingMap.AddMap(AllyLocationMap(MyLocation), -0.5f);
WorkingMap.MultiplyMap(InterestTemplate(MyLocation), 1.0f);
Location InterestingPlace = WorkingMap.GetHighestPoint();
```

We will see what can be done with these combinations in the next section.

30.6.3 Special Functions

There are a number of special functions that we must set up in order to make things easier for modular use later.

First, we can construct a general "normalization" function that takes a working map and normalizes its values to be between 0 and 1. The standard method of normalizing is to take the highest and lowest values present on the map and scale the contents such that they become 1.0 and 0.0, respectively. For instance, consider a map with a maximum value of 1.4 with a particular cell that had a value of 0.7. After normalization, the maximum value would be 1.0 (by definition) and the cell in question would now have a value of 0.5 (0.7/1.4).

The normalized map is convenient for times when we are interested in the general "terrain" of the map, but not its true values. We can then take that normalized map and combine it meaningfully with other normalized maps. We will investigate those further in the next section.

The other helper function is "inverse." In this case, we "flip the map contours upside down" in effect. This is done by subtracting the cell values in the map from 1.0. Therefore, an influence map of agents that would normally have high values at the points of greatest concentration and 0 values at the locations of no influence would now have a value of 1.0 at the places of no influence and its lowest points at the locations of the greatest influence.

The inverse function is helpful when combining maps from enemy factions. Instead of subtracting one faction's map from another, we can add one map to the inverse of the other. While, at first glance, this seems like it would yield the same result, the shift in values allows us to preserve convenient functions (such as retrieving the highest point) in our modular system.

30.7 Usage

The collection and storage of influence map data is useless without ways to use it. The power of the system is in how many ways the underlying data can be reassembled into usable forms. This information retrieval and processing can be divided into three general categories:

1. Gathering information about our location and the area around us
2. Targeting locations
3. Movement destinations

We address each of these in Sections 30.7.1 through 30.7.3.

30.7.1 Information

The most basic function that the influence map system can serve is providing information about a point in space. One function simply provides an answer to the simple question, "what is the status of this point?" The word "status" here could mean a wide variety of things depending on the combination of maps utilized in the query. However, other methods can query an entire area and answer the similar question, "what is the status of the (highest/lowest) point around me?" The latter can be done without specifying a point at all simply by looking at the surrounding area.

The first method—that of querying a specific point—is achieved by querying the value of a location through its associated influence map cell on one or more maps (Figure 30.6). For example, if we wanted to know the total threat from our enemies at the location we are standing, we would simply retrieve the value of the cell we are standing in from all of the threat maps that belong to enemy factions. Because the value that is returned represents the total threat at our location, it can be used in decisions such as when to relocate to a safer position. A similar query of the physical proximity map of our own faction would hint us as to whether or not we might need to move slightly to give space to our co-combatants. Note that this method does not require us to use a working map because we are only interested in the values of individual cells.

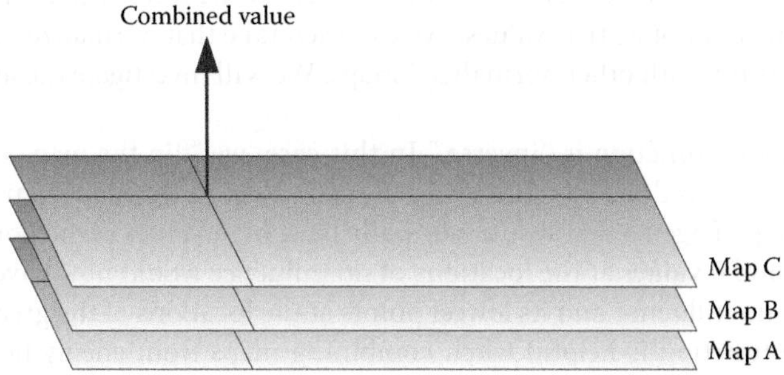

Figure 30.6

We can query a point on the map and retrieve data accumulated from a combination of maps at that point.

Another method for querying information is to look at the entire area surrounding us. For example, we may want to query the area to see if there are concentrations of enemies that are standing close together. To do this, we create a working map that is the same size as a personal interest template that, in this instance, might be how far we could attack in 1 s (our maximum threat range + our movement speed). We then populate that working map with the data from the proximity maps of our enemies. We then run a function that walks through the working map and returns the highest value (not the location). This value tells us what the maximum concentration of enemies is due to the fact that enemies closer together have their influence areas overlapping resulting in a higher sum as is shown in Figure 30.7. This might be useful in informing us that we might want to cast an area of effect spell. (Note that the location at which we would cast it is addressed in the next section.)

The usefulness of the modular nature of the map system becomes clear when we extend the aforementioned query to ask, "what is the highest concentration of all factions?" We could add all the factions together and find the highest value. Summing the enemy factions to the *inverse* of allied factions would give a number representing the highest concentration of enemies that isn't close to any allies. By mixing location and threat maps, we can extend the possible information we can get.

Often, it is good to prioritize information that is closer to the agent so that it doesn't make decisions that cause it to, perhaps, run past one threat to get to another. By multiplying the resulting working map by our personal interest template, we adjust the data so that closer cells are left relatively untouched, but cells on the periphery are reduced artificially—ultimately dropping to zero. In the example shown in Figure 30.8, the high point on the original map (a) is located at the edge of the personal interest map (b) surrounding the agent's location (dotted line). By multiplying the original map by the interest map, the resulting map (c) yields a different high point. While the *actual value* of this location is smaller than the high point in the original map, it is prioritized due to its proximity to the agent's actual location. Note that any points outside the radius of the personal interest map are reduced to 0 due to multiplying by 0.This is similar to the agent saying, "Yes, there is something interesting over there, but it is too far away for me to care."

30.7.2 Targeting

Another primary use for assembling information from combined influence maps is for use in targeting. In the aforementioned section, we mentioned that we could query the local area for the highest value. By using a similar process, we can acquire the actual location of the cell that produced that value. This is as simple as making a note of the cell in the working map that contains the highest value and then converting it back into a position in the world.

Possible uses for this include using the proximity maps for determining a location to cast an area of effect spell—a damaging one against enemies or a healing buff for allies. By finding the highest point on the working map, we know that it is the center of concentration of the forces of the faction we are checking. This means that the target will not be a character in the world but rather at a point that should be the "center of mass" of the group. Referring again to Figure 30.7, the "high point" identified on the map is the location of the highest concentration of agents.

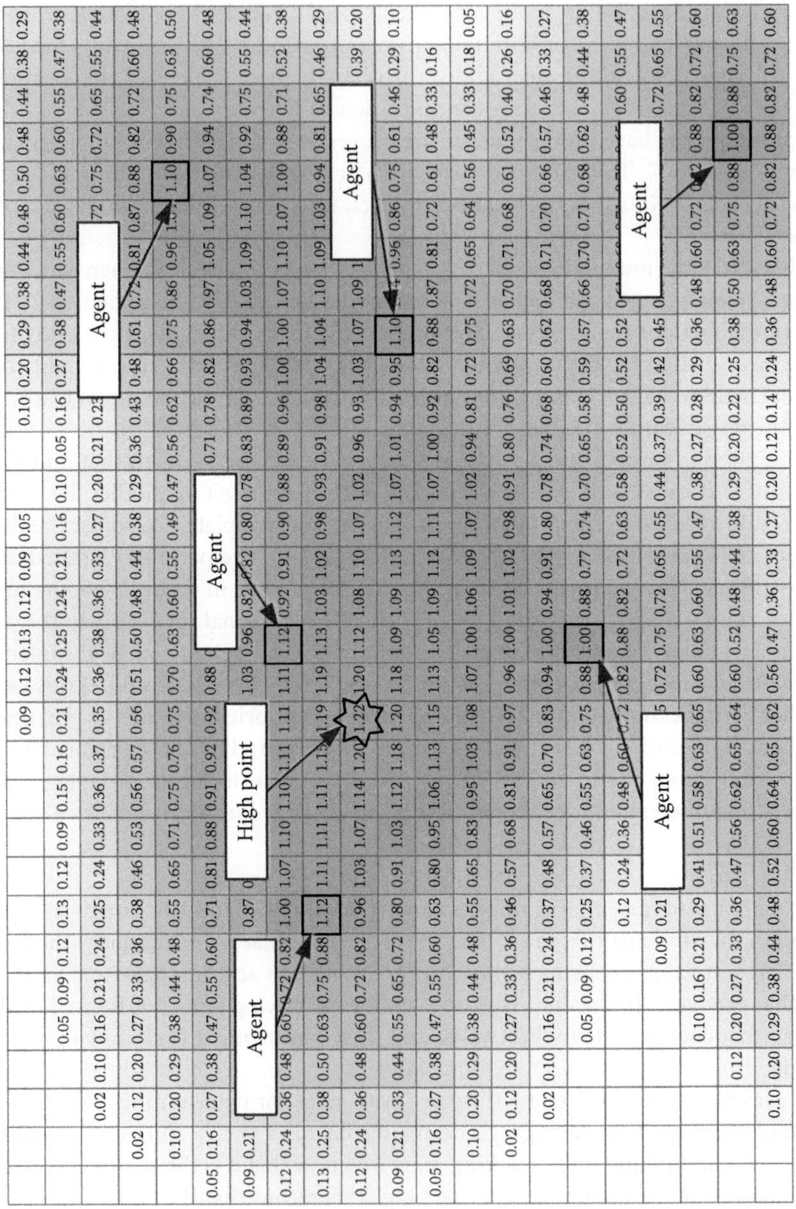

Figure 30.7

The "center of mass" of agents can be determined by finding the highest value on one or a combination of base maps.

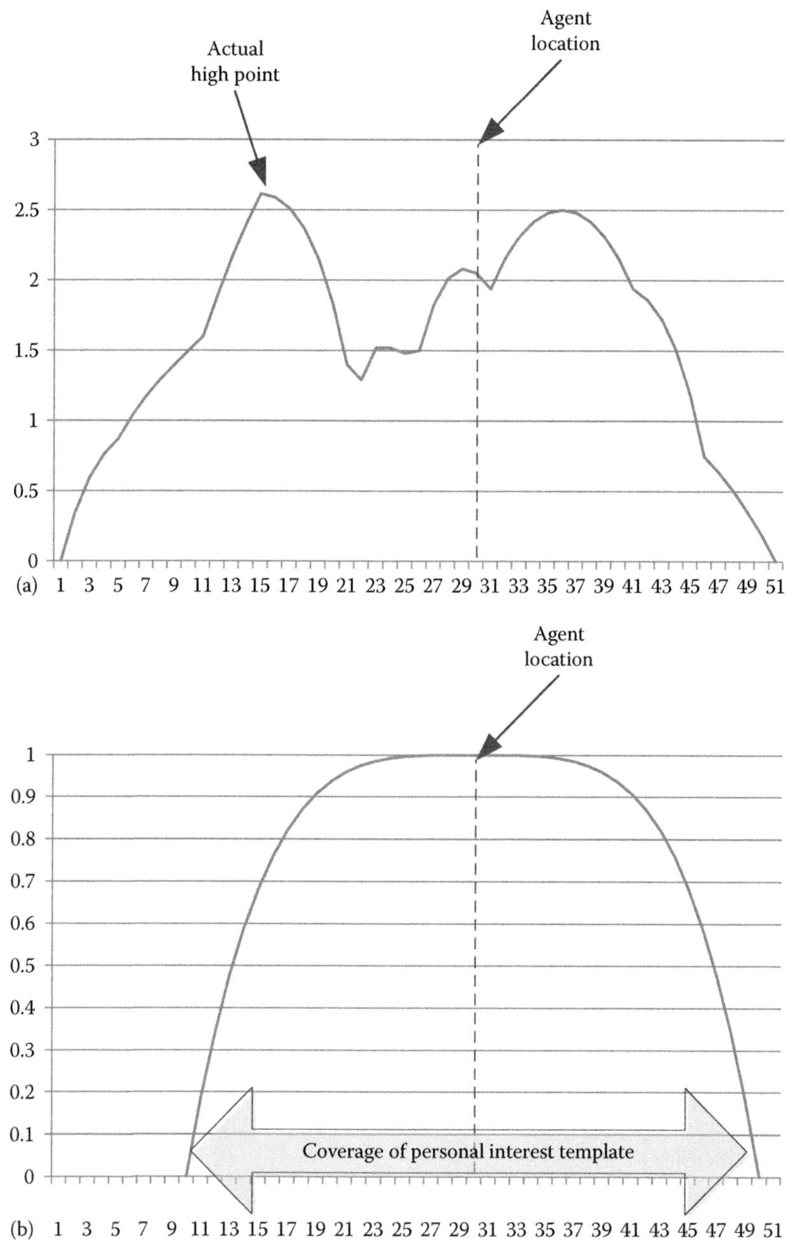

Figure 30.8

A complex influence map (a), when multiplied by a personal interest template (b),

(*Continued*)

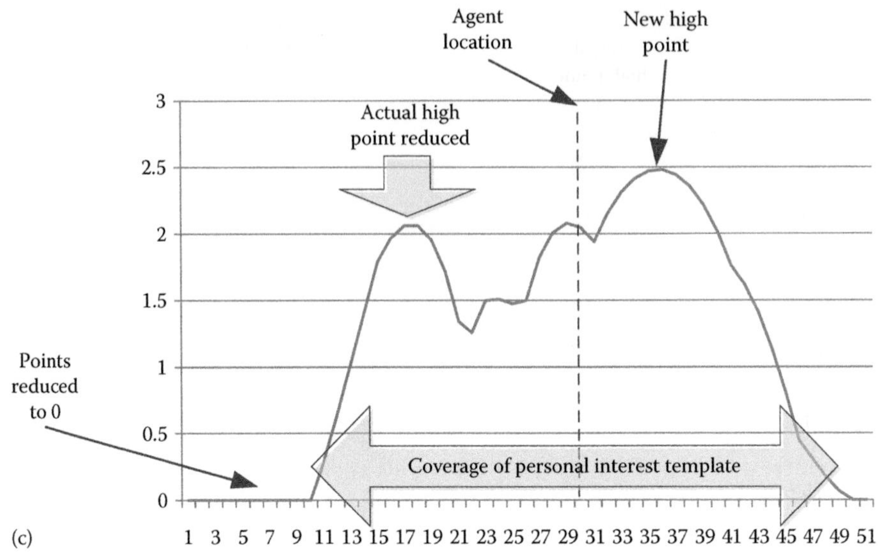

Figure 30.8 *(Continued)*

Might yield different high points (c).

Because of the modular nature of the system, we could add the enemy location maps together and then *subtract* the location maps for allies. The resulting high point would give a location of concentration enemies that is also *not near* allies. This might be useful in avoiding friendly fire, for example.

Another possible use would be identifying a position between the agent and the bulk of the enemies or even between the bulk of the agent's allies and the enemies. This might help identify where to place a blocking spell such as a wall of fire. This is accomplished by determining that point of the concentration of the enemies as we did earlier, but then using that as an endpoint for a line segment either between that point and the agent or that point and a corresponding one for the allies. In effect, this is determining the "threat axis" to be aware of. By selecting a location partway along that segment, you are able to identify a spot that would be good for a blocking spell (Figure 30.9) or for the positioning of forces, as we shall see in the next section.

30.7.3 Positioning

The third primary use for tactical influence maps is to inform movement commands. This is very similar to the use for targeting earlier. Upon deciding that it would like to perform some sort of movement (move toward a group, withdraw to a safe spot), the agent requests an appropriate destination location from the influence map system. As with the methods earlier, a working map is created and populated with data from the necessary maps, the personal interest template is applied (via multiplication), and the highest or lowest scoring location is returned.

Another use for positioning is to encourage spacing between agents—notably allied agents. By subtracting the location maps of the agent's faction—*and adding the agent's*

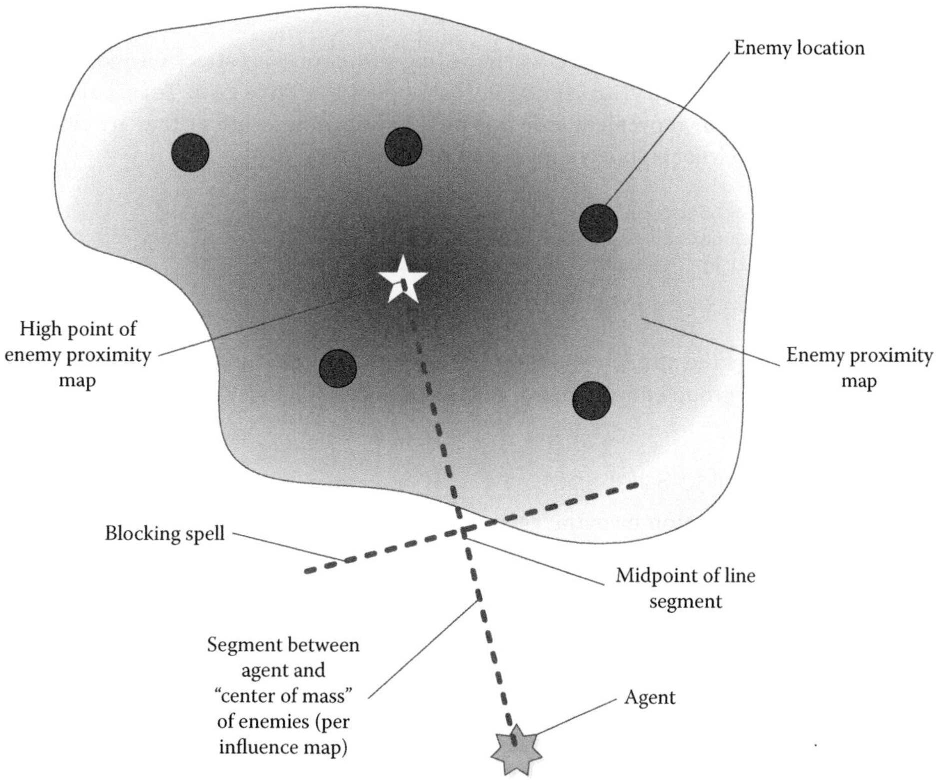

Figure 30.9

By determining the location of the high point of the enemy proximity map, we can select a location along the line between that point the agent to position a blocking spell, for instance.

own proximity template—the agent can adjust and take allied agents' positioning into account. This can be used on a stand-alone basis for a simple "spacing" maneuver (e.g., as part of an idle) or as a modifier to other positioning activities. At this point, the logic from the influence map request can be read as something similar to "find me a location that is away from enemy threats *but also spaced apart from my allies*."

30.8 Examples

The following are some examples of modularly constructed influence maps that can be used for common behaviors. Note that this assumes only one enemy and one allied faction. A separate code could be written to assemble all relevant factions.

The examples are written in a simplified structure for brevity and clarity. The actual implementation of the functions referenced here would be more involved and would differ largely depending on your base implementation. However, the actual modular functions to access the data should be little more complicated than what is shown here.

30.8.1 Location for Area of Effect Attack

This identifies if there is a point that is worth casting an area of effect attack on and retrieves the location. The `MultiplyMap` function that applies the `InterestTemplate` (of a size determined by our movement speed) is used to prioritize locations that are closer to the agent similar to what is show in Figure 30.8.

```
WorkingMap.New(MyLocation);
WorkingMap.Add(LocationMap(MyLocation, ENEMY), 1.0f);
WorkingMap.Multiply(InterestTemplate(MySpeed), 1.0f);

return WorkingMap.GetHighestLocation();
```

Note that to change the aforementioned code to find a position for an area of effect spell for allies (such as a group buff spell), we only would need to change the parameter `ENEMY` to `ALLY`.

30.8.2 Movement to Safer Spot

This identifies the location near the agent that has the least amount of enemy physical influence. This is good for finding a location for the character to move that is away from the immediate physical range of enemies.

```
WorkingMap.New(MyLocation);
WorkingMap.AddInverse(LocationMap(MyLocation, ENEMY), 1.0f);
WorkingMap.Multiply(InterestTemplate(MySpeed), 1.0f);

return WorkingMap.GetHighestLocation();
```

By using the inverse of the enemy location map, we are saying that the places where the cell values are low (or even 0)—that is, *away* from enemies—are now the highest points. Correspondingly, the highest points on the map are now the lowest due to the inverse. Since we are looking for place with the fewest enemies, we now can use the `GetHighestLocation()` function. Of course, the highest points would be modified somewhat after the application of the interest map, again as visualized in Figure 30.8.

Note that this code can also be used for moving away from allies (e.g., to keep spacing) simply by changing the parameter `ENEMY` to `ALLY`.

Additionally, by changing the code to use the threat map of enemies, we could find a location that had the least amount of enemy threat (but was also close to our location by application of the interest template). The new code would be as follows:

```
WorkingMap.New(MyLocation);
WorkingMap.AddInverse(ThreatMap(MyLocation, ENEMY), 1.0f);
WorkingMap.Multiply(InterestTemplate(MySpeed), 1.0f);

return WorkingMap.GetHighestLocation();
```

30.8.3 Nearest Battlefront Location

To determine a location that is in the area between our allies and our enemies, we multiply the enemy threat map by the ally threat map. The resulting map has high points along a line where the two maps overlap the most (Figure 30.10). By further multiplying this map by the interest template, we can find a location nearest to the agent that is "on the front lines."

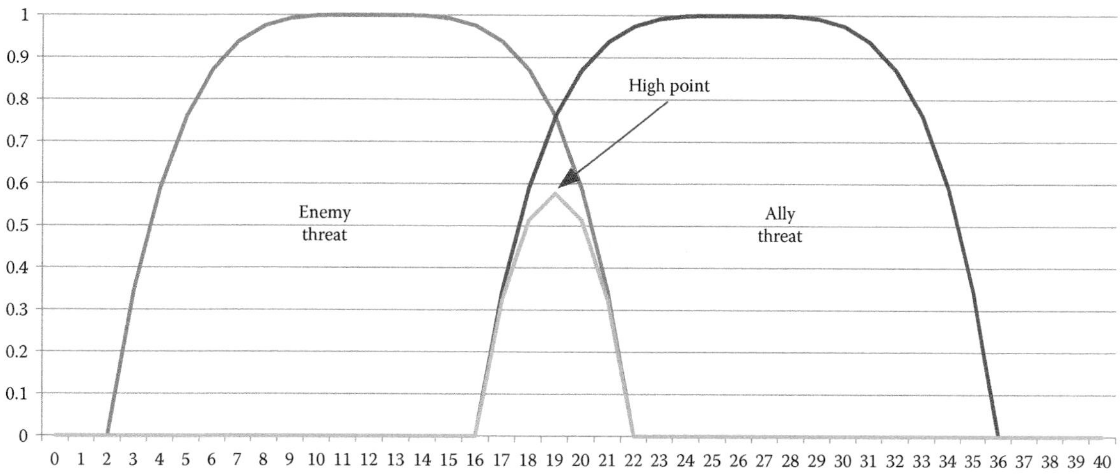

Figure 30.10

Multiplying enemy threat (or location) by ally threat (or location) yields high points along the front lines.

```
WorkingMap.New(MyLocation);
WorkingMap.Add(ThreatMap(MyLocation, ENEMY), 1.0f);
WorkingMap.Multiply(ThreatMap(MyLocation, ALLY), 1.0f);
WorkingMap.Multiply(InterestTemplate(MySpeed), 1.0f);

return WorkingMap.GetHighestLocation();
```

As we noted in the prior section, by subtracting our ally's proximity, we can find a point that is "on the front" but also away from our fellows. This leads to a behavior where allied agents will spread out along a battlefront by selecting a location that is not only in between the bulk of allies and enemies but also physically apart from their comrades. In order for this to work, we need to normalize the result of the map earlier and then subtract a portion of the ally proximity map. The version of the ally proximity map that we need must not include our own proximity. Therefore, a function is created that returns the ally proximity *without our own information*. This would simply be as follows:

```
AllySpacingMap.New(MyLocation);
AllySpacingMap.Add(LocationMap(MyLocation, ALLY), 1.0f);
AllySpacingMap.Add(LocationTemplate(MyLocation, MySpeed), -1.0f);

Return AllySpacingMap&();
```

We can then apply this spacing map into our original formula. The adjusted code would read as follows:

```
WorkingMap.New(MyLocation);
WorkingMap.Add(ThreatMap(MyLocation, ENEMY), 1.0f);
WorkingMap.Multiply(ThreatMap(MyLocation, ALLY), 1.0f);
WorkingMap.Normalize();
WorkingMap.Add(AllySpacingMap(), -0.5f);
WorkingMap.Multiply(InterestTemplate(MySpeed), 1.0f);

return WorkingMap.GetHighestLocation();
```

Note that we are multiplying the ally spacing map by a scaling factor of 0.5 before we subtract it in order to make it less of an impact on the positioning than the battlefront itself.

30.9 Conclusion

As we have demonstrated, influence maps can be a powerful tool for agents to understand the dynamic world around them. By providing a modular system that allows programmers to combine individual map components in a variety of ways, a wide variety of expressivity can be easily created and tuned with relative ease.

References

[Tozour 01] Tozour, P. 2001. Influence mapping. In *Game Programming Gems 2*, ed. M. DeLoura, pp. 287–297. Charles River Media, Hingham, MA.

[Woodcock 02] Woodcock, S. 2002. Recognizing strategic dispositions: Engaging the enemy. In *AI Game Programming Wisdom*, ed. S. Rabin, pp. 221–232. Charles River Media, Hingham, MA.

31

Spatial Reasoning for Strategic Decision Making

Kevin Dill

31.1 Introduction

In the real world, no military decision can be made without taking into account the characteristics of the space in which the decision is taking place. Individual soldiers will use cover and concealment, so as to maneuver on the enemy without being shot. Squad leaders will split their team, with one element pinning the enemy in place while the second maneuvers to attack from a flank. Platoon leaders emplacing a defensive perimeter will use their largest weapons to cover the most likely avenues of approach, and use resources such as minefields and barbed wire to constrain the enemy's maneuverability—forcing them to attack where expected. Beyond small unit tactics, spatial considerations are taken into account in decision after decision—from the placement of diapers in a toy store (at the back, so that parents have to take their children past the toys) to the placement of a city (in a good location for trade, with ready access to water).

While there are exceptions, game AI often does a poor job of thinking about space in these ways. A common justification is that the developer doesn't want to make the game too hard for the player—but there are any number of ways to balance the game, including simply making the enemies weaker or forcing them to make intentional mistakes that the player can exploit. Further, imagine the benefits of making the AI more spatially competent. As Koster so eloquently explained in *A Theory of Fun for Game Design* [Koster 04], one of the things that makes a game fun is *mastery.* Imagine an enemy that could use good spatial tactics and strategies against you in a difficult but not overwhelming way. If the player can learn from the strategies of their enemy, then they are being *shown* how to take advantage of the environment themselves, and we can gradually build upon that experience, imparting mastery step by step much like the game *Portal* gradually imparts mastery in the use of a teleportation gun.

In this chapter, we present a successful spatial reasoning architecture that was originally developed for the real-time strategy (RTS) game, *Kohan II: Kings of War* ("Kohan II") [Kohan II]. This architecture primarily addressed strategic needs of the AI, that is, the large-scale movements and decisions of groups of units across a map.

Spatial reasoning is, by its very nature, highly game- and decision-specific. The information that needs to be tracked and the techniques that will work best depend greatly on the specific nature of the experience that you're trying to create for your players. Further complicating the issue is the fact that the capabilities of your game engine will often drive you toward specific representations of space and away from others. As the approaches in this chapter were largely drawn from *Kohan II,* a tile-based strategy game, our solutions have that flavor about them. Nevertheless, many of the ideas discussed here are directly applicable in a wide range of domains, and others might spur your own ideas for spatial considerations. Our ultimate hope is to spark your imagination and get you thinking about (1) how space is important to your players' experience and (2) how you can represent and reason about that. From there, it's a small step to finding the right solutions for your own game.

It is worth noting that the *Kohan II* AI was discussed in *AI Game Programming Wisdom 3* [Dill 06]. While it's not necessary to read that chapter in order to understand this one, it will help to clarify the larger picture and in particular how some of the techniques discussed here might be used in the context of a utility-based AI.

31.2 Spatial Partitioning

Before any spatial reasoning can be done we need a *spatial representation,* which is created by breaking the game map up into meaningful *regions.* Regions will form the basis of most of the spatial reasoning techniques we will describe, including techniques for driving exploration, picking attack locations, path planning, and spatial feature detection.

The ideal subdivision is of course going to be game-specific, as you create regions that represent the spatial characteristics important to the decisions you want to make. With that said, here are some general characteristics of good regions as they are defined in Kohan II—just keep in mind that (with the possible exception of homogeneity, depending on your intended use) these are intended as fuzzy guidelines, not hard requirements:

- *Homogeneity*: It's often a good idea to have regions composed of a single "type" of space. For example, in a strategy game, your regions might divide space by terrain type, with each region being composed entirely of land, water, or mountain tiles, perhaps further subdivided to call out features like hilltops and roads that are of particular importance. Similarly, in a shooter with indoor maps, you might divide space into room and corridor regions, perhaps with smaller regions to represent areas of cover and concealment, potential snipe points, and so forth. The important thing is that each region should contain exactly one type of space—so a cover region should contain *only* cover, a hilltop region should contain *only* the hilltop, and so forth. This way, the AI knows that anywhere it goes in that region the expected characteristic will pertain.

- *Not too big*: If the regions are too large, then the reasoning becomes muddy and inaccurate—there isn't enough detail represented to make meaningful decisions. At the ridiculous extreme, we could treat the whole map as a single region—but this wouldn't be helpful to the AI at all.
- *Not too small*: If the regions are too small, then we can get buried in details. This can have profound performance implications, as many terrain reasoning techniques are search based and thus potentially expensive. More to the point, wherever possible (and this can be a difficult balancing act), we would like all of the features that go into making a decision about a region to be contained within that region or at least in a few adjacent regions. For example, if considering attacking a settlement in an RTS game, we'd like that settlement to be contained in a single region. If considering an army, we'd like the entire army to be contained in a single region. This is often not possible—armies typically move around and cross region borders freely, for example—so we will often need to consider characteristics of nearby regions when making decisions. Techniques exist for this, the most obvious being influence maps (which are discussed in detail in Section 31.4), but the fewer regions the army traverses, the better our decisions about it are likely to be.
- *Roughly equilateral/square/hexagonal/round*: Long, skinny regions tend not to be ideal—they can easily be too small in one dimension, and too large in the other. Of course, this is an ideal that depends very much on the situation. Long, skinny regions make perfect sense when representing long skinny things, such as a corridor in a building or the area along the side of a country road where the combination of a ditch and a stone wall may provide improved cover.
- *More-or-less convex*: Convexity is not an absolute requirement, even if you're going to use your regions for high-level path planning—in fact, it is often overrated. Nevertheless, if your spatial partition algorithm creates regions that are badly concave (e.g., a region shaped like a giant letter L or like Pacman with his mouth half open), you may want to consider taking a pass over all the regions and splitting these ones in half, particularly if they're large. As a rough rule of thumb, if the center of a region is not inside the region then the region is too concave.

31.2.1 Region Generation

There is no one right way to generate regions. When possible, it's a good idea to lean on the tools provided by your game engine. Techniques that you might consider include the following:

- *Designer defined*: For many games with predefined maps, designers can hand annotate the maps. This gives the most control over the player's experience and can produce very good results, but isn't possible on large open-world games or games with random maps.

- *Navmesh based*: If your game has a navmesh, then it's possible to simply use that, although this may not result in very good regions—many navmesh generation algorithms create regions that are long and skinny or that are widely varying in size. One partial solution is to automatically combine and/or subdivide the navmesh cells to produce better quality regions, perhaps sacrificing a bit of convexity to produce regions that are closer to round and of appropriate size. Of note, if you decide to head in this direction, consider using a technique such as conforming Delaunay triangulation for your navmesh generation—it will provide triangles that are closer to being equilateral (and thus not long and skinny) than many other approaches [Tozour 02, de Berg 08].
- *Tile based*: If you have a tile-based map (or can temporarily lay tiles over your map), you can use a flood-fill algorithm to create your regions. This is the approach that we used in *Kohan II*, so we will discuss it in detail.

For *Kohan II*, we used a greedy flood-fill-based approach to create rectangles from our grid tiles and then, in certain cases, combined adjacent rectangles to create our regions. It wasn't a perfect approach. It was time consuming (on a 2005 era machine, with a large map, it could take well over 20 seconds, so we ran it at load time only) and would sometimes create regions that were long and skinny or oddly shaped. Nevertheless, it was simple to implement and debug and makes a good basis for the rest of this chapter.

The logic for rectangle creation was as follows:

1. Start a new region that consists of a single tile. This tile should be one that has not yet been placed into a rectangle, and that is the farthest to the bottom and left of the map.
2. Using that tile as the bottom-left corner, find the largest homogenous rectangle that we can. We do this by alternately expanding the rectangle one row to the right and one row up, as long as this expansion results in a rectangle that is homogeneous.
3. If the resulting rectangle is "too big," divide it horizontally and/or vertically, creating two or more rectangles of a more reasonable size—for instance, if our maximum width is 16 tiles, then a 20×45 rectangle would be divided into six 10×15 pieces.

This algorithm results in rectangles of terrain that are homogeneous, generally roughly square (although this is not guaranteed), convex, and not too big. However, it can create a lot of very small regions along the borders of different types of terrain (e.g., along the edges of rivers or mountain ranges). These regions are not only too small, they also often aren't very interesting (not a lot of importance happens right on the edge of impassable terrain). Consequently, we would prefer to somehow get rid of them.

The first step to addressing this is to take a second pass over all of the rectangles looking for the undesirable ones. For example, we might search for rectangles that are less than two tiles wide in one direction or the other and that contain less than ten total tiles—although the details of how to tune that are of course game-specific. Whenever we find one of these rectangles, we try to attach it to an adjacent rectangle of the same terrain type. We only do this if the resulting region doesn't exceed some maximum height and width and if its center remains inside of its borders. The result is that we

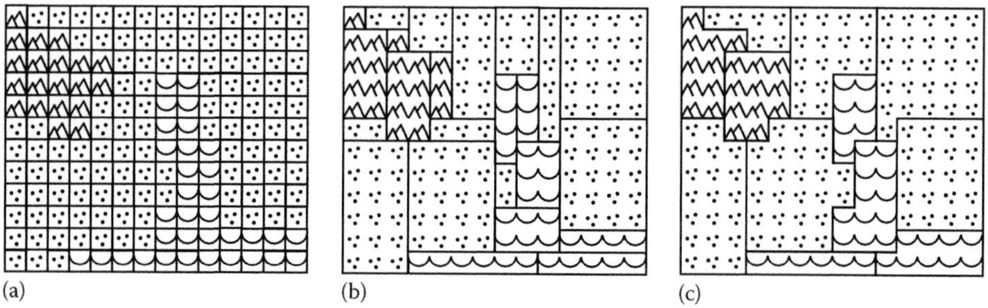

Figure 31.1

A hypothetical tile-based map with land, water, and mountain terrain (a) and the same map divided into rectangles (b) and regions (c).

get a smaller number of more useful, slightly larger, occasionally nonconvex regions. Figure 31.1 shows this entire process step by step.

In *Kohan II*, we retained all three representations. The tiles were useful for low-level path planning and collision avoidance, although we did allow movement within tiles. The rectangles gave a compact representation for the regions (a region consisted of a list of rectangles, and a rectangle simply stored the bottom-left and top-right tiles). Finally, the regions were used for a wide variety of spatial reasoning and decision-making tasks.

31.2.2 Static vs. Dynamic Regions

For many games, it is adequate to use static regions—that is, regions that don't change during gameplay. Static regions are generally baked into the map during development or, if you have random maps, created when the map is generated. Some games, however, have destructible or user-changeable terrain and, as a result, need to be able to update their regions as the map changes.

Dynamic region calculation is a difficult and thorny problem—think hard before deciding to include it in your game! With that said, it's not insoluble. For tile-based maps, a fast localized flood-fill-based solution can work—this is the approach that was taken by *Company of Heroes* [Jurney 07], which was probably the first game to solve this problem. If you're using a triangulation-based navmesh to provide your regions, it is possible to retriangulate the affected area reasonably quickly (e.g., Havok AI does this). Note that neither of these approaches is simple to implement or optimize, and no matter how much you optimize, neither is likely to run in a single frame. Thus, you're going to have to timeslice the calculations and also to figure out how the AI should handle the case where the regions have been invalidated but haven't yet finished recomputing. Regardless, dynamic recalculation of the regions is well beyond the scope of this article (but *Computational Geometry: Algorithms and Applications* might provide at least a starting point [de Berg 08]).

31.3 Working with Regions

So, now we have our regions… what do we do with them? Well, lots of things, but let's start with some examples that take advantage of the granularity and homogeneity of our regions—that is, of the fact that they're not too big, not too small, and made up entirely of a single type of space.

31.3.1 Picking Places to Scout or Explore

As discussed earlier, regions allow us to break the map into larger, less granular, spaces, which can greatly reduce the complexity of decision making. One area where this pays off is in selecting areas to explore or to scout for enemy forces. If we made this decision on a tile-by-tile basis, it would be entirely intractable—there are simply too many tiles to choose from. Instead, we can score the value of exploring a region using information such as the following:

- How much of it is already explored?
- How close is it to our current position?
- Does our current strategy prefer to explore close to the center of our territory (looking for resources) or far away (looking for enemy bases), and how does this region match that preference?

Scouting is similar to exploration, except that the decision is based on how recently that region has been scouted, its proximity to our territory, its proximity to known enemy territory or units, its strategic importance, and so forth.

Of course, once you've picked a region to explore or scout, you need a low-level AI that handles the actual motion over the tiles, perhaps spiraling outward until a new location is picked—but this is generally much more tractable than the high-level decision selecting a general area to explore.

31.3.2 Picking Places to Attack

Regions can also allow us to lump nearby structures or resources together and make decisions based on their aggregate value. For example, deciding where and when to attack is an important part of any strategy game. Lots of factors might go into this decision—the strength of our available units, the enemy strength in the area, the strategic value of the region, etc. Many of these factors are discussed elsewhere in this chapter, but the underlying basis for this evaluation is always going to be the economic and/or military value of the target being attacked.

What we want to avoid is launching multiple separate attacks against targets that are very close together, with each attack individually bringing enough units to defeat the enemy forces in the area. This results in sending far too many units to attack, thus depriving us of the opportunity to use those units in other ways. In order to do this, instead of attacking individual targets, we launch our attacks against *regions*. The value of attacking a region can be considered to be something like the sum of the values of all of the targets in that region, plus 25% of the value of targets in adjacent regions—or zero if there is an adjacent region that has a higher total value.

The result is that if we do launch multiple attacks, then those attacks will be spread out, hitting relatively distant targets. This forces the player to fight a battle on two fronts, which is generally a challenging (and enjoyable) experience.

31.3.3 Picking Unit Positions

In addition to their granularity, the homogeneity of the regions can help drive spatial decision making at the unit level. For example, imagine that our archer units have a bonus to their ranged attack value when they're above their enemies, that all units move slower when travelling uphill, and that spearman units have the ability to hide in tall grass and then spring out and ambush the enemy with a large bonus to their attack.

When picking a place to position a unit, we first need to identify the valid regions. Generally speaking, these are the regions that allow the unit to satisfy its high-level goal. For example, if the unit is participating in an attack, then the region must be close enough to attack the enemy, or if it's standing guard, then the region must be close enough to cover the target it's defending (and ideally located on a likely avenue of approach—more on that in Section 31.5.3). Next, we calculate a score for each of the valid regions based on a number of factors, including the proximity to the unit's current location, the cost of moving there, and the viability of moving there (e.g., it's not a good idea to move your archers through a mass of enemy swordsmen just to get to a good tactical position).

In addition to those factors, however, we can consider the value of the region itself. For example, archers might really like hilltop regions—not only do they get a bonus to their attack but they also have more time to fire at enemies coming up the hill to attack them. Spearmen might have a moderate preference for grassland regions, but only when guarding, since they won't have time to hide during an attack, and only when the region is on a likely avenue of approach, since they can only ambush enemies that go past them.

31.3.4 Path Planning

If our regions are created out of some smaller abstraction, such as tiles, then we can use the regions for hierarchical path planning, which will greatly speed up our path queries. To do this, we first find the shortest path through the regions (which is comparatively fast because the regions are moderately large so there are relatively few of them). Once we have the region path, we find the first region on the path whose region center is not visible from the current position of the unit we're planning a path for. On a tile-based map, we can do this with a series of tile walks, which are also quite fast (linear time on the length of the tile walk). A tile walk is similar to a raycast, except that instead of testing against the collision geometry, it simply determines which tiles are along the line. Finally, we calculate the low-level path (using the tiles) from the unit to that region center. This low-level path should also be very quick to find, because it's more or less straight (it typically has a single turn), which means that A* with a straight-line heuristic will find it in near-linear time (i.e., really, really fast—this is the best case scenario for A*).

One nice thing about this approach is that our regions (i.e., the nodes in our high-level abstraction) are homogeneous, which means that we can weight the high-level path based on the terrain type. For example, we can make a unit that prefers to travel through grassland, or to avoid hilltops, or both, by making regions of those terrain types more or less expensive to travel through. While hierarchical path-planning solutions have been around for some time, they don't typically use a homogenous abstraction, so they lose the ability to weight the path in this way—and thus the ability to choose their paths on the basis of anything other than shortest distance.

In the remainder of this chapter, we'll refer to the connectivity graph through the regions as the *region graph* and to a path through this graph as a *region path* or a *high-level path*.

31.3.5 Distance Estimates

One thing that we frequently want is an estimate of the distance between two distant objects. For example, if we are considering whether to attack an enemy settlement with a particular unit, then we will want to know the distance between that settlement and the unit. If we are considering exploring a particular region, then we will want to know the distance to that region not only from the exploring unit but also from each of our settlements. We could use the full path planner to find these distances, but doing so is likely to be prohibitively expensive, especially if we're going to be doing a lot of these checks (and we will almost certainly be doing a lot of these checks if we want to have good spatial reasoning). The obvious simplification is to use straight-line distance, but if your map is at all complex then straight-line distance often badly underestimates the actual distance.

The solution is to find the region path, which is fairly quick, and then calculate the distance from region center to region center along that path. The result isn't a perfect estimate—it will overestimate the distance to some extent. The good news, however, is that the extent to which it overestimates the distance is bounded by the size of the regions, so unless your regions are enormous, this estimate can be expected to be fairly good.

31.3.6 Region Path Caching

Given the frequency with which we'll be using distance estimates, even finding a region path may not be fast enough. In this case, if you can spare a few megabytes of memory, it's possible to cache the region paths as you discover them. In order to do this, you need to have your regions numbered from 0 … $n - 1$, where n is the number of regions in your game. You can then create an $n \times n$ lookup array. In this array, you store the first step to get from every region to every other region. So, for example, if the path from region 17 to region 23 is 17 → 12 → 23, then position [17][23] in the array would contain 12 (because the first step to get from 17 to 23 takes us to region 12). Similarly, position [12][23] would contain 23, position [23][17] would contain 12, and position [12][17] would contain 17.

If the region count is low enough, this "next step" lookup array could be precomputed fully at map generation time using an algorithm such as Floyd–Warshall [Floyd 62], which runs in $O(n^3)$ in the number of regions. If this cost is prohibitive, however, the contents of the array could also be computed in a just-in-time fashion. A single high-level path doesn't take long to calculate, so you can always run the path planner the first time you need a path between two particular regions and then store them in the path cache as you go. This works out well, because there are generally fewer units to work with (and thus, less work for the AI to do) early in the game, which gives us more time for path planning. In addition, even though the AI will ask for a lot of distance estimates all at once, many of them will start and end in the same general area. If the path planner uses the path cache to look up shortest partial paths, then groups of queries from similar locations will be very fast because most of the paths are just slight modifications of previous searches.

Clearly, one concern is that this array can get quite big if you have a lot of regions. If you have 2000 regions, and you store the region indices in 2-byte integers (since 1 byte isn't big enough), then the size of the array is $2000 \cdot 2000 \cdot 2 = \sim 8$ MB. That's not a completely unreasonable amount of memory on a modern system—although it's not viable on something like the Nintendo 3DS or a cell phone—but it's enough to catch the attention of the rendering team (who will no doubt want the space for more polygons). It's possible to optimize this a bit by compressing the region indices into less than 16 bits (e.g., we can handle 2000 regions with 11 bit indices), but this makes the code quite a bit more complicated for only an incremental savings.

Another trick is to only store the shortest path from the lower-numbered region to the higher-numbered region. Since the shortest path from region 17 to region 23 is the same as the shortest path from region 23 to region 17 (assuming that we don't have any unidirectional connections, like jump downs or one-way teleports), we can just store the first step from the lower-numbered region to the higher-numbered region. Working out the sequence of queries to rebuild the path is a bit tricky, but doable. The essence of it is that you work from both ends toward the middle, filling in pieces until you have the full path. So, in our example earlier, if we wanted to find the path from 23 to 17, first, we'd look up the first step from 17 to 23 (because we don't store the first step from 23 to 17) and find that it is 12. This tells us that we need to go from 23 → [unknown] → 12 → 17. Next, because 12 is less than 23, we look up the path from 12 to 23 and find that we can go directly there. Thus, our final path, as expected, is 23 → 12 → 17. If implemented properly, there should always be a single [unknown] location as we fill in the path—the trick is to look up the next step from the lower-indexed to the higher-indexed region adjacent to that location.

31.3.7 Recognizing Cul-de-Sacs and Chokepoints

Cul-de-sacs are areas that have only a single point of access (like dead-end streets). *Chokepoints* are narrow places in the terrain that connect two or more larger areas. Previous work has discussed a variety of ways to detect and make use of these features, but these approaches are often complex and computationally expensive [Forbus 02, Obelleiro 08] or require that the region graph be extremely sparse [Dill 04]. Unfortunately, most games have maps that are fairly open and easily traversable, which means that the region map is typically not sparse at all.

If your map has been divided into regions, then cul-de-sacs are dead simple to recognize. A cul-de-sac is simply a region that is passable (i.e., units can move through it), which has only one adjacent passable region. Looking back at the map in Figure 31.1c, there are three cul-de-sacs (though on a less constrained map, they would not be nearly so common): the southeast, southwest, and northwest land regions.

Detecting chokepoints is a bit more complicated. One approach is to look for a region R that separates the adjacent regions into two (or more) groups, which we will call *areas*, that are only connected through R. For example, in Figure 31.2a, region 2 is a chokepoint because you can only get from region 1 to region 3 by passing through it. In Figure 31.2b, it is not (at least, not according to this definition), because there is an alternate route around to the west. We can detect regions like this by doing a breadth-first search from each region adjacent to R and excluding R itself from the search. If the search from any adjacent region fails to find any other adjacent regions, then those two adjacent regions must be in different areas and R is a chokepoint.

There are two major problems with this solution. First, it is expensive to compute (unbounded breadth-first search from every region adjacent to every other region… yick!). Second, it is too strict. For example, in Figure 31.2b, region 2 is not considered a chokepoint, but in reality this region and the region directly to its west between them do a nice job of dividing the map into two areas. More generally, a region can be useful as a chokepoint even if there's an alternate route between the adjacent areas, as long as the alternate route is convenient or costly to take.

Fortunately, the solution to both of these problems is the same. We can simply limit the depth of our breadth-first search. This keeps the cost of the search down and also reflects

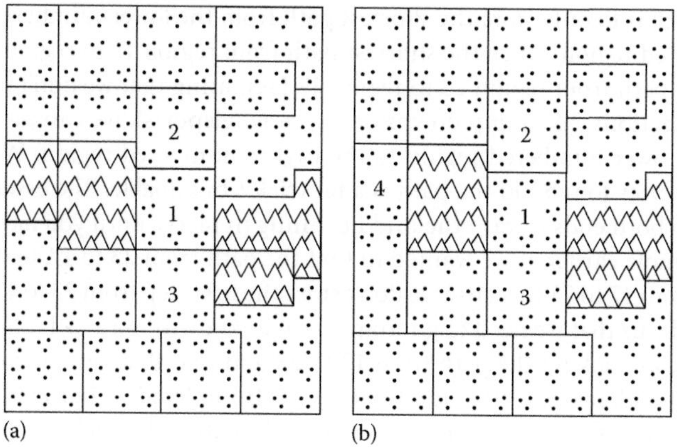

Figure 31.2

(a) Region 1 is a chokepoint because you can't get from region 2 to region 3 without going through it. (b) There are no chokepoints because there is an alternate route around the mountains to the west (through region 4).

the fact that a region can be a chokepoint merely by creating a local division between two areas—it doesn't have to create a global division between them. Finding the right depth for the search is another of those fuzzy, game-specific problems, but in general, a value somewhere between 5 and 10 is probably good for the sorts of maps we've been discussing.

Of note, both cul-de-sacs and chokepoints are generally only interesting if they are reasonably narrow. This is one of the reasons why we want to ensure that our regions aren't too large. As long as the regions have an appropriate maximum width, that width can serve as our definition of "reasonably narrow."

Once you have identified the chokepoints, there are all sorts of ways that you can put them to use. They are often excellent ambush points, for example. One trick is to keep track of how much enemy traffic goes through each chokepoint (or is likely to go through each chokepoint—more on this in Section 31.5.2) and place ambushes on the high-traffic spots. Furthermore, if you can identify a set of chokepoints that separate your territory from the territory of an enemy (i.e., they're along likely avenues of approach—again, more on this is discussed in Section 31.5.3), then they become excellent places to put defensive units and/or fixed defenses (such as forts or walls). This allows you to mass your defenses in fewer locations, giving you a better chance of defeating an incoming attack. At the very least, placing a few forces to stand guard there can warn you that an attack is on the way (in the Army, we called this an LP/OP, or listening post/observation post). Finally, if the chokepoints constrain movement then you might be able to mass your forces at the exit of a chokepoint and defeat the enemy as they come out of it. This tactical advantage may enable a small force to defeat a much stronger enemy—the Battle of Thermopylae, in which 300 Spartans famously held off a massive Persian army (for a time, at least), is perhaps the best known example of this.

On some maps, chokepoints can also be used to plan an attack. If the map is fairly constrained, you may be able to find the chokepoints closest to your target and stage your attacking forces into a multipronged attack, simultaneously striking from two or more different chokepoints. Alternately, you can launch a diversionary attack at one chokepoint and then send a much larger force against the other. As in real life, these sorts of maneuvers can be difficult to time and can go horribly wrong if they're detected in time—but when you're an AI opponent, allowing the player to defeat an overly clever maneuver might be the whole point!

Cul-de-sacs are generally less interesting than chokepoints precisely because they are out-of-the-way spaces that are not normally visited very often. On the other hand, they can be good places to hide economic buildings or other things that we don't want the player to see. We also might be able to optimize some aspects of our AI by excluding the cul-de-sacs from consideration.

One last note on chokepoints and cul-de-sacs: if a chokepoint only has two adjacent passable regions, and one of those regions is a cul-de-sac, then the chokepoint can also be considered part of the cul-de-sac. In other words, if the only place a chokepoint leads to is a dead end, then the chokepoint is really part of the dead end as well. Recognizing this can help to avoid placing units in a region that you think is a chokepoint when in fact nothing interesting is likely to happen there.

31.4 Influence Maps

Influence maps (as they are used in video games) have been around at least since the 1990s [Tozour 01]. They are typically used in the context of tile-based maps [Hansson 10] or on tile-like abstractions such as those proposed by Alex Champandard [Champandard 11]. With a few minor adaptations, however, they can be applied to regions with outstanding results.

31.4.1 Influence Map Basics

The key idea behind an influence map is that each unit has an *influence*, which is *propagated* out from the unit's position. The propagated influence of a unit decreases with distance in accordance with some formula, the simplest of which is simply to decrease the influence by some fixed amount for every tile that you traverse. The overall influence in each tile is the sum of the propagated influences of all of the units on the map.

As an example, consider Figure 31.3. In Figure 31.3a, we see a single lefty unit (whose icon and influence appear on the left side of the tile) with an influence of 5. This influence could represent any property that we wish to track over space, but for the purposes of our example let's assume that it is the combat strength of the unit. Influence propagates outward from the unit, so that adjacent tiles have an influence of 4, and the next tiles beyond those have an influence of 3, and so forth. Thus, on any tile, we can see the influence of this unit—which is to say, how relevant the unit is to combat decisions made with respect to that tile. In the tile where the unit is located, it exerts its full combat strength, but in more distant tiles, which it would have to travel for some time to reach, its influence is decreased.

In Figure 31.3b, we see how the influence of multiple units can be combined to give the overall influence of a player. Thus, instead of a single unit, we have three lefties, each with an influence of 5. The influence in any tile is simply the sum of the influences of the three units and represents the amount of combat strength we can expect that player to be able to bring to bear on a fight that occurs in that tile. There's no particular magic to calculating this—you can simply set all the influence values on the map to 0 and then go

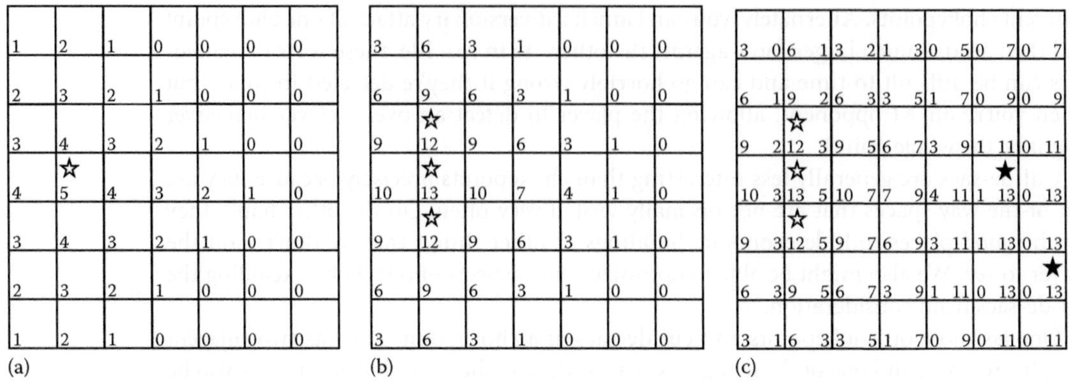

Figure 31.3

An example of an influence map with a single unit (a), three units belonging to the same player (b), and units belonging to two different players (c).

through each unit and add its influence to the map. Addition is commutative, so it doesn't matter what order you add the units in—the end result will be the same. Also of note, in this example we show each unit in its own tile, but the technique works exactly the same if you have multiple units in a tile—simply propagate their influence one at a time and the math will work.

Figure 31.3c is where things start to get interesting. Two righty units have come into the area. These units are a bit more powerful—perhaps they are cavalry units, rather than infantry—and so they each have an influence of 8. Righty influence propagates in the same way as lefty influence, and now we can see how much influence each side has and recognize areas that are contested (i.e., the areas where both sides have high influence, such as the tiles to the immediate right of the three lefty units), areas that are largely unoccupied (i.e., the areas where neither side has much influence, such as the upper and lower left-hand corners), and areas that are cleanly under the control of one side or the other (i.e., the areas where one side has high influence and the other low, such as the entire right side of the map).

Some authors suggest that when calculating the relative influence between two sides, you simply subtract enemy influence from friendly influence and look at the result—so, for example, the lefty influence in the tile with the middle lefty unit would be 8 (because 13 – 5 = 8), and the righty influence would be –8. This approach loses critical information, however. There is a big difference between a hotly contested tile and one that is far from the action, for example, and yet if you use subtraction to combine the scores, then in both cases you'll end up with an influence of 0.

Another point to consider is that if we keep the influences separately, we can recombine them in any way that we want as alliances change or as we consider different aspects of the situation. For instance, when considering my own attack power in a tile I might include 25% of the influence of my allies, since there is a reasonable chance (but not a certainty) that they will jump into the fight to support me, especially if it's a close thing. This single trick was the only thing that we did to encourage teamwork between AI players that were allies in *Kohan II*, and it resulted in really nice coordinated attacks and/or one-two punches (where one enemy would hit you, and then just as you defeated them another enemy would swoop in to finish you off).

31.4.2 Propagation Calculations

One detail that was glossed over in the aforementioned example is the rate at which influence decays while it propagates. In the example, we simply reduced the influence by 1 for each tile it propagated through—so, for example, the righty units (which were more powerful) exerted their influence over a larger area. This approach uses the formula in the following equation:

$$I_D = I_0 - (\text{distance} \cdot k) \tag{31.1}$$

where
I_D is the influence at some distance
I_0 is the initial influence that the unit will exert in the tile where it's located
Distance is the distance between those two tiles
k is a tuning constant (which can be adjust to make the AI behave appropriately)

It's worth noting that for tile-based influence, we sometimes use Manhattan distance rather than straight-line distance (i.e., we calculate the distance as the sum of the change in x and the change in y, rather than using the Pythagorean theorem to calculate it). This makes sense if our units only move along the axes, but it can also just be easier to compute. This is the approach that was used in Figure 31.3.

We should also note that influences that are less than 0 should be discarded, but for the sake of brevity we have removed the *max*() statement from this and all of the following formulae.

Although the simple distance-based approach given earlier is appropriate for some applications (such as border calculations, which we discuss in Section 31.4.5), we can do better when reasoning about combat strength. Conceptually, the influence in each tile represents the ability of a player's units to get to a fight in a given tile fast enough to have an impact on the outcome of that fight. The farther away the units are, the less impact they'll have, because a significant amount of fighting will already have occurred by the time that they arrive. Thus, the real limiting factor in how far the influence propagates is not simply distance but rather the travel time to arrive at a distant tile. We can model this with a formula like the one in the following equation:

$$I_D = I_0 \cdot \frac{max\_time - travel\_time}{max\_time} \tag{31.2}$$

where
max_time is the maximum travel time at which a unit is considered to exert influence (e.g., 60 seconds)
travel_time is the actual amount of time it will take to travel to the distant tile

The aforementioned formulae are *linear* and *continuous*, which is to say that if you graph them then you will get a single straight line. There are times when we want nonlinear formulae (the line isn't straight), noncontinuous formulae (there is more than one line), or both. For example, an artillery unit that can fire over several tiles might use a discontinuous formula. For tiles within its range of fire, it will exert full influence. Beyond that distance, its influence will depend on the time to pack and unpack the artillery piece, but the travel time will just be the time to get in range. In order to accomplish this, we will need two formulae. Tiles within firing range simply use $I_D = I_0$, while more distant tiles use a formula such as the one given in the following equation:

$$I_D = I_0 \cdot \frac{max\_time - (time\_to\_pack + time\_to\_get\_in\_range + time\_to\_unpack)}{max\_time} \quad (31.3)$$

Thus, the influence is constant and high out to some distance and then it drops to a significantly smaller value (because beyond that distance, the unit needs to pack and unpack as well as travelling before it can enter the fight).

Similarly, a commander unit might have a nonlinear influence that looks like an inverted parabola—that is, the commander remains strong in the vicinity of its troops (where it is highly effective) but then drops off more and more sharply with distance. We could model this with a formula such is the one in the following equation:

$$I_D = I_0 - (\text{distance})^k \quad (31.4)$$

Finally, the designers may want to be able to determine the influence themselves. If they are mathematically inclined, they may be able to help design these sorts of formulae—but if not, allowing them to give you a simple lookup table with the desired influence at any distance may be a good approach. Tables that are created in a spreadsheet and saved as .csv files can be easy for them to create and are also easy to parse in the code.

Ultimately, much of the intelligence in your influence maps comes from the way you choose to propagate the influence. For more detail on constructing AI logic out of mathematical formulae, much of which is directly applicable here, we highly recommend *Behavioral Mathematics for Game AI* [Mark 09].

31.4.3 Force Estimates over Regions

So far, we've talked about mapping influence over tiles, but it's straightforward to map the influence over regions instead. To do this, we first need to ensure that our propagation formula is based on distance (or travel time). All of the aforementioned formulae meet this requirement. Then, when propagating influence, we work our way through the region graph, just as we did through the tiles. In each region, we calculate the distance to the original region along the region graph (which we can track as we go—we don't have to recompute it each time) and use that value to calculate the local influence for that unit.

The only tricky bit in all of this is that we need to ensure that, as we walk the graph, we find the shortest path to each region. In order to do this, as we're walking the graph, when we're deciding which node to expand next, we always expand the node that has

Listing 31.1. The influence propagation algorithm. The regions variable is an array of region pointers, unit is a pointer to the unit whose influence we're propagating, and startRegion is a pointer to the region where unit is located.

```
for (int i = 0; i < numRegions; ++i)
{
    regions[i]->traversed = false;
}

heap<float, int> openList;
openList.push_back(0, startRegion->id);

while (!openList.empty())
{
    pair<float, int> nextRegionEntry = openList.pop();
    int nextRegionID = nextRegionEntry.second;
    Region* nextRegion = regions[nextRegionID];
    nextRegion->traversed = true;

    float distSoFar = nextRegionEntry.first;
    float influence = CalcInfluence(unit, distSoFar);
    if (influence <= 0)
        continue;

    nextRegion->influence += influence;

    Region* child = nextRegion->GetFirstChild();
    for (; child; child = child->GetNextSibling())
    {
        if (!child->IsPassable(unit) || child->traversed)
            continue;

        float dist = distSoFar + GetDist(nextRegion, child);
        openList.push_back(dist, child->id);
    }
}
```

the shortest total path from the starting region. Listing 31.1 shows pseudocode for this algorithm, and Figure 31.4 shows a new map with the influence for the lefty (white) and righty (black) players.

When calculating influence over regions, rather than over tiles, you lose some of the fine-grained precision. On the other hand, the resulting values are much easier to work with. If I have a settlement, three defensive units, and a fort all in close proximity, it's much easier to reason about how they interact if they're all in one region, or at least are in adjacent regions.

Another advantage of this approach is that even though we lose some precision, the resulting values can actually be more accurate. For example, note that the region with the three lefty units has their full influence—that is, the lefty influence in that region is 15. Compare this to Figure 31.3b, where the highest lefty influence was only 13. An influence of 15 is more accurate, since those units are close enough that they are able to—and are very likely to—support one another. Of course, there are border cases as well—for example, the two righty units in adjacent regions still end up with a maximum influence

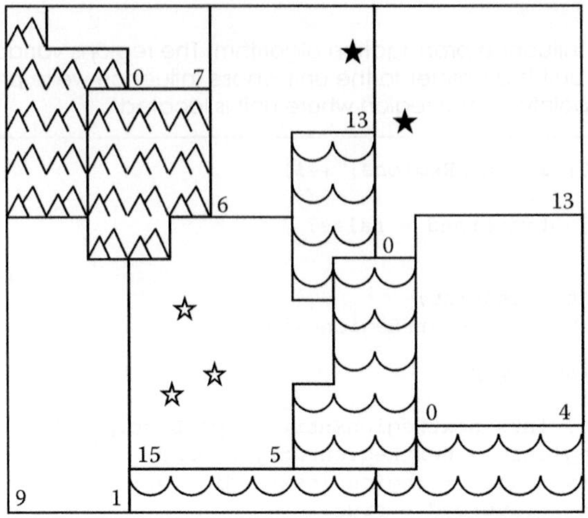

Figure 31.4

Influence propagation over the regions.

of 13, rather than 16. If these cases bother you, it's easy enough to check for them and adjust the influence values accordingly.

31.4.4 Illusion of Intelligence

One possible criticism of influence maps is that they are "cheating," in that they give the AI information that it could not otherwise have. In other words, even though the AI may not know the exact locations of the player's units, it knows generally where they are because it knows about their influence.

One solution is simply not to count influence for units that the AI can't see (or that it hasn't seen recently), but this approach has its own pitfalls. For example, this approach might make it easy to dupe the AI into attacking or defending in places where it shouldn't, which can then be exploited by the player. This will make the AI look stupid and will make the game less fun.

You could argue that the AI should scout better, but building a good scouting algorithm is a hard problem in its own right! Humans intuit how much force they should expect to face based on partial information—if they see two or three enemy units, they can make a guess as to how many they might not have seen and also as to what types of units the enemy is likely to have. Influence maps can provide a nice balance between a truly noncheating AI and an AI that doesn't blatantly cheat but does have a way to compensate for a human's innate intuition and stronger spatial reasoning skills. We don't allow the AI full knowledge, but we allow it enough knowledge to make the sorts of judgments that a human makes naturally.

More to the point, however, it's worth asking ourselves what our true goal is. Is it to build an AI that doesn't cheat or is it to provide a compelling experience for the player? One of the great advantages of basing your attack and defense decisions on influence maps is that it helps to *ensure* that the player's experience will be compelling. It is no fun to battle an enemy who doesn't fight back. It's a huge disappointment to build up your resources, amass an enormous army, and march on the enemy's stronghold—and discover that there are no defenders there, allowing you to win easily. It doesn't matter whether this occurs because the AI is truly stupid or because it made a poor choice and sent its units to the wrong place—it *looks* stupid and will rapidly erode the player's interest in your game.

Because the influence system gives the AI some warning that an attack is approaching—the enemy influence rises—we can avoid this hazard. When the enemy launches their massive attack, the AI will know that it's coming and will be able to ensure that there's something there to meet it. How the AI manages this is of course up to us (the solution used in *Kohan II* can be found in *AI Game Programming Wisdom 3* [Dill 06]), but now we have the information that we need to make a response possible.

Influence maps help to make our attacks appear more intelligent as well. Because the AI will tend to attack where the enemy is weakest, we get an enemy that is "smart" about where it strikes. This forces the player to maintain a broad defense, which adds to the challenge and sense of excitement. Furthermore, if we don't commit all of our forces to an attack immediately, but do require the ones who have actually engaged the enemy to remain where they are, then we get emergent skirmishes and diversionary attacks. The AI will initially attack with just a part of its total force. If the player rushes units from elsewhere to defend against the attack then the next attack may either be held back (because the player now has overwhelming force) or may go in at the new weak spot (which was exposed when the defensive units were pulled away). This result was actually a bit of a surprise for us on the *Kohan II* team—we didn't anticipate it—but it is borne out by the many reviews that said things like "the CPU uses smart battlefield tactics like trying to get the flank and attacking your weak spots" [Abner 04] or that it is "capable of drawing the player away or diverting his attention from a secondary attack." [Butts 04] The AI didn't explicitly reason about these things, they happened emergently as a result of our use of influence maps.

The best of all is that this cheating is hard for players to detect, because it's not blatant, it's not explicit, and it's not perfect knowledge. The AI sometimes does the perfect thing—but sometimes it doesn't. In Kohan II, we allowed players to go back and watch any game from beginning to end, from any viewpoint (i.e., they could turn fog of war off or even watch from the perspective of another player). We never heard complaints of the AI cheating, and indeed, some reviewers described the game as having a "noncheating AI." [Ocampo 04]

It might seem that this will make the AI too hard to beat but honestly, that's a good problem to have. There are a host of ways to tone down a difficult AI, but very few simple ways to increase the challenge when the AI isn't smart enough. What's more, players seem to genuinely enjoy the challenge of beating an AI that maneuvers well. Very nearly without exception, the reviews of *Kohan II* not only mentioned the AI but cited its ability to maneuver intelligently as one of the major strengths of the game.

31.4.5 Border Calculations

So far, we've talked about influence as a way to reason about combat power, but the same techniques can have much broader application. Space being limited, we will give one other example.

It is often beneficial to have a clear sense of what space is inside your borders, what space is clearly under somebody else's control, and what space is contested. This information can have broad-reaching implications. It can affect where you attack, where you position defensive forces, where you choose to expand, how many supporting forces you send to escort noncombat units such as builders or trade caravans, and so forth. On tightly constrained maps it's possible to extract this information directly from the region map [Dill 04], but as we discussed earlier, most strategy games have broader, more loosely constrained maps that don't yield well to this approach.

When a graph-based approach to border calculation is not practical, a less precise but more generalizable approach is to use influence. To do this, simply apply a certain amount of *border influence* to each major structure (e.g., buildings, bases, cities, settlements—whatever is important in your game). When propagating this influence, we want it to spread farther if the initial influence is higher. Thus, we can propagate it using the simple formula given in Equation 31.1.

Figure 31.5 shows an example in which the lefty and righty players each have one settlement. The lefty settlement is fairly small, and so it only has an influence of 15. The righty settlement is a bit larger and has an influence of 25. By examining the influence in each region, we can determine regions that are clearly controlled by the lefties (D and E), regions that are clearly controlled by the righties (C and F), and regions that are contested (A and B). From this, the lefties might identify region B as a good place to position defensive forces (it is contested, is reasonably close to their settlement, and is a chokepoint). Region A is less attractive for defensive forces, since it is a cul-de-sac with nothing in it, but it might be a good position for an ambush force. If the righties were to attack our settlement, forces hidden there could attack from behind and envelop them, blocking their line of retreat. Similarly, the lefties might identify regions D and E as good places to build economic structures, like mines or new settlements, which will need to be defended. Finally, they might pick region C as a good place to build an offensive fort, which will support an attack against the enemy, because it is the one where the lefties have the highest influence.

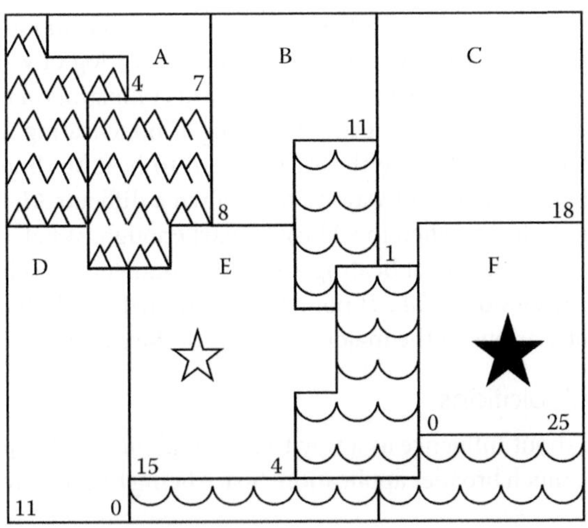

Figure 31.5

An example of how border influence could propagate over regions.

31.5 Spatial Characteristics

Much of the art of making your AI intelligent, whether in terms of spatial reasoning or in any other domain, comes from finding the right way to recognize and capture some distinction that you can then reason about. In this final section we will briefly discuss a number of easy-to-track distinctions that we can use to reason about space.

31.5.1 Scent of Death

One common trick, used in many games, is to keep track of how many things have died in each tile or in each region. We can use this in numerous ways, but two obvious ones are to prefer paths that avoid those regions and to only go into those regions in greater strength. So, for example, if we're considering building a gold mine in a region where we've previously lost a number of units, we might want to send extra defenders along to protect our builder unit (and our new gold mine).

A similar approach can be used to dynamically adjust the strength of enemy units who unexpectedly win battles. If, for example, we lose a battle that we expected to win, then we might increase the influence of the units that defeated us (or even increase the influence of all enemy units) in order to recognize the fact that this player is more wily and tactically competent than we expected. This will help to avoid sending losing attacks against the same target over and over without at least ensuring that each attack is stronger than the last.

31.5.2 High-Traffic Areas

It's often useful to know where other players are *likely* to travel. You can use this information to sneak around them, to ambush them, to place toll posts along their path, and so forth.

One way to gather this information is to simply keep track of the number of units of any given type (military units, caravans, etc.) that have moved through each region. This is guaranteed to be accurate (assuming that you cheat and log units that the AI didn't actually see) but only gives information about what has already happened—it doesn't necessarily predict the future.

Another approach is to plan region paths between all major sites, such as settlements, and keep track of the number of these paths that go through each region. This approach doesn't account for things like the likelihood of travelling between any two sites and can be exploited by players who deliberately choose obscure paths, but it can do a better job of predicting traffic that has not yet occurred.

31.5.3 Avenues of Approach

It is often important to be able to consider not only where the enemy is likely to attack but also *how they are likely to get there*—that is, the likely *avenues of approach*. For example, in real life, when a light infantry platoon is placed in a defensive perimeter, the commander will ensure that somebody is covering every direction, but they will place the heaviest weapons (e.g., the machine guns or grenade launchers) to cover the likely avenues of approach, while placing the lighter weapons (e.g., rifles) to cover the flanks and rear. This isn't foolproof, but it does make it more likely that the enemy will face your heaviest fire when they attack—or else that they'll be forced to work around your sides and attack through more difficult terrain. Likely avenues of approach are also good places to position

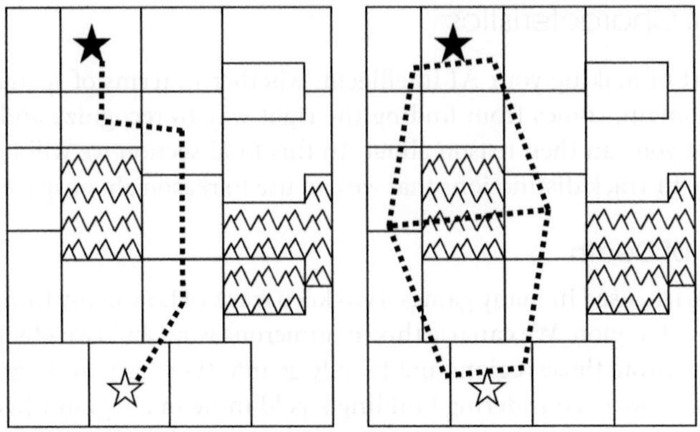

Figure 31.6

The avenues of approach between enemy settlements calculated using the region path (a) or two trapezoids (b).

LP/OPs, screening forces (i.e., defensive forces that will engage the enemy *before* they get to their target), and/or ambush forces (which can be used either to surprise enemies on their way in or to entrap them once they've engaged).

Of course, figuring out where the avenues of approach are is as much art as science, even in the real world. While computers aren't likely to do this as well as humans, there are some simple heuristics that you can use. The most obvious, shown in Figure 31.6a, is simply to calculate the shortest region path to nearby enemy sites or known enemy positions. The problem with this approach is that it doesn't catch alternate routes that might be used if enemy units don't start exactly where expected or deliberately take a longer path, such as the path to the west side of the mountains.

One alternative is to search some number of regions out from the shortest path. For example, if we search two regions out from the path in Figure 31.6a, then we would find the western pass through the mountains—but we would also identify a lot of inappropriate regions as avenues of approach (e.g., the cul-de-sac in the southeast corner of the map). We can add further complexity in order to try to identify and eliminate these regions, but that sort of special-case logic is prone to be brittle and difficult to maintain.

Another alternative, shown in Figure 31.6b, is to superimpose two adjacent trapezoids onto the map such that they stretch between the region you're defending and the nearby enemy position. These trapezoids should be narrower at the origin and destination and wider where they connect. Any region underneath these trapezoids can be considered an avenue of approach. This solution works well in this particular example, but one can easily imagine maps on which the only path goes well to the side of a straight line or even wraps around behind your defensive position, and so the actual avenue of approach is quite different from what the trapezoids suggest.

The best solution might be to combine the two techniques, for example, by only using the trapezoids if they cover every region on the shortest path or by warping the trapezoids to expand to the side of the shortest path, but this is certainly an area in which more work is merited.

It's also worth noting that while these examples have, for simplicity, only shown a single enemy location from which avenues of approach can originate, in reality, there are often multiple sources for enemy forces. In that case you may need to consider the approaches from all of them.

31.5.4 Flanking Attacks

In the infantry one learns numerous techniques for attacking an enemy position. Without question, when it is possible to achieve, the preferred approach is to first have one element of your force fix the enemy in place with suppressive fire (i.e., fire at the enemy position, keeping their heads down and preventing them from moving), while another element maneuvers around to their flank and then cuts across from the side to finish them off.

This tactic is rarely seen in video games and indeed runs a significant risk of making the enemy "too good" (especially since they typically outnumber the player as well). With that said, it certainly could add a significant element of both realism and stress to the game. It is actually not difficult to achieve. Divide the AI force into two groups. One group lays down suppressive fire, pinning the player in place. The other group calculates an area similar to the double trapezoid in Figure 31.6b. They then plan a path to the enemy that excludes the area inside of the trapezoids, which will bring them around the side of the enemy and across their flank. This approach was used by the human AI in *The Last of Us* and is described in more detail in Chapter 34, which discusses that game's AI.

31.5.5 Attackable Obstacles

Many fantasy strategy games have maps that are littered with lairs, lost temples, magic portals, mana springs, and other areas that your units can attack and exploit. At the same time, these games usually also feature enemy players who you need to overcome.

When assigning units to attack a distant target such as an enemy settlement, we don't want our units to get bogged down fighting smaller targets. At the same time, if a unit is going to have to path well out of the way of a spider lair, for example, then it might not be the most appropriate unit to use on that attack—or at the very least, we should probably deal with the spider lair first, so that our line of retreat will be clear.

In *Kohan II*, we solved this problem by not allowing a unit to be assigned to an attack if the region path between it and the target was not clear of enemies. This led to a new problem, however, which was that the player could prevent the AI from attacking a settlement simply by placing smaller, low-value forts in front of it.

We solved this second problem by adding a portion of the priority for attacking the distant target onto the intervening target any time that we found an intervening target that blocked one of our units from joining in an attack. As an example of this solution, consider Figure 31.7. The lefties have a priority of 100 to attack the righty settlement located in region F with their infantry units in region E, but there is a lost temple located in region C that will block their advance. As a result, we don't allow the AI to use those units in an attack on the settlement, but we do transfer 25% of the priority to attack the settlement to a goal to attack the lost temple. There was already a priority of 10 to attack the lost temple, so that priority is now increased to 35.

The end result is that if there is a good place to attack a high-priority target, such as an enemy settlement, then the AI will find it and perform the attack. If the high-priority

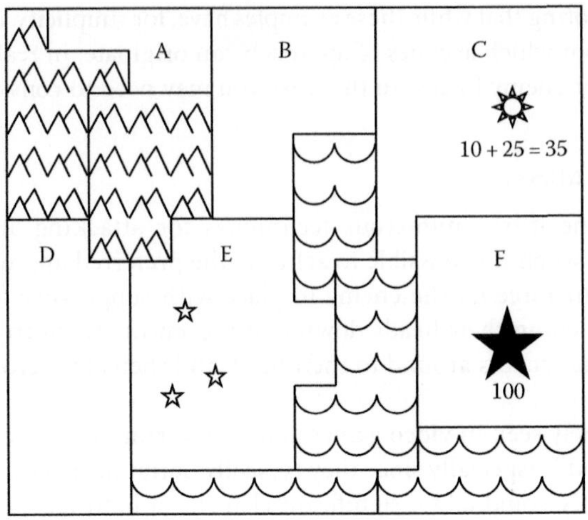

Figure 31.7

The lefties want to attack the enemy settlement in region F, but can't because of the lost temple in region C.

targets are all screened, then the AI will transfer the attack priority for hitting those targets to the screening obstacles and they will be attacked instead.

31.5.6 Counterattacks and Consolidation

In the infantry, one is trained that whenever you take an enemy position, the first thing you do is get into defensive positions and prepare for a counterattack. Only after some time has passed without counterattack do you move on to other tasks.

In strategy games, this same concept can serve us well. We can expect players to counterattack when we take territory away from them, if only because they may have defensive units that are late to arrive, and we can also enhance the player's experience by counterattacking when they take territory away from us. In the words of one reviewer, "[In] most RTS single player games… your armies run into predetermined clumps of foes and they duke it out. Once subdued, you can rest assured that the region is secured and pacified. Not in Kohan II. Fight over a town and take it; you'll find yourself beating a hasty retreat as a counter attack will soon follow unless you can consolidate your advance and secure your line of supply" [WorthPlaying 04].

Accomplishing this is relatively simple. Any time the enemy captures one of our settlements, we increase the priority for attacking the region that the settlement was in for the next several minutes. If we have enough remaining units to launch an attack (which we determine using the enemy influence in the region), then a counterattack will result. If we don't have the strength for a counterattack, as is often the case, then we'll preserve our forces for other goals—but if the enemy influence should drop too quickly (i.e., if the player pulls his units out of the region right after capturing it) then the counterattack goal will still be there for consideration.

We can brace against player counterattacks and follow-up attacks in a similar way. Any time that we win a fight against the enemy (whether offensive or defensive), we boost the priority for defending in the corresponding region. The influence map will tell us how much strength we need to bring to that defense, but boosting the priority lets the AI know that defending that specific area is particularly important because of the increased likelihood of further attack.

31.6 Conclusion and Future Thoughts

Spatial reasoning is a vast topic and this chapter has done little more than scratch the surface. We have concentrated most heavily on strategy game AI and particularly on techniques drawn from the RTS *Kohan II*, although ideas for other types of games are sprinkled throughout. For example, small unit tactics (such as those found in most first-person shooters) rely heavily on concepts such as cover and concealment, fire and maneuver, aggressive action, suppressive fire, lanes of fire, high ground, restricted terrain, kill zones, and so forth—and we have at best handwaved at those. Although true military tactics may be overkill for most games, they are a good place to begin—and they are full of spatial reasoning problems. The U.S. Army's FM 3-21.8, *The Infantry Rifle Platoon and Squad* [US Army 07], is publically available and is an excellent starting point for learning about how real-world forces operate.

Of course, many games are neither strategy games nor first-person shooters. Spatial reasoning solutions are as varied as the (often game-specific) problems that require them and the types of player experience that the game designers want to create. As with any aspect of game AI, it is best to start by thinking over the problem space. What would a human do? How would the human decide, and how can those decisions be simulated in code? What would those decisions look like to the enemy? What portion of that would make the game more compelling for our players and what would make it less? What would be fun?

In this chapter, we discussed some of the tools that can be used to help answer those questions, including techniques for creating a spatial partition, characteristics of a good spatial partition, a number of example uses of that spatial partition, influence maps and example uses of those, and a smattering of additional spatial characteristics that can be used to drive AI decisions. Although some of these concepts are directly applicable to broad classes of games, most require modification and customization to be truly useful. Our hope here is not to have provided a complete solution that can be dropped into any new game, but rather to have given a few ideas, starting points, hints, and most of all to have inspired you, the reader, to take space into account in more meaningful and compelling ways in your next game.

References

[Abner 04] Abner, W. 2004. Reviews: Kohan II: Kings of War. GameSpy.com. http://pc.gamespy.com/pc/kohan-ii-kings-of-war/549000p2.html (accessed May 18, 2014).

[Butts 04] Butts, S. 2004. Kohan II: Kings of War. IGN.com. http://www.ign.com/articles/2004/09/21/kohan-ii-kings-of-war?page=2 (accessed May 18, 2014).

[Champandard 11] Champandard, A.J. 2011. The mechanics of influence mapping: Representation, algorithm and parameters. http://aigamedev.com/open/tutorial/influence-map-mechanics/ (accessed May 18, 2014).

[de Berg 08] de Berg, M., O. Cheong, M. van Kreveld, and M. Overmars. 2008. *Computational Geometry: Algorithms and Applications*, 3rd edn. New York: Springer-Verlag.

[Dill 04] Dill, K. 2004. Performing qualitative terrain analysis in master of orion 3. In *AI Game Programming Wisdom 2*, ed. S. Rabin, pp. 391–398. Hingham, MA: Charles River Media.

[Dill 06] Dill, K. 2006. Prioritizing actions in a goal-based RTS AI. In *AI Game Programming Wisdom 3*, ed. S. Rabin, pp. 321–330. Boston, MA: Charles River Media.

[Floyd 62] Floyd, R.W. 1962. Algorithm 97. *Communications of the ACM* 5–6, 345.

[Forbus 02] Forbus, K.D., J.V. Mahoney, and K. Dill. 2002. How quality spatial reasoning can improve strategy game AIs. *IEEE Intelligent Systems* 17(4), 25–30. http://citeseerx.ist.psu.edu/viewdoc/download?doi=10.1.1.27.1100&rep=rep1&type=pdf (accessed May 18, 2014).

[Hansson 10] Hansson, N. 2010. Influence maps I. http://gameschoolgems.blogspot.com/2009/12/influence-maps-i.html (accessed May 18, 2014).

[Jurney 07] Jurney, C. and S. Hubick. 2007. Dealing with Destruction: AI from the trenches of COMPANY OF HEROES. In *Game Developer's Conference,* San Francisco, CA. http://www.gdcvault.com/play/765/Dealing-with-Destruction-AI-From (accessed May 18, 2014).

[Kohan II] Kohan II: Kings of war. [PC]. TimeGate Studios, 2004.

[Koster 04] Koster, R. 2004. *A Theory of Fun for Game Design*. Phoenix, AZ: Paraglyph Press.

[Mark 09] Mark, D. 2009. *Behavioral Mathematics for Game AI*. Boston, MA: Cengage Learning.

[Obelleiro 08] Obelleiro, J., R. Sampedro, and D. H. Cerpa. 2008. RTS terrain analysis: An image-processing approach. In *AI Game Programming Wisdom 4*, ed. S. Rabin, pp. 361–372. Boston, MA: Course Technology.

[Ocampo 04] Ocampo, J. 2004. Kohan II: Kings of war updated hands-on impressions. GameSpot.com. http://www.gamespot.com/articles/kohan-ii-kings-of-war-updated-hands-on-impressions/1100-6104697/ (accessed May 18, 2014).

[Tozour 01] Tozour, P. 2001. Influence mapping. In *Game Programming Gems 2*, ed. M. DeLoura. Hingham, MA: Charles River Media.

[Tozour 02] Tozour, P. 2002. Building a near-optimal navigation mesh. In *AI Game Programming Wisdom*, ed. S. Rabin, pp. 171–185. Hingham, MA: Charles River Media.

[US Army 07] US Army. 2007. *FM 3-21.8: The Infantry Rifle Platoon and Squad*. Washington, DC: Department of the Army. http://armypubs.army.mil/doctrine/DR_pubs/dr_a/pdf/fm3_21x8.pdf (accessed September 7, 2014).

[WorthPlaying 04] WorthPlaying.com. 2004. Kohan II: Kings of War. http://worthplaying.com/article/2004/11/26/reviews/20850/ (accessed May 18, 2014).

32

Extending the Spatial Coverage of a Voxel-Based Navigation Mesh

Kevin A. Kirst

32.1 Introduction

An AI navigation mesh, or *navmesh* for short, is a structure that can be used by an AI agent for pathfinding through a world. A voxel-based navmesh is one that is generated through the use of voxels. A *voxel*, representing a cube-shaped volume of space in a 3D grid, can be combined with other voxels to represent any volume of space. With voxels, a navmesh can be generated, which conforms greatly to the physical volume of a world, resulting in a navmesh that closely resembles the space in the world where an AI agent can physically fit. A voxel-based navmesh exists only where an AI agent can travel without colliding with or protruding into any physical body in the world.

A voxel-based navmesh is typically generated using parameters (notably height and radius) that describe the AI agent's dimensions while standing. This results in a navmesh that exists only where the AI agent can stand. Any space that is too low or too narrow for the AI agent to fit in while standing is excluded from the navmesh.

What follows is an explanation of how a voxel-based navmesh can be generated that includes the nonstanding spaces in the world: areas where the AI agent could fit if it were to crouch, lie prone, sidestep, swim, or otherwise contort its physical body appropriately.

Through appropriate markup, a more complete navmesh can be computed with a higher degree of spatial awareness. At a high level, an AI agent will continue to simply request a path from the pathfinder and travel along that path. Should that path take the AI agent through a small hole in the wall, the AI agent can use information embedded within the navmesh to dynamically contort its body to fit through the hole. Annotating navmeshes is nothing new; however, when combined with a voxel-based navmesh generator, the resulting procedurally built navmesh with extended spatial coverage can be used to give greater depth to an AI agent's ability to navigate through the world.

32.2 Overview of Voxel-Based Navmesh Generation

Before exploring this idea further, it's important to have a good understanding of the fundamentals behind a voxel-based navmesh. The goal here is to understand the steps involved in the generation process from a high-level perspective. This is important for understanding later how the process can be expanded to include other types of spaces in the navmesh. There are many articles on navmeshes and navmesh generation techniques (voxel based and otherwise). Greg Snook has done a wonderful job explaining the benefits and details of an AI navmesh [Snook 00]. David Hamm takes it one step further by discussing the benefits of utilizing an automatic navmesh generator while detailing the algorithm involved [Hamm 08]. There also exists a very well-respected voxel-based navmesh implementation known as *Recast*, written by Mikko Mononen, which is fully open sourced [Mononen 14]. This is a great resource containing example algorithms and a general code structure of a voxel-based navmesh generator.

32.2.1 Voxel-Based Navmesh Goals

Every voxel-based navmesh implementation out there is trying to solve the same problems and satisfy the same set of goals:

1. Maximize the coverage of the AI navmesh in the level.
2. Minimize the amount of human interaction required when placing the AI navmesh in the level.
3. Reduce the time spent when updating the AI navmesh during level iterations.

To maximize the AI navmesh's coverage, the navmesh needs to be extended across the entire level. The coverage will also need to be constrained by the physical world: ledges that are too high to jump over, slopes that are too steep to walk up, and walls that block the way forward should be omitted from the final navmesh.

To minimize the setup cost for building this AI navmesh in the level, the process needs to be automated as much as possible. The task should be no more difficult than painting the area where the AI agent can go in one broad stroke and having some automation fill in the blanks. To maximize the AI navmesh's coverage, this automation must be able to break apart the physical world and figure out what areas the AI agent can and cannot fit in the physical space (collision detection between the AI agent and physical objects) and ensure the navmesh extends only to the areas where the AI agent does physically fit.

To reduce the time spent in maintaining this AI navmesh, this automation process ought to continuously run and refresh the AI navmesh whenever the physical space in the level changes. Keeping true with the idea of automation, this process should happen seamlessly in the background without any additional interaction needed by the level designer. For example, if the designer drops a large object down in the middle of the room, puts up a new wall, or changes the degree of the slope in the terrain, then the AI navmesh needs to reflect these changes immediately after the action is carried out.

32.2.2 Enter Voxelization

Voxels are generated for the purpose of understanding algorithmically the space being constrained by the level's physical world. Figure 32.1 shows a simple in-engine scene. Figure 32.2 shows the same scene after voxelization.

Using these voxels, it is possible to calculate a set of planar polygons (hereafter referred to as only polygons), which cover the surfaces of the physical world and include in their areas as much of the navigable space as possible. These polygons are nontriangulated and consist of only a set of vertices that form the edges of the shape.

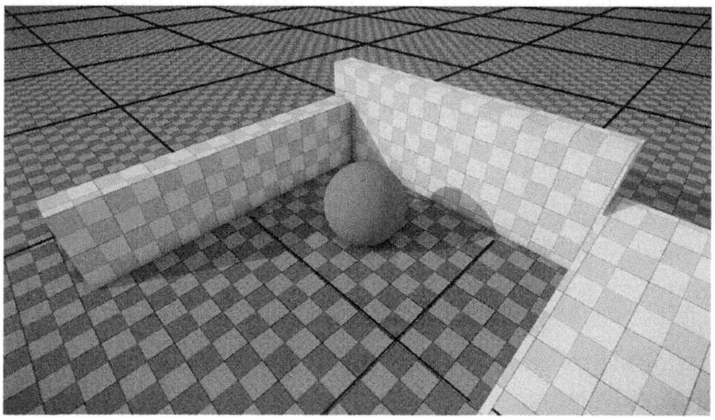

Figure 32.1

The world partitioned into grid for parallel voxelization.

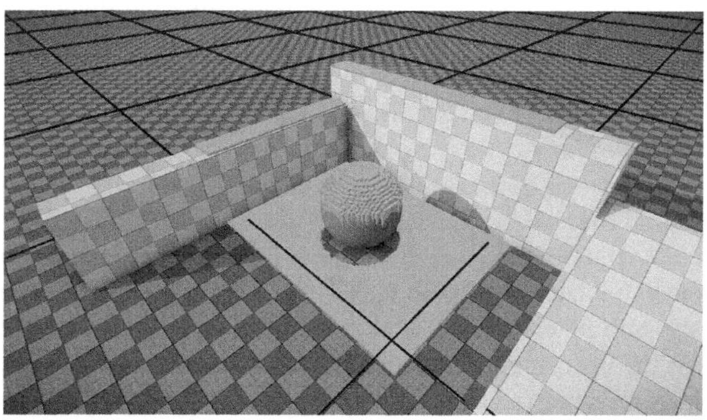

Figure 32.2

Voxels generated in a single grid, slightly overlapping the boundaries.

To generate the polygons, it must be determined which voxels form the edge of a polygon and how many polygons will be needed to cover the area. The area within these polygons will make up the AI navmesh in the level—anything outside these shapes are deemed nonnavigable by the AI agent. To find which voxels lay on the edge of a polygon (which subsequently will tell us how many polygons exist in the area), each voxel must be asked this single question: If an AI agent were to occupy the same space as this voxel, would that AI agent be able to legally move away from that space in any possible direction?

One obvious check for answering that question would be physical clipping. If the voxel is right up beside a wall and the AI agent stood centered on top of that voxel, then chances are the AI agent's arm or leg may be clipping into the wall. This is probably not ideal, and so it will be necessary to ensure that this voxel is left outside of all of the polygon shapes. We have another scenario: suppose the voxel is located just above the terrain on a slope with a steep gradient. Should the AI agent stand centered on top of this new voxel, then there is a strong certainty that the AI agent's feet may clip through the surface once it begins to play the run forward animation cycle. Since this is not ideal, it will again be necessary to ensure that this voxel is left outside of all of the polygon shapes.

To answer this question for each one of the voxels, a table of agent-driven parameters will be used. These parameters, when paired, describe two things:

1. The physical space that a single AI agent takes up (i.e., no other physical items should be within this space to ensure that the AI agent will not collide or clip through a nearby physical object while the AI agent plays any possible animations)
2. The maximum tolerance of the restrictions placed on the AI agent by motion-controlling animation

Listing 32.1 shows an example of what an agent-driven parameter table might look like.

The `radius` and `height` parameters are examples of description #1. With just these two parameters, it is ensured that the AI navmesh only covers areas where the AI agent can physically fit given its physics cylinder. The remaining parameters are examples of description #2. They do not describe anything about the physical world, but instead simply impose limitations on what would otherwise be legal navigable area. `maxStepHeight` can help in differentiating between a staircase and a large pile of rocks. `maxSlopeRad` can ensure the AI navmesh stays away from mountain slopes and sticks to just the rolling hills. Lastly, `minWaterDepth` and `maxWaterDepth` can be used to extend the AI navmesh a bit beyond the coastline.

With these parameters in hand, each of the voxels need to be flagged in one of three ways: **nonwalkable** (violates the parameters), **walkable** (passes the parameters), and **border** (passes the parameters but one of the neighboring voxels violates the parameters). Figure 32.3 shows the previous scene's voxels after they have been flagged. The nonwalkable and walkable voxels can safely be thrown away once all the voxels have been flagged. The remaining border voxels will be used to draw the outlines of the polygons—the voxels that neighbor one another are part of the same polygon. After going through all of

Listing 32.1. Sample agent-driven parameter structure.

```
struct SAgentParameters
{
    //Radius (in meters) of the AI agent's physics cylinder
    float radius;

    //Height (in meters) of the AI agent's physics cylinder
    float height;

    //Maximum height (in meters) of a step that the AI agent
    //can climb without breaking feet anchoring.
    float maxStepHeight;

    //Maximum angle (in radians) of a slope that the AI
    //agent can walk across without breaking animation.
    float maxSlopeRad;

    //Minimum height (in meters) from a sea floor where
    //the AI agent can stand and still keep its head above
    //water.
    float minWaterDepth;

    //Maximum height (in meters) from a sea floor where
    //the AI agent can stand and still keep its head above
    //water.
    float maxWaterDepth;
};
```

Figure 32.3

Flagged voxels. Lighter are walkable. Darker are border and nonwalkable.

these border voxels, one or any number of polygons may be determined, but it is important to remember which voxels belong to which polygon. Islands can form, as shown in Figure 32.4. These polygons may or may not be convex (some in fact might even have holes inside of them). This is perfectly okay, but should be remembered when moving on to the next step in the generation process.

Figure 32.4

Two polygons generated from the border voxels.

32.2.4 Triangulating the Polygons

To facilitate pathfinding through the navmesh, nodes need to be placed within the polygon shape to act as points along the calculated path. Any concave polygons, or polygons with holes, must also be handled correctly. No calculated paths should ever cut through a hole in a polygon or otherwise exit that polygon's borders and enter area not included in any of the other polygons. In order to use these polygons in the navmesh, they must be rendered convex. This can be done through a standard triangulation algorithm. Jonathan Richard Shewchuk describes a great triangulating algorithm that can handle both the convex, concave, and hole-filled polygons that may have been generated in the previous step [Shewchuk 02].

If the polygons shown in Figure 32.4 are triangulated without any additional modifications, the resulting triangle mesh would include an excessive number of small triangles in the parts around the polygon edges, due to the blocky border leftover from the voxelization process. See Figure 32.5 for an illustration of this point. This is not ideal, as it will result in placing a lot of nodes within a relatively small area, which is wasteful to both memory and computation time during pathfinding. What would be preferred is a polygon with a sloping side instead of a staircase side.

It is ideal if the polygon's border is simplified before it is triangulated, turning these staircases into slopes. Note that since the outside space is now entirely made up of nonnavigable areas for the AI agent, the polygon border should be simplified by shaving away interior space without including any nonnavigable exterior space. We are sacrificing coverage of the navigable area in exchange for an increase in performance. Figure 32.6 shows the same polygon border after it has been simplified.

The triangle list calculated through the triangulation algorithm will become the basis of the AI navmesh—the centers of each triangle representing a node and each neighboring triangle receiving a path connection between the two nodes. Figure 32.7 shows our previous scene's grid after triangulating the two polygons. Figure 32.8 shows the completed navigation mesh.

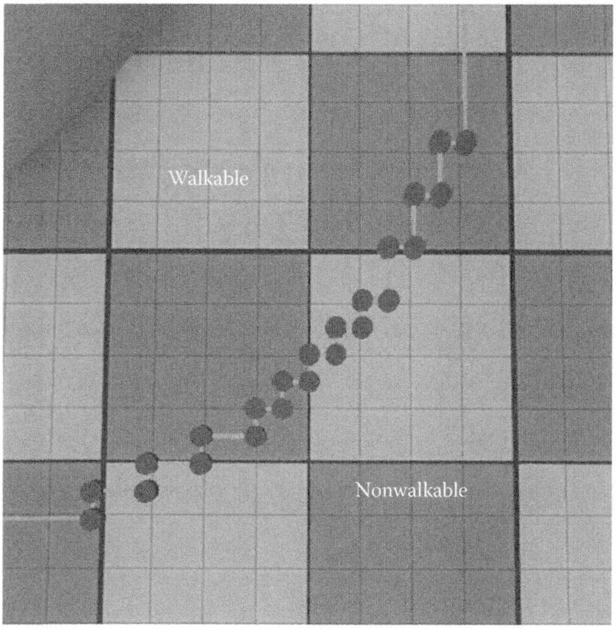

Figure 32.5

Polygon with a staircase side before simplification.

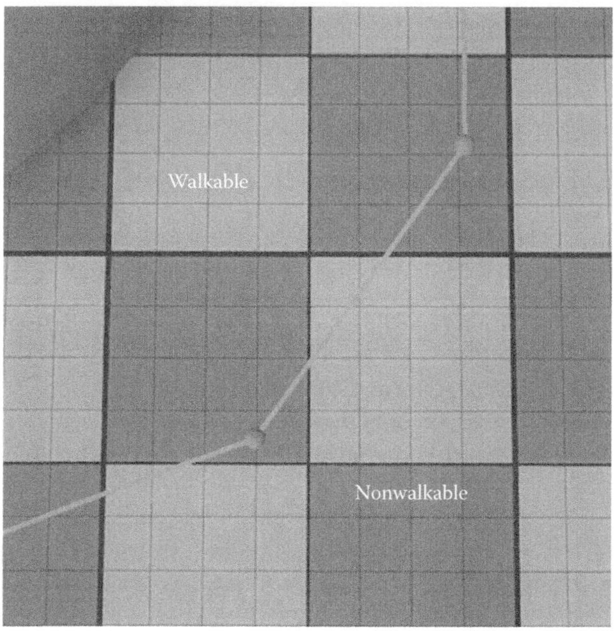

Figure 32.6

Polygon with a sloping side after simplification.

Figure 32.7

Simplified polygons after being triangulated.

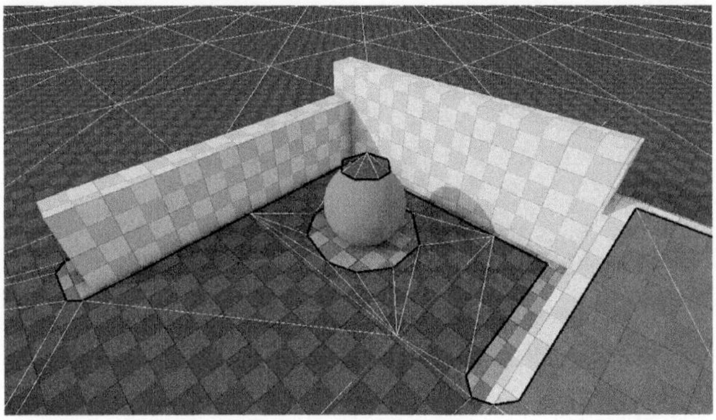

Figure 32.8

Completed triangulated AI navigation mesh.

32.2.5 Recap

Here's a quick recap of the voxel-based AI navmesh generation process.

1. Segment the world into individual cells using a grid. Overlap each grid on top of its neighbors slightly.
2. Using parallelization, perform the following on each cell:
   a. Voxelize the empty space in the cell (space not occupied by a physical body).
   b. Using the agent-driven parameters, flag all voxels as nonwalkable, walkable, or border.
   c. Throw away all nonwalkable and walkable voxels.
   d. Using the remaining border-flagged voxels, generate planar polygon shapes using the voxels as the edges.
   e. Simplify the polygon border shapes to prepare for triangulation, removing unnecessary vertices without increasing the area of the polygon.
   f. Triangulate the polygon and add the resulting localized triangle list to the master triangle list.

3. Once all cells have been processed, generate pathfinder nodes for all triangles in the master triangle list.
4. Create connections between the nodes that border each other—if they share the same triangle parent or if their parent triangles neighbor one another in the master triangle list.

This process gives us a workable AI navmesh that conforms to the physical world accurately, given a single static set of parameters based on an AI agent's physical state and motion behavior. As long as the AI agent does not deviate from its parameters, it will safely be able to travel anywhere along this navmesh without getting stuck or blocked by some physical body—as long as the physical bodies don't move around either! But if those physical bodies do move or change in some way, you could always regenerate the localized triangle list for the cells that contain that physical body and stitch the updated triangles back into the navmesh.

32.3 Extending the Navmesh's Spatial Coverage

Suppose an AI agent were to deviate from its physical parameters for a moment. Most action games support having an AI agent that can crouch down low, reducing its physical height. Suppose now the AI agent were to begin moving around while in this crouched state. As long as the new physical space that the AI agent occupies is less than the space used to generate the navmesh, there won't be any issues. Small objects can always fit in large spaces; therefore, the AI agent will still be able to safely travel everywhere along the navmesh. From that AI agent's perspective, the world has seemingly become much larger. Now, the space under a table looks easily passable. The AI agent could now fit through the air-conditioning duct opening. Even the holes blown out of the walls look passable from this state. But the navmesh was generated in a way that only considers where the AI agent could fit while standing. These new hiding places and shortcuts were passed over during the generation process. The voxels that filled these spaces were flagged as nonwalkable and were discarded.

32.3.1 Reintroducing the Discarded Space

It would be great if all of this discarded nonwalkable-flagged space could be reintroduced into the navmesh. But before that is done, it is important to flag this space with appropriate annotations. Without any additional metadata associated with the space, there is no way for the AI agent to determine if the space can be navigated while standing upright. Therefore, two rules must be satisfied:

1. The crouch-only triangles must be clearly separated from the stand-only triangles. Stand-only triangles should only exist in spaces where the AI agent can legally stand. Crouch-only triangles should only exist in spaces where the AI agent can legally crouch.
2. The crouch-only triangles must be flagged in some way, so that it is possible to later delineate what area is stand only and what area is crouch only on the navmesh.

The first rule is easily satisfied. The navmesh will be generated using the voxel-based generation process described earlier as usual; however, instead of discarding the nonwalkable

Figure 32.9

Crouch-only triangles (light) bordering stand-only triangles (dark).

voxels, these voxels will simply be set aside and sorted into a separate container for later revisiting. Once the generation process has finished constructing the localized triangle list for a cell, step #2 can be repeated in its entirety using the nonwalkable voxels that were set aside as a result of the previous pass' step #2a. That is, instead of voxelizing the cell space again, the nonwalkable voxels will be used as the starting pool of voxels, with all of their flags discarded. These voxels are then processed once again like before, but with a different set of agent-driven parameters—parameters that describe the AI agent's physical state and motion behavior from a crouching perspective. This will result in a new localized triangle list that spans across the remaining space in the cell where the AI agent can physically fit so long as it is crouched. And since the space in the cell where the AI agent could physically fit while standing is not being considered again (as those voxels were not included in the crouch-only pool of voxels), the edges of the newly calculated crouch-only triangles will exactly border the edges of the previously calculated stand-only triangles. Figure 32.9 illustrates this point.

Table 32.1 shows a side-by-side comparison of what the agent-driven parameters could look like for standing and crouching.

Notice how the `height` has decreased while the `radius` has stayed the same. While the AI agent is crouched down, the height of its collision cylinder has naturally lowered to match the difference in displacement from the floor to its head. The `maxWaterDepth` has also decreased proportionally. While crouched, the AI agent's motion behavior has been altered as well. The AI agent can no longer climb steep slopes like it used to and it cannot

Table 32.1 Standing and Crouching Agent-Driven Parameters

Parameter	Standing	Crouching
`radius`	0.4 m	0.4 m
`height`	2.0 m	1.2 m
`maxStepHeight`	0.5 m	0.25 m
`maxSlopeRad`	0.5 rad	0.35 rad
`minWaterDepth`	0.0 m	0.0 m
`maxWaterDepth`	1.5 m	0.7 m

raise its legs high enough to pass over certain steps. As a result, the `maxStepHeight` and `maxSlopeRad` values were decreased to better match its movement restrictions while crouched.

When these crouch parameters are used to flag the remaining voxel pool (remember the voxels in the pool were the ones that were flagged as nonwalkable by a standing AI agent), the voxels will then reflect if they are nonwalkable, walkable, or border for a crouching AI agent. For example, the voxels that were placed just above the floor but below the table were nonwalkable by a 2 m tall AI agent but are now clearly walkable by a 1.2 m tall AI agent. Voxels that are being found are now walkable, some of which are forming borders due to the absence of neighboring voxels that did not carry over from the previous pass. These newly flagged border voxels can generate new polygons, which once simplified and triangulated will fill a new localized triangle list full of crouch-only triangles.

If this localized triangle list were to be combined with the localized triangle list from the previous pass and merged into the master triangle list "as is," only the first rule will have been satisfied. The triangles from both passes will be clearly separated with no overlapping occurring. But the crouch-only triangles will have no distinguishing annotations associated with them that separate them from the stand-only triangles. An AI agent will still think it can traverse over these triangles while standing. These crouch-only triangles must be annotated in some way before being combined with the stand-only triangles, so that it is possible to distinguish between the two triangle types at path-planning time.

To satisfy the second rule, metadata are incorporated into the triangle data type. These metadata inform an AI agent of how it must alter its physical state or motion behavior in order to successfully travel over the triangle.

32.3.2 Using the Metadata

The last key of the puzzle involves getting the AI agent to make use of the metadata. When an AI agent requests a path of the pathfinder, triangle nodes in the navmesh become the vertices of the path. In the end, the AI agent is simply walking from one triangle node to another until the AI agent reaches the node from the last triangle (the one that contains the destination point within its area). The AI agent can always figure out which triangle it's currently standing over and which it's moving toward next, just by looking at the nodes in the path that it is following.

By including the metadata associated with the triangle in the path vertex, it then becomes possible for the AI agent to refer to the metadata while following its path. As an example, Listing 32.2 shows a simple structure describing a path vertex. The vertex is constructed from a triangle node. The metadata from that triangle node is included in the path vertex.

With the inclusion of the metadata in the path vertices, it is now just a matter of using the data at the right time. While the AI agent is following its path, it can look at the next path vertex and determine if it should be crouching or not. If the next path vertex has a true value for `bCrouch`, then the AI agent needs to set its stance to be crouching. If there is a false value for `bCrouch`, then the AI agent needs to set its stance to be standing. See Figure 32.10 as an example. A path can now be generated through standing-only space and crouch-only space interchangeably. The AI agent will set its stance correctly based on which area it is about to enter next.

Notice how the previous triangle node is passed in to the `SPathVertex` constructor if available. Figure 32.10 illustrates why this is needed. Six triangles are shown, forming

Listing 32.2. Path vertex structure which records if it came from a crouch-only triangle.

```
struct SPathVertex
{
    //Position of the path vertex
    Vec3 vPosition;

    //True if AI agent should crouch while navigating
    //to this vertex
    bool bCrouch;

    explicit SPathVertex(const STriangleNode &node,
        const STriangleNode *prevNode = 0)
    {
        vPosition = node.vPosition;
        bCrouch = node.bCrouchOnly;

        if (prevNode)
        {
            //Stay crouching if the previous triangle
            //was crouch-only
            bCrouch |= prevNode->bCrouchOnly;
        }
    }
};
```

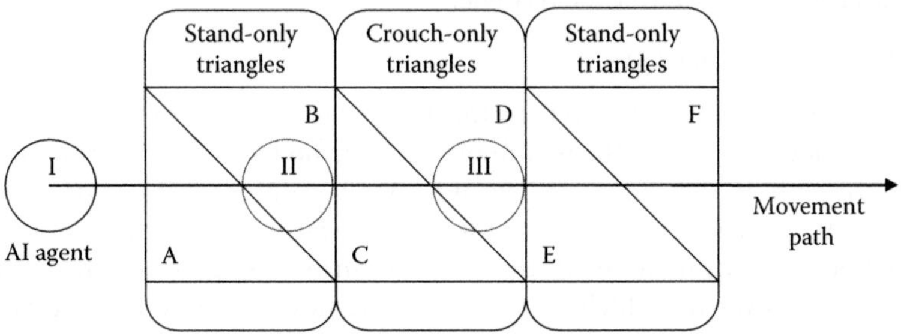

Figure 32.10

An AI agent's movement path on top of the navmesh. Six triangles are shown from the navmesh (A through F), with the middle two (C and D) being flagged as crouch only. Three points of interests are shown as circles labeled with the numerals I through III.

the navmesh. A movement path is passing through all six triangles (the nodes originating from the midpoints of the triangle segments), with the AI agent being located at the start of the path (point I). Note that triangle B is stand only, while triangle C is crouch only. When the AI agent has reached the path vertex from triangle B and begins to move toward the path vertex from triangle C (point II), the AI agent will begin to crouch. This is the correct behavior, as it gives the AI agent time to crouch before leaving the stand-only space of triangle B and entering the crouch-only space of triangle C. Now look at triangles D and E. Triangle D is crouch only, while triangle E is stand only. When the AI agent has reached the path vertex from triangle D and begins to move toward the path vertex from triangle E (point III), the AI agent will have begun to stand. This is because triangle E has a false value for `bCrouch`, and since the path vertex made using triangle E is the next path vertex, the AI agent ought to set its stance to be standing. But the AI agent is still within the crouch-only space of triangle D. The AI agent needs to exit this space before it can stand up. The safest way to know if the AI agent has cleared the crouch-only space of triangle D is to wait until the AI agent has reached triangle E and has moved on to the next path vertex from triangle F. To keep the AI agent crouching while navigating toward triangle E, we set its `bCrouch` value to be true, not because triangle E's metadata say so but because the previous node (triangle D) is crouch only.

32.4 Identifying Other Spaces

Crouch navigation is just one example of how the recycling process can be applied to a voxel-based navmesh generator. The following is an assortment of other possibilities that can be explored. Each one of these possibilities involves just adding another recycling pass of the leftover nonwalkable voxels using a different tweak to the agent-driven parameters and another entry in the triangle metadata.

32.4.1 Prone Navigation

Just like with crouch navigation, prone navigation works off the `height` parameter—just with a much lower value. For prone navigation, the agent-driven parameters might contain the values in Table 32.2.

The `radius` parameter has doubled that of the standing height. This is because, while in the prone position, the AI agent will be lying flat down on its stomach, and so from its pivot point located near its pelvis joint, the maximum radius of a circle that fully encloses the AI agent is half its standing height, or 1 m. The `height` parameter and the various motion behavior parameters are lowered and adjusted to fit the new height of the AI agent.

32.4.2 Swim Navigation

Swim navigation works off of the `minWaterDepth` and `maxWaterDepth` parameters. By using a `minWaterDepth` equal to the standing `maxWaterDepth` and a much larger value for the new `maxWaterDepth`, a navigation mesh can be generated along the sea floor of a very deep lake or even an ocean. The agent-driven parameters might contain the values in Table 32.3.

The `radius` and `height` parameters match those used in the proning parameters, as the AI agent will be swimming, which involves lying flat on its stomach.

Table 32.2 Proning Agent-Driven Parameters

Parameter	Standing	Proning
`radius`	0.4 m	1.0 m
`height`	2.0 m	0.5 m
`maxStepHeight`	0.5 m	0.1 m
`maxSlopeRad`	0.5 rad	0.15 rad
`minWaterDepth`	0.0 m	0.0 m
`maxWaterDepth`	1.5 m	0.35 m

Table 32.3 Swimming Agent-Driven Parameters

Parameter	Standing	Swimming
radius	0.4 m	1.0 m
height	2.0 m	0.5 m
maxStepHeight	0.5 m	48.5 m
maxSlopeRad	0.5 rad	2π rad
minWaterDepth	0.0 m	1.5 m
maxWaterDepth	1.5 m	50.0 m

The minWaterDepth matches the maxWaterDepth used in the standing parameters. This ensures only surfaces below sea level that are lower than the standing height of the agent up to its neck are considered. The maxWaterDepth parameter uses a value of 50 m, but this value can be however low or high as is necessary for the world. It will just cap how far out into the water the AI agent can swim, given how deep the water is at that point. The maxSlopeRad parameter is set to 360°. Since the AI agent will be swimming along the surface of the water, the slope of the ground or objects underneath the water surface is irrelevant, and using a value of 360° ensures any legal calculated slope will always pass.

The maxStepHeight parameter is a bit more interesting here and was calculated as

$$\texttt{maxStepHeight} = \texttt{maxWaterDepth} - \texttt{minWaterDepth} \tag{32.1}$$

Imagine a large cube resting on the sea floor 50 m below the water surface. If the height of that cube is less than 48.5 m, the AI agent can float on the water surface and not touch the top of the cube. If the height of the cube is greater than or equal to 48.5 m, then the AI agent could stand on the surface of the cube and be nearly or fully out of the water, meaning the height difference from the water surface to the top of the cube is too small for the AI agent to swim through.

Keep in mind that the AI navmesh is being generated along the sea floor and not the water surface. When constructing the path vertices along this section of the navmesh, the height of the vertex should be adjusted to match the height of the water surface, so that the AI agent does not attempt to follow a path underwater.

32.4.3 Sidestep Navigation

Sidestepping navigation involves moving one's body without extending one's legs forward. If one is moving to their left, then to sidestep, they would extend their left leg out to the left of their body and then retract their right leg so that it comes to rest beside their left leg again. This style of motion allows one to move through very tight spaces, as long as they can suck their gut in enough! For an AI agent, sidestepping translates into a navigation method that works with a much smaller radius. The agent-driven parameters might look something like Table 32.4.

These parameters are identical to the standing parameters, with the exception of radius, which has been halved to a mere 20 cm. If these parameters are used to generate sidestep-only triangles after a stand-only pass, the navmesh would be extended in tighter-fitting areas where the AI agent could still stand. An example of such an area

Table 32.4 Sidestepping Agent-Driven Parameters

Parameter	Standing	Sidestepping
`radius`	0.4 m	0.2 m
`height`	2.0 m	2.0 m
`maxStepHeight`	0.5 m	0.5 m
`maxSlopeRad`	0.5 rad	0.5 rad
`minWaterDepth`	0.0 m	0.0 m
`maxWaterDepth`	1.5 m	1.5 m

might be a narrow ledge along the parameter of a building or a room packed with boxes making a maze of walkways.

To navigate this space requires a more stylized approach for an AI agent. A unique set of locomotion animations that drive the AI agent's character to move forward by sidestepping is required. The collision cylinder around the AI agent might also need to be temporarily adjusted, so that the radius of the cylinder matches the maximum 20 cm space.

32.4.4 Multiple Generation Parameter Passes and Hierarchy

Due to the recursive nature of the multiple generation passes when using different parameters, the order in which the parameters are parsed is critical in determining the resulting navmesh. As each pass only considers those voxels that have previously been flagged as nonwalkable, the next set of parameters can only add (and consequently mark up) space that has not yet been included in the navmesh.

For example, consider generating the navmesh with standing, crouching, and proning parameters. If the hierarchy is standing, then proning, then crouching, the resulting navmesh will mostly consist of only standing- and proning-marked space. Since it is possible to prone anywhere where one can crouch (with the slight exception of the slightly wider radius for prone vs. crouch), all of the nonwalkable voxels from the stand-only pass will be consumed during the prone-only pass. The crouch-only pass will have very few nonwalkable voxels left for it to consider. Should the hierarchy be modified to consider crouching before proning, a better mixture of crouch-only and prone-only space will be distributed throughout the navmesh. Sometimes one method may be preferred over the other, and so there is no right or wrong answer for the order of hierarchy. This leaves the door open for many interesting combinations and resulting navmeshes to experiment with!

32.5 Playing with the Heuristic

Here is one additional footnote for consideration: it might be the case that having an AI agent that avoids crouching, proning, swimming, or whatever nonstanding navigation is preferable, if it is possible. Consider a table in the middle of the room. If the AI agent were to walk from one end of the room to the other, is it better for that AI agent to walk up to that table in the center, crouch down, crawl through the space underneath, emerge at the other end, and continue on? Or should that AI agent simply walk around the table?

Level of effort comes into play here. It requires far less energy to take the few extra steps and navigate around the table than it does to contort one's body to fit through the space underneath the table. Unless the point beneath the table top is the destination, there most likely isn't a logical reason for the AI agent to spend that extra energy to pass under it. This level of effort can be described through your pathfinding heuristic. By artificially scaling the pathfinding cost to move into a crouch-only triangle, an AI agent can usually be convinced that the pathway around the table is a far cheaper alternative than the direct path under the table.

32.6 Conclusion

Voxel-based navmeshes, when generated using the recycling strategy here described, can greatly enhance an AI agent's spatial awareness through its navigation. The examples that were covered (crouching, proning, swimming, and sidestepping) are just the tip of the iceberg of possibilities. Any tweak that is made to the agent-driven parameters to cover previously discarded areas can be merged into the navmesh, and with the addition of another aggregate in the triangle metadata, an AI agent can discern the information needed to contort their bodies to fit these newly covered spaces.

We have some parting food for thought: your triangle metadata can be used for much more than what has been stated thus far. Consider including other spatial information in your triangle metadata. For example, the triangles of your navmesh that lay under a forested area could include metadata flagging the area as forested. This information could then be read by an AI agent as it paths through the forest and used to modify its behavior, perhaps guiding it to take more advantage of the abundance of cover provided by trees as good hiding spots to seek or investigate. The navmesh will almost certainly be under an AI agent's feet at all times, so use it to your advantage! Store whatever information you can in the navmesh to help your AI agents understand the space they're in, and opportunity will surely come knocking.

References

[Hamm 08] Hamm, D. 2008. Navigation mesh generation: An empirical approach. In *AI Game Programming Wisdom 4*, S. Rabin, Ed. Charles River Media, Boston, MA.

[Mononen 14] Mononen, M. 2014. Recast navigation solution. https://github.com/memononen/recastnavigation (accessed September 10, 2014).

[Shewchuk 02] Shewchuk, J.R. May 2002. Delaunay refinement algorithms for triangular mesh generation. *Computational Geometry: Theory and Applications*, 22(1–3):21–74.

[Snook 00] Snook, G. 2000. Simplified 3D movement and pathfinding using navigation meshes. In *Game Programming Gems*, M. DeLoura, Ed. Charles River Media, Boston, MA.

SECTION VI
Character Behavior

33

Infected AI in *The Last of Us*

Mark Botta

33.1 Introduction

In *The Last of Us* a fungal infection has devastated human beings. The pandemic corrupts the mind and has left most of the population grotesquely disfigured and relentlessly aggressive. The survivors have been forced to struggle not only against those overcome by the fungus (known as the Infected) but also against predatory groups of survivors (known as Hunters). This chapter will focus on the AI behind the Infected. Subsequent chapters will discuss the AI for Hunters and buddy characters.

It was our goal to make the Infected feel fundamentally different than Hunters, despite the fact that they use the same AI system. This was done with a modular AI architecture that allows us to easily add, remove, or change decision-making logic. This allows us to create characters that interact with the world in highly varied ways while keeping the code as simple as possible. Simple code is more maintainable, which is crucial when rapidly iterating on new ideas. Developing the Infected required continuous experimentation to discover what worked best. The more quickly new ideas were implemented, the sooner the designers were able to provide feedback. Keeping that cycle of refinement short enabled us to make the Infected feel grounded, entertaining, and believable.

The best way to achieve these goals is to make our characters not stupid before making them smart. Characters give the illusion of intelligence when they are placed in well-thought-out setups, are responsive to the player, play convincing animations and sounds, and behave in interesting ways. Yet all of this is easily undermined when they mindlessly run into walls or do any of the endless variety of things that plague AI characters. Not only does eliminating these glitches provide a more polished experience, but it is amazing how much intelligence is attributed to characters that simply don't do stupid things.

33.2 The Infected

The Infected are humans who have succumbed to the parasitic *Cordyceps* fungus [Stark 13]. The infection ravages the body, leaving no trace of personality, compassion, or even self-preservation. The Infected are driven only by the instincts of the fungus.

Most survivors exist in prisonlike quarantine zones under martial law, but some choose to live outside of the quarantine zones, where they are free but constantly at risk of encountering the Infected or predatory gangs of Hunters.

We wanted the Infected to feel fundamentally different than the Hunters. Hunters work in groups, communicate with words and gestures, and protect each other. The player can see that their cold-blooded brutality is a means to survive. In contrast, the Infected seem chaotic and alien.

Table 33.1 summarizes the four types of Infected that represent the progression of the infection. Runners are the most common type. They are fast and often attack in uncoordinated groups. They can see and, like all Infected, their hearing is far more sensitive than that of the Hunters, making them just as effective in a dark room as they are on a sunlit street. Stalkers are similar to Runners but hide in dark areas and ambush prey. Clickers are visibly disfigured by the infection, with masses of fungus distorting their features and leaving them blind. They have developed a type of echolocation to compensate. They are slower than Runners but have a deadly frenzy attack and ignore melee attacks that don't use weapons. Bloaters are highly disfigured, blind, slow, and heavily armored. They grab and kill any character within reach, making melee attacks ineffective. They throw growths from their bodies that burst into disorienting clouds of irritating dust.

33.2.1 Senses

Our characters rely on their senses to reveal enemies and distractions in their environment. They track how and when they sense each entity and focus on the one that is the most threatening. All Infected, even Runners and Stalkers, rely primarily on hearing.

The sensory system does not reason about the actual audio heard in the game. Instead, logical sound events are generated specifically for this purpose. This gave the game designers more control, allowing them to specify which sounds are heard at what range

Table 33.1 Characteristics of Infected Character Types

Type	Runner	Stalker	Clicker	Bloater
Speed	Fast	Fast	Medium	Slow
Vision	Limited	Limited	Blind	Blind
Rarity	Common	Uncommon	Uncommon	Rare
Combat	Attack in groups	Ambush in dark areas	Melee frenzy, limited melee vulnerability	Armored, ranged attack, invulnerable to melee

by which character type. It also allowed sound designers to add or modify the game's audio without impacting the AI.

Wherever possible, we tried to correlate the logical sound events with actual audio, so that the player would be able to understand (and predict) the reactions of the Infected. There were exceptions, however. In particular, we wanted the AI to be able to sense nearby stationary targets, so we created a logical *breathing* sound that propagates over a very short range but has no audio.

Logical sounds are broadcast over a radius set by the designer, and any character within that radius—whether Infected or not—can hear it. Of course, not all characters hear equally well. We wanted the Infected to hear roughly six times better than the Hunters. We also wanted to be able to vary their hearing sensitivity based on their current behavior. For example, the Infected do not hear as well when they are unaware of the player. This makes it easier for the player to be stealthy, which slows the pace of the encounter, giving the player more opportunity to observe and plan. Thus, for a particular character type in a particular behavior, the radius of a logical sound is multiplied by a tunable value to give the effective radius within which that character will hear the sound.

Similar to actual audio, logical sounds are partially occluded by walls and obstacles. This was done to prevent the characters from hearing through walls as well as to reinforce the player's natural tendency to keep obstacles between them and the Infected. Each time a logic sound event is broadcast, rays are cast from each character within the sound radius to the source of the sound to determine the level of occlusion. The logical sound is broadcast to all characters in range that are not completely occluded.

In order to further differentiate the Infected from the Hunters, we wanted them to be more difficult to approach stealthily. It is a common video game trope to communicate stealthy movement to the player via crouch animations: when crouching, the player can approach another character from behind without being discovered. In *The Last of Us*, this was true of Hunters, but approaching the Infected with impunity while crouched made them feel considerably less dangerous. Our solution was to scale the broadcast radius of logical movement sounds with the speed of the player. This allows approaching the Infected more quickly from farther away but requires moving more slowly at melee range. To communicate this to the player, the Infected enter an agitated state when they start to hear noise, which gives the player a chance to respond before being discovered.

This raises an important point. Communicating the intent of the characters to the player is vital. We rejected some game features simply because they could not be communicated well. For example, Clickers make a barking sound that is an ornamental remnant of a more ambitious design. We originally wanted them to use a type of echolocation to build a local model of the environment (similar to how bats hunt and navigate). Each time that they barked, we would update their mental model of the local area by turning their vision on momentarily. This gave the character a sensory snapshot of threats in the world, but it did not communicate well and confused players that were *seen* by a blind character. We considered giving the bark a visual effect like a ripple of distortion washing over the environment but ultimately decided that this seemed too unrealistic. In the end, we abandoned this approach because it was complex and difficult to convey to the player.

33.2.2 Distractions

When Hunters see the beam of a flashlight or are hit by a brick, they can infer that somebody is nearby. The Infected lack this insight and react only to the stimulus itself. For example, they are drawn to the sound of a thrown object landing rather than deducing the existence of the character that threw it. This response empowered the player to manipulate the Infected and made bricks and bottles as valuable as any weapon.

This response was consistent with their instinctive behavior but it trivialized some encounters. This was particularly problematic when the player used a Molotov cocktail. The sound of the breaking bottle would attract all nearby Infected who would follow each other into the flames, become engulfed, and die. This was entertaining, but much too easy. We solved this by limiting the number of characters that could be affected by the flames. Molotov cocktails are expensive to craft and should be very effective, but not so effective that they take the challenge out of the game.

The Last of Us also allows players to create smoke bombs, which are used to break line of sight and mask the movement of the player. In principle, these should be ineffective against the Infected because they rely so heavily on their hearing, but again, that would take the fun out of the game. Instead, we had them occlude hearing as well as vision. Thus, after being attracted by the detonation of a smoke bomb, the Infected enter the cloud and become essentially blind and deaf. The player is rewarded with the opportunity to flee or to move among the distracted Infected strangling Runners and dispatching Clickers with shivs.

33.3 AI System

Our AI system makes a distinction between the high-level decision logic (*skills*) that decides what the character should do and the low-level capabilities (*behaviors*) that implement those decisions. This separation allows characters with different high-level skills to reuse the same low-level behaviors. For example, movement is encapsulated in the *move-to* behavior that is invoked by many different skills. Furthermore, in this behavior, the decision of where to go is independent of how the character decides to get there. One character may use the *move-to* behavior to move stealthily in the shadows, while another charges forward.

Skills decide what to do based on the motivations and capabilities of the character, as well as the current state of the environment. They answer questions like *Do I want to attack, hide, or flee?* and *What is the best place for me to be?* Once a decision is made, behaviors are invoked to implement it. For example, if movement is required, the skill may invoke the *move-to* behavior and then wait for it to succeed or fail.

The *move-to* behavior attempts to reach the destination using whatever capabilities are available to it. It answers questions like *Which route should I take?* and *Which animations should I play?* It generates paths, avoids obstacles, selects animations to traverse the environment, and ultimately reports the results to the parent skill.

33.3.1 Philosophy

As a general rule, characters don't need complex high-level decision-making logic in order to be believable and compelling and to give the illusion of intelligence. What they need is to appear grounded by reacting to and interacting with the world around them in believable ways. Of course, they also need to avoid doing stupid things. Characters in *The Last of Us* can see and hear threats and distractions, they can navigate by climbing over obstacles and jumping gaps, they can look around corners, they can respond to fire, and they can search for prey. By building a rich set of behaviors that allow characters to interact with the world and picking appropriate behaviors even in fairly simple ways, we create characters that draw the player into the drama of the moment, which sell the story and make the experience meaningful.

In order to be able to reuse skills as widely as possible, we needed to keep them flexible but well encapsulated and decoupled, so that each skill could be adjusted to fit its particular use without affecting other skills. This was very valuable in the late stages of development. Features changed quickly, and it was important to be able to insulate the rest of the code from unstable prototypes. Our modular approach also made it easy to completely remove any failed experiments without fear of leaving any remnants behind. This allowed us to experiment with major changes to the AI right up to the end of the project. For example, Stalkers were conceived of and implemented only a few months before the game shipped.

33.3.2 Data-Driven Design

One key to keeping the code general was to never refer to any of the character types in code, but instead to specify sets of characteristics that define each type of character. All of the Infected character types share a single C++ class and are differentiated only by the set of skills and the values of the tuning variables in their data files. For example, the code refers to the *vision type* of the character instead of testing if the character is a Runner or a Clicker. This may sound like a minor distinction, but it is central to our efforts to keep the code general. Rather than spreading the character definitions as conditional checks throughout the code, it centralizes them in tunable data. This gives designers control over character variations, rather than requiring them to request changes from the AI team, which would slow their iteration times considerably. Furthermore, when adding a new type of Infected or changing an existing type in a fundamental way, there is no need to hunt down all of the places in the code that refer to the character. There aren't any! Just add or remove skills, behaviors, and tuning variables, and everything is kept modular and flexible.

This approach requires constant vigilance. There were many occasions when we were tempted to add a check for a specific character type for *just one thing*. Unfortunately, that *one thing* tends to proliferate as code is extended and reused, or as features are added, or just for convenience when testing. The lesson here is to stay true to your design principles because that consistency will pay off in terms of stability and ease of implementing new features.

An additional benefit became clear when we added the difficulty levels to the game. Because of memory and performance restrictions, difficulty couldn't be tuned by adding more characters to encounters. Keeping all of the character-specific data tunable made it straightforward to configure the difficulty settings for each character type individually. For each character type, designers modified the thresholds at which the Infected would respond to stimuli. For example, at lower difficulty settings, Clickers respond to nearby stimuli by turning and barking, whereas at higher difficulty settings, they are less forgiving and will often chase the player at the slightest provocation.

33.3.3 Implementation

The AI for a specific type of character is implemented as a set of skills that invoke a hierarchy of behaviors. Both skills and behaviors are implemented as straightforward finite-state machines. Skills tend to be tailored to specific character types, while behaviors are more widely reused. For example, Hunters and Infected characters do not share any skills but they share most of their behaviors.

Each type of character maintains a prioritized list of skills. These are tested one at a time from highest to lowest priority to determine if they are valid to run. Testing stops when a valid skill is found. The last skill in the list must always be valid or the character could get into an uncontrolled state and become unresponsive, freeze, walk into a wall, or otherwise look stupid. Skills run until they are completed or are interrupted by a higher priority skill.

33.3.4 Debugging

Maintaining the separation between skills and behaviors has another benefit. We can debug a character by replacing the skills with logic that drives the high-level decisions from a game controller. Of course, nonplayer characters take input differently than a player character. For example, they move to specific locations as opposed to taking directional input from a thumb stick. Conversely, they have controls that the player character doesn't have. They can select from several demeanors (e.g., whether to appear aggressive or relaxed), they have numerous gestures for communication, they have to select look and aim points, and they have a rich set of behaviors to choose from. There are far more inputs available to nonplayer characters than there are buttons on a controller!

To support all of these inputs, an on-screen menu appears when a character is selected for debugging. From here, we can put the character into the desired state, select the desired behavior, and use a cursor to select a destination. We also have convenience options to teleport the character and repeat the last move command, making it much easier to refine animations and behaviors without needing to rely on waiting for the skills to use them.

33.4 Skills and Behaviors

Table 33.2 contains the skills used by each type of Infected, sorted by priority. Priorities specify which skills should be allowed to interrupt each other. For example, the *chase* skill is allowed to interrupt the *search* skill but can be interrupted by the *on-fire* skill. The *wander*

Table 33.2 Prioritized Skills for Infected Character Types

Runner	Stalker	Clicker	Bloater
On-fire	On-fire	On-fire	On-fire
Chase	Ambush	Chase	Throw
Search	Sleep	Search	Chase
Follow	Wander	Follow	Search
Sleep		Sleep	Follow
Wander		Wander	Sleep
			Wander

skill is the fallback for all types of Infected and is always valid. Conceptually, if the Infected aren't busy doing anything else, they'll be wandering around their environment.

Our goal was to share as much of the AI between the Infected characters as possible so that new character types could be added easily. When development started, it was unknown how many character variations there would be or how they would behave. We experimented with different types of game play and a variety of character types. Each variation went through several iterations before it showed promise and was kept for further refinement or until the potential was exhausted and it was cut. As a result, most of the skills are shared by all Infected character types. Only two skills are used by a single character type: the *ambush* skill used by the Stalker and the *throw* skill used by the Bloater. The Infected spend most of their time in the *wander* and *chase* skills. Similarly, most of these skills invoke behaviors that are also used by the Hunters. There are only two behaviors that are unique to the Infected: the *infected-canvass* behavior and the *infected-listen* behavior.

33.4.1 *Search* Skill

Hunters have a complex search skill that enables them to uncover all hidden locations in an encounter in a coordinated way. The Infected, on the other hand, are not particularly well organized or thorough, so an Infected-specific search skill was needed. The *search* skill becomes valid to run when an Infected loses track of the player during a chase. The search is not exhaustive; they eventually lose interest and resume wandering around. The intent of the skill is to keep the player moving as the character explores nearby hiding places.

Hiding places are polygons on the navigation mesh that are not visible from other parts of the navigation mesh. When the search begins, a graph of *search points* is generated that reveal hiding places. A search point is added at the center of the polygon containing the last known location of the target entity. A breadth-first traversal visits neighboring polygons until line of sight to the search point is broken. A new search point is added at the center of the parent polygon (i.e., the last polygon with line of sight to the previous search point). This process continues until the entire search area is visited or a fixed number of search points have been added. The result is a graph of points with visibility to each other and to all of the hiding places around them.

Points are selected on the search graph based on the predicted location of the player [Straatman 06]. This has the effect of propagating desirable search points over time, which the Infected explore in a natural-looking search pattern, and puts pressure on players who tend to stay put. When an Infected reaches a search point, it briefly investigates before moving on.

When investigating, we wanted the Infected to appear to move around frantically and cover as much of the immediate area as possible without looking planned or methodical. Also, since search points can be generated anywhere on the navigation mesh, the area to search could be an arbitrary shape and size and may contain obstacles like debris or furniture. The *infected-canvass* behavior was designed to meet these requirements. It works as follows (and is illustrated in Figure 33.1):

1. A logical grid is placed over the area covered by the *canvass radius* and centered on the Infected.
2. Obstacles and the area outside of the canvass radius are marked as *seen*, leaving an area of cells that need to be checked.

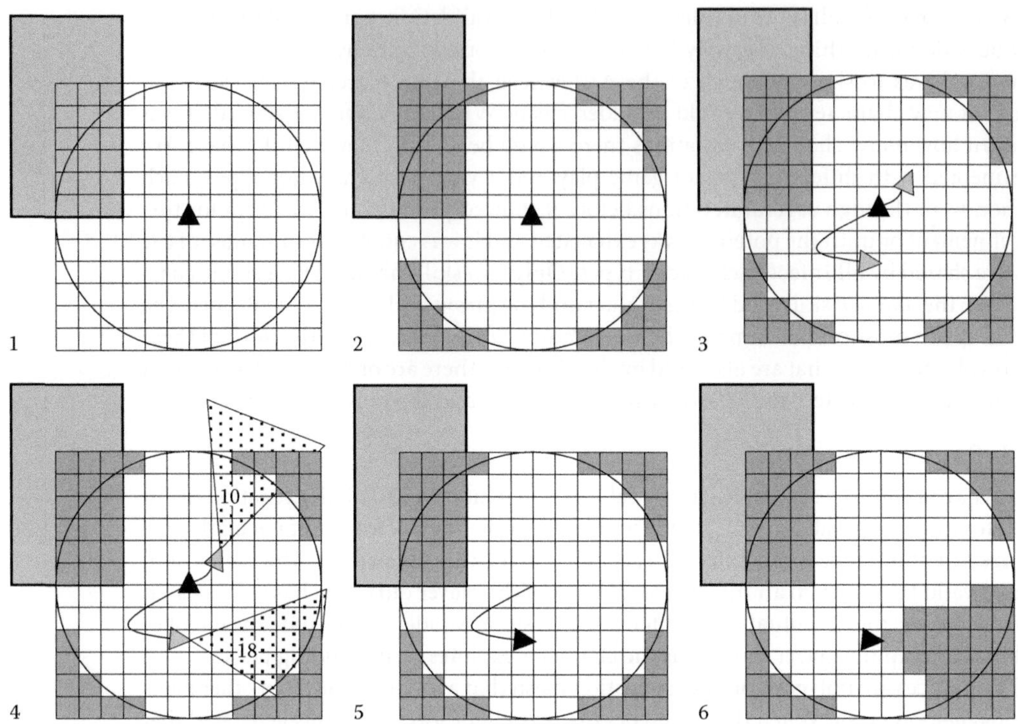

Figure 33.1

Selecting an animation in the *infected-canvass* behavior near an obstacle.

3. The invoking skill provides the behavior with a collection of animations that it can use. We determine the location and orientation that the character will have at the end of each of these animations.
4. The number of *unseen* cells in a sensory wedge in front of the character is counted for each animation. The wedge need not match the area covered by the actual senses. A larger wedge gives more coverage for a faster search and a smaller wedge gives a more thorough search.
5. Animations that result in more *unseen* cells are more desirable. Animations that were played recently are less desirable. The most desirable animation is played, moving the character.
6. When the animation has completed, the cells in the sensory wedge are marked *seen* and the process repeats at the new location from step 3.

The *Infected-canvass* behavior never explicitly selects the direction the character moves—it is based solely on the available animations. This made the code much simpler and animators were not restricted to producing animations in a fixed number of directions, which gave them the freedom to create a larger variety of expressive performances. Designers had control over the canvass radius and how long the character continues to canvass. For variety, the behavior includes sets of animations that move the character both near and far. In a small area, the character uses the near set of animations and turns quickly to look in all directions in an unpredictable (and seemingly random) order. In larger areas, the far set of animations are added to the mix, resulting in the character moving across the canvass area in short and long bursts. The process is not exhaustive, but it is convincingly frantic, it looks organic, and it is very flexible. The behavior was used by several other Infected skills in addition to the *search* skill.

33.4.2 *Chase* Skill

Most of the Infected have almost trivially simple combat tactics: when an entity is sensed, they get to it as fast as possible and attack it. This is done by the *chase* skill.

When an entity is first encountered, the Infected turns toward the stimulus and screams to alert the player that they have been discovered. The *chase* skill does this by invoking the *surprise* behavior that selects from a set of animations that orient the character in the appropriate direction.

Next, the *chase* skill invokes the *move-to* behavior, which provides an interface to the navigation system and is responsible for moving the character to a location or entity. As the entity moves through the environment, the *move-to* behavior continuously updates the path, leaving the parent skill to simply monitor for success or failure. This is one of the key advantages of the modular behavior system—it allows us to keep the high-level logic in the skills very simple.

During the chase, the character will occasionally pause to reorient, giving the player more opportunity to hide or prepare an attack. Instead of simply pausing movement, the *infected-canvass* behavior is used for a very short duration in a small area and with a special set of animations, which gives the Infected the appearance of frantically trying to reacquire the player during the chase.

33.4.3 *Follow* Skill

Unlike Hunters, the Infected do not communicate with one another. They share no information anywhere in the code. This is consistent with the idea that they are not intelligent and only respond instinctively to the stimuli in their environment. Consequently, if an Infected senses the player and starts to chase, any nearby Infected that do not directly sense the player are oblivious. Although this makes sense, in practice it made the Infected seem a bit too insensitive to their environment.

As an alternative, we added the *follow* skill, which allows one character to follow another that is chasing something. The following character does not receive any information about the entity being chased; it just has the compulsion to follow along. Conceptually, the Infected seek the opportunity to claim the unknown prey for themselves. As a result, when an Infected is alerted and starts chasing the player, it may pick up others along the way, but as the player expects, the alerted character will be the first to arrive.

33.4.4 *Ambush* Skill

The *ambush* skill is a combat skill used by Stalkers that replaces the *chase* skill used by all of the other Infected types. It was created late in the development of the game while experimenting with different character types. The character types we had were solid but we wanted more variety. We experimented with a light-sensitive character that the player could hold at bay with a flashlight. This showed promise but when the characters reacted quickly, they didn't feel dangerous, and when they reacted more slowly, the flashlight didn't feel effective. After a few iterations, we decided to take advantage of the dark in a different way. The idea was to have the character move from cover to cover, providing only glimpses to the player in dark environments. They would lay in wait until the player wandered too close, then attack and run back into cover. This simple concept proved very effective at heightening the sense of horror. In encounters with Stalkers, the player naturally became more defensive and approached each corner with caution. Keeping the Infected out of sight also served to hide the number of characters in the encounter, which made tracking down the last Stalker as tense as the first.

Ambush is the only Infected-specific skill that uses cover. Cover locations are selected using a system that evaluates points in the environment based on how suitable they are to ambush the player or to retreat after an attack. This system is shared with the Hunters and will be described in more detail in the chapter describing their AI.

33.4.5 *Throw* Skill

The Bloater is the only Infected character with a projectile attack. The fungus has swollen its body into a misshapen mass of armored plates and bulbous fungal growths. The Bloater rips these growths from various armored plates and throws them ahead of the moving player to produce a cloud of particles that briefly slow movement. The armor plates spawning these growths can be destroyed, and the *throw* skill plays animations that select from other plates until they are all destroyed and the Bloater dies. Until then, there is no limit to the number of growths a Bloater can throw, which prevents it from becoming less challenging as the encounter progresses.

33.4.6 *On-Fire* Skill

It may be odd to consider reacting to being engulfed in flame as an AI skill because, unlike other skills, it doesn't show intent and isn't a conscious decision. However, the goal here is not so much to show the intent of the character as it is to allow it to react to its situation and to make it more believable and entertaining.

The *on-fire* skill works by invoking the *infected-canvass* behavior briefly in a small area, with a custom set of animations. This causes the character to flail and dart around chaotically in an arbitrary environment without running into walls. It also provides emergent variation in the reaction because it combines several smaller reactions for the full effect. This is a great example of a case where we were able to reuse the same behavior with different contents (in this case, different animations) in order to achieve a very different, customized, and compelling result.

33.4.7 *Wander* Skill

The *wander* skill is the lowest priority skill for all of the Infected character types. It is the fallback that is used when nothing else is valid to run. When the Infected are not agitated, they will move throughout the environment either randomly or in predictable patterns. The challenge was to do this in such a way that the player is forced to make tactical decisions about when to move, distract, or attack.

Designers can specify whether the character wanders on a fixed route or randomly. Fixed routes require laying out a spline in the level editor and specifying environmental interactions at various points. These can be as simple as pausing and looking around or as complex as triggering a brief behavior (such as scavenging through debris) before returning to moving along the spline. Random wandering selects a random polygon on the navigation mesh as a destination. As the character moves, it keeps track of the polygons it visits. On arrival, it randomly selects a polygon that hasn't been visited and continues to wander. This has the effect of covering a large area in an unpredictable way.

Both types of wandering have their uses. A fixed route is predictable, which makes it useful for crafting stealth encounters where the player is encouraged to deduce the pattern and avoid it. Random movement is useful for covering a large area in unpredictable ways, offering the player a different challenge. In practice, fixed routes are used for the initial setup of an encounter, and random movement is used after leaving combat when the character may be far away from the original route.

33.4.8 *Sleep* Skill

Designers can configure the Infected to sleep when idle instead of using the *wander* skill. This is an idle state that greatly reduces the sensitivity of the senses, giving the player the opportunity to avoid, distract, or dispatch the character more easily. This skill was also useful for creating sentries at choke points throughout the game, since sleeping Infected stay where they are placed.

Sleeping characters react to disturbances in several ways. If the player moves too quickly or too near a sleeping Infected, it will stir briefly before settling back into slumber. This is feedback to inform the player that they should exercise more caution. If the player makes a loud noise from a great enough distance, the Infected will wake up and use the *infected-canvass* behavior to move about a small area searching for the disturbance before going back to sleep. If the player continues to disturb the character or is sufficiently loud, it will wake enraged and *chase* the disturbance. When the chase ends the Infected will wander through the environment instead of going back to sleep.

33.5 Conclusion

The Infected are a compelling part of a complex world. They are the result of design, art, sound, animation, and programming coming together to make characters that fit seamlessly into the environment, making the world more believable. They are entertaining characters and are worthy opponents that command respect but can be overcome with skill.

The capabilities provided by the behaviors allow the skills to focus on high-level decisions. This simplified the development process and enabled new ideas to be rapidly explored in order to refine the Infected into engaging opponents. Keeping the code simple and modular made it more maintainable and stable. This made it easier to isolate glitches that made the characters look stupid. Eliminating these problems went a long way toward making the Infected look smart.

Skills and behaviors are a small part of a complex AI character, but they provide the decision making needed to make the character respond convincingly to the player. Keeping it simple was the key. Using tuning values that were independent of the type of character allowed all of the Infected to share the same skills and behaviors but respond in ways that were unique and interesting.

References

[Stark 13] Stark, C. 2013. The creepy, real science behind "The Last of Us." http://mashable.com/2013/07/26/the-last-of-us/ (accessed September 10, 2014).

[Straatman 06] Straatman, R., A. Beij, and W. van der Sterren. 2006. Dynamic tactical position evaluation. In *AI Programming Wisdom 3*, ed. S. Rabin, pp. 389–403. Boston, MA: Charles River Media.

34

Human Enemy AI in *The Last of Us*

Travis McIntosh

34.1 Introduction

In the previous chapter, we discussed the overall design philosophy and the AI techniques behind the Infected. In this chapter, we will discuss a question that relates to the human opponents in *The Last of Us*. When we started prototyping the human enemy AI, we began with this question: *How do we make the player believe that their enemies are real enough that they feel bad about killing them?* Answering that one question drove the entire design of the enemy AI.

Answering that question required more than just hiring the best voice actors, the best modelers, and the best animators, although it *did* require all of those things. It also required solving an AI problem. Because if we couldn't make the player believe that these roving bands of survivors were thinking and acting together like real people, then no amount of perfectly presented mocap was going to prevent the player from being pulled out of the game whenever an NPC took cover on the wrong side of a doorway or walked in front of his friend's line of fire.

To begin with, our enemies had to be dangerous. If they acted like cannon fodder, the player would treat them like cannon fodder, so the player had to feel like each and every human they encountered was a threat. They also needed to coordinate, or at least to appear to coordinate. A roving band of survivors needs to work together to survive, just as Joel and Ellie must work together, and without some sort of coordination, they would appear subhuman. They also needed to care about their own safety. These were not suicide bombers. They were survivors. They should be as careful with their own lives as the player would be with theirs.

They needed to make good choices about where to go and when to go there, and more than that, they needed to be intelligent about *how* to get there. When they lost the player, they needed to communicate that fact to each other in a way that would be obvious to the player, and when their friends died, they needed to notice.

The design of *The Last of Us* also called for completely dynamic gameplay. Rarely were we guaranteed the location of the player when combat began, and at any point, the player could force the NPCs into a brand new setup from a different location. This meant that little of the NPC behavior could be scripted by hand. Instead, the NPCs had to be able to understand and analyze the play space, then adapt to the actions of the player.

Putting these concepts together with a number of visual and audio bells and whistles produced human enemies that could be enjoyable to play and just believable enough that, sometimes, every now and again, the player cared about who they were killing.

34.2 Building Blocks

Every AI system builds upon several key low-level systems. *The Last of Us* uses triangulated navmeshes, which are a fairly straightforward approach to navigation. The navmeshes are fairly coarse, and so we have a second-pass system that uses a 2D grid centered around every character on which are rasterized all static and dynamic blockers. This allows for short but very good paths, while the high-level system allows us to plan our overall route between distant points.

Pathfinding on navigation meshes is fast, especially utilizing the PS3's SPUs. We did between 20 and 40 pathfinds every frame utilizing approximately 4 ms of SPU time. Pathfinding through navigation maps (a fixed sized grid that surrounded each NPC for detailed path analysis), by contrast, was expensive enough that we limited the game to one per frame, with each NPC needing to wait for their turn.

One system that was new to *The Last of Us* was the *exposure map*. Early in the project, we found that in order for the AI to make good decisions about which path to take, we needed information about what the player could see and what he couldn't see. Exposure maps were our representation of this information.

We initially implemented visibility checks by casting rays toward the player from a number of different points on the NPC's current path and then using that information to decide whether the path was a good one or not. Unfortunately, this didn't work very well. Not only was it slow, but it didn't allow us to choose different paths based on the visibility information, which is what we really wanted. We then came up with concept of an exposure map, as shown in Figure 34.1. An exposure map is simply a 2D bitmap overlaid on the navigation mesh. In the exposure map, a one indicates visibility and a zero indicates occlusion.

In order to make calculating the exposure map fast, we embedded a simple height map inside of every navigation mesh. The height map used an 8-bit integer to represent the height of the world at every point on every navigation mesh. On the SPUs, we could then do very simple raycast out from the origin point in a 360° circle. Because we were working only in integer space and on the SPUs, we could parallelize this fairly easily. We then allowed the job to take multiple frames to complete. The end result is that we could continually calculate

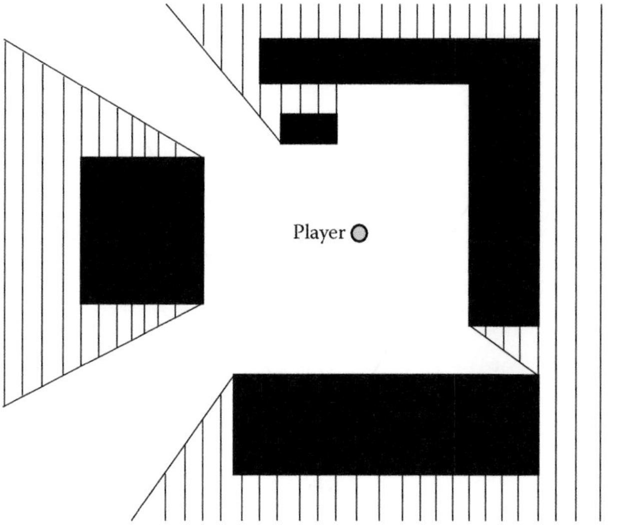

Figure 34.1

The exposure map covers everything an entity can see.

an exposure map for what the player could see, as well as an exposure map that showed everything any NPC could see as a simple bitmap using around 2–3 ms of SPU time.

Because the exposure map was, in fact, a bitmap, we often used it as a cost in our navigation function. The cost of traveling from one node to another was increased by integrating across this bitmap and multiplying by a scale factor. So, for example, we could use our standard pathfinding algorithm to find the best route from an NPC to the player, or we could add the exposure map as an additional cost and the path would minimize the NPC's exposure to the player's line of sight. Our first implementation of flanking was done using this exact algorithm, and it produced surprisingly good results in the static case.

34.3 AI Perception

One of the fundaments of AI in any game, especially a game focused on stealth, is AI perception. In the *Uncharted* series, AI used a few simple systems to determine their awareness of the world.

First, their sight we determined by a simple frustum and raycasts to check for occlusion. At the start of *The Last of Us*, we used this same system, as shown in Figure 34.2.

Problems arose in playtesting, however. Often, players right next to the NPC would be unseen, while NPCs too far away were noticed, simply because the cone we used for testing was not adequate to represent real vision. The fundamental issue was that, when close, we needed a larger angle of view, but at a distance we needed a smaller one. Using a simple rule—the angle of view for an NPC is inversely proportional to distance—we reinvented our view frustum to be much more effective, as shown in Figure 34.3.

Just because the player could be seen on one frame did not mean the NPCs had instant awareness of him. When an NPC saw the player, he would start a timer. Each frame the

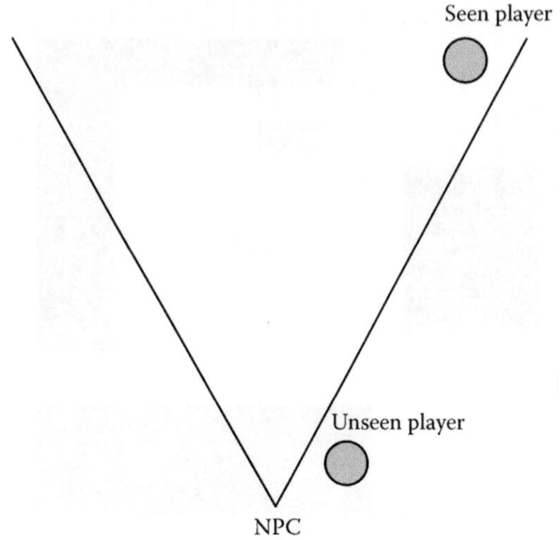

Figure 34.2

The simplest form of perception testing for NPCs had issues.

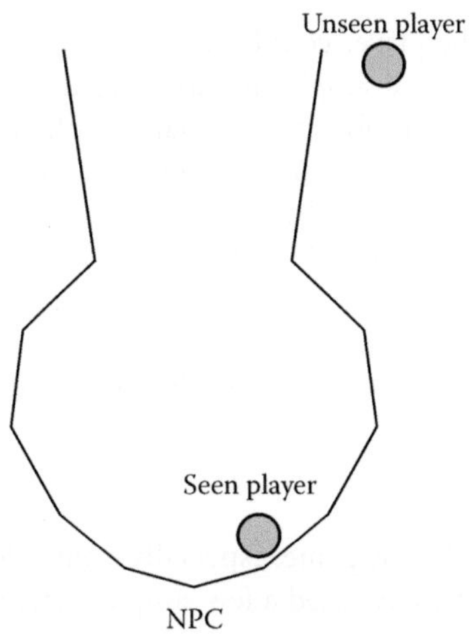

Figure 34.3

This more complex form of vision cone produced better results.

player was seen, the timer was incremented. Each frame the player was unseen, the timer was decremented. The player did not count as perceived until the timer reached a specified value (around 1 or 2 seconds for the typical NPC). When in combat, this threshold was much lower, and when the NPC had yet to perceive the player in its lifetime (i.e., the player is in stealth), this threshold was much higher.

We tried a number of different approaches to casting rays to check for occlusion. Our initial implementation involved rays to nearly every joint on Joel's body. Each joint was weighted, and the weighted average was compared against a threshold (typically 60%). If the sum was higher, then the player is counted as visible.

This produced mixed results. Although it was a decent approximation of when Joel was visible and eliminated the edge cases of being seen when just your head or finger was visible, players found it difficult to anticipate whether a given cover point was safe or not, because of the complexity of the casts.

After some experimentation, we found that we could use a single point on Joel's body instead. The location of that point would vary depending on whether we were in combat or stealth, as shown in Figure 34.4. If the player was in stealth, then the point is located in the center of the player's chest. If the player has engaged an NPC in combat, the point moved to the top of the player's head. This allows for player favoring perception in stealth while maintaining good visibility in combat.

Of note, the NPCs did not cheat with regard to knowing the player's location in most circumstances. When the player was perceived, the NPC would create an entity object with location and time stamp and then signal all other NPCs with the player's new location. If the player was not perceived by any NPCs, his location was never updated, instead remained in the previous location.

The combat cycle of *The Last of Us* was then as follows: The player showed himself, either visibly or by shooting his gun. The NPCs would surround him as best as they could and then began to advance on his position. If they had advanced as close as they could and they hadn't seen the player in a long enough period (10 s or more), a single NPC was chosen to approach the player's position to see if he was still there. If he was not, the NPCs then transitioned into the search behavior.

In our original focus tests, this combat cycle took far too long—nearly 2 min on average. Quite often, the player would have moved on long ago and would feel like the NPCs were not responsive. Our solution to this problem was to cheat. If the player moved further than 5 m from where the NPCs thought he was, he was considered to have snuck away, and we forced an NPC to approach his position immediately, so that they could enter search more quickly. This reduced the combat cycle to about 30 s and worked very well for pacing purposes.

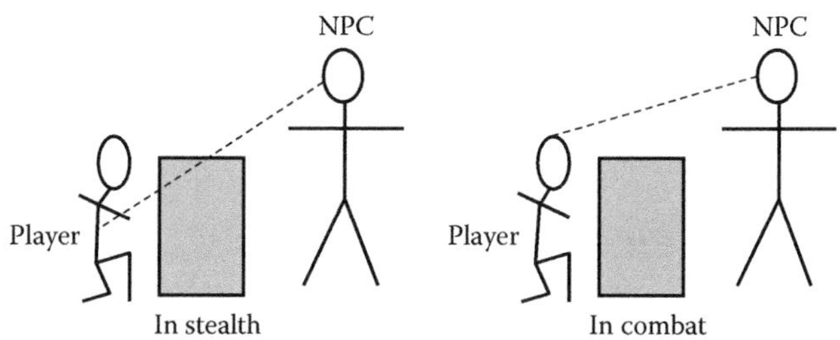

Figure 34.4

The left image shows that in stealth, the raycast point is placed on the player's chest, in order to favor the player. The right image shows that once combat has been initiated, the raycast point is placed much higher onto the top of the head.

34.4 Cover and Posts

Where to stand/take cover is one of the most fundamental decisions AIs need to make, and it is also one of the hardest. In order to properly rate and evaluate the best cover and open locations, you first need to gather a set of potential locations. We called these *posts.*

We had two distinct types of posts. The firsts were cover posts. These were gathered for each NPC in a radius around the NPC's location. Candidates were any cover spot facing away from the threat (all possible cover spots were precalculated by a tool analyzing the collision mesh). After we gathered the closest 20 cover spots for each NPC, we submitted them as a single job. Each frame, we would cast up to 160 rays to these different spots, each cover spot requiring 4 rays to determine whether the NPC could shoot and hit their target. When all of the rays for a given set of cover were complete, those covers where every ray was blocked were rejected, as shown in Figure 34.5.

We called the second type of post as an open post. Open posts were points in the world around the player. Primarily, these were used to find a good location for the NPCs to check the player's last known location when they were sent forward to begin a search. We again cast rays from these locations to the last known player position and rejected any whose raycast failed. In addition, we did a pathfind, limited to 20 per frame, from every NPC to every viable post for use in our post selectors.

Once we had a valid set of posts, we could then do analysis to select the location the NPC should use. Since every NPC behavior is significantly different, this used different criteria depending on what the NPC was doing at the time. We called these *post selectors.* Post selectors were defined in our LISP-based scripting language, with an example shown in Listing 34.1. We had 17 different post selectors when we shipped *The Last of Us.*

Each post selector defined what type of post it was interested in (in this case, cover and a number of different criteria). The criteria were different for each different selector and could easily be iterated on at runtime by reloading the script.

Of particular interest is the criterion **ai-criterion-static-pathfind-not-near-player**. Many times, during focus tests, players would complain that NPCs would rush forward to take cover. With some debugging, we determined that the issue was that a particular cover

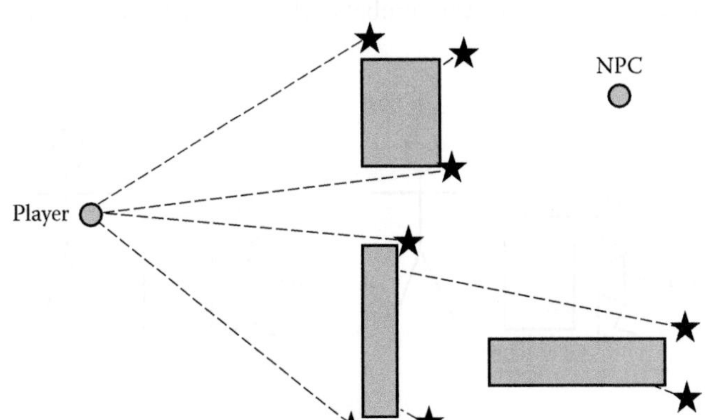

Figure 34.5

Any cover post whose raycast is blocked is rejected.

Listing 34.1. This script defines a post selector which locates a good place to hide.

```
(panic
  :post-type (ai-post-type cover)
  :criteria (ai-criteria
             (ai-criterion-path-valid)
             (ai-criterion-within-close-in-dist)
             (ai-criterion-available)
             (ai-criterion-static-pathfind-not-near-player)
             (ai-criterion-not-behind-the-player)
             (ai-criterion-distance
                :curve (new-ai-point-curve
                         ([distance 3.0] [value 0.0])
                         ([distance 5.0] [value 1.0])
                       )
             )
           )
)
```

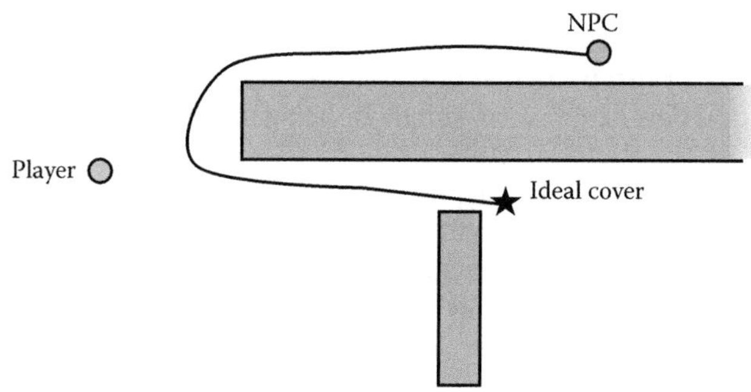

Figure 34.6

Sometimes the best cover could not be determined without a path. If the path to the cover required running toward the player for too long, as in this example, then the cover would be rejected.

was the best cover choice, but in order to pathfind there, the NPC would need to move toward the player, so that they could then move away again, as shown in Figure 34.6.

The solution was to write a criterion that used the pathfind information we had for every NPC to every viable cover. These paths were calculated in a round robin fashion and took about a 1/2 s to refresh, gathered at the same time as the cover-to-player raycasts. We would then analyze the path the NPC would take to each cover point, and if that path involved running toward the player for an extended period, then we would reject that cover.

There were, in fact, two major systems operating in parallel. The first system gathered pathfinding information, raycasts, etc. The second simply processed these data using the post selectors. Since the source data were all gathered on previous frames, these post selectors could be evaluated for very low cost on the SPUs. Each criterion would produce a float value normalized between zero and one; all of the criteria for a given post selector and a

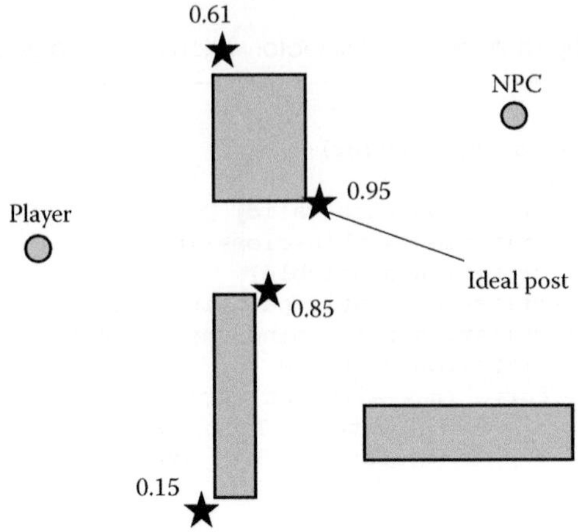

Figure 34.7

Every post is rated and the one with the highest number wins.

given post would then be multiplied together, and the resulting value would be that particular post's rating for that particular post selector. Next, all the posts would be sorted by rating, and the ideal post determined, simply by being the post with the highest rating, as shown in Figure 34.7.

Ratings would be different for each post per post selector and unique NPC. A post that was rejected for *panic* might be the ideal for *advance*. Note that all of the criteria for all of the posts and post selectors were evaluated continuously, so there was no delay when the NPC switched states—the ideal post for any given post selector was always available.

34.5 Skills, States, and Behaviors

The NPC's top-level states, which we called *skills*, were part of an FSM. Skills were prioritized, and each skill queried every frame whether it wished to run. The skill with the highest priority won. Examples of skills include *panic*, *advance*, *melee*, *gun combat*, *hide*, *investigate*, *scripted*, and *flank*.

Each skill included its own state machine. So, for example, *gun combat* could be in the *advance* or the *back away* state. Note that these were high-level states and didn't typically directly interface with the animation or pathfinding systems. Instead, a separate object known as a *behavior* would be pushed onto a behavior stack. Behaviors were on much lower level and were much simpler than the top-level states. Examples include MoveToLocation, StandAndShoot, and TakeCover.

34.6 Stealth

Stealth was handled by two separate skills. The *investigate* skill understood how to respond to a distraction sound and had a custom post selector. If the NPCs were in their standard scripted states—fully controlled by designer-created scripts that would tell them where to move, when to move, and even what audio dialog to play—then when an audio gameplay

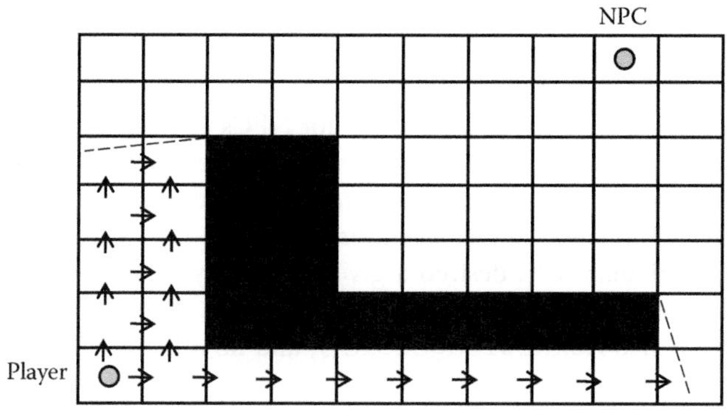

Figure 34.8

Search map locations spread out until within an NPC's line of sight.

event signaled a distraction, NPCs would request the role of an Investigator. Whichever NPC got that role would then walk to the ideal post as specific by the custom post selector and play an animation. If they found nothing, they would return to their previous location and pick up their script where it left off.

This was the case if the player had not been located yet. If the NPCs were already aware of the player, they entered the *search* state. *Search* involved procedurally partitioning the map and sending the NPCs to search it. Where to search was solved by the *search map*. The search map was a series of grid cells. If the player's location was known, all cells would be empty except the player's current location. Once the player's location was lost, however, the active cells would then bleed into their neighbors over time, and the potential location of the player would spread out to cover the map, as shown in Figure 34.8. Using the exposure map, any cells currently visible to an NPC would be cleared each frame. The result was a grid of cells that represented, roughly, the potential locations of the player from the NPC's perspective, who could then search in a relatively intelligent fashion.

34.7 Lethality

Games can create threatening enemies in a few ways. Enemies can take a lot of damage—in *The Last of Us* this broke immersion since you were supposed to be fighting humans. The number of enemies could be high—this directly contradicts our goal of making the player care about each and every kill. The enemies could deal a lot of damage—a possibility. The enemies could be very good at being hard to hit—another possibility.

We began by focusing on a concept we called *lethality*. Lethality meant that if a single enemy could kill the player, then every shot was frightening. One of the simplest and most successful things we did was make every shot the player received play a full body hit reaction. This meant that getting shot would not only deal significant damage but also take away control while the animation played out. In fact, it was the loss of control that most affected players. Those few moments of helplessness meant that every shot became a punctuation mark, a pause in the flow of the action that didn't let them forget their mistake.

Another way we made enemies lethal was by making sure to provide a threat whenever possible. This meant whenever an NPC had the ability to shoot the player, they would always choose to do that. With that said, it was only necessary for one NPC to be shooting the player at any given time; all other NPCs could spend their time taking cover, flanking, etc.

What this meant was that we needed a way for NPCs to coordinate with one another. We created a system we called the *Combat Coordinator.* The Combat Coordinator was simply a global object that managed each NPC's role. The roles include *Flanker, Approacher, Investigator, StayUpAndAimer,* and *OpportunisticShooter.*

Whenever a particular NPC desired a given role, they called the `RequestRole()` function on the Combat Coordinator. If that role was available, the function returned success, the NPC called `AcknowledgeRole()`, and no other NPC could take that role until they released it.

The purpose of the *OpportunisticShooter* role was to make sure there was at least one NPC focusing on shooting the player at any given time. If any NPC was able to see and shoot the player from their current location, they requested this role. Once they had the role, they instantly began shooting the player. This greatly increased the lethality of the NPCs. Note that when an NPC had this role, they would instantly stop whatever they were doing—even mid animation—and blend to standing and shooting at the player. In earlier playtests, they were noticeably slow in transitioning to shooting, with the result that oftentimes the player would be almost completely untouched when rushing.

34.8 Flanking

The role of the Combat Coordinator was not simply to be a gatekeeper to a few conceptual roles. In some cases, the coordinator would only allow a single, ideal NPC to take a given role. The best example of this is the *Flanker* role. Each NPC would run a pathfind in every frame to determine their best flank route. Each flank route would then be rated based on cost, and the coordinator would choose an ideal *Flanker* for the frame. If any NPC requested to flank the player but wasn't the ideal *Flanker,* their request would be rejected. Sometimes, as in the case of the *OpportunisticShooter,* we simply wished for the role to be taken as quickly as possible, so we would simply assign the role on a first come, first serve basis.

Although we originally used the exposure map to determine flanking, in practice this produced a number of issues. Because the exposure map changed as the player moved, often the flank routes could vary wildly from one frame to the next, and a corridor the algorithm identified as unexposed last frame could become exposed very quickly if the player was just around the corner.

The solution was to use a cost function based on the current *combat vector.* The combat vector was simply the current direction of combat from the player's perspective, calculated by averaging the NPC positions weighted by any shots that had been fired recently. Given the current combat vector, the cost function for flanking a given NPC was a fixed shape in the direction of that vector, as shown in Figure 34.9.

The closer to the center line (the line directly in the path of the combat vector), the higher the cost for pathfinding. The result of using this cost function was that flanking paths immediately attempted to move a large distance to the side and come around from behind, which was precisely what the player expected. In addition, the obstacles in the way were immaterial to how the cost function was created, and we instead let the pathfinding handle finding the path.

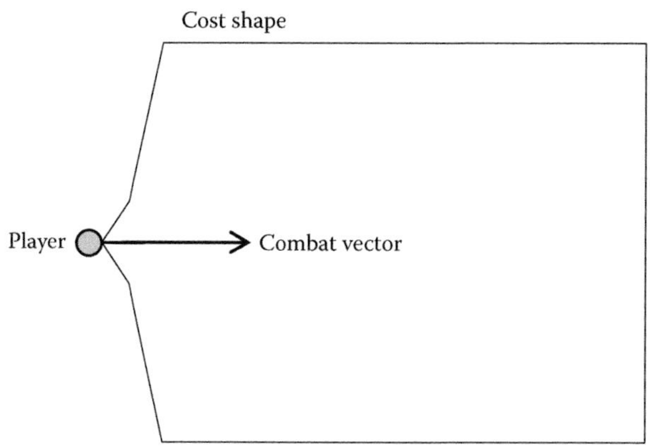

Figure 34.9

The combat shape rotates with the direction of the combat vector.

34.9 Polish

Once the AI decision making was in place, dialog could be layered in, animations could be polished, and setups could be scripted. Dialog in particular allowed the AI to communicate the decisions they make to the player, so that the NPCs could appear to be as intelligent as they sometimes were.

Then came focus testing, and more focus testing. Indeed, half of our implementation decisions were made in response to videos of players playing the game. In general, spatial analysis of the play space was perhaps the biggest win for us in terms of improving the AI's decision making. Combining that with the Combat Coordinator produced NPCs that made coordinated, informed decisions in a dynamic play space and appeared to be working together as a group.

34.10 Conclusion

In the end, we achieved our goal. The enemies had personality and had some sort of life, and most importantly, killing the enemies in *The Last of Us* was hard—not in the sense of difficulty but in a more emotional, more visceral sense. Because every enemy was a threat, every enemy felt more real and more alive, and because they felt alive, the player was able to build a small connection with them. The violence in *The Last of Us* was disturbing, not merely because of its graphic nature but because the player cared about the people they were attacking. The NPCs worked together, like real people. The NPCs fled and hid when threatened, like real people. The NPCs made good choices about where to go and how to get there, and most of the time they didn't destroy the illusion the player had immersed themselves in.

What we ended up with was not perfect by any means, but it answered the question of whether players cared about the people they were killing. They did.

35

Ellie: Buddy AI in *The Last of Us*

Max Dyckhoff

35.1 Introduction

In the last couple of chapters, you have read about the hunter and infected AI from Naughty Dog's third-person action adventure game *The Last of Us*. This chapter moves on to discuss the buddy AI.

The whole game focuses on relationships between characters and none more strongly than that of Ellie and Joel, the player's avatar. Ellie accompanies the player throughout most of the game, and we needed the player to love her companionship. We were acutely aware of the common pitfalls with AI companions: the risk of them turning into a tedious "escort" quest, generally getting underfoot, or turning into mindless drones with no agency in the world. We had to make sure that Ellie never annoyed or frustrated the player and that she remained a compelling entity throughout the game. Most importantly, we had to build a character that the player cared for.

Ellie is new to the world outside the military safe zone in which she grew up and new to the brutality and violence of the infected and humanity at large. She is seeing landscapes, cities, and actions as the player would, instead of through the world weary eyes of Joel. She is a young and fragile character in a dangerous world, and we wanted the AI to highlight this as well as support her growth and strength later in the game.

35.2 Starting from Scratch

The first decision we had to make was to start from scratch with just a few months of development remaining. Five months before we shipped, we had to present a press demo of the game, a combat encounter through a tight environment with a dozen or so infected. We wanted it to showcase how tense it would be fighting the infected and how having buddies with you would both aid you and increase the emotional impact of an encounter.

At that time, the two buddies in the encounter, Tess and Ellie, exhibited all the negative traits of buddy AI that we were trying to avoid: positioning themselves awkwardly, shooting at the wrong time, and generally getting underfoot. To avoid this, they had to be scripted for the entire duration, explained away using the video game trope of "staying back." Doing this completely removed them from the encounter and the player's attention; it was clear this was an unacceptable approach.

35.2.1 The Plan

The first thing we decided on was to keep buddies really close to the player. If a buddy is close to the player character, she is less likely to run into problems with enemy AI. Additionally, if she is far away from the player, she is easily forgotten, and the player will feel alone in the world, which is contrary to our storytelling goals for the game.

Once she reliably stayed close to the player, we started to give her utility in the form of both noncombat and combat behaviors. With these in place, she no longer felt like an escort quest. If she helps the player out of a tight situation, then the player feels thankful, grows to appreciate her presence, and has an improved opinion of the game in general.

Finally, we added touches to make her an interesting character, with a progression of combat vocalizations, a library of ambient animations for her to play, and a suite of noncombat conversation tracks. These systems are driven by the content creators, and with minimal effort, a character can become much more engaging.

35.2.2 Approach

One extremely important aspect of the development was how we thought about Ellie and the other buddies. We always treated her as an actual human being and spent time trying to get into her head, reasoning what she would do in a given situation and why. We tried to avoid the "gamification" of her AI as much as possible, restricting ourselves from cheating or doing things that would seem inhuman. We grew to genuinely care for Ellie and her well-being.

The decision to avoid cheating was extremely important. It's easy to cut corners by cheating, but even if the player never notices, it still moves you away from creating a living, breathing character, which was completely at odds with our goals for Ellie. There were exceptions, but we stuck to this policy as much as we possibly could.

35.3 Ambient Following

There are a lot of reasons for keeping a buddy character close to the player. Primarily, if she is sharing the same space as and behaving similarly to the player, then her actions can by definition be no more stupid than what the player is doing. If she has positioned herself correctly and is still seen by an enemy, then the player will have been seen too and consequently will attribute the failure to themselves rather than the buddy.

Additionally, a buddy that is close to the player has increased opportunity to trigger relevant dialogue. This dialogue can both serve as character exposition and provide gameplay utility. For example, rather than having the buddy run out from hiding next to the player when she is about to be seen by an enemy, she can vocalize the threat and allow the player to handle it. We can also vocalize exclamations of surprise or good fortune, augmenting the tension and reward of an encounter.

In the context of *The Last of Us*, when the player is separated from Ellie and no longer has her vocalizations of danger to rely on, the encounter becomes increasingly tense, and consequently, the relationship with the buddy is strengthened.

35.3.1 Follow Positions

To enable a buddy character to follow the player, or another character, we created a follow system that generated and evaluated positions near the leading character, and then moved the buddy there elegantly. The core of this was a follow region, a torus around the leader described by a set of parameters provided in data.

A number of candidate follow positions were generated inside this follow region and then evaluated for quality. The generation of the candidate follow positions was done by casting three sets of navmesh rays, as shown in Figure 35.1.

A first set of rays fan out from the leader position to the follow region in order to make sure that there is a clear line of movement from the buddy to the player. One candidate follow position is generated for each ray that reaches the follow region; see Figure 35.1a.

A second set of rays are then cast forward from each candidate position to make sure the position isn't facing a wall (Figure 35.1b). We tried allowing positions that would be close to a wall and just had the character face away from the wall, but in practice, a buddy moving right next to a wall feels unnatural.

Finally, rays are cast from the player's location to each "forward" location, to ensure that movement forward from this location wouldn't put an obstacle between the player and the buddy (Figure 35.1c). This ray may seem unnecessary, but in testing, we found that

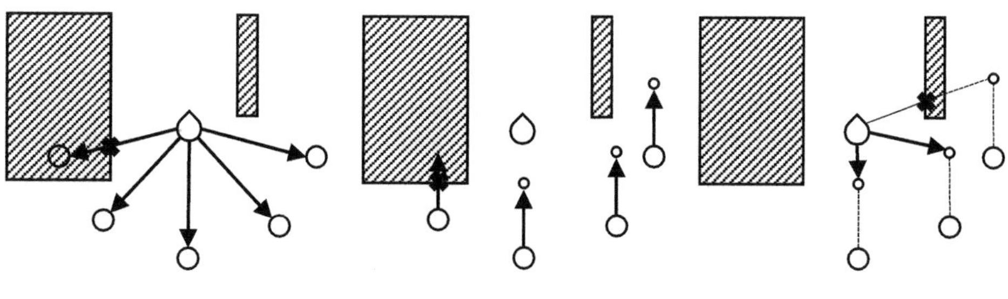

Figure 35.1

The generation of follow positions by casting a set of pathfinding raycasts. (a) Cast rays to generate candidate positions. (b) Cast rays to check forward direction. (c) Cast rays to check future position.

without it, Ellie would choose to stand on the other side of a doorway or fence. Adding this ray gave her a desire to stand in the same "room" as the player.

The resulting follow positions are then rated every frame, and an optimal position is chosen for the buddy to move to. These ratings are based on a number of criteria including

- Distance to the leader
- Staying on the same side of the leader
- Visibility of potential targets (either hiding or exposing)
- Not being in front of the player
- Distance to other buddies

35.3.2 Moving

Once we had chosen a position to move the buddy toward, we had to make sure she would perform the movement in a believable manner. We would watch her follow the player around a space, and if we saw a movement that seemed unnecessary or unnatural, we would pause the game and start investigating the cause.

From this, a lot of filters were added to the movement to make it appear more intelligent. First, we limited short-distance moves, only allowing them if they were absolutely necessary, for example, if her current location was exposed by an enemy. Then we prevented her from running past the leader character if possible, unless not doing so meant stopping in an undesirable location. It appeared very forced if she picked a follow position on the opposite side of the player and mechanically ran past the player. Allowing her to get "close enough" to her follow position, and not crowd the player, gave her follow behavior a very organic feel rather than the rigid behavior she had before.

Of course most of the time we are not generating follow positions around a stationary leader, as the player will be moving around the environment too. As the player moves, both the follow region and the generated follow positions move too. We regenerate follow positions each frame, but we include criteria in the position ratings to try and smooth out any noise.

In an ambient environment where the player is casually exploring a place, Ellie is allowed to saunter after the player without much urgency, while during combat, we like to keep her very close to the player. This meant creating a mapping from the desired movement distance to the buddy's movement speed to allow us to specify how urgently the buddy should move to her follow position. For short distances, a walk is sufficient; for extremely long distances, she must sprint; and in between, she may run.

Each movement mode (walk, run, and sprint) had a single fixed speed, which varied across buddies and was different from the player's movement speed. This meant that when following the player, she would approach some ideal distance from him and then oscillate between running and walking, which was clearly unnatural. To prevent this, we allowed the buddy to scale her movement animation speeds by as much as 25%, allowing her to stay in a given movement mode for longer. As she neared the threshold to start walking, she would scale back the speed of her run.

35.3.3 Dodging

We made the decision to have buddies not explicitly move out of the way of the player if they were there first. If the player and a buddy character are both stationary, we find that the player is not typically inclined to run straight at her, just as you would not run straight at a real-life friend standing near you. Instead of preemptively making her move, we assume the player is going to try and go around her and only at the last second make her play a canned animation dodging out of the way (along with a vocalization admonishing the player for encroaching on her personal space). This approach to dodging took what can frequently be a really frustrating and unrealistic behavior and turned it into a character element, making the player subconsciously respect Ellie and her choices.

35.3.4 Teleportation

One popular method to keep buddy characters near a player is teleportation, which can be effective but has a number of downsides. We decided very early on to never teleport the buddies for the purpose of keeping them near the player.

There were a number of reasons for this. The audio department didn't want the buddy's footsteps to suddenly appear closer to the player. We also didn't want to have situations where you know that Ellie is on one side of you and then suddenly she's on the other with no explanation for how she got there. You can write robust checks against this sort of issue, but if the player gets even a hint that teleportation is happening, it feels a little strange and can break the suspension of disbelief. We also just wanted to avoid it on principle, believing that if we aimed to make Ellie keep up with the player in all situations, then the end result would be more robust and believable. When we avoid cheating, we are forced to address the situations where we might cheat in a realistic way, and this creates small details in the character's behavior that make Ellie feel like a living, breathing character who is grounded in the world in which you are both participating.

Ultimately, the only time a buddy will teleport is when they need to immediately aid the player with a melee struggle, which is discussed later. We also considered allowing teleportation to bring Ellie closer to the player in cases where she was sufficiently far away, but in practice, this was rarely necessary.

35.4 Taking Cover

The follow system described earlier was largely used for ambient (i.e., noncombat) situations. Combat following, and particularly cover selection, requires something slightly different.

The Last of Us is a cover-based third-person game, so it was necessary to have the buddy characters take cover with the player efficiently. Our tools create "cover action packs" that represent places an AI character can take cover against a wall or similar obstacle, but ultimately this representation was too coarse for our needs. While enemy NPCs only require sparse information about where they can take cover, the player can take cover anywhere in the world. If we were going to keep the buddy characters nearby, then they needed to have the same ability.

35.4.1 Runtime Cover Generation

We used a hybrid approach to generate runtime cover, combining the system used by the NPCs with the dynamic system used by the player. We already have "cover edge" features generated by our tools, which are used to create the cover action packs that the enemy AI uses. These simply represent the intersection of a wall and floor collision plane, with a markup to indicate height and cornering.

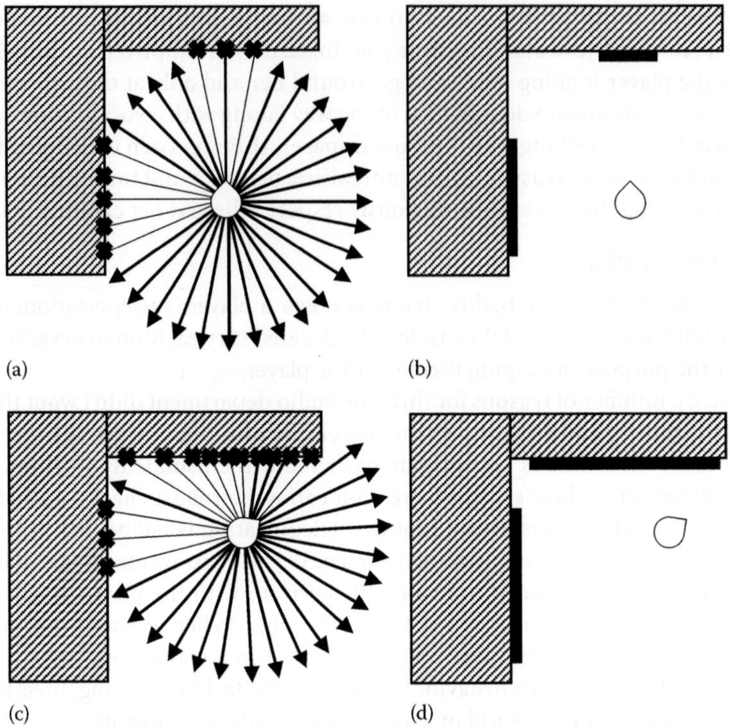

Figure 35.2

Generation of procedural cover edge features using collision raycasts. (a) Fire rays to find nearby collision. (b) Combine similar collision points to form cover edge features. (c) Fire rays again, when the leader moves. (d) Combine collision points with previous cover edge features to create larger edges.

To generate the runtime cover, first, we scan the environment around us and look for nearby cover edge features. We then augment this with a set of procedurally generated cover edge features. We cast a fan of raycasts from the leader's position against the collision geometry (see Figure 35.2a), compare the normal of the collision plane and location of each hit point, and then combine nearby points with a similar normal into procedural cover edge features (Figure 35.2b).

These two sets of cover edge features, one static and one procedural, are then combined and cached for future use. As the leader character moves, we perform the same tests (Figure 35.2c, d) and combine the results with the previous results. We only evict cover edge features from this cache when we start running out of storage. This combined set of cover edge features benefits from both the information derived by the tools and the runtime features, creating a more accurate set than either method alone. Unfortunately, the process was very computationally expensive, so doing it for all characters was unfeasible, and we had restrict it to just the buddy NPCs.

This set of cover edges is then rated to choose an ideal edge on which the buddy character should take cover. A large amount of time went into generating and tweaking the set of rating functions for cover edges, the most important being

- Visibility to enemies, a dot-product check
- Proximity to leader
- Predicted future visibility, derived by projecting enemy movement

35.4.2 Cover Share

Originally, the player was unable to share cover with a buddy; in fact, if the buddy saw the player approaching, she would pop out of cover, assuming that the player wanted to be in that location. This removed intentionality from the buddy's movement, much in the same way as dodging would, as discussed earlier. In order to solve this, we created an animation set in which Joel was able to enter cover on top of a buddy character, placing his hand on the wall next to her and shielding her with his body. The player was able to perform all the normal actions such as shooting or moving, and we didn't need to move the buddy at all.

One time, because of a bug, Ellie entered cover through Joel into this shared cover state. We realized it looked really believable, and with some small modifications to the animation set, we made it work all the time, allowing Ellie to take cover exactly where the player was.

We also added special dialogue lines, so the buddy character would comment on recent combat while sharing cover with the player. This cover share system really enhanced the bond with Ellie. It took our "stick close to the player" mantra to its logical conclusion, and it was virtually impossible as a player not to feel some compassion for Ellie when in cover share.

35.5 Combat Utility

Once we had the buddies following the player as robustly and smoothly as possible, it was time to move on to make them useful in combat. We always wanted Ellie and the other buddies to explicitly support the player rather than go off and do their own fighting. There were a number of ideals that drove our development of the buddy combat utility.

The game's difficulty was very carefully balanced, and we wanted to ensure the buddy performed consistently in a given encounter so that they wouldn't upset this balance. In particular, we didn't ever want a buddy to overpower an encounter and make the player feel useless. It was also important to make sure that the player saw the buddies doing things in combat. This is true of all AI characters but particularly so for buddies; they can be the most intelligent AI ever created, but if the player doesn't see what they are doing, then it is wasted effort.

There are also large sections of the game where Ellie is unarmed, but she still needs to interact in combat and support the player. This is where we started our development of combat behaviors.

35.5.1 Throwing

One of the most visceral combat actions Ellie performs is when she throws a brick at an approaching enemy. The logic to decide when to throw is very simple; we need to make sure that she isn't giving away the player's location but that she still throws the brick promptly enough to be effective. One of the primary triggers for the throw action is driven by hooking into the enemy perception and movement systems and predicting if they will be able to see the player in the near future.

These thrown objects stun the target for a few seconds, allowing the player to follow up in a number of ways: running away, melee attacking the enemy, grappling, etc. The throw action is put on a really long timer, to ensure it doesn't get overused. We always want it to be special and memorable when such an action occurs.

35.5.2 Grapples

Next, we added melee grapples, allowing an enemy to target and grab a buddy character. This was largely done through data by design, thanks to a verbose melee scripting system. We originally required the player to save Ellie every time she was grappled, but this quickly became tedious and clearly tipped us toward the "escort quest" design we were trying to avoid. Instead, we gave her a suite of animations allowing her to escape the grapple herself, after which she would reposition away from the temporarily stunned enemy, and we would disallow her from being targeted again for 15–30 s.

We kept the requirement for the player to save her in certain situations, but it was always done intentionally and infrequently. We would make sure she was visible and easily accessible to the player and that the player wasn't currently grappled himself. We wanted the player to want to protect Ellie, just not so often that it was irritating.

We also implemented the reverse situation; sometimes the player is grabbed by an enemy, and buddy characters are able to save you. People tend to feel really grateful if Ellie stabs a guy who has them in a headlock; this can take a desperate situation and turn the tables.

As mentioned earlier in this chapter, grapples are the only time we allow teleportation of a buddy. We decided that if the player is being grappled and we want Ellie to save them, then it's an acceptable time to teleport. During the grapple, the player has no camera control, so we can ensure it is facing in a direction that does not reveal the teleport.

35.5.3 Gifting

We already had one scripted sequence where one of the buddies, David, gave the player a box of ammo while fighting off infected at the start of the Winter chapter. Players reacted so well to this that we felt it should be something systematic that Ellie could do.

The game uses a complex drop system that works out what supplies should spawn in an area and what dead bodies should drop, and we just hooked straight into this to figure out what Ellie should give the player. We restricted it to ammo and health packs, meaning that the player would still need to scavenge for crafting items to apply as weapon upgrades. Because it was tied directly into the existing system, it didn't change the difficulty balancing that had already occurred, despite coming online very late in development.

We added another really long timer to her gifting, to prevent annoying the player. In the first playtest that we ran with gifting enabled, we noticed one player was stuck in a particular spot, and Ellie would give him ammo every minute. It not only highlighted that the level design needed some fixing, but it devalued the act of gifting. When properly tuned, it really helped to enhance the bond between her and the player; she would whisper and hand you something useful at exactly the right times.

35.6 Armed Combat

Having an extensive suite of unarmed combat behaviors, it was time to focus on making Ellie use a gun effectively and believably. For positioning, we used both the procedural cover edge features and the follow positions discussed earlier. Again we stuck with our mantra of staying near the player, and the settings for generation of follow positions were tuned to bring her closer to the player and allow her to move more responsively.

For the most part, we would try and mirror the player's decisions, crouching and taking cover or standing upright and out in the open in conjunction with the player's character. When in doubt, we would always prefer to select a cover location, as that was rarely a bad place to be.

Initially, we planned for the adult buddies like Tess and Bill to operate more independently in the environment, but in practice, it always felt like they were abandoning the player, and we didn't want that. Instead, they all behave like Ellie, although with more relaxed parameters for positioning and movement.

35.6.1 Shooting

The game heavily emphasizes stealth, so having a buddy give away your location is extremely infuriating and breaks all of the trust that the buddy has gained. Thus, knowing when (and when not) to shoot is absolutely key.

The first thing we did was reverse the logic for shooting; instead of being happy to shoot most of the time—like the enemy NPCs—Ellie wants to not shoot. This not only makes sense for AI reasons but also for real-world reasons; she is a young girl and hesitant to use a gun. We then built logic to give her permission to fire.

If the player is actively firing a weapon or engaging in noisy melee combat, then Ellie is allowed to fire upon her target. In addition, we model the intentions of enemy NPCs and allow her to fire if the player is in immediate danger. Finally, if the player was trying to sneak away from an encounter, we tried to recognize this by comparing the player's location with the enemy NPC's perception of where the player was. If these were significantly different, then we considered the player to be back in stealth, and shooting would no longer be allowed.

35.6.2 Balancing

After we enabled gun usage, suddenly Ellie was a killing machine. She did the same damage as the player and was pretty accurate. Fortunately, we had a lot of knobs to control her damage output: damage values, accuracy, firing rate, and so on.

We didn't want to change damage, because that makes an NPC feel broken. If it takes the player three shots to down an enemy, it should take the buddy the same number of shots (with some small margin of error). We also didn't want to change the fire rate or accuracy too much. That would make her face down an enemy with her gun pointing at it and shoot so infrequently or inefficiently that again she felt broken. We made minor changes to fire rate and accuracy to bring them to a believable limit on a per encounter basis, but the buddies were still far too effective.

In order to address this, we decided that if the player isn't going to see the hit, then it isn't necessary for a buddy to do any damage. This meant the player would hear a normal burst of gunshots, but the composition of the encounter didn't change. In practice, players rarely realized that the buddy wasn't doing any damage, so we were able to retain game balance without breaking the player's immersion in the game.

With that said, we didn't want Ellie to feel completely useless, so we tried to identify key moments when it would be good for her to hit and damage a target. In particular, if the player hasn't seen her shoot anyone recently, or if the player is in immediate danger from a charging enemy, low health, a grapple, or something similar, then this is a good time for Ellie's shots to start landing.

Despite all of these changes, we still found the need to lower her fire rate below "realistic" levels to balance damage, so we gave her a "furtive" idle animation that makes her look nervous when she wasn't shooting. This really helped pad out the gaps between shots, and the animation also helped to build her character.

35.6.3 Cheating

Throughout development, there was one prominent decision that we had to make: specifically, whether or not enemies could see Ellie and be alerted by her. For the majority of development, they were able to see her, and this drove us to make her as stealthy as possible, perfecting the AI as much as we could. In practice, it worked about 90%–95% of the time, and we were very proud of how close we got to perfect buddy stealth, but ultimately we had to make a decision one way or the other. Neither option was ideal: either buddies would occasionally give away the player's location, or enemies would never be able to see buddies unless they were actively in combat.

In the end, we decided that the only viable option was to make buddies invisible to enemy NPCs if the player was being stealthy. The result is that sometimes a buddy will run past a bad guy in clear view and not be seen, but as discussed, we had done a lot of work to make sure this wouldn't happen frequently. It breaks realism but considers the alternative. If Ellie was seen even once and gave away the player's location, then the bond between them would become fractured, and we wanted to avoid that at all costs.

35.7 Finishing Touches

Having a robust, well balanced, and ultimately fun buddy AI up and running, it was finally time to add the little touches that would really make Ellie and the other buddies come alive. It's important to recognize that much of what makes a character really deep and compelling has nothing to do with AI; it is having a large library of content to draw from.

35.7.1 Vocalizations

We realized very early on that there needed to be close integration between the combat AI and the dialogue system. This enabled us to easily have a buddy comment on specifics of the recent combat, such as the types of kill she had witnessed or if she had saved you during the fight.

Completely by coincidence, we noticed that Ellie's vocalizations would frequently mirror what the player was exclaiming. After a particularly gruesome battle, it wouldn't be uncommon for the player to utter profanities, followed shortly by Ellie playing an identical vocalization. This made an entirely unplanned connection between the player and Ellie.

35.7.2 Callouts

Next, we added callouts of unseen threats, either whispered or yelled depending on the severity of the situation. This system tries to model the player's view of the world and keep track of threats that they aren't aware of, and will then have a buddy comment on the threat at an appropriate time.

One very important thing we discovered when testing this new callout system is that it is absolutely imperative to ensure that whenever a buddy calls out an enemy, the enemy is there for the player to see. We were a little overzealous with our callouts originally, and Ellie would call out someone who she had only just caught a glimpse of or who may have ducked behind a wall again. When the player heard her warn about an enemy that they were unable to spot, it reflected badly on Ellie's intelligence, so we iterated hard to eliminate bad callouts. This is a classic example of a situation where the requirements for AI are actually more stringent than they would be for human intelligence.

When the system was working and tuned, it really helped give the player a better view of the world. We had a pretty minimal HUD—no minimap in the corner showing enemy locations—so any additional information you could get about the encounter was invaluable. Ellie was acting as an information source for the player, and it really improved the bond.

35.7.3 Ambience

Huge portions of the game have no combat, and we needed Ellie to be interesting and alive during these sections. There are lots of scripted dialogue interactions with the player, of which some are explicitly triggered through the controller and others are triggered dynamically after combat encounters.

We also created a suite of idle animations for her to play, things as simple as cleaning her knife, tying her shoelace, or straightening her hair. Fortunately, it was really easy for animators to get content like this into the game.

Finally, we added an "explore" system for buddies where designers would instrument the world with points of interest and cinematic interactions for her to use. The designers loved this and very quickly made the open spaces a lot livelier with buddies searching them, looking in cabinets, and so on. It's a really basic system, it only took a day or so to implement, but it felt great going into a space and having Ellie start wandering off looking at things. She shared in the player's wonderment at this abandoned world. We got a lot of good feedback about the sections where Ellie would explore, and designers loved having this tool to flesh out their spaces.

35.8 Conclusion

After all of this, buddy AI in *The Last of Us* was a complete success and really enhanced the game. Our hard work paid off and strengthened the bond between Ellie and the player, and the half dozen additional buddy characters that the player encounters throughout the game are unique and believable entities in the world.

Just 5 months of development from a very small team—just one core engineer with backup from the rest of the character engineering team—meant that we had to have laser focus on what we needed to accomplish. We learned that the key to good buddy AI development and AI development, in general, does not lie in the complexity of the systems driving it but in the nuances of the character performance.

Getting into the right mindset was absolutely key for this. It sounds clichéd, but from day one, we tried to approach Ellie's character, and all the other buddies, as living, breathing characters in a world we were creating. Trying to empathize with their situation and reason about how they would operate in this world was central to everything we did.

The core of Ellie's AI is a robust and believable following system. Even before Ellie was able to shoot or do anything in combat, she felt great just by moving intelligently, taking cover in good locations, and staying out of the player's way. After that was in place, we did everything possible to eliminate the traditional annoyances associated with buddy characters, coupled with giving her agency in the world through her combat abilities.

The majority of the development time was spent on iteration, rather than building new systems. We had an almost manic obsession with fine-tuning the details of follow positioning, firing parameters, and ambient dialogue triggers. Having the tools available to iterate on and debug AI is absolutely essential, and it enabled prototyping new behaviors and tweaking things as we were watching them.

Another key to success was to put the buddies' combat abilities behind really big timers. In a long game, you don't want to tire the player out with witty banter, overzealous gifting, or special moves. If Ellie saved you from a melee grapple just once during the game, you would remember that moment fondly and talk about it. If she gave you a health pack around every corner, you wouldn't think of her as helpful, but it would become just another pickup, devaluing the act and her presence.

Finally, making the decision that a buddy would never break stealth was an extremely important one to make. Ultimately, we are making a game here, and your buddy AI can be as intelligent or realistic as possible, but if they ruin what the player is trying to do just once, it's all in vain.

36

Realizing NPCs

Animation and Behavior Control for Believable Characters

Jeet Shroff

36.1 Introduction

A core goal for game developers is to build nonplayer characters (NPCs) that are believable to the player. Believability does not necessarily imply realism, but in order to be believable, these characters must move convincingly, bound by their physicality and environment. They must look, act, and react meaningfully, both individually and in groups. Their actions and intentions must be clearly understood by the player. NPCs that maintain the illusion of believability compel the player to interact with them, further sell the fantasy, and ground the player within the game world. The process of clearly visualizing and communicating not only the NPCs' actions but also their intentions can be referred to as behavior realization.

Animation plays a central role in bringing NPC behaviors to life. By focusing on realizing NPC behaviors with improved animation fidelity, in combination with systems that help control how behaviors are varied, assigned, and executed by NPCs, we can ensure the authenticity of our characters.

This chapter will discuss a wide range of animation techniques that can be used to provide improved realization of NPC behaviors while simultaneously addressing the cost of production and memory budgets. In addition, it will look at ways to control the execution of behaviors in an effort to provide the player with a consistently positive and believable experience.

36.2 Character Movement

Nearly all NPCs have to be able to move in some way. Believable movement does its best to respect the laws of motion, factoring in inertia and momentum. In addition, characters that play animations that convey their intention while moving increase their authenticity by providing the player an awareness of their mental state and context. In this section, we will look at a few techniques to help accomplish this while still keeping our memory and production costs low.

36.2.1 Movement Models

Many game engines use a game-driven approach to character movement, where the animation does not define the motion of the character. Instead, movement is driven by an AI controller that evaluates the position of the character and requests the physics system to move the character's physical representation. The controller also feeds this information to the animation system, which plays animations that match the movement. For example, if the AI controller wishes to move the character forward, a forward moving walk or run animation might be selected by the animation system. Such animations would be authored as moving on-spot animations. This is a fully game-driven approach to character movement.

The alternative is to allow the animation to drive the character's movement. This is referred to as animation-driven movement and is achieved through the use of a *root* or *reference node* within the character's skeleton. The root node is a bone that represents the translation and rotation of the character's motion during the animation. The animation contains transform data for this bone for each frame of animation, just like it does for every other bone. This node is generally placed on the ground, centered directly under the hips of the character, as shown in Figure 36.1.

Every frame, after updating the animation pose, the position and orientation of the root node is passed to the physics system, which updates the position and orientation of the character's capsule (as shown in Figure 36.2). This is referred to as "extracting motion from the animation."

Both these techniques have their advantages. Game-driven movement provides us with maximum level of flexibility as it drives the character independent of animation. Animation-driven movement ensures that the character's overall motion matches that of the animation, providing the best visual results. In addition, this approach better conveys a character's change in momentum along with intention of motion when necessary. For example, a well-authored transition animation that drives the character fully through animation can convey the energy and acceleration or deceleration needed for the character

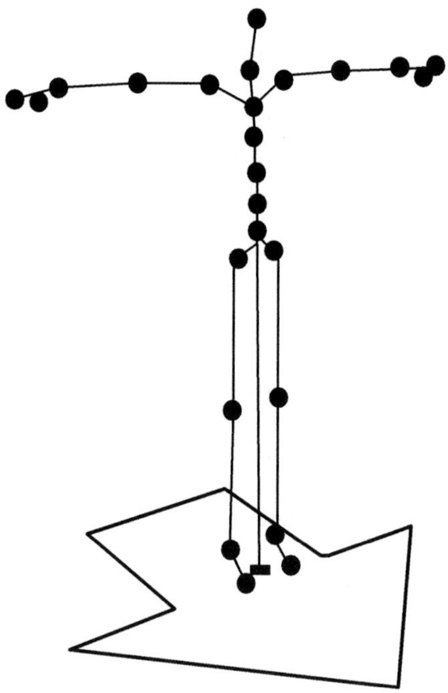

Figure 36.1

The arrow represents the root node and where it lies in the hierarchy of the rig.

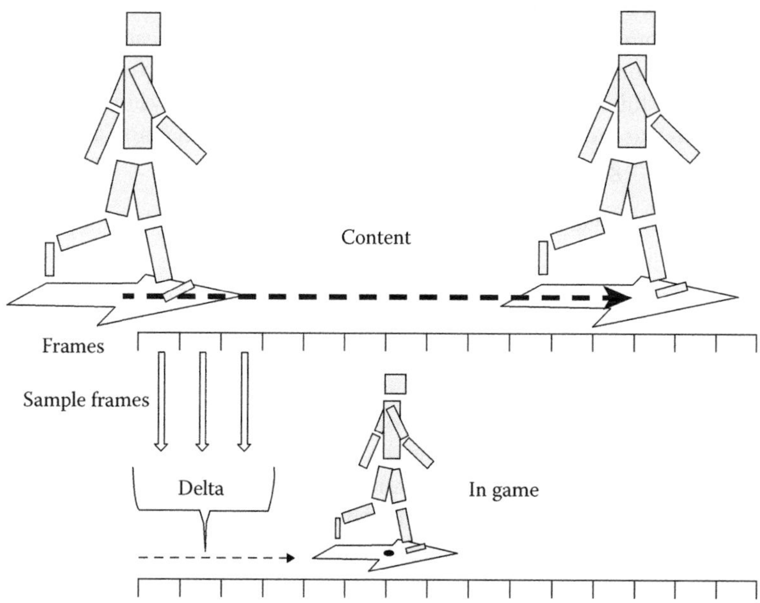

Figure 36.2

Motion extraction of the root node.

during such movement. Effective realization requires both control and fidelity, which we can achieve through a combination of both of these techniques.

36.2.2 Decoupling Extracted Motion

When combining game- and animation-driven movement, it is important to ensure that the extracted motion is decoupled from the animation update. In other words, instead of directly updating physics (and the character's capsule) with the animation's motion when the animation pose is updated, we can separate the animation from the motion update. This allows us to modify the extracted motion in order to better control the character and also to increase animation coverage (i.e., to cover a wider range of motion using a given animation set).

We want to limit our modifications and base them on the original extracted motion. This avoids visual inconsistencies (such as keeping our characters from significantly sliding when moving) and also preserves specific movement characteristics such as weight and energy. In other words, it allows us to stay true to the intentions of the animation and to avoid changes that might be noticed by the player.

36.2.3 Motion Correction

Character motion can be represented and updated using three core components: the displacement direction (i.e., the world space direction that the character is moving), the orientation of the character (i.e., the world space direction that the character is facing), and the speed at which the character is moving. Each frame, after the motion has been extracted, the change in displacement direction, orientation, and speed is read and applied to our character's physical representation by passing that information to the physics system. If no change is made, then the character is being driven fully via animation.

Each of these components can be corrected independently of each other, to match a specific game situation. This corrected change is then used to update physics and the character's motion. The following sections will describe a variety of ways in which we can correct motion as well as techniques that use a combination of game- and animation-driven movement to provide greater animation coverage.

36.2.4 Correcting Displacement Direction and Orientation

The animations within a movement system can be categorized as either looping, transition, or one-off (nonlooping) animations. Some examples of looping animations include forward- and backward-moving (or "backpedal") cycles. The displacement direction and orientation for these animations typically remain at the same offset to each other throughout the course of the animation. For example, the displacement direction and orientation in a looping backpedal animation point in opposite directions throughout the entire animation. Looping animations are also created so that the start and end frames are identical, so that you can play them over and over again to make the character move continuously.

In contrast, transition animations may update the offset of the displacement direction and orientation throughout the course of the animation to account for the change in the transition of movement that is needed. For example, a transition animation from standing to walking might rotate the character to face the displacement direction and also move and accelerate the character in that direction. Looping, transition, and one-off animations can all use motion correction to extend their coverage.

36.2.4.1 Looping Animations

The displacement direction and orientation of looping animations can be corrected to match a target direction. The target direction is set up by the path following or movement controller. In the case of following a path facing forward, the character will need to align their displacement direction and orientation to be along the path, so that they do not veer off the path or unintentionally strafe sideways.

A wide range of smoothing algorithms can be used to drive the orientation and displacement direction toward the one needed by the path. The most basic approach would be to use a simple interpolation. On analyzing the path, every frame, the controller sets up the target directions that are needed. Then new directions are evaluated that smoothly drive the current directions to the targets. These directions are passed on to physics. Other algorithms that factor in angular acceleration, along with the curvature of the path, can be used to provide more believable results. For example, we can use sets of tunable acceleration curves to control the rate of correction of the character's displacement direction and orientation for different circumstances. The speed of the character must also be modified to account for the radius of the turn (as shown in Figure 36.3), but speed adjustments will be discussed in a later section. Since the animation is updated independently of the corrected motion, we can add a procedural lean to account for these corrections and visually communicate this change to the player.

In order to be able to correct the displacement direction and orientation of our animations, we must impose certain constraints on the way the root node is animated. In the case of these looping animations, the animations should be animated within one plane (such as the XZ plane; in our examples we will always assume that Y is up). In addition, we

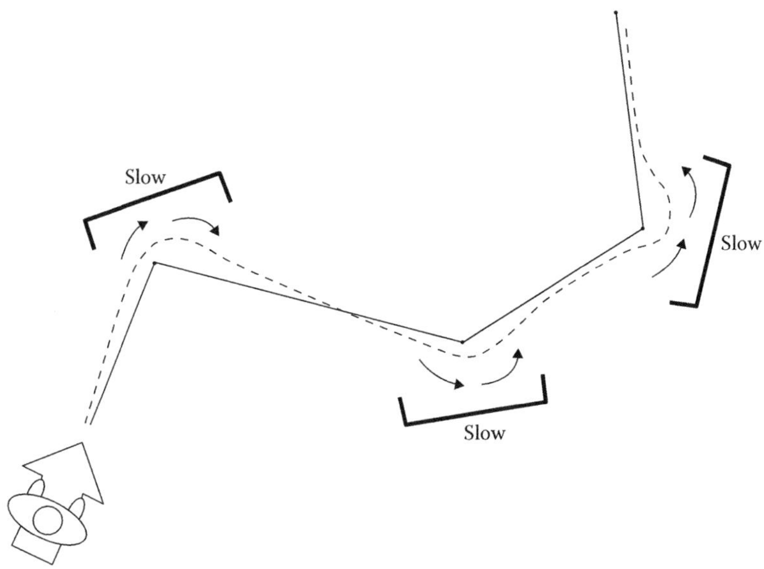

Figure 36.3

Following a path while facing forward using motion correction.

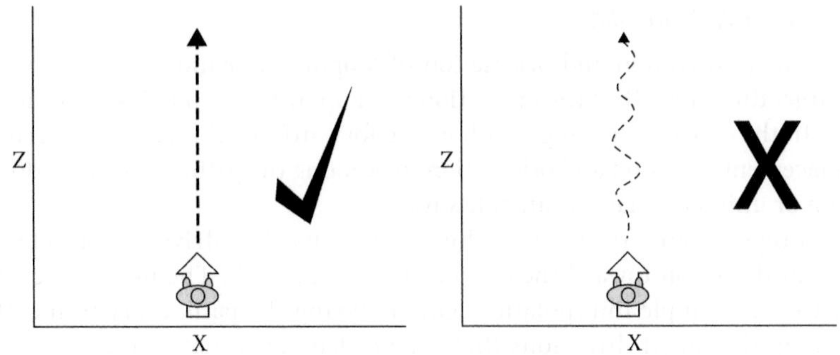

Figure 36.4

Root node motion for cyclical movement animations.

also need to minimize the curvature within the translation for the root node, as shown in Figure 36.4. Transition animations require a different set of constraints.

36.2.4.2 Transition and One-Off Animations

Transition animations, such as starting to move, planting to turn, and stop animations help to communicate a character's change in momentum to the player. Using a naive approach, we often need a wide range of animations to cover all cases. For example, a given starting to move animation can only rotate a character by a fixed amount. Blending animations together may help to alleviate the amount of coverage needed, but persistently blending motion-based animations can lose the subtle nuances of motion particularly authored for specific directions. Motion correction can be used in this case to generate a wider range of coverage while preserving the fidelity of the original content.

Let us continue with the example of starting to move. When starting to move from an idle, we want the character to be able to move in any direction without getting stuck in the transition animation for too long. To account for this, we can use motion correction to perform an additional rotation after the orientation is calculated from the extracted motion. This correction adjusts for the difference between rotation in the animation and the rotation required to face the target direction, which is fixed in this case. On each frame, we add the appropriate portion of this difference as a delta to the animation rotation to ensure that the character ends up facing the intended direction. When using this approach, it is important to ensure that the animation is built with a little shuffling or movement in both feet. This helps to hide the fact that the feet will slide as the character turns. Ensuring that the difference is spread evenly across every frame of the rotational component of the animation and imposing a constraint that the root node be rotated at a constant rate during the animation, we can also help to minimize the sliding that one might notice.

Using this approach, we were able to create 360° of coverage using just three start animations: a 0° direction, a 120° to the right direction, and a 120° to the left direction. This provided surprisingly good results, even though we might think more coverage would be necessary. With that said, if the fidelity is not good enough, more coverage can easily be added by adding just a few more transitions (for instance, 60° to the right and left transitions). This is illustrated in Figure 36.5.

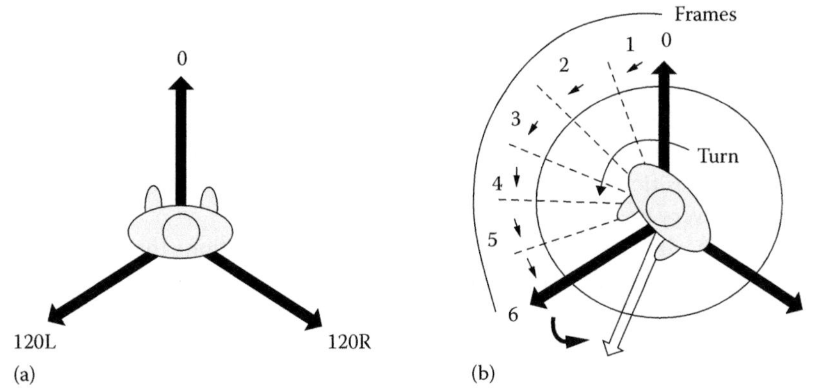

Figure 36.5

Motion correction applied during starting to move animations. (a) Original start animations, 0, 120R, and 120L. (b) Intended angle in white is 155L. Select the 120L animation, add on the difference of 35 degrees, and spread uniformly across the 6 frames of rotation to end up at 155 degrees from the original facing angle at the end of the rotation.

As each of our three components can be updated independently, it is worth noting that in this case, the displacement direction can be corrected as described in the previous section via the controller, the speed can be fully driven by the animation, and the orientation can be corrected using the aforementioned technique. Within the same animation, toward the end of the rotational segment, the orientation can be blended to be corrected by the same smoothing technique used in looping animations to match the requested direction. In cases where target direction is varying during the course of the animation, we can use a combined technique of orientation smoothing along with the delta rotational adjustment per frame. Different combinations of either movement model with motion correction can be used for many forms of transition animations, such as stop animations or plant and turn animations, as well as one-off animations such as rotating or reacting in place animations.

Displacement direction or orientation correction can also be used to add variety to the trajectory of one-off animations such as a hit reaction or death animations from an explosion. In the case of explosion animations, we can also add a random upward component to the extracted motion, which changes how high the character's body flies. As with the orientation changes described earlier, the upward component should be distributed across the course of the animation. All of these techniques can create variety and increase coverage from a small set of animations.

Finally, motion correction can also be applied to one-off animations where the end position of the character is set by the game. This can be used for animations like entering a vehicle or interacting with a specific object. As with the adjustment on the start animations, we can calculate the difference between the end position of the one-off animation and the intended target position and then apply an appropriate-sized delta, each frame, to align the character's displacement direction and orientation accordingly. Speed adjustments can also be made to match this correction.

36.2.5 Correcting Speed

Looping animations are typically authored to have a fixed speed throughout the animation. As mentioned earlier, in some cases, we may want to temporarily alter that speed. For example, when following a path, we might want to slow the character down as he or she goes around a tight turn. Similarly, we might want to alter the speed of the player character to match the position of the thumb stick. We want to do this without creating custom animations for every possible speed.

One approach, shown in Figure 36.6, is to take two animations that were authored at different speeds and blend them together in order to achieve the desired result. While common, this approach can impose restrictions on the authoring of the animations themselves and typically results in a loss of animation fidelity. In reality, moving at different speeds introduces a wide range of subtleties in body movement and stride (distance between each step) of a character. In order to ensure that these cycles blend well with each other, these differences usually have to be heavily dampened or eliminated. In addition, in most cases, these animations need to be authored with the same number of steps, which is limiting both from a stylistic and a motion capture perspective. The bottom line is that the subtleties of motion are lost during the persistent blend of all these animations. Another approach is to drive the character's speed through the game, while correcting the animation's playback rate to match this speed. This maintains the original posing, weight, and motion of the character from the source animation. By limiting the correction to the

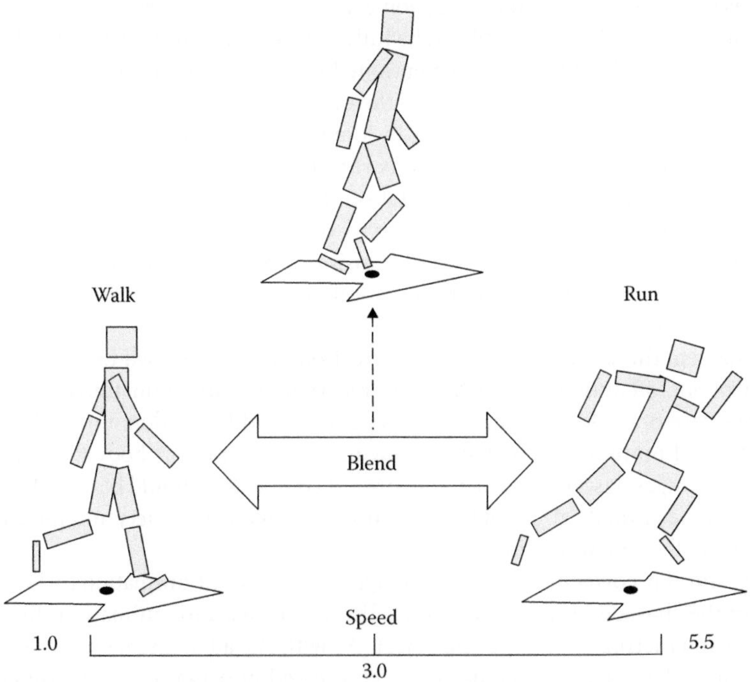

Figure 36.6

Blending animations together to create coverage for speed.

extracted motion and adjusting the playback rate of the animation to match the correction, we can satisfy both the fidelity and coverage concerns.

During gameplay, the target speed is calculated for the character each frame. If this speed is faster or slower than the current speed of the character, every frame, the AI controller calculates a "next" speed that approaches the target speed using smoothing or an acceleration/deceleration curve (similar to what we did for displacement direction and orientation). Since the motion is decoupled from the pose, we can pass this speed on to the physics system to move the character. At the same time, we visually match the speed of the character by adjusting their animation playback rates. As the character speeds up or slows down, we will need to transition between animations (e.g., from walk to run to sprint).

We control this by specifying a set of speed ranges. Each speed range specifies a looping animation that we have identified as a speed that our character typically moves at (i.e., their usual run speed, walk speed, sprint speed). The speeds of these animations become our *reference speeds*. The animation is then played back at a lower or higher rate to account for the difference between the current speed and the reference speed. Since this is simply a visual match with decoupled motion, the reference speed for an animation can be adjusted, even if it doesn't really move at that speed in the animation, to best match the character's movement in game. To ensure smooth motion, we allow the speed ranges to overlap, so that there are transition areas where we change from one animation to another as the speed smoothly moves up or down to the next reference speed. Each frame, we check which animation or animations are appropriate given the current speed. If only one animation is appropriate, then that is what we play. When we are in a transition where two animations are appropriate, we blend them together. Note that this is the only time when these scaled animations are blended together. The amount of overlap is defined by the available coverage. This technique is illustrated in Figure 36.7.

We can minimize the amount of time that the character remains within an overlapping range by ensuring that the AI controller always tries to set the target speed to be a reference speed. This avoids the persistent blend and ensures that the character plays the core looping animation at the reference speed, as it was originally intended as much as possible. As the overlap between these ranges is fairly small, we rarely notice the difference in the actual movement and animation sampling.

Transition animations, such as start or stop transitions, can also be speed corrected to visually match the target speed of motion. In these cases, the speed is not constant throughout the animation, so specific reference speeds are defined for the varying acceleration and deceleration segments within the animation. Further improvement can be made by removing the need for the reference animations to have the same number of steps. This allows for more freedom when capturing and creating data. For example, a walk animation requires far more steps to look natural than a run, since the walk is at a much slower pace and begins to look mechanical when looped, while a highly intentional run is far more forgiving. In order to do this, we need two variants of the animation: the base version and a variant that is intended specifically for blending. When in an area of the speed range that overlaps, we play the blending variant, but as soon as we are out of the overlap range, we go back to the better-looking base version. We can use an animation technique known as pose matching (described later) to allow us to smoothly blend between the base version and the blending variant as needed.

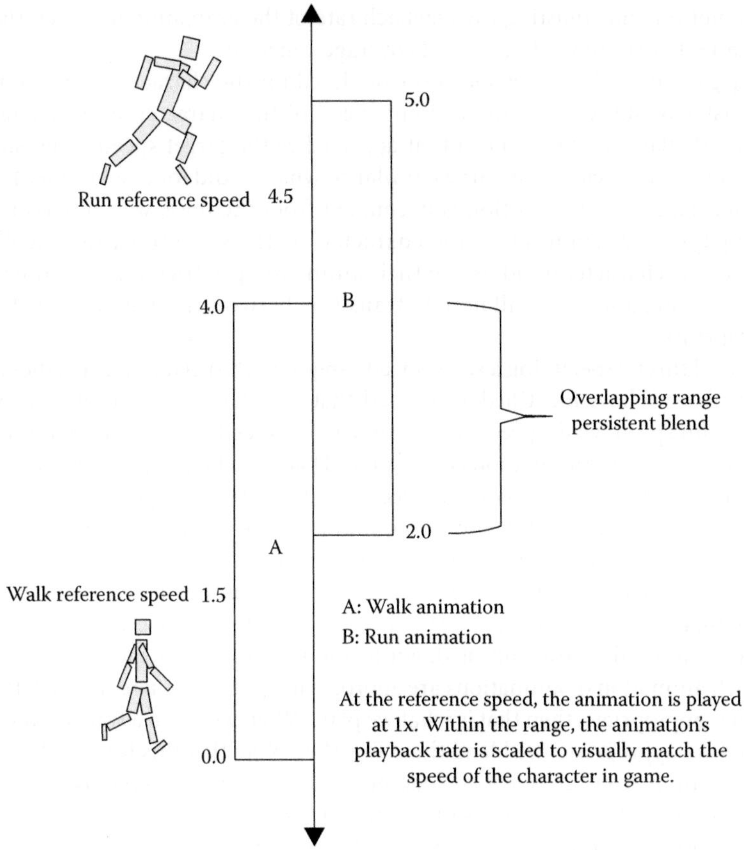

Figure 36.7

Using ranges to scale the playback rate of animations to visually match the character's motion.

Using speed correction along with speed ranges can yield a higher level of quality while still allowing for the smooth transitions that we can get by blending the transitions as we speed up or slow down.

36.3 Interrupting and Blending Movement

One of the challenges when transitioning between moving animations is that if the time between footfalls, or the motion of the arms, or some other significant feature in the two animations is not precisely in sync, the character's appendages may scissor, freeze, windmill, or otherwise move implausibly. For example, the time between footfalls when running is generally longer than the time in between footfalls when walking. Thus, at one second into a run animation, the right foot may be descending, headed toward a foot plant. In the walk animation, the right foot may already have planted, and the left foot may be swinging forward. If you try to blend these two animations simply based off of time, you'll get odd results because the feet are doing different things. This is particularly common when we must interrupt an animation at any point.

36.3.1 Pose Matching

Pose matching is a technique that addresses this problem. Instead of blending animations based on elapsed time, we blend the two animations based on their pose. In most moving animations, the pose can be defined by phase. In this case, the phase of an animation is defined as the time in the swing cycle of each foot, as shown in Figure 36.8, going from 0 to 1. With that said, for any given set of animations, the definition used should depend on the feature that you are trying to match. Phase information can be generated offline and stored as metadata, keeping runtime calculations to a minimum.

States can define whether to apply pose matching when they blend in from another state or only when they blend out to another state. Looping animations, for instance, will choose to pose match when a character transitions to and from them, since they include phase information for the entire cycle. Certain transition animations, however, may only choose to apply pose matching when transitioning out of the state. This is necessary because pose matching on entry may cause us to skip the most important parts of the animation.

36.3.2 Pose-Only and Per-Bone Blending

Interrupting movement to come to a stop also poses a unique set of challenges. Stop animations are transitions that are used to convey the shift in momentum and deceleration needed when a character comes to a stop. Often, our games require that the characters come to a stop on a dime, especially when dealing with the player releasing game pad input. Stopping in an instant is an animator's nightmare. Coming to a complete stop immediately is both physically impossible and visually unnatural. This problem is exacerbated by the fact that if you're using motion capture, the data will

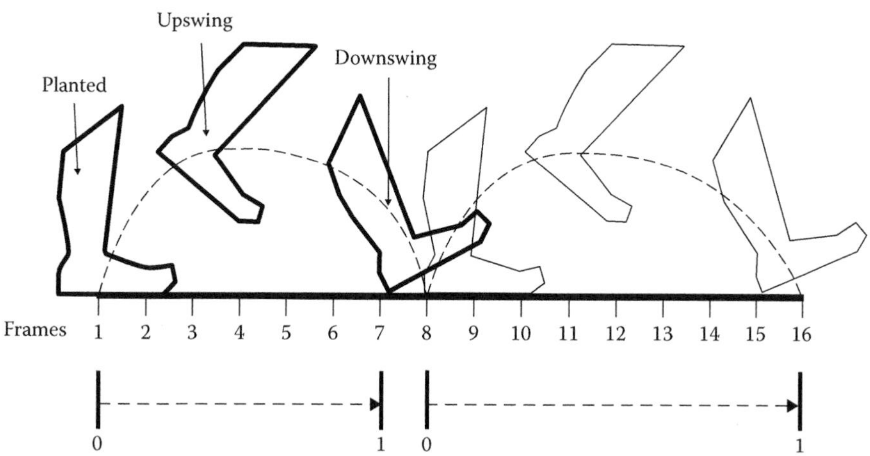

Figure 36.8

Phase match information, going from 0.0 to 1.0 with respective frames.

always have some motion in it. A simple animation technique that helps to improve the quality of this is pose-only blending.

When we transition from a movement animation to our stop animation, we can blend the pose and the root node separately. In the case of an instant stop, we do not include any of the root node translation, which ensures that the character will stop instantly, but we still blend in the pose from the movement animation, which helps to create the illusion of deceleration and alleviates the visual harshness of the sudden transition. In order to work, this requires that the root node for the stop animations be authored without any translation.

This idea can be further extended not just to blend the root node without any blending but also to blend different sets of bones at different rates. This is known as per-bone blending. Using this technique, we can create the illusion of momentum or motion lag, for example, by blending in the upper- and lower-body parts differently.

36.4 Combining Actions

NPCs often need to do more than one thing at the same time. For instance, they might need to carry and aim their weapons while running or talk on a cell phone while riding a bicycle. In the case of carrying or aiming weapons, having to create content for each different weapon type is also cumbersome and expensive. Memory limitations make this approach further challenging. In this section, we will discuss techniques for realizing these features using specific combat-based examples.

36.4.1 Animation Masking

Sharing animation data among features is a great way to save on animation memory. Animation masking is one way to do this. We can use bone masks to split animations into combinations of masked animations that can be recombined as needed. This allows us to ensure that there is never any duplication of animation data. Data that can be shared is exported out as a mask only once. This mask is then reused as needed. Masks should be generated offline. We can think of our final animation pose as being built at runtime from a combination of these bone masks.

Figure 36.9 demonstrates this idea using the example of an idle animation. The original idle animation can be thought of as using no mask, including all bones shown at the very top. However, as we build content to hold a two-handed weapon such as a rifle, we realize the upper-body portion of the animation needs to be different, but the lower-body portion of both of these animations is the same. So we mask the original animation into two: a lower-body mask (A) and an upper-body mask (B). We then share the lower-body mask for both animations and need only a rifle holding upper-body mask (C) to create the rifle holding idle. When a significantly different weapon type is introduced, such as an RPG, we only need to change the arms of the upper-body two-handed rifle mask (C). And so we further mask that to separate the arms into their respective masks (E) and (F), along with the armless upper-body animation (D) to account for the two different weapons. This allows us to minimize our use of animation memory.

We can further optimize this by masking out bones that do not require key frame data for every frame of the animation. These often include the face and finger bones. They can be exported as simple poses, so that we only include data for those animations that require their bones to move.

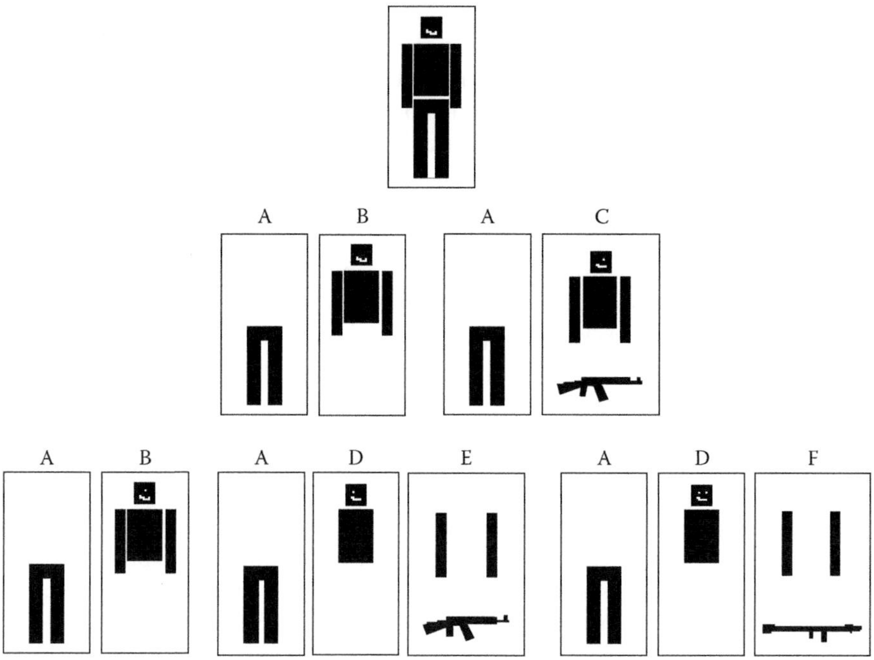

Figure 36.9

Masking animations for an idle with weapons.

36.4.2 Animation Mirroring

In order to save additional memory, we can make use of animation mirroring. Mirrored animations are animations that can be played symmetrically on either side of a plane, for example, animations that can be played either to the right or left, requiring the same movements in either direction (looping animations where the character is aiming either to the left or right side or one-off animations such as entering or exiting a vehicle from either side). Content is built only for one side and mirrored during runtime to get the coverage for the other side.

36.4.3 Animation Layering

Animation layering is a technique that can be used to play secondary actions that do not need to be synchronized with the base action. Animation layers can be thought of as tracks that can play an animation. You can think of the main layer as being the base animation that is played on the character. Once the base animation has been selected as either a no mask or combined with a set of masked animations, additional layers of animation that do not need to be synchronized with the base animation can be sequentially blended together with this pose to create the final pose of the character. When a layer's blend weight is 1.0, it means that the animation that is being played on that layer is completely overriding the animation on the layer beneath it. This is exactly what is needed when we want to play an animation that can cover and override multiple base animations. This saves us additional authoring time and memory.

For example, we could have an animation that uses a single arm to detonate an explosive or both arms to reload a weapon. This technique also works very well for things like facial animation and conversational gestures. These animations can generally be used across several base animation states. Animation data per layer are applied sequentially in the local space of the character. To ensure that these animations work well, we must enforce the bone masks to be flexible enough to be applied independently of the base animation state. We can do this by limiting the masks to head or arm-only animations, thus preserving the base pose as best as possible.

These techniques are not limited to weapons or combat alone. The important takeaway here is that when it comes to dealing with large feature sets, it is important to think of ways to reuse animation content as widely as possible.

36.5 Tracking

NPCs often need to be able to track another object—for instance, by looking at another wandering NPC or aligning a weapon to aim at a specific target. Furthermore, we often need our NPCs to be able to track an object in all directions. Tracking an object while aiming a weapon without breaking the original pose or sticking the weapon through any part of the character's body is a difficult problem to get right. In this section, using aiming as an example, we can look at some techniques to solve this problem.

36.5.1 Additive Aiming Poses

Additive animations are animations that are applied as additional offsets to an existing animation. These animations are created by taking the difference between two animations to generate offsets per frame. We can apply these offsets onto the base animation to generate a different pose. Many games use additives to provide extra runtime animation noise. This adds variety and communicates a character's context to the player, for instance, additional breathing when a character is tired or leaning when making a hard turn.

There are two different ways we can generate and apply additive offsets: either as additive pose offsets (as a single frame) or as additive animation offsets (animations that are synced with the original animation). In either case, these additive offsets are created offline.

When using additive pose offsets, we must specify the animation pose and a reference pose that we can use to generate the offsets for that pose. For example, in the case of a leaning pose additive, we would provide the maximum leaning pose as the animation pose and the straight pose as the reference pose. When we generate the additive pose offset for this, we would get the additive offsets necessary to add to the straight pose to create the maximum leaning pose. We should ensure that the additive animation pose is built directly from the reference pose. This ensures a controlled and high-fidelity final pose when applying the offsets at runtime.

Coming back to the example of aiming, animators can create aiming poses for the maximum angles needed for aiming. We then use a reference pose of the base animation to generate the offsets for each maximum angle. Finally, a persistent blend of these pose offsets is used at runtime to create the final pose with the weapon aimed correctly. We should make sure this blended additive is applied last within the animation blend tree.

This minimizes the adulteration of the pose. If further precision or fidelity is required, we can add more pose offsets at specific angles until we get the quality results that we need.

It is often a good idea to use this solution only for vertical aiming, that is, upward and downward, and instead to use inverse kinematics (IK) for our horizontal aiming. This dual aiming system will be discussed in greater detail later.

Additive pose offsets work exceptionally well for looping animations where the overall pose does not change significantly throughout the course of the base animation. Using additives for aiming provides the animator more control and allows the character to still hit key-authored poses, resulting in higher quality. In addition, using additive poses is a great way to minimize the amount of memory and time needed to create fully synced aiming animations for every base animation that would need to support aiming.

36.5.2 Additive Aiming Animations

The pose-based additive aiming solution does have a limitation. Additive pose offsets don't quite work when the pose itself changes significantly during the course of the base animation. An example of such an animation would be a hard landing animation from a long fall. Since there is a significant squash component during the beginning of the animation, followed by a stretch component after which the hips and head stabilize, we would require different offsets along the course of the animation to ensure that we maintain the intended aiming direction. To solve this problem, we can use synced additive animations that are authored at the required maximum aiming angles. We then can generate offsets frame by frame for the whole animation. As before, we then blend in a weighted offset to create the angles we need. This solution should only be used for animations that require it, because it requires significantly more memory. When it is required, we can decrease the memory requirements by only creating an additive pose for every X frames of the base animation (where X is typically something like 10) and apply the offsets accordingly. This still provides the animators enough control to create high-quality aiming offsets, while dramatically reducing the size of the additive animations.

36.5.3 Inverse Kinematics

Although we could use additives for both vertical and horizontal aiming, doing so would require a lot more poses to ensure coverage of every possible aim angle. In addition, it can limit the animators to altering only very specific sets of bones in each directional offset to ensure that they don't conflict with each other. Finally, if you need additive animations (rather than just poses), authoring the animations to meet these constraints can be painfully time-consuming.

As an alternative, IK works relatively well for horizontal aiming because the core rotation for aiming horizontally can be limited to a smaller set of bones. To make this work well, the locomotion system should select its movement animations based on the horizontal aiming range. Within a range, the horizontal aiming coverage needed is reasonably small and thus easily achievable through the use of IK. We can also choose to use a cheaper version of this for horizontal tracking when pointing or looking at an object. This rule generalizes that when using IK, it is important to select the right animations and bones to apply the IK to.

In addition to horizontal tracking, we use IK in other situations such as a postprocessing for foot or hand placement and for adding procedural variation to the pose.

36.6 Behaviors

The animation techniques described previously increase the fidelity of character realization of each individual NPC. However, maintaining the believability of our world requires us to think beyond that, looking at how often a character executes a specific behavior, how varied it is, and how it is distributed across multiple NPCs.

36.6.1 Creating Variety

Too often in games, we see an NPC play the same animations or behavior over and over again. One solution is to have a lot of animation and behaviors to pick from, but this can be expensive from both an authoring and memory standpoint. The ideas presented in this section can help to create the illusion of variation without requiring prohibitively large amounts of content.

36.6.1.1 Contextual One-Off Animations

Games generally make use of a large number of looping animations to communicate fundamental NPC actions such as idling or moving. While it's important to include variations of these animations, they tend to be longer in length compared to other animations in the game. If we were to create a lot of variation for each of these cycles, we would quickly run out of both development time and memory. Consider walking, for example. People within a similar context (the same height, age, and mental state) walk in a similar fashion. Either changes to this cycle will not be very noticeable or they will look unnatural. It is the smaller nonlooping actions and movements, such as changes in stride, shifts in weight, or looking around, that differentiate how one walks from another.

Contextual one-off animations add variety and help to break up looping animations. By matching the context of the looping animation, they further communicate a character's behavior to the player. These animations do not interrupt the underlying behavior, but instead desynchronize and vary them. Continuing with the example of walking, examples of some contextual one-offs might include stopping to scratch your leg, shifting your weight from side to side, and an animation to smoke (played as a mask on a different layer to save memory). These one-offs can be motion corrected to match both the current speed and the trajectory of the motion. For full-body one-offs, we use phase matching to transition seamlessly in and out of the one-off animation and back to the underlying looping animation. Most importantly, the contextual one-offs contain only the change we want to make to the base animation, so they are much smaller and can be reused across different contexts, which significantly increases the amount of variation we can create given a particular animation budget.

36.6.1.2 Micro Behaviors

Just as we can break up looping animations with smaller one-offs to create the illusion of variation within them, we can also extend this idea to vary behaviors themselves through the use of micro behaviors. Micro behaviors can be thought of as smaller subbehaviors that can run their logic in parallel with a core behavior, simply to provide variation. These behaviors can also temporarily interrupt a core behavior to perform a specific action, returning back to the core behavior after completion. Similar to animation one-offs, we can make use of a wide variety of micro behaviors to support the core behavior and break up behavior synchronization.

For example, imagine a combat situation with two NPCs that are executing a cover behavior. While in cover, they are peeking and shooting, evaluating for better cover, etc. One of the NPCs decides to reposition, and before the character performs this action, it shares this information with all other NPCs that are part of that scene. The cover behavior (i.e., being executed by all NPCs in cover) can include a micro behavior that reads this and plays a one-off animation to order an NPC to reposition. This doesn't need to be synchronized and runs independently on each NPC. The behavior logic chooses how often to select these micro behaviors. What's more, like contextual one-offs, micro behaviors can often be reused across multiple behaviors.

Another advantage to micro behaviors is that, in addition to creating variety, they can be used to clearly communicate the NPC's intent, making the reasoning behind the core behaviors apparent to the player. This is a crucial part of behavior variation. We often focus on tweaking values or adjusting utility formulae to make the NPC execute a behavior slightly differently. While this form of variation in behavior is important, if we don't clearly support this, it may be barely noticed by the player. Making the reasoning behind the behaviors obvious to the player allows the player to interact with them in meaningful ways. If the player doesn't understand what's happening, it might as well not be happening at all.

36.6.1.3 Using Additives with Idles

Idle animations suffer from the same issues described previously. They are cyclical and long. Additionally, they require a lot of variation to be compelling enough to notice. To deal with this problem, we can use a set of noise-based additive animations on a large number of idle poses (single-frame animations). These additive animations are played on a different animation layer and are unsynchronized with the base idle pose to add extra variation. This can create a large amount of variation from single-frame idle animations, which can save a great deal of animation memory and production time.

36.6.2 Behavior Distribution

One often overlooked aspect of NPC behaviors is how behaviors are distributed among a group of NPCs. NPCs whose behaviors are synchronized to happen at just the same time easily break the player's suspension of disbelief. In this section, we will look at ways to assign and distribute NPC behaviors.

36.6.2.1 Action Tokens

We often need to control how often a specific action occurs. For example, while a group of NPCs are executing their cover behavior, we might need to control how often an NPC throws a grenade. We can use the concept of action tokens to help with this. Each action that can be executed by multiple NPCs is assigned a particular number of tokens, and before an NPC can execute an action, they must acquire one of these tokens. For example, characters that want to shoot at the player when moving all can share a set of "move and shoot tokens." These tokens are used to limit the number of characters that can be moving and shooting at the same time.

The token system should support designer-specified parameters for each type of action. For example, the designers might want to specify the minimum amount of time that an NPC must wait after releasing a token before acquiring it again and whether the number of tokens should scale based on the number of characters in the scene. Using these sorts of parameters, we can control not only how often an action occurs but also how it is distributed across multiple characters.

36.6.2.2 Blackboards

In order to facilitate communication between logic that is spread across different behaviors for an individual character as well as among multiple characters, we can make use of data blackboards. These data blackboards can be defined at a global, group, or local level. All characters have access to the global blackboard, characters that are part of a specific context, have access to that context's group blackboard (e.g., all of the passengers in a vehicle might share a group blackboard), and finally each individual character always has access to its own local blackboard. Through the blackboards, we can communicate and manage actions and behaviors for the NPCs within a specific scene, while still keeping the logic independent of each other.

36.6.2.3 Action Ranking

In addition to action tokens, we can evaluate and assign a unique rank to each character within a specific situation. For example, all NPCs that are currently engaged in combat can be given a combat action rank. We can then assign specific actions or behaviors to characters with different ranks or rank categories.

These action ranks can be used to ensure that the NPCs that are most relevant to the player are the ones that execute the most interesting behavior. We can use a simple utility-based formula to determine the ranks. Factors such as the distance to the player, whether the character is visible to the player, whether the player is aiming at the character, and event-based values such as hearing gunfire or receiving damage from a bullet can be used to calculate the action rank. The event-based stimuli can be limited to influence the action rank for a set period of time (which should be specified by the designer).

Some behaviors can be scripted to execute unique rank-specific micro behaviors to further add variation within the scene. For example, a character holding a high action rank may be allowed to taunt the player. In addition, we can use ranks to specify unique behaviors for particular characters before allowing their systemic AI to run. For example, we can require high-action-ranked NPCs to stand and shoot the player for a few seconds, when the player first initiates combat with a particular group of NPCs. This gives the player a few targets to engage with first, while the others scatter for cover, rather than just allowing everyone to rush for cover.

36.6.2.4 On-Screen Realization

In order to make our behaviors more player centric, we can distribute behaviors based on what the player is actually seeing. For example, we can use on-screen realization as part of our utility ranking to ensure that NPCs that are on-screen receive a higher action ranking than those offscreen. We can also use on-screen realization to influence behavior execution. For example, we can ensure that NPCs that are on-screen choose cover or goal positions that do not cause them to run offscreen (which is often annoying to the player).

36.7 Conclusion

AI character development must include a strong focus on the synergy between animation and behavior. Having the right mindset and focus on realizing characters ensures that our NPCs make appropriate and intended decisions while still maintaining a strong sense of believability. This effort contributes significantly to the overall player experience.

Using animation techniques that focus on creating coverage while preserving the original authored animations, using a minimal amount of content, and reusing animation content, we can strive to maintain a high level of overall fidelity while keeping our memory budget in check. When it comes to motion, our emphasis is on displaying behavioral intent, variation, and preservation of momentum.

Finally, it is important to focus on solutions that explicitly manage variety and that distribute behaviors between characters. This level of realization control, centered on the player, guarantees a consistently positive experience.

37

Using Queues to Model a Merchant's Inventory

John Manslow

37.1 Introduction

Queues frequently appear in game worlds. Sometimes they are obvious—like the queues formed by cars in a traffic jam or patients waiting to see a doctor. At other times, they are more difficult to identify—like the queues formed by items in the inventory of a merchant. M/M/1 queues arise when objects are added to, and removed from, a collection at random time intervals and can be used to model such processes even when the order of the objects is not important.

This chapter will describe how to use the statistical properties of M/M/1 queues to efficiently simulate how they change over time. To provide a practical example, the chapter will show how to represent the inventory of a merchant as a set of M/M/1 queues and demonstrate how to efficiently generate realistic and mutually consistent random realizations of the inventory that take account of the levels of supply and demand. The book's website (http://www.gameaipro.com) includes a full implementation of everything that is described in the article.

37.2 M/M/1 Queues

An M/M/1 queue is a process in which objects are added to, and removed from, a collection at random intervals. The name M/M/1 is actually a form of Kendall's notation [Zabinsky 13], which is used to classify queues and indicates that additions and removals are memoryless (the time of one addition or removal does not affect the time of another) and that the queue consists of only a single collection. The random timings of the additions and removals mean that the number of objects in the collection—the length of the queue—changes randomly with time. Although this makes it impossible to predict the length of the queue with any certainty, it is possible to model it using two probability distributions, the stationary distribution and the transient distribution.

The stationary distribution models the length of queue that one would expect to see if the queuing process had been running for a very long time before it was observed. It is therefore useful for describing the length of a queue when it is encountered by the player for the first time. If objects are added to a queue at an average rate of *add_rate* per unit time and removed from it at an average rate of *remove_rate* per unit time, then its stationary distribution is

$$p(n) = \left(1 - rate\_ratio\right) \cdot rate\_ratio^{n} \tag{37.1}$$

where

$$rate\_ratio = \frac{add\_rate}{remove\_rate} \tag{37.2}$$

and $p(n)$ is the probability of the length of the queue being n items.

Note that, for a queue to be of finite length, it is necessary for *rate_ratio* to be strictly less than one. In other words, if the merchant's inventory isn't going to grow without bound, things need to be leaving the store faster than they are coming in. In general, the average length of an M/M/1 queue is 1/(1 – *rate_ratio*), and the probability of observing an empty queue is 1 – *rate_ratio*.

Players naturally expect to encounter queues of specific lengths and not strange quantum queues in weird superpositions of states. It is therefore necessary to create a specific realization of a queue when the player first observes it by sampling from its stationary distribution. A simple way to do that is to generate a random number x that is greater than or equal to zero and less than one and, starting at $n = 0$, add the values of $p(n)$ until their sum exceeds x and then take n to be the length of the queue. This approach is implemented in `MM1Queue::GetSample`.

The transient distribution describes the length of a queue that has already been observed and is therefore useful when a player encounters a queue for anything other than the first time. If, t units of time ago, the player observed a queue to be of length m, its transient distribution is [Baccelli 89]

$$p\left(n \mid t, m\right) = e^{-(add\_rate + remove\_rate) \cdot t} \cdot \left[p_1 + p_2 + p_3\right] \tag{37.3}$$

where

$$p_1 = rate\_ratio^{\frac{n-m}{2}} \cdot I_{n-m}(at) \tag{37.4}$$

$$p_2 = rate\_ratio^{\frac{n-m-1}{2}} \cdot I_{n+m+1}(at) \tag{37.5}$$

$$p_3 = (1 - rate\_ratio) \cdot rate\_ratio^{n} \sum_{j=n+m+2}^{\infty} rate\_ratio^{-\frac{j}{2}} \cdot I_{n+m+1}(at) \tag{37.6}$$

and

$$a = 2 \times remove\_rate\sqrt{rate\_ratio}, \tag{37.7}$$

$I_n(\cdot)$ is the modified Bessel function of the first kind, which is computed by `MathUtilities::Iax`, and $p(n \mid t, m)$ is the probability that the length of the queue is n, which is computed by `MM1Queue::GetStateProbability`. Once again, it is necessary to create a specific realization of the queue, and that can be done using the procedure that has already been described, but substituting $p(n \mid t, m)$ for $p(n)$. This approach is implemented in the overload of `MM1Queue::GetSample` that takes time and count parameters.

Because both the stationary and transient distributions are derived from a statistical model of the queuing process, samples that are drawn from them naturally satisfy all common sense expectations as to how queues change over time. In particular,

- Queues with high rates of addition and low rates of removal will usually be long
- Queues with low rates of addition and high rates of removal will usually be short
- The effects of player interactions will disappear with time—slowly for queues with low rates of addition and removal and quickly for queues with high rates of addition and removal
- Queues will change little if the time between observations is short, especially for queues with low rates of addition and removal
- Queues will change a lot if the time between observations is long, especially for queues with high rates of addition and removal

The first row of Table 37.1 gives the stationary distribution for a queue with $add\_rate = 0.5$ (one addition every other unit of time on average) and $remove\_rate = 1.0$ (one removal per unit of time on average). Assuming that the player observes the queue to be of length two at time zero and adds four objects to it, the following rows show the transient distribution 0.01, 0.1, 1, 10, and 100 units of time later. It is important to note that these rows show how the transient distribution would evolve if the queue remained unobserved and hence no concrete realizations were produced. For example, 10 units of time after the player had observed the queue, there would be a 0.103 probability of the queue being 3 objects long.

Table 37.1 An Example of an Equilibrium Distribution and Transient Distributions

	Queue Length, *n*								
Time, *t*	0	1	2	3	4	5	6	7	8
0.00	0.500	0.250	0.125	0.063	0.031	0.016	0.008	0.004	0.002
0.01	0.000	0.000	0.000	0.000	0.000	0.010	0.985	0.005	0.000
0.10	0.000	0.000	0.000	0.000	0.004	0.087	0.865	0.043	0.001
1.00	0.000	0.002	0.010	0.042	0.131	0.284	0.349	0.142	0.033
10.00	0.315	0.186	0.131	0.103	0.082	0.063	0.046	0.031	0.020
100.00	0.500	0.250	0.125	0.063	0.031	0.016	0.008	0.004	0.002

The transient distribution makes it possible to model how the length of a queue changes after it has been observed but provides no way of determining how many of the individual objects that were originally in the queue are still there when it is observed again. That kind of information is useful when the objects are uniquely identifiable. For example, cars parked on a street will have different colors and be different makes and models, and people waiting in a hospital will have different clothing and facial features.

If the objects are processed on a strictly first-come, first-served basis, then the number that remain in the queue from the previous observation can roughly be estimated by taking the original length of the queue and subtracting a sample from a Poisson distribution that represents the number of objects processed since the queue was last observed.

If the objects are processed in a random order, the number that remain can be approximated by taking a sample from the same Poisson distribution and then using it in conjunction with a binomial distribution to estimate the number of objects in the original queue that were processed. Technically, this is equivalent to assuming that the length of the queue remained the same between the two observations, but it produces realistic-looking estimates even when that is not actually the case. Implementations of both techniques can be found in the `Inventory::GenerateRealization` overload that takes the time parameter.

Before finishing the discussion of M/M/1 queues, it is important to highlight the fact that the expressions for the stationary and transient distributions assume that the average rates at which objects are added to, and removed from, the queue are constant. This assumption holds for many natural processes but breaks down when additions or removals occur in bursts. Such bursts will occur in relation to the numbers of cars waiting at an intersection, for example, due to the presence of a neighboring intersection or the effects of traffic signals. In such cases, the theoretical deficiencies of M/M/1 queues will often not be apparent to the player and can be ignored, but, in some cases, it will be necessary to use an alternative model [Zabinsky 13].

This section has described the basic properties of M/M/1 queues, given expressions for the stationary and transient distributions of queue length, and shown how to sample from those distributions to generate consistent realizations when queues are encountered by the player. The following section will describe how M/M/1 queues can be used to model the inventory of a merchant to produce random inventories that are consistent with each other, with the levels of supply and demand of each type of item in the inventory and with the player's observations and interactions with the merchant.

37.3 Modeling a Merchant's Inventory

In a large, open world game with dozens of merchants, hundreds of NPCs, and tens of thousands of individual inventory items, it is impractical to explicitly model economic activity in real time in enough detail to track the inventory of each merchant. Fortunately, to make the world believable, it is sufficient to generate random inventories each time a merchant is encountered provided that they are consistent with players' common sense expectations as to how they should change with time.

In terms of the numbers of each type of item in an inventory, those expectations are essentially the same as those for the lengths of queues that were given earlier. This strongly suggests that a merchant's inventory can be modeled in the following way:

1. Create one M/M/1 queue for each type of item the merchant can have in his or her inventory.
2. Set the average rate at which each type of item is added to its queue to be equal to the average rate at which the merchant will buy it.
3. Set the average rate at which each type of item is removed from its queue to be equal to the average rate at which the merchant will sell it when he or she has it.
4. When the player first encounters the merchant, create his or her inventory by sampling from the stationary distribution for each type of item.
5. On all subsequent encounters, create his or her inventory by sampling from the transient distribution for each type of item.

Even though real merchants do not buy and sell at random, steps 2 and 3 ensure that the merchant's inventory is generally consistent with the levels of supply and demand for each type of item, and step 5 ensures that players see an inventory that is consistent from one visit to the next.

Table 37.2 gives an example of how the numbers of three inventory items—truffles, arrows, and swords—vary with time, which, in this example, is measured in game world hours. Truffles are assumed to have limited supply (only one is added to the inventory every 1000 h on average) but high demand (one is sold every hour on average), arrows are assumed to have high supply (one is added every hour on average) and high demand (one is sold every 0.98 h on average), and swords are assumed to have low supply (one is added every 200 h on average) and low demand (one is sold every 100 h on average).

Table 37.2 An Example of How a Simple Three-Item Inventory Changes with Time

	Item		
Time (h)	Truffles	Arrows	Swords
0	0	83	1
0 after player interaction	5	33	1
1	3	33	1
48	0	37	1
100	0	26	0
200	0	47	0

The numbers of truffles, arrows, and swords at time zero—when the player encounters the merchant for the first time—are obtained by sampling from each type of item's stationary distribution. The player sells the merchant five truffles and buys 50 arrows and then explores the environment for 1 h. He or she then returns to the merchant, and a new inventory is generated by sampling from each type of item's transient distribution. This reveals that the merchant still has three truffles left and the number of arrows and swords hasn't changed. Returning to the merchant after 48 h reveals that all truffles have been sold and the merchant has 37 arrows. The code that was used to generate the numbers in this example is included on the book's website.

The basic inventory model that has been described so far can easily be enhanced to simulate more complex behavior. For example, a merchant might buy 50 arrows every Monday but only if he has fewer than 50 arrows in stock. This kind of behavior can be closely approximated by sampling from the distribution for the number of arrows in the merchant's inventory from the previous Monday and adding 50 if the sample is less than 50. The resulting number can then be used as a "virtual observation" when sampling from the current transient distribution to obtain the current number of arrows—the game simply behaves as though the player had been present the previous Monday and seen how many arrows the merchant had.

Similar logic can be used if the merchant always buys enough arrows to bring his or her stock up to 50, if the arrow vendor comes randomly rather than every Monday, or if the supply of arrows is not entirely dependable. The merchant buying additional stock is only one type of special event that affects the numbers of items in his inventory. Another might be the death of a nobleman, causing the merchant to suddenly acquire a large number of luxury items at the resulting estate sale or the commander of a local garrison buying up all of the armor. Such events can be modeled in a similar way to the merchant's buying behavior; a virtual observation of the affected inventory item can be created for the time of the event and used in the transient distribution when the player encounters the merchant.

Other events might cause permanent changes in the levels of supply and demand, and they can be simulated by changing *add_rate* and *remove_rate*. For example, a new mine might open up, leading to an increase in the supply of iron. This effect can be simulated by making a virtual observation of the amount of iron that the merchant had in stock when the mine opened by sampling from a distribution with the old values of *add_rate* and *remove_rate*. That observation would then be used in the transient distribution with the new values of *add_rate* and *remove_rate* when the player encountered the merchant. If the levels of supply and demand change multiple times between encounters, the effects of the changes can be simulated by multiple virtual observations that are obtained using the previous observation, the previous values of *add_rate* and *remove_rate*, and the sampling from the transient distribution. The game would thus behave as though the player had observed the level of stock of the affected type of item each time its supply and demand changed.

In some cases, it is desirable to ensure that a merchant always has a certain minimum number of items of a particular type in stock. If a game directs the player to travel a long way to buy special items, for example, it would be very frustrating to arrive at the destination only to discover that the items were not available. This problem can easily be solved by adding a constant to the number of items generated by the stationary distribution on the player's first encounter. If the merchant should generally maintain a certain minimum stock level, then adding a constant is unsatisfactory because it does not adequately model the dynamics of how stock changes in response to interactions with the player—if the player buys all the stock, for example, the amount of stock needs to recover in a convincing way.

The simplest solution to this problem is to model the merchant regularly buying new stock, as was described earlier. Alternately, it is possible to create a reserve of items that can only be purchased by the player and model how it recovers over time if the player makes a purchase that depletes it. This is done by estimating the number of items that could have been added to the reserve since it was depleted if the merchant repopulated it by buying items at a rate of *add_rate* and selling nothing. If the reserve could only have been partially repopulated, the reserve is the full extent of the inventory, and no sample from the transient distribution is required. If the reserve could have been fully repopulated, however, the time when the process of repopulation would've been completed is calculated, and the number of nonreserve items is obtained by sampling from the transient distribution using a virtual observation of zero nonreserve items backdated to when the reserve would've reached full strength. This technique is implemented in the overload of `Inventory::GenerateRealization` that takes the time parameter.

Finally, some types of items, such as arrows, are naturally traded in batches, and it is unlikely that a merchant would buy or sell only a single instance of such types. This effect can be approximated by using stationary and transient distributions to represent the numbers of batches held by the merchant rather than the numbers of individual items. When the number of batches changes from the player's last observation, the number of items can be generated randomly by assuming that a particular number of batches would correspond to a particular range of numbers of items. For example, if each batch of arrows is of size 25, then one batch would correspond to between 1 and 25 arrows, two batches, 26 and 50 arrows, etc. If a sample from the distribution specified a stock level of two batches, the actual number of items would be chosen randomly from the range 26 to 50.

In general, the properties of M/M/1 queues that were described earlier make it possible to guess values for parameters like *add_rate* and *remove_rate* to simulate specific behaviors. It is, however, important to validate those behaviors using a simple test application like the one included on the book's website that allows the behaviors to be quickly and efficiently evaluated over a wide range of timescales.

37.3.1 Computational Considerations

A game might contain many thousands of different types of items that could potentially be found in an inventory, so the question naturally arises as to whether it's computationally practical to sample from such a large number of queues. Fortunately, for types where *rate_ratio* is small (i.e., for types that are unlikely to appear in the inventory or to only be present in small numbers—such as truffles and swords), samples can be obtained at a rate of hundreds of thousands per second per core on a typical desktop PC. Where *rate_ratio* is close to one—as was the case with the arrows—samples can only be obtained at a rate of thousands per second, so the approach described in this chapter might not be suitable for inventories where hundreds of different types of items are likely to be present in hundreds or thousands. Such inventories are likely to be the exception, however, and it is important to remember that samples are only required when a player encounters a merchant—there's no ongoing computation—and that samples for each type of item are independent, and hence the process of sampling can, if necessary, easily be distributed across multiple cores and multiple frames.

37.4 Conclusion

This article has described M/M/1 queues and showed how they can be simulated in a consistent and computationally efficient way by sampling from their stationary and transient distributions. It has shown how they can be used to represent the inventory of a merchant in such a way that it remains consistent with each item's supply and demand, the player's observations of the inventory, and the player's interactions with the merchant. This provides a simple and efficient way to simulate how the inventory of a merchant changes with time.

References

[Baccelli 89] Baccelli, F., Massey, W. A. 1989. A sample path analysis of the M/M/1 queue. *Journal of Applied Probability*, 26(2): 418–422. https://www.princeton.edu/~wmassey/20th%20Century/sample%20path%20MM1.pdf (accessed July 20, 2014).

[Zabinsky 13] Zabinsky, Z. 2013. Stochastic models and decision analysis, University of Washington, Seattle, WA. http://courses.washington.edu/inde411/QueueingTheory.pdf (accessed July 20, 2014).

38

Psychologically Plausible Methods for Character Behavior Design

Phil Carlisle

38.1 Introduction

If you have ever worked with 3D game character artists, you'll have heard them talk obsessively about silhouette and how a character reads. They do this because they understand that for video games especially, there is the issue of viewpoint. As players move around a world in 3D, they can change their viewpoint with respect to the character considerably, changing distance and angle. Artists want their work to be understood by players, so they try and maximize that understanding by taking care to make a "readable" character. A readable character is one that can be viewed from different directions and at different distances and still remain recognizable.

As behavior designers, we have very similar issues to deal with; we have to make our behaviors "readable" by players in different situations and have our players recognize and understand the behavior. The aim of this chapter is to encourage you to think about this aspect of your behavior design and to ground you in a sample of the psychological aspects that come into play from the player's perspective. Using a number of studies performed by groups of undergraduate game design students as examples, the intention is to raise awareness rather than to be academically rigorous. As psychology is a very complex field, it is recommended that these studies not be taken at face value, but instead should be used to consider how psychology might inform the development of character behavior, by adding methods of evaluation and ways of thinking about player understanding.

38.2 Perception and Abstractions

When working on character behaviors, one of the principal tools at our disposal is the use of animation and movement. By the use of movement, we can convey to the player different behavioral meanings based on the nature of the movement, but how do players actually perceive movement?

In the 1970s, psychologist Gunnar Johansson ran a series of studies involving point-light animations [Johansson 73]. He took a number of his students and dressed them completely in black clothing. He then attached small reflective markers to various joints and got the students to act out particular motions while filming them such that only the markers were visible. The resulting films bear a striking resemblance to modern motion-capture data; an example of his work can be viewed online [Maas 11].

Johansson was interested in our perception of motion. What he found was that from these relatively sparse data, his test subjects were able to describe what types of objects were involved and in some circumstances what gender the subject was. He varied the angles of the motions and otherwise manipulated the viewpoints in order to study where perception broke down. Interestingly, when he tested occluding some of the markers, the participants were able to perceive the motion until a relatively high percentage of the markers were obscured. Similarly, he altered the orientation and found that perception broke down only in fairly extreme circumstances (e.g., when the subject was turned upside down).

What this perception study showed is that humans (and presumably other animals) have a capability to take relatively sparse or abstract motions and parse them into familiar mental models of motion. We can think of this process as *shape fitting*, taking motion, and mapping it to known patterns of movement and then attributing that movement to some previously learned behavior.

It seems likely that this capability is actually a very useful one in terms of neuroevolution; for instance, it might be used to spot a prey animal from a distance by its movement pattern or for selecting a weaker prey animal from a herd.

So what does this all have to do with character AI? The basic premise proposed here is that when we create behavior, we should take care that the motion the behavior exhibits matches motions that can then be shape fitted by players into mental models that allow them to associate the motion of the character with learned patterns.

Just to highlight this point, consider a character behavior in the abstract for a moment. If we want to portray an aggressive character, what styles of movement would we most likely select to show that aggression? One suggestion would be that short, fast movements would be better for showing aggression than long, slow movements. Why would this be the case? One possibility is that we have evolved a capability to detect sharp fast movements as aggressive in response to the types of movements we might have seen from predator animals. For example, think of a cat trying to attack a mouse; how does the movement change as the cat approaches? Think of the explosive force used for when the cat "pounces" on the mouse.

This sharp fast movement happens in other animals too. Fish, insects, and snakes all exhibit striking motions. Most 3D animators know this instinctively, but this notion of movement speed was actually outlined much earlier in traditional stop-motion animation as the principle of force described well in *The Illusion of Life* [Thomas 81] and essentially deals with the biomechanical effort involved in specific motions. The act of stalking in the cat movement might be seen as aggressive by a viewer who had previously seen the cat hunting. From the perspective of the prey, however, the slower movement is less threatening, which suggests that viewpoint has a large impact on the way movement is perceived and is informed by the previous experience of the viewer.

Another interesting aspect to come out of Johansson's work is the fact that some motions suggest particular feelings or relationships. In one study, the motions of two point lights were arranged such that a synchronized circular motion was used, as shown in Figure 38.1. Where the point lights gained close proximity and mirrored the motion of each other, this was perceived by viewers as having affinity between the points. Similarly, points that moved in contrary motions were perceived to have animosity.

In order to cement this notion of perception of motion in the abstract, let us present another study that will also ease us into another aspect of psychology.

In 1944, Fritz Heider and Marianne Simmel presented a paper called *An Experimental Study of Apparent Behavior* [Heider 44]. In it, they describe a study where they presented viewers with a film showing a number of abstract shapes (lines, circles, triangles) with corresponding motions filmed using stop-motion animation. They asked the participants to explain what they saw in the film. In almost all of the cases, the participants explained the film in terms of what the "characters" were doing. They described the scene with explanations such as the following: "A man has planned to meet a girl and the girl comes along

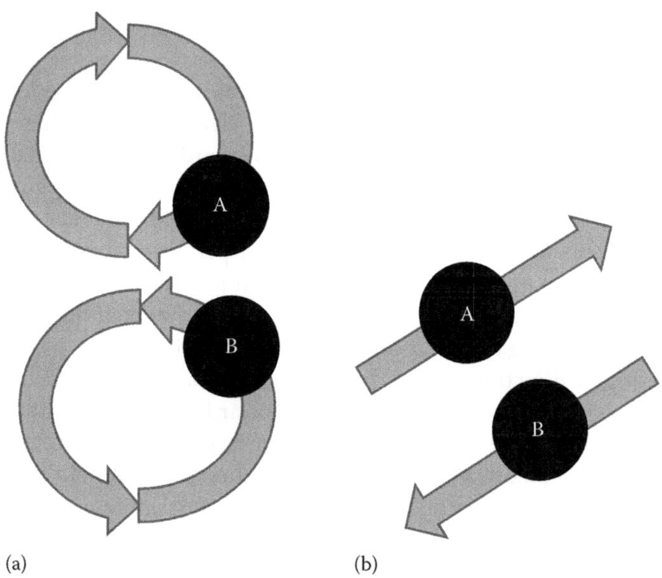

Figure 38.1

An example of complementary (a) and contrary (b) motions used in the study.

with another man. The first man tells the second to go; the second tells the first, and he shakes his head. Then the two men have a fight, and the girl starts to go into the room to get out of the way and hesitates and finally goes in," clearly showing that they had generated an internal narrative to explain what they saw. Indeed it is hard not to see the same footage [Smith-Welch 08] and offer a similar explanation.

The fact that viewers of a film are able to take abstract shapes with motion and construct an internal narrative should really drive home the point that we need to consider the qualities of motion inherent in behavior when we are trying to design characters. Once again, this points to the ability to map relatively abstract movements to known behavioral patterns. As character designers, this should give us some ideas on how to shape the understanding of a character's behavior from a player's perspective. Altering the qualities of movement and the viewpoint they are seen from could allow us to alter how a character is perceived to our advantage, much like an author setting up a reader's mental view of a character before getting them to perform an action.

38.3 Developmental Psychology and the Teleological Stance

The process by which we are able to translate movements into mental models and the specifics of that process is an ongoing area of research. The term "shape fitting" relates it to the processes used in computer vision, but this is merely a shorthand description for a complex set of processes. It is quite useful to review this aspect within the literature on developmental psychology. A useful starting point is the *Blackwell Handbook of Childhood Cognitive Development* [Goshwani 10]. In particular, the chapter by Gergely [Gergely 10] describes an early infant process that allows inference about actions through a naive theory of rational action, basically a process of mapping movements to intended actions that is referred to as the teleological stance. As infants grow, they develop more capabilities in terms of the ability to read a given motion and infer its intention, so developers of games for infants should probably consider the stages of development their target audience has reached.

This ability to read the intentions of others uses gaze direction as a key component. Children follow the gaze direction of their parents in order to learn what is important for them to be aware of [Goshwani 10]. Over time, they develop the capacity to model the knowledge of others, using gaze as a significant aspect of that model. For example, as a child grows, they begin to understand that another person might have knowledge of a particular object or they might not. They learn that if the other person has actually seen the object (i.e., directed their gaze toward it), then they know about the object. Thus, they learn that the stronger the gaze, the more important the object.

This aspect of gaze direction is important for us as behavior designers because it is one of the primary tools we can use to direct the player toward the correct reading of behavioral intent. The player can read the behavior quite differently if they see that the character is not aware of an interacting object; in other words, if we direct the gaze of the character away from an object, we can alter how the player reads any corresponding interaction with it.

Consider Figure 38.2 as an example. In the leftmost pair, we have no way of determining the gaze direction. If you focus on that pair exclusively, you are unlikely to ascribe any intention to the objects. In the middle pair, the gaze is pointing inward; this is likely to indicate antagonism or aggression, unless we have previously seen context in which the pair had displayed positive affect, in which case we might view them as being in a friendly

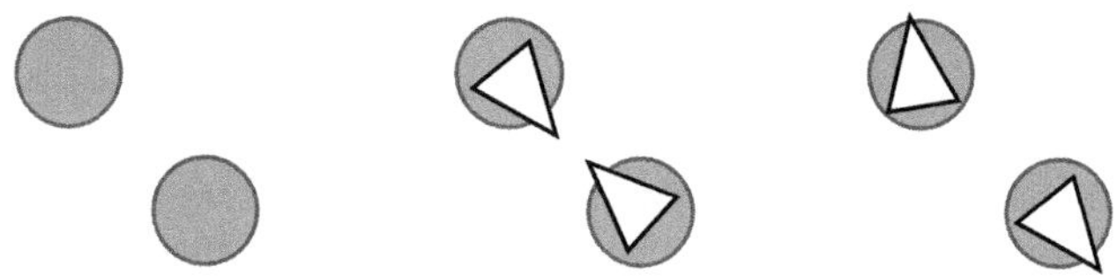

Figure 38.2

A simple example of how perceived gaze direction can influence our reading of a situation.

chat or a conspiratorial congress. The final pair we might well view as being unaware of each other, unless we had seen previous context that suggested they knew each other, might then change the reading of the pair to one of a social rebuff. However, if you interpret the "characters" in the figure, you should be aware that the only condition that is changing is the perceived gaze direction of each pair. This effect is happening even within a very abstract scene but can be particularly strong when seen in motion.

38.4 Attribution Theory

The work by Heider, Simmel, and others eventually led to the field of psychology known as attribution theory [Kelley 67]. For behavior design, this concept of *attribution* is an important one. The basic idea is to consider how we attribute the intention of an action. We commonly think of actions as internal (i.e., the character intended to do it) or external (it was done to the character or caused by other factors). As behavior designers, we should be able to influence a player's view of the behavior such that they ascribe the action as being intentional by the character or unintentionally happening to the character. For instance, we might hint at the incompetence of a character, which leads the player to likely ascribe positive actions as being external; in other words, if something good happens, it happens by chance and not skill.

An interesting aspect of the Heider/Simmel study was that the narrative given to explain the scene changed when the scene was presented in reverse; each viewer was presented with both a "forward" normal viewing of the film and a "reverse" viewing, in which the film was played backward. In many areas, the narrative broke down because the context of the motions was changed. For instance, the larger triangle in the forward presentation is seen as dominant or bullying through the remaining narrative due to an early segment where it performs a fast motion toward the smaller triangle and pushes it a short distance; however, in the reverse presentation, the first aggressive "push" movement is not seen, and thus the narrative of dominance is changed. This implies that in order for a viewer to correctly attribute a behavior, that behavior must be seen within a context that is temporally plausible; in other words, the order in which we present behavioral movements is important. It can be useful to recreate this aspect of the study with your own section of a film, playing the film in the reverse and thinking about how the behaviors are affected. Are some behaviors still understandable? Do you read the motivations of characters differently? What is causing that effect?

We can consider a simple illustration of this effect. Think of a cat trying to catch a mouse; imagine the cat slowly creeping up behind the mouse, keeping close to the ground, slowly moving up, and then suddenly moving with rapid force during a "pounce" behavior.

Now consider the behavior with the order of actions reversed. Instead of a creep-then-pounce, think how a pounce-then-creep would look.

The concept of attribution of behavior is an interesting one, in that it poses questions about awareness and intent. If we are constantly evaluating the motions of others in a bid to understand their intention in terms of our own beliefs about them, then perhaps we can start to manipulate that evaluation in order to achieve a desired effect. One of the key aspects we need to think about is the attribution of intent. Does a behavior we want to portray show intention for the character or not? For example, imagine two characters and a ball. Character A throws the ball at character B; only character B is facing away from A and is not aware of the ball, so consequently B gets hit on the head. In this simple scene, we can actually influence different readings of the inference of the viewer.

Consider the case where we have previously shown character A throwing balls at other characters. In this case, it is likely a viewer would ascribe the ball-throwing behavior as an intentional act. The viewer will have learned that character A throws balls and thus would see the ball-throwing action as fitting in with what they know about A's likelihood to intentionally throw a ball at another character.

Now imagine the same scene, but instead we have previously seen character B being hit by several other characters throwing balls. In this case, we are more likely to attribute the behavior to be a lack of awareness by B than any particular malice by character A.

The fact that a simple ball-throwing behavior could be understood differently depending on our understanding of the attributed qualities of the participants is an important point to note in any character behavior design. We can begin to manipulate a player's reading of a given character by reinforcing their mental attribution processes if we can set up scenes in a manner that takes into account the teleological stance of the behavior and reinforces a given view of the character.

38.5 Problem of Characters as Tokens

Before we get on to discussing the practical application of these psychological principles in terms of behavior design, it is worth noting an issue that most character designers face. A number of years ago at the University of Bolton, we ran an (unpublished) undergraduate study into the methods that players use to select companion characters in games. In this particular study, the test involved choosing companion characters for further gameplay from a roster of characters, which were presented in different ways. The characters themselves were portrayed using different clothing and gender options, with the aim of the study being to understand more about the effect of the communication mode (text, cinematic) on the choice. One of the more surprising results from the study came from the qualitative interviews conducted with participants after they had made the character choice. Although this was not the aim of the study, we found that most players chose characters not based on their narrative delivery method, but instead on a measure of perceived usefulness in the game. In essence, they had ignored the "character" of the choice and had instead chosen based on the utility value. This was not a choice that was based on evidence (no statistics were provided for comparing the characters) but rather on a simple perceived value, that is, "they looked like they would be good in a fight."

The fact that players understand that characters in games are also part of the game mechanics suggests an underlying problem in terms of making more believable characters, in that for all our best efforts, we may never be able to break that relationship in the player's mind. It might well be that games with more focus on the story and setting of the game could convince players to choose characters for their narrative value; however, it is worth considering what aspects of a character players are likely to base their choices on at the design stage. Is the player presented with information on the character that will explicitly state their utility? How can we identify players who make choices based on other aspects of character and perhaps alter our offering of choices based on that identification?

38.6 Practical Application of Psychology in Character Behavior Design

In another study, an undergraduate group was interested in how the perception of a character shaped a player's view of their own performance. They conducted an experiment in which test subjects played an online game against a series of three "bots" where each bot was represented with a different narrative designed to relate to easy, medium, and hard opponent difficulty levels. What the test subjects were not aware of was that each of the three "bots" was actually being controlled by a human player, who was deliberately playing to a script that essentially reduced the combat to the same level of difficulty for each play session. What the study found was that the players were more likely to score their own performance highly if they managed to win against the "hard" enemy. Similarly, they sought to attribute a loss to the difficulty level of the opponent. This study essentially showed that players can be influenced to feel differently about their own performance depending on the narrative context of their actions. If the context is one where the player feels they are likely to lose, then they ascribe a loss to the game, whereas if they win they are more likely to ascribe the win to their own mastery or skill, no matter of the actual difficulty involved in the action.

In practical terms, this means we can start to encourage players to feel more skillful by presenting them with challenges described as hard, but which are biased toward them winning. This can be as subtle as describing enemies in a manner that inflates their ability with respect to other agents, for example, calling an agent a major instead of a soldier. We can also influence a player's perception by making sure they see a character fail at a task; from that point, it is more likely they will perceive that character as more likely to fail other tasks.

Similarly, we can influence a player's perception of character interactions within a group by carefully manipulating their motions. Considering the case where a player is controlling a group of role-playing characters, we can make two characters within that group appear more friendly toward each other by simply biasing their movements to be more complementary (i.e., often aligned in the same direction, being in close proximity). We can increase the perception of animosity by making sure that the characters avoid close proximity and bias their movements such that they never mirror each other.

38.7 Conclusion

When designing the behaviors of characters in a game, it can be too easy to focus on the individual behavior and lose sight of the overall readability of the character. If we want to create characters that players understand and believe in, we must embrace the aspects of psychology that inform how a player perceives them.

In this chapter, we have tried to offer some simple psychological theories that you can investigate and use to your advantage when considering your initial character designs. Hopefully, this chapter has convinced you that many of the psychological tools you can use to affect players' perceptions function at a high level of abstraction and can often be implemented with very minimal development cost.

Psychology itself is an ongoing area of research and we are only just beginning to investigate the psychology involved in games. From a practical point of view, many of the psychological effects described in this chapter are quite subtle or do not apply universally to all player types. Even with these caveats, it is well worth the time for a designer to familiarize themselves with psychology and its measurement as part of the design toolset. We have seen many of our students gain design roles within the game industry due in large part to their experience working on an aspect of game psychology that is under researched, offering a unique experience and perspective that many employers seem to find valuable.

References

[Gergely 10] Gergely, G. 2010. Kinds of agents: The origins of understanding instrumental and communicative agency. In *Blackwell Handbook of Childhood Cognitive Development* (2nd edn.), ed. U. Goshwani, pp. 76–105. Oxford, U.K.: Blackwell.

[Goshwani 10] Goshwani, U. ed. 2010. *Blackwell Handbook of Childhood Cognitive Development* (2nd edn.). Oxford, U.K.: Blackwell Publishers.

[Heider 44] Heider, F. and Simmel, M. 1944. An experimental study of apparent behavior. *The American Journal of Psychology* (University of Illinois Press) 57(2): 243–259.

[Johansson 73] Johansson, G. 1973. Visual perception of biological motion and a model for its analysis. *Perception and Psychophysics* (Springer-Verlag) 14(2): 201–211.

[Kelley 67] Kelley, H. H. 1967. Attribution theory in social psychology. *Nebraska Symposium on Motivation* (University of Nebraska Press) 15: 192–238.

[Maas 11] Maas, J. 2011. Johansson: Motion perception. https://www.youtube.com/watch?v=1F5ICP9SYLU (accessed June 1, 2014).

[Smith-Welch 08] Smith-Welch, M. Youtube.com. https://www.youtube.com/watch?v=sZBKer6PMtM (accessed June 2, 2014).

[Thomas 81] Thomas, F. and Johnson, O. 1981. *The Illusion of Life: Disney Animation.* New York: Hyperion.

SECTION VII
Analytics, Content Generation, and Experience Management

39

Analytics-Based AI Techniques for a Better Gaming Experience

Truong-Huy D. Nguyen, Zhengxing Chen, and Magy Seif El-Nasr

39.1 Introduction

Recently, it has become increasingly common to gather gameplay data through telemetry logs. These data can provide valuable insight into the player's interactions with the game and are typically used by designers to balance the game, but they can also be used to algorithmically adjust game systems in order to create better engagement. Specifically, gameplay data analytics can provide ways to (1) algorithmically adapt game content and mechanics on the fly; (2) recommend games to play on game portals, such as Steam; and (3) match teams in multiplayer games.

Adapting game content and design to the user's behaviors and responses has gained momentum in the recent years [Piggyback 09; Newell 08]. Titles that adjust difficulty and/or game mechanics based on the user's skill level and performance include *Fallout 3* [Bethesda 08], *Fallout: New Vegas* [Bethesda 10], *Left 4 Dead* [EA 08], *Left 4 Dead 2* [Valve 09], and *Resident Evil 5* [Capcom 09]. Difficulty adjustment can increase engagement and thus increase user retention. While there are many different methods to develop adaptive games, in this chapter, we will focus on AI algorithms that use a model of the user to adjust game content or mechanics in real time.

Matching teams within multiplayer games is another trend that has gained momentum [Dota Team 13; Lefebvre 14; GO 13]. Notable examples include *Defense of the Ancients 2*, often better known by its acronym *DotA 2* [Valve 13]; *League of Legends*, a.k.a. *LoL* (all seasons) [Riot 09]; and *Counter Strike: Global Offensive* (CS:GO) [Valve 12]. In these examples, user performance and skills can be gauged through data collected during play (i.e., telemetry data), and team matching can be done based on this analysis.

We reviewed numerous articles in both industry and academia that report the use of analytics to drive better experiences through adaptation, recommendation, or team matching. The approaches taken can be categorized into five groups:

1. *Skill-based adaptation*: Techniques that aim to adapt the game mechanics to the user's skill level. The goal is to maintain a level of challenge that will not overwhelm players with overly hard tasks but will keep them challenged and engaged.
2. *Emotion-based adaptation*: Techniques that change aspects of the game to influence the emotional process of players based on their affective states. The goal can be to evoke certain kinds of emotions or to modulate the player's emotions for a more relatable game experience.
3. *Style-based adaptation*: Techniques that adjust elements in the game (e.g., content) based on the player's play style.
4. *Game recommendation*: Techniques that reach beyond the scope of just one game, recommending games to play based on the player's past choices. Recommendation systems develop a model of the player's preference based on their game choices, rating scores, etc. Using this information and information from other players collectively, such systems can suggest games that players may enjoy, which results in a better experience, more engagement, greater retention, and higher ratings.
5. *Team Balancing*: In games that allow team-based battles, matching appropriate team members/opponents based on their skills can directly impact the experience. Most automated matchmaking systems implemented in commercial titles, such as that of *DotA 2*, *LoL*, or *CS:GO*, match teams with similar skill levels against each other [Dota Team 2013].

In this chapter, we will discuss these systems through a review of two sets of works. First, we will discuss algorithms and techniques that will allow us to model users in terms of performance, preference, or behaviors. This work is the focus of game analytics. Game analytics is a set of techniques drawing from data mining, machine learning, and statistics to generalize or understand play-related data collected through play sessions. Second, we will discuss examples to show these approaches in action, in particular for adaptive games. We will show how game content and mechanics can be modeled and adjusted algorithmically in order to tune them to a user model driven from analytics results. We will draw on examples from academia and industry, indie and AAA titles, as well as single-player and multiplayer games to show how such techniques can be used across a wide variety of game types.

39.2 Game Analytics Approaches to Modeling User Performance, Skills, and Behaviors

Game analytics refers to the process of collecting data pertinent to how players interact with the game world, analyzing that data to uncover implicit patterns and trends, and finally converting the data into useful knowledge [Seif El-Nasr 13]. Play data collected for this purpose are usually referred to as *game telemetry*, which is raw, time-stamped stream of actions taken and player-related events happening in the game. Usually, such data are logged and transmitted for storage in a remote database, thus the name telemetry.

39.2.1 Game Metrics

Once we have the telemetry data, we next need to define a set of features that will allow us to evaluate the player's experience, skills, behaviors, and/or preferences. These features are called *game metrics* and are defined as quantitative measures of one or more attributes of interaction in the context of the game. For example, completion time for each level can be a metric. Depending on the game genre, different metrics can be derived from the telemetry data. Examples of metrics for popular genres include

- *First-person shooters*: Types of weapons used, types of item/asset used, character choice, route choice, loss/win quota, team scores, vehicles used, strategic point captures/losses, jumps, crouches, and special moves
- *Strategy games*: Types of commands given to units, upgrades purchased, win/loss ratio, team/race/color selection, maps used, map settings, match/game settings, and time spent on building tasks versus unit tasks
- *Platformers*: Jumping frequency, progression speed, items collected, power-ups/abilities used, and damage taken/sources of damage
- *Role-playing games (RPGs)*: Character progression, quest completions, quest time to complete, character ability/item use (including context of use), combat statistics, AI-enemy performance, story progression, nonplayer character (NPC) interactions, damage taken and sources of damage, and items collected

39.2.2 Analysis Techniques

Given these metrics, several techniques can be used for analysis of these data to derive a user model in terms of performance, skills, and behavior. Analysis techniques usually fall under two categories: individual and community based.

39.2.2.1 Individual Analysis

Individual analyses operate on data pertaining to a *single* player, aiming to learn the different processes that drive the targeted player's in-game actions. Here are the common goals of individual analysis:

1. Adapt game difficulty to the skill of an individual player so that the player is faced with an appropriate level of challenge.
2. Predict the player's gameplay behavior to tune the design increasing player retention.

3. Generate personalized game content to satiate the player's appetite, including narratives, maps, and skins.
4. Develop game AIs that match the player's play style and skill level.

We will discuss how these goals are achieved using concrete examples, most of which start from player models. *Player modeling* is defined as the development of computational techniques to model players' cognitive, behavioral, and affective (i.e., emotional) state based on play data or theory [Yannakakis 13]. The development of a player model is usually done using machine learning algorithms, such as artificial neural networks (ANNs), support vector machines (SVMs), or Bayesian networks. In some other cases, simple models using numeric vectors, updated with hand-tuned rules, are also adopted.

ANNs [Bishop 06] are supervised learning algorithms inspired by animals' nervous systems. They are constructed as a network of *neurons* (represented as nodes), divided into one input layer, zero or more hidden layer(s), and one output layer. Each neuron processes its input using an activation function, usually either a sigmoid or a step function. Nodes between adjacent layers are connected by directed links pointing from lower-layer (i.e., closer to the input layer) source nodes to higher-layer target nodes, with the output of the source nodes fed as part of their target node's input. More specifically, the input of a target node is a linear combination of all its source nodes, with coefficients defined by the links' weights.

Before using these algorithms for prediction, ANNs need to be trained, which is an automated process that configures all of the links' weights so that, for each set of input layer values, the values in the output layer approximate those defined in the training data set.

In the context of player modeling, ANNs are often used as a compact predictor that maps from game states/situations to the corresponding player actions [Togelius 07; Tang 09]. Togelius et al. [Togelius 07] presented an approach to model players' driving styles in racing games using ANNs. The player model starts with some default values and then is progressively trained during play using data collected at 30 waypoints along the track. The input features include

1. The speed of the car
2. The angle between the car's heading and the direction to the current waypoint
3. The distance between the car and nearby walls

The output is one of nine action commands in controlling the car, including the arrow keys and combinations of them.

A multiobjective evolutionary algorithm is then used for training the network to optimize three fitness functions matching the observed human's behavior in terms of distance traveled, speed, and maneuver direction. The algorithm represents each ANN candidate as a vector of weight parameters and thus as one individual in a set of candidates. Through generations of evolution (consecutive selection with respect to each fitness function, then multiplication, and mutation), an ANN that approximately optimizes the three aforementioned objectives is achieved and used as the player model.

An *SVM* [Burges 98] is a supervised learning technique that uses a discriminative classifier able to categorize incoming data. Given labeled training data, the algorithm outputs the hyperplane that best separates it. This hyperplane can then be used to categorize new samples. It can, thus, model the player's play style in a similar manner to ANNs, taking as input a game state and returning the most probable action the player would take.

Missura and Gartner [Missura 09] used SVMs to classify players' play styles in a 2D shooting game where the goal is to destroy alien spaceships. The data used for modeling are gathered from multiple plays of 17 test players, who can set the difficulty level while playing. Each play record, which is at most 100 s long, is first normalized into a fixed-size sequence of time-stamped feature tuples, which record the game state at 100 ms intervals. The features used included the score, the player's health, and the current selected difficulty level. The play records are split into two parts. The input data to the SVM are the first 30 s (without the difficulty information) of play, while the training labels are identified through cluster analysis, namely, K-means [Bishop 06], on the remaining 70 s play data. The SVM is trained to divide its input data into the categories generated by the K-means clustering. Thus, we end up with a predictive model that is able to classify new players into one of K player types based on their health and score over the first 30 s of play. The difficulty is then adjusted according to the average difficulty in that player type. One advantage of this approach is that player types are not crafted by hand but are generated from the training data. Once a player has been categorized as a particular type, his or her difficulty level can be adjusted automatically to be the average difficulty selected by the cluster that the player belongs to.

Bayesian networks [Neapolitan 04] provide a means for representing independency relationships among events' occurrences, as well as a mechanism for inferring the occurrence states of pertinent events under uncertainty. A Bayesian network consists of a collection of nodes, along with directed links that connect them. Unlike ANNs, links here represent the probability that the target node will be true (or false) if the source nodes are observed to be true (or false). In the field of player modeling, Bayesian networks can cope with uncertainty in the player model, allowing for inference on a set of *class variables* given a subset of the input *observation* features, rather than a complete representation of them.

Yannakakis et al. [Yannakakis 05] used Bayesian networks to capture the relationship between a player's behavior statistics and the parameters that affect game content generation. They developed a modified version of Pac-Man where, much like in the original, the player's goal is to collect pellets while avoiding being killed by ghosts. Unlike the original, Yannakakis' version has ghost generators that take as input two parameters: e_v (the ghost evaluation parameter) and p_m (the ghost diversity parameter), which directly affect how competitive the game is. The game uses a Bayesian network in which the class nodes are e_v and p_m, and the observation nodes are score, time-played, numeric measure of player aggressiveness, the initial interest in the game, and the relative interest difference after 10 games. Interest is computed as the linear combination of three metrics quantitatively calculated from game data, which are the challenge metric (based on the difference between maximum and average player's lifetime over 50 games), diversity metric (based on the standard deviation of player's lifetime over 50 games), and aggressiveness metric (based on the stage grid-cell visit average entropy of the ghosts over 50 games). Training data were generated using three different AI players, each with a different strategy that represents a different player type. Each of the AI players was run against multiple predefined configurations of (e_v, p_m). After being trained against the results of these sessions, the Bayesian network was able to infer from an incomplete set of observations (score, time, aggressiveness, etc.), a setting of (e_v, p_m) that will maximize the player's interest.

Numeric weight vectors provide a simple yet popular alternative to machine learning techniques for modeling players. The weight vector indicates how confident the system is in categorizing the player to an archetype. Thue et al. [Thue 07] adopted this method to adjust storylines in an RPG developed using the *Aurora Neverwinter Toolset* [Atari 02]. Thue's archetypes categorized players as Fighters (who prefer combat), Power Gamers (who prefer gaining special items and riches), Tacticians (who prefer thinking creatively), Storytellers (who prefer complex plots), and Method Actors (who prefer to take dramatic actions). The player model expressed a 5D weight vector, with each dimension representing how closely the player's actions resemble those expected from one of the five base types. During the development phase, designers manually identify all actions that are associated with the various archetypes. When the player takes one of these actions, the weight vector is updated accordingly. For example, a player might start with a weight vector of <Fighter = 1, MethodActor = 81, Storyteller = 1, Tactician = 1, PowerGamer = 41>, meaning he is classified as most strongly as a Method Actor but is also something of a Power Gamer. After he asks for a reward for helping an NPC, the vector is updated to <Fighter = 1, MethodActor = 81, Storyteller = 1, Tactician = 1, PowerGamer = 141>, in order to account for the fact that this player has shown an interest in gaining riches. These techniques (and a number of variants on it) are discussed in more detail in Chapter 42.

39.2.2.2 Communal Analysis

In contrast to individual analysis, communal analysis aims to uncover the general patterns or trends of a subset of, if not all, players collectively. Typically, the goal is to cluster player behaviors to recognize different distinct groups; a player group could be a community in a game or a set of players who share similar playing styles. Communal analysis relies on data mining techniques, including clustering algorithms, such as K-means [MacQueen 67], C-means, principle component analysis (PCA) [Jolliffe 02], nonnegative matrix factorization (NMF) [Lee 99], archetypal analysis (AA) [Cutler 94], and other variants of these algorithms.

Clustering algorithms: Given a set of data points, clustering algorithms aim to group similar data points together to form several representative groups such that the number of groups is much smaller than that of the data points. The resultant group data can then be used for classification (K-, C-means, and NMF) or data compression tasks (PCA).

Although all clustering algorithms share the same goal, their requirements and outputs may vary. In particular, while K-means and C-means both assign one unique group label to each data point, C-means additionally restricts the cluster centers to be among the actual data points instead of just averages, that is, medians in place of means. NMF, unlike K-means and C-means, allows data points to fuzzily belong to multiple clusters by representing them as linear combinations of different cluster centers. Moreover, it requires that all data points, group centers, and each data point's membership to groups contain only nonnegative values, making both inputs and clustering results interpretable by human experts. While having similar outputs as NMF, which are basis vectors able to compose the bulk of input data points, PCA aims to capture the main directions of fluctuation or variance exhibited by the input data points. Intuitively, these fluctuations are the most representative components of the point set.

Unlike clustering analysis, whose goal is to find *average* points of a data set, *AA* looks for *extreme* points called *archetypes*. As such, any point in the data set can be interpreted as a combination of these archetypes. In practice, cluster analysis tends to yield similar basis vectors for different groups, which renders the player styles hard to distinguish from one another even for domain knowledge experts. On the contrary, because of the extremeness, archetypes are data points that have the most prominent characteristics and thus easy to interpret by a human. AA is commonly used to find extreme profiles (outliers) and can be used to detect bots, cheating, or extreme player behaviors. In AA, each archetype is a linear mixture of the data points. Each data point is clustered as a combination of all archetypes. AA, however, comes with significant computation cost, which makes it not ideal for large data sets, as its underlying algorithm involves solving many constrained quadratic optimization problems consecutively.

Simplex volume maximization (SIVM) is a variant of AA that was proposed in order to cope with large data sets [Thurau 10]. It exploits the fact that optimal basis vectors maximize the volume of the simplex they construct as vertices. Similar to AA, basis vectors in SIVM are as far (extreme) as possible to each other to maximize the volume of such simplex. The computation needed to find basis vectors in SIVM is however much lower than that in AA due to its algebraic derivation.

To cluster players of *Battlefield: Bad Company 2* [EA 10], Drachen et al. [Drachen 12] applied both K-means and SIVM to the game telemetry of 10,000 players [Drachen 12]. The telemetry data collect 11 game metrics that are closely related to

- Character performance (e.g., score, skill level, accuracy)
- Game asset use (kit stats, vehicle use)
- Playtime

Mixing different unnormalized data metrics may skew the results of clustering, because the metrics tend to contribute unevenly in dissimilarity measurement. The authors employed variance normalization to preprocess the telemetry data from different metrics before running K-means or SIVM. The presence of ratio data (e.g., kill/death ratio, win/loss ratio) may result in zero values in denominators, which required the authors to implement several smoothing algorithms. The two clustering algorithms yielded seven player profiles, among which the three player prototypes (Assassins, Veterans, and Target Dummies) are shared by both algorithms although the percentage of each may vary (see Tables 39.1 and 39.2). For the remaining clusters, SIVM results in profiles that exhibit a higher degree of difference than K-means.

Later, Drachen et al. conducted comprehensive experiments to a data set of 70,000 players' from World of Warcraft [Drachen 13]. The data set included playtime and leveling speed. They compared different clustering algorithms to develop a model of players' performances. Specifically, they used SIVM, K-means, C-means, PCA, and NMF. Results show that the rendered basis vectors are more intuitively interpreted when using SIVM, K-means, and C-means than PCA and NMF. K-means and C-means are the only two among the five algorithms that hard-label players (i.e., each player could only be assigned to one cluster, rather than being assigned with a linear combination of weights from all clusters). Since SIVM is a variant of AA, which represents data points by extreme archetypes, it results in the most distinguishable basis vectors.

Table 39.1 Behavior Clusters Resulted from SIVM (%P Is the Percentage of Players)

Title	%P	Characteristics
Assault Recon	1.4	Active kill and death statistics (high KpM and DpM), low hit accuracy, average scoring ability, second highest kill/death ratio overall
Medic engineer	0.8	Using vehicles more often, high skill level and hit accuracy, good at scoring
Assault specialist	5.0	Focus on assault, but low score, high death statistics and playtime, low skill level, kill/death ratio, and hit accuracy
Driver engineers	1.1	Extremely obsessed in driving vehicle; high playtime, score, and hit accuracy; lowest death statistics; inactive in killing enemies
Assassins	61.6	Highest kill/death ratio, lowest playtime, active kill statistics while keeping from dying efficiently
Veterans	2.01	Highest score, playtime, and rounds played, overall high values
Target Dummies	28.1	Lowest kill/death ratio, low scoring ability, minimal scores for all features but playtime and rounds played

Table 39.2 Behavior Clusters Resulted from K-Means (%P Is the Percentage of Players)

Title	%P	Characteristics
Snipers	7.4	Median scoring ability, overall low-middling values, high death statistics, extremely high hit accuracy
Soldiers	27.9	Median scoring ability, overall low-middling values, high DpM
Assault engineer	13.1	Similar to Soldiers but better skill value, high kill/death ratios
Target Dummies	26.0	Lowest scores for all values (including playtime) except high death statistics
Trainee Veterans	10.7	Similar to Veterans, but second rank in most features, lower playtime
Assassins	10.9	Highest rank in kill/death ratio, most active kill statistics, low playtime
Veterans	4.1	High playtime, second rank in most features, highest overall skill level

39.3 Game Analytics and Adaptive Techniques

We will examine three classes of adaptive techniques:

1. *Skill based*: Adjusting the level of *difficulty* or *challenge* to match the player's skill level
2. *Emotion based*: Personalizing the game content to the player's *affective state*
3. *Style based*: Adapting the game's content and/or mechanics to the player's preferred style

Of these three categories, skill-based adaptation is the most popular in tailoring players' gaming experience, while emotion-based and style-based customization techniques are gaining more attention.

39.3.1 Skill-Based Difficulty Adaptation

The goal of skill-based difficulty adaptation is to tailor the difficulty level of the game, in an evolving manner, to match the player's skill level. Two common approaches to implementing this are to adjust the behavior of AI-controlled characters and to adjust the layout of the game map (e.g., by adding or removing obstacles in a racing game or side-scroller). The techniques used to control these adjustments include weighted behavior selection, reinforcement learning (RL), and artificial evolution.

Weighted behavior selection techniques select suitable AI behavior or content from a library of predefined templates according to an online-adapted weight vector. Dynamic scripting (DS) [Spronck 06] is an example of a weighted behavior selection technique that has demonstrated to balance the competitiveness of the AI to different skill levels in *Neverwinter Nights* [Spronck 04]. The idea is to dynamically build scripts by probabilistically selecting rules from a rule library after each combat. The failure or success of a script in combat results, respectively, in an increase or decrease in the selection probabilities of the rules used. In other words, if a script is successful, then the rules from that script will be more likely to be selected in the next fight. The rule library that DS operates on is typically constructed manually, although some evolutionary algorithms can be used to enrich it automatically [Ponsen 05; Ponsen 07].

RL [Sutton 98] algorithms can be used to fine-tune AI behavior by rewarding beneficial actions and punishing detrimental or failed ones. Depending on the defined reward function, the resulting system may adapt to make NPCs more competitive or more collaborative. For example, Andrade et al. [Andrade 05] used RL techniques to learn the effectiveness (i.e., the amount of damage inflicted) of each action in one-on-one fighting games, such as Ultra Street Fighter IV [Capcom 14]. Using this analysis, when faced with a particular action from the player, the AI responds not with the best action, but rather with one that has an equal chance to beat/be defeated by the player's action. The authors showed that the technique provides manageable challenge to simulated players of different skill levels. Although it was only evaluated with an experimental fighting game, the technique seems promising for adoption in commercial fighting games.

Artificial evolution techniques use population-based evolutionary algorithms [Simon 13] to adaptively create entities that optimize some fitness function. This is through reproduction, mutation, recombination (crossover), and selection of individual entities in the population. When used for skill-based adaptation, the entities are modifications to the game, while the fitness function indicates the quality of each individual.

The general process starts with an initial population of candidate entities and repeatedly applies the following operators:

1. *Reproduction*: Breed new individuals by random recombination and mutation.
2. *Selection*: Retain best-fit individuals and discard worst fits.

When used to adjust the difficulty/challenge of a game, these techniques encode the desired quality of the adapted entities as the (multiobjective) fitness function used for selection.

Togelius et al. [Togelius 07] proposed a multiobjective evolutionary algorithm called *cascading elitism* to build racing tracks that optimize three *fun* criteria: (1) provide the right amount of challenge on average [Malone 80], (2) provide a varying amount of challenge [Koster 13], and (3) provide sections that encourage fast driving (such as straight lines). First, each track is represented as a vector of 30 numbers, encoding the control points of 30 connected Bezier curves with the tail segment attached to the start to form a closed shape. This track is then modified using an evolutionary process called *cascading elitism* that seeks to optimize three fitness functions to match different aspects of the observed human's behavior:

1. Total progress (i.e., the number of waypoints passed within 1500 time steps)
2. The speed at which each waypoint was passed
3. The deviation of direction

Representing each ANN candidate as a vector of weight parameters in a generation of individuals, cascading elitism undergoes N steps of selection ($N = 3$ in Togelius' work), each of which selects the individuals that perform best on one of the fitness functions. Specifically, out of a population of 100 genomes with different ANN configurations, the 50 genomes that score highest on the first fitness function are selected first. Next, the 30 genomes that score highest on the second fitness function (out of the 50 from the first step) are picked. Finally, the 20 genomes that score highest on the third fitness function are selected. These surviving 20 individuals are then copied five times each and then mutated into the next generation.

39.3.2 Emotion-Based Adaptation

The goal of emotion-based adaptation is to tailor the game according to the current detected affective state of the player. As such, many of these techniques involve the use of some sensor to automatically record physiological responses of players [Yannakakis 08; Yannakakis 10; Tognetti 10; Ambinder 11], while others try to infer the players' currently experienced emotion based on their behavior in games [Pedersen 09; Shaker 10; Booth 09]. Recently, with the prominence of game consoles coming with some sort of motion-sensing input devices (Kinect in Xbox One or PlayStation Camera in PlayStation 4), there have been works devoted to affect modeling using video data as well [Zeng 09; Kleinsmith 13; Meng 14].

Given the player sentiment data, there are generally two approaches in constructing adaptation rules: the first being via heuristics, possibly informed by psychological facts and theories [Booth 09], and the second resulted from offline study on playtesters. Works following the second approach usually generate rules using supervised learning algorithms, such as ANNs, to model the relationship between game parameters/player in-game behavior and emotion indices. Emotion indices are informed by either postsurvey self-reports [Yannakakis 06; Pedersen 09; Shaker 10] or physiological data recorded from biofeedback devices [Tognetti 10; Yannakakis 10; Ambinder 11]. The knowledge is then used to modulate the game while play so as to evoke author-intended sentiments from players. We will focus on the adaptation techniques, rather than affect modeling techniques, so while we will touch on the latter for a better understanding of the adaptation approaches adopted, surveying emotion modeling is beyond the scope of this section.

Left 4 Dead [EA 08], a postapocalyptic zombie-themed survival game published by Electronic Arts and Valve in 2008, is among the first AAA titles that publicly report their use of players' inferred affective state to adapt gameplay [Booth 09]. In particular, the system keeps track of a measure called the survivor intensity (SI) that associates with each player's *emotional intensity* when battling zombies. The SI value is updated according to heuristic rules. For example, a heuristic rule indicates that SI value increases when player receives damage (e.g., injured by zombies, incapacitated, or pushed off of a ledge) and decays over time otherwise. It is, therefore, implicitly assumed that players experience more trauma and anxiety when taking more damage in this game setting. Taking SI as input, the adopted adaptive dramatic pacing algorithm follows a cyclic finite-state machine (FSM) to spawn zombies. The FSM consists of four states, the transitions between which are determined by SI values:

1. *Build up*: Continuously spawning zombies until SI exceeds a peak value
2. *Sustain peak*: Trying to maintain SI peak for 3–5 s
3. *Peak fade*: Imposing minimal threat until SI falls below peak range
4. *Relax*: Continuing with minimal threat for 30–45 s or until players have traveled far enough

While SI is arguably tied to players' skill level (i.e., the more skilled they are, the harder for SI to increase over time) and quantities of zombies to game difficulty, the fact that the game does not blindly increase or decrease its difficulty according to the exhibited skillfulness but follows a *drama peak* principle makes it more of an emotion-based adaptive system than a skill-based one. After all, the algorithm's goal is to keep players entertained and not overly exhausted with fighting zombies instead of maintaining the challenge level.

Additionally, Valve has reportedly started looking at biofeedback input to inform gameplay adaptation for their future titles [Ambinder 11]. Specifically, the team has conducted experiments to assess the effectiveness of adaptation based on physiological signals using Left 4 Dead 2's (L4D2) platform. While there are many input possibilities such as heart rate, skin conductance level (SCL), electroencephalography, and body temperature, the experiment focuses on indexing player's arousal based on SCL information. The authors modified the AI Director in L4D2 to take SCL-based arousal values instead of heuristic rules based on SI values and let playtesters try both versions. Preliminary post-surveys showed that adapting the gameplay using biofeedback data has improved both the participants' fun factor and sense of challenge. The team subsequently conducted similar experiments with Alien Swarm [Valve 10], which showed similar positive results. The team, however, acknowledged some major hurdles before such techniques become practical. First, because biofeedback signals vary from player to player, the adaptation algorithm requires a lot of tweaking to work desirably. Second, most state-of-the-art methods for collecting physiological data are intrusive to the gaming process, as they require additional wiring or device attachment to the player's body. Finally, it could be hard to associate the stimuli with in-game events due to a known delay in bodily response. That said, there have been some attempts in releasing commercial gaming systems that include physiological signal recorders as part of the package. One notable example is Wild Divine with their Iom, a USB-based biofeedback reader [Wild Divine 14]. The device attaches to the three fingers of the player to measure her heart rate and SCL, which are used as input to meditation game series named The Journey to Wild Divine.

In the academia, Tognetti et al. [Tognetti 10] showed that by using a biofeedback device, namely ProComp Infiniti device by Thought Technology, more objective measures based on biological signals can be achieved, analyzed, and used for adaptation. In the work, they propose to use *linear discriminant analysis* to model player experience from recorded physiological responses such as blood-volume pulse (BVP), electrocardiogram, galvanic skin response, respiration, and temperature. The technique yields comparable performance to other modeling techniques [Yannakakis 08] while incurring lower computation overhead. Additionally, the technique is demonstrated in The Open Racing Car Simulator [Torcs 07], an open-source racing game platform used mainly for research.

Changing the player's view in the game world is another approach to influencing their affective state [Yannakakis 10]. The idea is to first train a predictive model that maps each configuration of camera control parameters and biosignal features to an affective state value. The investigated biosignal features are BVP, skin conductance, and heart rate, recorded using an IOM biofeedback device, a highly unobtrusive device. Predictive models used are based on ANNs trained using an evolutionary algorithm with the goal of matching players' reported emotional preferences and the ANN output. Next, these models are then evaluated and adjusted to satisfaction before being integrated into the content generator as a fitness function to predict the effect of candidate outputs. The technique was evaluated in a test 3D predator/prey game.

39.3.3 Style-Based Adaptation

Style-based adaptation techniques aim at tailoring the game experience to fit the preferred play style of players. Unlike skills that can be used to compare players' expertise with the game, that is, their chance in beating AI NPCs or other fellow players, play styles refer to in-game behaviors that differ due to personal choice or interests. As such, players with similar experience and skill levels can exhibit very different styles in interacting with the game world. For instance, in Assassin's Creed [Ubisoft 07], players can either exterminate opponent NPCs in a high-profile noisy fight or assassinate them silently. While the game promotes low-key stealth behavior, either style choice is valid for advancing in the game.

It is worth noting that many skill-based techniques can be adapted for use with the style-based adaptation approach by appropriately changing the evaluation functions in finding best-suited candidates [Lopes 11]. Targets for style-based adaptation usually include game content [Thue 07] or interface components [Magerko 08].

In order to deliver players a highly personalized story-based experience, Thue et al. [Thue 07] propose to decompose the gameplay into story events or *encounters*, which are selected appropriately from a library at run time based on the observed play style of the player. Each encounter comes with a set of preconditions for happening and a set of *branches* or available actions that players can take in that situation. In commercial games whereby a main storyline needs to be in place to reflect the overarching story of the game, these encounters that can be flexibly presented to players can be thought of as side quests, that is, optional play that potentially increases fun and replayability. The encounter selection system, namely, PaSSAGE, takes as input a player model that fuzzily categorizes players as one of five archetypes according to Robin's laws [Laws 02]: Fighters (combat inclined), Power Gamers (item collectors), Tacticians (creative thinkers), Storytellers (who like complex plots), and Method Actors (who likes to connect the in-game drama to their own selves). This model is constructed in real time based on predefined recognition rules and their in-game behavior. Next, PaSSAGE consults a library of encounters, each of which has been annotated to appeal to specific play styles, to find the one with a story branch that fits the current player model the most. The selected encounter then goes through a refinement phase in which various parameters are determined so that its instantiation is consistent to the modeled play style and current story line. Finally, the selected encounter is actualized when its preconditions (such as the appearance of required actor types) are satisfied. For instance, when an encounter of exchanging conversation with a friendly trader is selected for a Power Gamer player type, the system will populate the dialog with lines that mention locations for valuable items (which preferred by Power Gamers) and waits until a trader is nearby before conducting the encounter. In contrast, the same encounter will inform Fighter types of where to find monster hoards instead. PaSSAGE was evaluated with 90 university students by letting them play a scenario of the *Red Riding Hood* story, built using the *Aurora Neverwinter Toolset*. Participants reported to perceive more fun and sense of agency in playing the adaptive scenario over the fixed one.

In a similar manner, Magerko et al. [Magerko 08] advocated for generating highly personalized game interfaces in learning games based on the detected player–learner type, be it Explorer, Achiever (interested in quickly collecting awards/badges), or Winner (seeking to complete the level thoroughly). In particular, Explorers are presented with bonuses and trivia, but less information on how they are performing, such as leader board or timer. Winners and Achievers on the other hand are shown the leader board more frequently, with Winners having the option to access trivia questions or tutorials, while Achievers the timer.

39.4 Game Analytics and Recommendation Systems

Reaching beyond the scope of personalizing a single game, many publishers are interested and in fact already striving, for example, Steam [Orland 10] and PlayStation Store [Lempel 10], to personalize the gaming experience of visitors/members of their game networks by introducing players to games that they are likely to enjoy. As such, the goal of these recommendation systems is to apply analytics technologies to player's behavior and build preference models that can inform the recommendation process.

The idea is inspired by major Internet and e-commerce websites, such as Google News [Das 07], Amazon [Linden 03], or Netflix [Amatriain 12], which suggest new products to site visitors based on their purchase and viewing history. Recommendation systems [Schafer 99] have been used in many prominent game release networks, such as PlayStation Store [Lempel 10] and Steam [Orland 10], to suggest titles that players are more likely to enjoy, but the input for these algorithms is not the players' in-game behavior, but their preferences expressed out of game (such as their ratings of played titles). The goal of these automated recommendation systems is to predict, among yet-to-play titles, which game a specific player with some history of played games will enjoy the most. While automated recommendation is a popular research topic [Bobadilla 13], we would like to highlight a technique that is reportedly behind the success of Amazon [Linden 03; Mangalinda 12] in marketing highly relevant products to customers. The algorithm belongs to the class of item-based collaborative filtering (CF) algorithms [Sarwar 01; Linden 03; Su 09].

CF is based on the observation that people who have behaved similarly in the past tend to act similarly in the same setting. This observation extends to purchase behavior on products (a game or some movie). This means we can deduce the rating of user *X* on product A from that of user *Y*, who has a similar rating history on similar or same products and who has already rated product A. A predicted positive rating entails that *X* has a high chance of enjoying A (i.e., will probably rate A positively after purchasing it), thus suggesting A to *X* is worthwhile [Su 09]. This approach, *user-based CF*, can be summarized as a two-step process:

1. Compute the similarity in rating behavior between users.
2. Given a product A, approximate *X*'s rating of A based on those of the users' most similar to *X*.

Product A is then suggested to *X* if *X*'s predicted rating for A is sufficiently high. The metric function to compute similarity in step 1 is often chosen to be the cosine of the angle between two rating vectors of the involved users, that is,

$$\text{Similarity}\left(\vec{X},\vec{Y}\right)=\cos\left(\vec{X},\vec{Y}\right)=\frac{\vec{X}\cdot\vec{Y}}{\left\|\vec{X}\right\|*\left\|\vec{Y}\right\|} \tag{39.1}$$

in which $\vec{X},\vec{Y}$ are respective rating vectors of user *X* and *Y* on all items in the item catalogue.

Unfortunately, this user-based approach does not scale well with the number of customers and items, as it has to examine every combination of customers and item ratings during the training phase (step 1). In order to overcome this problem, Amazon [Linden 03], and subsequently Steam [Orland 10], adopted an item-based variant of CF, which builds similarity relationships between items, instead of users. The algorithm *item-to-item CF* replaces the two steps in user-based CF with the following:

1. Compute similarity in rating scores between items.
2. Given a user *X*, approximate *X*'s rating of product A based on ratings of *X* on items that are similar to A.

In other words, if we combine the ratings of users on catalogued items as a matrix with columns being items and rows being users, user-based CF operates row-wise, while item-to-item CF operates column-wise. Because the similarity metric now works on items' rating vectors, users who never rate anything they purchase can still be recommended suitable items as long as there are ratings on pertinent items from other fellow shoppers who purchased similar items.

With the recent explosive growth of social networks (such as Facebook and Twitter), players now have many channels to voice their preferences. As such, many game publishers such as Steam have incorporated data gleaned from these sources in their recommender systems [Orland 10; Williams 13].

39.5 Game Analytics and Team Matching Techniques

In many games that feature an online player versus player game mode, such as those in the *multiplayer online battle arena* genre [Ryan 12] or the *real-time strategy game* genre [Dor 14], the fun factor no longer lies solely in the hands of game designers. While game mechanics and aesthetics still need to be sufficiently rich, it is the human factor and social interactions in those virtual matches that make playing exciting or boring [Madigan 13]. If games such as DotA or LoL are going to retain players over the long run, it is crucial for them to match teams up appropriately.

We surveyed the matchmaking systems in DotA [Dota Team 13], LoL [Zileas 09; Pereira 13; Lefebvre 14], and *CS:GO* [Totilo 11; GO 13; Rose 14]. In all of these games, the common approach is to

- Represent players' skill level using an aggregating score system. Examples include the matchmaking rating (MMR) in DotA, the Elo rating system in LoL (seasons 1 and 2) and CS:GO's initial launch, the League Point and Matchmaking Rating in LoL (season 3), and the Skill Groups in CS:GO (current). Players' scores are updated after finishing each battle
- Elicit additional matchmaking constraints from players, for example, LoL's Team Builder [Pereira 13; Lefebvre 14] allows players to join specific queues for the specific champions (in-game characters) that they want to play
- Rule-based heuristics to match players with similar skill scores while satisfying the players' matchmaking conditions

While differing in their aggregating formulae, the adopted score systems always take into account performance-based metrics, such as win/loss statistics, at the team level and performance statistics, such as kill/death, at the individual level [Dota Team 13; Setola 13]. Score update rules are designed such that beating stronger opponents yields a larger score increase, while losing to weaker opponents yields a larger score decrease.

The key goal that drives the design of matchmaking rules is to form teams that are equally balanced, both internally and externally. The assumption is that players enjoy fighting against others with similar skill level because of the uncertainty in the battle outcome and that they prefer to play with others at a similar skill level so that they will feel needed, but not like they're having to hold the team up [Zileas 09; Dota Team 13]. For instance, to achieve such a balance, DotA 2 adjusts the involved players' MMRs before starting the match by (1) boosting the MMRs of all players in low-ranked teams to match the opponents' average MMR and (2) reducing the MMR difference gap among team members in the process. LoL does something similar in that team members' ratings are also boosted to more balanced state before starting a match, but refuses to provide more details on these trade secrets [Zileas 09]. Note that this is only an example and there could be other ways to achieve skill balance when matching teams, which are often classified information to avoid players from gaming the system.

39.6 Conclusion

In this chapter, we discussed analytic approaches for developing player models using individual and communal analysis. We then illustrated, using both academic and industry examples, how the resulting player models can be used to adjust the gaming experience and increase engagement. We gave examples for adapting various aspects of the game based in the modeled skill level, affective state, and play style. Lastly, we analyzed in detail the techniques used behind many real-world systems for product recommendation and team matching.

There are several areas that we see as opportunities for growth in leveraging game analytics to enhance players' experiences. In particular, recommendation systems do not leverage player styles and temporal analysis of their game behaviors; instead, the techniques adopted by the industry have been approaches used by Amazon and Netflix, which do not tend to have depth of behavioral data to stimulate its decisions. It should be possible, for example, to leverage game analytics and collective intelligence algorithms to make better predictive algorithms for recommendations based on behavior data and game buying behavior in addition to review data.

Another area that has received very little attention is the development of adaptive algorithm to adjust content based on interest or play styles. While there has been much work on modeling players' interest, styles, and personality in regard to behaviors and while there have been designers who have advocated for more personalized designs leveraging personality theory [VandenBerghe 12], there has been very little work in procedural content personalization based on style. This is an area that deserves more attention and can lead to better and more sustained engagement, especially for social games that currently do not have high sustained engagement [Playnomics 12].

In conclusion, we hope that this chapter has provided readers with a broad overview of an area that is currently up and coming in both research and industry works. We also hope that the discussion has sparked some interest in using these algorithms in more creative and innovative ways to advance current game designs and AI systems in games.

References

[Andrade 05] Andrade, G., G. Ramalho, H. Santana, and V. Corruble. 2005. Extending reinforcement learning to provide dynamic game balancing. In *Proceedings of the Workshop on Reasoning, Representation, and Learning in Computer Games, 19th International Joint Conference on Artificial Intelligence* (*IJCAI*), Edinburgh, Scotland, UK, pp. 7–12.

[Amatriain 12] Amatriain, X. and J. Basilico. 2012. Netflix recommendations: Beyond the 5 stars. Netflix. http://techblog.netflix.com/2012/04/netflix-recommendations-beyond-5-stars.html (accessed August 18, 2014).

[Ambinder 11] Ambinder, M. 2011. Biofeedback in gameplay: How valve measures physiology to enhance gaming experience. In *Game Developers Conference,* San Francisco, CA.

[Atari 02] Atari. 2002. Neverwinter nights. http://www.ign.com/games/neverwinter-nights/pc-12077 (accessed August 18, 2014).

[Bethesda 08] Bethesda Softworks. 2008. Fallout 3. http://www.ign.com/games/fallout-3/xbox-360-882301 (accessed August 18, 2014).

[Bethesda 10] Bethesda Softworks. 2010. Fallout: New Vegas. http://www.ign.com/games/fallout-new-vegas/pc-14341979 (accessed August 18, 2014).

[Bishop 06] Bishop, C. M. 2006. *Pattern Recognition and Machine Learning,* Vol. 1. New York: Springer.

[Bobadilla 13] Bobadilla, J., F. Ortega, A. Hernando, and A. Gutiérrez. 2013. Recommender systems survey. *Knowledge-Based Systems* 46: 109–132.

[Booth 09] Booth, M. 2009. The AI systems of left 4 dead. In *Keynote, Fifth Artificial Intelligence and Interactive Digital Entertainment Conference* (*AIIDE 09*), Palo Alto, CA.

[Burges 98] Burges, C. J. C. 1998. A tutorial on support vector machines for pattern recognition. *Data Mining and Knowledge Discovery* 2(2): 121–167.

[Capcom 09] Capcom. 2009. Resident evil 5. http://www.ign.com/games/resident-evil-5/xbox-360-760880 (accessed August 18, 2014).

[Capcom 14] Capcom. 2014. Ultra street fighter IV. http://www.ign.com/games/ultra-street-fighter-4/xbox-360-20002351 (accessed August 18, 2014).

[Cutler 94] Cutler, A. and L. Breiman. 1994. Archetypal analysis. *Technometrics* 36(4): 338–347.

[Das 07] Das, A. S., M. Datar, A. Garg, and S. Rajaram. 2007. Google news personalization: Scalable online collaborative filtering. In *Proceedings of the 16th International Conference on World Wide Web,* Banff, Alberta, Canada, pp. 271–280.

[Dor 14] Dor S. 2014. A history of real-time strategy gameplay from decryption to prediction: Introducing the actional statement. http://www.kinephanos.ca/2014/real-time-strategy/ (accessed August 18, 2014).

[Dota Team 13] Dota Team. 2013. Matchmaking. http://blog.dota2.com/2013/12/matchmaking/ (accessed August 18, 2014).

[Drachen 12] Drachen, A., R. Sifa, C. Bauckhage, and C. Thurau. 2012. Guns, swords and data: Clustering of player behavior in computer games in the wild. In *2012 IEEE Conference on Computational Intelligence and Games* (*CIG*), Granada, Spain, pp. 163–170.

[Drachen 13] Drachen, A., C. Thurau, R. Sifa, and C. Bauckhage. 2013. A comparison of methods for player clustering via behavioral telemetry. *Foundations of Digital Games* 2013: 245–252.

[EA 08] Electronic Arts. 2008. Left 4 dead. http://www.ign.com/games/left-4-dead/xbox-360-875936 (accessed August 18, 2014).

[EA 10] Electronic Arts. 2010. Battlefield: Bad company 2. http://www.ign.com/games/battlefield-bad-company-2/xbox-360-14293277 (accessed August 18, 2014).

[GO 13] GO. 2013. Competitive skill groups FAQ. http://blog.counter-strike.net/index.php/2012/10/5565/ (accessed August 18, 2014).

[Jolliffe 02] Jolliffe, I. T. 2002. *Principal Component Analysis.* New York: Springer.

[Kleinsmith 13] Kleinsmith, A. and N. Bianchi-Berthouze. 2013. Affective body expression perception and recognition: A survey. *IEEE Transactions on Affective Computing* 4(1): 15–33.

[Koster 13] Koster, R. 2013. *Theory of Fun for Game Design.* Sebastopol, CA: O'Reilly Media, Inc.

[Laws 02] Laws, R. D. 2002. *Robin's Laws of Good Game Mastering.* Austin, TX: Steve Jackson Games.

[Lee 99] Lee, D. D. and H. S. Seung. 1999. Learning the parts of objects by non-negative matrix factorization. *Nature* 401(6755): 788–791.

[Lefebvre 14] Lefebvre, E. 2014. League of legends introduces the new team builder queue. http://massively.joystiq.com/2014/03/27/league-of-legends-introduces-the-new-team-builder-queue/ (accessed August 18, 2014).

[Lempel 10] Lempel, E. 2010. Next PS3 firmware update adds playstation store recommendations. Sony Network Entertainment. http://blog.us.playstation.com/2010/07/26/next-ps3-firmware-update-adds-playstation-store-recommendations/ (accessed August 18, 2014).

[Linden 03] Linden, G. D., B. Smith, and J. York. 2003. Amazon.com recommendations: Item-to-item collaborative filtering. *IEEE Internet Computing* 7(1): 76–80.

[Lopes 11] Lopes, R. and R. Bidarra. 2011. Adaptivity challenges in games and simulations: A survey. *IEEE Transactions on Computational Intelligence and AI in Games* 3(2): 85–99.

[MacQueen 67] MacQueen, J. B. 1967. Some methods for classification and analysis of multivariate observations. In *Proceedings of the Fifth Berkeley Symposium on Mathematical Statistics and Probability,* University of California Press, Berkeley, CA, Vol. 1, pp. 281–297.

[Madigan 13] Madigan, J. 2013. Modifying player behavior in League of Legends using positive reinforcement. http://www.gamasutra.com/view/news/184806/Modifying_player_behavior_in_League_of_Legends_using_positive_reinforcement.php (accessed August 18, 2014).

[Magerko 08] Magerko, B., C. Heeter, J. Fitzgerald, and B. Medler. Intelligent adaptation of digital game-based learning. In *Proceedings of the 2008 Conference on Future Play: Research, Play, Share,* Toronto, Ontario, Canada, pp. 200–203.

[Malone 80] Malone, T. W. 1980. What makes things fun to learn? Heuristics for designing instructional computer games. In *Proceedings of the Third ACM SIGSMALL Symposium and the First SIGPC Symposium on Small Systems,* New York, pp. 162–169.

[Mangalinda 12] Mangalinda, J. 2012. Amazon's recommendation secret. http://fortune.com/2012/07/30/amazons-recommendation-secret/ (accessed August 18, 2014).

[Meng 14] Meng, H. and N. Bianchi-Berthouze. 2014. Affective state level recognition in naturalistic facial and vocal expressions. *IEEE Transactions on Cybernetics* 44(3): 315–328.

[Missura 09] Missura, O. and T. Gärtner. 2009. Player modelling for intelligent difficulty adjustment. In *Proceedings of the 12th International Conference on Discovery Science,* Porto, Portugal, pp. 197–211.

[Neapolitan 04] Neapolitan, R. E. 2004. *Learning Bayesian Networks,* Vol. 38. Upper Saddle River, NJ: Prentice Hall.

[Newell 08] Newell, G. 2008. Gabe Newell writes for edge. http://www.edge-online.com/features/gabe-newell-writes-edge/ (accessed August 18, 2014).

[Orland 10] Orland, K. 2010. Valve launches game recommendation feature for steam. Gamasutra. http://www.gamasutra.com/view/news/122261/Valve_Launches_Game_Recommendation_Feature_For_Steam.php (accessed August 18, 2014).

[Pedersen 09] Pedersen, C., J. Togelius, and G. N. Yannakakis. 2009. Modeling player experience in Super Mario Bros. In *IEEE Symposium on Computational Intelligence and Games* (*CIG*), Milan, Italy, pp. 132–139.

[Pereira 13] Pereira, C. 2013. League of legends' team builder lets you preselect your role. http://www.ign.com/articles/2013/10/15/league-of-legends-team-builder-lets-you-preselect-your-role (accessed August 18, 2014).

[Piggyback 09] Piggyback. 2009. *Resident Evil 5: The Complete Official Guide.* Roseville, CA: Prima Publishing.

[Playnomics 12] Player Engagement Study Q3. 2012. Playnomics report. http://www.insidesocialgames.com/wp-content/uploads/2012/10/Playnomics_Q3-report_Final-copy.pdf (accessed August 19, 2014).

[Ponsen 05] Ponsen, M. J. V., H. Muñoz-Avila, P. Spronck, and D. W. Aha. 2005. Automatically acquiring domain knowledge for adaptive game AI using evolutionary learning. In *Proceedings of the National Conference on Artificial Intelligence,* Pittsburgh, PA 20(3): 1535.

[Ponsen 07] Ponsen, M. J. V., P. Spronck, H. Muñoz-Avila, and D. W. Aha. 2007. Knowledge acquisition for adaptive game AI. *Science of Computer Programming* 67(1): 59–75.

[Riot 09] Riot Games. 2009. League of legends. http://www.ign.com/games/league-of-legends/pc-14287819 (accessed August 18, 2014).

[Rose 14] Rose, M. 2014. How counter strike global offensive turned itself around. http://kotaku.com/how-counter-strike-global-offensive-turned-itself-arou-1575373000 (accessed August 18, 2014).

[Ryan 12] Ryan, C. 2012. Multiplayer online battle arena explained. http://www.alteredgamer.com/pc-gaming/43646-multiplayer-online-battle-arenas-and-dota-explained/ (accessed August 18, 2014).

[Sarwar 01] Sarwar, B., G. Karypis, J. Konstan, and J. Riedl. 2001. Item-based collaborative filtering recommendation algorithms. In *Proceedings of the 10th International Conference on World Wide Web,* Hong Kong, pp. 285–295.

[Schafer 99] Schafer, J. B., J. Konstan, and J. Riedl. Recommender systems in e-commerce. 1999. In *Proceedings of the First ACM Conference on Electronic Commerce,* Denver, CO, pp. 158–166.

[Seif El-Nasr 13] Seif El-Nasr, M., A. Drachen, and A. Canossa. 2013. *Game Analytics: Maximizing the Value of Player Data.* New York: Springer.

[Setola 13] Setola, H. 2013. Valve's counter-strike "Global Offensive" is a failing strategy. http://www.gizorama.com/feature/opinion/valves-counter-strike-global-offensive-is-a-failing-strategy (accessed August 18, 2014).

[Shaker 10] Shaker, N., G. N. Yannakakis, and J. Togelius. 2010. Towards automatic personalized content generation for platform games. In *The Sixth AAAI Conference on Artificial Intelligent and Interactive Digital Environment* (*AIIDE 10*), Stanford, CA.

[Simon 13] Simon, D. 2013. *Evolutionary Optimization Algorithms.* Hoboken, NJ: John Wiley & Sons.

[Spronck 04] Spronck, P., I. Sprinkhuizen-Kuyper, and E. Postma. 2004. Difficulty scaling of game AI. In *Proceedings of the Fifth International Conference on Intelligent Games and Simulation* (*GAME-ON 2004*), EUROSIS, Belgium, pp. 33–37.

[Spronck 06] Spronck, P., M. Ponsen, I. Sprinkhuizen-Kuyper, and E. Postma. 2006. Adaptive game AI with dynamic scripting. *Machine Learning* 63(3): 217–248.

[Su 09] Su, X. and T. M. Khoshgoftaar. A survey of collaborative filtering techniques. *Advances in Artificial Intelligence* 2009: 4.

[Sutton 98] Sutton, R. S. and A. G. Barto. 1998. *Reinforcement Learning: An Introduction.* Cambridge, MA: MIT Press.

[Tang 09] Tang, H., C. H. Tan, K. C. Tan, and A. Tay. 2009. Neural network versus behavior based approach in simulated car racing game. In *IEEE Workshop on Evolving and Self-Developing Intelligent Systems, 2009* (*ESDIS'09*), Nashville, TN, pp. 58–65.

[Thue 07] Thue, D., V. Bulitko, M. Spetch, and E. Wasylishen. 2007. Interactive Storytelling: A player modelling approach. In *Proceedings of the Third AAAI Conference on Artificial Intelligent and Interactive Digital Environment* (*AIIDE 07*), Stanford, CA, AAAI Press, pp. 43–48.

[Thurau 10] Thurau, C., K. Kersting, and C. Bauckhage. 2010. Yes we can: simplex volume maximization for descriptive web-scale matrix factorization. In *Proceedings of the 19th ACM International Conference on Information and Knowledge Management,* Toronto, Canada, pp. 1785–1788.

[Togelius 07] Togelius, J., Nardi, R. D., and Lucas, S. 2007. Towards automatic personalised content creation for racing games. In *Proceedings of IEEE Symposium on Computational Intelligence and Games (CIG)*, pp. 252–259.

[Tognetti 10] Tognetti, S., M. Garbarino, A. Bonarini, and M. Matteucci. 2010. Modeling enjoyment preference from physiological responses in a car racing game. In *Proceedings of IEEE Symposium on Computational Intelligence and Games* (*CIG*), Copenhagen, Denmark, pp. 321–328.

[Torcs 07] Torcs. 2007. The open racing car simulator. http://torcs.sourceforge.net/ (accessed August 18, 2014).

[Totilo 11] Totilo, S. 2011. An hour with counter-strike: GO. http://kotaku.com/5834542/an-hour-with-counter-strike-go (accessed August 18, 2014).

[Ubisoft 07] Ubisoft. 2007. Assassin's creed. http://assassinscreed.ubi.com/en-US/home/index.aspx (accessed August 18, 2014).

[Valve 09] Valve. 2009. Left 4 dead 2. http://www.ign.com/games/left-4-dead-2/xbox-360-14352241 (accessed August 18, 2014).

[Valve 10] Valve. 2010. Alien swarm. http://store.steampowered.com/app/630/ (accessed August 18, 2014).

[Valve 12] Valve. 2012. Counter-strike: Global offensive. http://www.ign.com/games/counter-strike-global-offensive/mac-116695 (accessed August 18, 2014).

[Valve 13] Valve. 2013. DotA 2. http://www.ign.com/games/dota-2/mac-89236 (accessed August 18, 2014).

[VandenBerghe 12] VandenBerghe, J. 2012. The 5 domains of play: Applying psychology's big 5 motivation domains to games. Presentation at the *Game Developer Conference*, San Francisco, CA.

[Wild Divine 14] Wild Divine. 2014. Wild divine website. http://www.wilddivine.com/ (accessed August 18, 2014).

[Williams 13] Williams, R. 2013. Valve launches beta for steam reviews, allowing you to share your recommendations with the world. http://hothardware.com/News/Valve-Launches-Beta-for-Steam-Reviews-Allowing-You-to-Share-Your-Recommendations-With-the-World/ (accessed August 18, 2014).

[Yannakakis 05] Yannakakis, G. N. and M. Maragoudakis. 2005. Player modeling impact on player's entertainment in computer games. In *User Modeling 2005*, eds. L. Ardissono, P. Brna, and A. Mitrovic, pp. 74–78. Berlin, Germany: Springer.

[Yannakakis 06] Yannakakis, G. N. and J. Hallam. 2006. Towards capturing and enhancing entertainment in computer games. In *Advances in Artificial Intelligence*, eds. G. Antoniou, G. Potamias, C. Spyropoulos, and D. Plexousakis, pp. 432–442. Berlin, Germany: Springer.

[Yannakakis 08] Yannakakis, G. N. and J. Hallam. 2008. Entertainment modeling through physiology in physical play. *International Journal of Human-Computer Studies* 66(10): 741–755.

[Yannakakis 10] Yannakakis, G. N., H. P. Martínez, and A. Jhala. 2010. Towards affective camera control in games. *User Modeling and User-Adapted Interaction* 20(4): 313–340.

[Yannakakis 13] Yannakakis, G. N., P. Spronck, D. Loiacono, and E. André. 2013. Player modeling. In *Artificial and Computational Intelligence in Games,* S. M. Lucas, M. Mateas, M. Preuss, P. Spronck, and J. Togelius, Eds., *DFU* Vol. 6, Dagstuhl, Germany, pp. 45–59.

[Zeng 09] Zeng, Z., M. Pantic, G. I. Roisman, and T. S. Huang. 2009. A survey of affect recognition methods: Audio, visual, and spontaneous expressions. *IEEE Transactions on Pattern Analysis and Machine Intelligence* 31(1): 39–58.

[Zileas 09] Zileas. 2009. LOL matchmaking explained. http://forums.na.leagueoflegends.com/board/showthread.php?t=12029 (accessed August 18, 2014).

40

Procedural Content Generation

An Overview

Gillian Smith

40.1 Introduction

Procedural content generation (PCG) is the process of using an AI system to author aspects of a game that a human designer would typically be responsible for creating, from textures and natural effects to levels and quests, and even to the game rules themselves. Therefore, the creator of a PCG system is responsible for capturing some aspect of a designer's expertise—a challenging task for an AI!

PCG has been used in many games for several different purposes. Two popular motivations are replayability and adaptability. PCG can provide large amounts of content, so that each time the player starts the game, they will have a different experience. In combination with an AI system that can infer player skill, PCG can be used as a form of dynamic difficulty adjustment, shifting the content the player will see in order to adapt to their skill level.

One of the first examples of PCG was in the game *Elite* [Braben 84], where entire galaxies were generated by the computer so that there could be an expansive universe for players to explore without running afoul of memory requirements. However, unlike most modern games that incorporate PCG, *Elite*'s content generation was entirely deterministic, allowing the designers to have complete control over the resulting experience. In other words, *Elite* is really a game where PCG is used as a form of data compression. This tradition is continued in *demoscenes*, such as *.kkrieger* [.theprodukkt 04], which have the goal of maximizing the complexity of interactive scenes with a minimal code footprint. However, this is no longer the major goal for PCG systems.

Regardless of whether creation is deterministic, one of the main tensions when creating a game with PCG is retaining some amount of control over the final product. It can be tempting to use PCG in a game because of a desire to reduce the authoring burden or make up for missing expertise—for example, a small indie team wanting to make a game with a massive world may choose to use PCG to avoid needing to painstakingly hand-author that world. But while it is relatively simple to create a system that can generate highly varied content, the challenge comes in ensuring the content's quality and ability to meet the needs of the game.

There are several major approaches to PCG that offer different means for this control, as well as supporting different extents to which the control can take place. There are also many reasons for why PCG may be used in a game, which can help inform a game designer's and/or developer's choice about what technique to use when creating the system. *Civilization* [MicroProse 91], *Rogue* [Toy 80], *Minecraft* [Persson 11], and *Borderlands* [Gearbox Software 09] are all examples of popular games that use PCG, but with completely different approaches and purposes.

For the sake of scope, this chapter focuses on creating content that a player somehow interacts with as part of gameplay—think levels and quests, rather than textures and trees that involve procedural modeling [Ebert 03]. It will also avoid a discussion of procedural generation of game rules—that is, research that is really still in its infancy as of this book's publication [Smith, A. 10, Togelius 08]. The focus is on the procedural creation of content (e.g., what would be created by a level designer) rather than on storytelling and NPC behavior, though there are many relationships between these systems. However, while we won't delve into systems that create game rules, for many PCG systems, it is still necessary to find ways to formally specify aspects of the game's rules in order to guarantee that playable content will be generated.

This chapter will give an overview of PCG, survey different techniques for creating content generators, examine how PCG fits into a game's design, and give some advice for how to choose an appropriate method for a game. At the end, there are pointers to literature and resources where the reader can find more details on PCG and learn how to stay up to date on PCG research.

40.2 Technical Approaches to Content Generation

While there are no off-the-shelf tools or frameworks for creating your own PCG system, there are several common approaches and methods for knowledge representation. This section will give an overview of these approaches and methods and discuss some tradeoffs between them.

40.2.1 Algorithms and Approaches

One of the primary considerations when choosing an approach to designing a content generator is the extent and kind of control needed. Approaches to PCG range from purely bottom-up, simulation-based methods that only permit control over the initial state of the world and the operators for changing it to top-down, constraint-driven methods that let the system meet firm authoring constraints but may be more expensive to create and debug.

40.2.1.1 Simulation Based

Simulation-based approaches to PCG start with an initial world and a set of operators that can alter that world and then run a simulation for a predetermined period of time. For example, a simulation-based approach to creating terrain might start with a single landmass in an ocean, a climate/rainfall model, and an erosion model to create a new terrain with rivers, lakes, cliffs, and beaches. *Dwarf Fortress* [Bay 12 Games 06, Adams 15] is a game that takes this approach to generation, with a full simulation that creates landmasses, caves, and a history for the world. Simulation-based approaches do not permit any control over the final output of the system without using a generate-and-test paradigm (described further in the section on constructionist systems). While simulation can be a slow process with limited control, it has two potential benefits that may make it a good choice: (1) it provides you with a content history that can be referred to or replayed, and (2) it can be run during gameplay to create a world that reacts to the player's choices and actions.

40.2.1.2 Constructionist

A constructionist approach is one that pieces together premade building blocks according to an algorithm especially constructed for the game. This algorithm has design knowledge implicitly baked into it—any intelligence in the process exists only in the choices made by this one algorithm, rather than more explicitly stated as an optimization function or as a set of design constraints. For example, many *Rogue*-like level generators [Rogue Basin 12] use constructionist approaches that build different rooms and then construct corridors between them. Constructionist approaches are typically ad hoc, specialized for one particular game with little applicability beyond it, and accessible primarily to developers, rather than designers and artists.

Constructionist approaches often rely entirely on their knowledge representation (see below). Many, though not all, approaches involve taking large, preauthored pieces of content and placing them next to each other randomly, as in endless runner games like *Robot Unicorn Attack* [[adult swim] games 10] or *Canabalt* [Saltsman 09]. This kind of constructionist approach is perhaps more accurately named *content selection*, where there is no attempt to make intelligent choices in the *process* that is followed, but there is very tight designer control over the building blocks.

Constructionist systems are difficult to control and difficult to get good variation from; it's easy for all the content to start to feel the same if there's a limited set of building blocks to choose from. Large branching control flow structures can also be difficult to debug, especially if the bug lies in a piece of code that is executed very rarely. And you can spend a huge amount of time tweaking your algorithm to get content that is *just right* in one situation, without realizing that you're simultaneously breaking the content for some different situation.

Designing your own algorithm from the ground up does have some benefits, however. From a design perspective, content selection is a lightweight approach that is good enough for some games, especially where there aren't a lot of constraints on what constitutes playability (e.g., a simple platforming game such as *Canabalt* just needs the platforms to be reachable, whereas a lock-and-key puzzle game such as Joris Dormans's *Zelda*-like game [Dormans 10] has deeper constraints).

40.2.1.3 Grammars

A grammar-based approach starts by specifying the possibility space of content (or *generative space*) as a formal grammar. Next, an interpreter for that grammar (which will parse and process the rules to create content) is built. This explicit separation of grammar rules from content assembly offers more organization than a constructionist approach, where the rules are often implicitly defined in the code, and can also be useful to technical designers who may be able to edit the grammar rules without needing to touch the content assembly system. Grammars have been used to create levels for platforming games [Smith, G. 11c] and action-adventure games [Dormans 10], as well as in tools for rapidly designing buildings [Müller 06]. Shape grammars are also a useful kind of grammar for creating visual content [Stiny 80].

When used in a process in which content is tested against requirements and discarded if it doesn't pass the tests, this approach strikes a balance between bottom-up emergence from designer-specified rules (in the form of the grammar) and top-down control over content (in the form of the acceptance rules for the generated content). It still allows a computer to explore the design space and come up with surprising and varied results.

Authoring the rules for a grammar-based system is done by breaking down your desired content into increasingly small pieces. The grammar will then specify rules as nonterminal and terminal symbols. Nonterminal symbols can be expanded into more nonterminals and terminals, specified by a set of rules. Content creation begins with a single nonterminal symbol, the start symbol, and then repeatedly replaces nonterminals with new symbols (which may be terminals, nonterminals, or a mix of the two) according to a set of expansion rules until only terminal symbols remain. There may also be more than one rule per nonterminal symbol, thus allowing nondeterministic content to be created. Some rules might be weighted toward being selected more frequently than others, which can provide some additional control over the kind of content that will be produced.

The grammar's interpreter is responsible for selecting the next rule to expand. It can be tempting to combine the grammar rules and the interpreter into one big branching control flow, and for simple grammars this can suffice. However, the power of grammars often lies in the ability to quickly add or change rules and see the impact on content, and grammars often change and grow to meet changing design constraints. Thus, it is a good idea to keep the interpreter and the grammar separate.

A grammar can produce huge amounts of content often very quickly. Unfortunately, grammars are prone to *overgeneration*, where they may create content that was not intended when the grammar rules were designed. If the grammar is too loosely constrained, there is no guarantee that everything it can create will be *good* content. Fixing overgeneration in the grammar rules can sometimes restrict the abilities of the grammar too much, leading to *undergeneration*—all the content may now be considered good, but it will also feel too similar and predictable. Thus, choosing to overgenerate and then running a suite of tests on the results can ensure that surprising content is still generated, but unacceptable content is discarded.

In order to achieve this, there must be defined some simple-to-measure acceptance criteria (e.g., that a level must have at least 15 features) with which the bad content will be culled. These criteria also offer an opportunity to explicitly define criteria that are difficult, or even impossible, to specify in the grammar rules, and provide some ability to have top-down design constraints while still benefiting from the emergent content that comes from using bottom-up rules for generation.

The strength of a grammar-based approach lies in the combination of simple, easy-to-author rules that provide emergent and interesting content with a generate-and-test paradigm that lets the generator meet soft constraints. Grammar rules are also easy to use to express design patterns. Since grammars usually generate content very quickly, generating a great deal of content and throwing much of it away are not expensive. As an example, *Launchpad* [Smith, G. 11c] is an unoptimized level generator for Mario-like platforming levels. Its grammar-based representation is capable of creating ten thousand candidate levels in only a few seconds. The speed of this approach is dependent in large part upon the complexity of the grammar rules, but since it is possible to specify recursive rules, speed is also dependent upon the allowed recursion depth. The weakness of grammars is their difficulty in meeting hard design constraints and in debugging the rule system, which can become quite complex.

40.2.1.4 Optimization

An optimization-based generator involves a search process (often unbounded) that seeks out the optimal combination of components according to some evaluation function. This evaluation function is usually specified as a formula that attempts to calculate the desirability, and the search attempts to maximize this value. Alternately, there can be a *human in the loop*, with a human player or designer selecting their favorite content from among the candidates.

Evolutionary algorithms are a popular approach to optimization-based content generation in academic research. They attempt to mimic natural evolution. An initial population is created and then bred and mutated into a new population that can be evaluated by the fitness function (or by the human in the loop). The best candidates are bred and mutated once again, and their children are evaluated. This cycle continues until there is a piece of content that is a good fit to the evaluation function or until a maximum number of candidate generations have been created, at which point the candidate with the best evaluation score is chosen.

As a simple example of an evolutionary algorithm, consider the problem of procedurally generating a maze. An evolutionary algorithm might start with a population of a thousand completely random mazes. It would then calculate the fitness score for each maze based on how well that particular candidate meets the evaluation criteria and would generate a new population of mazes by *breeding* highly rated mazes together—perhaps by combining the left and right halves of two different mazes into a new one. This process would be repeated either until a predetermined amount of time has passed or until a maze that meets the acceptance criteria has been generated.

There are a lot of nuances to creating genetic algorithms. Optimization-based approaches are also highly sensitive to the knowledge representation used (e.g., representing a maze as a set of walls with endpoints and lengths or as a grid with open and closed cells) [McGuinness 12], as well as to the particular implementation of the algorithm.

What should the mutation and breeding operators be? How should the evaluation function be crafted? How should the percentage of the population that is chosen to breed versus mutate be selected? Should some of the candidates be saved for the next generation without breeding (known as elitism)? There is a survey article on search-based methods for PCG that provides a good entry point to the literature [Togelius 11].

All optimization-based approaches to PCG must have an evaluation function—some way of quantifying the overall goodness of an arbitrary piece of content. These evaluation functions can be fairly simple approximations, such as the distance from the actual distribution of components in the content to the desired distribution of those components. However, it can be difficult to capture everything important about the content in one evaluation function. *Player experience modeling* [Yannakakis 11] is an attempt to treat the evaluation function more abstractly by learning a model of individual player preferences by having them play some of the content and then applying the model as the fitness function to create personalized content. A simpler use of player modeling is to use the human as the evaluation function. *Galactic Arms Race* is a game that takes a *human-in-the-loop* approach and uses an inferred simple model of player preference (those weapons the player uses most often are most desirable) to generate new weapons that are personalized to a particular play style [Hastings 09].

The use of an optimization-based approach relies on a comfort with the notion that there is such a thing as an optimal piece or pieces of content and that it is possible to express this mathematically. Note that this evaluation function does not necessarily need to be reduced to a mathematical definition of *fun*. It can instead be a set of desired properties that the system should aim for. If the generator is being designed with a concrete goal that can be expressed mathematically, then this approach may be a good one. It can also work quite well if there is a way to involve a human in guiding the generation process at runtime. Another benefit is that, like the generate-and-test approach used with grammars, optimization-based approaches can be useful for soft constraints—properties of content that are desirable but not crucial to the function of the game. However, evolutionary algorithms that do not have a human-in-the-loop can be slow, and player experience modeling requires the player to be put through training levels, which can be time consuming for the player and must be designed into the game.

40.2.1.5 Constraint Driven

Constraint-driven methods are declarative approaches in which hard design constraints are specified, and then a constraint solver is used to find all potential solutions that meet those constraints. All of the content is expressed as variables with ranges of potential values, with constraints dictating the relationships between these variables. This entirely top-down approach allows the specification of knowledge about what the content *should* look like separately from the underlying search algorithm.

Constraint satisfaction has been used for generating room interiors [Tutenel 09] using semantic constraints, which introduce knowledge about what objects are and how they relate to others (e.g., a table should be surrounded by chairs). Numerical constraint solving has been used for placement of platforms and other level geometry in platformer levels [Smith, G. 11b]. Answer set programming, a method for specifying constraint problems in first-order logic, has been used for levels in an educational puzzle game [Smith, A. 12] as well as the real-time strategy game *Warzone 2100* [Smith, A. 11].

The challenge in constraint satisfaction for content generation comes from fully specifying all of the constraints. Commonsense constraints, such as the idea that two objects cannot occupy the same position at the same time, must be specified along with more game-specific constraints. However, constraints are a powerful method for expressing a design space, and this approach works well when there are many constraints that *must* be met in order for the content to be acceptable. Runtime performance for constraint satisfaction approaches to PCG varies drastically based on the size of the problem, how the problem is described, and the number of constraints. Many solvers, such as answer set programming, work by reducing the problem to a Boolean satisfiability problem, which is an NP-complete problem. However, for small-to-medium-sized domains, such as mazes, grid-based puzzle games [Smith, A. 11], and even simple platformers [Smith, G. 11b], constraint-based content generation can produce results in a matter of seconds, or a few minutes at worst. What's more, adding constraints can actually improve the runtime performance of some constraint-based systems, as it allows the system to rapidly eliminate portions of the search space that don't contain satisfactory solutions.

40.2.2 Knowledge Representation

Many of the approaches described in the previous section can be further varied by changing the knowledge representation—that is, the building blocks that the content generator will piece together. Here, there are four major kinds of building blocks that trade off authoring control against risk of the player recognizing common patterns. They are presented in order from most to least human authoring.

40.2.2.1 Experiential Chunks

An experiential chunk captures a sufficiently large amount of content that, on its own and outside the context of the entire piece of content, it could still be experienced by the player as its own entity. An example would be the level chunks used in *Robot Unicorn Attack*. One advantage of this representation is that there is a great deal of artistic and design control over the appearance of the generated content, but there is a significant chance that the player will begin to notice the same chunks repeated again and again. Raph Koster notes that game players are pattern recognition machines [Koster 04], and this is certainly true for PCG. Unless pattern recognition is desired, experiential chunks should be either avoided or tempered by using a mixture of approaches to designing the generator (see Section 40.2.3). Experiential chunks are usually used with constructionist algorithms, but can also be used with grammars.

40.2.2.2 Templates

Templates are a more generalized form of experiential chunk, where the design team can still control the content, but leaves blanks for the AI to fill in automatically. Templates are like the *Mad Libs* of PCG and, unless care is taken to construct the template and the rules for what content can fill in the gaps, can have the same quirky consequences as the word game. However, templates can strike a nice balance between authorial control and variety for high-fidelity games.

Templates are a kind of high-level design pattern, and the design pattern literature can be a good place to draw inspiration for templates for a generator. Bjork and Holopainen's book [Bjork 04] is a good collection of general patterns, but there are also patterns specific to genres such as first-person shooters [Hullett 10], role-playing game levels and quests [Smith, G. 11a, Onuczko 05], and 2D platformers [Smith, G. 11c], to name a few examples.

40.2.2.3 Components

Like templates, components are patterns that have been designed by a human. However, unlike templates and experiential chunks, components cannot stand on their own to be experienced as content in their own right. For example, enemies in a first-person shooter have general behavior dictated by a human designer, but cannot exist without the broader context of the level that they inhabit. Using components reduces the risk that content patterns will be seen by the player. However, it also means that the generation algorithm needs to play a much stronger role, as it will be almost entirely responsible for the quality of the content that is produced. Component patterns can work well with all of the generation approaches mentioned in this chapter.

40.2.2.4 Subcomponents

A subcomponent representation uses the smallest possible assets. Subcomponents do not have embedded semantic information about what the content is or how it should be used. They can be imagined as the same kind of building block that humans use to construct their levels, such as art assets from a tileset. Very few generators use this approach to content generation because it is difficult for the generator to understand how to piece things together without some amount of semantic information about the content, and thus it's more common for generators to use a component representation. For example, it is helpful for a generator to understand the concept of a *room* or a *chest* and how they are allowed to fit together. However, *Galactic Arms Race* [Hastings 09], an experimental game that creates particle system weapons, is one example of a game that uses this representation.

40.2.3 Mixing and Matching

These approaches and knowledge representation techniques can be combined to produce more sophisticated systems and to meet the demands of the game's design. For example, using content selection to create levels at runtime that use pregenerated pieces of content (i.e., experiential chunks) provides the reduced authoring burden and high variety of PCG while still allowing for a lightweight generation algorithm; furthermore, the use of pregenerated content pieces can provide more varieties among the chunks than would be easy for human designers to create. *Polymorph* [Jennings-Teats 10] is an experimental adaptive level generator that uses this approach to create levels that are customized to a player's abilities. Each pregenerated chunk is tagged with a difficulty score, and as the player progresses through the level, chunks with an appropriate difficulty score (based on an estimate of player skill level via observing their failures) are placed in front of the player.

Using different content generation techniques at different layers of abstraction can help balance out human authoring with algorithm complexity. For example, a constructionist, template-based approach to create a dungeon crawler level could be combined with a constraint solver to place items into the rooms in the slots that are left unfilled. This would allow for tight control over the room's overall appearance and ensure that gameplay requirements are met, but still provide a high level of variety in the room's contents. This hypothetical generator is similar to the generation approach taken in the

Tanagra level design assistant [Smith, G. 11b], where reactive planning is used in conjunction with a numerical constraint solver to create platformer levels in collaboration with a human designer.

Mixing-and-matching paradigms can be very powerful, but it does have one major drawback: in general, different layers of the generator will not be able to easily communicate with each other. In our dungeon crawler example given, if the constraint solver is unable to place items into the room to meet all design constraints, the generator must go back and choose another set of room templates, then ask the constraint solver to try again. This is because the constraint solver does not have the power to alter room layout, and the room layout algorithm does not have any knowledge of the kind of constraints that the solver cares about. In a purely constraint-based system, the room layout would potentially be able to shift to meet constraints on the level components.

40.3 Understanding PCG's Relationship to a Game

Now that we have an understanding of the different ways to build a PCG system, let's look at how to understand the role that PCG will be taking in the game. This is largely a set of design decisions, but it has a lot of impact on the way that the AI system should be constructed.

40.3.1 PCG's Mechanical Role

There are several important aspects of PCG's mechanical role within the game, including how it is integrated in to the overall game, if and how the player will interact with it, and how well it can be controlled by designers and players.

40.3.1.1 Game Stage

Does content generation need to happen *online*, while the player is playing? Or can it occur *offline*, while the level is loading or even while the game is being developed? If the generator must run online and frequently, then performance is one of the largest concerns, and it may be necessary to compromise quality to some extent. On the other hand, a generator that runs offline can be slower, but it needs to be able to create content that is flexible enough to support the variety that is inherent in player behavior (i.e., content can't be crafted as a response to the player's actions), and it also has to store and load generated content efficiently.

40.3.1.2 Interaction with the Generator

In games where the player does interact with the generator (as opposed to just with the generated content), there are three main types of interaction the player may have: *parameterized*, *preference*, and *direct manipulation*.

Parameterized control lets the player set some parameters that influence the generator before they interact with content. For example, the *Civilization V* level generator allows the player to set parameters such as world age, temperature, and landmass type.

Preference control means that the player can (directly or indirectly) specify preferences for what content they will see next while they are in the game. For example, *Galactic Arms Race* infers player preferences based on their behavior, allowing them to provide indirect control over the kind of weapons that they will see next.

Direct manipulation lets the player directly interact with the content while the generator runs in the background to assist the player. This kind of control appears in *Spore's* creature creator, where the player builds a model of a creature while the content generator supports the player's choices and augments them by supplying textures and animations.

40.3.1.3 Control over Player Experience

While it is possible to build a content generator that simply stitches together preauthored chunks of content (i.e., a constructionist approach), it is often desirable to have tight design control over particular aspects of the player's experience. This control can come in two forms: *compositional* and *experiential.*

Compositional control means that the generator can make design guarantees about the presence of particular components in the final product, for example, a platformer level generator that can guarantee that 50% of the challenges in a level will be due to gaps or a quest generator that can guarantee the quest will involve the player finding two angry shopkeepers.

Experiential control means that the generator has an understanding of some aspect of the player's in-game experience beyond just component placement, for example, a platformer generator that can guarantee level pacing independently from what components are present or a quest generator that can guarantee that a quest will have a particular difficulty associated with it.

40.3.2 Player Interaction with PCG

The *dynamics* of PCG (borrowed from Hunicke et al.'s mechanics, dynamics, and aesthetics framework for analyzing games [Hunicke 04]) are the styles of play that arise from the player's interactions with the generated content. Understanding these patterns can help in selecting which techniques to use and the range of content to create.

40.3.2.1 PCG Relationship to Other Mechanics

We can first consider the role of PCG in the game relative to the other game mechanics. Will the player's experience revolve around the generated content, or are we creating decorative, incidental content that only augments the player's experience? Some games use PCG to frame player experience: *Civilization V* is a game where procedurally generated maps give the player something surprising to explore in the early phase of the game, but most of the player's strategies revolve around other aspects of the game (e.g., build order and military strategy)—and indeed, many scenarios with fixed, designer-generated maps exist. Endless runner games such as *Canabalt*, on the other hand, have generators that the player's experience is entirely dependent upon. These games have no mechanic other than to interact with the generated content. Understanding the extent to which your generator will influence the player's experience can help you decide how to focus your efforts, how important design guarantees are, and how to ensure that there is sufficient variety for players.

40.3.2.2 Reacting

PCG is often used to create surprising or unexpected content, forcing the player to react to unforeseen circumstances rather than allowing them to regurgitate memorized actions. This reaction may be related to exploration, as in *Spelunky* [Yu 09], or it may be a test of reaction time, as in *Robot Unicorn Attack*. Reaction comes from the random elements of PCG, but you may wish to be able to control this somewhat. If the game would benefit from the player being able to practice some aspects, but still be a test of reaction in others, then using experiential chunks may be a good choice for your knowledge representation.

40.3.2.3 Strategizing

The use of a content generator that runs online and can be controlled (either directly or indirectly) by the player leads to situations where the player forms strategies about how to interact with the generator. If this style of play is desirable, then consider what these strategies should be when designing the generator. For example, if the player should be able to strategize around the composition of challenges in levels, as in *Endless Web* [Smith, G. 12], then the generator must be designed such that this can be explicitly controlled.

40.3.2.4 Searching

Players can do two kinds of searching as a result of PCG. The first is when the content being generated is a world: players will search through it and explore it, looking for surprises and interesting moments, as in *Minecraft*. The second is when the content is smaller and can be found in the environment, when players may search for interesting or unique content, as in *Borderlands*. The lesson to be learned from this dynamic is the same no matter the kind of searching: the generator should produce content that can be surprising and exciting for the player to find. A generator may be able to produce millions of unique pieces of content, but the quantity is meaningless if those million pieces all *feel* the same to the player. Introducing surprise and variety can be difficult. It may come from incorporating small, hand-authored pieces of content into the generator for the player to find or from careful construction of grammar rules and weights.

40.3.2.5 Practicing

Many games use PCG to allow the player to practice game strategies. *Civilization V* (and other strategy games with generated maps) is a particularly good example of this dynamic—the other mechanics of the game provide multiple strategies for success, and the procedural placement of land and resources means that the player can practice selecting from among those strategies and adapting them to many different, but controlled, environments. In such games, especially multiplayer games, the ability for the generator to make design guarantees about resource availability, playability, and balance may be of high importance. Constraint-based generators, or generators that use generate-and-test to approach design requirements, are good techniques for games that need such guarantees.

40.3.2.6 Community

Finally, PCG can be used to vary the player's experience so as to make it impossible to write a walkthrough for your game. This leads to players having different experiences from each other. When crafting a PCG system, it is common to think of a single player's experience with the generated content, but for some games, it is also important to think about the *community*'s experience with that content. Fans of games such as *Dwarf Fortress* engage in long, drawn-out discussions and debates based on the results the generator provides, telling stories of their own experiences in their own unique world.

40.4 Choosing an Approach

This section discusses how to get started with PCG and how to choose an approach, as well as the kinds of design considerations that need to be taken into account.

40.4.1 Getting Started

There are two ways to start building a PCG system: from the bottom up or from the top down. Doing both of these at the same time may be helpful, as one method may inspire decisions you make in the other.

A top-down approach starts by mapping out the kinds of content you want to be able to create and developing specific examples of what the generator should be capable of. It can be particularly helpful to start by designing examples of content that represents the extremes of what the generator could produce: *What are the easiest and hardest levels, or the quirkiest weapons, or the ugliest and prettiest flowers?* If there are parameters that the player should have control over (e.g., the size of the map or the shape of the robot), these are useful starting points for building examples of what the generated content should look like. From these examples, start distilling patterns: these will be the building blocks in the generator.

A bottom-up approach works up from the tools. For example, if you think a grammar approach is an interesting choice, start writing some production rules and see what kind of content you can get out of it. Keep adding rules, and tweaking the ones that you already have, until it starts to feel like you are getting what you want. If a constraint system interests you, start writing simple playability constraints, look at how they can go wrong, and then iterate on them, adding more or changing the ones you have until you get the sort of content that you want to see.

For both approaches, remember that the algorithms you use and building blocks you are piecing together define a large probability space, where each point in that space is an individual piece of content. The space may have some strange twists and turns—there may be kinds of content that you can never produce without changing your knowledge representation or your algorithm, and there may be kinds that you overproduce until you rein in the generator. Rather than thinking about how to create a single perfect piece of content, think about the space of potential content that can come out of your generator.

40.4.2 Game Design Constraints

One of the difficulties that comes with PCG is the need to relinquish some amount of authorial control. The ability for the human designer to control the content that the player will see is limited by the need to allow it to be generated dynamically. With this in mind, when selecting PCG techniques, you should consider (1) what kind of design control is needed and (2) if there is a need for tight design guarantees or if it is sufficient to come close. For example, a level generator probably has a need to absolutely guarantee that levels are playable, but it may be sufficient for the levels to just come close to meeting difficulty or pacing requirements. For that matter, even the playability guarantee might not be required if the player is given tools to morph the environment or if the playability issues occur infrequently. These constraints may be dealt with in a different way depending on how important they are. For example, the *Launchpad* level generator [Smith, G. 11c] guarantees level playability by baking it in to the generation algorithm, allowing only legal placement of level geometry, but it does not guarantee that the desired frequency of different level components will be perfectly met due to its use of generate-and-test for that design constraint.

Other potential game design constraints arise when there is a need to obey rules imposed by some other aspects of the design. For instance, if there is an overarching game narrative that all generated levels must fit into, then there must be a way to express the important aspects of narrative as a constraint or rule for the generator.

40.4.3 Relationship with Art

Assuming that some or all of the content that a PCG system produces is visual in nature, the PCG system must be designed in concert with artists. Unless all of the content, including textures, will be generated by the computer (a difficult challenge), artists must create modular assets for the generator to use.

Art is one of the main motivations behind the different kinds of building blocks being chosen: experiential chunks are good when the art direction mandates a rich and detailed world and the artists want tight control over its appearance. Each chunk needs to be designed so that it can fit with others, but otherwise they can stand alone. At the other extreme, a subcomponent representation is useful for a game that uses a tile-based representation, such as a 2D sidescroller, so each subcomponent has a single tile art asset that can be associated with it.

It may still be important for the generator to incorporate some sense of art direction, so that the structure of generated content is suitable to be skinned by human-created art assets. For instance, in a *Mario*-like game, a long, flat platform punctuated by only coins and gaps may be playable and even provide an enjoyable challenge, but will likely not be visually interesting.

40.4.4 Engineering Constraints

Finally, there are important engineering constraints to consider when building a generator. Algorithm speed and efficiency are a big concern. While none of the approaches presented here are *unusable* for content generation, some are certainly better than others for specific domains. Simulation-based and evolutionary approaches tend to be fairly slow unless they are running alongside the player in real time. Constraint-based approaches are more difficult to predict. Depending on the number of variables and the kind of constraints that are expressed, constraint systems can actually solve some content generation problems quite quickly. Grammars usually generate content very quickly, but may need slightly more expensive generate-and-test loops to cull undesirable content.

There is also the concern of how long it will take to create the system and, importantly, test and debug it. Content generators are massively emergent, so bugs can be hard to find, even when following debugging practices such as generating from known random seeds. Constraint-based systems reduce concerns about whether the system will accidentally create unplayable content, but can be more difficult to author and debug. Most current constraint solving methods cannot tell you which combination of constraints is causing an unsatisfactory answer, though it is possible to build in debugging methods. On the other end of the spectrum, approaches that build content from relatively simple rules, such as simulations and grammars, do not make it so easy to make design guarantees but can be easier to author.

40.5 Tuning and Debugging a Content Generator

Because of their emergent nature, debugging PCG systems usually requires more than simply spot-checking different pieces of content that are produced. Standard practices for debugging systems that use a lot of randomness apply, for example, keeping track of random seeds so that bugs can be reproduced more easily and logging decisions made during generation (if possible, given the method used) to get an explanation from the system of what it's doing. For complex PCG systems, however, this alone is not enough to get a sense for what the system is doing and how changes made to the generator influence the content being produced.

Expressive range refers to the shape of the space of content that a PCG system can produce, as well as how easily that space can be controlled [Smith, G. 10]. A good method for understanding expressive range is to define important, measurable qualities (*metrics*) of the content being generated and produce a graph or other visualization of those metrics to see what kind of content is being created. By generating a large amount of content and evaluating each piece using those metrics, it is possible to get a view of the generator's performance. A first step is to look just at the minima, maxima, and medians for each metric—this will show examples of content that are at the extremes of the generator's abilities. For example, this is a quick way to see what the *easiest* and *hardest* levels are (for some approximation of difficulty), as well as the level at average difficulty. The metrics can be simple approximations, such as assigning scores to different level components based on their difficulty and averaging them together. More sophisticated metrics, including automated playtesting techniques [Salge 08], are also possible.

We can also use expressive range analysis to see if the generator seems biased to making any particular kinds of content by looking at the data in a histogram. Are there some bins that have more content in them than others? The generator may be biased toward creating that content over other kinds. A heatmap visualization can be applied to a 2D histogram to visualize *hot spots* in the generator and quickly see changes in the expressive range from different versions of the generator.

By investing in creating a system like this up front, it is possible to see how small changes to the generator lead to changes in the qualities of the content, be rerunning the metrics and seeing new expressive range charts. Expressive range can also be used to compare different generators [Horn 14].

40.6 Conclusion

This chapter has given an overview of techniques for content generation and discussed their trade-offs, described the many roles that PCG can have in a game and how to use those roles to guide decisions about which technique is best, and given some advice for getting started and for debugging your PCG system. This is only an overview of the field of PCG, and there are many more resources available for learning specific techniques or finding how other games have implemented their own content generators. Consequently, this chapter will close with a list of resources to point you toward more information.

40.6.1 Tools and Frameworks

While most off-the-shelf tools are not appropriate for use in large game projects, these tools and frameworks can be used as a prototype for your generator, to experiment and see what is possible:

- *Context Free Art* [Context Free Art 2014] and its cousin *StructureSynth* [Christensen 10] are accessible and well-documented tools for using shape grammars. They are intended for use by digital artists, but can be used to mock-up game content generators.
- *Choco* is a free and open source Java-based numerical constraint solver [Choco Team 2008].
- The *Potassco* suite of tools, particularly *clingo*, is a good tool for getting started with answer set programming [Gebser 2011].

40.6.2 Reading and Community

- *Procedural Content Generation in Games: A Textbook and an Overview of Current Research* is a book with chapters written by prominent researchers in the PCG community [Shaker 14].
- The PCG wiki is a community effort to create a central repository for articles and algorithms [PCG Wiki 14].
- The PCG Google group is an active community of developers and academics who share an interest in PCG [PCG Group 14].
- There is a great deal of academic research into PCG. Common venues for PCG research are the *Foundations of Digital Games* (FDG) conference, the *Procedural Content Generation* (PCG) workshop, and the *Artificial Intelligence in Interactive Digital Entertainment* (AIIDE) conference. Papers from AIIDE are available for free online through AAAI's digital library. Many FDG and PCG papers are archived in the ACM digital library.

References

[.theprodukkt 04] .theprodukkt. 2004. .kkrieger (PC Game).

[Adams 15] Adams, T. 2015. Simulation principles from Dwarf Fortress. In *Game AI Pro²: Collected Wisdom of Game AI Professionals*, ed. S. Rabin. A K Peters/CRC Press, Boca Raton, FL.

[[adult swim] games 10] [adult swim] games. 2010. Robot unicorn attack (PC game).

[Bay 12 Games 06] Bay 12 Games. 2006. Slaves to Armok: God of Blood Chapter II: Dwarf Fortress (PC Game).

[Bjork 04] Bjork, S. and Holopainen, J. 2004. *Patterns in Game Design* (*Game Development Series*), 1st edn. Charles River Media, Hingham, MA.

[Braben 84] Braben, D. and Bell, I. 1984. Elite (BBC Micro). Acornsoft.

[Choco Team 08] Choco Team. 2008. Choco: An open source java constraint programming library. *White Paper, 14th International Conference on Principles and Practice of Constraint Programming, CPAI08 Competition*, Sydney, New South Wales, Australia.

[Christensen 10] Christensen, M. H. 2010. StructureSynth. http://structuresynth.sourceforge.net (accessed June 22, 2014).

[Context Free Art 14] Context Free Art. 2014. Software. http://www.contextfreeart.org (accessed June 22, 2014).

[Dormans 10] Dormans, J. 2010. Adventures in level design: Generating missions and spaces for action adventure games. *Proceedings of the 2010 Workshop on Procedural Content Generation in Games (Co-located with FDG 2010)*, Monterey, CA.

[Ebert 03] Ebert, D. 2003. *Texturing & Modeling: A Procedural Approach*. Morgan Kaufmann, San Francisco, CA.

[Gearbox Software 09] Gearbox Software, and Feral Interactive. 2009. Borderlands (XBox 360). 2K Games.

[Gebser 11] Gebser, M., Kaminski, R., Kaufmann, B., Ostrowski, M., Schaub, T., and Schneider, M. 2011. Potassco: The potsdam answer set solving collection. *AI Communications* 24(2): 105–124.

[Hastings 09] Hastings, E., Ratan, J., Guha, K., and Stanley, K. 2009. Automatic content generation in the galactic arms race video game. *IEEE Transactions on Computational Intelligence and AI in Games* 1(4): 245–263. doi:10.1109/TCIAIG.2009.2038365.

[Horn 14] Horn, B., Dahlskog, S., Shaker, N., Smith, G., and Togelius, J. 2014. A Comparative evaluation of procedural level generators in the mario ai framework. *Proceedings of the Foundations of Digital Games 2014*, Fort Lauderdale, FL.

[Hullett 10] Hullett, K. and Whitehead, J. 2010. Design patterns in FPS levels. *Proceedings of the 2010 International Conference on the Foundations of Digital Games (FDG 2010)*, Monterey, CA.

[Hunicke 04] Hunicke, R., LeBlanc, M., and Zubek, R. 2004. MDA: A formal approach to game design and game research. In *Proceedings of the 2004 AAAI Workshop on Challenges in Game Artificial Intelligence*. San Jose, CA: AAAI Press.

[Jennings-Teats 10] Jennings-Teats, M., Smith, G., and Wardrip-Fruin, N. 2010. Polymorph: A model for dynamic level generation. *Proceedings of the Sixth Conference on Artificial Intelligence for Interactive Digital Entertainment*, Palo Alto, CA.

[Koster 04] Koster, R. 2004. *A Theory of Fun for Game Design*, 1st edn. Paraglyph Press, Scottsdale, AZ.

[McGuinness 12] McGuinness, C. 2012. Statistical analyses of representation choice in level generation. In *2012 IEEE Conference on Computational Intelligence and Games (CIG)*, Granada, Spain, pp. 312–319. doi:10.1109/CIG.2012.6374171.

[MicroProse 91] MicroProse. 1991. *Sid Meier's Civilization (PC Game)*.

[Müller 06] Müller, P., Wonka, P., Haegler, S., Ulmer, A., and Van Gool, L. 2006. Procedural modeling of buildings. *ACM Transactions on Graphics* 25(3): 614–623.

[Onuczko 05] Onuczko, C., Cutumisu, M., Szafron, D., Schaeffer, J., McNaughton, M., Roy, T., Waugh, K., Carbonaro, M., and Siegel, J. 2005. A pattern catalog for computer role playing games. In *Game on North America*, Montreal, Canada, pp. 33–38.

[PCG Group 14] Procedural Content Generation Google Group. 2014. https://groups.google.com/forum/#!forum/proceduralcontent (accessed June 22, 2014).

[PCG Wiki 14] The Procedural Content Generation Wiki. http://pcg.wikidot.com/ (accessed June 22, 2014).

[Persson 11] Persson, Marcus. 2011. Minecraft (PC Game).

[Rogue Basin 12] Rogue B. 2012. Articles on implementation techniques. http://roguebasin.roguelikedevelopment.org/index.php?title=Articles#Implementation (accessed April 28, 2014).

[Salge 08] Salge, C., Lipski, C., Mahlmann, T., and Mathiak, B. 2008. Using genetically optimized artificial intelligence to improve gameplaying fun for strategical games. In *Proceedings of the 2008 ACM SIGGRAPH Sandbox Symposium on Video Games (Sandbox'08)*, pp. 7–14. Los Angeles, CA: ACM.

[Saltsman 09] Saltsman, A. 2009. Canabalt (PC Game). Adam atomic. http://www.adamatomic.com/canabalt/ (accessed August 14, 2014).

[Shaker 14] Shaker, N., Togelius, J., and Nelson, M. 2014. *Procedural Content Generation in Games: A Textbook and an Overview of Current Research*. Springer. http://pcgbook.com.

[Smith, A. 10] Smith, A. M. and Mateas, M. 2010. Variations forever: Flexibly generating rulesets from a sculptable design space of mini-games. *Proceedings of the IEEE Conference on Computational Intelligence and Games (CIG)*, Copenhagen, Denmark.

[Smith, A. 11] Smith, A. M. and Mateas, M. 2011. Answer set programming for procedural content generation: A design space approach. *IEEE Transactions on Computational Intelligence and AI in Games* 3(3): 187–200.

[Smith, A. 12] Smith, A. M., Andersen, E., Mateas, M., and Popovic, Z. 2012. A case study of expressively constrainable level design automation tools for a puzzle game. *Proceedings of the 2012 Conference on the Foundations of Digital Games*, Raleigh, NC.

[Smith, G. 11a] Smith, G., Anderson, R., Kopleck, B., Lindblad, Z., Scott, L., Wardell, A., Whitehead, J., and Mateas, M. 2011. Situating quests: Design patterns for quest and level design in role-playing games. In *Proceedings of the International Conference in Interactive Digital Storytelling*, Vancouver, British Columbia, Canada.

[Smith, G. 10] Smith, G. and Whitehead, J. 2010. Analyzing the expressive range of a level generator. *Proceedings of the Workshop on Procedural Content Generation in Games, Co-located with FDG 2010*, Monterey, CA.

[Smith, G. 11b] Smith, G., Whitehead, J., and Mateas. M. 2011. Tanagra: Reactive planning and constraint solving for mixed-initiative level design. *IEEE Transactions on Computational Intelligence and AI in Games (TCIAIG)*, Special Issue on *Procedural Content Generation* 3(3): 201–215.

[Smith, G. 11c] Smith, G., Whitehead, J., Mateas, M., Treanor, M., March, J., and Cha, M. 2011. Launchpad: A rhythm-based level generator for 2D platformers. *IEEE Transactions on Computational Intelligence and AI in Games (TCIAIG)*, 3(1), pp. 1–16.

[Smith, G. 12] Smith, G., Othenin-Girard, A., Whitehead, J., and Wardrip-Fruin, N. 2012. PCG-based game design: Creating endless web. In *Proceedings of the International Conference on the Foundations of Digital Games* (*FDG '12*), pp. 188–195. Raleigh, NC: ACM. doi:10.1145/2282338.2282375.

[Stiny 80] Stiny, G. 1980. Introduction to shape and shape grammars. *Environment and Planning B* 7(3): 343–351.

[Togelius 08] Togelius, J. and Schmidhuber, J. 2008. An experiment in automatic game design. In *IEEE Symposium on Computational Intelligence and Games, 2008 (CIG'08)*, Perth, Australia, pp. 111–118.

[Togelius 11] Togelius, J., Yannakakis, G. N., Stanley, K. O., and Browne, C. 2011. Search-based procedural content generation: A taxonomy and survey. *IEEE Transactions on Computational Intelligence and AI in Games* 3(3): 172–186.

[Toy 80] Toy, M., Wichman, G., Arnold, K., and Lane, J. 1980. Rogue (PC Game).

[Tutenel 09] Tutenel, T., Smelik, R., Bidarra, R., and de Kraker, K. J. 2009. Using semantics to improve the design of game worlds. In *Proceedings of the Fifth Artificial Intelligence in Interactive Digital Entertainment Conference (AIIDE09)*, Palo Alto, CA.

[Yannakakis 11] Yannakakis, G. N. and Togelius, J. 2011. Experience-driven procedural content generation. *IEEE Transactions on Affective Computing* 2(3): 147–161. doi:10.1109/T-AFFC.2011.6.

[Yu 09] Yu, D. 2009. Spelunky (PC Game).

41

Simulation Principles from *Dwarf Fortress*

Tarn Adams

41.1 Introduction

Dwarf Fortress is a game built on simulation, generating unique game worlds for the player to experience through procedural content generation (PCG) [Dwarf Fortress 14]. Over the development, four guiding principles kept the game simulation robust and easy to work with. This chapter shares those principles with you.

Dwarf Fortress procedurally generates the entire world from scratch. The process begins with an elevation map, generated based on a randomized fractal. Next, it creates several map layers, which include temperature, rainfall, drainage, vegetation, and salinity. With the raw components of the map defined, the next step classifies each tract of land into different biomes (plant and climate types, such as woodlands or savannas). In the next phase of the simulation, temporary rivers wear down the mountains, followed by permanent rivers that flow from high ground to low ground. Plant and animal populations are then introduced, followed by world-specific fantasy creatures. At this point, the world creation is complete and the simulation of civilization begins. Through this process settlements are raised, trade routes are formed, and wars are waged. At a designated point in time, the simulation stops and the player begins the game in a unique living world.

41.2 Principle 1: Don't Overplan Your Model

Developers often make the mistake of overplanning their model. It's a problem with mechanics in general, but especially with simulation-based PCG, since you can't always predict the results and you don't necessarily want to. It can be extremely rewarding to play your own game and enjoy what emerges from the simulation. As a general strategy, it's best to get something running as soon as you can and then work from there until you're satisfied. Rather than overplanning the model, build it up through iteration.

41.3 Principle 2: Break Down and Understand the System

If you just focus on the end result, it's not clear what's required to make it look and work correctly. Instead, break down and understand the system you are modeling in terms of its basic elements and interactions. Not only will you develop a richer interplay of objects, but certain problems solve themselves. As a simple example, when creating terrain, it is tempting to spawn particular biomes or allow a fractal to directly define the biomes. However, *Dwarf Fortress* achieved much better results by handling fields separately: temperature, rainfall, elevation, drainage, etc. The interplay of those fields determined the final biome, resulting in a more natural, internally consistent solution.

41.4 Principle 3: Don't Overcomplicate

There's no reason to have 50 variables modeling one aspect of a game's behavior if they don't all have a meaningful impact on the game. Operate at the level of what the player sees or one layer below. Don't get carried away and create a lot of worthless noise. Not only do uselessly complicated systems hinder tuning, but they can have a paralyzing effect during development. Use complexity only where it's needed, otherwise strive for simplicity.

41.5 Principle 4: Base Your Model on Real-World Analogs

It's helpful to base your simulation on reality. If you have a real-world analog in mind, you can correct defects using a broader understanding of the fundamentals. In *Dwarf Fortress*, for example, the world maps improved greatly when rain shadows were taken into consideration (mountains block rain-producing weather systems, casting a shadow of dryness on the other side). Oddly enough, drainage was another nonobvious consideration that helped smoothly delineate forests from swamps. We know the real world works, so if you fall back on reality, you can usually get the simulation to work as well, given adequate memory and CPU time.

41.6 Conclusion

Regardless of what you're simulating, the preceding four principles should help you craft the game you actually want. When starting out, don't overplan the model. Build the model up over time, break down the components, and try to fully understand the underlying system. Base the model on real-world analogs so that you can benefit from systems that are known to work. Allow the individual elements to combine, producing results which can be varied, surprising, and yet still responsive to your adjustments. By keeping it simple, you can avoid black box simulations and ultimately stay in control of your game.

For further information and a great wealth of PCG tips and tricks, please see the chapter "Procedural Content Generation: An Overview" in this book or visit the PCG Wiki [PCG Wiki 14].

References

[Dwarf Fortress 14] Dwarf Fortress. 2014. http://www.bay12games.com/dwarves/ (accessed September 10, 2014).

[PCG Wiki 14] Procedural Content Generation Wiki. 2014. http://pcg.wikidot.com/ (accessed September 10, 2014).

42

Techniques for AI-Driven Experience Management in Interactive Narratives

Vadim Bulitko, Greg Lee, Sergio Poo Hernandez, Alejandro Ramirez, and David Thue

42.1 Introduction

Recently, there has been a trend to include open-world gameplay in story-rich video games (e.g., [Petit 14]). Giving the player agency can lead to his or her affecting the original story in a way that the game designers may not have anticipated. To illustrate, imagine a game version of the *Little Red Riding Hood* story [Perrault 1697, Grimm 1812]. Suppose that the player, controlling Red, kills the wolf early in the game. The rest of the story is then broken, since the wolf is unable to eat the grandmother.

This chapter describes several artificial intelligence (AI) techniques that can help game designers provide players with more agency while still maintaining a desired narrative feel for their games. In the example of Red killing the wolf, the AI techniques can automatically revise the story upon the wolf's demise (e.g., another predator appears) so that certain authorial goals are maintained (e.g., the grandmother is eaten).

42.2 AI-Driven Experience Management

The task we consider in this chapter is that of managing a player's experience, driven by AI. This is an expansive area in which several approaches have been proposed, and it offers several avenues to explore [Riedl 13]. The key idea is to create an AI game master (AI GM), which is bundled with every copy of the game. As the player proceeds through the narrative, making narrative choices, the AI GM monitors the player's actions and dynamically modifies the story in a way that the story designer would have wanted. In this chapter, we use the terms *story designer* and *story author* interchangeably, and this view of interactive storytelling is also known as *delayed authoring* [Thue 08].

For the sake of consistency with existing literature, we also use the terms *AI GM* and *AI experience manager* interchangeably throughout the chapter. Computationally, we view experience management as an optimization problem where the AI GM attempts to optimize the player's experience according to a designer's specified objectives [Thue 12]. We detail our approach in the following sections.

42.2.1 Player in a Game Environment

If a game narrative is going to be modified by AI, it first needs to be represented in a computer-readable format. This means that the narrative state (e.g., Red just met the wolf) and all actions available to change the state (e.g., shoot the wolf or reason with the wolf) need to be formally described. While numerous methodologies have been used to represent game worlds in an AI-readable format, in this article, we will use the Planning Domain Definition Language (PDDL) [McDermott 98]. Listing 42.1 illustrates the PDDL encoding of the action *eat*, which one game character may do to another in the *Little Red Riding Hood* story.

Note that the action is represented in a programming-like notation with variables (e.g., `?eater`) and predicates (e.g., `alive`). It says that the `eater` can eat the `eatee` if the `eater` is a predator, the `eatee` is a person, the `eater` knows the `eatee`, and the `eater` is hungry. They both must be alive and the `eatee` cannot yet be eaten. Once the action is applied, the `eatee` is eaten and is located inside the `eater`, and the eater is no longer hungry. Table 42.1 illustrates an application of this action.

Listing 42.1. An action template that can be instantiated into an in-game action.

```
(define (action eat)
    :parameters (?eater ?eatee)
    :precondition (and (knows ?eater ?eatee)
                       (predator ?eater)
                       (alive ?eatee)
                       (alive ?eater)
                       (not (eaten ?eatee))
                       (hungry ?eater)
                       (person ?eatee))
    :effect (and (eaten ?eatee)
                 (in ?eatee ?eater)
                 (not (hungry?eater))))
```

Table 42.1 Changes in Game Narrative State Caused by an Action

Current State	Action	New State
(person red)		(person red)
(alive red)	(eat wolf red)	(alive red)
(predator wolf)		(predator wolf)
(alive wolf)		(alive wolf)
(hungry wolf)		**(not (hungry wolf))**
(knows wolf red)		(knows wolf red)
(knows red wolf)		(knows red wolf)
		(in red wolf)
		(eaten red)

In this example, the action's variables `eater` and `eatee` are bound to the wolf and Red, respectively. The current state is shown in the first column of Table 42.1. It is represented with a series of facts (e.g., Red is a person and the wolf is a predator) and satisfies the preconditions of the action. Once the action is applied in the current state, the new state is generated with the new facts shown in bold.

42.2.2 AI Manager Modifying Narrative

Once the narrative state and the player's actions are represented in a computer-readable format, the AI can reason over the narrative and modify the game world in response to the player's actions on the fly. To do so, the AI GM needs to know what the author wants to happen in the story.

Traditionally, games encode nonlinear narrative as story graphs (or story trees). The game engine selects the appropriate branch based on story tokens (e.g., whether the player saved Ashley or Kaiden in *Mass Effect* [BioWare 07]). An alternate approach to specifying the author's wishes is through PDDL-described game facts. Figure 42.1 depicts a skeleton of the interactive narrative for the *Little Red Riding Hood* [Ramirez 13] where the story author has two goals: (1) a predator should eat both Red and her grandmother, and (2) Red should give her grandmother a cake (shaded nodes in the story graph on the left).

When the player kills the wolf, both `(eat predator red)` and `(eat predator granny)` are invalidated as the wolf is dead and unable to eat anyone. The AI manager can then engage an automated planner to satisfy these goals from the current state. Given the action templates that are available, the planner may come up with two stories. In one, another predator (named Grendel) greets the player and takes over from the deceased wolf. In the other, a magic fairy resurrects the original wolf who can then resume his eating duties.

42.2.3 Choosing between Stories

Whenever several stories are available that satisfy the authorial goals, the AI GM needs to decide which one to run. To choose among them, the game master can rely on the author's specification of an ideal player experience. For instance, suppose that the author wants to maximize the player's enjoyment of the story. Suppose also that on the basis of the player's previous actions, the AI experience manager believes the player to have an inclination

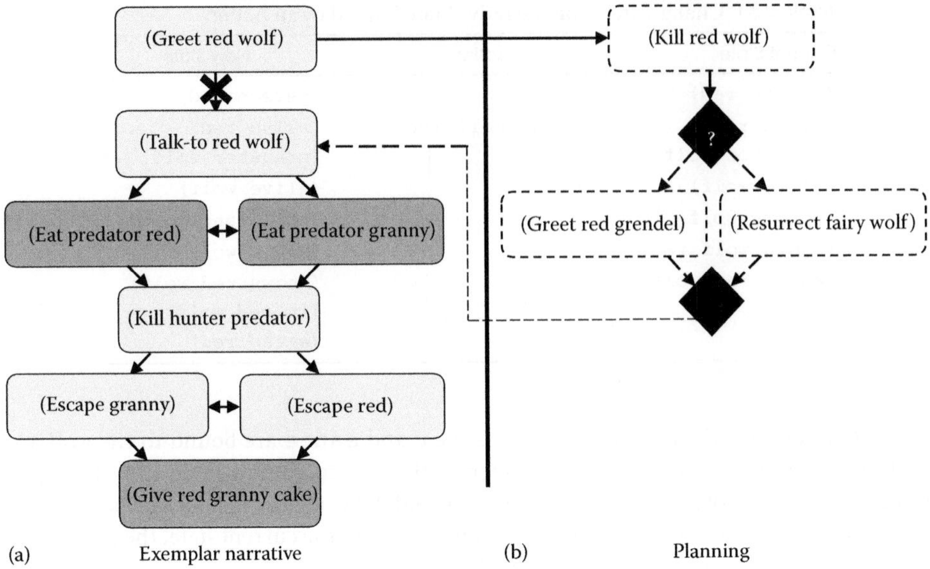

Figure 42.1

Author's desired events (a) and AI experience manager's actions (b). The arrows show possible temporal relations between the events.

toward combat. Then in deciding between two possible narratives in Figure 42.1, the manager may decide that introducing Grendel—effectively a bigger, meaner version of the original wolf—is a more suitable option than presenting a resurrecting fairy. The manager then runs the narrative content with Grendel until the player takes the next action and once again prompts the manager to modify the game world. We give examples of how an author can describe an ideal player experience in the following sections.

42.3 AI-Driven Experience Management: Common Techniques

The previous section introduced AI-driven player experience management. The interactive narrative was encoded in a computer-readable format, story branches were either pre-authored or automatically planned out, and a specification of the player's ideal experience was used to select among them. Figure 42.2 shows how these steps are related to gameplay, with the AI GM monitoring and updating the game to manage what happens next.

In this section, we detail computational techniques that power those steps. In doing so, we provide the game designer with a set of tools that he or she can mix and match to suit the needs of his or her particular game.

42.3.1 Technique: Narrative Generation

Given a formal representation of the story world and a history of the player's actions, the AI GM can automatically compute possible narratives that (1) are consistent with the player's actions and (2) satisfy any future authorial goals. One approach to doing so is to use an automated planner. In the past, narrative-centric planners have been used

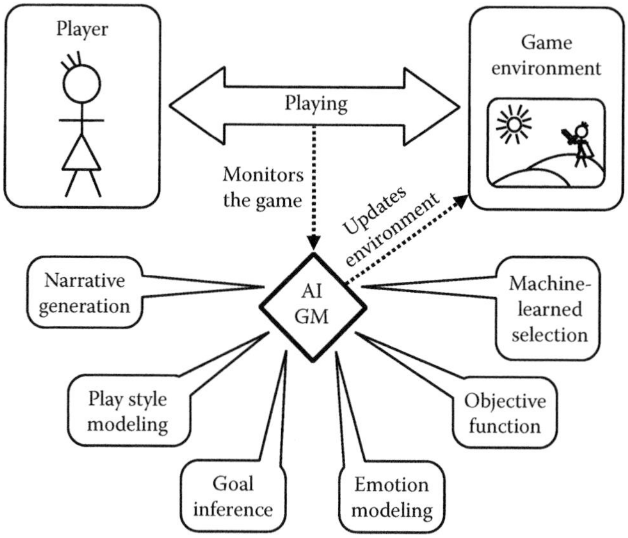

Figure 42.2

A high-level view of AI experience management.

(e.g., *Longbow* [Young 94]). More recent systems attempt to use general-purpose off-the-shelf planners such as *Fast Downward* [Helmert 06].

Since a planner cannot produce the actual high-quality writing or multimedia content to go with the narrative stubs generated in PDDL, the corresponding narrative pieces need to be pregenerated during game development and then fleshed out by human writers and artists. Then, during the game, the AI planner is effectively *selecting* from a library of narrative fragments in order to assemble start-to-finish narratives on the fly while satisfying the world consistency (e.g., the wolf is dead) and authorial constraints (e.g., the grandmother needs to be eaten).

42.3.2 Technique: Play Style Modeling

Knowing something about the player can be helpful when choosing between narratives. One approach is to model the player as a vector of numbers, each number indicating the player's inclination toward a certain play style. The play styles can be taken from player archetypes such as the canonical RPG types [Laws 01]. For instance, the vector could be (F: 0.9, M: 0.2, S: 0.1, T: 0.4, P: 0.3), which indicates that the player has often played as a fighter (0.9) but less so as a method actor (0.2), storyteller (0.1), tactician (0.4), or power gamer (0.3). These values are maintained by the AI GM when it observes the player's actions in game [Thue 07]. A simple way to implement this is to annotate each action template (e.g., Listing 42.1) with a vector of updates to the model. For instance, whenever the player kills anyone, the model's estimate of his or her fighter inclination could increase by 0.3.

The player's play style inclinations may change over time. Thus, the model should track the player's current/recent inclinations. This can be handled by gradually moving all vector components toward their neutral values over time.

42.3.3 Technique: Goal Inference

Knowing something about the player's inclinations toward different play styles can help the AI manager infer the player's current goals. For instance, if the player controlling Red has previously shown an inclination toward fighting, it is likely that he or she will try to kill Grendel.

We can implement this type of inference by having the game designer encode potential player goals in PDDL and specify a correlation between play styles and goals. To illustrate, suppose that when Grendel is first introduced, any player may intend to either kill Grendel (goal #1) or avoid him (goal #2). Then, the correlation can be specified as in Table 42.2.

This means that someone purely interested in fighting would have a strong (0.9 out of 1) intention to kill Grendel and a weak intention (0.1) to avoid him. In practice, a player is usually inclined toward a mix of different play styles. Thus, the goal intentions of a given player are computed as a matrix product of the correlation matrix and the player model (F: 0.9, M: 0.2, S: 0.1, T: 0.4, P: 0.3):

$$\begin{pmatrix} 0.9 & 0.7 & 0.2 & 0.4 & 0.6 \\ 0.1 & 0.3 & 0.6 & 0.8 & 0.1 \end{pmatrix} \times \begin{pmatrix} 0.9 \\ 0.2 \\ 0.1 \\ 0.4 \\ 0.3 \end{pmatrix} \approx \begin{pmatrix} 1.31 \\ 0.56 \end{pmatrix} \tag{42.1}$$

Note that both the correlation matrix and the player model shown in Equation 42.1 are transposed to make the matrix product work. The result shows us the player represented by our current player model has a weight of 1.31 to fight Grendel and a weight of 0.56 to avoid it. We also normalize the vector to keep all intention values between 0 and 1. The normalized result is approximately (0.7, 0.3), indicating that this player is likely intending to kill (and not avoid) Grendel [Poo Hernandez 14].

42.3.4 Technique: Emotional Modeling

One way for the game designers to specify an ideal player experience is to give the desired emotional arc. For instance, many games follow the classic Aristotelian tension arc [BioWare 07, BioWare 09, Bethesda 11], while some experiment with periodic functions. A commercially deployed example of the latter is Valve's *Left 4 Dead*, which uses an AI Director to keep the player on a sinusoidal tension curve by dynamically shaping the zombie influx [Booth 09].

Table 42.2 Play Style and Goal Correlation Example

Play Style Inclination	Goal 1: Kill Grendel	Goal 2: Avoid Grendel
Fighter	0.9	0.1
Method actor	0.7	0.3
Storyteller	0.2	0.6
Tactician	0.4	0.8
Power gamer	0.6	0.1

While *Left 4 Dead's* AI Director models the player along a single emotional dimension (tension), the appraisal-style models of emotions [Lazarus 91] are able to infer the player's emotions in several dimensions [Ortony 90]. For example, CEMA [Bulitko 08] is a lightweight subset of EMA [Marsella 03] that focuses on just four emotions: joy, hope, fear, and distress. Thus, the player's emotional state is represented with four numbers, each expressing the current intensity of the corresponding emotion. Thus, (J:0.8, H:0.6, F:0.2, D:0) would represent a player who is presently joyful (0.8) and hopeful (0.6) but slightly fearful (0.2) and not distressed (0).

To compute the numbers, an appraisal-style model needs to know the player's goals and the likelihood of accomplishing them. To derive the player's goals, one can use the technique of goal inference presented earlier in the article. The likelihood of accomplishing the goals can be computed based on the player's character attributes (e.g., a stealthy character will probably be able to avoid Grendel).

To illustrate, consider a player whose goal intentions to kill Grendel and avoid dying are computed as (0.7, −0.3). Suppose this player has a 50% chance of killing Grendel and a 10% chance of dying. A desirable but uncertain goal elicits hope and hence the system models the player as being hopeful at the intensity of $0.5 \times 0.7 = 0.35$. According to appraisal-style models, once a desirable goal is certain, it no longer elicits hope; instead, it elicits joy. Since the goal of killing Grendel is uncertain, there is no joy from it (yet). Dying is undesirable to this player (values for undesirable outcomes are expressed by negative numbers, −0.3 in this example), and hence it elicits the emotion of fear with an intensity of $0.1 \times 0.3 = 0.03$. There is no distress yet since the player is not certain to die. Hence, the player's emotional state is computed as (J:0, H:0.35, F:0.03, D:0) [Gratch 06].

42.3.5 Technique: Objective Function Maximization

Player inclinations and emotional state models can be used by the AI GM to select among alternative narratives, with the goal of achieving the author's notion of an ideal player experience. A simple way of doing so is to annotate each narrative with its suitability with respect to different styles of play. For example, introducing Grendel may be most suitable for a fighter, whereas a resurrecting fairy may appeal to a storyteller. Computationally, the suitability of a narrative is a vector of numbers, one for each style of play. For instance, a simple annotation for the *introduce Grendel* narrative can be (F: 0.9, M: 0, S: 0, T: 0, P: 0), whereas the *introduce magic fairy* narrative can be annotated as (F: 0, M: 0, S: 0.9, T: 0, P: 0). Given several annotated alternative narratives, the manager can take a dot product between the player inclination model and each annotation. The narrative with the highest dot product is then presented to the player [Thue 07, Ramirez 13]. In our example, the player's play style inclinations are modeled as (F: 0.9, M: 0.2, S: 0.1, T: 0.4, P: 0.3), which means that the dot product for *introduce Grendel* is 0.81 (Equation 42.2), whereas the dot product for *introduce magic fairy* is 0.09 (Equation 42.3). Hence, our player will face Grendel after killing the wolf:

$$\begin{pmatrix}0.9 & 0 & 0 & 0 & 0\end{pmatrix}\cdot\begin{pmatrix}0.9 & 0.2 & 0.1 & 0.4 & 0.3\end{pmatrix}=0.81 \tag{42.2}$$

$$\begin{pmatrix}0 & 0 & 0.9 & 0 & 0\end{pmatrix}\cdot\begin{pmatrix}0.9 & 0.2 & 0.1 & 0.4 & 0.3\end{pmatrix}=0.09 \tag{42.3}$$

A more advanced approach is to use the play style inclinations to infer the player's intentions. Those can then be used to predict how the player's emotional state will be affected by each of the alternative narratives. The narrative that manages to bring the player's emotional state the closest to the target emotional state (as specified by the author) is then presented to the player. To illustrate, suppose the author wants their players to experience the following emotional state (J:0, H:0.4, F:0.03, D:0) at this point in the story. The narrative introducing Grendel is predicted to put the player in the emotional state (J:0.8, H:0.6, F:0.2, D:0), whereas the narrative introducing the magic fairy is expected to elicit the emotional state (J:0, H:0.35, F:0.03, D:0). The Euclidean distance between the expected emotional state (J:0.8, H:0.6, F:0.2, D:0) and the target emotional state (J:0, H:0.4, F:0.03, D:0) is 0.83:

$$\sqrt{(0.8-0)^2+(0.6-0.4)^2+(0.2-0.03)^2+(0-0)^2} \approx 0.83 \tag{42.4}$$

On the other hand, the distance between the emotional state (J:0, H:0.35, F:0.03, D:0) and the target emotional state (J:0, H:0.4, F:0.03, D:0) is only 0.05. The AI manager tries to minimize the distance and thus will select the narrative with the magic fairy.

42.3.6 Technique: Machine-Learned Narrative Selection

Yet another alternative for selecting narratives is to use machine learning during the development stage to automatically acquire a mapping from game and player states to the set of alternative narratives. One such mapping is a ranking function, similar to how Internet search engines map user queries to a ranked list of web pages. This approach is appropriate when training data are available. For instance, if human game masters could be observed and their narrative selection recorded, then the resulting corpus of data could be used to machine-learn an AI approximation to a human game master. We describe an implementation of this approach in the following section.

42.4 Implementations

Over the last seven years, our research group at the University of Alberta has implemented AI experience managers using different combinations of the techniques given earlier. In the following sections, we briefly review these implementations and describe how they were tested.

42.4.1 PaSSAGE

Player-Specific Stories via Automatically Generated Events (PaSSAGE) [Thue 07, Thue 11] is an AI experience manager that combines two techniques: (1) play style inclination modeling and (2) maximizing a simpler version of the aforementioned objective function. We deployed PaSSAGE in the domain of RPG-style games, using off-the-shelf game engine technology from both *Neverwinter Nights* [BioWare 02] and *Dragon Age: Origins* [BioWare 09]. Our first test bed, *Annara's Tale*, is an adaptation of the *Little Red Riding Hood* that included five different endings, eight substantially different paths through the story, and three points at which PaSSAGE could choose between story branches. Our second test bed, *Lord of the Borderlands*, is an original story that included 16 different endings, 32 substantially different paths through the story, and two points at which PaSSAGE could influence what happened next. When compared to a uniform random manager (which still obeyed the game's authorial constraints), PaSSAGE scored higher with respect to player-reported fun with high confidence (as tested with 133 undergraduate students). While preliminary, this result shows promise for applying PaSSAGE in both current and next generation games.

42.4.2 PAST

Player-Specific Automated Storytelling (PAST) [Ramirez 12, Ramirez 13] added narrative generation to PaSSAGE. Specifically, instead of hand-scripting the narrative continuations (as was done in PaSSAGE), PAST used the automated planning module from the Automated Story Director [Riedl 08] to compute narratives that were consistent with the player's actions and the authorial goals.

We evaluated PAST with a text-based choose-your-own-adventure version of the *Little Red Riding Hood* story. Within each game, the player made four consecutive narrative choices. For each player choice, PAST computed several alternative accommodations (i.e., alternate stories based on a virtual domain description aligned with authorial goals) and selected one using a play style model similar to the one in PaSSAGE. More than 30 different narrative trajectories were available to the players. Players' self-reported perception of fun and agency indicated positive trends [Ramirez 13].

42.4.3 PACE

Player Appraisal Controlling Emotions (PACE) [Poo Hernandez 14] is our latest AI experience manager. It uses the four techniques of narrative generation, play style modeling, goal inference, emotion modeling, and the second, more advanced type of the objective function. Unlike PAST, we used a PDDL-compatible off-the-shelf automated planner to compute possible narratives. PACE uses the full objective function to predict the player's emotional state along each of the alternative narratives. It selects the narrative that brings the player closest to the target emotional trajectory.

PACE is currently being deployed within the novel video game *iGiselle*: an interactive reimaging of the classic Romantic ballet *Giselle* [Gautier 41]. In *iGiselle*, the player assumes various ballet poses (read by Microsoft Kinect) to control their avatar and make narrative choices. The narrative is presented via a combination of still images, prerecorded voiceovers, videos, and music.

42.4.4 SCoReS

Sports Commentary Recommendation System (SCoReS) chooses stories for sports broadcasts [Lee 13]. It uses machine-learned narrative selection to pick the piece of color commentary most suitable to the state of a sports game at any given moment. It was evaluated in the domain of baseball and received positive feedback from both the users and human expert color commentators.

42.5 Conclusion and Future Work

We have presented the task of managing a player's narrative experience in a video game. In doing so, we decomposed the problem into several steps and presented specific techniques that can be used to implement an AI GM for a particular video game. We then briefly described four such game masters that we have developed in our research group.

Future work will continue implementing and testing these types of approaches within different games. We also hope to build a narrative space exploration tool that will combine the narrative generation technique with player models data-mined from existing game telemetry. Game designers could then use this tool to interactively explore and shape a narrative space in the early stages of a game's story development.

References

[Bethesda 11] Bethesda. 2011. The Elder Scrolls V: Skyrim. http://www.elderscrolls.com/skyrim.

[BioWare 02] BioWare. 2002. Neverwinter Nights. http://www.bioware.com/en/games/.

[BioWare 07] BioWare. 2007. Mass Effect. http://www.bioware.com/en/games/.

[BioWare 09] BioWare. 2009. Dragon Age: Origins. http://www.bioware.com/en/games/.

[Booth 09] Booth, M. 2009. The AI systems of Left4Dead. Keynote. *Fifth Artificial Intelligence and Interactive Digital Entertainment Conference.*

[Bulitko 08] Bulitko, V. et al. 2008. Modeling culturally and emotionally affected behavior. *Proceedings of Artificial Intelligence and Interactive Digital Entertainment Conference*, pp. 10–15. AAAI Press.

[Gautier 41] Gautier, T. et al. 1841. *Giselle.*

[Gratch 06] Gratch, J. and S. Marsella. 2006. Evaluating a computational model of emotion. *Journal of Autonomous Agents and Multiagent Systems* 11:23–43.

[Grimm 12] Grimm, J. and W. Grimm. 1812. Little red cap. In *Kinderund Hausmärchen*, 1st edn., Vol. 1.

[Helmert 06] Helmert, M. 2006. The fast downward planning system. *Journal of Artificial Intelligence Research* 26:191–246.

[Laws 01] Laws, R. D. 2001. *Robin's Laws for Good Game Mastering.* Austin, TX: Steve Jackson Games.

[Lazarus 91] Lazarus, R. S. 1991. *Emotion and Adaptation.* New York: Oxford University Press.

[Lee 13] Lee, G., V. Bulitko, and E. Ludvig. 2013. Automated story selection for color commentary in sports. *IEEE Transactions on Computational Intelligence and AI in Games* 6(2):144–155.

[Marsella 03] Marsella, S. and J. Gratch. 2003. Modeling coping behavior in virtual humans: Don't worry, be happy. *Proceedings of Second International Joint Conference on Autonomous Agents and Multiagent Systems*, pp. 313–320.

[McDermott 98] McDermott, D. et al. 1998. PDDL-the planning domain definition language.

[Ortony 90] Ortony, A., G. L. Clore, and A. Collins. 1990. *The Cognitive Structure of Emotions.* Cambridge, U.K.: Cambridge University Press.

[Perrault 97] Perrault, C. 1697. Little Red Riding Hood.

[Petit 14] Petit, C. 2014. Balancing freedom and story in *Dragon Age: Inquisition.* Gamespot. http://www.gamespot.com/articles/balancing-freedom-and-story-in-dragon-age-inquisition/1100-6419121/ (accessed May 4, 2014).

[Poo Hernandez 14] Poo Hernandez, S., V. Bulitko, and E. St. Hilaire. 2014. Storytelling with artificial intelligence. *Proceedings of the 10th AAAI Conference on Artificial Intelligence and Interactive Digital Entertainment,* North Carolina State University, Raleigh, NC, p. 7.

[Ramirez 12] Ramirez, A. and V. Bulitko. 2012. Telling interactive player-specific stories and planning for it: ASD + PaSSAGE = PAST. *Proceedings of the Eighth AAAI Conference on Artificial Intelligence and Interactive Digital Entertainment,* Stanford University, Palo Alto, CA, pp. 173–178. AAAI Press.

[Ramirez 13] Ramirez, A., V. Bulitko, and M. Spetch. 2013. Evaluating planning-based experience managers for agency and fun in text-based interactive narrative. *Proceedings of the Ninth AAAI Conference on AI and Interactive Digital Entertainment,* Noreastern University, Boston, MA, pp. 65–71. AAAI Press.

[Ramirez 14] Ramirez, A. and V. Bulitko. 2014. Automated planning and player modelling for interactive storytelling. *IEEE Transactions in Computational Intelligence and AI in Games* 12, in press.

[Riedl 08] Riedl, M. et al. 2008. Dynamic experience management in virtual worlds for entertainment, education, and training. *International Transactions on Systems Science and Applications* 4(2):23–42.

[Riedl 13] Riedl, M. and V. Bulitko. 2013. Interactive narrative: an intelligent systems approach. *AI Magazine* 34(1):67–77.

[Thue 07] Thue, D. et al. 2007. Interactive storytelling: A player modelling approach. *Proceedings of the Third AAAI Conference on AI and Interactive Digital Entertainment,* Stanford, CA, pp. 43–48. AAAI Press.

[Thue 08] Thue, D. et al. 2008. Making stories player-specific: Delayed authoring in interactive storytelling. *Proceedings of the First Joint International Conference on Interactive Digital Storytelling,* pp. 230–241. Springer, Berlin, Germany.

[Thue 11] Thue, D. et al. 2011. A computational model of perceived agency in video games. *Proceedings of the Seventh AAAI Conference on Artificial Intelligence and Interactive Digital Entertainment,* Stanford, CA, pp. 91–96. AAAI Press.

[Thue 12] Thue, D. and V. Bulitko. 2012. Procedural game adaptation: Framing experience management as changing an MDP. *Proceedings of the Fifth Workshop in Intelligent Narrative Technologie,* Stanford, CA. AAAI Press.

[Young 94] Young, M. R. 1994. A developer's guide to Longbow discourse planning system. University of Pittsburgh Intelligent Systems Program Technical Report 94-4, Pittsburgh, PA.

Index

A

B

C

D

E

F

G

H

J

K

L

Q

R

S

Printed and bound by CPI Group (UK) Ltd, Croydon, CR0 4YY
23/10/2024
01777689-0002